UNFAITHFUL:
THE HISTORY OF THE
ADULTERY FILM

Anthony Balducci

Slingshot Books

NEW PORT RICHEY, FLORIDA

Anthony Balducci/Slingshot Books
New Port Richey, FL

Unfaithful: The History of The Adultery Film/ Anthony Balducci. -- 1st ed.
ISBN 979-8-218-23126-2

Dedicated to Michael Balducci

CONTENTS

Introduction

People enjoy a good Hollywood love story. Boy meets Girl. Boy and Girl fall in love. But, oh, Girl has a Husband. Or, maybe, Boy has a Wife.

A story needs to have conflict. It follows that a marriage story will present a conflict between husband and wife - unfaithfulness, debt, infertility, alienation, or abuse. The relentless strife that threatens married couples in Hollywood films is discussed by a young husband and wife in *Saturday's Children* (1940).

> Bobby: Rims, did you ever see a scene in a picture where the whole world was against two people trying to pull them apart?
>
> Rims: I think there was one picture in which I didn't see it.

The most dramatic as well as the most versatile conflict comes from unfaithfulness. So, it figures that this would be the most common marital problem in films. The Internet Movie Database (IMDb) has a helpful keyword search. When I last checked, the keyword "adultery" turned up 7,033 film titles. Everything considered, adultery has been a major subject for filmmakers.

Hollywood filmmakers have long preferred to accentuate the pitfalls of marriage while ignoring the important and often sublime benefits of marriage. Baseball would look like a pretty bad idea if films about baseball almost always highlighted the worst players. *The Pride of the Yankees* (1942) would not make you love baseball if it did nothing but show you Lou Gehrig's fumbles and fouls. Wikipedia reports, "As a theme [adultery] brings intense emotions into the foreground, and has consequences for all concerned. It also automatically brings its own conflict, between the people concerned and between sexual desires and a sense of loyalty."[1]

In jungle films, people are always stumbling into quicksand. It is as if the jungle floor is teeming with patches of liquefied soil. Jeffbert, a long-term member of the Science Fiction and Fantasy Chronicles forum, wrote, "This is the thing that most terrified me as a child. That the ground itself could simply swallow me, was just too much."[2] Daniel Engber of Slate wrote, "Quicksand once offered filmmakers a simple recipe for excitement: A pool of water, thickened with oatmeal, sprinkled over the top with wine corks. It was, in its purest form, a plot device unburdened by character, motivation, or story. . ."[3] Adultery turns up more often in the melodrama film than quicksand turns up in the jungle film. Melodrama fashions marriage into a dangerously exotic landscape. But adultery, unlike quicksand, cannot exist in a film without character, motivation and story. What type of person cheats on their spouse? Why do they do it? How does this dire violation of the marriage pact come about? Should we be terrified that the ground in a marriage may open up and swallow us whole?

Take, for instance, the motivation for the ruinous infidelity in Gustave Flaubert's famous 1856 novel "Madame Bovary." Roxana Robinson of The New Yorker wrote:

> More surprisingly, for a novelist, [Flaubert] blames [Emma Bovary's] downfall on novels. When she was at convent school, Emma was spiritually inclined; she considered a religious vocation. But she lost interest in the Church when she began reading contraband romances that had been smuggled inside in an old lady's pockets. Emma learned that she could escape from the real world into fiction. She

learned about midnight trysts, stolen brides, passion and glamour. She learned that romantic love was a crack-cocaine high, tingling, ardent, and never-ending. This was an adolescent's dream, impossible to realize, but no one told Emma that. (Her mother was dead.) She believed it; it became her ideal; it ruined her life.4

In M-G-M's 1949 film adaptation of *Madame Bovary*, Flaubert (James Mason) similarly speaks of Emma's motivations while defending himself in court against an obscenity charge. He questions how a "kitchen drudge" could come to embrace elaborate fantasies about the common canoodling of a man and woman. Where exactly did she get these "[r]idiculous dreams of high romance and impossible love"? His answer:

Novels, novels. She lived in a world of love, lovers, sweethearts, persecuted ladies fainting in lonely pavilions, horses ridden to death on every page, gentlemen, brave as lions, gentle as lambs, always well-dressed and weeping like fountains. Oh, love in Italy! Oh, love in Spain!

What else inspires ridiculous dreams of love and romance? Movies, movies. Let us examine these movies and identify possible fault, absurdity, or harmful influence.

Hal Erickson of AllMovie Guide praised the adultery film *Stormy Waters* (1941) as "a heavy-breathing French melodrama. . . replete with two-fisted action, star-crossed romance and intense emotional turbulence."5 The adultery film is not guaranteed to present two-fisted action, but it could be relied upon to provide heavy-breathing melodrama, the sure and steady encroachment of doom, and "intense emotional turbulence."

The melodrama is, by definition, the domain of the adultery story. Wikipedia reports:

Melodramas are typically set in the private sphere of the home, and focus on morality and family issues, love, and marriage, often with challenges from an outside source, such as a "temptress", or an aristocratic villain. . . Melodramas put most of their attention on the victim and a struggle between good and evil choices, such as a man being encouraged to leave his family by an "evil temptress". . . Melodrama generally. . . emphasiz[es] "forbidden longings.6

The melodrama traffics in heightened emotions. Richard Dyer, Professor of Film Studies at the University of Warwick, referred to melodramas as "dramas of passion, turbulence and ferocity."7 The headline used to advertise Cecil B. DeMille's adultery tale *The Cheat* (1915) read "A Drama of Intense Emotional Appeal." This is drama driven by hyperbole and excess, with the strongest of emotions lying firmly at its core.

The adultery film took the form of lurid and often fatal melodrama. Adulterous passion, which unmoored a person from their moral obligations, often had dark consequences. The adultery film is, in this way, a horror film. Adultery is a dastardly villain around every corner and a boogeyman under every bed.

A wide variety of classic films touch upon the subject of extramarital affairs. An adultery subplot can be found in the sweet romantic Christmas comedy *The Shop Around the Corner* (1940). The story unfolds at a shop that sells novelties and leatherware to a high-class clientele in Budapest. Lighthearted comedy flourishes against a background of elegant shops and quaint cafes. But, amid the film's holiday cheer and sweet-natured romance, adultery rears its ugly head. The shop owner, Mr. Matuschek (Frank Morgan), is informed by a private investigator that his wife is having an affair with one of his employees. He mistakenly suspects the upstanding Alfred Kralik (James Stewart) to be his wife's lover and fires him just days before Christmas. *The Godfather* (1972) makes time between the intermittent shooting, stabbing and garroting for a quick bit of extramarital hanky-panky. During the lavish celebration of his sister's wedding, gangster Sonny Corleone (James Caan) sneaks away from his wife to have rough sex in an upstairs bedroom with the maid of honor.

The number one rule of marriage can be summed up in two words: marry wisely. But that means strictly applying reason when choosing a spouse. A person needs to determine if a potential spouse shares their values and objectives. The courtship ritual allowed a person and their family to evaluate potential matches and determine if a marriage was a good idea. According to the article "The History of Dating in America":

> The courting script was usually contained to "calling," in which the man was invited into the woman's parlor for conversations over tea and involved a large degree of supervision. Reputation was also an essential form of social currency that required intimate guarding. . . During the courtship process, it was typical for the intended couples to divulge their perceived character flaws to ensure that a long-term commitment would be logical and feasible.[8]

But a new perspective became popular. Alain de Botton, the author of "The Course of Love," wrote: "Romanticism emerged as an ideology in Europe in the mid-eighteenth century in the minds of poets, artists and philosophers, and it has now conquered the world. . ."[9] He continued:

> For Romanticism, the marriage of reason was not reasonable at all, which is why what it replaced it with – the marriage of feeling. . . What matters is that two people wish desperately that it happen, are drawn to one another by an overwhelming instinct and know in their hearts that it is right. The modern age has had enough of "reasons', those catalysts of misery, those accountants' demands.[10]

Here, according to de Botton, was the key principle of romantic love:

> Romanticism believed that choosing a partner should be about letting oneself be guided by feelings, rather than practical considerations.[11]

He further noted:

> The feelings of love that we are familiar with at the start of a relationship are expected to prevail over a life-time. Romanticism took marriage (hitherto seen as a practical and emotionally temperate union) and fused it together with the passionate love story to create a unique proposition: the life-long passionate love marriage.

The ultimate belief of the romantic is that pure love, something apart from reputation, discussion or logic, is the most precious product of the soul. It is foolish to believe that love wasn't always an important factor in marriage. The poet did not invent love. Love comes naturally from the human heart. But love should never be the one and only element of a marriage.

The romanticism trend allowed the artist to lay out a new design for marriage and for marriage, now defined as a passionate love story, to be a suitable subject for melodrama. Marriage, in this impractical state, could inspire a man and woman to pick bad partners or impose impossible demands on their union.

David Lutz wrote in "The Institution of Marriage and the Virtuous Society":

> The transition from a traditional to liberal society has been accompanied by a transformation in our understanding of marriage from an institutional model to a romantic model. While romantic love is a powerful motivator to form personal relationships, it often fades when those relationships become

rocky. Traditional marriage is a social institution with moral obligations; it forms the core of families, promotes social stability, and endures, fluctuating emotions notwithstanding.[12]

Marriage is the ultimate duty. Duty, which arises out of moral obligations and legal responsibility, stands apart from naked lust and unabashed romance, which are key elements of a melodramatic tale.

David Kelly, an English professor at Sydney University, wrote:

Tony Tanner [author of "Adultery and the Novel: Contract and Transgression"] argued that as the literary form of the novel emerged and evolved concurrently with the bourgeois construction of modern European society it came to concern itself with the contractual character of bourgeois life, exploring and testing this through elements of theme, character and narrative form. In particular, the novel increasingly came to focus upon the marriage contract and. . . infractions of that contract.[13]

American author Tom Perrotta pointed out that the most popular novels of the 19th century often featured unhappy wives who sought romance outside their marriage. The novels included Leo Tolstoy's "Anna Karenina," Gustave Flaubert's "Madame Bovary," D. H. Lawrence's "Lady Chatterley's Lover" and Nathaniel Hawthorne's "The Scarlet Letter."

In the late 1920s and early 1930s, Hollywood filmmakers made it a practice to attract audiences with lurid content. In place of a strong story or compelling characters, filmmakers often relied on explicit depictions of sex and crime. In 1934, The Motion Picture Production Code was instituted to restrict filmmakers from indulging further in this troubling trend. The framers of the Code published the rationale for their regulations in a statement titled "Reasons Underlying the General Principles." As the framers saw it, a film can lower moral standards if wrongdoing is "made to appear attractive and alluring"[14] or the viewer is made to sympathize with the wrongdoing. They noted, "Sympathy with a person who sins is not the same as sympathy with the sin or crime of which he is guilty. We may feel sorry for the plight of the murderer or even understand the circumstances which led him to his crime: we may not feel sympathy with the wrong which he has done."[15] The framers importantly stated, "Even if later in the film the evil is condemned or punished, it must not be allowed to appear so attractive that the audience's emotions are drawn to desire or approve so strongly that later the condemnation is forgotten and only the apparent joy of sin is remembered."[16]

The Motion Picture Producers and Distributors of America were aware that films could depict marital relations in a way that could damage the public's perception of marriage. Frank Capra called Hollywood "this enormous thing that has the tremendous power to move and influence."[17] In 1927, the organization resolved that "special care be exercised" in the manner in which marriage was treated. Later, it was stated in the Production Code:

The sanctity of the institution of marriage and the home shall be upheld. Pictures shall not infer that low forms of sex relationship are the accepted or common thing. Adultery, sometimes necessary plot material, must not be explicitly treated, or justified, or presented attractively.[18]

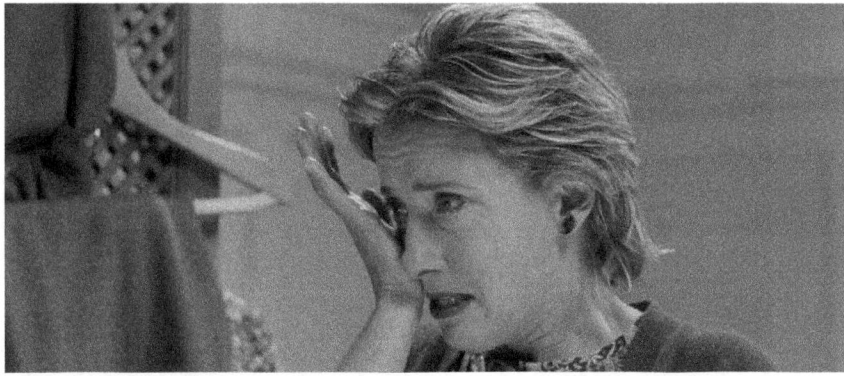

Emma Thompson cries about her cheating husband in *Love Actually* (2003)

The Production Code was explicitly designed to prohibit a film like the post-Code *Love Actually* (2003). Colleen Hehir of Odyssey wrote:

> *Love, Actually* is probably the worst offender out there for romanticizing cheating. A man is in love with his best friend's wife and he thinks it's ok to profess his love to her? And she thinks its ok to return the favor by kissing him on the stoop of her home, which she shares with her husband? And, to top it all off, we all find it incredibly romantic somehow??
>
> Why and how do these plots with unfaithful and repulsive people draw us in and keep our attention? As with many cruel and vile acts, we as a collective people have been desensitized to realities of our world through the so-called entertainment funneled into our homes. From simple adultery being viewed as exciting and even somehow wrapping up in a grand, romantic gesture to a gruesome murder being displayed in any given detective show or horror film, the desensitization of our populations is startling and unsettling.
>
> Cheating and adultery are not exciting, or sexy, or invigorating, at least not for the vast majority. And almost anyone who has been cheated on can attest to the fact that being cheated on certainly is neither invigorating nor exciting, but upsetting, hurtful, and damaging.[19]

This sort of film indeed threatens to numb a person's moral sense. Russian writer Leo Tolstoy recognized this as a problem in 1890. He wrote, "[Marital infidelity] should not be extolled, as it is now, in novels, poetry, songs, operas, etc."[20]

Adultery was certainly romanticized by Hollywood. This is certainly indicated by something a young wife tells her husband in *Saturday's Children*. "You know," she says, "sometimes I almost wish I was somebody else's wife. . . [Then] you'd always want to see me, and we'd have to scheme to meet places and you'd hate the old brute that owned me."

Adultery happens to good marriages. A stable and loving marriage can have a sameness at times. An affair can be, by comparison, fresh and exciting. A marriage can be perfectly sustained by intimacy, tenderness, passion and respect. But do many marriages possess every one of those qualities at all times? It is worrisome that a film can fan the flames of discontent and temptation. Adultery is not beautiful. Adultery is not glamorous. Adultery is not exotic. Adultery is, if we're honest, ugly. And we know, as we watch cinema's adulterers go to extreme lengths to preserve their illicit relationship, that their many misdeeds - sometimes murder - are pretty bad, right? Or do movies blur the moral line in these matters?

Of course, some adultery movies are more sensitive, which we will see in Chapter Thirteen. It is interesting to see a caring and dutiful person engage in a moral struggle with these issues.

Ann Sothern and Kirk Douglas in *A Letter to Three Wives* (1949)

Too often, films about marriage are untrue to rudimentary human instinct. A husband and wife don't have basic marriage skills if they don't know how to avoid drama. A healthy and mature couple will not issue ultimatums. They will not trample across the most sensitive fault lines in their relationship. They will not walk out of their home and make it impossible for their spouse to negotiate a truce. A movie husband and wife act in support of the screenwriter's need to coax out drama. They will let the pettiest misunderstanding tear them apart. Movie marriages are not model marriages. Movie marriages are often the weakest and most unpleasant sort of marriages.

Can we look at the marriage melodrama as a cautionary tale? In a cautionary tale, the protagonist acts as the reader's surrogate and suffers the consequences that the reader would suffer if he acted wrongly in a situation. The writer means for the reader to learn from the protagonist's mistake. A dramatist's study of a marriage can, if reasonable and realistic, improve our perspective on marriage. It could even help us to better understand the wrong or right of our own particular marital arrangement. But the marriage melodrama is rarely reasonable, rarely realistic and, as a result, rarely helpful.

The earliest known film about adultery is a three-act Biograph melodrama called *The Unfaithful Wife* (1903). It is a simple plot, though barely a plot. A young husband returns home unexpectedly and catches his wife with another man. He angrily forces the man out of his home. But, later, the husband finds his wife and the man together again at a dance hall. He wildly attacks the rogue and is promptly ejected from the dance hall for creating a disturbance. At home, the husband pleads with his wife to give up her lover, but she refuses and laughs at him. He becomes crazed. He brings out a revolver and shoots the woman. As she lies dead on the floor, he raises the gun to his head and shoots himself. We will see in films again and again that adultery is a road to madness and death.

Another early adultery film was Vitagraph's *The Deceiver* (1908), which involves an opera singer who carries on an affair with a married woman.

Let's look at a few other early adultery films. In the silent era, the adultery film was pure melodrama. The situations are extremely exaggerated, characterized by fiery lust and bloodthirsty revenge. Adultery provided an ideal motive for a lurid revenge plot.

The Great Breach (1909), a short film produced in France by Pathé Frères, is set in Spain during Napoleon's invasion of Spain in the early 19th century. The story opens with a Spanish nobleman, Count de Feredia (Philippe Garnier), being arrested as a prisoner of war. The Moving Picture World reported:

> Having given his word of honor not to attempt to escape, the Spaniard seeks to beguile the hours among the gay throngs along the avenues where he sees and meets the Countess de Merret, the beautiful wife of the Sub-prefect. Condemned to a monotonous and uneventful life in the quiet province and married to a man in whose stern character [fails] to respond to the joyousness of her own nature, the Countess discovers in the person of Feredia a congenial companion. . .[21]

The Countess (Véra Sergine) brings Feredia home to her boudoir. When her husband (André Calmettes) arrives home unexpectedly, the Countess quickly hides her new lover in the closet. Wikipedia notes:

> Pressured by her suspicious husband, Madame de Merret [swears] upon a crucifix that there [is] no one in the closet, but threaten[s] in turn to leave her husband if he were ever to open the closet out of suspicion. In response, Monsieur de Merret [sends] for a mason to wall up the closet, trapping the lover inside.[22]

The Countess is terrified as she listens to muffled noises coming from the closet. The Moving Picture World reports:

> For twenty days thereafter the Sub-prefect sits at the bedside of his wife, who has succumbed to the frightful ordeal. . . Slowly, with infinite effort, the Countess drags herself from her bed and tottering to the relentless barrier, taps a feeble, last farewell with [an] ebony crucifix, the fateful gift of her lover slowly dying behind the wall.[23]

The Countess had secretly arranged for the mason to break a hole in the wall. She peers into the hole and, according to Wikipedia, "catches a final glimpse of the maddened eyes of her lover."[24]

The film is based on the 1831 short story "La Grande Bretèche" by Honoré de Balzac. It is generally believed by literature historians that the story was the inspiration for Edgar Allen Poe's story "The Cask of Amontillado." D. W. Griffith had produced a less faithful version of "La Grande Bretèche" the same year. The film, *The Sealed Room* (1909), ends with Griffith's vengeful husband walling up the entire chamber so that his wife and her lover are both suffocated. These macabre revenge stories went into a dormancy for four decades, but returned in full force in the 1960s. *Tales of Terror* (1962), a horror anthology film by Roger Corman, includes an extensively reworked adaptation of "The Cask of Amontillado."

In *The Unfaithful Wife* (1915), an Italian nobleman is entombed while still alive by his wife and her lover. Oscar Cooper of Motion Picture News: "He awakens, struggles out of the coffin, and then deliberately plans revenge, ultimately killing the lover in a duel, and sealing up the unfaithful wife in the very tomb where the two had, a few months before, laid him."[25] Cooper believed that, in playing a character motivated by blind vengeance, Mr. Mantell becomes trapped in "a quagmire of melodramatic posing."[26]

In *Above All Law* (1922), an Indian prince (Conrad Veidt) discovers his wife has been unfaithful and determines to bury her alive in an extravagant tomb.

The movie cuckold was a master at perverse revenge schemes. In *Le Cake-walk forcé* (1907), Mr. Walter catches his wife at home with a lover, Robert (René Gréhan). The husband holds a gun on the scoundrel as he forces him to sign the following agreement: "I agree to dance the cake-walk whenever Mr. Walter wishes."

Mr. Walter stalks Robert and, whenever he sees the man with friends or family, he forces him at gunpoint to spring into action with enthusiastic high-stepping. Eventually, Robert tires of being humiliated and obtains his own gun, which he uses to make Mr. Walter dance the cake-walk in a sprawling rain puddle. The man stomps around in the water far less artfully than Gene Kelly would later do in *Singing in the Rain*.

Here is Moving Picture World's plot summary for *Broncho Billy's Mexican Wife* (1912):

> Broncho marries a Mexican girl. . . Later a Mexican singer wins her love and, to get Broncho out of the way, she has him arrested and jailed on the charge of having assaulted her. In a frenzy of rage, Broncho secures the sheriff's revolver, escapes from jail and tracks the pair at his shack. Meanwhile the Mexican singer's sweetheart, jealous of his attentions to Broncho's wife, reaches the shack first and, when Broncho bursts in, gun in hand, he finds the pair dead on the floor, her knife having found both their false hearts.[27]

On the lighter side, Italian comedian Ernesto Vaser makes a pass at a man's wife in a movie theatre in Itala's *Al cinematografo guardate - ma non toccate* (1912).

For *The Cameraman's Reverence* (1912), Russian animator Ladislas Starevich manipulated embalmed insects to create a humorous stop-motion tale of marital betrayal. The story involves Mr. Beetle sneaking away from his wife to enjoy a rendezvous at the Hotel d'Amour with, as described by The Internet Movie Database, "a statuesque dragonfly dancer."[28] Unknown to the couple, the dancer's jealous grasshopper boyfriend follows them to the hotel and films their encounter. An IMDb reviewer, Red-Barracuda, described the climax as follows:

> The Beetles then make up and go to the cinema but lo and behold the projectionist is our grasshopper friend and he splices in footage of the adulterous Mr. Beetle in action. Mrs. Beetle goes crazy and batters him over the head with an umbrella. The fight escalates and ends up in the projection booth catching fire and the Beetles are imprisoned for their actions. In jail they start to make up with one and other.[29]

The plot of *The Ne'er to Return Road* (1913) was typical for its time. Hanson discovers his wife at a dance hall with a lover, Henry Clark (Barney Furey). Enraged, he kills Clark without hesitation or regret.

The characters in a Keystone comedy were notoriously lacking in morals. In *The Man Next Door* (1913), Ford Sterling is reading a book by a window when he notices a neighbor's pretty wife. He thinks nothing of expressing his admiration of the woman with a lascivious grin. Lon Davis, the author of "CHASE! A Tribute to the Keystone Cop," wrote that Sterling became popular at Keystone playing "a shifting array of philanderers."[30]

In Keystone comedies, married men stroll through parks in search of an extramarital romp. Take for example *Getting Acquainted* (1914). In a park, Charlie Chaplin woos a married woman (Mabel Normand) while the woman's husband (Mack Swain) seeks the affections of Charlie's wife (Phyllis Allen). It was as if the bucolic park setting unleashes a mad impulse to commit adultery.

Pa Droppington (Chester Conklin) is smitten by a cabaret dancer in Keystone's *Droppington's Family Tree* (1915).

Adultery was a good excuse for a slapstick brawl. In *Poor Jake's Demise* (Imp, 1913), Jake gets upset when he comes home and catches his wife with another man. In a wild fury, he throws the man through the parlor window. Later, when he sees the man again at a bar, he lets loose on him with a seltzer bottle.

Damaged Goodness (1917) is a short comedy produced by Victor Film Company. A husband learns that his friend plans to dope his coffee so that he can steal his wallet and run off with his wife. The husband pretends to pass out after drinking the coffee. Les Adams of IMDb wrote: "The car breaks down and the bachelor learns that his friend's wife is no bargain. The husband catches up with them and the bachelor agrees to return his wallet if he will also take his wife back. The husband only wants his money back."[31]

In *Humbugs and Husbands* (1918), Larry Semon is visiting a pretty young wife when her cowboy husband arrives home suddenly. He ducks beneath a table, where he cowers as the husband sits at the table for a drink. He struggles to keep still while the husband's spurs repeatedly poke him in the backside. An important element of the adultery film was the fear of exposure.

The Brute (1914) deals with an abusive husband. Black Barton (William Parsons) is unable to control his drinking and often gets violent with his wife (Anne Schaefer) and children (Paul Willis and Janet Vallet) after a day at the saloon. One night, his wife is visited by a childhood friend (William Desmond Taylor). Barton arrives home and jealously spies the visitor through a window. His wife is laughing while watching the visitor play with the children. Barton enters the home and the laughing stops. His wife suddenly looks miserable and the children cower in fear. Barton realizes at this moment that his family cannot be happy with him around. So, he walks to a cliff and leaps to his death.

A defiant and independent wife is at the center of *The Right and the Wrong of It* (1914). Elsie Maynard (Anita Stewart) is bored being married and returns to her old job as a secretary. Her husband, John (E. K. Lincoln), becomes enraged and makes plans to run off with a simple country girl, Dora (Lucille Lee Stewart). But Elsie finds out that she's pregnant and the couple is so excited by the news that they decide to stay together.

Sessue Hayakawa and Fannie Ward in *The Cheat* (1915)

Cecil B. DeMille dug deeply into the melodrama of the adultery film with *The Cheat* (1915). A married society woman, Edith Hardy (Fannie Ward), embezzles money from a Red Cross fund that she manages to buy expensive clothing. A Burmese ivory trader, Hishuru Tori (Sessue Hayakawa), is willing to pay off her debt in exchange for sexual favors.

The Evil Men Do (1915) is melodrama run amok. Beatrice Elton (Marie Weirman) is heartbroken when her childhood sweetheart, David Horton (Maurice Costello), marries Margaret Forsythe (Mary Anderson). David realizes that he married poorly as Margaret's extravagant spending dissipates his finances. Once she sees that her husband has nothing left to offer her, Margaret runs off with a handsome army officer, Captain Clifford (Thomas R. Mills). The officer soon becomes bored with Margaret and deserts her. He meets Beatrice and, not long after, he and Beatrice marry. Margaret tracks down Clifford with a mad obsession to murder him. The couple struggles with a gun and the gun accidentally fires and kills Margaret. Beatrice leaves Clifford, making him so distraught that he kills himself. The film winds through a series of tragedies, including bankruptcy, abandonment, murder, and suicide.

Forbidden Fruit (1915) features another woman who is pressured to exchange sexual favors with an unscrupulous businessman. Ruth Ancaster (Paula Shay) breaks off her engagement with Edward Hemingway (James Cooley), who has cheated on her with other women. She instead marries Edward's best friend, Henry Stuart (Everett Butterfield). Edward resents Ruth for leaving him. He confronts Ruth, telling her that he will turn in her husband for forgery unless she has sex with him.

The Soul Market (1916) involves a coerced marriage. An actress, Elaine Elton (Olga Petrova), is pursued by two passionate suitors. One of the suitors, Oscar Billings (Arthur Hoops), is a powerful businessman who owns several theaters. Pamela Short of IMDb summarized the core of the plot:

> [Oscar] tells Elaine that she will never work again if she refuses to become his wife. Elaine gives in and marries Oscar, but then murders him because of his numerous affairs, after which she herself dies while trying to escape from the police.32

Elaine wakes up and realizes that she had a nightmare.

When False Tongues Speak (1917) involves a treacherous husband. Mary Walton (Virginia Pearson) organizes a settlement home in the slums to distract herself from her husband Fred (Carl Harbaugh) and his various infidelities. Fred wants his wife to leave him so that he can marry his latest mistress. He hopes to find evidence that his wife is cheating on him with Eric Mann (Carl Eckstrom), who has been helping her at the settlement home. The plot is resolved in a tidy manner, with Fred suddenly being killed by a burglar.

The bonds of matrimony are deeply folded into the bonds of humanity, as revealed in *J'accuse!* (1919). During the First World War, François Laurin (Lazare Séverin-Mars) finds himself serving alongside Jean Diaz (Romuald Joubé), a poet who he suspects had an affair with his wife Maria (Maxime Desjardins). In time, the men become close friends. Both men suffer injuries in battle. François dies in a field hospital. Jean, in poor health, returns to his mother's home. He has a grand vision of dead soldiers rising from their graves before he falls dead himself.

An Englishman (Ivor Novello) commits adultery with a Sicilian woman (Desdemona Mazza) in the 1920 French film *The Call of Blood*.

In *Heart's Haven* (1922), a young businessman (Robert McKim) is driven to despair by his unfaithful wife (Claire Adams). Laurence Reid of Motion Picture News wrote, "[T]he youth finds true love with [another] girl when his wife runs away and is killed in an accident."[33]

His Secretary (1925) has a lighter touch. After catching her husband John (Willard Louis) kissing his pretty secretary, Mrs. Sloden (Mabel Van Buren) demands that her husband find himself a less attractive secretary.

Gloria Swanson and Lew Cody in *Don't Change Your Husband* (1919)

Exchange of Wives (1925) brings adultery to the middle-class suburbs. John Rathburn (Lew Cody) is bored with his wife, Margaret (Eleanor Boardman), and takes an interest in Elise Moran (Renee Adoree), a lively lady who lives next door with her unadventurous husband Victor (Creighton Hale). Meanwhile, Margaret and Victor discover that they are more compatible with each other than they are with their spouses.

Cody was dubbed the "He Vamp" by the magazine Motion Picture Classic in 1920. Imogen Sara Smith wrote, "Cody specialized in playing smooth cads and lounge lizards; he has 'Other Man' embroidered on him like a monogram, and a reptilian face that betrays little feeling."[34] Cody's He Vamp can be seen in full force in *Don't Change Your Husband* (1919), *So This is Marriage* (1924) and *Husbands and Lovers* (1924). The plot of *Husbands and Lovers* was ideal for Cody. A neglected housewife, Grace (Florence Vidor), transforms herself into a flapper, drawing inappropriate attention from her husband's smooth-talking best friend Rex Phillips (Cody).

Cody said that he was unwilling to play the old-fashioned stage villain. "[This villain] was everything bad and nothing good," he said. "There was no in-between. But they were not the real sort of people that we meet in drawing rooms or at a dance."[35]

Corinne Griffith regrets marrying Kenneth Harlan in *The Marriage Whirl* (1925)

Three Women (1924) features Cody as, according to Exhibitors Trade Review's George T. Pardy, a "squire of dames." Edmund Lamont (Cody) looks to pay off his debts by marrying a wealthy widow, Mabel Wilton (Pauline Frederick), but he becomes more interested in Mabel's lovely daughter, Jeanne (May McAvoy). Lamont loses interest in Jeanne once they are married. Seeking new thrills, he carries on an affair with a fun-loving flapper, Harriet (Marie Prevost). Jeanne, neglected by her husband, falls in love with a young doctor, Fred Armstrong (Pierre Gendron). She asks Lamont for a divorce so that she can marry Fred, but he hasn't gotten to spend all of her money yet and he coolly refuses her request. Mabel frees her daughter from her unscrupulous husband by fatally shooting him.

The "marry wisely" lesson applies to *The Marriage Whirl* (1925). Marian (Corinne Griffith) marries Arthur on the condition he stop going to parties and settles down. Frank Fob of IMDb wrote, "It isn't long before he becomes restless, though, and takes up with a flashy [cabaret] dancer [Nita Naldi]. Feeling neglected, Marian meets up with a former boyfriend, Bob. Complications ensue."[36]

The best-known adultery film of the silent era is *Sunrise* (1927), which is based on the 1917 novella "The Excursion to Tilsit" by German author Hermann Sudermann. Kelly provided the set up to the story:

> The Woman from the City [Margaret Livingston] urges The Man [George O'Brien] to murder his wife
> - a fair, meek, dutiful and loving mother - to sell his farm, and to come with her to the city. . .[37]

The seduction scene can linger the most in the viewer's mind. The evil seductress is proud to see how her legs look in her black stockings. She takes a long puff on her cigarette before she steps outdoors into the night. She stands outside The Man's cottage and whistles for him. The sound of the whistles torments him. He is gloomy and distressed, but he cannot resist the siren's call. He acts like he's in a trance as he leaves his home to meet her. The camera tracks him through a foggy, moonlit marsh in a scene that can best be described as nightmarish. Filmsite notes:

. . . [T[he thicket of vegetation opens up on both sides to reveal her dark figure waiting for him and sil-houetted against the moon. She twirls a flower in her hand and then tosses it away (a symbol of nature and the country that she despises). The temptress primps in a mirror held in her purse and applies make-up.[38]

As soon as reaches her, The Man seizes her in his arms and kisses her. Filmsite continues, ". . . [S]he steals his sanity and soul as she literally pulls him down into the swamp."[39] Roger Ebert wrote, ". . . [W]hen his wife returns to the table with their dinner, he is gone, and the movie juxtaposes her embracing their child and the woman from the city embracing him."[40]

The Woman asks him to sell his farm and come to the city with her. He is worried what he should do about his wife. The Woman laughs. "Couldn't she get drowned?" she asks.

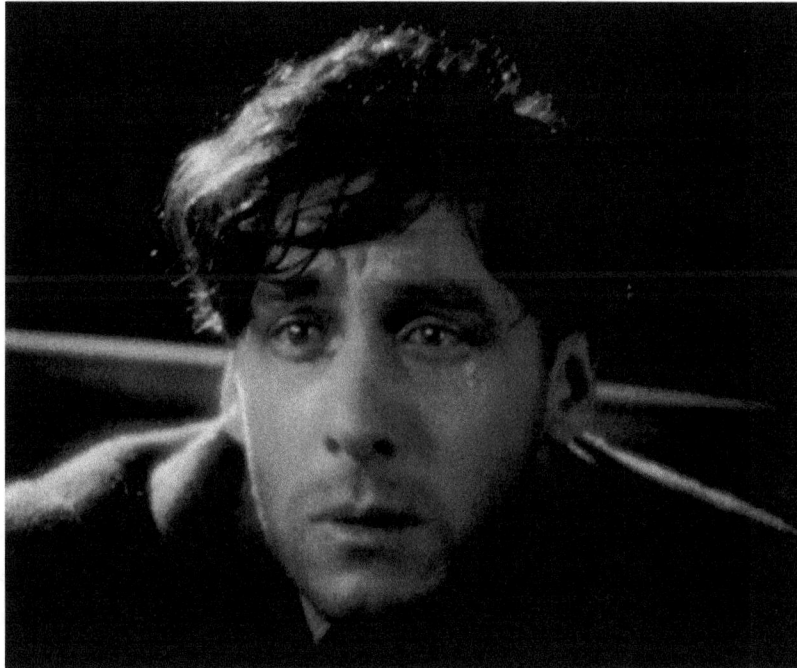

George O'Brien in *Sunrise* (1927)

Later, when The Man is back home, The Woman lingers in his mind as a frightful phantom grasping at him. Nothing exists between this man and woman other than lust. Lust without moral restraints has brought about a fever dream.

The Man takes The Wife out on a lake with a rowboat. He stares at his wife with a dark look in his eyes. He stands unexpectedly and lumbers towards her. She senses that she is in danger. She cowers beneath her husband, pleading for her life. Church bells break him out of his deadly trance. He sits down again and quickly rows the boat to the village.

The TV Guide website noted:

The sequence where the man and his wife reconcile after watching the wedding in a church, and the street traffic dissolves into a field of flowers as they're lost in the reverie of their kiss, is one of the most sublime moments in cinema.[41]

The couple finds that their renewed commitment makes them stronger than ever. Martin Scorsese said, "The broken couple is reunited. Fear and guilt fade away. They become invulnerable. Nothing can harm them anymore."[42]

The couple celebrates their reunion at a carnival. Their ebullience is ideally expressed in a gleaming fireworks show. Emotions, just as the chemical elements in fireworks, are combustible materials. Love, kindness and generosity can mix together like carbon, sulphur and potassium. At one time, Chinese people believed that fireworks could expel evil spirits and bring about luck and happiness.

On their journey home, a storm capsizes their boat. The raging storm fits well into a story about raging passions. Again, the passion that arises out of love or hate is elemental. It embodies the powers of nature in the same way that a storm does. Storms got stirred up in later adultery films, including *When Tomorrow Comes* (1939), *Stormy Waters* (1941), *Day of Wrath* (1943), *I Know Where I'm Going!* (1945) and *The Ice Storm* (1997).

The Man swims to shore, but his wife goes missing. He encounters the city woman, who assumes that he murdered his wife. He begins to strangle the evil temptress, but his maid calls out that his wife has been found. He rushes to his wife and is overjoyed to find that she is still alive. The film ends with the wife awakening in bed next to her husband and child.

In the original story, the man drowns when the sailboat is overturned. The author saw the need to punish the errant husband despite his repentance.

Ebert wrote in his review of *Sunrise*, "[S]ilent films had a language of their own; they aimed for the emotions, not the mind, and the best of them wanted to be, not a story, but an experience."[43]

The Way of Lost Souls (1929)

Louise (Paola Negri) works as a prostitute in a seaport town. Today, she hangs out at a seedy bar, perpetually perusing the room in search of a potential customer. She spots John (Hans Rehmann), the lighthouse keeper. It's time to get to work. She spits on her palms, straightens her jacket, and swaggers toward him. He ignores her, his only concern being to eat his sandwich. She tickles his nose with her feather boa and, when this fails to illicit a response, hops into his lap. But he remains uninterested. She finally walks away and is confronted by her disappointed pimp, Max (Warwick Ward). John intervenes when Max gets rough with Louise. The pimp pulls out a knife, but John knocks him cold with a swift and powerful punch to the jaw. Louise begs John to take her away from her wretched life. "Take me, take me," she cries out. He refuses.

John finds himself in peril when his boat is overturned in a storm. He prays, "Save me, Lord! And I will save the more unfortunate of your creatures." The storm instantly settles. The dark clouds part, allowing a bright shaft of light to shine down from the heavens. John now understands that he owes a debt to God. So, he marries the unfortunate Louise and takes her to live with him in his lighthouse. It takes time for her to adjust to being a housewife, but she comes to find happiness in her new life.

Just when everything is going well, Max shows up at the lighthouse while Louise is alone. Louise begs him to go away, but he refuses. He admits to being wanted by the police (although he doesn't say why). Louise hides him to avoid John finding out he'd been there. But John catches Louise with Max and assumes that Louise kept him from the police because she loves him. He becomes enraged. "Go away, whore!" he commands. John grapples with Max, who stabs him to get away. The police arrive and capture their fugitive. Meanwhile, Louise rows out into a turbulent sea. A wave overturns her boat and she drowns.

The silent film era was near its end when *The Way of Lost Souls* was released. The film features the sort of pure and shameless melodrama that was to become somewhat rare in the coming years.

Chapter One:
The Social Damage of Adultery

Charlton Heston and Susan Hayward in *The President's Lady* (1953)

Let us start with a woman who was branded "The Adulteress" in 1880s America: Rachel Donaldson Jackson. Andrew Jackson, the seventh president of the United States, regarded Rachel as the great love of his life. His 34-year marriage to Rachel is fondly dramatized in *The President's Lady* (1953), which featured Charlton Heston as Jackson and Susan Hayward as Rachel. The Jacksons' story clearly shows that adultery could become a public issue.

Rachel originally married Lewis Robards, a land speculator, in 1785. The wedding ceremony took place in Harrodsburg, Kentucky, after which the couple settled on a farm. Robards had money troubles, which put a strain on their marriage. In later years, he was more prosperous as a militia captain and a merchant. But financial woes followed him throughout his life.

Robards was an abusive husband. Ann Toplovich of the Tennessee Historical Society exhaustively investigated the subject. She noted: "[His brother] George's wife Elizabeth Sampson would support some of the more damning stories about Lewis in the Nashville Committee affidavits of 1827 – that he was violently jealous and that he frequented the slave quarters at night."[44] The film shows Robards (Whitfield Connor) telling a young slave woman (Vera Francis) that Rachel suspects them of carrying on together and it would be best for her to stay at his cousin's home until her suspicions died down.

Serious marital problems were evident by 1787. Rachel developed a relationship with a boarder, Peyton Short, who was heir to a plantation fortune. John Overton visited his brother James, who was also a boarder at the Robards' home. He found that Robards was angry because he believed that his wife was engaged in an affair with Short. His brother informed him that "great uneasiness had existed in the family for some time before my arrival."[45] Robards wrote to Rachel's mother that he was no longer willing to live with Rachel and he intended to send her back to her family in Nashville.

Toplovich wrote:

There was something to Robards's suspicions. Short later confessed to his friend Henry Banks that he had great "sympathy" for Rachel and determined to marry her after her separation from Robards. He planned on converting his inheritance into money or slaves "and if Mrs. Robards would accept him as a husband, to go with her to the Spanish Dominions on the Mississippi; and there to settle himself for life." As fate would have it, Robards intercepted the letter from Short that held this offer and pursued Short to Virginia. In Richmond, Short offered Robards either the satisfaction of a duel or a pay off with money. Robards settled for $1,000.[46]

In late summer of 1788, Rachel's brother Samuel came for her and they traveled to their mother's home in Nashville. The Robards contended Rachel had simply gone to visit her family, but Jackson always insisted that Robards had thrown her out. It became important in the debate that transpired years later whether Rachel was cast out by her husband or whether she deserted her husband.

Rachel stayed at her mother's home. One of her mother's boarders at the time was a 21-year-old attorney, Andrew Jackson. Toplovich wrote, "By the summer of 1789, Rachel's friendship with Jackson caused such gossip that Short heard Rachel was involved with him and he married another woman. That same summer witnesses saw stormy arguments between Robards and Rachel as well as altercations between Robards and Jackson – in a blackberry patch, in an orchard."[47]

Jackson traveled to nearby Natchez, a Spanish territory, to pledge his allegiance to the King of Spain and thereby obtain citizenship rights outside of the United States. This was an obvious ploy on his part, for Rachel's marriage to Robards was not legally recognized by Spanish authorities and Jackson could now elope with his married lover to Natchez without fear of legal consequences. In July 1790, Jackson and Rachel traveled to Natchez with several people, including military officer Hugh McGary. Toplovich wrote, "[McGary] gave Robards the eyewitness he needed to Jackson and Rachel's 'bedding together.'"[48] Jackson said that he and Rachel had married upon their arrival in Natchez, although no record of a marriage has ever been found.

Robards accused Jackson of stealing Rachel and committing adultery by living with her. Despite Jackson's legal maneuvering, allegations of Rachel's abandonment still had to be settled in Tennessee. Jackson claimed that, prior to their departure from Nashville, he was told by friends that Roberts had obtained a divorce. He was, he said, surprised to learn that no divorce had occurred. Regardless of the legal and ethical questions, Toplovich notes that "the vivacious Rachel shed herself of a problem husband."[49]

Let us assume for the moment that Jackson had married Rachel while she was still married to Robards. It certainly raises a question of bigamy. But, at the time, bigamy was common in backcountry areas of the United States. People often abandoned a legal spouse and remarried. Toplovich wrote, "From the founding of the American republic, the new states wrestled with their citizens' desires to be freed from failed marriages."[50] She added:

[Charles Woodmason] noted that "colonists formed and dissolved cohabitational relationships without observing mar-tial formalities." However, as long as the community accepted their unions, backcountry folk cared little for these condemnations from Anglican ministers. . . As early as 1778, the North Carolina state assembly passed a law regulating the "rites of matrimony" in an attempt to curtail extra-legal, self-declared unions.[51]

Robards took the matter of Jackson and Raquel's cohabitation to court. Toplovich wrote, "The divorce and trial were undoubtedly the talk of Kentucky – news and gossip traveled fast where marital scandal was involved. . . [T]here is clear evidence that members of the wider Tennessee community saw Rachel as a fallen woman and Jackson as a rake for many years afterward."[52] Robards finally secured a divorce in 1794, after which Rachel married Jackson in a private ceremony. In the meantime, Rachel was branded an adulteress. Gossip on the matter plagued the woman for the rest of her life. In 1806, Charles Dickinson was killed by Jackson in a duel for calling Rachel a bigamist. Accusations of adultery were renewed when Jackson campaigned for president in 1828. Charles Hammond of the Cincinnati Gazette wrote on March 23, 1827:

> [N]o man can succeed to a place of high trust who. . . stands condemned as the seducer of other men's wives, and the de-stroyer of female character. . . [Should we] give sanction to conduct, which is calculated to unhinge the fundamental principles of society?. . . Let all inducements to the maintenance of conjugal fidelity be broken down: let all veneration for the marriage state and covenant be destroyed; and let me then ask, what there is in social life worthy of regard?. . . Show to the world your abhorrence of a man, who disregards the laws which even savages revere."[53]

Rachel died three months before Jackson's inauguration. Jackson engraved on her tombstone: "A being so gentle and so virtuous, slander might wound but could not dishonor."

Toplovich wrote:

> In the face of the hard legal evidence that Andrew Jackson had eloped with Rachel while she was still very much married and that they had indeed lived in adultery, the Jackson partisans prevailed with their position that marriage should be "romantic and private with a distinct preference for heartfelt sentiments over precise legal forms". . . [T]oday they are legendary lovers. If Andrew Jackson is admired for anything, even by his most determined critics, it is for his devoted marriage to Rachel and his vigorous defense of her reputation.[54]

The Divine Lady (1929) dramatizes an 18th-century affair that is one of the most notorious tales in British history. Lady Hamilton, the beautiful wife of Sir William Hamilton, developed a romantic relationship with Vice-Admiral Horatio Nelson, who himself was married to the loving and devoted Fanny Nisbet.

Lady Hamilton became Nelson's political facilitator. Ellen Eineck, a curatorial assistant at London's National Maritime Museum, wrote:

> It is believed that Emma's influence helped to have British ships resupplied before the Battle of the Nile in 1798. Nelson had attempted to re-provision his fleet at Syracuse in Sicily. He was refused entry by the governor, as it was against the terms of the treaty between Naples and France. Nelson asked Sir William for help, though Flora Fraser argues that it was Emma who advanced his cause. She persuaded Maria Carolina [Queen of Naples] to have her husband provide the fleet with the necessary document. . . Emma's intervention proved crucial.[55]

In his will, Nelson left instructions for Lady Hamilton to receive money and asked that his mistress be allowed to sing at his funeral. But the woman was denied money, which she desperately needed at the time, and was barred from attending the funeral.

Nelson and Hamilton's affair was dramatized again in *That Hamilton Woman* (1941).

Other adultery stories had great historical value.

Ernst Lubitsch's *Passion* (1919) relates the story of Madame DuBarry (Pola Negri), the mistress of Louis XV of France, during the time of the French revolution. This, too, was a great scandal in its day.

So, marriage is at once private and public. We marry in public before family and friends because the institution has a public interest.

The Baker's Wife (1938) was based on the novel "Blue Boy." The author, Jean Giono, based the bucolic setting ("made up of meadows and fair orchards"[56]) on his own childhood town. A picturesque and normally peaceful village is sent into an uproar when the baker, Aimable (Raimu), learns that his young wife Aurélie (Ginette Leclerc) has run off with a handsome shepherd (Charles Moulin).

The village is a microcosm of society. Society as a whole benefits from a faithful marriage. Stable families provide a solid foundation on which a society thrives. Leo Tolstoy called marriage "the keystone of the whole edifice of life."[57] The village understandably suffers as the baker is too distraught to make bread for the residents.

The town leaders realize that they need to take action. They divide the surrounding countryside into six sections, each of which is assigned to a patrol group. Dozens of men scour the area as if it's a military exercise. Once a patrol group spots the couple, a priest and a schoolteacher are dispatched to approach the baker's wife and offer her their counsel.

Wikipedia reports: "[Aimable] forgives her . . ., though he can't resist a few choice words about randy young shepherds who charm you, love you and leave you. Together they light the oven, so that the village will have bread in the morning."[58]

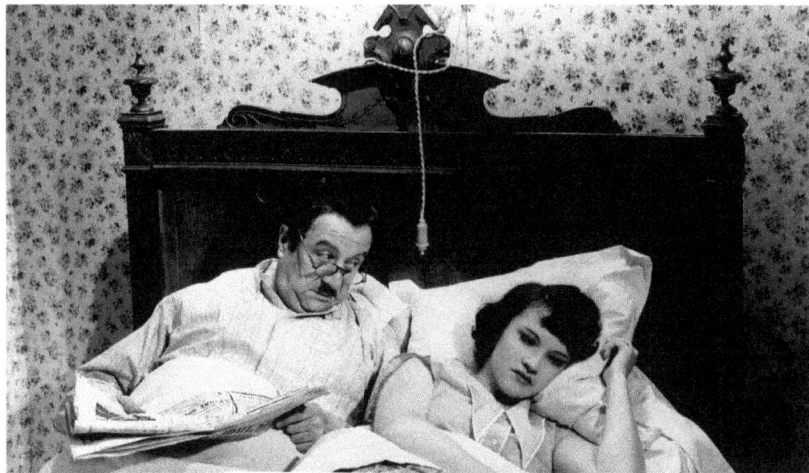

Raimu and Ginette Leclerc in *The Baker's Wife* (1938)

The vast majority of adultery films are personal stories, but an adulterous affair can often sprout tentacles that reach out and touch many other people. In one way or another, everyone has a stake in the success or failure of a marriage. The state of society is in many ways shaped by marriage trends. Good marriages and strong families support the well-being of communities. In 1890, Tolstoy wrote:

> . . . [I]t is necessary that the violation of a promise of fidelity, given at marriage, should be punished by public opinion certainly in no lesser degree than are punished the violations of monetary obligations and mercantile frauds. . .

Screenwriters have managed for more than one-hundred years to examine and debate the importance of marital fidelity.

Chapter Two:
Understanding Adultery

Frank Pittman, author of "Private Lies: Infidelity and the Betrayal of Intimacy," conducted a study of adultery. He wrote that thirty of the forty unfaithful men and women in his sample found that sex at home was acceptable, but they complained of having little or no intimacy. Pittman wrote, "Affairs were thus three times more likely to be pursuit of a buddy than the pursuit of a better orgasm."[59]

In *Little Children* (2006), Brad Adamson (Patrick Wilson) isn't drawn into an affair with Sara Pierce (Kate Winslet) out of sexual arousal. An unseen narrator of says:

> It didn't seem to matter that Sarah wasn't his type, wasn't even that pretty - at least not compared to [his wife] Kathy, who had long legs and lustrous hair and perfect breasts. Sarah was short, boyish, and had eyebrows that were thicker than Brad thought necessary. But even so, she'd walked into his arms that day as if she were fulfilling a secret wish he hadn't remembered making.

The couple is held together mostly by an emotional connection.

Adultery can often start with emotional bonds, which is something that becomes obvious in *The Bishop's Wife* (1947). Dudley (Cary Grant), an angel, has come to earth incognito to assist a troubled bishop. He manages during his visit to form a close bond with the bishop's wife, Julie (Loretta Young). This creates a conflict for him after he finishes his mission and prepares to leave. He doesn't want to part from Julie.

> Dudley: Few people know the secret of making a heaven here on Earth. You are one of those rare people.

Julia: I think you ought to go.

Dudley: No. Please, Julia. Don't send me away.

Julia: What are you saying, Dudley?

Dudley: I'm tired of being a wanderer. I'm tired of an existence where one is neither hot nor cold, hungry nor full.

Julia: No. No. No, you must go away. And never come back.

Julia understands that a serious line has been crossed. The feelings that Dudley has expressed are frightfully wrong.

In *Day-Time Wife* (1939), Jane Norton is shocked to learn that her husband Ken is romancing his secretary. She tells her friend Blanche:

If a woman can't hold her man, then it's her own fault. But I'm going to hold mine. . . [I]f I find the cause, then I'll know the cure. Blanche, I'm going to do some research that even the Carnegie Institute never heard of. I'm going to find out just what it is that secretaries have that wives haven't.

In the end, Blanche is eager to know what Jane has learned. What advantages does the secretary have? Jane says, "Blanche, there's a little of the wandering minstrel in every man. And if you don't hold his interest, he's bound to go whistling under other people's balconies." We sat through 72 minutes to learn that a wife has to keep her marriage exciting to keep her husband from straying. This is not a profound, or necessarily accurate, revelation.

Surely, we need a more dogged investigator on the case. A promising candidate is Marilyn Parker (Linda Watkins), who goes undercover to investigate adultery in *Good Sport* (1931).

Marilyn is astonished to learn her husband Rex (Alan Dinehart) will be accompanied on a three-month business trip to Europe with a pretty mistress, Peggy Bums (Greta Nissen). She can't understand how this could have happened. Why would a husband turn to a mistress? How could a husband deceive his wife? What motivates a woman to go with a married man? She is determined to find answers. She infiltrates a nest of gold diggers to understand their motivations and methods and figure out the reason they could make a man stray from a happy marriage.

The mistresses occupy a torrid underworld in which they enjoy nonstop liquor-fueled parties. Marilyn participates in the party life. In the process, she falls in love with bachelor millionaire, Boyce Cameron (John Boles). But she is determined to remain a faithful wife and wards off his advances. Meanwhile, Rex returns from Europe with news that his business has suffered grave set-backs and he is about to lose his fortune. Marilyn is willing to help her husband by selling off her personal property. She figures that they'll do better to weather this crisis without the mistress. But, when she goes to confront the woman, she finds Rex in her apartment. She decides at this point to leave Rex for Boyce.

A similar plot turned up many years later in *Ni tuyo, Ni mía* (2020). The plot summary according to IMDb is as follows: "Amanda realizes that her perfect husband is having an affair. Instead of confronting him, she teams up with his husband's lover to understand what went wrong and win him back."[60]

Joan Bennett and John Boles in *Careless Lady* (1932)

Careless Lady (1932)

The film manages, in its own farcical way, to delve into the psychology of adultery. Is there something in the psychology of a man that can draw him to a married woman?

Sally Brown (Joan Bennett) is convinced by a friend that men find virgins to be unexciting. She wants men to think that she's experienced without them thinking she's *too* experienced. So, she pretends to be a married woman by embarking on an ocean voyage as the fictions Mrs. Illington. Men do in fact find her more interesting now. A perennial IMDb reviewer, Martin Hafer (also known as planktonrules), wrote:

"There is a problem, however. . . soon Mr. Illington (John Boles) arrives. . . and he's quite amused to discover he has a wife!"[61]

Linda Darnell, Ann Sothern and Jeanne Crain in *A Letter to Three Wives* (1949)

A Letter to Three Wives (1949)

Erickson wrote:

Three wives, played by Jeanne Crain, Ann Sothern and Linda Darnell, are about to embark on a boat trip when each receives a letter, written by a mutual friend named Addie, informing her that Addie is about to run off with one of their husbands. In flashback, each wife wonders if it is her marriage that is in jeopardy.[62]

In this situation, an adultery film is fashioned into a fabulous whodunit without the gruesome presence of a murder victim. Still, Addie's letter is treated by the wives as a death notice. The film climaxes with most of the main characters meeting up at a nightclub. The scene essentially serves as a post-mortem. Rita Phipps says, "There's a fine, relaxed atmosphere at this table - as if there were a body hidden under it." The film's portrayal of the three marriages allows the viewer the opportunity to examine factors that could cause a husband to stray from their marriage. Deborah Bishop (Crain), who was raised on a farm, doesn't feel that she can ever be accepted among her husband's more sophisticated friends. Rita Phipps (Sothern), who has a busy job writing radio soap operas, is so preoccupied with her work that she regularly neglects her husband George (Kirk Douglas). It bothers George even more that she earns more money than he does. He tells her, "I'll admit it has upset my male ego from time to time." Lora Mae Hollingsway (Darnell) has never made her husband Porter (Paul Douglas), the owner of a department store chain, feel that she truly loves him. Porter believes that she unfairly pressured him to marry her. This is reflected in his marriage proposal: "Okay, you win, I'll marry you." The fact that Lora Mae has never been outwardly affectionate to him confirms to her well-to-do mate that she married him for his bank account. He sees her as manipulative and mercenary. He says that she is "plenty smart" and "made a good deal" in marrying him.

Porter: To you, I'm a cash register. You can't love a cash register.

Lora Mae: And I'm part of your inventory. You can't love that either.

We hear dialogue from Rita's hokey radio melodrama, *Linda Gray, Registered Nurse*. Ms. Gray says, "What small-town American girl would not be at a proposal of marriage from a gentleman as distinguished as you. But I must decline, with thanks. We have Lady Bruce to consider, invalid though she is and though you've been married in name only for many years she is your wife in sickness as she was in health and must not be cast aside."

But *A Letter to Three Wives* is not a melodrama. Joseph L. Mankiewicz, the film's writer and director, is seeking a more natural and truthful exploration of marital infidelity. He is, in fact, mocking the old adultery melodramas for being so absurd.

We never see the interloper, Addie, although we hear a lot about her. Also, interestingly, she narrates the first act of the film.

Porter is the husband who ran off with Addie, but he realized that he made a mistake and came back home to Lora Mae. We hear a sadness in Addie's voice-over as she provides a brief sign-off: "Hi-ho."

The film suggests that a husband and wife must maintain a delicate balance of power and provide one another with attention, affection, trust and affirmation.

Black Ice (2007)

The original Finnish title: *Musta jää*

Saara (Outi Mäenpää) has a busy practice as a gynecologist. She takes her focus away from her work long enough to realize that her husband Leo (Martti Suosalo) is dating a younger woman, Tuuli (Ria Kataja). Saara adopts a false identity so that she can befriend Tuuli and figure out what it is about this woman that appeals to her husband. She becomes deeply committed to helping Tuuli when she learns that the woman is pregnant with Leo's child.

The Other Man (2008)

Peter Ryman (Liam Neeson) suspects that his deceased wife Lisa (Laura Linney) had an affair. He snoops around on her computer and finds photos of her naked with another man. Lisa carried on the affair in Milan, where she often went on business. Flashbacks explore Peter and Lisa's marriage. Lisa felt guilty about her infidelity and wanted to confess to Peter about it. But she couldn't do it. She told Peter, "I do love you, you know. You do know that, don't you?" Peter cared for Lisa while she was dying and kept up her spirits. He told Lisa, "Write down somewhere we've never been that I could take you to." She selects Lake Como, a popular retreat for wealthy people in Italy. Knowledge of the affair taints Peter's memories of their marriage. The mourning widower wonders if his wife truly loved him. He needs answers. He flies to Milan to meet Lisa's lover, Ralph Cortés (Antonio Banderas). He follows Ralph to a cafe and, without revealing his identity, starts a friendly conversation with him. He gets him to talk at length about his twelve-year affair with Lisa. Lisa had ended their relationship without telling Ralph that she had contracted cancer. He has no idea that she's dead. Peter learns that Lisa and Ralph frequented Lake Como. Was Lisa at her happiest being with Ralph in Lake Como? Peter's daughter, Abigail (Romola Garai), is worried about her father and catches up with him in Milan. She finds her father in great turmoil. His feelings of hurt and confusion have grown to frightening proportions. Peter realizes that Lisa reached a level of passion with Ralph that she never reached with him. He tells Abigail, "We never spent days and nights in bed together." He continues, "I was always faithful to her. I thought we were close. I thought we told each other everything. But she was a different person. She must have been." Abigail tries to reason with him, but he is overwhelmed with emotion. She finally breaks down in tears. "I can't take it anymore!" she shouts. "Just let it go!" Peter plans to murder Ralph, but he changes his mind at the last moment. In the end, Peter resolves his anger and toasts Lisa at a memorial dinner. Lisa remains a mystery at the end of the story. She left behind several clues of her affair - photos, a phone message, a note. Why? The strange, downhearted and confusing film was a bomb at the box office.

Chapter Three:
The Open Marriage

Bette Davis and Monroe Owsley in *Ex-Lady* (1933)

The vow to forsake others, part of the "Declaration of Consent," is a key to a strong marriage. But, in an open marriage, a husband and wife consent to having sexual relationships outside of the marriage. Jessica Burke of The Federalist spoke to a woman who persuaded her husband to engage in an open marriage. As it turned out, the woman deeply regretted taking this path. She said, "[It] caused a lot of pain, so I'm still not even sure why I fought for it the way I did. . . I really just felt like it was right, like it was important to my growth. It was like I was choosing to take a stand for my own pleasure and sticking to it. It was strong, that feeling."[63]

The idea of a free and open marriage was explored in films during the 1930s.

Smart Woman (1931)

Nancy Gibson (Mary Astor) returns home after visiting her sick mother in Paris. She learns that, in her absence, her husband Donald Gibson (Robert Ames) has taken up with a mistress, Peggy Preston (Noel Francis). Nancy refuses to make a fuss about her husband's infidelity. She chooses instead to be a modern wife and welcome Peggy to her home for the weekend. But Nancy is a smart woman (see the film's title) and she is not about to let her marriage be undone so easily. The free thinking that she alleges is merely a ruse, for Nancy has every intention to regain her husband's affections and get rid of the brazen homewrecker. In the meantime, Nancy and Peggy exchange a lot of modern talk, for instance:

Nancy: It's so nice and modern not to care whose husband belongs to who.

Peggy: And, after all, people can't help being in love, can they?

Nancy: That's the only trouble with being in love. People can't help it.

She pretends that she herself has fallen for a man that she met in Europe. She invites Sir Guy Harrington (John Halliday), who she met on the voyage home, to spend the weekend at her home and act as if he's in love with her.

Consolation Marriage (1931)

Sports reporter Steve Porter (Pat O'Brien) excitedly returns from a job overseas expecting to marry heiress Elaine Brandon (Myrna Loy). But Elaine greets him in the foyer of her opulent home to reveal a change of plans. She met another man while he was away and she and the man are now married. Elsewhere, shopkeeper Mary Brown (Irene Dunne) bids farewell to her lover Aubrey (Lester Vail), a classical pianist who is off to marry a high-society woman who has the resources and connections to advance his career. The jilted lovers are brought together by their mutual heartbreak. Mary is feeding milk to her new puppy when Steve gets an idea. He says, "Why don't we get married and give him a couple of good parents? Why not? What could we lose? Sure, getting married is no big leap for a couple of booby prizes like us. Might even give us a chuckle or two."

Marrying for "a chuckle or two" means marrying without passion or devotion. The two agree that their hearts belong to their lost loves, who are their only true loves. It is a rather childish view of romantic love. But their alleged lack of passion and devotion doesn't stop them from having a baby together.

In the second act, the film turns into another open marriage story. Steve's old lover returns to him, which puts the marriage in jeopardy. But Mary is unfazed. She tells her old friend Jeff (John Halliday), "You know how it is with Steve and me, Jeff. If either of us strays [to our lost love], well, it's just a case of return to owner and no questions asked." The wife and mistress have a friendly conversation.

Then, Mary's old lover returns. Mary is prepared to leave her husband and child for him. She explains to her baby (really to the audience) her philosophy:

I want to go away with someone who loves me very much - someone who wants me more than anyone will ever want me again. And, if I go, what difference would it make to you? None. You won't suffer. A baby doesn't need its mother half as much as a mother likes to think. After all, a baby is only an episode in a woman's life - an episode that grows up and goes on and forgets. Twenty years from now, if I told you I'd given up happiness for you, you'd call it pretty old-fashioned. You'd think I was blaming you. And I might be. You'd say, 'Why didn't you go?' Now wouldn't you? I'm going. No, I'm not going to cry. That would be the usual thing. And I'm not doing the usual thing. I'm doing what millions of women have wanted to do and didn't have the courage."

She changes her mind and returns home. She and Steve talk and agree to stay together. She now tells her baby:

You didn't hear what mamma said, did you? She didn't mean it, darling. No, no, she was just talking. Just raving. You, an episode? Why, you're everything! You're the world! I love you!

This last-minute turnaround allows Mary to embrace common traditional values before the final fade-out. In general, film historian Jeanine Basinger questioned if this sort of abrupt reversal within the last five minutes of a film should define a character more than everything else we have been shown in the previous eighty-five minutes.

Illicit (1931)

An ad read, "Can a woman hold a man without marriage?"

Anne Vincent (Barbara Stanwyck) rejects a marriage proposal from her boyfriend, Dick Ives II (James Rennie). She has no interest in having a husband or having children. She sees Dick as an ideal playmate and that's all that she really wants. Her fear is that their marriage will replace love with duty. As she sees it, the obligations that marriage imposes on a husband and wife will make it impossible for them to truly enjoy their relationship. Dick is tired of arguing with Anne about getting married. The two separate for a while, but they decide they love each other and want to stay together. Erickson wrote, "Sure enough, when Annie and Dick do tie the knot, they immediately begin fooling around with others."[64] Anne tells Dick, "Something's gone. I don't know. The spark's gone out of it. We used to be gay and young together. Now we're only gay when we are around other people." An old boyfriend, Price Baines (Ricardo Cortez), is still in love with Anne and thinks that she should leave her husband for him. He tells her, "When you have all you can stand of marriage, I'll be waiting as always. I love you, Ann. I always have and I always will." He leans close to her, desperate for a kiss, but she draws away from him. Resentful of Anne's relationship with Price, Dick begins to date an old friend, Margie True (Natalie Moorhead). In the end, Anne and Dick drop their lovers and commit themselves to their marriage.

In contrast to these open marriage stories, *Heller in Tights* (1960) presents a couple that is extremely tight-knit and generally excludes others from their relationship. Lust can be rather trivial thing when set against the great love and loyalty that this couple feels towards one another. But the couple isn't married. So, at least according to this film, fidelity doesn't only exist when a couple has a legally binding agreement.

Ex-Lady (1933)

Helen Bauer (Bette Davis), a successful commercial artist, regards marriage as too restrictive to suit the liberal attitudes of modern folk. She lives happily with her boyfriend, Don Peterson (Gene Raymond). Ignoring her protests about marriage, Don eventually convinces her to marry him. Later, Don is enticed into an affair by a married woman, Peggy Smith (Kay Strozzi). Meanwhile, Helen begins dating a playboy, Nick Malvyn (Monroe Owsley). In the end, the couple agrees to end their extramarital relationships and give their marriage another chance.

Here is the debate that Helen and Don have when Don asks Helen to marry him.

Helen: I went away from home to be on my own. I don't want to be like my mother, a yes-woman for some man. I want to be a person on my own. If I like to live a certain way, and have a certain kind of furniture, do a certain kind of work, and wear a certain kind of clothes, I want to do it. And not have somebody tell me I ought to do something else.

Don: No one is going to tell you.

Helen: Oh, yes, you are. If you're married. That's what being married means. You must do what the other person wants. You must please them. Marriage means. . . Oh, I've said it 50 times, Don. It's dull. I'm not going to say it again. . . We have a different sense of values. I don't want babies. When I'm 40, I'll think of babies. In the meantime, there are 20 years in which I want to be the baby and play with my toys, and have a good time playing with them.

Don: A career.

Helen: Oh, it isn't just that. Sure, I want to do good work. But it isn't that. I want to stay young for a while and have a good time. And not be dull and set. I don't want to be a wife.

When Ladies Meet (1933)

A novelist, Mary Howard (Myrna Loy), is having an affair with her married publisher, Rogers Woodruf (Frank Morgan). A great debate about adultery is waged from beginning to end in the film.

Mary's best friend, Bridget "Bridgie" Drake (Alice Brady), suspects that Mary has been dating Rogers, who has been a frequent visitor to her home. Mary vehemently denies it. "What do you think I am?" she asks. "He's a married man." Bridgie casually responds, "Of course, he is. The good ones always are. Someone has always beaten you to it." Mary becomes annoyed, but Bridgie persists on the subject. She says that Rogers is "terribly attractive" and "life is flying by terribly fast." "Why not?" she asks. "Why control yourself? Nobody else does." Mary expresses concern for Rogers' wife. "Well," says Bridgie. "you don't know her and they say she's an awful dub." Bridgie is not the best person to dispense advice on love. She, herself, keeps company with a gigolo boyfriend, Walter Manning (Martin Burton).

Mary struggles to work through her awkward situation by writing about a nearly identical situation in her book. She sees the mistress in her book as an intelligent modern woman. She wonders if she wouldn't be able to go to the wife "without subterfuge or hypocrisy" and just say, "I love your husband?" Rogers questions if this is very realistic. This discussion about her novel leads into a discussion about their own affair. Mary laments that she cannot stop thinking about Rogers' wife, who has been married to Rogers for eight years and has had two children with him. She says, "If she loves you half as much as I do. . . Oh, it's heartbreaking business, Rog." Rogers maintains that the great love that he feels for Mary has "the right of way absolutely above anything." She cannot accept this. Rogers argues:

You accuse me of being cruel. Good heavens, Mary, up till the time a man's 25, he's not supposed to make anything but mistakes about anything but women. If he marries one and it's wrong. . . Sweetheart, you're not going to spoil our chance of a little happiness by this quibbling.

Mary happens to meet Rogers' wife, Claire (Ann Harding) at a party. Both women are entirely unaware of who the other woman is. Mary gets into describing the plot of her new book. She says:

Well, after a year, Aileen goes to the wife and tells her the whole thing. And they simply talk it out together. They both loved him, both lived with him. One phase of his life belonged to one woman another to the other.

Mary believes that the wife can be "big enough and intelligent enough to face this without letting it destroy either of them."

Like Rogers, Claire regards the story as unrealistic. She admits that her own husband has had multiple affairs. "Of course," she says, "each one thinks that she is the love of his life and that he's going to divorce me and marry her but he doesn't seem to, somehow." She admits that, though she is sometimes exhausted by his infidelities, she has come to accept them in order to preserve their marriage. She says:

> I've made him my man. I built my life around that. . . When the first one happened, it nearly killed me. I thought the end of everything had come. Then when the second one bobbed up, it took the sting out of the first because I knew then that - that one didn't mean any more to him than the other. I can always tell when an affair is waning. He turns back to the old comfortable institution of marriage as naturally as a baby turns back to a warm bottle.

Mary returns to the plot of her book.

Mary: If she came to you honestly and told you how much she loved him, what would you do?

Claire: I'd loathe her with a deadly hate that would shrivel her up. I'd call her a vile, brazen. . . Those two women could never talk to each other. I mean I-I couldn't. No wife could.

Claire suddenly learns that Roger is Mary's publisher. She now realizes that Mary is her husband's current mistress.

Claire: I suppose you've done the girl so well because you believe she's right? You'd do it yourself.

Mary: Yes. I believe that love like that comes before everything. She didn't go after this man, or take him away from anybody. He was just there. So what could they do? It came, it was. That's all.

Claire: You can't hope to hold him with just yourself. I don't care how beautiful or clever or wonderful you are, he has to have something in him that will make him stick. Nothing else can pull a man and a woman through the ghastly job of living together.

Claire has an angry confrontation with Rogers. She says:

> All I know is that you've convinced one of the finest girls I've ever met that you love her in the same great way that she loves you. . . Always before I was glad to get you back and thankful that it was over. Always thinking of you, never of her. Now, I've seen her and something's happened to me. I've seen all of her, her heart and her soul. And I know so well how you've made her love you like that. No, it's. . . it's the last time for me, Rogers.

She tells him that she no longer loves him and their marriage is "all over." Rogers sputters hopelessly as his wife berates him. She continues:

> Never again, Rogers, never. I've eaten a lot of humble bread during the years I've been with you, an awful lot. For the sake of the children, for the thing we called home, for a lot of reasons. Chiefly because I've loved you very deeply. And always I thought the time would come when we put the silly, bad things behind us and then maybe we'd have a little happiness. But there's something so brutal in the way you've treated this girl. She wasn't playing any cheap game with you, Rogers. As some of the others were. And you're not worth a minute of one anxious hour that either one of us have given you. There's only one thing the matter with you - you're too smart. You think the simple things are silly. Real love and home - the good, old stuff.

Here we have a pre-Code film with a strong positive view of marriage. The film was based on a 1932 play by Rachel Crothers. Crothers came from a Christian conservative family. Her mother and father both achieved success as doctors. Her mother, Marie, took great pride in being one of the first women physicians in Illinois. Her parents made sure that their daughters were well-educated and could pursue useful careers. Crothers never married or had children. Her focus was always on her career. Between 1903 and 1937, she wrote thirty plays. She believed that women deserved greater acceptance in the workplace. Still, she was critical of radical feminism and thought that it was important for women to become wives and mothers. She addressed the importance of family in two plays - "He and She" from 1920 and "Susan and God" from 1937.

Frank Morgan, Ann Harding and Myrna Loy in When Ladies Meet (1933)

By Your Leave (1934)

Henry Smith (Frank Morgan), an insurance salesman, is bored with his life. He proposes to his wife, El-len (Genevieve Tobin), that they set aside their marital commitments for a week, during which time they can embark on separate vacations and have fun with other partners. Henry insists, "I need my ego restored. I have to get a new slant on things." He claims that this could strengthen their marriage. "If I kissed another girl," he says, "I'd probably remember how much sweeter it is to kiss you." He admits, though, that it could also endanger their marriage. Yet, he smiles when he says this. It is the danger of the arrangement that ex-cites him. He is careful to stipulate, "No questions asked when it's all over." Ellen feels hurt and abandoned, but her pride prevents her from admitting this. She agrees to the proposal. Oddly, the couple spends their vacation in town, which imposes many restrictions on their pursuits.

Henry starts out his vacation by getting drunk. This is hardly a way for him to restore his ego and get a new slant on things. He goes on a date with a Broadway dancer, Merle (Shirley Chambers). But Merle finds Henry to be nervous and fussy and wants nothing to do with him. One of Henry's old friends, Freddie Wil-kins (Glenn Anders), sees an opportunity to seduce Ellen. To keep Henry out of the way, he introduces him to a prostitute, Andree (Marion Nixon). But Henry is more nervous with the uninhibited and accommodating Andree than he was with Merle. So, he abruptly ends their date and hurries home.

Meanwhile, Ellen meets a suave and wealthy explorer, David McKenzie (Neil Hamilton), who takes her to dinner at an elegant restaurant. McKenzie invites Ellen to join him on his yacht in the morning. Ellen has already fallen in love with David. She returns home to pack her bags, but she finds Henry anxiously waiting for her. Henry has been broken by his extramarital adventure. He is scared, embarrassed, and contrite. Ellen agrees to stay with Henry, who clearly needs her, but she is wistful and doubtful about giving up her trip with David. She brings out a pith helmet that she bought for the dashing explorer and sadly gives it to Henry instead. Henry looks silly trying on the ill-fitting helmet.

It weakens the story to depict Henry as a skittish and stammering fool. How would a man as skittish as this get the idea for a free-love vacation? Tobin portrays a far more sympathetic, serious and sensitive character. It doesn't seem that Ellen belongs with Henry.

Ann Harding and Herbert Marshall in *The Lady Consents* (1936)

The Lady Consents (1936)

The title says it all. Anne Talbot (Ann Harding) graciously agrees to divorce her husband Mike (Herbert Marshall) so that he can marry another woman, Gerry Mannerley (Margaret Lindsay).

Gerry is busy touching up her face at a make-up table when she is approached by Anne's best friend, Susan (Ilka Chase). Susan advises Gerry to leave Mike alone and move on to another man. But Gerry doesn't see a problem with her vying with Anne for Mike. She explains, "Ann's a civilized woman just as I am." Susan is appalled by this woman's shameless indecency. She looks upon Gerry as she would a lunatic axe murderer and hurries off as quickly as she can.

Mike doesn't have much to say to his wife on the matter. He tells her, "What can I do, Anne? I can't bear hurting you." A divorce soon follows.

Anne plays pool with her former father-in-law, Jim (Edward Ellis). She insists that nothing is more important than Mike's happiness.

> Jim: You make me sick. Honest you do. Letting that dame get away with it.
>
> Anne: I tried, Jim, the only way I knew how. If Mike wants to go, I don't want to keep him.
>
> Jim: You're a liar, Anne.
>
> Anne: Perhaps.
>
> Jim: I wish I'd throttled him in his cradle.
>
> Anne: Oh, don't wish that, it's not his fault. He probably didn't want to fall in love with her. Those things just happen.

Anne attends Mike and Gerry's wedding. She expresses her good wishes as Gerry is putting on her wedding gown. It is an odd scene. But Gerry explains, "You and I are showing the world how civilized woman should behave."

Anne proves to be as clever as Mary Astor was in *Smart Woman*. She makes exorbitant alimony demands that threaten to drain Mike's financial resources. Fearful that Mike will be unable to provide her with a luxurious lifestyle, Gerry panics and abandons her marriage. Now, as she expected, Anne is able to reconcile with Mike.

In real life, Marshall was not a steadfast husband. He was married five times and became notorious for his many extramarital affairs. A strong tension often existed between the values of the average film fan and the values of the average Hollywood star.

X, Y and Zee (1972)

Zee and Robert Blakeley (Elizabeth Taylor and Michael Caine) have an open marriage. But it strains the boundaries of their marriage when Robert starts to date a beautiful boutique owner, Stella (Susannah York). Zee shows just how unappealing she is in her loud and rude efforts to sabotage the relationship.

Husbands and Lovers (1991)

A married couple, Stefano (Julian Sands) and Alina (Joanna Pacula), lose passion for one another when they find they cannot have children. They decide that it may save their relationship to have an open marriage. But Stefano regrets this arrangement when Alina divides her time between him and her new musician lover, Paolo (Tchéky Karyo).

La Separation (1994)

Pierre (Daniel Auteuil) and Ann (Isabelle Huppert) have the sort of "modern marriage" that was mocked in *Smart Woman* and *The Lady Consents*. Pierre is determined to react in a civil manner when his wife Anne tells him that she's having an affair. The couple continues to live together as if nothing is amiss even though

Anne occasionally goes off to meet her lover. Eventually, Pierre realizes that this arrangement is putting an intolerable strain on him. He demands that Anne leave their home immediately. But Anne refuses. She insists that this is her home, too, and she does not want to be away from their two-year-old son. Yes, the couple has a child, though his welfare isn't considered much by his self-absorbed parents. For much of the film, the couple is unemotional about the cruel infidelity that has thrust itself between them and has destroyed their marriage and psychological well-being.

David Parkinson of Radio Times wrote:

> Although a masterclass in actorly restraint, this examination of a disintegrating relationship is too studied and civilised for its own good. . . [D]irector Christian Vincent makes Huppert's Anne seem unnecessarily callous and fails to prevent Auteuil from becoming increasingly pathetic. . . [D]isappointingly detached melodrama. Impressive, but too impassive.[65]

The film is, in the end, boring and pointless.

Afterglow (1997)

Lucky Mann (Nick Nolte) became unhappy in his marriage when his wife, Phyllis Hart (Julie Christie), got pregnant from an extramarital affair. He has since had multiple affairs, which Phyllis has come to accept. Marianne Byron (Lara Flynn Boyle) hires Lucky to convert a home office into a child's room. Marianne is desperately trying to have a baby. But it has become obvious to Marianne that her husband, Jeffrey Byron (Jonny Lee Miller), doesn't share her interest in parenthood and has been avoiding having sex with her. So, she has sex with Lucky instead. Jeffrey is attracted to Phyllis and takes her to a resort. But the pair argue and never have sex. Phyllis is devastated when she learns that Marianne is pregnant with Lucky's child. She remains painfully silent when Marianne misleads Jeffrey into believing that the child is his.

The Man from Elysian Fields (2001)

A failed novelist, Byron (Andy Garcia), becomes an escort to wealthy women. One of his clients, Andrea Alcott (Olivia Williams), is married to a famous novelist, Tobias (James Coburn). Tobias is a dying old man who is struggling to finish his last novel. Tobias, who can no longer satisfy Andrea sexually, is willing to allow Byron to have sex with his wife. Byron stays in this relationship mainly because he wants to collaborate with Tobias on his novel. Meanwhile, Byron tries to keep the arrangement secret from his wife Dena (Julianna Margulies), but she finds out about it and leaves him. Byron is the principal author of the novel, which becomes a bestseller. Tobias has died by this time and Andrea refuses to acknowledge Byron's work or pay him royalties. She tells him that he should have secured a contract with Tobias. It is only now that Byron sees the truth. Andrea only pretended to love him. She really only loved Tobias and was determined to protect his legacy. Byron writes his next book as a deeply felt apology to Deena. Deena shows up at a book signing and seems to be willing to forgive him. Margulies' performance as Byron's aggrieved wife is the highlight of the film.

5 to 7 (2014)

Brian Bloom (Anton Yelchin), a young writer, meets a beautiful French woman, Arielle Pierpont (Bérénice Marlohe). Brian and Arielle are instantly attracted to one another. Arielle tells Brian that she is married to a diplomat, Valéry (Lambert Wilson), but she and her husband agree that they can engage in extramarital affairs between 5 and 7 p.m. on weeknights. Brian reveals the situation to his parents. His father, Sam (Frank Langella), is appalled. He says that it makes him feel as if his pancreas is about to explode. His mother, Arlene (Glenn Close), greatly differs in her opinion. She says, "There are two forces on earth you don't want to be fighting - mother nature and love." Brian can no longer accept the two-hour-a-day arrangement. He loves Arielle and he wants to marry her. He presents her with an engagement ring, which she joyfully accepts. Valéry shows up at Brian's apartment. He is angry that Brian got Arielle to violate the terms of their open marriage. He roughly slaps him. But then he gives Brian a check for a quarter of a million dollars and tells him to make sure that Arielle has a good life. Arielle realizes in the end that she cannot leave her husband and children. Years later, Brian and Arielle meet again by chance outside the Guggenheim Museum. Brian introduces Arielle to his wife, Kiva (Jocelyn DeBoer), and their two-year-old son. He sees that Arielle still wears the ring that he gave her.

Was Brian's mother correct that a person should never resist the forces of lust and romance? We don't know if Venus struck Brian and Kiva with a lightning bolt when they first met. We don't know if they have passionate sex every night. But we can look at this couple with their son and see a happy and sound family. Greater forces than lust and romance bind a husband and wife together. Greater forces uphold a family.

Chapter Four:
The Interloper

At first, the adultery film was most often in the style of the Victorian melodrama. It was standard in the Victorian melodrama to feature a sneering villain - selfish, avaricious, deceitful. The early adultery films made no exception. The adultery story could not occur without a sinister outsider encroaching on the marital home and creating a crisis between a husband and wife.

A young man observes in *Folly to Be Wise* (1952):

> Look, say a gent gets sweet on another gent's Judy. The gent what owns the Judy, he's got two or three things he can do. He can go about blinding and belly-aching. He can clock the other guy and give his Judy something to remember, but that don't get you anywhere. No, the only thing in my experience, is to sit down over a pint of wallop and say, "Here, chum, how about it?" There's plenty of other judies in the world yapping about, leaving their hair combings all over the place, what you want to come messing around my Judy for? She takes a bit of getting used to, I warn you. And I've got used to her. If you look at it reasonable, judies is things that most blokes can do with in moderation. I mean, there's things you've got to do, you've got to eat, you've got to sleep, but you ain't got to go running after other blokes' judies.

But that's exactly what these blokes did. IMDb member Jim Tritten said of one such character: "He is a cad, a bounder, an unmitigated reprobate who steals other men's wives."[66]

An actress tries to seduce a drama critic in *Please Don't Eat the Daisies* (1960). He explains as bluntly as possible that he's a married man and, sorry, not available to her. She is undeterred, responding, "Anyone's available who isn't dead." Marriage is no boundary for an immorally lustful person.

The vamp, or vampire, was at the center of the first big wave of adultery films. A seductive woman was first described as a "vampire" in Rudyard Kipling's 1897 poem "The Vampire." Selig produced an adaptation of the Kipling story in 1910. The vamp is depicted as a demonic force. The Film Index noted of *The Vampire*: "[A] young husband becomes ensnared in the coils of the Vampire (a destroyer of souls). Clandestine meetings are arranged and the cunning, unscrupulous, satanic actions of the Vampire compels the poor weakling, Temple, to falter and fall before her charms."[67]

Rosemary Theby revived the vamp character in Vitagraph's *The Reincarnation of Karma* in 1912.

The Supreme Test (1912) suggests that a man can escape from the wiles of a vamp. A siren, Lois Whitehall (Frances Marion), lures a young husband, Raymond (Whitney Raymond), away from his wife, Eva (Eva Prout). Raymond becomes furious when he learns that Lois was merely trifling with his affections. Upon returning home, Raymond is distraught to receive news that Eva died in a train wreck. He is about to commit suicide when Eva, who in fact missed the train, walks into their home alive and well. Overcome with joy, he begs his dear wife for forgiveness.

One wife found a way to outfox a vamp in *The Masked Dancer* (1914). Alphonso (George Cooper), a dance hall manager, learns that mining engineer Henry Martin (George Holt) has discovered a rich vein of gold. He persuades a pretty employee, Dolores (Beatrice Dominguez), to persuade Henry to gamble away his gold nuggets. But Henry's wife, Alice (Myrtle Gonzalez), lures Henry away from the deceitful vamp by arriving at the dance hall dressed as an exotic masked dancer.

The Kalem Company exploited the vamp in a series of films starting with *The Vampire* (1913). A vampire, played by Alice Hollister, poses as a wood nymph to lure a young artist to his death. The Moving Picture World reported: "The beauty and amazing grace of this monster fascinates the artist who, despite his struggles, is enmeshed by her terrible wiles. It is a feature so surcharged with realism the beholder chafes under a sense of helplessness at being unable to render aid to the doomed victim."[68] Hollister went on to play similar roles in *The Vampire's Trail* (1914), *The Mystery of the Yellow Sunbonnet* (1914), *The Curious Case of Meredith Stanhope* (1915), *The Destroyer* (1915) and *The Siren's Reign* (1915).

IMDb describes the plot of *The Siren's Reign* as follows: "An upright young man marries a siren, a drunken, unfaithful woman, who mothers his child, and then ruins him financially and morally."[69]

IMDb describes the plot of *The Destroyer* (1915) as follows: "An actress weaves her web, like a disgusting spider, around a susceptible young man, lures him away from his sweetheart, and eventually destroys him."[70] The actress, Cherie (Hollister), compels Dick (Harry F. Millarde) to rob money from his wealthy father's safe. When his father learns that his son has stolen from him, he disowns him. The Moving Picture World reported:

> Dick hastens to Cherie to seek consolation. He finds Macklyn, a rival for her favor, present. When the woman hears Dick has been disinherited, she scornfully orders him to leave her apartment. With this evidence of the woman's character, Dick vows never to see her again. He eventually tries to get back into Helen's graces, but the girl's love for him has died. Dick drifts lower down life's ladder. Months later, Cherie and Macklyn alight in front of a fashionable jeweler's. A beggar accosts them just as they leave their automobile and whines a request for money. Macklyn scornfully drops a coin into the man's hand. Cherie, however, recognizes the wretch. She contemptuously draws away from him. It is Dick.[71]

The Two Roses (1914) was described by The Moving Picture World as follows:: "A well-sustained story of a young married man who is lured from his cold, undemonstrative wife by a designing woman [appropriately named Eleanor Tempest]. . . The heartless woman is fatally injured in an auto accident and her last wish is that the husband return to his wife."[72] The Moving Picture World added in a separate review, "[T]he fury of selfishness and infidelity takes possession of [a man's] soul. The Vampire triumphs and purity is crushed."[73]

The Siren (1914) showed that the formula for the vamp film was already firmly established. According to Motography, the film casts Mistin Guett as a "treacherous flirt"[74] with "alluring charms and enticing ways."[75] This siren, the magazine states, "pretends to love and encourages the attentions of every man she meets until finally the mother of one of her victims, goaded almost to insanity by the knowledge of how her son's head had been turned by the deceitful woman, attacks her and puts an end to her life of wantonly playing with men's hearts."[76]

At the core of these stories was an obsessive passion. In *A Siren of the Desert* (1914), a husband is unable to keep away from a charming singer at the local dance hall.

Ellaline Terriss portrays a vampire in *The Flame of Passion* (1915). The Moving Picture World reported that the film's hero must find a way to escape the siren's "deadly fascination" and "villainous scheming."[77]

An ad for *The Ring of the Borgias* (1915) noted, "[T]he ignoble vampire, like the sinuous snake, gather[s] her victim in its coils. . ."[78]

Theda Bara specialized in playing femme fatales who got pleasure from luring weak-willed men away from their wives. Bara brought the vamp to its greatest height in *A Fool There Was* (1915). The ultimate goal of the vamp was to sexually dominate the men and lead them to ruin.

A Fool There Was (1915)

John Schuyler (Edward José), an eminent attorney, is called to a diplomatic mission in England. En route aboard an ocean liner, he meets a notorious woman known only as The Vampire (Bara). Fritzi Kramer of Movies Silently wrote, "Theda boards the ship but her abandoned lovers are all about. Apparently, she drove one man to become a beggar, another one rots in prison. How she accomplished this is left vague."[79] One of The Vampire's victims follows her onto the ship with the intention of shooting her. She carelessly waves a flower in the air and says, "Kiss me, my fool." Kramer wrote, "The fool promptly shoots himself in the head, presumably to free himself from the vampire's curse."[80]

The Vampire selects Shuyler as her next victim. As a result, Schuyler loses his job, abandons his wife and child, ruins his friendships, and becomes an alcoholic. AFI reports:

> In the end, his strength and spirit broken, John crawls to the vampire to beg her to leave him in peace, but she laughs and gives him the order "kiss me, my fool." He tries to stand, but instead, collapses and dies.[81]

Bara followed *A Fool There Was* with *Kreutzer Sonata* (1915). Raphael Friedlander (Henry Bergman) pays Gregor Randor (William E. Shay) to marry his daughter Miriam (Nance O'Neil), who has become pregnant with a man unwilling to marry her. Gregor has no real interest in Miriam and engages in an affair with Miriam's younger sister, Cilia (Bara). Miriam shoots her cheating husband and her wicked adulteress sister in a jealous rage. Leo Tolstoy's 1889 novella *Kreutzer Sonata* involves a wife who has an affair with a violinist. The husband finds his wife and the violinist together and, enraged, slays his wife with a dagger. He lets the violinist escape. He says: "I wanted to run after him, but remembered that it is ridiculous to run after one's wife's lover in one's socks; and I did not wish to be ridiculous but terrible."[82] The fact that he caught his wife with another man prompts the jury to acquit him of murder. Tolstoy is better known for his adultery novel "Anna Karenina." The author, himself, believed in sexual abstinence. In his view, a man can hinder his lofty pursuits by becoming infatuated with an object of carnal love and giving himself over to "animal excesses."[83]

The melodrama was increased for Bara's *The Devil's Daughter* (1915). Bara's evil continued to show no bounds. Resentful that a lover abandoned her, Gioconda Dianti (Bara) vows to use her powers of seduction to ruin the lives of as many men as she can. She meets a sculptor, Lucio Sattella (Paul Doucet), on the beach and agrees to model for him. Though married, Lucio is drawn into a passionate relationship with Gioconda. He is so enthralled by Gioconda that he agrees to abandon his wife, Silvia (Doris Heywood), and his three-year-old daughter Beata (Jane Lee). Lucio, distraught with guilt, tries to commit suicide. Silvia nurses him back to health only to have him return to Gioconda. Silvia confronts Gioconda at the art studio, where the sphinx statue for which Gioconda modeled is prominently on display. Gioconda responds with insults. Silvia attacks her. The women struggle. Silvia bumps into the statue, which topples over and falls on her hands. No one fares well in this story. Silvia never regains the use of her hands and becomes a bitter woman. Lucio becomes a raving maniac. Gioconda, too, descends into madness.

Theda Bara

Bara's next film was *The Clemenceau Case* (1915). Iza Clemenceau (Bara) cheats on her husband Pierre (William E. Shay) with a wealthy Russian Duke, Sergius (Frank Goldsmith). When her husband kills Sergius in a duel, she spends no time mourning his loss. Instead, she takes an interest in a sculptor, Constantin Ritz (Stuart Holmes). She has no trouble making Constantin forget his lovely young wife. Pierre sees that Iza is determined to ruin Constantin's life just as she ruined his. To save Constantin, he plunges a knife through her heart.

Bara is a bigamist in *Lady Audley's Secret* (1915). When her first husband catches up to her, she shoves him down a well.

Bara is again out for revenge in *The Serpent* (1916). Vania (Bara), a peasant girl, vows revenge on a duke who assaulted her and murdered her lover. Years later, Vania achieves fame as an actress, which has placed her in the same social circles as the Duke. Vania has changed so much that the Duke fails to recognize her. She soon sets out to seduce the Duke's son, Prince Valanoff (Carl Harbaugh), who was crippled in the war. Valanoff is a fragile and vulnerable young man. Once the couple marries, Vania sets out to seduce the Duke. She carefully arranges for Valanoff to catch her making love to his father. The prince is so distraught by this great betrayal that he commits suicide. Vania's revenge is complete.

Bara's screen image had softened by the time that she made *The Siren's Song* (1919). Marie Bernais (Bara), a village girl, becomes romantically involved with a rich merchant, Gaspard Prevost, who is already married. She becomes increasingly uncomfortable with the arrangement and leaves Gaspard to sing uplifting tunes to soldiers.

The Bara imitators were many. Louise Glaum was clearly a Bara imitator in *The Wolf Woman* (1916), *Honor Thy Name* (1916) and *Sweetheart of the Doomed* (1917). Valeska Suratt became a Bara-like vamp in *The Siren* (1917).

Scriptwriters created a trend of dedicated doctors who neglect their wives. Suratt plays a neglected doctor's wife, Emma Rolfe, in *Wife Number Two* (1917). Despondent over a failed affair, Emma resolves to drink acid to end her life. She finds a quiet place beside a river to perform the deed, but she cannot bring herself to raise the fatal drink to her lips. She is about to return home when the river bank gives way beneath her and she drowns in the current.

Suratt is an agent of others more unscrupulous than her in *The New York Peacock* (1917). Mr. Martin (Eric Mayne), a manufacturer, has set up a deal with a munitions firm in New York City. He entrusts his son, Billy (Harry Hilliard), with delivering a $100,000 bank draft to secure the agreement. Billy bids a fond farewell to his wife before departing on his trip. In the meantime, a broker's secretary tips off the manager of a gambling house that Billy will be arriving in town with a large sum of money. A fake broker's representative comes to meet him and brings him to the gambling house, where he meets Zena (Suratt). He is captivated by Zena, who urges him to gamble on the roulette wheel. Billy loses all of his money and is too embarrassed to return home. Billy's father becomes worried about him and travels to New York City to seek him out. It takes the father exposing Zena's treachery to convince Billy that he should accept that he acted foolishly and return home.

Suratt matches Bara's flamboyance in this film. She wears a big spider web hat and a gown adorned with peacock feathers. Motography noted:

> If a garish display of jewelry and eccentric manners and dress are the substance of the fatal lure of the "vamp," we must unreservedly hand Miss Suratt the prize for attaining the supreme rung of vampiredom in this picture. . . [W]ithout these embellishments, we suppose the "vamp" would lose her serpentine hold on her victims, as well as her hold of fascination upon audiences.[84]

But Suratt's Zena isn't entirely evil. She actually falls in love with Billy. So, did love reform her? Edward Weitzel of The Moving Picture World reported:

> The siren, after falling on the floor and dissolving into tears as she clasps a photograph of the lost one to her breast, springs up at the entrance of an old admirer, throws the photograph and her grief over her left shoulder and suggests it's about time she had her supper.[85]

The vamp was softening after two years of relentless evil.

Olga Petrova, Metro Pictures' first star, became Bara's most serious rival. But Petrova didn't only play femme fatales, as is evident in *What Will People Say?* (1916). AFI provides the set-up:

> Persis Cabot [Petrova], a society girl brought up in the lap of luxury, does not wish to give up her luxurious life style, even though she passionately loves poor Army captain Harvey Forbes. Her millionaire father, on the verge of financial ruin, encourages her to marry Willie Enslee, whom she does not really love but who is extremely wealthy and can keep her in the manner to which she has grown accustomed.

Persis regrets marrying Enslee when she discovers that he has a mistress. She asks her husband for a divorce so that she can marry Harvey, but he becomes upset and stabs her with a letter opener. Persis recovers from her wound and obtains a divorce.

Before Ernst Lubitsch became famous for his naughty adultery farces, he directed an adultery melodrama called *Intoxication* (1919). IMDb summarized the plot as follows: "Gaston finally succeeds as a dramatist and decides to leave his wife and child for another woman. When the child dies, the finger is pointed at him and he winds up as a destitute. . ."[86]

Why Change Your Wife? (1920) was another adultery film by DeMille. But, this time, the wife is far more sympathetic. Beth Gordon (Gloria Swanson), a dowdy wife, loses her husband Robert (Thomas Meighan) to a sultry and manipulative shop girl, Sally Clark (Bebe Daniels).

Thomas Meighan and Gloria Swanson in *Why Change Your Wife?* (1920)

The Common Sin (1920) features an evil mistress. Frederick Searles, a Wall Street financier, goes bankrupt through a series of bad investments. His wife, desperate to maintain their luxurious lifestyle, pressures her eldest daughter Needa (Grace Darling) to marry wealthy John Davis Warren, ignoring Warden's reputation for brutality and drunkenness. Needa is heartbroken to break up with her true love, Hugh Stanton (Rod La Rocque), but she sees it as her duty to help her family. Warren's mistress (Nita Naldi) worries that she will lose Warren when she receives news that Needa is pregnant. She puts the idea into Warren's head that Needa may be carrying Stanton's baby. Warren beats Needa, which causes her to lose the baby. Needa leaves Warren immediately. Warren blames Mrs. Barnes for breaking up his marriage and tells her that he no longer wants to see her. Enraged, the woman brings out a gun and shoots him. Upon learning that Warren has died, Needa realizes that she is now free to marry Stanton.

In the Heart of a Fool (1920)

Laura Nesbit (Mary Thurman) is engaged to marry Grant Adams (James Kirkwood Sr.), the editor of the local newspaper. Grant gets upset with Laura for flirting with a shady young lawyer, Tom VanDorn (Philo

McCullough). Margaret Muller (Anna Q. Nilsson) sees this as the right time to get Grant's attention. Grant goes on a date with Margaret and is shocked to find out weeks later that she is pregnant. He marries Margaret for the sake of the baby. Laura in turn marries VanDorn, but their marriage ends when VanDorn also becomes entangled with Margaret. Obviously, Margaret has become skilled at breaking up relationships. Laura cares for Grant when he is injured in an accident. This brings the couple back together again.

The Wild Goose (1921)

Frank Manners (Holmes E. Herbert), is busy with his work as an architect, unaware that he has reason to be concerned about affairs at home. Ogden Fenn (Norman Kerry) seduces Manners' wife, Diana (Mary MacLaren), who is described by Janiss Garza of AllMovie as "willful and frivolous."[87] Diana runs away with Fenn, taking along her young daughter Tam (Rita Rogan).

Garza continued:

> Manners is infuriated and sets out to shoot them, but he is stopped by Mrs. Hastings, a family friend who has grown to love him herself (Dorothy Bernard). She convinces him to put aside his wrath and think of Tam. Meanwhile, Mr. Has-tings (Joseph Smiley) has come to realize that his wife loves Manners and sees all the misery that Fenn is causing. He goes to the bungalow where Fenn and Diana are staying, and forces Fenn into the car with him. He drives the car at breakneck speed, killing them both. Mrs. Hastings brings the wayward Diana and her husband back together.[88]

Laurence Reid of Motion Picture News wrote:

> *The Wild Goose* is a study in the eternal triangle of a wife who delights in trespassing until such time as she reflects upon her conduct and returns a repentant figure to be forgiven. . . The other man, as usual, is a "snake in the grass," and shows his cowardice in the pinches. . . The only reason why the wife trespasses is planted in a sub-title which says that she is an impulsive grown-up child. . . The picture seldom rings true and looks especially false in the dramatic scenes.[89]

The cad, unlike the vamp, is more interested in securing money than corrupting souls. But he generally suffers a worse fate than his female counterparts. The cad dies in a car crash in *The Wild Goose*. The cad suffers fatal trauma after falling from a balcony in *A Private Scandal*. The cad is trampled to death in an elephant stampede in *Old Loves and New* (1926). And then we have *Foolish Wives* (1922), in which the cad winds up as a corpse floating around in a sewer.

Foolish Wives (1922)

A fake count, Count Wladislaw Sergius Karamzin (Erich von Stroheim), seduces rich married women to extort money from them. These seductions are not sufficient to satisfy his great sexual appetite. He prowls around town in search of other lovers. One lover is a hotel maid, Maruschka (Dale Fuller), and another is a mentally disabled young woman, Marietta (Malvina Polo).

Erich von Stroheim and Helen Hughes in *Foolish Wives* (1922)

Maruschka becomes crazed when Karamzin loses interest in her and retires to his hotel room with Mrs. Hughes (Miss DuPont). She quickly gets to work setting the room on fire. The couple rushes out on the balcony and cries out for help. Once the firemen have opened up a safety net below them, Karamzin elects to jump from the balcony first. Wikipedia reports, "Karamzin's public displays of selfishness and cowardice ensure that he is shunned by the high society by whom he craves to be accepted."[90] Marietta's father, Cesare (Cesare Gravina), seeks out Karamzin for disgracing his daughter and savagely murders him.

Husbands or Lovers (1924)

Nju (Elisabeth Bergner), a bored wife, is lured away from her husband Ehemann (Emil Jannings) by an enigmatic poet (Conrad Veidt), whose eyes exert a hypnotic power over her. Ehemann demands that the poet stay away from Nju, but the poet is not intimidated by the outraged husband and dares to insult him in front of his wife.

The film wasn't distributed in the United States until 1927. The Moving Picture World critic found it to be a predictable and outdated melodrama. He wrote, "The outcome is inevitable and the 'how' is not interesting. . . [Veidt] is theatrical and impossible and by no means suggests his brilliant performances in other films. It is all artificial and unreal. . ."[91] Tastes were definitely changing.

After Marriage (1925)

David Morgan (George Fisher), a wealthy young, marries a poor girl, Lucille Spencer (Helen Lynch). His father, James (Herschel Mayall), strongly disapproves of the marriage. David is suddenly enticed by the charms of a beautiful actress, Alma Lathrop (Margaret Livingston). Alma, a full-fledged vamp, already has

David's father as a sugar daddy. She manages with her seductive ways to create a romantic rivalry between father and son. Emotions get heated. The father attacks Alma, who draws a gun and kills him.

Variety (1925)

A murderer, Boss Huller (Emil Jannings), breaks a ten-year silence in prison to explain to the warden the great injustice that drove him to murder. A flashback reveals Huller operating a low-budget side-show with his wife (Maly Delschaft). He was once a trapeze star in the circus and misses the fame and glamour that he enjoyed during his prime years. But then he meets a lovely young woman, Berta-Marie (Lya De Putti), and is inspired to revive his old act with Berta-Maria as his partner. He abandons his wife and child to tour with his new act. A trapeze star, Artinelli (Warwick Ward), hires Hull and Berta-Marie to join his show. He pretends to be dazzled by their acrobatic skills when, in fact, he is only dazzled by Berta-Marie's beauty. He seduces Berta-Marie and gets her to abandon Huller. Huller is devastated. He goes to Artinelli's apartment to confront the man for robbing him of his happiness. He takes out a knife and fatally stabs Artinelli while Berta-Marie watches in horror. As Beta-Marie cries hysterically, he leaves the apartment without a word. He trudges lifelessly down a long staircase pursued by the distraught young woman, who falls in her haste and tumbles helplessly down the steps.

This is not technically an adultery story as Huller never marries Beta-Marie. But the Hull character is indistinguishable from Jannings' standard cuckold role.

The film presents a dark world lacking in morals. This is the type of environment in which adultery thrives. Take for instance *It Always Rains on Sunday* (1947). According to film historian Imogen Sara Smith, the film depicts post-war East End London as "a world where everything is slightly crooked."[92] The crooked people perpetuate regular incidents of adultery. Smith pointed out, "[Record store owner] Morry is trying to carry out an extramarital dalliance in the listening booth in the back of his shop. Rose is trying to hide her fugitive lover in the bedroom."[93]

Variety shares plot elements with a 1917 Denmark film, *The Clown*. *The Clown* has a simple story. A clown, Joe Higgins (Valdemar Psilander), is abandoned by his bareback rider wife, Daisy (Gudrun Houlberg), for the devilish Count Henri (Robert Schmidt). Heartbreak, suicide and murder follows.

The Battle of the Sexes (1928)

J. C. Judson (Jean Hersholt), a middle-aged real estate tycoon, is devoted to his wife and children until he falls into the clutches of a cunning gold digger, Marie Skinner (Phyllis Haver). Judson's wife (Belle Bennett) has him leave their home after she catches him dancing with Skinner in a nightclub. But, in the end, Judson expresses remorse for his actions and his wife agrees to take him back.

The word "gold digger" first appeared in print in Virginia Brooks' 1915 book "My Battles with Vice." A gold digger ensnares men for their money. She demands lavish gifts from suitors. Merriam-Webster defines a gold digger as "a person whose romantic pursuit of, relationship with, or marriage to a wealthy person is primarily or solely motivated by a desire for money."[94]

Recaptured Love (1930)

A middle-aged married man, Brentwood Parr (John Halliday), leaves his wife Helen (Belle Bennett) and son Henry (Junior Durkin) to marry a nightclub singer, Peggy Price (Dorothy Burgess). As it turns out, his new wife is only interested in spending money and going to parties. Soon, Brentwood learns that Peggy is having an affair with another man (Richard Tucker). He quickly returns to Helen and begs her to take him back.

A Lady to Love (1930)

The 1924 Pulitzer Prize-winning play "They Knew What They Wanted," written by Sidney Howard, was adapted into three films: *The Secret Hour* (1928), *A Lady to Love* (1930) and *They Knew What They Wanted* (1940). Let's focus on *A Lady to Love*.

Tony (Edward G. Robinson) is captivated by a waitress, Lena (Vilma Bánky), who he meets while visiting San Francisco. He writes her a letter proposing marriage. He fears that a woman as pretty as Lena will not find him to be good-looking enough, so he sends the letter with a photo of his handsome hired man Buck (Robert Ames).

Lena is quick to arrive at the vineyard, but she is shocked to meet Tony. "Who's that old man?!" she asks. Tony's age is not the only issue. Tony, who crashed his car on the way to meet Lena at the train station, is bedridden with two broken legs. He is far from the fit and strapping man that she expected. Lena, pained by the idea of returning to her waitress job, reluctantly agrees to marry Tony.

Films at the time took an unsympathetic view of a woman willing to enter into a loveless marriage for a life of luxury. These women, in their obsession with jewels and furs, come across as greedy and cold-hearted. At the same time, though, you had the woman who isn't greedy, cold-hearted or materialistic, but she is still willing to forsake love for financial security. Wikipedia defines a gold digger as "someone who engages in romantic relationships for money rather than love."[95] Is the woman who marries a man purely for home and security less a gold digger than the woman who marries a man for ostentatious possessions? It is, in either case, a woman who cares about a man's money rather than the man himself. An old woman tells Gene Kelly in *Living in a Big Way* (1947):

> . . . My dear stubborn young man, most women marry for security. Not only for themselves, but for their offspring. That was a little trick we learned, way back, before ideals and hoop skirts and lipstick and all the rest of it. We taught men the idea of romantic love, but that was only another illusion we created to keep them in line. We're a cold-blooded lot, Gogarty.

An attraction inevitably develops between Lena and Buck, whose virile looks are what brought her to the vineyard. The crippled Tony is not able to consummate the marriage on the wedding night. A grief-stricken Lena turns to Buck instead. Their night of passion leaves Lena pregnant. Buck, unwilling to take responsibility for a baby, leaves the vineyard.

Lena comes to love Tony while nursing him back to health. She has finally found happiness, but Buck suddenly returns and demands that Lena resume their affair.

In the play, the waitress (named Amy) has sex with the hired hand (named Joe) the night before she marries Tony and she never carries on the relationship after that. So, she is a faithful wife. Trouble doesn't arise until the newlywed bride learns that is pregnant with the hired hand's baby.

They Knew What They Wanted unfolds to reveal, in the words of Erickson, "the grim consequence of a misbegotten mail-order marriage."[96] Amy Peters (Carole Lombard) vows to be loyal to her new husband (Charles Laughton) though she finds him physically unappealing. But, regardless of her vow, she eventually succumbs to her attraction to Joe (William Gargan).

The Secret Hour is tamer than the play and the two other film versions. The waitress, Amy (Pola Negri), agrees to marry Tony (Jean Hersholt), but she falls in love with Tony's foreman Joe (Kenneth Thomson) and sneaks off to marry him. Amy and Joe return to the vineyard and let Tony know that they are now husband and wife. Erickson wrote, "[T]he good-hearted Tony can't bring himself to send Amy away or break up his friendship with Joe, so he agrees to bless their marriage."[97] So, the film has no infidelity and no bastard child.

Passion Flower (1930)

Katherine "Cassy" Pringle (Kay Johnson), the daughter of a wealthy businessman, shocks her father Leroy (Winter Hall) when she announces her plan to marry the family chauffeur, Dan Wallace (Charles Bickford). She receives support from her cousin, Dulce Morado (Kay Francis), who is secretly attracted to the chauffeur herself.

The film presents a thoughtful though not necessarily sympathetic perspective of the other woman. Dulce opposed her cousin marrying the chauffeur until she got an eyeful of him. As her attraction for Dan grows, she finds herself reevaluating her life. She admits to her Uncle Leroy that she regrets having married her husband, Tony (Lewis Stone), for his money.

> Dulce: If Cassy loves [Dan], what difference does it make what he is?
>
> Pringle: You didn't think love was so important when you married Tony Morado.
>
> Dulce: No. I married him because he was the richest man I knew. I know better now.

Better, she thinks, to marry for love. She tells Katherine, "Love is a rare thing. If you throw it away, it may never come again." Dulce is swept away by her attraction for Dan. She claims to be motivated by love, but the way she slinks around Dan suggests that lust is truly at the core of her actions. She speaks of her desire for happiness, but it is a happiness that she likely expects to find in sexual fulfillment. As she once associated her well-being with money, she now associates her well-being with sex.

Hafer wrote, "I happened to see [*Passion Flower*] and three other Kay Francis films recently when they were shown on TCM. And, surprisingly, all four films were about adultery and three of them had Kay playing a horrid skank!"[98] It's not really surprising that all four of Francis' films were about adultery. Francis specialized in women's melodramas and woman's melodramas relied extensively on adultery storylines. What were the other three films that Hafer saw that day? Presumably, those films were *Transgression* (1931), *Jewel Robbery* (1932) and *Divorce* (1945). Hafer had no reason to have sympathy for Francis in any of those films.

Dulce takes no blame for her wrong decision. She says, "There are too many roads in the world already. They're confusing. Sometimes it's hard to tell which one to take."

Tony becomes aware of the affair and confronts Dulce. He feels sorry for his wife, who he sees as confused and misguided. He warns her that her actions will likely cause harm to herself and others. Dulce tells him that she is so unhappy in her current situation that any change has to be an improvement.

Dulce: I've done a lot of thinking myself, lately. I've thought myself around in circles. And I always come back to the place I started. I deserve some happiness out of life, don't I? But I'm not so noble I can give up the one thing in life that I want more than anything else in the world and I won't.

Tony: You are letting yourself in for a lot of heartache, Dulce.

Dulce: Well, it will be *my* heartache. And that's certainly better than nothing at all.

Dulce confronts Cassy. She says:

Oh, Cassy. I know you have every right to loathe and hate me. But I want you to know that it isn't just a trivial thing with me. I did fight against it. Cassy. Cassy, look at me. You do believe that, don't you? I would crawl on my knees if that would do any good. If there were anything. . . Dan and I love each other, Cassy. We can't help that. Love isn't a thing you can control. If it happens, you just can't help it.

She maintains that she had no control in this situation. She says, "I feel rotten about it, Cassy. Every day. Well, it's stronger than I am, I guess."

In the end, Dan makes his way back to Cassy and Dulce finds herself defeated and alone.

Laughter (1930)

Peggy (Nancy Carroll), a dancer with the Zeigfeld Follies, gives up her free and easy lifestyle to marry an elderly millionaire, C. Mortimer Gibson (Frank Morgan). She finds herself bored beyond endurance after a year of marriage. Her marriage no longer seems important when an old boyfriend, Paul Lockridge (Fredric March), comes back to town. Paul tells Peggy, "You are rich - dirty rich. You are dying. You need laughter to make you clean." The suicide of an acquaintance makes her realize that it is important to find laughter in life.

It is a film without nuance or ambiguity. This relationship between husband and wife has less passion than the relationship between a financial adviser and a client. Morgan is given little to do in the role of the boring millionaire. The normally robust actor is lifeless in the few scenes that he has been given. The audience cannot be expected to care about the bland and lifeless Gibson. Instead, the sympathy of the audience is directed towards the gold digger desperate for good times.

Five and Ten (1931)

Jennifer Rarick (Marion Davies) is in love with Berry Rhodes (Leslie Howard), who is engaged to marry Muriel Preston (Mary Duncan). Muriel confronts Jennifer. She says, "You don't seem to realize that Berry's engaged to me, Miss Rarick. And in our set it isn't very sporting to play around with a man who belongs to someone else." Jennifer is more defiant after Berry's marriage to Muriel sours. She tells her, "He loves me. You know he loves me. No matter what you think. We've been fair to you. I told Berry that I wouldn't see him again until you saw things fairly and gave him up. But I won't bother to be fair any longer."

In a subplot, Jennifer's mom Jenny (Irene Rich) takes up with a gigolo because her husband John (Richard Bennett) is too preoccupied with his work.

Jennifer accepts defeat in her efforts to take Berry from his wife. She boards a ship to sail to Europe and get away from her sorrows. But, just then, Berry arrives to let her know that he has filed for divorce and will join her in Europe once the divorce is final.

Pre-Code films like *Laughter* and *Five and Ten* present the collapse of a marriage as a happy ending.

Transgression (1931)

A husband, Robert Maury (Paul Cavanagh), needs to live in India for a year to handle business matters. He has his wife, Elsie (Kay Francis), live with his sister in Paris while he is away. Elsie meets a Spanish nobleman, Arturo de Borgus (Ricardo Cortez). She is thrilled by Arturo's flirtations, but repeatedly resists the Lothario's tireless efforts to seduce her during her husband's year-long absence. Arturo senses that Elsie's resistance is weakening after she receives a letter that her husband is finally coming home. She realizes that she must now chose between her husband and Arturo. She chooses Arturo. Elsie writes a letter to let her husband know that she has fallen in love with another man. She visits Arturo ready to succumb to his seductions. But a peasant, Carlos (Agostino Borgato), suddenly breaks into Arturo's home. Carlos accuses the Lothario of seducing his 16-year-old daughter and getting her pregnant. The man is insane with grief as his daughter died during childbirth. He shoots and kills Arturo. The scene is much like a scene from *Foolish Wives*. Elsie is unable to intercept her letter to Robert, but Robert forgives her and holds her in a firm and loving embrace.

Ricardo Cortez and Kay Francis in *Transgression* (1931)

The film is a remake of *The Next Corner* (1924), which also starred Cortez as Arturo. Janiss Garza of AllMovie wrote of that film's plot: "American engineer Robert Maury (Conway Tearle) travels to Paris with his wife, Elsie (Dorothy Mackaill). He leaves her there while he goes to Argentina on business. Elsie, like most neglected wives (at least in films), uses this opportunity to get into mischief. . ."[99] An ad for the film featured the headline: "The daring story of a young married woman who played with the fire of forbidden love and was caught in the flames."[100]

The Iron Man (1931)

A prizefighter, Kid Mason (Lew Ayres), is too distracted by his demanding gold digger wife Rose (Jean Harlow) to train properly. Rose leaves her husband, realizing that his repeated losses in the ring are not going to provide her with the opulent lifestyle that she desires. This allows him to focus on his training and become successful, which oddly serves to bring back the woman who had once been the obstacle to his success. Wikipedia reports:

> [Rose] worms her way back into his life, despite the misgivings of manager George Regan (George Armstrong). Eventually, she cons Mason into dumping Regan and replacing him with her secret lover Lewis (Miljan), even though he has almost no experience in the fight game.[101]

The role of Rose is a dry run for Harlow's more popular gold digger role in *Red-Headed Woman* (1932).

Just a Gigolo (1931)

Lord Robert Brummell (William Haines) poses as a gigolo. He proclaims to a prospective lover, "Say 'yes' to life. Say 'yes' to love. Say 'yes' to me." Life is home, family, and career achievements. Or is it sexual pleasure? Marriage is not meant to serve a sensualist's lust. It is impossible for a person who is shallow, selfish and given over to the pursuit of pleasure to make a good marital partner. Say "no" to the gigolo.

Bachelor's Affairs (1932)

Bachelor's Affairs takes the opposite perspective that *Laughter* takes. What is it like for a man married to a young fun-loving gold digger? A middle-aged millionaire, Andrew Hoyt (Adolphe Menjou), impetuously marries a beautiful young gold digger, Eva (Joan Marsh). Their four-week honeymoon is filled with nonstop activity, mostly bicycling, horseback riding and dancing. There are presumably other more private activities that we don't get to see. This level of activity and excitement leaves Hoyt exhausted. Eva, who is not too bright, is guided in her gold-digging ways by a wiser older sister, Stella (Minna Gombell).

Andrew reassesses the marriage after the honeymoon. He can see that he is ill-suited as a husband to this sassy young woman, described by Picture Play Magazine as "frolicsome."[102] Eva's lack of intelligence makes her a purely physical creature with no capability for reason or judgment. Andrew finds it impossible to hold a simple conversation with her. He must accept that he is too old for his untutored and hyperactive wife. He schemes to get her into a romance with a younger, more tolerant and more durable man, Oliver Denton (Arthur Pierson). Everything is working as planned until he discovers that Oliver has a wife that he never bothered to mention. He pays Oliver's wife $5,000 to rush to Reno for a divorce.

Minna Gombell and Joan Marsh in *Bachelor's Affairs* (1932)

Kim Luperi, of the "I See a Dark Theater" blog wrote, "[T]he sanctity of marriage. . . is non-existent here."[103]

Scott Nye of Letterboxd was present for a rare showing of this film at UCLA. He wrote, "Joan Marsh does a hell of a Jean Harlow, and there's enough fine comedic tension to keep this cooking for an hour."[104]

Those We Love (1932)

May (Mary Astor) and Fred (Kenneth McKenna) are happily married with a young son, Ricky (Tommy Conlon). But Valerie (Lilyan Tashman), a woman in the neighborhood, turns up at their home while Fred is alone and attempts to seduce the unsuspecting husband. She is in the mold of the old-fashioned temptress. She clasps his hand. "Freddie," she says, "don't be scared. There can't possibly be any harm in holding hands." He quips, "Famous last words." He is surprised when the woman suddenly kisses him. He never acquiesces to her seductions, but his wife misunderstands when she catches Valerie taking a bath in their home. After May leaves him, Fred becomes so resentful that he sleeps with Valerie out of spite. But his wife forgives him in the end.

The number of adultery films was at its greatest peak from 1932 to 1934. This was, without question, the Golden Age of the Adultery Film.

Love Bound (1932)

John Randolph (Montagu Love) is blackmailed by his gold digger mistress, Verna Wilson (Natalie Moorhead). When he refuses to pay her, she takes him to court. frankfob2 of IMDb wrote, "His son [Jack Mulhall], discovering that the woman is part of a ring of blackmailers and that she is planning to flee the country, takes along his hulking chauffeur and follows her onto an ocean liner."[105]

One Hour with You (1932)

IMDb: "An unhappily married couple try to come between a happy one."[106]

Bad outside influences can damage the strongest marriage, which is demonstrated in *One Hour with You*. Dr. Andre and Colette Bertier (Maurice Chevalier and Jeanette MacDonald) are preparing to celebrate their third wedding anniversary. The couple has had a happy marriage, but a pair of insidious people turn up and threaten to spoil everything. Colette's old friend, Mitzi Olivier (Genevieve Tobin), is unhappily married to Professor Olivier (Roland Young). The Oliviers are routinely unfaithful spouses, each guilty of multiple affairs. They could not possibly have a positive influence on the Bertiers. Mitzi resolves to seduce Andre. She flirts with Andre first in the backseat of a cab and later during a medical examination. He resists her flirtations. But, as John Oswalt of IMDb points out, "she is persistent, and very cute, and he succumbs."[107] Meanwhile, Professor Olivier wants to wriggle out of his marital vows to run off with the maid. As Andre becomes preoccupied with Mitzi, his best friend Adolph (Charles Ruggles) is overcome by his burgeoning lust for Colette and makes a play for the charming wife.

Maurice Chevalier and Jeanette MacDonald in *One Hour with You* (1932)

Red-Headed Woman (1932)

The vamp was updated for the pre-Code era with *Red-Headed Woman*. Jean Harlow plays much the same gold digger role that she played the year before in *The Iron Man*. She seeks out weak-willed men who she can manipulate to her own advantage. She is not an exotic sort of vamp like Theda Bara, who wore chic, sultry and outre costumes. In 2002, Doyle auctioned a black and white beaded chemise dress that was worn by Bara. Here is Doyle's description of the dress: ". . . [T]he bodice top and skirt covered with tiers of long silver bead fringe, looped on bodice and swinging free on skirt, the torso solidly beaded with white pearlescent and black beads in a dramatic burst pattern centered with elliptical shape worked in rhinestones and square paillettes with a bead tassel dangling from middle."[108] Harlow, outfitted in standard secretary garb, is a stealth predator.

Men are pushovers for the alluring Lil Andrews (Harlow). Lil seduces her married boss, Bill Legendre Jr. (Chester Morris), to join her in an indiscreet tryst. She continues to use her wiles to break up Bill's marriage to his loving and devoted wife, Irene (Leila Hyams), and persuade the smitten Bill to marry her. Lil wants to be accepted into high society, but Bill's family and friends remain loyal to Irene and shun the uncouth home-wrecker. Bill's father, Will Legendre, Sr. (Lewis Stone), finds Lil's handkerchief at the home of coal tycoon Charles B. Gaerste (Henry Stephenson). He tells his son that he shouldn't trust Lil. Bill hires a private investigator, who returns with photos of Lil canoodling with Gaerste's French chauffeur, Albert (Charles Boyer). Lil is so enraged to catch Bill with Irene that she pulls out a gun and shoots him. Bill survives being shot and is a better man for the experience. He gladly divorces Lil and remarries Irene.

Jean Harlow in *Red-Headed Woman* (1932)

IMDb's nnnn4508919131 wrote of the film: "Made before censorship came into effect in Hollywood, this movie is able to shock viewers even today. . . Sex is out in the open and immorality is the name of the game."[109]

Wikipedia describes the film's tart ending as follows: "Two years later, [Bill] sees [Lil] again, at a race-track in Paris, in the company of an aged Frenchman. . . Lil and her elderly companion get into a limousine driven by Albert."[110]

The Beautiful Sailor (1932)

The original French title: *La belle marinière*

Marinette Bosquet (Madeleine Renaud) leaps into a river to drown herself. Pierre (Jean Gabin), the captain of a barge, quickly spots her and rushes to her rescue. Pierre and Marinette marry soon after and spend the early days of their marriage boating along the canal routes. Meanwhile, Marinette becomes close to

Pierre's crew mate and best friend, Sylvestre (Pierre Blanchar). It isn't long before the couple falls in love. This causes the friends to fight, after which Sylvestre moves off the barge. Pierre and Sylvestre see each other again weeks later and renew their friendship. But the old problem remains. Marinette realizes that she still loves Sylvestre and sneaks off the barge in the early morning to go away with him.

Cynara (1932)

The title is based on a poem by Ernest Dowson that contains the line: "I have been faithful to thee, Cynara, in my fashion."

A barrister, Jim Warlock (Ronald Colman), develops a fascination for beautiful young Doris Lea (Phyllis Barry) while his wife is away in Venice. The affair is instigated by Jim's lecherous best friend, John Tring (Henry Stephenson). Tring tells Jim, "There seems to be no color in your life. No variety. You have settled down to a routine. You are becoming smug. Don't you ever feel like kicking over the traces?" Smirking, Tring raises a glass of wine and announces, "I'll drink a toast to the last of the virtuous men."

Jim and Tring are dining at an Italian restaurant when Tring becomes interested in two shop girls seated at a nearby table. He jovially invites them to join them for dinner. One of the young women is Doris, who takes a liking to Jim almost immediately and has no concern with the fact that he is married. Before the couple parts, she writes out her phone number for him. Jim tears it up once she is out of sight. But Tring lets Doris know that Jim will be a judge for a beauty contest and she can see him again if she signs up as a contestant. So, the couple meets again at the beauty contest. After Jim awards her the cup, Doris turns away, trips and falls. She says that she twisted her ankle and can't walk, which prompts the gallant man to carry her home. But minutes later, when they argue, she has no problem striding indignantly across the room. Had she faked twisting her ankle to get him to take her home? There's no suggestion that she faked tripping and falling. The fact is that this interloper never comes across as cold and calculating, nor does she act greedy and materialistic. She is hopelessly in love. She is starry-eyed. This makes her, in spite of her foolishness, sympathetic. She reassures Jim, "You needn't be afraid. I've always dreamed of someone like you. Just like you. I'd never be a nuisance. I'd go away whenever you told me to." She says of his wife, "She needn't know. It won't hurt her if she doesn't know."

Jim grows increasingly uncomfortable with the relationship. He reminds Doris that she promised to quietly go away if their relationship became a problem for him.

Doris: I said when the time came to say goodbye, I'd go without a word. And I meant it when I said it.

Jim: But Doris, nothing has changed.

Doris: Oh, Jim, everything has changed.

When Jim ends their relationship, she commits suicide. Jim is treated harshly at the inquest for her suicide.

Usually, the best friend tries to be the conscience of the protagonist. But not in this instance. Tring goes to see Clemency, but she doesn't look happy to see him.

Tring: Oh, I'm in disgrace. Mephistopheles. I was afraid of that. You think it was my fault. Does *he*?

Clemency: No, he doesn't.

Tring: Well, he might. I did take him to that restaurant. I did speak to the girls. And of course I did nudge the laws of chance a bit. Yes, so far as fate ever has one eye open, I suppose I am guilty.

Tring, though, puts the most of blame on Doris.

Tring: She broke the rules.

Clemency: What are they?

Tring: To play for the stake you've settled on. Women always want to change the stakes in the middle of the game. You can't raise a man ten shillings on a one shilling limit.

Cynara's director, King Vidor, would revisit the subject of adultery twice within the next three years. He set the other adultery films, *The Stranger's Return* (1933) and *The Wedding Night* (1935), in the less glamorous environs of farm country.

Downstairs (1932)

Wikipedia reports:

It stars John Gilbert as a charming but self-serving chauffeur who wreaks havoc on his new employer's household, romancing and fleecing the women on the staff, and blackmailing the employer's wife.[111]

Gilbert is a traditional melodrama scoundrel.

Flesh (1932)

Ricardo Cortez plays the oily Nicky. Nicky abandons Laura (Karen Morley) when he finds out that she's pregnant with his child. She marries the big-hearted, dull-witted Polakai (Wallace Beery) because she knows that he will care for her and her baby. Polakai, a waiter in a beer garden, finds his extraordinary strength useful in tossing out drunken patrons. He also applies his muscles to a flashier sideline as a wrestler. In time, his success as a wrestler provides Laura with a comfortable lifestyle. But Nicky comes back into her life for a share of her comforts. Despite her better judgment, she is unable to resist his charms and renews her relationship with him.

Erickson wrote: "John Ford directed *Flesh* in a heavy Germanic fashion reminiscent of the Emil Jannings 'cuckolded husband' melodramas of the 1920s."[112] Jannings' *Sins of the Fathers* (1928), with its beer garden setting, most resembles *Flesh*. Greta (Ruth Chatterton), described by AFI as "an unprincipled adventuress,"[113] seduces Wilhelm Spengler (Jannings), a middle-aged restaurant owner, away from his ill wife (ZaSu Pitts). His wife, heartbroken to lose her husband, soon dies. Greta convinces Wilheim that he can make more money as a bootlegger. Wilheim becomes rich by illicitly manufacturing and distributing liquor. He can afford to send his son, Tom (Barry Norton), to a fine college. But Tom celebrates his graduation by freely imbibing his father's liquor, which causes him to go blind. The legal authorities finally catch up to Wilheim and put him in prison. Greta and her boyfriend promptly run off with Wilheim's money. Surprisingly, although Wilheim has suffered much from his involvement with Greta, AFI reports a (sort of) happy ending:

> [Wilheim] wins an early release for good behavior and becomes a waiter in a beer garden. One day he comes across his son, cured of blindness, and they are happily reunited.[114]

Ricardo Cortez and Karen Morley in *Flesh* (1932)

Skyscraper Souls (1932)

This is a quintessential pre-Code film, with no moral person in sight. David Dwight (Warren William), a bank owner, is an atrocious womanizer. He is unwilling to divorce his estranged wife, Ella (Hedda Hopper), because maintaining his marriage allows him to hold his many mistresses at bay. Ella is perfectly happy with the arrangement as David provides her with a generous allowance. David is dating his secretary, Sarah Dennis (Verree Teasdale), who is unaware of his marital arrangement and expects him to eventually obtain a divorce. Meanwhile, he turns his interest to young and pretty Lynn Harding (Maureen O'Sullivan), who also works for him. Lynn resists David's advances in the office, but David figures that the young woman will be more compliant in a more private and relaxed setting. He has her deliver a report to his penthouse, where he is waiting with a bottle of champagne. Lynn agrees to have one glass of champagne. Rather than weaken her defenses, the champagne puts her to sleep. When Lynn awakens an hour later, she is only interested in getting out of the penthouse and going home. Unfortunately, her boyfriend Tom (Norman Foster) is spying on her and sees her being escorted to the lobby by David.

Warren William and Alice White in *Employee Entrance* (1933)

Employee Entrance (1933)

Kurt Anderson (Warren William), an ambitious man, has risen rapidly to the general manager position in a major department store. He has advanced in his career by making himself into an unstoppable force. He is equally forceful in his relations with women. The scoundrel is willing to press his attentions on a married woman even if the woman protests vigorously. William plays virtually the same ruthless businessman that he played the prior year in *Skyscraper Souls*. He, too, likes to get young female employees drunk so it will be easy for him to seduce them. At a company ball, the lecherous Anderson gets his assistant's wife, Madeline West (Loretta Young), drunk.

Madeline: Oh, wait a minute! Maybe I shouldn't have any more. I feel kind of foggy.

Anderson: Go ahead and get foggy. You're among friends.

Madeline: Can I depend on that?

Anderson: Absolutely.

When she gets groggy, he gives her a key to his hotel room and recommends that she go to the room for a rest. He tells her, "When you feel better, come on back. I'll wait right here." But he gives her time to fall asleep before he arrives at the room and slips into bed with her.

Anderson continues to pursue Madeline at the office the next day. She is clear that she doesn't want to be involved with him.

Madeline: Don't touch me! Why don't you leave me alone?

Anderson: Because you're an attractive woman - one of the most attractive I've ever seen. There's something in us right now that pulls us together. We haven't anything to say about it. If I just lay my hand on you now -

She pulls away, but he is undeterred. She remains so distraught that she attempts suicide.

Enraged by his wife's suicide attempt, Martin West (Wallace Ford) storms into Anderson's office and shoots his lecherous boss. Anderson survives, having suffered a minor wound, and refuses to call the police.

William played a scoundrel in other films, including *The Dark Horse* (1932), *The Match King* (1932) and *Bedside* (1934). Adultery was part of the scoundrel's modus operandi. In *The Match King*, William is a business schemer fooling around with his partner's wife.

Luxury Liner (1933)

Sybil Bernhard (Vivienne Osborne) runs off with a wealthy financier, Alex Stevanson (Frank Morgan). Her jilted husband, Dr. Bernhard (George Brent), learns that his wife and her lover have booked passage on the luxury liner Germania. He rushes aboard the ship, determined to locate his wife and persuade her to change her mind. A flaw of the film is that Sybil presents no appealing qualities. Why is Bernhard so desperate to get her back? Why is the wealthy financier interested in her? It is understandable when, early on, Stevanson loses interest in Sybil and expresses regret for having run off with her. He quickly turns his attention to a charming opera singer, Luise Marheim (Verree Teasdale).

The Woman I Stole (1933)

A ruthless oil baron (Jack Holt) seduces his general manager's wife (Fay Wray).

East of Fifth Avenue (1933)

Often, ugly surprises await those newlyweds who have married impulsively. Vic Howard (Wallace Ford) meets and marries Edna (Mary Carlisle) while on a business trip. It doesn't go well when he takes his new bride back home to New York City. She learns to her dismay that he lives in a low-rent boarding house. She learns, too, that her husband lives off money he earns from gambling, mostly from backroom poker games and horse racing. How do you marry someone without knowing how they make their living? Vic finds that his bride is lazy, shallow, and flighty. An aspiring poet, Paul Baxter (Walter Byron), is quick to take advantage of the situation by whispering sweet words into Edna's ear. Paul is just as lazy, shallow and flighty as Edna, which makes them a perfect match. To make Edna happy, Vic earns a sizable bankroll at the racetrack hoping to buy a garage, which will assure him a steady income. But Edna steals the money and runs off to Tahiti with Paul. The future of the runaways shows little promise. Edna lazily lays across Paul's lap eating chocolates while Paul haughtily recites his bad poetry. Edna must have doubts by now because we see her wince at Paul's latest couplets. Meanwhile, Vic is reunited with an old girlfriend who truly loves him.

A Lost Lady (1934)

Days before Marian (Barbara Stanwyck) is to wed Ned Montgomery (Phillip Reed), a man angrily approaches Ned outside a nightclub and accuses him of dallying with his wife. With Marian looking on, the man pulls out a gun and fatally shoots Ned.

Marian is distraught over Ned's death and travels to a resort in the Canadian Rockies for a rest. She is out hiking in the mountains when she falls off a ledge and twists her ankle. She is rescued by genial Dan Forrester (Frank Morgan). Dan looks after Marian, not only making sure that her ankle heals but also lifting her spirits.

Dan is an older man who has attained great prominence as an attorney. He comes to love Marian and asks her to marry him. Marian agrees. She is willing to marry this caring, reliable older man out of sheer gratitude. After all, it was his affectionate care that lifted her out of her depression. But she is also willing to marry him because, after the trauma she suffered, she is desperate for comfort and security. She is honest with him that she doesn't love him.

The rakish Frank Ellinger (Ricardo Cortez) is cheeky, charismatic and persistent as he entices Marian to embark on an affair. Marian has an attraction to Frank that defies good judgment. But we already know that her late fiancé, Ned, was rakish as well. This must be the type of man who appeals to her. But it's certainly not the type of man that a woman can rely upon. Would Frank have had the patience and compassion to have sat at Marian's bedside and guided her through her recovery as Dan had? Yet, Marian is willing to give up a strong marriage for the passion and romance that Frank promises.

Dan is crushed when Marian tells him that she is leaving him for Frank. He frets so much over her decision that he is unable to sleep all night. He goes to court the next day to present a case, but he is tired and ill-prepared. During the hearing, he suffers a heart attack. Marian remains at Dan's bedside during his recovery, caring for him in the same way that he once cared for her. Marian realizes as she fusses over Dan that she truly loves him.

Cortez had much experience playing the other man, having played similar roles in *Transgression* (1931), *Illicit* (1931) and *Flesh* (1932).

The film is loosely based on Willa Cather's 1923 novel "A Lost Lady." Britannica notes:

. . . [Marian Forrester] is portrayed through the adoring eyes of young Niel Herbert. He initially views Marian — the beautiful, gracious, and indomitable wife of an industrial magnate and Western pioneer — as the personification of ladylike propriety. In truth she is somewhat less perfect than he pictures her. . .[115]

SuperSummary reports:

Niel becomes disillusioned when he discovers that Frank Ellinger shares Mrs. Forrester's bedroom while her husband is away. This realization that his ideal woman is unfaithful to her husband causes a loss of innocence for Niel.[116]

The twelve-year-old boy goes up to the window of Mrs. Forrester's bedroom to lay flowers on the sill. The book reads, "[H]e heard from within a woman's soft laugh; impatient, indulgent, teasing, eager. Then another laugh, very different, a man's."[117]

Her husband, Captain Forrester, loses much of his fortune when a bank in which he is heavily invested goes bankrupt. SuperSummary continues:

Captain Forrester suffers a stroke due to the stress of his financial loss. The Forresters are forced to retire to Sweet Water, to the dismay of Mrs. Forrester, who cherishes the much more sophisticated society in Colorado.[118]

Britannica reports, ". . . [A]fter her husband's death she drinks too much and looks to other men for emotional and financial support."[119]

Brian Aherne and Madge Evans in *What Every Woman Knows* (1934)

What Every Woman Knows (1934)

Maggie (Helen Hayes) was jilted by a minister, who suddenly fell in love with another woman and married her. Her father, Alick Wylie (David Torrence), feels sad for Maggie. He says, "It's an ill breed of men these days that don't know a fine woman when they can have one." Maggie assumes that the minister's new wife has lots of charm. Her father asks her to explain what she means by "charm." She says, "It's a sort of bloom on a woman. If you have it, you don't need anything else. And, if you don't have it, it doesn't much matter what else you have. Some women, the few, have charm for all. And most have charm for one. And some have charm for none." Maggie, who sees herself falling into the last category, is resigned to remaining unmarried for the rest of her life. But her father and brothers, David (Donald Crisp) and James (Dudley Digges), feel obligated to find her a husband.

Wylie suspects that a burglar has been breaking into their home at night. He and his sons excitedly lay in wait for the burglar's return. An intruder does, in fact, show up. But the intruder, John Shand (Brian Aherne), has no interest in robbing them. He was recently forced to drop out of college due to a lack of money and he has been trying to further his education by reading the books in Wylie's extensive library. Wylie takes a liking to the ambitious young man. He offers to pay for him to return to college if he allows Maggie the option to marry him in five years.

John accepts the arrangement and marries Maggie five years later. He is successful in pursuing a career in politics. But his success has a bad effect on his marriage. After he attains prominence in Parliament, he drifts away from Maggie for an affair with a countess' niece, Lady Sybil Tenterden (Madge Evans). Lady Sybil is one of those women with lots of charm. The Indianapolis Times referred to her as a "designing young siren."[120]

In time, John comes to realize that he cannot do without Maggie, whose steadfast support and guidance had much to do with his career success. The message of the film is that a marriage cannot be built on love or lust alone. It has to have a practical element. And maybe love develops out of that.

Devotion and support could be more important than passion and sex. It was stated in the article "The History Of Dating in America": "[In the 1700s,] a marriage built solely on the forces of emotion and mutual affection was scorned and perceived as irresponsible. Rather, love was regarded as the product of a constructed arrangement, eventually achieved by couples with aligned resources and values."[121]

A woman addresses this issue on her deathbed in *Green Dolphin Street* (1947). The woman, Sophie Patourel (Gladys Cooper), wants to make her feelings to her husband Octavius (Edmund Gwenn) and daughter Marguerite (Donna Reed) clear before she dies. She says:

> When I married you, Octavius, I did not love you. The marriage was forced on me by my parents. Against my will. I was in love with another man. I came to you, Octavius, with a broken heart, hating you. But from the very beginning, you were kind to me, thoughtful, generous. And soon I began to realize that your love was bigger than anything I had ever felt. I was humble and frightened in its presence, but still I did not love you. But as the years went on, something began to grow in my heart. At first, respect. Then gratitude. And the dashing young prince I'd once loved faded from my dreams. And suddenly, before my eyes, you, Octavius - feeble-sighted, without much hair, no longer young, but more splendid than any dream any girl ever had. Do you know what I'm saying? Do you, Marguerite? I've come to love your father with a love so deep, so great that nothing on earth can compare with it.

Evelyn Prentice (1934)

Evelyn Prentice (Myrna Loy), the neglected wife of a prominent attorney, falls prey to a hustler, Lawrence Kennard (Harvey Stephens), who blackmails her for the return of her love letters to him. In his office, she grabs a gun from an open drawer and demands the letters. He struggles with her for the gun, which fires accidentally. Evelyn flees the scene in a panic. Kennard is found dead by the police the next day. When Kennard's girlfriend Judith Wilson (Isabel Jewel) is accused of the crime, the guilt-ridden Evelyn begs her husband John (William Powell) to defend her. As the evidence mounts against Judith, Evelyn realizes that she will need to confess. But, instead, Judith confesses! Evelyn had not shot Lawrence when the gun fired. He simply stumbled, fell, and hit his head. After Evelyn rushed out of his office, Judith came into the room, picked up the gun, and fired it at Lawrence.

Bette Davis and Ann Dvorak in *Housewife* (1934)

Housewife (1934)

Nan (Ann Dvorak) feels great love for her husband, Bill Reynolds (George Brent), but she believes that he has failed to realize his full potential. She is convinced that her husband's timidity and lack of ambition are holding him back in his job at an advertising agency. She urges him to quit his job to start a rival agency. Bill has great success building up his new business. The new confident and ambitious Bill arouses the interest of Pat Berkeley (Bette Davis), an advertising copywriter who knows Bill and Nan from high school. Bill and Pat's relationship grows more intimate, but Bill fools himself into thinking they are nothing more than good friends. Pat is immoral and predatory in her stealth pursuit of the naive Bill. Nan is concerned about the relationship, but she chooses to dismiss her concerns as being nothing more than foolish jealousy. This proves to be a mistake as, soon, Bill asks Nan for a divorce. When she refuses, he storms out of the house. He is in a blind rage as he starts to drive off and runs his car into his son Buddy (Ronnie Cosby). The stunned couple renews their bond as they see Buddy through his recovery.

Age of Indiscretion (1935)

A secretary, Maxine Bennett (Madge Evans), comforts her boss Robert Lenhart (Paul Lukas) when his greedy wife Eve (Helen Vinson) leaves him and his son Bill (David Holt) for a more prosperous man. The couple soon falls in love and finds happiness together. But Eve's wealthy new mother-in-law, Emma Shaw (May Robson), demands that Eve obtain custody of her son. Robert and Maxine fight together against Eve's high-priced lawyers to hold onto Bill.

Private Worlds (1935)

A subplot of *Private Worlds* involves a young woman, Claire Monet (Helen Vinson), making advances on a married doctor, Dr. Alex MacGregor (Joel McCrea). Alex's wife Sally (Joan Bennett) becomes distressed by Claire's attentions, which places a serious strain on the marriage.

Dangerous Waters (1936)

A ship captain, Jim Marlowe (Jack Holt), impulsively marries Joan (Grace Bradley). Joan is a frisky young woman who has managed to conceal her wild past from her husband. She has no interest in remaining faithful to one man. She works hard to seduce Jim's first mate, Dusty Johnson (Robert Armstrong). Dusty resists at first, but he eventually succumbs to her charms. Jim is enraged when he catches Dusty and Joan kissing. But, in the end, Joan gets drunk and admits to persistently flirting with Dusty until she "broke [him] down."

School for Husbands (1937)

Marion Carter (Diana Churchill) and Diana Cheswick (June Clyde) are enthralled by Leonard Drummond (Rex Harrison), a rakish novelist who is notorious for his many careless love affairs. Marion says that, unlike their husbands, Drummond is interesting and understands women. But she is worried that Diana is falling prey to his charm and needs to be rescued before she does something stupid. Marion gets Drummond alone to talk to him and make him see the folly of his philandering. She explains that an extramarital affair, unlike a marriage, isn't real. She says, "I am sorry for you. Because I think you'd be so much happier if you loved one woman instead of so many." Drummond comes to find the feisty and strong-willed Marion more exciting than the compliant Diana. Marion's husband Geoffrey (Henry Kendall) and Diana's husband Morgan (Romney Brent) are worried to see Drummond mixing with their wives. Geoffrey and Morgan pretend to go on a trip to Paris intending to catch Drummond with either Marion or Diane. Their plans go wrong when their car breaks down during a storm and they are unable to get back home. Marion suddenly gets the foolish idea to use Drummond to make Jeffery jealous.

Her Husband's Secretary (1937)

Carol Kingdon (Jean Muir) and Diane Ware (Beverly Roberts), who work together as secretaries, become best friends. Diane is ruthless and selfish. She recommends Carol to get ahead by seducing her married boss.

> Carol: I hope you don't let anybody hear you talk like that. They'll think you're really as cold-blooded as you sound.
>
> Diane: Well, why not? After all, he's a big shot. He's rich, intelligent, fairly attractive, and as susceptible to flattery as most men.
>
> Carol: And married.
>
> Diane: Don't be noble. Do you want to be a secretary your whole life?

Carol: No wonder wives think we're pirates!

Clara Blandick, Warren Hull, Beverly Roberts and Jean Muir
in *Her Husband's Secretary* (1937)

Diane only cares if a man has money. She thinks that Carol is foolish to marry a modest construction worker, Bart (Warren Hull). It turns out, though, that Bart comes from a wealthy family. Bart's father, Dan (Harry Davenport), summons his son to his deathbed to ask him to take over the family business. On Carol's recommendation, Bart hires Diane as his secretary. Carol becomes suspicious when Bart starts to spend more time at the office. She has every right to be suspicious. Bart and Diane travel to the Oregon woods to spend the weekend together in a cozy cabin. Carol, who has followed them, arrives at the cabin unexpectedly. She argues with Diane, slaps her across the face, and then storms out. A forest fire forces Bart and Diane to evacuate the cabin, but Bart trips over a log and hits his head on a rock. Diane panics seeing Bart unconscious and flees for her life. She encounters Carol driving along the road and pleads with her to hurry her away from the fire, but Carol insists on Diane leading her back to Bart.

The Sisters (1938)

Tom Knivel (Dick Foran), a young bank president, briefly strays from his good marriage. bkoganbing of IMDb wrote: "Foran falls victim to the town tart briefly, one of many men in the area."[122]

Man-Proof (1938)

Mimi Swift (Myrna Loy) loses playboy Alan Wythe (Walter Pidgeon) to heiress Elizabeth Kent (Rosalind Russell), whose wealth means more to Alan than anything Mimi has to offer. But Mimi refuses even after Alan and Elizabeth marry to give up her man.

Mimi insists that Alan made a mistake marrying Elizabeth and she has "a right to [him]." Her mother Meg (Nana Bryant) tells her flatly, "You ought to lay off Alan." But Mimi refuses to take her mother's advice. She later tells her:

I promised you I'd try to get interested in something else. Well, it didn't work. And now if Alan loves me as much as I love him - and I think he does - he can't keep on with Elizabeth. But whatever happens, everything's going to be above board. That's why I'm telling you all this, and I'm going to tell Elizabeth.

Mimi, as a self-righteous homewrecker, represents a new breed.

Elizabeth arrives and catches Alan with Mimi. She offers her view on the situation. She says:

I knew, oh, right away that Alan didn't love me. Women can hide the way they feel, but men can't. So, I was very unhappy for a time. I could only think that he was still in love with you, Mimi, that he'd only married me because I was a rich girl. . . And then I began to realize something else, and it was strange. He was trying to be in love with me. So hard. The effort was desperate. And I knew that Alan had never been in love and never would be. But in his not wanting to be like that, that made a difference. And instead of hating him for being ordinary, I felt sorry for him, because I had on my hands a very lonely man.

Alan agrees that he has been selfish and needs to do better to save his marriage. He leaves Mimi to return to Elizabeth.

The Women (1939)

Mary Haines (Norma Shearer) is stunned to learn that her husband Stephen is having an affair with a perfume counter girl, Crystal Allen (Joan Crawford). Mary is not going to accept this without a fight. She confronts Crystal to demand she stop seeing her husband. But Crystal is unmoved by Mary's demands.

Crystal: Listen, I'm taking my marching orders from Stephen. He seems to be satisfied with this arrangement. So don't force any issues unless you want to cause plenty of trouble.

Mary: You've made it impossible for me to do anything else.

Crystal: You're very confident, aren't you?

Mary: Yes. Because I know Stephen couldn't love a girl like you.

Crystal: If he couldn't, he's an awfully good actor. Look, what have you got to kick about? You've got everything that matters. The name, the position, the money.

Mary: My husband's love happens to mean more to me than those things.

Crystal: Oh, can the sob stuff, Mrs. Haines. You noble wives and mothers bore the brains out of me. I'll bet you bore your husband, too.

Mary: You're a hard one, aren't you?

Crystal: I can be soft on the right occasion. Look, what did you expect me to do? Burst into tears and beg you to forgive me? Isn't that what you really came in here for?

Mary: Not after seeing you. You're even more typical than I dared hope.

Crystal: Honey, that goes double. Get this. I'd break up your snug little roost if I could but I don't stand a chance. Don't think it's because your husband isn't crazy about me. It's because he lets old-fashioned sentiment put the Indian sign on him.

Mary: I'm glad you understand the strength of sentiment, Miss Allen, because its beauty is something you'll never know.

Crawford takes the boldness and shrewdness of a gold digger to new heights.

The film includes a second confrontation between a wife and a mistress. Sylvia Fowler (Rosalind Russell) learns that Miriam Aarons (Paulette Goddard) is having an affair with her husband. The outcome of this confrontation isn't so much about insults and recriminations as it is about slaps and hair-pulling. The catfight between Sylvia and Miriam is the comic highlight of the film.

Joan Crawford and Norma Shearer in *The Women* (1939)

Crystal persuades Stephen to divorce Mary. The story advances two years. As Stephen's wife, the former counter girl is living in luxury. But she has become bored with Stephen and has found herself a new lover, Buck Winston. Buck is a radio star married to the wealthy Countess de Lave (Mary Boland). Mary still loves Stephen and feels sorry for him when she learns of Crystal's affair. She resolves to expose the affair and get her ex-husband back.

The nail salon's most dynamic nail polish color is Jungle Red. At first, Mary is not bold enough to wear such a color. But the time has come for Mary to fight to get her man back and she approaches this opportunity as a changed woman. She holds up her hands to show off her new crimson nails. She announces with a wicked grin, "I've had two years to grow claws, mother. Jungle Red!"

Crystal lets Mary know that she can have Stephen. She intends to upgrade her lifestyle by marrying Buck. But the film has a sweet ending, as described by Wikipedia: "The weeping Countess reveals that she has been funding Buck's radio career and that without her, he will be penniless and jobless."[123]

Gone with the Wind (1939)

Ashley Wilkes (Leslie Howard) loves Scarlett O'Hara (Vivien Leigh), but her passionate personality and thoughtless actions have convinced him that she would not be a suitable wife for him. He explains to Scarlett, plainly, that they are too different from one another. Ashley instead marries his cousin Melanie, who he sees as a more ideal match. Scarlett tries on more than one occasion to persuade Ashley to leave Melanie. At one point, she asks Ashley to run away with her to Mexico. Ashley speaks to her of honor, but she doesn't care about honor and prefers to kiss him instead. He does not resist her at first. But, then, he violently pulls away from her. "We won't do this," he insists. "I tell you, we won't do it!" Scarlett cries out, "Say it. You love me." He responds, "All right, I'll say it. I love your courage and your stubbornness. I love them so much that, a moment ago, I could have forgotten the best wife a man has ever had. But, Scarlett, I'm not going to forget her!"

Scarlett takes an interest in her sister Suellen's fiancé, Frank Kennedy, as he has become a successful merchant and has the money that she needs to save her plantation. She lies to Frank that Suellen doesn't really love him and uses her charm to convince him to marry her instead.

Purity and Precision, a website that offers a Christian perspective on films, emphasizes that Scarlett never treats marriage with the sanctity it deserves. The site points out: "After their marriage, Rhett and Scarlett agree to cease physical relations with each other indefinitely, on the understanding that Rhett may go to a brothel on a regular basis."[124]

Lana Turner and James Craig in *Marriage Is a Private Affair* (1944)

Marriage Is a Private Affair (1944)

Erickson wrote:

Lana Turner is the bride, John Hodiak the groom. James Craig is the odd man out, who pursues Turner when Hodiak is off fighting the war. Bored by domesticity, Turner welcomes Craig's attentions, but impending motherhood straightens out her priorities. Nearly two hours of celluloid are expended on a story that any other studio would have zipped out in seven reels.[125]

Theo West (Turner) believes that it is easy to "slip" when it comes to marital fidelity. Her father, Ed Scofield (Morris Ankrum), is the voice of morality. He tells her, "Darling, I hope if you marry again, it won't be with the idea that you can call it off like a ballgame." The man feels guilty about divorcing her mother when she was still a child. He blames the divorce for making his daughter feel uncertain in her own marriage. He says, "That won't be your fault. But mine. . . mine and your mother's. We tore the certainty out of you."

Craig plays the other man in two other films, *The Heavenly Body* (1944) and *While the City Sleeps* (1956). Many films in this period dealt with wartime affairs. We will return to this subject in Chapter Nineteen.

Divorce (1945)

Diane Carter (Kay Francis) is a serial divorcee (she's gotten divorced four times!). Anxious to marry yet again, she pays a visit to a high school sweetheart, Bob Phillips (Bruce Cabot). He's married, but that doesn't bother her. She manages with little effort to break up the marriage. Bob finally sees that Diane has no morals when she tries to involve him in an illegal property deal. Sandra Brennan of AllMovie perfectly summarizes the ending: "The man figures out her game and leaves her in favor of his former wife."[126]

Suspense (1946)

A mysterious drifter, Joe Morgan (Barry Sullivan), gets a job as a peanut vendor with an ice skating show operated by Frank Leonard (Albert Dekker). Morgan quickly takes an interest in Leonard's lovely young wife, Roberta Elva (Belita), who is also the show's star. He catches her leaving the theatre and strikes up a conversation with her. She is taken aback by his flagrant flirting.

Morgan isn't content to hawk peanuts. While sweeping up peanut shells, he watches the skaters rehearse a number for the show. Harry Wheeler (Eugene Pallette), Leonard's assistant, complains that the number isn't exciting enough. He says, "Our box office is sagging from broken-down circus routines." The cocky peanut vendor steps up to the stage with an idea to add excitement to the number - Roberta leaping through a ring of swords. His dynamic suggestion earns him an immediate promotion to a management position. Leonard says, "We could use some new blood around here." Morgan doesn't accept the job humbly. "Mr. Leonard," he says, "let me be the first to congratulate you. You've just made a very smart move." He is even less humble approaching Roberta about his new position. "I've been promoted, baby," he announces to her. She tells him that he's a "fresh character" and demands that she call her "Mrs. Leonard." He is undeterred. He kisses her. "You must be crazy," she says. "You think you can get away with anything, don't you?" He insists that "there are some things that are worth taking chances for."

Roberta eventually succumbs to Morgan's persistent enticements. She feels horribly guilty when she realizes that her husband, who went missing, was murdered by Morgan. Morgan has taken wife-stealing to a psychopathic level.

The Egg and I (1947)

City folk Bob and Betty MacDonald (Fred MacMurray and Claudette Colbert) move to upstate New York to become chicken farmers. But even the MacDonalds, who occupy their days with the humble business of egg production, aren't safe from the wiles of a glamorous homewrecker. It is obvious to Betty that Harriet Putnam (Louise Allbritton), the owner of the state-of-the-art Bella Vista Farm, is out to steal her husband.

One night, while Betty is alone preparing dinner, an old woman comes to the door. The woman tells Betty that she once lived in her home. It becomes evident that the woman isn't in her right mind when she matter-of-factly introduces Betty to a husband who is nowhere to be seen. She then, according to AFI, "regales [Betty] with stories about vicious giant chickens."[127] The sheriff shows up looking for the old woman, who escaped from a mental health facility. He explains that the woman went insane after her husband ran off with another woman. Betty, fearful of turning into this old woman, immediately packs her bags and leaves.

Not surprisingly, the couple reconciles in the end.

The film's adultery-and-chicken premise is not really unusual. Lady Chatterley bonds with her lover over the care of chickens. Also, a sophisticated city woman attempts to lure a farmer away from his wife in *Sunrise*.

Louise Allbritton, Fred MacMurray and Claudette Colbert in *The Egg and I* (1947)

The Private Affairs of Bel Ami (1947)

Georges (George Sanders) is an ambitious man. He abandons his loving girlfriend, Clotilde de Marelle (Angela Lansbury), to marry a rich widow, Madeleine (Ann Dvorak). But his social climbing does not end with the widow. He frames Madeleine for adultery so that he can marry Suzanne Walter (Susan Douglas), the daughter of a wealthy newspaper publisher.

The Arnelo Affair (1947)

Anne Parkson (Frances Gifford), an interior decorator, feels neglected by her lawyer husband. To relieve her boredom, she begins a flirtation with Tony Arnelo (John Hodiak), a nightclub owner who has hired her to redecorate his club. Anne realizes that a romance is developing between them. She hopes to distance herself from Tony by convincing her lawyer husband, Ted (George Murphy), to take her on vacation. But her husband tells her that he is too busy for a vacation. Anne is determined not to get drawn into an affair with Tony. Tony murders his troublesome former girlfriend, Claire Lorrison (Joan Woodbury). He figures that he can force Anne to leave her husband if he threatens to frame her for the murder.

The titular affair isn't much of an affair. Anne and Tony never even kiss.

Wild Harvest (1947)

Joe Madigan (Alan Ladd) heads an itinerant combine crew, a top-notch team that includes his best friend Jim Davis (Robert Preston).

A farmer's niece, Fay Rankin (Dorothy Lamour), shows up looking for a man to take her off the farm. She fails at seducing Joe so she decides instead to ply her wiles on the more gullible, easygoing Jim. Fay and Jim marry, but Fay still has her eyes on Joe. One night, she visits Joe in his tent and tries to seduce him to steal a portion of the harvest.

Joe: You forgot one thing.

Fay: What's that, Joe?

Joe: You're married.

Fay: Ha, that's a joke!

Joe: Well, Jim's not laughing.

Fay: Maybe I don't care.

Joe: Maybe I do.

Joe calls her "cheap, poisonous and crooked."

Desire Me (1947)

Paul Aubert (Robert Mitchum) speaks with great affection of his wife, Marise (Greer Garson), while being held in a German prisoner-of-war camp. A fellow prisoner, Jean Renaud (Richard Hart), falls in love imagining Paul's ideal wife. When the war ends, Jean visits Marise in Normandy and lies by saying he saw her husband shot dead while escaping the camp. He manages, in his false efforts to comfort her, to misappropriate her trust and affection.

A 1928 German film, *Homecoming*, provided a sad and tender take on essentially the same tale. Two German soldiers, Karl (Gustav Fröhlich) and Richard (Lars Hanson), escape from a Russian prisoner-of-war camp. Richard becomes exhausted and collapses, but Karl refuses to abandon him and continues the journey carrying his friend. When Karl leaves Richard alone to look for water, Russian soldiers arrive and recapture Richard. Karl makes it to Hamburg and visits Richard's wife, Anna (Dita Parlo). Richard spoke often of Anna in the camp and Karl feels like he already knows her. Anna lets Karl live in a spare room. The couple falls in love. Richard arrives home just in time to see Anna and Karl kiss for the first time. He draws a pistol, planning to kill Karl, but he changes his mind. Instead, he leaves and gets a job on a freighter.

Daybreak (1948)

Eddie (Eric Portman), the owner of a barge, hires Olaf (Maxwell Reed) to work as a deckhand. Loading freight doesn't interest Olaf as much as eyeballing Eddie's wife, Frankie (Ann Todd). Eddie often has to go out of town for days. Olaf uses Eddie's absences as an opportunity to make sexual advances toward Frankie. Olaf comes upon Frankie dancing to a record (Nigel Tangye's "Daybreak"). He tells her that he shares her fondness for music and dancing. The two dance. Without warning, he wraps his arms around her and kisses her. She pulls away violently. The record is what got this started. She must be rid of it now. She snatches the record off the player and breaks it in half. She then tosses the broken pieces into the ocean. She doesn't believe that Olaf will keep away from her and doubts that she will be able to rebuff his aggressive advances much longer. She is afraid to tell Eddie about what's going on. She instead asks him to bring her along on his business trips. But he turns her down.

One night, while Eddie is away, Olaf shows up on the barge and demands that Frankie have a drink with him. Eddie returns unexpectedly and catches the two drinking together. "What's been going on here?" he asks. He gets into a fight with Olaf. Olaf knocks him overboard. Eddie disappears in the water and never resurfaces. The police presume that Eddie drowned and arrest Olaf for murder. Frankie is distraught after speaking to the police. Before the police are off the barge, she takes a pistol out of a drawer and shoots herself. The police rush to her and find her dead. Eddie climbs ashore the next morning. He stays hidden while Olaf is on trial for his murder. In the end, Olaf is convicted and sentenced to hang. Eddie wants to see Olaf hung, but he comes forward in time to save the brute's life. In despair, he goes off on his own and hangs himself.

An innocent married couple is led to death by an evil interloper, who is left free to destroy other married couples. Not surprisingly, this downer of a film failed dismally at the box office.

East Side, West Side (1949)

Jessie Bourne (Barbara Stanwyck) is alone at home while her husband Brandon (James Mason) is drunkenly flirting with other women at a nightclub. Brandon approaches a pretty young lady, Rosa Senta (Cyd Charisse). Rosa, who is aware of his reputation as a philanderer, wryly asks him about his wife. He insists that he's a reformed man and simply wants her to sit with him for a drink. She agrees.

Rosa: I'm curious about guys like you.

Brandon: Yeah? What are you curious about, with guys like me?

Rosa: Well, doesn't your wife dance?

Brandon: Brilliantly.

Rosa: Yeah. She's prettier than I am, she dresses better, and she's probably a lot smarter. Everything I can do, chances are she can do better. So, what do you want to be sitting here with me for? What is it with guys like you? What goes on in your fuzzy little heads?

After dawdling for a bit, he answers, "Before I reformed, I suppose my thinking went something like this. Just because a man has one perfect rose in his garden at home, it doesn't mean that he can't appreciate the flowers of the field."

Little does Brandon realize that he is about to be lured into an affair by an old girlfriend, Isabel (Ava Gardner), who has recently returned to town. Isabel is aggressive in her pursuit of him. He rejects her advances at first. "I don't like revivals," he says flatly. He makes it clear to her that he loves his wife and that he's happy with his marriage. But she persists. She asks him if he didn't love her, too. He avoids the question. She says:

Maybe it wasn't love. Maybe it was only chemistry, or the right combination, or a miracle. But most people drag through their whole lives without finding it. We both know that, don't we, Bran?

He is unable to resist her for long.

Brandon is not at all sympathetic. None of the people around him are willing to conceal their disdain for his inveterate unfaithfulness. His own mother (Gale Sondergaard) has harsh words for him. The sad truth is Brandon, more than anyone else, hates himself for having the affair. He tells his wife, "You're everything that's good in my life. Don't you think I know that? This other thing is like a sickness." Jessie, according to the DVD press material, "bears her husband'sindiscretion with a gallant dignity."[128]

In *The Vampire's Trail* (1914), a wife confronts the scheming actress who stole her husband. According to The Moving Picture World, the actress "shrinks in fear from the enraged wife."[129] This scene plays out much differently in *East Side, West Side*.

Isabel: All right, you're late, and I am going to a cocktail party, so I'll wind this up fast. I'm back, and I'm going to stay back. . . It would just be simpler if you would let him go. But if you don't, I want to tell you what to expect. This time it's going to be different. This time he's not going to sneak a few minutes with me when he can get away from you. This time, you'll see him only when I don't want him. Is that clear?

Jessie: You're not difficult to follow.

Isabel: Sorry I'm not more subtle, but you must remember, I haven't had your advantages.

It clearly bothers Isabel that Jessie has had a much easier life than she has had. She says, "When your mother sent you to Miss Cavanaugh's School for nice young ladies, I was slinging hash." But Isabel believes that she has earned what she has.

Isabel: Like all your kind, you think by marrying a man you've done enough. Well, there's one thing Miss Cavanaugh forgot to teach you, something I learned, how to keep a man, how to keep him wanting you.

Jessie: My husband doesn't want you. He's finished with you. He told me so, last night.

Isabel: I'll call him and he'll come running.

Jessie: Do you know how he thinks of you?

Isabel: Roughly.

Jessie: As a sickness.

Isabel: And what do you stand for, health? Sacred and profane love, huh?

Jessie: If Bran wants you, why doesn't he leave me? I'd let him go. He knows that. But he begs me to stay with him. Why?

Isabel: He's told me why, over and over again. For the same reason he married you.

Jessie: Because he loves me.

Isabel: Because he wanted a checkrein, a control, a straightjacket. And that's what you are to him, because he's a little afraid to be himself.

Jessie: You're a little afraid, too, aren't you?

Isabel: Of what? Of you?

Jessie: Why else did you call me? Because you're not sure of yourself. Because you know you've lost Bran, this is one last desperate try, isn't it? You're afraid and unhappy, and perhaps that's only fair. You've caused me a great deal of unhappiness in the past. But if I were in your place, I would remember something Miss Cavanaugh didn't forget to teach me. How to lose, gracefully.

Gardner is a brazen homewrecker much like Joan Crawford was in *The Women*. The worst interloper has a sense of entitlement. *Madame Bovary*'s Rodolphe believes that a fit man like himself, not a "fat fellow" like Charles Bovary, deserves a woman as attractive as Emma.

Born to be Bad (1950)

Donna Foster (Joan Leslie) lets Christabel (Joan Fontaine) move into her home so that she can attend a nearby business college. Christabel flirts with Donna's wealthy fiancé, Curtis Carey (Zachary Scott), at a party for Donna's friend, painter Gabriel Broome (Mel Ferrer). Christabel comes up with a simple but effective strategy to steal Curtis away from Donna - use Curtis' wealth to create a wedge between the couple. She easily instills doubt in Curtis' mind by implying that Donna has been too receptive to his expensive gifts. She in turn tells Donna that, by accepting expensive gifts from Curtis, she is giving her groom-to-be the impression that she only wants to marry him for his money. Now it is time for the *coup de grâce*. She convinces Curtis to ask Donna to sign a prenuptial agreement, knowing that this will enrage Donna and cause her to break up with him.

Christabel is as ambitious, scheming and amoral as *The Women*'s Crystal Allen. The way that she goes about breaking up a happy engagement is worse than the way that Crystal breaks up a happy marriage. Like Crystal, she schemes and manipulates to get her man and attain a luxurious lifestyle. Her closets are bursting with fancy new clothes. But, also like Crystal, she becomes bored as a member of high society and figures to entertain herself by having a lover on the side. Nick Bradley (Robert Ryan), an aspiring author, refuses to be her lover. He tells her, "Sorry, I'm not cut out to be a backstreet boy. And I don't make dates with other men's wives unless they bring written permission from their husbands." But she has found a new lover with

Broome. She tells Curtis that she is going to visit her sick aunt when in fact she is meeting Broome at a vacation resort. Her aunt, who is truly sick, dies while Christabel is canoodling with Broome. Her stern uncle, John Caine (Harold Vermilyea), is repulsed as he exposes her vile lie to Curtis.

Zachary Scott and Joan Fontaine *in Born to be Bad* (1950)

Wikipedia summarizes the conclusion: "Curtis reunites with Donna after sending away Christabel with nothing more than a few expensive furs. She gets into an accident and is hospitalized, but promptly begins a flirtation with her doctor, showing that she is truly incorrigible."[130]

Christabel is a 1950s update of the vamp. Theda Bara dominated men with exotic allure, brazen eroticism and otherworldly charm. Harlow stalked high-powered businessmen as a humble secretary, dressing and acting in a way that made her indistinguishable from the typical secretary. But she revealed an overt sexuality once her prey was within her grasp. Christabel is more sly than that. She is able to subtly seduce a man largely with psychological manipulation.

The Riding School (1950)

The original French title: *Manèges*

The Riding School is a grim film from beginning to end. The film opens with a grief-stricken man, Robert (Bernard Blier), visiting his dying wife, Dora (Simone Signoret), at a hospital. The hospital is dark and silent with only a single nurse on duty. Robert thinks back on their marriage. We witness their marriage in a flashback. Robert works hard running a riding school while Dora devotes most of her time going on shopping sprees with her mother (Jane Marken). He always looks upon her adoringly and she always responds with a strained smile. It is a smile lacking in warmth or affection. It is a smile of placation. It isn't long after they wed that her extravagant spending places the man into grave debt, but he is so smitten with her that he doesn't care. "It didn't matter," he says in a voice-over. "You could have taken it all. I wish I could have given you more." She gets him to hire a horseman that, she says, her mother knows. He is, in fact, a lover, François (Franck Villard). She is unhappy to learn that Robert has gone broke and has to shut down the riding school. She goes out one day and gets struck by a car, which is how she ends up in the hospital. Her prognosis improves after she is visited by a specialist. The specialist is confident that surgery will save her life. Dora tells her mother that it is time Robert knows the truth. "Tell him," she says to her mother. Mother is happy to comply. She says:

> You really thought she loved you? You always believed it. But no, it's not so! Neither of us could stand you from the beginning. We were in rags, we had to pull through. And so, we found you. Oh, we had trouble hooking you in. But we got you eventually. We started to reel you in. And you. You came right along blindly, like a fool. You gave us a good laugh. Really, you can only laugh!

She lets him know that they find him to be dumb and ugly. They never tired of laughing about him behind his back while bilking him out of his money.

Jane Marken, Simone Signoret and Bernard Blier in *The Riding School* (1950)

We see another flashback, this one from Dora's perspective. When her husband goes broke, her mother needs to find her a new sucker to seduce. Dora briefly dates Eric (Jean Ozenne), an affluent man who leads her to believe that he will marry her and usher her into high society. But he is only after a sexual conquest and dumps her once she acquiesces to his romantic overtures. The next sucker is a greengrocer. But Dora isn't interested in him. She realizes by now that she is in love with François. Dora tells her mother that this is the first time that she has ever felt love for a man. It doesn't matter to her that François is a man without money. This revelation upsets her mother, who calls her daughter "silly." She insists that love is "the best way to ruin yourself." François is amused when she tells him about the greengrocer. He says that he hopes she likes to peel oranges. She really wants to run away with François. But François, who has found a wealthy woman willing to fund a comfortable lifestyle for him, is no longer interested in Dora. She is devastated. She is on her way to visit the greengrocer when she has her accident.

Dora comes out of surgery permanently paralyzed. Robert abandons Dora and her mother upon hearing the news. The ending is something out of a Grand Guignol horror show. The sort of gruesome ending where the adulteress ends up maimed turns up in other adultery films, including *Freaks* and *Ethan Frome*.

Mel Gordon wrote in "Theatre of Fear & Horror": "Both in the silent and sound eras, Todd Browning created the films that borrowed most heavily from the Theatre of the Grand Guignol. Especially in *The Unholy Three* (1925), *The Unknown* (1927), *Freaks* (1932), and *The Devil Doll* (1936), Browning established a particular, unhealthy atmosphere that closely resembled pure grandguignolesque."[131] Wikipedia reports, "Examples of the old Grand Guignol horror shows included *Le Laboratoire des Hallucinations* by André de Lorde: When a doctor finds his wife's lover in his operating room, he performs a graphic brain surgery, rendering the adulterer a hallucinating semi-zombie. Now insane, the lover/patient hammers a chisel into the doctor's brain."[132]

Evelyn Keyes, Van Heflin and John Maxwell in *The Prowler* (1951)

The Prowler (1951)

Webb Garwood (Van Heflin), a police officer, responds to a prowler complaint from Susan Gilvray (Evelyn Keyes). He immediately finds himself attracted to Susan, both for her looks and her wealth. He returns the following night, saying that he wanted to make sure that she is doing alright. He makes further visits, getting increasingly amorous with the lonely married woman. On his fourth visit, he becomes aggressive, grabbing her in his arms and kissing her. She doesn't resist. Webb shows up the next night and shoots Susan's husband John (Sherry Hall), claiming that he assumed the husband was a prowler. Not long after, Garwood proposes marriage to Susan, who foolishly accepts.

Webb and Susan pretend to have met each other for the first time at the trial. They marry soon after. But Susan learns that she is four months pregnant. The fact that John was infertile means that he couldn't be the father. This panics Garwood, who realizes that the pregnancy will throw suspicion on him. He takes Susan away to a ghost town, where she can have her baby in secret. Webb has to call in a doctor when Susan experiences problems with the delivery. Webb figures to murder the suspicious doctor, but the doctor gets away and calls the police. The police arrive and shoot Webb as he attempts to escape.

UNFAITHFUL: THE HISTORY OF THE ADULTERY FILM · 77

My Forbidden Past (1951)

Barbara Beaurevel (Ava Gardner) is in love with a married man, Dr. Mark Lucas (Robert Mitchum), but the good doctor insists on being faithful to his wife, Corinne (Janis Carter). Barbara is self-righteous about taking Mark away from his wife. Years earlier, she was set to elope with Mark to South America before her sly and meddling cousin, Paul (Melvyn Douglas), made her fearful that her elopement would aggravate her Aunt Eula's heart condition. He insisted that she would never live down the scandal if she caused her aunt's death. Paul is the darkest of villains despite his jolly manner. Barbara figures to break up Mark's marriage by having Paul seduce Corinne, who is a shameless social climber. But his seduction takes an unexpected turn. Corinne slaps Paul for laughing off her proposal of marriage. Paul reacts by angrily pushing Corinne, causing her to fall and strike her head on a metal basket. He panics when he checks on Corinne and realizes that she's dead. Paul gets away without anyone seeing him. A prosecutor brings Mark before a grand jury to indict him for Corinne's murder. Barbara tells the grand jury the truth even though it means being disowned by her scandal-shy aunt. Mark is proud of Barbara for facing up to her mistakes. He encourages her to remain on this path. While escorting her out of the building, he says, "You might turn out to be quite a woman."

Janis Carter, Robert Mitchum and Ava Gardner in *My Forbidden Past* (1951)

Good Lord Without Confession (1953)

The original French title: *Le bon Dieu sans confession*

The film opens on a funeral, with the memories of mourners depicted in flashback. François Dupont (Henri Vilbert) is a wealthy businessman trapped in a loveless marriage. He meets Janine Frejoul (Danielle Darrieux) and is immediately enchanted by her beauty. She looks sweet and innocent, but she gladly uses her deceptive appearance to take advantage of the man's generosity. Wikipedia reports, "Dupont, blinded by his passion, covers her with gifts, settles her debts, maintains her property, buys her horses."[133] Meanwhile, Janine is seeing a lover, Maurice Frejoul (Ivan Desny). In time, François realizes that he must end the affair to preserve his relationship with his three children. With his daughter pregnant, he can now look forward to being a grandfather. But he never gets a chance to break off with Janine. François, overstressed by both his personal problems and work problems, has a heart attack during an argument with his business partner.

A Lion is in the Streets (1953)

Hank Martin (James Cagney), an ambitious politician, is a man possessed by both angels and devils. He means to do what is right, but he can be tempted away from his moral instincts and good motives by a propitious proposal. Martin was based on real-life Louisiana governor Huey Long. Long biographer Thomas O. Harris viewed Long as being "neither saint nor devil, he was a complex and heterogeneous mixture of good and bad. . ."[134] Martin loves his wife Verity (Barbara Hale) and strenuously resists the charm of young and sultry Flamingo McManamee (Anne Francis). But, eventually, Flamingo's kisses and caresses are more than he can resist.

Wicked Woman (1953)

A trashy waitress (Beverly Michaels) tries to convince her married boss (Richard Egan) to leave his alcoholic wife (Evelyn Scott) and run off with her to Mexico.

The Girl on the Pier (1953)

An ex-convict, Nick Lane (Ron Randell), visits his former criminal associate Joe Hammond (Campbell Singer) at his pier-side waxworks museum. He wants to know what Nick did with the loot from a robbery. Nick develops an interest in Joe's wife Rita (Veronica Hurst), who is already having an affair with a band singer on the pier. Joe demands that Rita keep away from Nick, but his demand falls on deaf ears.

Nick is curious to know the reason that Rita hasn't been a faithful wife.

Nick: What's the trouble? Does he knock you about?

Rita: No. Sometimes I think it'd be better if he did. At least things would be lively.

Nick: He cooled off?

Rita: No, he's never been any different. And the only things he thinks about is money and booze.

Nick: He's no fun for a hot tomato like you. Why'd you marry him?

Rita: Oh, the old story. I was in a show that folded. I was down on my luck.

Nick: And he was up on his?

Rita: Oh, he was kind at first. He said he was lonely. I guess we were both feeling sorry for ourselves.

Nick: Did you love him?

Rita: It's not hard to kid yourself that you love someone when the wind's blowing cold and you're hungry.

The Earrings of Madame de... (1953)

Furs and jewelry are symbols of status and security. These are the gold digger's badges of success. A valuable piece of jewelry is at the center of *The Earrings of Madame de. . .* A fur is at the center of *BUtterfield 8* (1960). Let's start with *The Earrings of Madame de. . .*

The film's clever plot, with its various twists and turns, can, on first viewing, distract attention from the characters. It is the depth and sophistication of the characters that is truly the film's greatest strength.

A French army general, André (Charles Boyer), is married to Louise (Danielle Darrieux), a beautiful woman who likes to live extravagantly. Even though her husband provides well for her, she has amassed debts that she cannot afford to pay. Rather than reveal her situation to her husband, she secretly sells her costly heart-shaped diamond earrings to her jeweler, Mr. Rémy (Jean Debucourt). She later pretends that she lost the earrings at the opera. The earrings, which André gave to his wife as a wedding present, have a great sentimental value to him. He conducts an exhaustive search for them. He searches the opera house in a desperate effort, but the earrings are nowhere to be found. He sifts around in the back of his wife's coach on his hands and knees. His dignity has given way to the sentiment that he feels for the earrings. The jeweler is fearful of a scandal when he sees the theft reported in the newspaper. He approaches André and urges him to buy back the earrings. André buys the earrings but, rather than return them to his wife, gives them to his mistress Lola (Lia Di Leo), who is relocating to another city. Lola sells the earrings to settle a gambling debt. The next owner of the earrings is Fabrizio Donati (Vittorio De Sica), an Italian baron, who happens by coincidence to meet Louise and fall in love with her. He ends up presenting the earrings to her as an expression of his affection. She sees this as an act of fate. In her mind, fate must have wanted her to pawn the earrings so that she would receive her most precious belonging from her true love, Donati. She will now wear these earrings always. Of course, she now must explain to her husband how her lost earrings have suddenly returned. She slips the earrings inside a glove and, while her husband is present, pretends to find them suddenly. André is unhappy with her deception. André and Louise encounter Donati at a social function. The baron has a mishap with his horse and is thrown to the ground. Louise is so frightened that Donati may be seriously injured that she faints. André sees this reaction and realizes that his wife is in love with this man. André deduces that the earrings were a gift from the baron. At a formal ball, he approaches Donati and tells him about Louise's lie about losing the earrings at the opera. Donati is appalled by Louise's dishonesty and ends their relationship. Louise, who truly loves Donati, is heartbroken. André tells Louise that his niece, who recently had a baby, is more deserving of the earrings. The niece is enthusiastic to receive the earrings as she is able to sell them to the jeweler to settle her husband's debts. Louise, for whom the earrings now represent Donati's love, is desperate to get them back. She sells off jewels and furs to afford the earrings. She confesses to André that she loves Donati and had to have the earrings. André feels that he has no choice now but to challenge Donati to a duel. Louise, who knows that her husband is an excellent shot, pleads with him to call off the duel. When he refuses, she prays at the church for God to spare her lover. She rushes off to stop the duel but, as she approaches, she hears a shot fired. The shot is not returned, which means that the opposing party has fallen. Louise collapses. Her nanny (Mireille Perrey) fears that she is dying and runs off screaming for help.

Danielle Darrieux and Vittorio De Sica in *The Earrings of Madame de...* (1953)

Little did Louise know that, by pawning her earrings at the beginning of the film, she would set off a chain of events that would end with the death of the one man she truly loved.

The film's director, Max Ophüls, had ended a previous film *Letter from an Unknown Woman* with a tragic duel. This is also reminiscent of William Wyler's *Jezebel* (1938). *Jezebel*'s main character, Julie Marsden (Bette Davis), is, like Louise, spoiled, vain and frivolous. She, too, causes the death of a lover.

Wikipedia describes the film's ending as follows: "Ultimately it is seen that Louise has left a burning candle at the shrine, along with her prized earrings, and a card reading that they are a gift from her."[135]

Ophüls saw Louise as an empty person leading a meaningless life. He said that what stood out for him in the source novel was "the senselessness of that woman's life."[136]

Terrell-46 of IMDb wrote:

What a pleasure it is to see subtle and experienced actors as Charles Boyer, Danielle Darrieux and Vittorio De Sica take their roles and bring them to life in such a way that we are forced to continually readjust our feelings toward their characters. When Boyer as the General comments to his wife that "a liar should have more sangfroid," he manages without effort to show amusement, indulgence, perhaps love, but also a little distaste, all in one line reading.[137]

Seeing Louise off at a train station, Boyer moves towards his wife as if he is about to kiss her lovingly on the lips. Before this moment, he has not been shown kissing his wife. But, then, he simply takes her hand and gently kisses it. Passionate expression has no place in this shallow and one-sided relationship.

Gloria Wandrous, the main character of *BUtterfield 8*, is a promiscuous young woman. It is indicated in the novel that Gloria once participated in an orgy. John Chamberlain of The New York Times said that the novel provided "the ultra-ultra in fictional depiction of the willful degradation of sex."[138]

The film has an intriguing opening. Gloria (Elizabeth Taylor) wakes up in bed naked. She wraps a sheet around herself and staggers around the bedroom in search of a cigarette. There are no cigarettes to be found, so she has a glass of Scotch instead. She needs to get dressed, but she lifts her peach gown off the floor and frowns to realize that it was torn during the previous night's revelry. From the novel:

. . . [W]hen she took a second look at the evening gown she remembered more vividly the night before. The evening gown was torn, ripped in half down the front as far as the waist. "The son of a bitch."[139]

The "son of a bitch" is a wealthy businessman, Weston Liggett, who slipped Gloria into his apartment while his wife was out of town. Henry Gonshak, Professor of English at Montana Tech, wrote:

Elizabeth Taylor in *BUtterfield 8* (1960)

. . . [T]he young woman has nothing to wear, so she cavalierly rifles through the clothes closets of Liggett's wife, draping herself in one of Mrs. Liggett's elegant fur coats, which causes Liggett to spend much of the novel desperately trying to retrieve his wife's garment.[140]

Liz Locke of Cinema Sips wrote, "[Gloria] find[s] $250 on the nightstand, but instead of taking the money, she scrawls 'no sale' on his mirror in pink lipstick, steals his wife's mink coat, and walks out with a bottle of scotch."[141]

Death of a Scoundrel (1956)

Sabourin (George Sanders) seduces Edith van Renssalaer (Coleen Gray) to gain control of her stock holdings in her husband's department store.

Baby Doll (1956)

A man makes sexual advances on a young married woman.

A Certain Smile (1958)

Luc Ferrand (Rossano Brazzi), a suave middle-aged man, has habitually cheated on his wife Françoise (Joan Fontaine) during their many years of marriage. He is predatory in his bold seduction of his nephew's fiancée, Dominique (Christine Carère). The film is based on a novel by French author Françoise Sagan. In the novel, Dominique feels no guilt or shame about the affair. She later tells Françoise, "I was a woman. I had loved a man. It was a simple story. There was nothing to make a fuss about." Sagan's characters were often amoral. In her best-known novel "Bonjour Tristesse," a philanderer quotes Oscar Wilde: "Sin is the only note of vivid color that persists in the modern world." Dominique is a gullible romantic in the film. She pleads with Françoise for her forgiveness. Françoise is exhausted by Luc's cheating. "I loathe it," she says. "I hate it. Every time it happens, I die a little." In the end, she leaves Luc.

It Started with a Kiss (1959)

In Spain, celebrated bullfighter Antonio Soriano (Gustavo Rojo) brazenly expresses his attraction to Maggie Fitzpatrick (Debbie Reynolds), the newlywed bride of Air Force staff sergeant Joe Fitzgerald (Glenn Ford). Soriano casually informs Joe, "[This is] the oldest war in life. . . two men and one woman."

Only Two Can Play (1962)

An affluent woman, Liz Gruffydd-Williams (Mai Zetterling), develops an attraction for a married librarian, John Lewis (Peter Sellers). She lures him into an affair by getting her councillor husband to recommend him for a promotion.

Lewis visits Liz at her home for a romantic evening, but the couple has barely started to kiss when Liz's husband arrives home unexpectedly and John has to escape through a bedroom window. John and Liz next attempt to consummate their romance by driving out to the countryside and parking in an empty field. A shabby herd of cows suddenly wanders onto the scene and mill lazily around the car. In a panic, Lewis accidentally switches on the car radio. The noise arouses a farmer, who comes storming out of his home with a shotgun. Lewis drives off quickly.

Once John is approved for the promotion, Liz takes on a dominant attitude with him. This is made clear when she has him hold her dog for her. Then, she instructs him to buy a new suit. "This one doesn't fit you," she says. "I want you to look nice. Would you do that for me?" He decides that the price that he has to pay for his new job is too high. He refuses the job and contritely returns to his wife, Jean (Virginia Maskell).

Liz is different than the vamps of the past. Theda Bara received satisfaction from sucking out a man's soul and leaving him reduced to a shell of his former self. Liz wants to turn John into an empty puppet to do her personal bidding. This is certainly a form of soul-stealing. But she wants him to be successful. He will not end up in beggar rags like the many men who previously fell victim to vamps.

We will again examine the unconsummated affair in *Il seduttore* (1954) and *The Facts of Life* (1960).

This Is My Street (1964)

Harry (Ian Hendry), a flashy nightclub owner, repeatedly attempts to seduce his landlady's married daughter, Marge (June Ritchie). Marge strongly resists him at first, but he is persistent. She becomes more receptive after he helps her to find her young daughter, who wandered off to a scrapyard. Marge, an attractive woman, is accustomed to men making passes at her. Mr. Fingus (Derek Francis), her boss, has long pestered her for a date. But Harry is able to charm her like no one else could. Marge is suddenly overwhelmed by pent-up emotions when she embarks on a relationship with Harry. But Harry loses interest in her once he meets her younger sister, Jinny (Annette Andre). Distraught, Marge attempts to kill herself by sticking her head in a gas oven. Fortunately, her mother smells the gas and takes away her daughter before she succumbs to the deadly fumes. The family turns on Harry, evicting him from the home. Harry has to face Jinny about the affair. He blames the affair on an uncontrollable lust. He explains to Jinny, "I had to have her. It's as simple as that." Marge recovers. She is on her way home when she is approached by Harry, who is bold enough to ask her out for a drink. Marge refuses and continues to her home. She smiles warmly when she sees her daughter outside the front door. She hugs and kisses her daughter before carrying her into their home.

The film has a classic ending. The interloper is banished, order is restored, and the errant wife rediscovers her love for her family.

Harry is comparable to the titular character of *Alfie* (1966), which we will examine later.

June Ritchie and Ian Hendry in *This Is My Street* (1964)

The World of Henry Orient (1964)

Henry Orient (Peter Sellers), an egotistical concert pianist, is a highly neurotic and highly compulsive interloper. He knows that it's dangerous to go after married women, but he lacks the willpower to stop himself.

His compulsion forces him to live in constant fear of an enraged husband breaking down his door and beating him within an inch of his life.

The Man Who Had Power Over Women (1970)

A talent agent, Peter Reaney (Rod Taylor), is thrown out by his wife, Angela (Penelope Horner). Angela accuses Peter of being a cheap and self-loathing drunk. Peter's best friend, Val Pringle (James Booth), invites Peter to move into his home. Flirtations begin almost immediately between Peter and Val's wife, Jody (Carol White). The couple stares longingly at one another for the first hour of the film before they finally get around to kissing. Val dies ten minutes later when a truck makes a sharp swerve and dumps a load of toilets on him. The film is somewhat like *Other Men's Women* except the husband does not have a heroic death.

Two Males for Alexa (1971)

The original Spanish title: *Fieras sin jaula*

Alexa (Rosalba Neri) marries a wealthy older man, Ronald Marvelling (Curt Jürgens). She understands that she is forfeiting love and romance for money and security, but she accepts this as a fair deal. But then she meets Peitro (Juan Luis Galiardo). Peitro, who is aggressive and unscrupulous, is able to break down Alexa's resistance and lure her into an affair. Ronald learns about Alexa's affair. He figures out a bizarre revenge scheme. Ronald is not a cackling, sadistic madman like the husband in *Nightmare Castle* (1965) (as we will learn in Chapter Five). He conveys desperation and anguish over Alexa's infidelity. He storms into their bedroom while the couple is having sex, pulls out a gun, and shoots himself in the head. Immediately, steel shutters seal the doors and windows, trapping them in the room with the bloody corpse. A tape recorder activates. Ronald announces in a chilling recording that Alexa will soon join him in death and they can be united forever. The film features flashbacks as Alexa reflects on her affair. She realizes that Peitro is responsible for drawing her into their romance. As the last of the room's oxygen dwindles, she takes a knife in hand and stabs Peitro in the stomach.

Shampoo (1975)

A hairdresser, George Roundy (Warren Beatty), enjoys having casual sex with his lovely female clients. But Felicia Karpf (Lee Grant), a wealthy married woman, becomes desperately attached to him. George has a steady girlfriend, Jill Haynes (Goldie Hawn), who is beginning to doubt George's fidelity. George has ambitions to open his own salon and hopes for Felicia's husband Lester (Jack Warden) to fund the venture. George learns that Lester is dating one of his old girlfriends, Jackie Shawn (Julie Christie). Jackie is the one woman that George ever truly loved and George is determined to renew their relationship.

Love Among the Ruins (1975)

Jessica Medlicott (Katharine Hepburn), a grand dame, acquires the service of an esteemed barrister, Sir Arthur Glanville-Jones (Laurence Olivier), to defend her in a breach of promise suit against a gold-digging young lover, Alfred Pratt (Leigh Lawson). Arthur has vivid memories of a brief love affair that he himself had with Jessica forty years earlier, but she doesn't remember him at all. Arthur sees a parallel between the circumstances of this case and the circumstances of their long-ago breakup. Jessica abandoned Arthur to marry a much older man who was wealthy and could provide her with a lavish lifestyle.

> Arthur: The young men who were your admirers might have accused you of bartering your youth for an old man's gold, as they say in melodramas.
>
> Jessica: What is your point? It's true, he was older than I and he was rich. . . Giles Medlicott loved me.
>
> Arthur: And you?
>
> Jessica: I loved him too. In time.
>
> Arthur: But not when you married him?
>
> Jessica: Why should you have to know that? I loved him when he died, isn't that enough? Long before he died. I made him happy.

Jessica's meeting with Alfred was arranged by Alfred's mother, Mrs. Fanny Pratt (Joan Sims), who sent of picture of Jessica to her son. The picture, according to the young man, aroused in him a great passion. He responded with a letter that let Jessica know how beautiful he thought she was. But Arthur recognizes Alfred's alleged passion ("a mad, flaming passion," he calls it) and his lavish flattery about Jessica's beauty as the worst hokum. He sets out to expose Alfred in court as a gold digger. In a fine summation speech, the barrister paints the gold digger as the lowest form of human life. He says:

> Indeed, were we to accept my learned friend's attempts at retouching and restoring nature's canvas, we would see before us here a picture of perfect suitability, of two lovers ideally matched, unquestionably equal. Gentlemen, look at this woman. Look at her. Oh, pray, do not be misled by the costume, which would, of course, be most appropriate were this the eternally youthful nymph of Mr. Devine's wayward and, not to say, wanton imaginings, but which, in the circumstances, is, at the very least of it, silly and unsuitable and, at the very worst of it, pitiful and ridiculous. No, gentlemen, I invite you to look beneath the costume, in a manner of speaking, just as I invite you to look beneath the young man's mask of pious and sincere devotion. Gentlemen, can you, in all conscience, see these two at the altar? On their honeymoon? In a cottage? Outdoors, running, gaming, sporting, in the hundred ways that are the province of bride and groom? Tell me, are there children in that fantasy? A daughter to perpetuate her mother's beauty? A son to carry on the name of Pratt? No, gentlemen. It is, by heaven, it is unlikely as it is unseemly and unnatural to imagine this shackled for life - for what is left of her life, to this. Here is an individual so low that he will bargain away his youth, the brave, young manhood, for a mess of pottage and 30 pieces of silver and the feeble, impotent embrace of this crumbled, pathetic ruin of a once great lady.

Arthur continues with his brutal assessment of the situation. Jessica furiously protests when he refers to her as "a senile great-grandmother." The judge has her removed from the courtroom. Arthur continues:

> The Alfred Pratts of this world, to the world's misfortune, always appear in pleasing shapes and sizes, the better to seduce the unwary and vulnerable, clothing their malicious motives in fine words. The finest word that we've heard from the mouth of that clever lad and the one most degraded by the mere fact of his having spoken it, is that most precious of words in the language: love. Love. Dr. Johnson,

in all his perversity, tells us that love is the wisdom of the fool and the folly of the wise, or to those who would prefer to believe with Dryden, that love is the finest frailty of the mind, but however we define it, we cannot mistake it for a hypocrisy, for cupidity, for cunning. We cannot look upon greed and call that love. We cannot and must not reward so vile a counterfeit.

The Inheritance (1976)

Irene (Dominique Sanda) reveals that, as a child, she could dream of nothing but becoming rich. She says, "My parents would have thought me crazy had they known me for what I really was." She has no compunction about using her beauty and wits to manipulate men into serving as benefactors. Her ungoverned lust for money makes her a poisonous woman. She is prepared to connive and wheedle for a sizable share of her dying father-in-law's fortune. Eventually, she cuckolds her husband Pippo (Gigi Proietti) with both his brother Mario (Fabio Testi) and his father Gregorio (Anthony Quinn). Proof of her poisonous touch is the fact that all three of the men are dead by the end of the film. The father dies of heart failure while the two cuddle and kiss in bed. The spurned Mario shoots himself in front of her. The cuckolded Pippo dies in an asylum crying out her name.

Submission (1976)

The original Italian title: Scandalo

Eliane (Lisa Gastoni), a married pharmacist, is seduced by her shop assistant, Armand (Franco Nero). Armand enjoys dominating and humiliating Eliane. As he loses interest in Elaine, he seduces Elaine's daughter, Justine (Claudia Marsani).

Swing Shift (1984)

Kay Walsh (Goldie Hawn) has an affair with Lucky Lockhart (Kurt Russell) while her husband is at war. Lucky is indeed manipulative.

Lucky: It's your own life. You've got a right to be happy.

Kay: I can't. I'm married. Don't you understand that? Don't you get it? Please. . . go away.

Lucky: Come on, I'll give you a ride home.

Kay: No.

Lucky: Come on, Kay.

The film presents neither consequences nor lessons for adultery.

The Boss' Wife (1986)

Joel Keefer (Daniel Stern), a married stockbroker, is stalked by his boss' amorous wife Louise (Arielle Dombasle) during a team-building corporate weekend.

Arielle Dombasle and Daniel Stern in *The Boss' Wife* (1986)

Dangerous Liaisons (1988)

The story involves the moral degeneracy of wealthy Parisian nobility during the 18th century. The Vicomte de Valmont (John Malkovich) finds it thrilling to seduce married women. He feels an extraordinary attraction to Madame de Tourvel, the deeply religious young wife of a Parliament official. Marquise Isabelle de Merteuil (Glenn Close) wagers Valmont that he will not be able to make Tourvel into one of his conquests. Merteuil is one of Valmont's former lovers. Like Valmont, she has a cruel and cunning nature and enjoys using deceptive practices to corrupt innocent people. But Valmont's latest plan goes awry. After he beds Tourvel, Valmont is startled to find that he truly loves the woman. Tourvel feels very differently about their sexual liaison. She is so ashamed that she falls deathly ill and has herself taken to a monastery to recover. Merteuil is jealous to see Valmont desperately in love with another woman. She discloses to Danceny that Valmont slept with his wife, Cécile. Danceny challenges Valmont to a duel. Valmont, who cannot live without Tourvel, purposely runs into Danceny's sword, assuring his own death. As he is dying, he asks Danceny to give Tourvel a message. He says, "I'm glad not to have to live without her. Tell her, her love was the only real happiness that I have ever known." Before he takes his last breath, he gives Danceny letters from Merteuil, which expose incriminating information about the marquise. Tourve quietly dies at the monastery. Word of Merteuil's letters spread among the Paris elite. In the final scene, a crowd boos Merteuil at a theater.

*Zandalee (*1991)

Thierry (Judge Reinhold) introduces his wife Zandalee (Erika Anderson) to an old friend, Johnny (Nicolas Cage). Johnny is brash, immoral, and devious. He is attracted to Zandalee and it doesn't matter to him that she is married to his friend. Johnny offers the most asinine justification for adultery. He tells Zandalee, "Nobody will be hurt from it. Because it is what it is. Just as simple as that. You want it and I want to give it. A perfect relationship." Frankly, the entire story is asinine. Thierry realizes that Zandalee and Johnny are having an affair. He becomes drunk and angry during a speedboat ride with the couple. He drives the boat at a dangerous speed. Suddenly, the boat lurches. He falls overboard and drowns. Johnny makes extra money selling cocaine, but his guilt over Thierry's death drives him into consuming much of his cocaine supply. He is unable to pay for the cocaine, which angers his cocaine supplier. The supplier intends to kill Johnny in a drive-by shooting, but Zandalee steps in front of Johnny to intercept the bullet. IMDb describes the overwrought ending as follows: "Johnny, now alone, as he cradles and holds Zandalee's dead body. The movie ends with him walking in front of the church with the lifeless Zandalee in his arms."[142] Throughout the film, Johnny illogically swings back and forth between being a manipulative crumb and compassionate saint. It is odd that, after callously causing the death of Thierry and Zandalee, he ends up crying outside of a church.

Sleep with Me (1994)

Best friends Joseph (Eric Stoltz) and Frank (Craig Sheffer) vie for the affection of lovely Sarah (Meg Tilly). Sarah chooses to marry Joseph, but Frank refuses to accept his rejection and continues to pursue Sarah.

Into My Heart (1998)

Ben (Rob Morrow) has been friends with Adam (Jake Weber) since childhood. They have a close and durable relationship, yet this doesn't stop Ben from having sex with Adam's wife Nina (Claire Forlani). It exacerbates the matter that Ben gets Nina pregnant. Adam has difficulty coping with this double-edged betrayal. He becomes so distraught that, one night, he quietly leaps off a tower. He amazingly survives the fall and is rushed to the hospital. Nina is devastated. She sobs in Ben's arms. She desperately clutches him. And, then, she kisses him. It is a passionate, sucking-off-his-face kiss. Ben has to pull away to take a breath and takes this opportunity to declare his love for Nina. Suddenly, Nina is appalled. Snogging is acceptable to her under the circumstances, but a declaration of love is entirely off limits. "Jesus Christ," says Nina, "don't. This is over. You know that. I am so evil. His best friend. What were we doing? What the fuck were we doing?"

Ben has a loving and tender girlfriend, Kat (Jayne Brook), who learns about the affair and doesn't understand why Ben would do something as horrible as this. "What do you want me to say?" Ben asks Kat. "I don't know why I did it!" This enrages her. She shouts, "I mean, what are you? A two-year-old? You just take whatever you want? Fuck everyone else!" Ben is at a loss for words. He literally hangs his head in shame.

Ben: I'm sorry! I'm sorry if I hurt you!

Kat: What? If you hurt me? Are you insane?

Ben: What do you want from me?

Kat: Don't fuck other people! Don't break my h. . . my heart. How's that? God, you piece of shit! You know. . . I can, uhh. . . I can almost. . . I can almost understand you doing this to me. But how. . .? I mean, did. . . did you want to possess him? Somehow? Some, some part of him you couldn't have? Huh? So you fuck his wife, is that it?

Adam dies. Nina goes off on her own. Kat leaves Ben. The story advances several years. Nina has remarried. She is accompanied by her child and her husband when she and Ben meet again by chance in a restaurant. She looks him deeply in his eyes and asks him how he's doing. Ben replies, "I try to do good things." It is a genuinely moral film that depicts adultery as something sad and depraved.

Faithless (2000)

The original Swedish title: *Trolösa*

Marianne (Lena Endre) once found her husband, Markus (Thomas Hanzon), to be sexually exciting, but her passion for him has cooled. A family friend, David (Krister Henriksson), has an easy time enticing her into an affair. David is, by his own admission, deeply flawed. He explains, simply, that he is "rotten." But this doesn't bother Marianne. Markus, a well-known orchestra conductor, is leaving for a tour of the United States. Marianne sees this as a perfect time for her and David to enjoy a romantic getaway to Paris. But David's rottenness spoils their good time. Marianne explains what went wrong to a friend, Bergman (Erland Josephson). She says, "Suddenly he asks me about my past lovers. He asks with a smile, indifferently. . . I don't sense the risk. I innocently tell him details of my modest erotic biography. David is asking funny, knowing questions. We're both laughing. And l get bolder. Then, after dinner - we'd drunk more than usual - all hell breaks loose." He frightens her during a jealous rampage. The rampage culminates in him beating Marianne. Markus hears rumors of the affair and catches Marianne and David together. He takes an overdose of sleeping pills to end his life. Marianne talks to Margareta (Juni Dahr), who worked in Markus' orchestra, about Markus' suicide. Margareta was close to Markus. She admits that they were lovers. She says that Markus changed after he learned of the affair. She says, "He became harrowed, rancorous, frightened." Marianne and Markus' warmhearted young daughter has been traumatized by her father's death. The affair has had a destructive effect on several people.

Speaking of Sex (2001)

A marriage counselor, Dr. Emily Paige (Lara Flynn Boyle), is treating Melinda (Melora Walters) and Dan (Jay Mohr), who have lost interest in sex. She advises Melinda to see a depression expert, Dr. Roger Klink (James Spader), but Roger foolishly violates professional ethics by falling love with Melinda and having sex with her.

Say Nothing (2001)

IMDb: "An unfulfilled married woman [Nastassja Kinski] becomes intrigued by an alluring suitor [William Baldwin] whose attention soon becomes obsessive."[143]

Who Loves the Sun (2006)

The film is set at the picturesque Falcon Lake. Daniel Bloom (Adam Scott) acts as best man when his best friend, Will Morrison (Lukas Haas), weds Maggie Claire (Molly Parker). Understandably, Will is appalled when he catches Maggie and Daniel having sex in a boathouse. Will quietly packs and leaves town. Maggie doesn't see Will again until she returns to town five years later. Will is delighted to meet Maggie at the dock.

But she doesn't say hello. She doesn't hug him. She slaps him. She believes that Will was wrong to leave without talking with her. She doesn't seem to accept the greater wrong that she, herself, committed. Daniel still loves Maggie. He regularly wrote to her in the past five years, but she never responded to the letters. Maggie tells Daniel that she regrets their romp in the boathouse. She says, "It wasn't worth it, Daniel. It wasn't anywhere near worth it." Yet, she lets him kiss her, which Daniel sees. Will asks Maggie why she cheated on him. She says simply, "I wanted to. Of course, afterwards, it seemed like a terrible mistake. But, at the time, I just, I wanted to." Daniel is told by Will's father, Arthur (R. H. Thomson), that Daniel was conceived out of an extramarital affair between his long-lost father and Will's mother, Mary (Wendy Crewson). The fact that he and Will are half-brothers forces him to reconsider their relationship. Maggie tells Mary about the boathouse incident. This must be a painful memory as she suddenly breaks down crying. But the fact that Maggie has acted childishly flighty and conceited for much of the film makes it difficult to understand her tears. Moments later, Daniel enters the room and confronts his mother about her affair. She breaks down crying, too. The selfish and thoughtless behavior of these women has caused pain and hardship for several men. Will's father was so upset by the affair that he left town and has never been seen again by family and friends. Yet, it is the women who cry. Maggie and Will settle their differences and have sex for the first time in five years. Maggie quietly leaves town early the next morning. What else would a flighty woman do?

Rendez-Vous (2015)

A Dutch couple, Simone (Loes Haverkort) and Eric (Mark van Eeuwen), inherit a decrepit country home in the South of France. They pack up their children and their belongings to start a new life in France. During the renovation, Simone embarks on an affair with one of the construction workers, Michel (Pierre Boulanger). She looks ready for sex the moment that she first sets eyes on Michel. It is an extremely stealth affair. Michel barely talks. He often sneaks up behind Simone. One night, he silently walks in on her while she's in the shower. Is he a lover or a stalker? The pair have clandestine meetings, creeping around at night in dark rooms. They have sex in an abandoned building. The film captures a sinister and creepy mood. Simone was traumatized as a child because her mother abandoned her family to run off with a lover. And, yet, she herself now pursues a lover. How does this make sense? The story takes a turn when Simone learns that she is pregnant. The builder, Peter (Peter Paul Muller), uses photos of Simone with Michel to blackmail her. It turns out that the lover is his stepson and the two regularly scheme to blackmail foolish wives. Peter drains money out of Simone by prolonging the renovation. Simone becomes frustrated with Peter's extortion efforts. She impulsively shoves him, causing him to crack his skull on a tree stump. Michel admits to the blackmail plot to get her released from jail. Eric cannot bring himself to talk to Simone. He remains standoffish as they arrive home. In the final moments of the film, Simone tenderly rubs her pregnant belly and smiles. We have no redemption here. The film has a promising start, but Simone proves to be an unsympathetic and incredibly foolish protagonist. She has a good husband. She has two beautiful young children. Yet, she becomes swoony meeting Michel and never once looks back once she and Michel become lovers. A good person has an internal system to maintain their moral bearings. But Simone has none. She never, for a single moment, shows devotion to her family.

Hot, Exotic Locales

Illicit love affairs thrive in hot, exotic environments. It is not a good idea to drag a wife away from familiar and friendly surroundings to a place where she constantly feels alone and out of place. Let's look at stories of illicit love in sweltering foreign places.

Exile (1917)

Vincento Perez (Wyndham Standing), the governor of a Portuguese colony, schemes to cheat silk dealers out of money. A government engineer, Richmond Harvey (Mahlon Hamilton), threatens to expose the governor. Desperate, Perez sends his wife Claudia (Olga Petrova) to seduce Harvey. A rebellion is staged by the natives, who capture the governor and hang him. IMDb summarizes the neat and simple ending as follows: "Claudia is rescued by Harvey and the two face a happy future together."[144]

Vengeance (1930)

John Meadham (Jack Holt) has become tired of running a trading post in West Africa. Weekly Kinema Guide alternately referred to the film's setting as a "heat-soaked place"[145] and a "fever-stricken desolation."[146] His London bosses send a replacement, Charles Summers (Philip Strange), who is obnoxious in his usual manner. Meadham and Summers disagree on the way to run the trading post and quickly become adversaries. Meadham soon takes an interest in Summers' abused wife, Margaret (Dorothy Revier). The love triangle is interrupted by a native uprising. Meadham risks his life to rescue Summers from the natives. A. F. Botsford of The Royal Theatre found the film to be "rather sordid and depressing."[147]

The Road to Singapore (1931)

Dr. George March (Louis Calhern) moves to Singapore with his new wife, Philippa Crosby (Doris Kenyon). Another new arrival to the community is the notorious Hugh Dawltry (William Powell). Dawltry, a bona fide playboy, has dedicated his life to seducing women and enjoying to excess the finest of liquor. He fled London to escape bad publicity after his seduction of a married woman entangled him in a divorce scandal. He is shunned by respectable members of his community for having broken up the marriage. March says, "He's strictly taboo!"

Philippa arrives at the dock on a rainy afternoon. Dawltry comes alongside her in a rickshaw and holds an umbrella over her head. "You will find it gets rather damp," he says. "Will you join me?" Philippa is wary of Dawltry at first and is unsure if she should accept his invitation. But she is finally overcome by his charm.

Dawltrey dances with Philippa during a party at the clubhouse. George is a clumsy dancer, stomping on his wife's feet. Dawltry, in contrast, moves elegantly across the dance floor. The couple becomes less inhibited with their flirtations once they settle onto a secluded patio. Dawltey leans down and kisses Philippa. He should know by now to avoid married women considering that his last dalliance with a married woman turned him into a social pariah. But he can't help himself. He confesses to Philippa, "I've never known anything deeper than a conquest." He has real feelings for this woman, which is something new for him.

Doris Kenyon and William Powell in *The Road to Singapore* (1931)

The film is engaged with the idea that the wife of a dull, work-obsessed man is bound to be susceptible to the seductions of a devil-may-care playboy. It is a simple premise already used by other adultery films. But, usually, the neglected wife is a do-nothing society woman. This type of wife has no baby that needs her care, no meal that has to be cooked, and no floor that needs to be scrubbed. Her life is devoted to play. She therefore cannot do without a playmate. These are vain and empty women who are wives in name only. A woman content to spend her days at cafes, beauty salons and dress shops is not a true marital partner. Philippa is different than those women. She gave up being a nurse when she married George. Why did she trade a life of tending to the ill and saving lives for an idle existence? It is never explained. Philippa is not occupied with either babies or beauticians. She is caught in a sweltering netherworld with little to do to pass the time.

Dawltry speaks of a goddess who snuck off to earth to taste sin but found love instead. This is meant to describe Philippa, but it probably describes him more.

George returns early from a medical call and learns that Philippa is spending the night in Dawltry's bungalow. He angrily confronts the couple. A defiant Philippa lets her husband know that she is leaving him.

Philippa: I came out here in search of love and happiness. I found instead a machine. A machine of cold steel. As cold as the instruments you use to probe into the bodies of unconscious patients on operating tables. Nursing hasn't changed me from a woman. But surgery in the tropics has changed the man I came to marry. So I turn to Hugh Dawltrey for the love and affection you didn't give me.

George: If I didn't know that you were suffering from a pathological complaint common to the tropics, I should think you were neurotic. It's just a physical heatwave. And that cad took advantage of it.

Philippa: Not of me, George. You did that! All you wanted was a wife. Any woman would have done as well. And some other woman can take my place from now on. . . You will get over it. You may even find another sacrococcygeal tumour to comfort you.

Dawltry said that he's willing to take George's wife away from him to stop her from "shrivel[ing] up and rot[ting] in this hole like the rest of you."

This is definitely a pre-Code film. The wife has no shame about her interest in another man. The lovers end up together. Dawltry and Philippa board a ship together to leave Singapore.

Of course, some might regard a skillful surgeon who saves lives as more valuable to society than a drunken playboy. But the drunken playboy ends up as the hero of the story nonetheless.

Gene Raymond, Clark Gable and Mary Astor in *Red Dust* (1932)

Red Dust (1932)

Dennis Carson (Clark Gable) owns a rubber plantation in French Indochina. Vantine (Jean Harlow), a prostitute, takes refuge on the plantation to escape arrest by the Saigon police. Dennis hires surveyor/engineer, Gary Willis (Gene Raymond). Vantine falls in love with Dennis, but Dennis loses interest in her once Gary's elegant and lovely wife Barbara (Mary Astor) arrives. He sends Gary on a surveying trip to give himself the opportunity to seduce Barbara. Vantine is brokenhearted seeing Dennis romance Barbara, but she's helpless to do anything about it. Dennis convinces Barbara to leave Gary, but he changes his mind after he spends time with Gary in the swamp. Gary tells Dennis that he loves his wife and has plans for their future together. Dennis starts to wonder if the plantation is a good place for Barbara. He remembers his mother being ravaged by the brutal conditions of the plantation and dying while he was only a boy. He tells Gary, "Her grave is on the hill at the far edge of the compound. You know, I faintly remember asking my father if he was digging a well." To convince Barbara to leave, he tells her that he doesn't really love her and becomes openly affectionate with Vantine. Barbara is so enraged that she shoots him. Fortunately, the bullet only grazes his side. Vantine tells Gary that Barbara was forced to shoot Dennis to ward off his unwanted advances. She says:

You oughta be proud of her. This bozo's been after her every minute. And tonight he comes in drunk and tries to break into her room and she shoots him. The way any virtuous woman, with a beast like that. If I were you, Mr. Willis, I'd take her away from here, and the quicker the better.

Vantine carefully cleans out Dennis' wound. The film ends with Dennis recuperating while Vantine reads him a children's bedtime story. She says, "A chipmunk and a rabbit. Hey, I wonder how this comes out?"

Irresistible passion motivates the characters in this story. This film takes the perspective of the scoundrel, although this scoundrel has a bit of a conscience.

The film was remade in 1953 as *Mogambo*. The ending of *Mogambo* is slightly different. Marswell (Gable again) struggles to admit his feelings for Honey Bear (a Vantine substitute played by Ava Gardner). Honey Bear decides to return to her showgirl job in New York City. She is setting off in a canoe when Marswell suddenly shouts out a proposal of marriage to her. Honey Bear, her pride still hurt, rejects the proposal at first. But then she changes her mind, wildly jumping into the water to get to Marswell. The film ends with the couple in a loving and soggy embrace on shore.

White Heat (1934)

William Hawkes (David Newell), the owner of a sugar cane plantation in Hawaii, visits San Francisco for a planter's convention. During his visit, he meets and falls in love with Lucille Cheney (Virginia Cherrill). Hawkes acts quickly to marry Lucille before he is due to return to Hawaii. Lucille becomes lonely and bored being away from her family and friends. She begins an affair with Chandler Morris (Hardie Albright). This doesn't turn out well, as described by Les Adams of IMDb: "[Hawkes] catches Lucille and Chandler together and a fight ensues, Lucille, in an effort, to save her lover throws a kerosene lamp into the ripe sugar cane and fire spreads in all directions."[148] We will see a similar climax in *Days of Heaven* (1978)

The Painted Veil (1934)

Dr. Walter Fane (Herbert Marshall) has dedicated himself to bacteria research in the hope of finding cures for a variety of lethal infections. His work takes him and his wife, Katrin (Greta Garbo), to China. Katrin is left alone most of the time. She finds companionship with Jack Townsend (George Brent), who works at the British Embassy. Walter is unhappy to learn that Katrin is having an affair, but he has no time to address the situation due to an outbreak of cholera. Katrin works alongside her husband in tending to the victims of the epidemic. Walter and Katrin grow close during their diligent efforts. A village found to be the source of the epidemic is burned by authorities. The residents riot against their homes being destroyed. Walter is stabbed during the riot, which devastates Katrin. Katrin sits by Walter's bedside during his recovery. She realizes now that she loves him and ends her relationship with Townsend.

A 1957 remake, *The Seventh Sin*, has a darker mood. Film noir was in its waning days, but it still exerted a significant influence on this film. The doctor's wife was now a bit of a femme fatale. Carolyn Carwin (Eleanor Parker) is married to Dr. Walter Carwin (Bill Travers). She agreed to marry Walter while on a rebound from a breakup and has come to see their marriage as a mistake. She is having an affair with a French shipping executive, Paul Duvel (Jean Pierre Aumont). Walter learns of the affair and confronts Carolyn about it. He, too, realizes now that their marriage was a mistake. He admits that he knew Carolyn was vain, shallow and frivolous before he married her, but he loved her too much for it to matter. He is willing to consent to a divorce if Paul agrees to marry her. But Paul prefers to remain with his wife. So, Carolyn accompanies Walter to the mainland of China to battle a cholera epidemic. Walter dies after contracting cholera (as in the original novel). Carol returns to Hong Kong without knowing what will become of her.

The Heart of the Matter (1953)

IMDb: "An unhappily married British security officer stationed in Sierra Leone during World War II falls in love with a young Austrian woman and starts an affair."[149]

A husband and wife, Harry and Louise Scobie (Trevor Howard and Elizabeth Allan), have grown cold towards each other since the death of their child. While his wife is away, Harry falls in love with a young widow, Helen Rolt (Maria Schell). He is overcome with guilt. Being a strict Catholic, he is more concerned with being disloyal to God than being disloyal to his wife. He confesses to a priest about his predicament, but Catholicism offers him no comfort and no easy solution. His talk with the priest leaves him feeling far more guilty and upset.

A clerk, Wilson (Denholm Elliott), is in love with Louise and believes that he deserves to be with Louise more than Scobie.

Wilson: You sent Louise away because you were afraid of me.

Harry: No hat, you see. . . It's the sun, old boy!

Wilson: She couldn't stand your stupid unintelligence. You don't know what a woman like Louise thinks.

Harry: I don't suppose I do, but then nobody wants anyone to do that, do they?

Wilson: I kissed her, I kissed her that day. . .

Harry: It's a colonial sport, my dear fellow.

Louise talks to Harry about Wilson.

Louise: Don't you mind him making love to me?

Harry: Is it our fault that we fall in love?

Helen later says, "Nothing is your fault. All your promises belong to your wife. Nothing you said to me is a promise." The solemnness of a promise comes up again when Scobie speaks to an oily blackmailer, Yusef (Gérard Oury). The blackmailer tells him, "The penalty of the blackmailer, Mr Scobie, is that he has no debts of honour. Nothing you say to me is a promise." Just as no debt of honor can exist between a blackmailer and his victim, perhaps no debt of honor can exist between illicit lovers.

The Comedians (1967)

Brown (Richard Burton), a hotel owner in a collapsing Haiti, is having an affair with an ambassador's wife, Martha Pineda (Elizabeth Taylor). The ambassador, Manuel (Peter Ustinov), is aware of the affair. He mournfully reflects on his marriage. He remembers Martha and himself being happy in Rio, but he sees that they lost those good feelings once they came to the grim spectacle of Haiti.

Heat and Dust (1983)

Olivia (Greta Scacchi) marries Douglas Rivers (Christopher Cazenove), a civil servant in Britain's colonial administration, which means that she must now live in India. Douglas leaves Olivia alone much of the time. In her lonely hours, she becomes enthralled by the exoticness of India. The Nawab of Khatm (Shashi Kapoor) invites British officials and their wives for a dinner party at his palace. Olivia attracts the attention of the rakish Nawab. She is vain and superficial in her reaction. From the novel:

> His eyes often rested on her, and she let him study her while pretending not to notice. She liked it - as she had liked the way he had looked at her when she had first come in. His eyes had lit up - he checked himself immediately, but she had seen it and realised that here at last was one person in India to be interested in her in her way she was used to.[150]

The Nawab easily seduces Olivia and they engage in an illicit affair. Olivia gets pregnant. Douglas is excited by the news. He says, "You know, [the Rivers babies] are all very blond. We all have white blond hair 'til we're about 12." She tells the Nawab about her pregnancy. He reacts with delight as he is sure that he is the father. Olivia, afraid to give birth to Nawab's non-blonde child, visits a midwife who can induce premature labor. But she has a bleeding problem afterward and has to go to a hospital. It is obvious to her doctor that she did not have a natural miscarriage. She is abandoned by Douglas and his friends. Douglas is brokenhearted, but the narrator tells us that he eventually remarried. The Nawab buys Olivia a house in the Kashmir mountains. He visits her infrequently until he suffers a fatal heart attack. Olivia, despondent and outcast, lives as a recluse for the remainder of her life.

Cairo Time (2009)

Juliette Grant (Patricia Clarkson) travels to Cairo for vacation. Her husband, Mark (Tom McCamus), meant to be with her, but he has been delayed on business. He asks an Egyptian friend, Tareq Khalifa (Alexander Siddig), to take care of Juliette until he arrives. As Tareq escorts Juliette around to the exotic sights of Cairo, the couple develops feelings for one another. The affair doesn't get physical until late in the film, at which time the couple embraces and kisses. But they decide to go no further. The film ends. The sanctity of marriage is preserved, though just barely.

A hot, exotic locale also plays a role in *The Letter* (1940) and *Temptation* (1946), which we will examine in Chapter Five.

The House Guest

Other Men's Women (1931)

In early sound films, the interloper in an adultery film was a charming rogue played by the likes of George Brent and William Powell or a more ruthless Lothario played by the likes of Ricardo Cortez and Warren William. But *Other Men's Women* presents the cad as someone foolish and ordinary. He is, simply, a working-class galoot.

Bill White (Grant Withers) and Jack Kulper (Regis Toomey) become best friends while working together as train engineers. When Bill gets thrown out of his boarding house, Jack allows his friend to stay with him and his wife Lily (Mary Astor). Bill and Lily start out with a playful relationship. Lily is convinced that she can reform Bill out of his bad-boy ways and get him to settle down with a wife. But the two soon fall in love. The couple cuts their love affair short after they share an impetuous kiss in the kitchen.

Sheila O'Malley of The Shelia Variations blog wrote:

> . . . Bill demands that Lily tell Jack what has happened. He cannot betray his friend. They must go to him and confess, and she must leave Jack so that they can be married. Lily, a good girl, is devastated. She loves Bill but she cannot hurt Jack.[151]

Bill confesses to Jack about the kiss. Jack becomes angry. Bill tells him that it's fine to speak badly of him, but he shouldn't blame Lily for what happened. "She's okay," he insists. Jack says, "She was until I brought you into the house. What did you do to her? You made her a dirty, rotten. . ." Bill smacks him before he can finish the sentence. This sparks a fistfight. Jack falls during the struggle and strikes his head hard enough to lose consciousness. It is learned when Jack is revived that the head injury has left him blind.

Grant Withers and Mary Astor in *Other Men's Women* (1931)

Bill, desperate to redeem himself, is willing to sacrifice his life to stop a flood threatening the town. He has the idea to weigh down a locomotive with cement blocks and then drive it over the weakened bridge, hoping that it will cause the bridge to collapse and create a pile of rubble that will block the flood waters. Jack learns of his daring plan and, despite his blindness, stumbles through a raging downpour to find Bill. He explains to Bill that his blindness has made him a burden to Lily and he can better afford to risk his life. Bill refuses to listen to Jack, so Jack knocks him out and puts him off the train. He stops the flood as planned and loses his life in the process. Bill and Lily are now free to pursue their relationship.

This pre-Code film is subversive in its endorsement of adultery. The story puts across the idea that a wife has a right to trade out her man if a better one comes along. The husband is the guilty party because he has been unable to fulfill his wife's emotional needs and has failed to be an exciting partner for her. Even worse, he seems to be condemned by the filmmaker for letting himself be so overwhelmed with jealousy that he becomes violent. He is, in effect, blinded by jealousy. He, himself, says, "I got what's coming to me."

But is Bill White a better man? Bill is, without question, irresponsible. He drinks too much. His landlady has tolerated Bill being overdue on the rent, but she finally kicks him out for passing out drunk while leaving the water running in the bathtub. Bill backs out of marrying Marie (Joan Blondell) on their wedding day. She becomes furious, accusing him of taking a "run-off powder" on her. Jack takes Bill into his home when he has nowhere else to go. Rather than be grateful, he has an affair with the man's wife. Men sleep with their best friend's wife in other films. We explored this earlier in the chapter with *The Beautiful Sailor* (1932), *Into My Heart* (1998) and *Who Loves the Sun* (2006). But at least the other men weren't guests in their friend's home. Certainly, a guest sleeping with his host's wife infringes upon the rules of hospitality.

So, was Jack wrong to become angry? The argument could be made that the affair ended before it began and Jack should have left well enough alone. But was the affair finished? Lily still loved Bill and had lost affection for her husband. Bill was still around and had it in his mind that Lily should leave Jack for him. Under the circumstances, Jack had a perfect right to get angry with Bill. In the end, though, he turned his frustration and confusion onto himself. He decided that he was wrong for neglecting his wife and fighting with his friend. He felt bad knowing that his unhappy wife would never leave him now that he was blind. In his mind, he had to nobly sacrifice his life to redeem himself and set everything right. It is not an easy plot turn to accept.

A similar story exists in 12th-century literature written about King Arthur. Arthur admires Lancelot, a soldier known for his unfaltering bravery, expert sword skills and great virtue. He welcomes Lancelot into his court and allows him to join his fellowship of knights. But Lancelot finds his loyalty to Arthur tested when he falls in love with Queen Guinevere. The story is dramatized with several key changes in *Lancelot and Guinevere* (1963). According to Arthurian legend, the couple ends up guilt-ridden over their illicit affair. Lancelot relinquishes his knighthood and becomes a monk. A blogger at A Land of Myth and A Time of Magic noted, "[A]fter Arthur's death, Guinevere joins a convent in penitence for her infidelity."[152] But, unlike the classic tale, the film has a happy ending. Arthur is slain in a civil war. Lancelot redeems himself by avenging Arthur's death. He locates Guinevere in time to stop her from taking vows as a nun. The lovers are reunited. The story was later the basis of *Lancelot du Lac* (1974). The illicit love affair was set to music with *Camelot* (1967).

A House Divided (1931) shares a number of key plot elements with *Other Men's Women*. The film was based on "Heart and Hand," a 1927 short story written by Olive Edens for McCall's Magazine. The story was simple. A young mail-order bride, Ruth Preston, shows up in a small fishing village to meet her groom-to-be, Hal Law. Hal, a middle-aged fisherman, is a recent widower. He sends his adult son, Tommy, to greet Ruth when she arrives on a passenger ship. Hal has no interest in getting to know Ruth. He has a parson at his home ready to marry them. But she is afraid of the brutish man. From the short story: "She ran to Tommy, shrank behind him, her terrified face peering from around his shoulder." Hal is unsympathetic. He tells her, "You took on a bargain, and you live up to it, my lit'l girl." Tommy is determined to protect Ruth from his father. He insists that his father leave her alone. But Hal, unwilling to be denied his bride, bristles at his son's interference. He lunges at Tommy. Suddenly, he gets his foot caught against a table leg and comes crashing to the floor. Hal, his back injured, is unable to move. A doctor determines that Hal has become permanently paralyzed. The once robust man becomes confined to his bed. Tommy and Ruth marry and settle in a nearby home. Tommy regularly visits his father to care for him. Hal gradually softens his attitude. He finally finds peace when Tommy visits him with his new son.

The story is brief (roughly 5,000 words) and contains little action. Two pivotal action scenes were created to enliven the film adaptation. Inexplicably, the character names were changed by the screenwriters.

The film opens on a funeral. Seth Law (Walter Huston) is assisted by his son Matt (Douglass Montgomery) in carrying his wife's coffin to her grave. After the burial, Seth gets drunk at a bar. Matt is appalled to watch his father singing and dancing while his mother is fresh in the ground.

Ruth Evans (Helen Chandler) is persuaded to marry Seth based on a gentle and sensitive letter that she receives from him. But the letter was actually written by Matt. Matt is still grieving the death of his mother and is upset that his father is determined to remarry so soon after her death. Seth insists that he needs a new wife to cook and clean for him. But Seth is surprised to see how young and pretty Ruth is and realizes that she might serve him best in the bedroom. Seth and Ruth are married in a hasty ceremony. Ruth tells Seth that she is afraid of him, but he seems to enjoy her fear and becomes even more aggressive. He glares at her with a wicked grin, insisting that she will soon bear him a son. Unlike the short story, father and son get into a rough fight. Rather than trip and fall, Seth crashes through a balcony rail and falls to the bottom of a staircase. A doctor tells Seth that he'll never be able to walk again. But Seth is determined to prove the doctor wrong and begins to regain movement. He crawls around his home defiantly, swearing that he will walk again and will consummate his marriage. Ruth and Matt agree to go away together. Ruth waits for Matt in a boat, but storm winds and rough waves set the boat adrift. Seth and Matt set out in boats to rescue Ruth. Matt swims out to Ruth's boat while Seth's boat capsizes and Seth drowns.

The film was directed by William Wyler, who would explore adultery themes more deeply with *Dodsworth*, *The Letter* and *Carrie*.

Other Men's Women is similar to *A House Divided* in three ways. First, a man fights an intimate relation for usurping his rights and authority as a husband. Second, the husband falls during the fight and suffers a debilitating injury. Third, the husband performs a redemptive act of heroism during a storm and loses his life for his efforts.

A House Divided is in other ways like *A Lady to Love* and Eugene O'Neill's 1924 play "Desire Under the Elms." In *A Lady to Love*, a homely grape grower entices a mail-order bride by sending her a photo of his handsome hired hand. So, the prospective bride is deceived by a photo in one film and a letter in another. The grape grower and the hired hand have a warm relationship, making them more like a father and son than Seth and Matt. The groom-to-be is a jolly man, which makes him far more appealing than the mean and brutish Seth. This assures a happier resolution.

A House Divided is most similar to "Desire Under the Elms," which was adapted into a film in 1958. Ephraim Cabot (Burl Ives) is much like Seth Law. He is a cruel and greedy farmer who treats his family like slaves. He has already worked two wives to early deaths. He now has his mind set on finding himself a third wife. Two of his sons abandon the farm to seek success in California. His youngest son, Eben (Anthony

Perkins), is determined to eventually own his father's farm. His mother told him before she died that it was his birthright to inherit the farm. Ephraim brings home a new wife, Anna (Sophia Loren). Anna is young, beautiful and headstrong. She freely admits to Eben that she only married Ephraim for his money. Eben and Anna have an affair, which results in Anna becoming pregnant. Ephraim is proud thinking that the baby is his. Eben becomes distraught over the situation. He argues with Anna and tells her that he wishes the baby was dead. He says that he never wants to see her again. Anna feels distressed to have lost Eben and murders the baby in the hope of getting him back. The sheriff comes to arrest Anna for the murder. Eben feels responsible for what happened and tells the sheriff that he participated in the crime. Ephraim is content to see the lovers taken to jail. He is pleased to know that no one will get his prized farm after he dies.

Burl Ives, Sophia Loren and Anthony Perkins in Desire Under the Elms (1958)

Dramatists often create their own version of the Russian nesting doll. This is the case with stories about a son who has an affair with his stepmother. O'Neill's play owed a great debt to the ancient Greek myth about Hippolytus. Hippolytus is the chaste son of King Theseus. Hippolytus, as a hunter, worships Artemis, the goddess of the hunt and wild animals. Aphrodite, the goddess of love, is offended that Hippolytus refuses to honor her and resolves to elicit revenge on the defiant man. She casts a spell to make Hippolytus' stepmother, Phaedra, fall in love with him. Hippolytus rejects Phaedra's advances, which causes her to hang herself. Phaedra leaves behind a suicide note that accuses Hippolytus of raping her. Theseus summons Poseidon, the god of the sea, to murder his son as punishment. Theseus learns of Hippolytus' innocence just before his son dies in his arms.

A son cuckolds his father with his stepmother in other films, including *The Second Wife* (1998) and *Forty Shades of Blue* (2005). Italian beauty Maria Grazia Cucinotta is at the center of *The Second Wife* as a young single mother, Anna. Anna marries a rough-mannered, middle-aged truck driver, Fosco (Lazar Ristovski). The new wife is left alone when Fosco is sent to prison for stealing ancient relics from graveyards. She receives comfort from Fosco's sensitive adult son, Livio (Giorgio Noè). It isn't long before the two fall in love.

Autumn Leaves (1956) shows that a father, too, can transgress the moral standards of the home. A newly-wed husband, Burt Hanson (Cliff Roberton), comes home early from work and catches his pretty wife in bed with his father (Lorne Greene). The shock is more than he can bear. He flees his home in a daze. Repressing his memory of the experience simply makes him more anxious and perplexed and drives him to neurotic behavior. He unexpectedly shows up in Los Angeles, 2,000 miles away, where he meets Milly Wetherby (Joan Crawford). Milly falls in love with Burt. She becomes concerned when Burt's unconscious disturbances cause him to engage in irrational and unpredictable acts, including shoplifting. She urges Burt to get medical help. Milly is enraged when she confronts Bert's father and his now ex-wife. She tells them, "You committed the ugliest of all possible sins and drove him into the state he's in now. . . He's decent and proud! Can you say the same for yourselves? Where's your decency? In what garbage dump?" Virginia becomes indignant, accusing Milly of being crazy. But this doesn't deter Milly, who brings her admonishment to a blistering crescendo. She declares, "You, his loving fraud of a father! And you, you slut! You're both so consumed with evil! Your filthy souls are too evil for hell itself!"

Regardless of the circumstances, a disloyal friend or a disloyal family member is the worst sort of interloper.

Importantly, we learn from *Other Men's Women* that an interloper can be a seemingly innocent house guest. Let's examine other house guest films.

Bed and Sofa (1927)

The set-up for *Other Men's Women* is the same as the set-up for the 1927 Russian film *Bed and Sofa*, but the two films have very different outcomes.

Volodia (Vladimir Fogel) arrives in town with no place to stay. His old friend, Kolia (Nikolai Batalov), graciously invites Volodia to sleep on a sofa in a one-bedroom basement apartment that he shares with his wife, Liuda (Lyudmila Semyonova). Liuda, who is unhappy with household drudgery and a bossy husband, finds herself attracted to the friendly, helpful Volodia. The plot then takes a strange twist.

Wikipedia reports:

When Kolia returns from [a] trip, he finds himself to be the one relegated to sleeping on the couch. Initially outraged, he calms down and the three settle into a polygamous, domesticated routine. However, now that Volodia has taken over the role of "husband," he unfortunately begins acting like one. . . In fact, he is even less sensitive and more dictatorial than Kolia.

Meanwhile, the two men are bonding, joking and playing checkers while Liuda pouts. She begins sleeping with both men (at different times). Eventually, the inevitable happens, and she becomes pregnant, and since no one knows who the father is, both men insist she have an abortion.[153]

Liuda, unwilling to get an abortion, leaves the men to raise her baby on her own. She is joyful looking out of the train window and watching the city of Moscow rush past in a blur. Back at the apartment, Volodia questions if he and Kolia haven't been scoundrels. Minutes later, they are lounging about and contemplating eating bread and jam. It looks as if the men are content to return to their easygoing lives as bachelors.

Vampire (1915)

An injured motorist, Jane Lagrange (Olga Petrova), is brought to a nearby resort to recover. TV Guide notes:

> Once she's out of danger, Jane proves to be a most bewitching "guest," and before long she has wrapped every one of the male hotel patrons around her little finger. She has a particularly powerful effect over married men, who need only take one look at Jane before deciding to desert their wives and families.[154]

She, as the typical vamp, is loved by all but loves no one in return. She has created such a great uproar at the resort that the manager demands that she leave. But then she meets the one man who is able to win her heart and she cannot bring herself to deceive him.

Adam Had Four Sons (1941)

David Stoddard (Johnny Downs) sends his new wife, Hester (Susan Hayward), to live on the Stoddard family estate while he is away at war. During her stay, she seduces her brother-in-law, Jack (Richard Denning).

Most house guests that we encounter in our regular lives are friendly and respectful. A few may have an odd annoying habit or two, but it isn't something that we can't tolerate for the duration of their visit. But a house guest is different in films. They are often a disruptive force that creates great emotional shocks and ruptures. Take, for instance, *Boudu Saved from Drowning* (1932) and *The Man Who Came to Dinner* (1942). A group of bachelor professors enjoys having a sassy nightclub singer as a guest in *Ball of Fire* (1942), but the positive upheaval that she creates is a rare case.

Guest in the House (1944)

Dr. Dan Proctor (Scott McKay) takes his fiancé, Evelyn Heath (Anne Baxter), to meet his family. Evelyn displays neurotic tendencies. She sits alone in her room listening to sad music on a phonograph. She shrieks at the sight of a pet bird. Dan's older brother Douglas (Ralph Bellamy) opens a window to let the hyperventilating Evelyn get air, but this makes Evelyn panic even more. She cries, "Don't! Don't, Douglas, don't!. . . I don't want you to. Don't you see them, those leaves there. In the moonlight, they look like birds trying to get in." Douglas tells her that she shouldn't have such bad thoughts. "Look," he insists, "that's first-class moonlight." Dan explains to Douglas that an alcoholic father caused Evelyn much fear and grief during her childhood. Douglas feels sympathetic towards her and treats her with kindness. Evelyn is attracted to Douglas and schemes to steal him away from his wife, Ann (Ruth Warrick). The manipulative Evelyn manages during her stay to sabotage relationships, create dissension, use gossip to rid herself of a perceived rival, and separate Douglas and Ann by instigating an argument between them. Ann calls out Evelyn for her manipulations. Evelyn becomes hysterical and accuses Ann of being jealous of her. Later, Evelyn becomes distressed by the sight of the empty birdcage, assuming that the bird has gotten free. The simple truth is that the bird died. AFI reports: "When Evelyn becomes hysterical, [Aunt] Martha [Aline MacMahon] taunts her that the bird is flying free in the house. Panicked, Evelyn runs out screaming and plunges to her death from a cliff."[155]

Anne Baxter and Aline MacMahon in *Guest in the House* (1944)

Baxter, who later received an Oscar nomination for her role as a bad house guest in *All About Eve* (1950), had a good dry run as the hellishly insane house guest of *Guest in the House*.

The Man in Grey (1943)

Clarissa (Phyllis Calvert) and Hesther (Margaret Lockwood) are classmates at Miss Patchett's Establishment for Young Ladies. Clarissa is kind to the vain and mean-spirited Hesther while other students wisely snub her. Hesther is unable to fit in at the school. Eventually, she runs off to marry an ensign.

After leaving the school, Clarissa meets Lord Rohan (James Mason). Rohan's mother, Lady Rohan (Helen Haye), believes that Clarissa will make a suitable wife for her son. Rohan tells his mother that he would prefer to marry a woman as black-hearted as himself, but his mother bristles at the notion and insists that Rohan marry the virtuous Clarissa to remain in her good graces. Clarissa is similarly opposed to a marriage between herself and Rohan. She feels no love for this wicked and brutal man just as he feels no love for her. But family pressure comes to bear on her as well. Clarissa agrees to marry Rohan to please her godmother, who admires Rohan for his wealth and status. Rohan agrees to marry Clarissa for her health and beauty, which makes it likely that she will produce a fine heir.

Phyllis Calvert and Margaret Lockwood in *The Man in Grey* (1943)

Suddenly, Clarissa's old friend Hesther comes back into her life. Hesther tells Clarissa that she has become destitute due to the death of her husband. Clarissa graciously has Hesther come live in her home, not knowing that Hesther is a ruthless schemer who will take this as an opportunity to steal her husband. Clarissa is warned not to trust Hesther by various people, but she insists that Hesther is her best friend and stubbornly ignores the many warnings. Hesther works efficiently to contrive an affair with the cynical and dissolute Rohan. Rohan, who is no fool, can see through Hesther's lies and looks into her past. He tells her, "And as for this husband whom you so wistfully described as having passed away in your loving arms, he died of jail fever in fleet prison after you'd deserted him in favour of a more wealthy protector." But the lies only make Hesther more attractive to him. He says, "I never thought to find a woman with a spirit as ruthless as mine. You take what you want until the devil were the consequences. So do I."

Hesther sees that Clarissa has taken a liking to her friend, Peter Rokeby (Stewart Granger), and thinks that she can instigate an affair between the couple by convincing Clarissa to give Rokeby a job on her estate. Hesther's plan works. Clarissa and Rokeby fall in love and plan to run off together. Rohan finds out Clarissa's plan and challenges Rokeby to a duel. Rokeby is defiant. He tells Rohan:

You damned arrogant swine. It's time someone told you the truth about yourself. Just because you've had everything poured into your lap and better men to do your bidding, you think you're some kind of being apart. Well, you're not. You're just a well-bred scoundrel whose treatment of his wife has been beyond contempt. You tricked her into marrying you to perpetuate your rotten line. You gave her no love, no understanding and now you betray her in her own home with a friend she trusts. All London condemns you for it and will applaud her for leaving you.

Rohan's expert skills with a sword make it unlikely that Rokeby will survive the duel. But the duel is broken up by one of Rohan's friends. Rokeby is persuaded by a trusted confidante, Mrs. Fitzherbert (Nora Swinburne), to flee the country on his own and wait for Clarissa to divorce her husband. Clarissa gets sick standing in the rain while biding Rokeby a sad farewell. Hesther is expected to nurse Clarissa back to health, but she works to make Clarissa sicker. She gives Clarissa a heavy dose of sleep medication to put her into a deep sleep. Then, she puts out the fire and opens the window to let in the cold wind. The chill assures that Clarissa is dead by morning.

Rohan learns from a faithful servant boy, Toby (Scott Antony), that Hesther murdered Clarissa. He becomes enraged. "You killed a Rohan," he shouts. "He who dishonors us dies!" He looms over Hester and, undeterred by her pleas, beats her to death with his cane.

Rohan is more sympathetic in the novel. He is cold, not cruel. He in fact warns his wife about Hesther's scheming. Less sympathetic are Rokeby and Clarissa. Tony Williams, film studies professor at Southern Illinois University, wrote:

> The novel's Rokeby is little more than a buccaneer gentleman of fortune who sleeps with Clarissa and dies on board ship before he can regain his fortune. The book's Clarissa is less virtuous than her screen counterpart. She accrues gambling debts and becomes pregnant by Rokeby.[156]

Patricia Roc and Margaret Lockwood in *The Wicked Lady* (1945)

The Wicked Lady (1945)

Caroline (Patricia Roc) invites her friend Barbara (Margaret Lockwood) to her wedding to Sir Ralph Skelton (Griffith Jones). Barbara works quickly to seduce Ralph away from Caroline before the wedding. Barbara and Sir Skelton marry, with the degraded and demoralized Caroline serving as maid of honor. Barbara has succeeded in becoming Lady Skelton, but she finds herself bored. She has an affair with Kit Locksby (Michael Rennie). But that's still not exciting enough for her. One night, she gambles at cards with her sister-in-law, Henrietta (Enid Stamp-Taylor). Henrietta wins Barbara's jewels, including a precious ruby brooch. Barbara gets a wild idea. The gentry of the area have been falling victim to a notorious highwayman, Captain Jerry Jackson. Barbara masquerades as Jackson to hold up Henrietta's coach and rob Henrietta of her brooch as well as the rest of her jewelry. She finds so much excitement in the act that she continues to rob coaches. Meanwhile, she becomes romantically involved with the real Captain Jerry (James Mason).

Williams wrote, "Barbara's cross-dressing as a highwayman and enjoyment of a man's life with Jerry Jackson contrast with the boring world of Sir Ralph."[157]

Barbara falls in love with Locksby. She is willing to reform for him, becoming his wife and having children with him. She just needs to be rid of her husband. She plans to hijack Ralph's coach disguised as the highwayman and shoot her husband during the robbery. But Kit accompanies Ralph in the coach. He is fast with his gun and is able to shoot Barbara before she can harm Ralph. Barbara is brought home to die in her bed. She is visited by Kit. Williams wrote, "Her intended mate retreats in horror after she reveals her deadly past. Shocked by her wicked deeds, Kit leaves her to die alone as the camera cranes overhead, framing her dying posture through a window."[158]

James Mason, Julie Newmar and Susan Hayward in *The Marriage-Go-Round* (1961)

The Marriage-Go-Round (1961)

Paul and Content Delville (James Mason and Susan Hayward), a happily married middle-aged couple, welcome their daughter's friend, a Swedish girl named Katrin Sveg (Julie Newmar), to stay at their house for a few days. Katrin has a big surprise for her hosts. She tells Paul that she admires him for his extraordinary intelligence and wants to have a baby with him.

Death Smiles on a Murderer (1973)

The original Italian title: *La morte ha sorriso all'assassino*

Greta von Holstein (Ewa Aulin) is injured in a carriage accident. A wealthy young couple, Eva and Walter von Ravensbruck (Angela Bo and Sergio Doria), come to her aid and bring her back to their estate. Greta has no memory of who she is. Eva slips into the bathroom while Greta is bathing in the tub. Excited to see her lovely guest naked, she has sex with her. Eva becomes outraged when she discovers that Greta has also been having sex with Walter. She takes Greta to the cellar and walls her up alive inside a small concrete room. But, as it turns out, Greta is not truly alive. She is the undead. Greta died in childbirth three years earlier, but her brother Franz (Luciano Rossi) used a mystical amulet from the ancient Incas to return her to life. Greta returns as a rotting corpse to murder Eva.

Poison Ivy (1992)

Sylvie Cooper (Sara Gilbert) attends a private school with the enviably beautiful Ivy (Drew Barrymore). She invites Ivy to stay at her home during a school break. Ivy wastes no time in seducing Sylvie's stepfather, Darryl (Tom Skerritt). Determined to take the place of Sylvie's stepmother, Georgie (Cheryl Ladd), she murders the woman by pushing her off a balcony.

The Governess (1998)

Charles Cavendish (Tom Wilkinson) has an affair with his family's governess, Rosina da Silva (Minnie Driver).

Disobedience (2017)

Ronit (Rachel Weisz), a rebellious woman who has been estranged from her rabbi father Rav Krushka (Anton Lesser), visits her orthodox Jewish family upon learning of her father's death. She stays at the home of a childhood friend, Dovid Kuperman (Alessandro Nivola), who was her father's chosen successor. Within a couple of days, Ronit manages to have separate affairs with both Dovid and his secretly lesbian wife Esti (Rachel McAdams).

A Private Scandal (1921)

A good guest is to be found in *A Private Scandal*. Janiss Garza of AllMovie wrote:

> Philip and Carol Lawton (Ralph Lewis and Kathlyn Williams) adopt Jeanne Millette, a French war orphan (May McAvoy). Her loyalty to the Lawtons, and to their little daughter, Betty (Gladys Fox), is unshakable.[159]

Philip is a horse-racing enthusiast whose interest in thoroughbred horses exceeds his interest in his wife. The neglected wife romances a neighbor, Alec Crosby (Lloyd Whitlock), and makes plans to run away with him. Lawton becomes suspicious when he finds Crosby at his home, but Jeanne protects Carol by claiming that Crosby is her lover and he has come to the home to see her. This creates difficulty between Carol and her boyfriend, Jerry Hayes (Bruce Gordon). But the flimsy ruse doesn't hold up for long. When Lawton catches Crosby sneaking out of his home, he lunges after him and the two men get into a fistfight on a balcony. The fight ends with Crosby falling from the balcony to his death.

We will further examine the neglected wife trope in Chapter Twelve.

Grand Guignol

Ethan Frome (1993)

"Ethan Frome," a book from classic literature, involves an affair that develops after a woman invites her lovely young cousin to live with her and her husband. Zeena, a severe hypochondriac, is bedridden and in need of a caretaker. Her cousin, Mattie, is willing to serve dutifully in this role. Zeena never considers that her husband might fall in love with her new caretaker.

Strangely, it wasn't until the 1990s that a producer got the idea to adapt the novel into a film.

Zeena (Joan Allen) sees that Ethan (Liam Neeson) and Mattie (Patricia Arquette) have fallen in love and demands that Mattie return home to Stamford, Connecticut. Ethan accepts that Mattie must leave, but he defies Zeena by taking Mattie to the train station. Ethan laments that they never went sledding as they planned. He says, "How'd you like me to take you down now?" Mattie laughs. She tells him that there isn't time. But he insists. "There's all the time we want," he says. "Come along!" They have fun riding the sled, but riding down the hill gives Mattie a dark idea. The couple dreads having to part. Mattie believes that, rather than be miserable for the rest of their lives, they should end their lives now by riding the sled directly into a large elm tree. From the novel:

> Her pleadings. . . came to him between short sobs. . . "Come!" Mattie whispered, tugging at his hand.[160]

Ethan complies, not saying a word. He is steering the sled towards the tree when he suddenly envisions Zeena's face before him. He panics and swerves from his course. The sled crashes. From the novel:

> The stillness was so profound that he heard a little animal twittering somewhere near by under the snow. It made a small frightened cheep like a field mouse, and he wondered languidly if it were hurt. Then he understood that it must be in pain. . .[161]

It turns out that the small, frightened *cheep* is coming from Mattie, whose spine was broken in the crash.

The story ends with a frighteningly dark and morbid twist. A visitor to Ethan's home hears a woman's voice coming from a bedroom. It is an unpleasant voice. It is a woman complaining. The reader likely assumes that this is Zeena, who spent her days lying in bed and complaining to her caretakers. But it turns out that the woman is Mattie, who was paralyzed in the sled crash. Mattie, who was once sunny and personable, is now bitter and dour. Ethan was proven correct in his belief that Zeena only imagined her illness. Zeena is now robust in caring for Mattie. Their roles have perfectly reversed. Wikipedia notes:

> Ethan and Mattie have gotten their wish to stay together, but in mutual unhappiness and discontent, with Mattie helpless and paralyzed, and with Zeena as a constant presence between the two of them.[162]

It is a Grand Guignol ending, similar to the endings of a few other adultery films, including *Freaks* (1932), *Manèges* (1950) and *The Cook, the Thief, His Wife & Her Lover* (1989).

Rita Kempley of The Washington Post wrote:

The public television types at American Playhouse have made a watery gruel of Edith Wharton's popular 1911 novella, "Ethan Frome." A tragedy of wasted lives and romantic longing as written, it has become a wan, rather silly cautionary tale on the perils of forbidden sex and unsafe sledding in late-19th-century New England.[163]

Freaks (1932)

Cleopatra (Olga Baclanova), a carnival's trapeze star, becomes interested in a sideshow midget, Hans (Harry Earles), when she learns that he is due to inherit a fortune. Cleopatra schemes with her strongman lover, Hercules (Henry Victor), to marry Hans and then murder him for his money. The charming woman has to no more than offer Hans a bit of sweet-talk to seduce him away from his fiancée, Frieda (Daisy Earles), a fellow midget in the show. Olga drunkenly humiliates Hans at the wedding reception, making it clear to Hans that she does not love him. Hans realizes that Olga is trying to poison him and pretends to be taking the poison. He plots with his friends to get revenge on his treacherous bride. Wikipedia notes:

> The freaks... capture Cleopatra and sometime later, she is shown to be a grotesque, squawking 'human duck' on display for carnival patrons; her tongue has been removed, one eye has been gouged out, the flesh of her hands has been melted and deformed to look like duck feet, her legs have been cut off, and what is left of her torso has been permanently tarred and feathered.[164]

The Cook, the Thief, His Wife & Her Lover (1989)

A vicious crime boss, Albert Spica, (Michael Gambon), is enraged when he learns that his wife, Georgina (Helen Mirren), is having an affair with a gentle-mannered bookseller, Michael (Alan Howard). "Georgie!" Albert bellows. "I want my wife! Georgie! I'll bloody find her. I'll find them. I'll bloody find them. I knew it. Scheming tart! I'll bloody find them and I'll bloody kill him! And I'll bloody eat him! I'll kill him and I'll eat him!"

Albert has Michael beaten into a bloody mess. But this isn't enough for him. As he stomps around the bookstore ranting and raving, one of his henchmen stuffs pages of a book down Michael's throat until the bloodied man chokes to death.

As revenge, Georgina has her lover's corpse served to the gluttonous Albert at his favorite restaurant. She holds a gun on Albert, demanding that he eat the corpse as he once threatened to do. Once Albert eats a mouthful of the corpse, Georginia calls him a cannibal and shoots him.

Chapter Five:
Murder

Erickson wrote in a review of *Pitfall* (1948): "If adultery has been committed, can murder be far behind?"[165]

The Greek play "Agamemnon," written by Aeschylus in 458 BCE, involves an adulterous affair that leads to murder. World History Encyclopedia summarizes the plot as follows:

> In Agamemnon, the Greek king of Argos and commander of the forces against King Priam's Troy has returned victorious after ten grueling years. With him is his newly acquired concubine, the beautiful prophetess Cassandra, daughter of King Priam and a priestess at the shrine of Apollo. In his absence, his "devoted" wife Clytemnestra has taken a lover Aegisthus, Agamemnon's first cousin. The scheming couple, hoping to rule Argos together, decides to kill the returning king and his mistress.[166]

An adulterous wife schemes with her lover to murder her husband in *The Unfaithful Wife* (1915).

The cheating wife is nothing more than a wanton hussy in *The Death Dance* (1918), which focuses on the evil machinations of a lustful woman. First, the woman leaves her husband for another man. Then, she becomes bored with her new man and turns her attention to a handsome businessman who she finds more appealing. She conceives of two murders - a murder to dispose of the businessman's lover and a second murder to free herself from her own lover.

So many more murders were to come.

Her Private Affair (1929)

Vera Kessler (Ann Harding) is neglected by her husband, who is busy with his prosperous law practice. Vera becomes vulnerable to the devilish charms of Arnold Hartman (Lawford Davidson). She writes love letters to Hartman. The couple makes plans for a romantic evening at his home. Vera arrives at Hartman's home, but she comes to her senses before anything happens and leaves. Hartman threatens to show her letters to her husband unless she makes a substantial payment to him. Hartman laughs when Vera draws a gun on him and demands that he turn over the letters. He insists that he is going to make love to her. He grabs her roughly, at which time the gun goes off by accident. He falls dead. Ludwig Grimm (Elmer Ballard), Hartmann's butler, is charged with the murder. Vera remains painfully silent during the trial. She is relieved when Grimm is acquitted, but she can no longer live with her guilt and finally confesses to the crime.

Up for Murder (1931)

A newspaper reporter, Bob Marshal (Lew Ayres) is assigned to escort society columnist Myra Deane (Genevieve Tobin) to a ball. He enjoys their time together and develops feelings for Myra. As a show of his affection, he buys Myra a bracelet as a birthday present. When a co-worker warns him that Myra is dating the boss, he becomes upset and makes a surprise visit to her apartment. The apartment is an extravagant place, far more than Myra could afford on her salary. Myra tells Bob that his visit is inconvenient and asks him to leave. Bob is appalled when his married boss, William Winter (Purnell Pratt), saunters into the room. Bob insists that he loves Myra and that Winter should leave. Winter scoffs at the idea of leaving. He makes it perfectly clear to Bob that he is the one paying the rent on the apartment. Bob gets into a scuffle with Winter, who falls and hits his head on a table. Bob and Myra are shocked to discover that Winter has died.

Bob turns himself over to the police for Winter's murder. Myra, fearing that a scandal could ruin her reputation, is unwilling to testify on Bob's behalf. But she realizes that she can no longer be silent when Bob is convicted and sentenced to death. She tells the defense attorney that Winter's death was an accident, which enables the attorney to get Bob's conviction overturned. Wikipedia reports an upbeat romantic ending: "Bob receives a package with the bracelet inside, along with Myra's invitation to return it to her in person."[167]

The Man Who Committed Murder (1931)

This German film was the fourth film adaptation of Claude Farriere's 1906 novel "L'Homme qui assassina." Marquis de Sévigné (Conrad Veidt), a military attache stationed in Turkey, learns that an English consul (Heinrich George) has been mistreating his lovely wife, Lady Falkland (Trude von Molo). The marquis visits the wife and falls in love with her. Soon, the two are plotting the death of the consul.

24 Hours (1931)

Jim Towner (Clive Brook) is wrongly accused of killing his mistress, nightclub singer Rosie Duggan (Miriam Hopkins).

The Crime of the Century (1933)

Dr. Emil Brandt (Jean Hersholt) will do anything to hold onto his young wife, Freda (Wynne Gibson). Brandt figures to put his hypnotism skills to use when a bank official comes under his care. Once he has the patient under a trance, he instructs him to rob $100,000 from the bank vault. He intends to murder the bank official once he has delivered the money to him. Meanwhile, Freda learns about his scheme and arranges for her boyfriend Gilbert Reid (Gordon Westcott) to grab the money instead.

The Kiss Before the Mirror (1933)

Walter Bernsdorf (Paul Lukas) follows his wife Lucy (Gloria Stuart) to her lover's home. He is creeping through the garden when he spots Lucy through a window undressing. He loses control. He raises a gun and fires three shots at his wife. She instantly falls dead.

Walter gives his account of the murder to his attorney, Paul Held (Frank Morgan). He canceled a lecture so that he could come home early and spend the evening with his wife. He found her standing before the mirror in her dressing room. He says:

> [S]he was admiring herself. She was just about to dress. She penciled a thin line on her eyebrows, applied lipstick to her lips, everything as if she was in love with herself. And yet, with a certain purpose, she made herself perfect! As she lightly powdered her breast, she smiled knowing she was particularly beautiful then. . . [S]he was radiantly happy. She was humming a tango. Oh, I can hear it now. . . Unspeakable joy overpowered me that this beautiful woman belonged to me. I walked over to her, embraced her suddenly, and kissed her neck and her shoulders. . . And here, the tragedy begins. She

shook me up angrily and said I had ruined her hair. . . I saw her face in the mirror as strange, full of hate and dislike. . . That mirror showed me the whole lie of my existence. I realized what a pitiful fool I was. She didn't love me at all. She covered the traces of my kiss with her powder puff, and I knew she was preparing for a lover. She finished dressing,. . . said goodbye, and walked off. I stared into the empty mirror. . .

Frank Morgan and Nancy Carroll in *The Kiss Before the Mirror* (1933)

Molly of Dreaming in the Balcony wrote: "[Walter]'s wife's mirror is adorned with a gilded cupid. Another cupid sits haughtily upon a mantle. Women it seems are too often guided by Cupid's whims."[168]

Paul returns home to his wife, Maria (Nancy Carroll). He has a nearly identical experience when he sees his wife elaborately preparing herself in front of a mirror. He, too, tries to kiss her and is rebuffed. She wants to look good for someone, but not him. He suddenly realizes that Maria is cheating on him. He now understands how crazed Walter became and he, himself, contemplates killing his wife. He later says that blood pounded in his temples and a thousand serpents crawled through his heart. Like Walter, he follows his wife and sees her meet a lover (Donald Cook). He now understands Walter's mad jealousy, which allows him to better defend his client in court. Obscure Hollywood reports, "Paul is pleading his own defense in anticipation of killing [Maria]. . ."[169]

As the trial is winding down, Walter warns Paul not to do anything rash. He tells him that he would regret harming Maria. Obscure Hollywood notes: "Walter's inconsolable sorrow teaches Paul that murdering his wife will not resolve his anger and grief."[170]

The film ends favorably for the main characters. Walter is acquitted of murder. Paul and Maria reconcile.

Upperworld (1934)

Upperworld provided Warren William with his only opportunity to play a sympathetic adulterer. He appears in the role of Alexander Stream, a railroad tycoon who feels neglected at home. His wife, Hettie (Mary Astor), is busy with social functions and has little time left for him. Alexander falls in love with a chorus girl, Lilly Linda (Ginger Rogers), who he sets up in a luxury suite. Alexander has fun being with Lilly. In one scene, the two engage in a jolly duet of "Who's Afraid of the Big Bad Wolf?" Lilly secretly has a boyfriend, Louie Colima (J. Carrol Naish), who tries to blackmail Alexander. Alexander and Louie get into a fight. Louie fires a gun at Alexander, but his shot misses and hits Lilly. Alexander takes Lilly in his arms and can see that she's dead. He grabs a gun that Lilly left on a chair. He fires at Louie, killing him. Alexander goes on trial for murder, but he is acquitted. Hettie forgives Alexander and promises to spend more time with him. The final scene shows Alexander and Hettie on a cruise ship heading for a romantic vacation in Europe.

The Lower Depths (1936)

A young thief, Wasska Pépel (Jean Gabin), has an affair with his landlord's wife, Vassilissa Kostyleva (Suzy Prim). Vassilissa asks Wasska to kill her husband. "He's old and evil," she insists. "It would be a good deed." But he is disgusted by her. "That's a nice combination," he says. "A husband in the ground and a lover in the joint." He tells her that she is "heartless" and he wants a "clean break" from her. Wasska falls in love with Vassilissa's younger sister, Natasha (Junie Astor). Vassilissa holds a grudge against Wasska for abandoning her. The landlord, Kostylev (Vladimir Sokoloff), is worried about an upcoming inspection of his building, but he expects the inspection to go well if Natasha seduces the inspector. Natasha refuses to cooperate, which prompts Vassilissa and Kostylev to beat her. Wasska intervenes, pummeling Kostylev. Other lodgers join Wasska in his attack on the hated landlord. "Let me at that bastard!" one man cries out. Kostylev is beaten to death. Vassilissa, out for revenge, identifies Wasska to the police as the man who murdered her husband. The police learn from an eyewitness that Kostylev was beaten during a brawl and Wasska was not personally responsible for his death. Wasska finds Natasha waiting for him when he leaves prison. The couple agrees to leave the town and start a new life together somewhere else.

Confession (1937)

The film opens with Vera Kowalska (Kay Francis), a cabaret singer, on trial for murder. A flashback reveals the motive behind the murder. Vera was once a promising young opera singer. A Lothario pianist, Michael Michailow (Basil Rathbone), finds her attractive and sets out to seduce her. Vera, who is devoted to her husband Leonide (Ian Hunter) and their two-year-old daughter Lisa, has no interest in Michael. Undeterred, he persists in his advances. One night, he slyly sets about getting her drunk at a party. Once he has her giggling and barely able to stand, he offers to escort her home. Vera makes it clear that she is anxious to get back to her daughter's nursery, but she wakes up in Michael's bed the next morning without remembering how she had gotten there. Michael continues to pursue Vera, sending love letters to her home. Worried that her husband might find one of the letters, she goes to Michael's apartment to demand that he leave her alone. Leonide, who has become suspicious, follows Vera and is enraged to catch her alone with Michael. He obtains a divorce and legally bars Vera from seeing her daughter. Fifteen years later, Michael re-enters Vera's life by chance. The pianist happens to see Vera's daughter Lisa (Jane Bryan), now a lovely 17-year-old music student, at a train station. He becomes enchanted with her as he once became enchanted with her mother. Still practicing his sly womanizing ways, he arranges to tutor Lisa with the true intention of seducing her. Vera is shocked to see Michael kissing Lisa at the cabaret where she sings. Determined to protect Lisa, she shoots Michael dead before he can escort her daughter back to his home. In her trial, Vera is allowed by the judge to testify privately in his chambers. She is able to produce her divorce papers to verify her story. She is found guilty, but the judge pardons her. Lisa does not realize that Vera is her mother, but she understands that this woman acted to protect her. She tearfully approaches her to thank her.

This was a reoccurring plot. It turned up in a number of films, including *The Ransom* (1916), *Playing with Fire* (1916), *Millie* (1931) and *Madame X* (multiple versions).

Let's first look at the plot of *The Ransom*. Janet Osborne (Julia Dean), aspires to be an actress despite the protests of her stern husband, Mark (J. Albert Hall). Janet is bedded by a wily theatrical agent, Geoffrey Allen (Kenneth Hunter). Mark learns of this infidelity and throws Janet out of their home. He demands that she never return home and keep away from their young daughter, Marcia. Years later, Janet is working as a maid. She learns that Marcia (Louise Huff), now a young woman, has become involved with Allen. She tries to warn Marcia about the agent, but Marcia doesn't realize that the worn and frazzled maid is her mother and thinks that she's crazy (people actually call the addled old woman "Crazy Jane"). So, Janet gets a pistol and shoots Allen. Moving Picture World noted: "Janet falls dead, having ransomed her soul to save her daughter from the life she has herself led. . . [Marcia] never knows that 'Crazy Jane' was her mother."[171]

The same basic story elements are present in *Playing with Fire*. Jean Servian (Olga Petrova), a cameo cutter, is losing her sight. Geoffrey Vane (Arthur Hoops), a wealthy widower who collects cameos, has great affection for Jean and asks her to marry him. Jean, fearful that blindness will end her livelihood, is receptive to the marriage proposal, but she feels obligated to tell Vance that she doesn't love him. Vane is content to have the lady's gratitude. He arranges for Jean to be treated by a top eye specialist, who is able to fully restore her sight. Their marriage is not passionate, but it is serene, orderly, and satisfying to both parties. Unfortunately, a villainous interloper is about to enter the scene. Jean's friend, Rosa Derblay (Catherine Doucet), introduces Jean to her artist brother, Phillip (Pierre LeMay). Rosa is called away and leaves Jean and Phillip alone. Phillip invites Jean to his studio to see his paintings. Once Jean enters the studio, Phillip locks the door behind her and rapes her. Years pass. Jean's stepdaughter, Lucille (Evelyn Brent), becomes engaged to Philip. Jean intervenes in a violent argument between Philip and Lucille and accidentally shoots and kills Philip. Jean is put on trial for murder, but she is acquitted at the outcome. Pamela Short of IMDb wrote, "[Geoffrey] easily forgives his wife for her past indiscretion."[172]

Night Club Scandal (1937)

Dr. Ernest Tindal (John Barrymore) murders his unfaithful young wife and contrives evidence to implicate her lover, Frank Marlan (Harvey Stephens).

The Toy Wife (1938)

After finishing school in France, Frou-Frou Brigard (Luise Rainer) returns to her family's plantation in Louisiana. The young woman is intrigued by stories that she has heard about New Orleans. She says, "New Orleans, where flowers bloom all the year. And it is fun even to walk over the streets." She is anxious to see if the stories are true and pretends to have a toothache so that she can call upon a dentist in the fair and festive city. She comes upon a party as she tours the city and meets Andre Vallane (Robert Young), a carefree young man who identifies himself as a "dishonored gambler."

Melvyn Douglas and Luise Rainer in *The Toy Wife* (1938)

Back home, Frou-Frou becomes acquainted with Georges Sartoris (Melvyn Douglas), a prosperous attorney. Frou-Frou's older sister, Louise (Barbara O'Neil), is in love with Georges and hopes to marry him. She reveals her feelings to no one, but she expects Georges to know how she feels about him. Much to Louise's surprise, Georges develops an attraction for Frou-Frou. But Frou-Frou is no interloper. She makes no advances on Georges. It is Georges who pursues her. He, in fact, pursues her vigorously. Frou-Frou senses that Louise has feelings for Georges. So, she directly asks her sister if she loves him. Her sister, unwilling to stand in the way of Georges' happiness, denies that she has feelings for the man. She makes it clear to Frou-Frou that she has no claims on Georges and any other woman is free to marry him. The friendly, high-spirited Frou-Frou fails to see that she is being manipulated by two lovers, neither of whom can acknowledge their deep feelings for the other.

Frou-Frou is only 16 years old when she agrees to marry Georges. This young woman has to care for a baby and run a plantation at the same time. It is no wonder that she would be overwhelmed by her duties.

Georges installs Louise in the home to take charge. Relieved of her household duties, Louise passes through her days with nothing to do and comes to feel useless in her own home. The final blow comes when she sees that her son prefers Louise over her. To keep busy, she takes to acting in an amateur play with Andre. Andre is still in love with Frou Frou and uses this opportunity to renew their relationship. He asks Frou Frou to run away with him. She sees it as best for everyone if she leaves her husband and child in Louise's care. Frou Frou and Andre flee together to New York City. But Georges is enraged.

In time, Andre must return to Louisiana for money though he knows that he will have to confront Georges in a duel. He realizes that Frou-Frou still loves her husband and will be devastated if he is killed in the duel. He figures to at least give the man a chance. So, though he is an expert swordsman, he chooses pistols over swords for the duel. As a result of this selfless act, he is puts himself at a disadvantage and is killed by Georges.

Frou-Frou becomes gravely ill and asks Louise to bring her son Georgie (Alan Perl) to see her. Georges will not allow this.

Georges: I'm *ashamed*. Ashamed of the thing she's made of our marriage. Of the thing she's made of herself. I tell you, she's out of my life forever.

Louise: Poor Frou Frou. How much she has to forgive us.

Georges: To forgive *us*?

Louise: Yes. Once you called her a "toy-wife." Well. . . wasn't a pretty toy-wife what you wanted? You say she was selfish, shallow, foolish. But I know a woman. . . who loved you. Who was neither selfish nor shallow. And not often foolish. Who had all the proper sensible virtues that.men associate with womanhood. But was that what you wanted? No. . . no, you never even looked at her except as a friend. As someone to persuade the toy-girl to have you for a husband.

Georges: Louise.

Louise: Yes. I was that woman. Are you surprised? No wonder. You never even saw me for her.

Georges: We've both known for a long time that you were the woman I should have married.

Louise: Frou Frou saved me from that. Now that I've seen the cruelty towards the one you've wronged in your heart as much as she's wronged you. I give thanks on my knees I'm not the wife of such a man.

Georges: Louise!

Louise: Do you think I could have told you that I ever loved you if you hadn't killed that love at last? Forever. Goodbye, Georges.

Georges relents and Frou-Frou is able to see Georgie before she dies.

The Trip to Tilsit (1939)

The film, like *Sunrise*, is based on Hermann Sudermann's novella "The Excursion to Tilsit."

Endrik Settegast (Fritz van Dongen) is a fisherman in a village across the bay from the city of Tilsit. He is married to Elske (Kristina Söderbaum) and has a small son, Jons (Joachim Pfaff). Elske is beloved by family, friends and neighbors, all of whom are distressed to know that Endrik has been spending time with another woman. The woman, Madlyn Sapierska (Anna Dammann), is a dark and moody city woman. We get to hear the great disdain that the townsfolk feel towards the illicit lovers.

Madlyn confronts Elske at her home.

Madlyn: We should talk like women who understand and respect one another. Even if something difficult comes between them.

Elske: There's nothing to be said, Miss Sapierska. I'd rather discuss these things with En - with my husband.

Madlyn: But surely you know, Mrs. Elske, that your husband no longer belongs to you. Surely you noticed his ties to you are broken. He wants to get out.

Elske: If my husband no longer loves me, let him tell me in person. He won't need you for that!

Madlyn insists that she loves Endrik. She insists that Endrik will be happier with her. She tells Elske, "I want you to set Endrik free." She sees herself as the greatest of romantic figures - the woman in love. She sees herself as a freedom fighter committed to liberating an unhappy and oppressed man. Elske cannot bring herself to tell the woman what she really is. She says, "[Endrik] knows best whether he belongs to his child's mother, or. . . to a. . ." She asks the woman to leave. Madlyn says:

> You hate me. Perhaps you're obliged to hate me. Now that I'm leaving, know this: I'll never give up Endrik. Never. I will bear every sacrifice and shame to keep him as long as he loves me.

She doesn't believe that Elske is justified to hate her. "Am I evil because I love you?" she asks Endrik. In her mind, love and happiness is more important than duty and family. Their love for each other means that he belongs to her. "You're mine," she tells him. Madlyn is not demonic like the vamp in *Sunrise*. She is sadly needy and misguided.

Elske is overjoyed when she learns that Madlyn has finally been convinced to leave town. But, unknown to Elske, the determined woman is unable to stay away for long.

The drama intensifies during a pair of dinner scenes. Mr. Schleif (Albert Florath), a wise old teacher, is present at the first dinner. He acts as the film's voice of morality. He confronts Endrik about his unfaithfulness. Endrik reacts with a frightening hostility. Elske panics as she believes that he might physically attack the genial old man. We have a different third party in the second dinner scene. Their young son, Jons, mentions seeing father out on a boat with Madlyn. Elske now knows that Madlyn is back in town. It is a heartbreaking moment as the innocent, good-natured little boy is thrust unwittingly into the center of this marital maelstrom.

Madlyn is pushed to a murderous rage after Elske's father, Erwin Bohrmann (Eduard von Winterstein), confronts her in the street and strikes her repeatedly with a dog whip. She demands vengeance. She shrieks, "I'll kill her! I'll kill her!" She snarls, "If I'm beaten like a dog, I can fight like a dog." Her rage transfers to Endrik, who is now convinced that he must murder his wife.

Endrik plans to sell his most valuable belongings so that he will have money to start a new life with Madlyn. He believes that he can get a good price for his horse in Tilsit. Elske is appalled as she feels a strong attachment to the horse, which was a wedding present.

Elske and Endrik travel together across the bay in their small sailboat. Endrik intends to drown Elske during the trip, but he cannot bring himself to do it. Instead, he realizes that he loves his wife.

Elske and Endrik spend a joyful day in Tilsit. On their trip home, the couple gets caught in a storm. The sailboat overturns in raging waters. Endrik manages to swim to shore, but Elske is nowhere to be found. Endrik fears that Elske has drowned and cannot see how he'll be able to live without her. The horse swims to shore with Elske attached to its reins. Madlyn happens to be the one person around to witness this. Seeing Elske lying on the shore near death arouses remorse and compassion in her. She rushes off desperately to get help.

So, the husband is reformed and rekindles his commitment to his wife. The mistress is reformed and redeems herself by bringing medical aid to the bedraggled wife. The husband and wife are lovingly reunited for a happy ending.

Sunrise is surreal. *The Trip to Tilsit* possesses an unsettling realism that highlights the cruelty and madness behind adultery.

21 Days Together (1940)

Larry Durrant (Laurence Olivier) engages in a romantic relationship with Wanda (Vivien Leigh), a married woman who is estranged from her husband Henry Wallen (Esme Percy).

Henry shows up abruptly. He claims that Wanda abandoned him three years earlier. He promises not to make trouble for her if she pays him a small sum. Larry becomes indignant and demands that Henry leave, but the unwelcomed visitor charges at him with a knife. The two men struggle for the knife. Henry falls back and hits his head on the fireplace. He is dead. Larry hides the body and goes to his brother Keith (Leslie Banks), an eminent attorney, for advice. Keith is less concerned with his brother's welfare than he is about own reputation and how the arrest of his brother might spoil his chances to become a judge. He advises his brother to flee the country. But Larry cannot bring himself to flee once he learns that another man has been arrested for the murder.

Earthbound (1940)

The ghost of a murdered man (Warner Baxter) works with his widow (Andrea Leeds) to expose his scorned mistress, Linda Reynolds (Lynn Bari), as his killer.

The Letter (1940)

The film was based on the 1927 play "The Letter" by W. Somerset Maugham. It earned William Wyler his third Oscar nomination for Best Director.

Bette Davis and Herbert Marshall in *The Letter* (1940)

A married woman, Leslie Crosbie (Bette Davis), shoots her lover Hammond when he ends their relationship. Neil Sinyard, author of "A Wonderful Heart: The Films of William Wyler, wrote:

> A shot rings out. . . A cockatoo flies. . . from its perch. . . [A] man stagger[s] onto the veranda, clutching at the banister before falling to the ground. He is followed by a woman. . . with a gun in her hand.

The man dies and Leslie is arrested for murder. Leslie claims that she shot him in self-defense.

As she awaits trial, Leslie often steadies her nerves by doing needlework. Alexander Walker, author of "Bette Davis: A Celebration," described Leslie's needlework as a "study in neurotic compulsion."[173] She looks prim and proper knitting a coverlet for the marital bed that she has profaned. It is a cold facade. Charles Higham and Joel Greenberg, authors of "Hollywood in the Forties," saw "her lace stitched oval by tiny oval" as "a symbol of. . . her ability to build piece by piece a complex pattern of deceit."

Meanwhile, Hammond's widow has a letter that Leslie wrote demanding that her husband come to see her the night that he was murdered. Mrs. Hammond demands $10,000 for the letter. Leslie's attorney, Howard Joyce (James Stephenson), arranges payment to stop the letter getting into the hands of the prosecutor.

Leslie is acquitted at the end of a brief trial (five minutes of the film's running time). Her husband, Robert (Herbert Marshall), hosts a party to celebrate the acquittal. Leslie finally breaks down and confesses to Robert. She says:

> We used to meet each other constantly once or twice a week. Not a soul had the smallest suspicion. Every time I met him, I hated myself, and yet I lived for the moment when I'd see him again. There was never an hour when I was at peace, when I wasn't reproaching myself. I was like a person who is sick with some loathsome disease and doesn't want to get well. Even my agony was a kind of joy.

Joyce is incredulous when he tells Leslie, "He's going to forgive you."

The party fails to hold Leslie's interest. She doesn't feel that she has anything to celebrate. She retreats into her bedroom so that she can be alone and cry. She tries to distract herself with her needlework, as we have seen for much of the film, but she has too much on her mind to be distracted for long and carelessly tosses the needlework aside.

Robert enters the room, uncertain of what to say. She apologizes to him for the trouble that she has caused. "I've failed you," she says. He makes his position clear to her. He will be able to forgive her as long as he knows that she loves him. She says that she loves him, but he tries to kiss her and she quickly pulls away. "No!" she cries. She breaks down and confesses, "With all my heart, I still love the man I killed!"

The Production Code demanded that Leslie be punished for her crime. Her punishment comes in the final scene. Leslie walks out into the garden, where she is confronted by Hammond's Eurasian widow (Gale Sondergaard) and the widow's henchman. At Mrs. Hammond's command, the henchman grabs Leslie and stuffs a cloth in her mouth. Mrs. Hammond steps forward with a knife and stabs Leslie.

The moonlight shines on Leslie's lifeless body. A tracking shot moves from the body to her bedroom. Farran Smith Nehme of Self-Styled Siren blog points out that the camera comes upon "a breeze stirring the still-unfinished lace."[174] The camera then takes us back outside to the moon. The moon was a motif of the film. William Wyler biographer Jan Herman found that Wyler used the moon as "a recurrent visual symbol of sin.[175]

Nehme addressed the racial issues of the film. She wrote:

The Letter gives you a very clear bead on the Malayans' contempt for their foolish, deceitful, greedy "betters," and it gives you plenty of reasons to share their opinion, even as the British toss off insults: "Too bad rubber won't grow in a civilized climate."[176]

The film was based on an actual event that occurred in 1911. Ethel Proudlock, the wife of an English headmaster, shot her lover to death in Malaya. She, too, claimed in court that the man attempted to rape her. She was not incriminated by a letter. A letter wasn't necessary, for the inconsistencies of her testimony were enough to elicit a guilty verdict. But a number of petitions were submitted to induce the court to free Proudlock. The court finally agree to release the murderess after she had spent five months in prison. Much is made about race in the film. It is therefore interesting to note that Proudlock was, like Hammond's widow, Eurasian.

The Letter (1929), an earlier film adaptation of the Maugham play, climaxed with a brutal confrontation between Leslie (Jeanne Eagels) and Robert (Reginald Owen).

Robert: I want to know whether you've been my wife. . . or just a common whore.

Leslie: Don't say that!

Robert: I want the truth.

Leslie: You want the truth? Very well. You shall have it. Geoffrey Hammond was my lover.

Robert: Go on.

Leslie: He was my lover for years. We were constantly together. Until about a year ago when he began to change. And, then, I couldn't believe it as he was everything in the world to me.

Robert: God.

Leslie: He was my whole life until I heard about that Chinese woman. Then I couldn't believe that. I could not believe he didn't still love me. So I sent for him. You have the letter. So finally he came. I told him that I knew about that Chinese woman. He denied it. I knew he was telling a lie. Finally I made him admit that it was the truth. And then he said to me that, if he had to choose between me and the Chinese woman, he would choose her! Oh, God, I don't know what happened after that. I went absolutely mad, grabbed the revolver. And I fired at him and I fired and I fired and fired until the gun was empty.

Robert: And I gave you my name. Worked and slaved for you.

Leslie: I know. I know. I know I have been vile but I have no excuse to offer. And don't forget this. You got me to this filthy Godforsaken place and kept me here for seven years. To live among a lot of dirty natives and dowdy planters' wives. With my youth going. Eating my heart out with loneliness. Trying to make a go of it. And I did try. I did try for your sake. And what did I get from you? Nothing. Nothing. Your whole life was just wrapped up in rubber.

Robert: Rubber? That was my business.

Leslie: Yes.

Robert: Working to make money to give you the things you wanted.

Leslie: What I wanted. What I wanted? I am flesh and blood. What I wanted was love, affection. . . happiness. You took everything for granted. Once you got me out here to this Godforsaken place, all you thought about was rubber. All that was on your mind was rubber. All day long I was alone. All night I had to listen to you talk of rubber, rubber, rubber. *Rubber!* Is it any wonder that when a man came along and talked to me of love and romance and music that I fell into his arms? Well I did. And it is done now. So what are you going to do about it?

She expects Robert to send her away, but he explains that their legal bills depleted their savings and he has no money to send her away.

Robert: You are going to stay here. Right here in this house. With your memories.

Leslie: Ha! So I am to be punished? I am to be punished, am I?

Robert: Yes.

Leslie: I am to live here in this house with my memories. Very well. Alright. If you and your smug respectability are going to punish me. And that is to be my punishment. That I am to remain here in this house with my memories. Alright. I will give you something to remember. I, with all my heart and soul still love the man I killed! Ha ha! Take that, will you. With all my heart and all my soul, I still love the man I killed.

The confrontation is muted in the remake. The husband is now too weak-willed to become angry. Yet, it is more powerful now when Davis cries out, "With all my heart, I still love the man I killed!" Davis delivers the line in an entirely different way than Eagels does. Eagels is defiant and cruel. She wants more than anything to hurt her husband. Davis delivers the line in way that, according to Wyler, creates "a desperate moment of honesty and self-flagellation."[177]

Temptation (1946) is, in ways, similar to *The Letter*. As we will see, love letters are again used for blackmail purposes.

Ruby (Merle Oberon), a glib and haughty gold digger, marries wealthy Egyptologist Nigel Armine (George Brent). Nigel, who is eager to dig around for mummies, brings Ruby to his estate in Cairo. Bored, Ruby offers to recover a friend's illicit love letters from an unscrupulous playboy, Mahoud Baroudi (Charles Korvin). Their meeting quickly leads to an affair.

Ruby doesn't seem to want to do wrong, but she cannot help herself. She regards an immoral life or a dangerous life better than a boring life. She speaks of boredom as if it is a lethal malady. But boredom is a condition that only possesses an empty and useless person.

Ruby's housemaid Marie (Lenore Ulric) is a voice of morality. She waits up for Ruby while she's out with Baroudi. She has a lecture for her mistress: "It's two o'clock. Aren't you ashamed of yourself? And you look bad. Where is this going to lead us?" She warns her that she will soon end up in divorce court. Ruby assures her that, now that her husband is due to return home, she will end the affair. Marie says, "It may not be as easy as you think." Ruby demands that Marie leave the room and let her be alone. The maid parts with a warning: "One day you may be alone and old."

Baroudi coerces Ruby to slowly murder Nigel with small doses of a powdery poison. Nigel becomes sick and is confined to his bed. Marie realizes that Ruby is poisoning Nigel and heatedly confronts her mistress. She beseeches her to break away from Baroudi. "This man Baroudi," she says, "he will destroy you." Ruby becomes hysterical and demands that Marie leave her alone. Marie, finally defeated, announces that she is leaving Cairo and moving back to Paris.

Ruby visits Baroudi to tell him that she cannot murder Nigel, but Baroudi demands that she finish the job. She chooses to poison Baroudi instead.

Nigel gets better and goes hiking with Ruby. Ruby is in good spirits and seems to have made a new commitment to her marriage. But she is suddenly caught in a rockslide and dies. So, contrary to Marie's ominous prediction, she does not end up old and alone.

The 1909 novel on which the film is based had been made into a film on four previous occasions: *Bella Donna* (1915), *Bella Donna* (1923), *Infatuation* (1925) and *Bella Donna* (1934).

They Drive by Night (1940)

Joe Fabrini (George Raft) refuses the affections of Lana Carlsen (Ida Lupino). She is attracted to Joe, but Joe makes it clear that he doesn't date married women.

Lana: What's the matter with me?

Joe: Nothing. . . except you got a husband, Mrs. Carlsen. And it happens that he's a good friend of mine. Understand?

Lana: Oh, you've been listening to some narrow-minded people.

Lana murders her husband Ed (Alan Hale Sr.) thinking he is the only thing standing between her and Joe.

The Suspect (1944)

Mild-mannered shopkeeper Philip Marshal (Charles Laughton) is constantly being tormented by his horror show of a wife, Cora (Rosalind Ivan). He meets sweet and tender Mary Gray (Ella Raines), who possesses an all-around beauty that Cora so dismally lacks. The couple develops a deep love for one another and Philip wants to divorce his wife to marry Mary. Philip sets out to arrange the divorce in a civil and reasonable manner. He tells Cora:

Cora, if we could come to some sort of understanding, it might help us. Now, listen, if we face things honestly, we'd admit that we have never been happy together. We haven't been happy not once in all the years we have been married. It's not anyone's fault. We have tried to rub along together. Over and over again, we've tried. And it isn't that I do this or that you do that. Don't you know that, when two people are shut up together and they don't love each other, everything they do becomes hateful just because they do it. . . All I say is that we have some good years ahead of us, both of us. Why can't we live them happily apart from each other?. . . Let me go, Cora.

But Cora is not about to let him go. And, worse, she promises to ruin him and his lady friend with exposure and scandal.

Philip feels the solidness of a cane's handle before following Cora upstairs. The next morning, Nora is found dead. It seems that she tripped on loose carpeting at the top of the staircase and broke her neck while tumbling down the steps. But was Philip involved in her fall? Did he shove her? Did he attack her with the cane?. And, really, what if he did? It's hard to imagine that anyone watching the film could blame him. hitchcockthelegend of IMDb wrote:

How delightfully off, that a film that features a wife murderer. . . should be so restrained and actually beautiful. *The Suspect* in principal is about a decent man pushed to do bad things by his awful life when hope then springs from an unlikely source. The moral shadings here are most intricate, Laughton's Philip Marshal is a completely sympathetic and fascinating character, the makers deftly toying with our perceptions in the process. . . Murder as justifiable homicide? Ridding the world of bad people is OK?[178]

When in the throes of a bad marriage, a man is capable of doing anything.

A homicide detective, Inspector Huxley (Stanley Ridges), suspects that Marshall murdered wife, but he is unable to prove it.

Marshall's black-hearted neighbor, Gilbert Simmons (Henry Daniell), visits him at his home. Simmons, who displays a malignant grin, obviously has no good reason to visit. He demands that Marshall pay him money or else he will make up a story that he overheard Marshall arguing with his wife on the night of her death. When Marshall questions his morals, he shamelessly confesses to being a "complete rotter." Marshall promptly disposes of the grinchy blackmailer by poisoning him.

Marshall makes arrangements for him and Mary to move to Canada. Inspector Huxley realizes that he has one last chance to trap Marshall before he leaves the country forever. So, he frames Simmons' good-natured wife Edith (Molly Lamont) for Simmons' poisoning. Huxley knows that Marshall is basically good and cannot allow Edith to be hung for a crime she didn't commit. Marshall makes sure that Mary is safely on the ship for Canada before he leaves her to turn himself in to the police.

The murder of Cora Marshall has much in common with the real-life murder of Cora Crippen. The Crippen murder case was the basis of two other films, *We Are Not Alone* (1939) and *Dr. Crippen* (1962). As depicted in the latter film, Cora Crippen is in no way an ideal wife. Over the years, she has had flagrant affairs with multiple men. She has admirers hanging around her home and getting underfoot. We will look at a similar wife, Vera Sargeant, when we examine the 1945 British film *They Were Sisters*. Crippen (Donald Pleasence) becomes so repulsed by Cora that he refuses to sleep with her and moves into a separate bedroom. Crippen falls in love with his beautiful young secretary, Ethel Le Neve (Samantha Eggar), and begs Cora for a divorce. Cora threatens to expose her husband to scandal unless he gives up his beloved mistress. This is a grave threat as a scandal is likely to ruin his professional reputation and prevent him from continuing in his job. The same malicious strategy was employed by the wives in *The Suspect* and *Carrie* (1952).

Coral Browne is grandly shrewish in the role of Cora. She is just as chilling and repulsive as *The Suspect*'s Rosalind Ivan and *Carrie*'s Miriam Hopkins. But, unlike Hopkins and Ivan, she gets a surprisingly tender and tearful scene in which she pleads with her husband for his affection. She laments, "I have to beg you to even touch me." Crippen comforts her as she sobs.

Cora: Am I so repulsive?

Crippen: No, of course it isn't that.

Cora: Well, what is it, then? When was the last time you came to me as a husband of your own free will? When was the last time you kissed me? Let alone made love to me?

Crippen: You say yourself you don't lack for male admirers.

Cora: You're my husband. I want my husband to admire me. Look, if you're ill, why don't you say so? At least, I'd understand that.

Crippen: No, I'm not ill. It isn't that.

Cora: I don't care about the boys. I wouldn't want any other man if you would only treat me like a woman occasionally.

Crippen: You'd always want other men.

Cora: I wouldn't. I wouldn't. No, stay with me tonight. Stay with me and I'll get rid of them tomorrow.

On the day of his execution, Crippen tells the warden, "[Cora] wasn't a bad woman, really, but coarse and dirty. Love, to her, was a matter of appetite, whereas. . . to me, it. . . Well, I found what I wanted in Ethel." He sounds a lot like Mellors from "Lady Chatterley's Lover."

Fred MacMurray, Barbara Stanwyck and Edward G. Robinson in "Double Indemnity," with Jean Heather, Tom Powers, Byron Barr, Richard Gaines, and Fortunio Bonanova. Directed by Billy Wilder. A Paramount Picture.

Fred MacMurray and Barbara Stanwyck in *Double Indemnity* (1944)1

Double Indemnity (1944)

Linda Rasmussen of AllMovie describes the first two-thirds of the film in a single sentence:

Phyllis Dietrichson (Barbara Stanwyck) seduces insurance agent Walter Neff (Fred MacMurray) into murdering her husband to collect his accident policy.[179]

But, then, Phyllis and Walter begin to mistrust one another. And a wily insurance investigator, Barton Keyes (Edward G. Robinson), suspects foul play and comes poking around.

Double Indemnity has been thoroughly dissected by many film historians for its dark and psychosexual elements.

Summer Storm (1944)

The film is an adaptation of Anton Chekhov's 1884 novel "The Shooting Party."

Olga Kuzminichna (Linda Darnell), a beautiful peasant girl, agrees to marry a middle-aged Russian civil servant, Anton Urbenin (Hugo Haas). But Olga is an unenthusiastic bride. She flees her wedding reception rather than kiss her new husband.

The newlywed bride attracts the lustful attentions of two men, Count Volsky (Edward Everett Horton) and Judge Fedor Petroff (George Sanders). Fedor finds the imaginative young woman fascinating. Olga tells him that her mother was killed by lightning. But she does not see this as a tragic fate because she believes that a person killed by lightning goes straight to heaven. In the novel, Olga says:

> My mother was going through the fields, crying. She had a very bitter life in this world. God had compassion on her and lulled her with His heavenly electricity. . . Do you know? People who have been killed by a storm or in war, or who have died after a difficult confinement go to paradise. This is not written anywhere in books, but it is true. My mother is now in paradise.

Olga expects to die this way herself. She imagines wearing a beautiful silk dress on the day of her death. She says, "I'll walk to the summit of the hill and wait for the lightning."

Fedor plans to marry Nadena Kalenin (Anna Lee), but Nadena catches him kissing Olga outside of the wedding reception and promptly ends their relationship.

> Fedor: [Y]ou must listen to me. Even the drunkards and petty thieves who come to my court are given a fair trial.
>
> Nadena: I'm not judging you, Fedor. You are not on trial. You're free to do as you wish.
>
> Fedor: One incident. One moment of insanity. And you would cast aside the whole of our future?
>
> Nadena: That wasn't a mere incident, Fedor. It was something in you which is stronger than either of us. We could never be happy together.

Fedor admits to himself that Olga has cast a spell on him. "I have known love," he tells her. "This is something different." He knows that his obsession for Olga has made him twisted and degraded.

Fedor asks her why she married Anton when she clearly doesn't love him. She says, "Because I hated dirt. I hated being poor. At least he was better than what I left." But her social climbing isn't over.

Olga takes carriage rides with Count Volsky and accepts valuable gifts from him. At the count's home, she puts on the wedding gown of his late wife. She tells him that she would love to have the occasion to wear it the public. He recognizes this as a marriage proposal and accepts. Fedor is shocked to learn of the impending marriage. He stabs Olga to death in a jealous rage. The police arrest Anton for the murder.

Fedor visits a church, where he finds Nadena praying. He apologizes to his former fiancée for hurting her. He says, "I'm not myself. There's something in me. Something strange that drives me on. . ."

Olga has an opportunity on her deathbed to expose Fedor as her assailant. But she doesn't. Is she too delirious, or is she more concerned with her ascent into heaven (she describes seeing the "heavenly electricity"), or is she trying to protect Fedor? It is not clear.

Anton is convicted of murdering Olga and sentenced to spend the rest of his life in a labor camp.

The Russian Revolution leaves Fedor stripped of his title and property. Fedor and Volsky live together in impoverished conditions. A guilt-ridden Fedor secretly admits to murdering Olga in a manuscript, which he presumably doesn't expect anyone to read until after he has died. But Volsky, who hasn't read the manuscript, assumes that Fedor has written an uncontroversial memoir and expects that it might be worth money to Nadena, who now owns a publishing company. Nadena is upset by what she reads. She prepares to mail the manuscript to the public prosecutor, but she still has feelings for Fedor and cannot bring herself to turn him over to law enforcement. Instead, she persuades Fedor to take the package and mail it himself. "One last chance," she says. "To let me love you again." Fedya complies with her wishes. But then he panics and attempts to steal the package back from the postman. Police officers chase him and shoot him as he flees into a bar. Wikipedia reports:

> As he dies, he, too, claims to see the "heavenly electricity." As Fedya's corpse is carried away, the police discover on him only Nadena's dance card from [Olga and Anton's] wedding banquet, on which he wrote "I Love You." It ends up discarded on the floor, swept up with the garbage and dumped in a trashcan.[180]

Pillow of Death (1945)

Wayne Fletcher (Lon Chaney Jr.) wants to get rid of his wife Vivian (Victoria Horne) so that he is free to marry his secretary, Donna Kincaid (Brenda Joyce). He smothers Vivian to death with a pillow. The police suspect that Vivian was murdered by Fletcher, but they need to find proof. Fletcher is unable to sleep. He tells Donna that he is being tormented by Vivian's ghost. One evening, he hears Vivian's voice beckoning him to leap out of a window. The voice insists that suicide is the only way for him to avoid arrest. Fletcher struggles to resist the voice, but its hold on him is too strong. He bolts across the room and dives through the window to his death.

The Great Flamarion (1945)

Connie Wallace (Mary Beth Hughes) works her seductive wiles on a vaudeville sharpshooter, The Great Flamarion (Erich von Stroheim). It is her intention to persuade armed and ready Flamarion to murder her alcoholic husband, Al Wallace (Dan Duryea). She promises to marry him once Al is gone. Flamarion shoots Al during their stage act. It is decided in court that the shooting was a timing error caused by Al's drunkenness. Connie tells Flamarion that it would arouse suspicion if they are seen together. She advises that they separate for now. She promises to meet him in Chicago in three months. But she never shows up. She is on a theatrical tour in Central America with her true lover, Eddie Wheeler (Stephen Barclay). Flamarion is a broken man when he finally catches up to Connie at a vaudeville house. Connie is still not faithful. That evening, Eddie discovered that Connie is having an affair with an acrobat. Flamarion sneaks into Connie's dressing room while Connie is getting ready to perform. She panics, grabs a gun, and shoots him. But Flamarion manages to stagger forward and attack her. He grabs her by the throat and strangles her. Flamarion lies in the arms of Tony (Lester Allen), an old clown friend, as he takes his final breath.

Mildred Pierce (1945)

Mildred Pierce (Joan Crawford) is a divorced waitress with two young daughters. She has ambitions to rise above her financial difficulties by opening her own restaurant. She meets Monte Beragon (Zachary Scott), a nearly broke society playboy who owns a building that can be converted into a restaurant. Mildred and Monte develop a romantic relationship. Mildred becomes interested in marrying Monte for his social status. Monte becomes interested in marrying Mildred for a share in her prosperous business. The couple's calculated marriage remains loveless. In time, Monte has an affair with Mildred's spoiled daughter, Veda (Ann Blyth), who recently turned 19. Mildred catches the pair together and intends to shoot Monte, but she changes her mind and flees in tears. Mildred's all-consuming adoration of Veda makes this situation horribly painful for her. But she has long indulged Monte and Veda, nursing these treacherous vipers in her midst. Veda asks Monte to divorce her mother so that they can marry, but Monte tells her that he will never marry her because she is a "rotten little tramp." Veda snatches up her mother's gun and fatally shoots Monte. Mildred tries to conceal Veda's guilt, but the police aren't fooled and arrest her.

We previously examined the melodrama's stepmother/stepson affairs (which date back to the Greek myths about Hippolytus and Phaedra), but it was unique during this period for a film to show an affair between a stepfather and stepdaughter.

The Dark Corner (1946)

A snooty art collector, Hardy Cathcart (Clifton Webb), arranges the murder of his wife's lover, Tony Jardine (Kurt Krueger), and frames Jardine's former business partner, Brad Galt (Mark Stevens), for the deed.

Black Angel (1946)

Cathy Bennett (June Vincent) is determined to prove that her husband is innocent of murdering his mistress, cabaret singer Mavis Marlowe. At first, the obvious suspect is her former husband, Marty Blair (Dan Duryea), an alcoholic piano player. But Marty has an alibi - he was passed out in bed after a drunken binge. This has been verified by his friend, Joe (Wallace Ford). Joe says:

> Marty was right here in this room when his wife was killed. . . See that bolt? It was locked when you came in, wasn't it?. . . I always lock it when he's on a real tear. He was on one that night, and I locked him in. . . a good two hours before the murder.

Marty agrees to help Cathy to find the real killer. It turns out, though, that Marty killed his wife while suffering from "alcohol amnesia." How did he get out of his room? It was simple - he paid the building's superintendent to unlock the door. It's not a plot twist that will cause anyone to gasp. Still, it works. Erickson wrote of Duryea, "His [sympathetic] performance makes the plot twist at the end both startling and believable."[181]

The Postman Always Rings Twice (1946)

Films became darker and more cynical after World War II. This is definitely the case with *The Postman Always Rings Twice*, which is based on 1934 bestselling crime novel by James M. Cain.

A drifter, Frank Chambers (John Garfield), takes a job at a roadside inn owned by Nick Smith (Cecil Kellaway). Frank cannot take his eyes off Nick's beautiful young wife, Cora (Lana Turner). While they are alone in the kitchen, he grabs her and kisses her passionately. She reacts nonchalantly, reapplying her lipstick. She avoids him for the next two weeks, but they are unable to remain apart.

Cecil Kellaway, John Garfield and Lana Turner in *The Postman Always Rings Twice* (1946)

Frank: You must have had to fight off a lot of guys.

Cora: A lot of guys? All the guys. I don't especially like the way I look sometimes, but I never met a man since I was 14 that didn't want to argue about it.

Frank: Sure. By the time Nick came along, you were ready to marry anybody that owned a gold watch.

Cora: Seemed the best thing to do from my angle. And as for him, I told him. . . I told him I didn't love him.

Frank: He said that would come in time.

Cora: Yeah.

Frank: But it didn't.

Cora: But I meant to stick by him. And that's why. . .

Frank: That's why you married him and retired. The undefeated champ.

Frank makes a humorous observation about adultery.

Cora: Too bad Nick took the car.

Frank: Even if it were here, we couldn't take it. Not unless we want to spend the night in jail. Stealing a man's wife, that's nothing, but stealing his car, that's larceny.

After a while, the couple conspires to murder Nick for a hefty insurance payout.

Cora: Listen, Frank, I'm not what you think I am. I wanna keep this place and work hard and be something. That's all. But you can't do it without love. At least a woman can't. I've made a big mistake in my life. And I've got to be this way just once to fix it.

Frank: They hang you for that.

Cora: Not if we do it right. You're smart, Frank. You'll think of a way. Plenty of men have.

Frank: He never did anything to me.

Cora: But, darling, can't you see how happy we would be together here? Without him?

Frank: Do you love me, Cora?

Cora: That's why you've got to help me. It's because I do love you.

Frank: I guess you do. You couldn't get me to say yes to a thing like this if you didn't.

Garfield often appeared in films as cynical, embittered and combative. These qualities are further emphasized in this film. But his character is childlike, too.

Kellaway seems out of place running a roadside gas station. He might be more believable as a roadside librarian. He also doesn't seem to be the type of man who would be interested in buddying around with a rough-mannered vagabond. An earlier Italian version of Cain's story, *Ossessione* (1943), had a realism lacking in the Hollywood version. Further details of the murder plot and its outcome will be provided in a discussion of *Ossessione*.

Pursued (1947)

Pursued shows how adultery can shatter families and communities. Grant Callum (Dean Jagger) has a mysterious motive for wanting to see Jeb Rand (Robert Mitchum) dead. His motive is eventually revealed: revenge. We get a flashback. Grant's brother becomes enraged to learn that his wife (Judith Anderson) is having an affair with Jeb's father. Callum shows up at the Rand home, but Rand is faster with a gun than he is and is able to kill him in self-defense. Upon hearing of his brother's death, Grant becomes obsessed with getting revenge. But he won't be satisfied to just kill Rand. He believes that he will not obtain justice unless he slaughters his brother's killer along with the man's entire family. Jeb, a four-year-old boy at the time, is able to stay hidden during the killings. He is adopted by Ma Callum, who becomes his protector and takes him away so that he'll be safe. Grant remains determined to see Jeb, the last of the Rands, dead.

It takes Grant six years to track down Jeb. Jeb is riding his prized colt through desert land when Grant, hidden in shrubbery on a hilltop, takes a shot at him. The shot misses Jeb, but it strikes the colt and kills it. "The score isn't settled for [my brother's] death," he tells Ma soon after. "I swore I'd kill every Rand on earth and he's the only one left." Years later, Grant turns Ma's son Adam (John Rodney) against Jeb. The animosity between the two young men reaches a fever pitch.

One morning, a gunman shoots at Jeb from a hilltop. Jeb quickly takes cover behind a rock and fires back at his unknown assailant. The gunman is hit and falls. When Jeb goes to investigate, he finds Adam dead. Mrs. Callum's daughter, Thor (Teresa Wright), has loved Jeb for many years, but she cannot help but hate him now for killing her brother. She agrees to marry him with the intention of killing him on their wedding night. Eventually, she learns about the Rand family's slaughter and realizes that Jeb is the victim in this situation.

Grant, supported by various cousins that he has managed to round up, captures Jeb and prepares to hang him. This is a Hollywood story of the Old West, where bloodthirsty frontier justice is the rule. The western films of this era were not complete without a cattle stampede, or a bank robbery, or a vigilante mob hanging someone. Thor pleads with her mother to stop the hanging. Mrs. Callum calmly raises her rifle and shoots Grant. With Grant lying dead on the ground, the cousins give up hanging Jeb and quietly leave.

There is more than a bit of *Wuthering Heights'* Heathcliff in Jeb. Like Heathcliff, Jeb is taken into a foster home as a child. Like Heathcliff, he falls in love with a daughter in his adoptive family and develops a hostile relationship with a son. Like Heathcliff, he earns a fortune after he goes off on his own.

Dear Murderer (1947)

Dear Murderer is a twisted and twisty film. Lee Warren (Eric Portman) gets rid of his wife's latest lover by staging his murder to look like a suicide, but he soon learns that his wife has already moved on to another lover. When the police find evidence that the man was murdered, Lee sets out to frame his wife's new lover for the crime.

The Two Mrs. Carrolls (1947)

Geoffrey Carroll (Humphrey Bogart), a moody painter, marries a woman who inspires him in his work. But that inspiration doesn't last and he is desperate to find a new woman to stir his creativity. When he meets Sally Morton (Barbara Stanwyck), he realizes that he has found his next muse and needs to get rid of Mrs. Carroll. He uses small doses of poison to gradually murder his wife. A year later, he starts a new marriage with Sally. All is well until he meets the beautiful Cecily Latham (Alexis Smith), who is an even greater inspiration than Sally. He is now determined to murder Sally so that he and Cecily are free to marry.

The Lady from Shanghai (1947)

Michael O'Hara (Orson Welles) is a deckhand on a yacht owned by Arthur Bannister (Everett Sloane). O'Hara becomes infatuated with Bannister's wife, Elsa (Rita Haywood). Elsa uses her seductive ways to draw Michael into a murder plot. The greedy and unscrupulous characters ensure that the film is filled with double-crosses, fake-outs, manipulations, secret alliances and, most of all, murder. In the midst of various twisty schemes, Michael is framed for the murder of Bannister's partner, George Grisby (Glenn Anders).

Like *The Lady from Shanghai*, *A Life at Stake* (1954) involves a duplicitous husband and wife drawing a man into a deadly plot designed to earn them a sizable payoff. This film, like the former, starts with the wife seducing the man. Doris Hillman (Angela Lansbury) approaches an unemployed architect, Edward Shaw (Keith Andes), to become her partner in a real estate development business. She tells him that she is funding the new business with money provided by her wealthy husband. But her real interest is in an insurance policy that names Edward as a key man to the business. The policy will pay out a large sum of money to Doris if the business were to suddenly lose Edward in a fatal accident. Her plan is to drug her new partner and send him over a cliff in his car.

The Unfaithful (1947)

This remake of *The Letter* brings the story close to home, transferring it to a friendly suburb of Southern California. Chris Hunter (Ann Sheridan) had a brief affair while her husband, Bob (Zachary Scott), was in military service overseas. Her lover is a high-strung sculptor, Michael Tanner (Paul Bradley). Tanner becomes unhinged when Bob returns home. He arrives uninvited at Ann's home and becomes belligerent. Ann panics when he attacks her and stabs him with a knife that is lying around. *Unfaithful* upturned the character motivations of *The Letter*. Now, it was the murdered man who was dangerously obsessed and possessive. He was not going to let Chris return to her husband. The incriminating letter of the original story is replaced by an incriminating sculpture, which Tanner created in Chris' distinct likeness. Larry Hannaford (Lew Ayres), Chris' friend and attorney, refuses to hear Chris' explanation for the affair. He tells her, "I don't want to hear all the petty details. I've heard the same story in a dozen courtrooms. I know all the shabby tricks and tearful excuses." But, fortunately, Chris is heard out by Bob.

Chris: There wasn't time. We knew each other only two weeks before we married. Then you were gone.

Bob: It didn't take you long to forget.

Chris: I didn't forget. I didn't want to. But you were 6,000 miles away and I was alone. There was nobody. Larry, Paula. Her friends now and then. During the day there were things to do. But at night I sat alone. I ate alone. I went to the movies alone. I took a walk alone. . . You won't understand. No man could. But ask any woman who has sat and waited. Who tried to hang on to something real when there seemed to be nothing real.

Bob: Millions of women waited. They waited decently and loyally. They didn't cheat.

Chris: I'm not making excuses. There is no excuse possible. I'm just trying to tell you what happened to me. How it happened. I was willing to wait. I thought I was prepared for it. The men I met around town didn't worry me. I was on guard against them. But this man didn't seem to be like that. . . He asked me to stay for dinner. I hadn't heard from you in weeks. I was worried and blue. I stayed just to have someone to talk to. Just to get away from myself for an evening. Instead, I. . .

Bob: You don't have to go on.

Her sister-in-law, Paula (Eve Arden), tells Bob that he was wrong. He married Chris after knowing her for two weeks and then shipped out immediately afterward. Paula tells him:

How long was that supposed to last her? What you wanted was a whirl and a memory. You wanted a beautiful woman waiting for you. You didn't want anyone making time with her while you were away. So you hung up a "No Trespassing" sign like you'd stake a gold claim. You didn't marry her. You just took an option on her. . . Do you think a woman can make a career out of looking at a picture? She needs more than a wedding ring and a letter a week to hang on to.

The Paradine Case (1947)

Attorney Anthony Keane (Gregory Peck) is entranced by his latest client, Magdalene Paradine (Alida Valli). Many other men have been entranced by her in the past. At an early age, Maddalena used her beauty and charm with men to escape from poverty. In recent years, she came to marry and care for a highly honored retired colonel, who lost his sight in recent years.

Keane has an ideal marriage. His wife, Gay (Ann Todd), is good-natured and wants to think the best of people. At first, she is sure that Maddalena didn't murder her husband.

Gay: I don't believe she did it.

Keane: Do you mind telling me why? As her defending counsel, I might be able to use any bit of evidence.

Gay: Well, nice people don't go about murdering other nice people.

Keane: So you think she's nice?

Gay: Her photograph looks nice. And anyone who wasn't nice wouldn't have married that poor blind man.

Others are also sympathetic to this fair lady. Judge Lord Thomas Horfield (Charles Laughton) is irritated when his wife, Lady Sophie Horfield (Ethel Barrymore), asks him to show mercy toward Maddalena. Horfield responds, "You always forget that punishment is part of the scheme. An extremely necessary part of it." Lady Horfield asks, "Doesn't life punish us enough, Tommy? Doesn't it? Why should we hurt each other? We've no right to be cruel. If I'm certain of anything, I'm certain of that."

 Keane's passion for Maddalena is obvious. Whenever he visits her in prison, the prison matron (Elspeth Dudgeon) is compelled to watch over them as sternly and suspiciously as a prom chaperone. Keane is reprimanded by Judge Horfield for becoming too impassioned in his defense of Maddalena. Most of all, Gay can see that Keane fancies Maddalena. She can imagine Keane running off with Maddalena if she is exonerated. She vows not to stand in his way if that happens. "After all," she says, "I don't own him. I only love him." She speaks frankly to Keane when she sees that he is developing a dangerous obsession. She says:

I won't deny there have been moments when I've wished the worst for her. It's not easy to face the thought of losing you. We've been really married, really truly married, as few people have been. . . But I've come to a conclusion, Tony. I want her to live. I want very much for her to live. And I hope she gets free, scot-free, free to kill or take other wives' husbands or do anything else that comes into that beautiful head of hers. You can't really care what happens to her. But I do. I care very much. Not for any noble reasons. I do hate her. But because I want all this business over and done with, and an end to your being all mixed up, part lawyer, part lover.

Keane bristles at being called "part lover." "What nonsense!" he grumbles. Gay continues:

Nonsense. All right, frustrated lover, then. Yes, and part husband still. Because you're not finished with me. You wouldn't have come back home today if you were. I've seen your torture, and I've loved you all the more for letting it torture you. I know the depth of your feelings. I know it, and I'm counting on it. All I ask is that she lives, so the fight can be an even one. Because if she dies, you're lost to me forever. I know you'll go on thinking that you love her. You'll go on imagining her as your great, lost love. May I tell you something, Tony? You don't love her. No, you don't. I may not be the cleverest woman in the world. There are lots of things I don't know. But there's one thing I know better than anyone else: I know you.

Keane becomes convinced that the true killer is Colonel Paradine's valet, André Latour (Louis Jourdan). He is determined to break down Latour in court. But his harsh interrogation of Latour drives the valet to commit suicide. Maddalena is heartbroken when she learns of Latour's fate. In her grief, she confesses on the witness stand that she poisoned her husband. She says that she seduced Latour, who felt guilty for betraying his master and would have nothing to do with her afterward. She becomes enraged at Keane, who she blames for Latour's death. "I loved Andre Latour," she says, "and you murdered him." Keane becomes dispirited. He turns over the case to a fellow barrister and leaves the courtroom. Gay finds him at the home of a friend and colleague, Sir Simon Flaquer (Charles Coburn), and encourages him to continue as a barrister.

Repeat Performance (1947)

Sheila Page (Joan Leslie) is married to an alcoholic playwright, Barney (Louis Hayward), who is obsessed with fellow playwright Paula Costello (Virginia Field). In a rage, she shoots Barney. Suddenly, she finds herself transported in time to a year earlier. She now has the chance to relive the last year and avoid becoming a murderer.

Shed No Tears (1948)

Edna Grover (June Vincent) tells her husband Sam (Wallace Ford) that she has a plan to fake his death so that they can collect on a $50,000 life insurance policy. Sam pretends to die in a hotel fire. While Sam is in hiding, Edna collects the insurance money and runs off with her lover, Ray Belden (Mark Roberts). Tom (Dick Hogan), Sam's adult son from a previous marriage, suspects that Edna murdered his father. He hires a private investigator, Huntington Stewart (Johnstone White), to collect evidence that can be used against her. Sam is shocked to find out about Belden. He is in an unbalanced state of mind as he tracks down Belden and murders him. Stewart figures out that Sam is still alive and blackmails him. Edna meets with Sam at a hotel. She attempts to shoot Sam after he admits to killing Belden, but she struggles with Stewart and falls out of a window. Tom blames himself as he watches his father being arrested. But Sam reassures Tom that everything has turned out for the better. Better? Really?

White Heat (1949)

Crime boss Cody Jarrett (James Cagney) learns while in prison that his top henchman, "Big Ed" Somers (Steve Cochran), is having an affair with his wife.

Tension (1949)

Claire (Audrey Totter) murders her lover in a fit of rage and tries to blame the murder on her meek pharmacist husband, Warren Quimby (Richard Basehart).

The Hidden Room (1949)

The film is, in a way, a throwback to silent film melodramas. Dr. Clive Riordan (Robert Newton) kidnaps his wife's lover, Bill Kronin (Phil Brown), at gunpoint. It is his plan to hold Riordan captive in a hidden room while the police search for the missing man. Once the police lose interest in finding him, he will shoot him and dissolve his body in acid.

Forbidden (1949)

Jim (Douglass Montgomery) resents that his selfish and domineering wife, Diana (Patricia Burke), forced him to give up his modest job as a chemist to sell hair tonic at a fair. The experience has demoralized him. But then he meets a sweet young woman, Jane (Hazel Court), who restores his confidence and makes him feel happy for the first time in years. He asks Diane for a divorce, but she refuses. He becomes desperate. He sets out to substitute Diane's prescription pills with a chemical concoction that is sure to kill her. But then he changes his mind and rushes home to save her. He finds his wife dead and panics. He hides her body, but he learns afterwards that she never took the pills and died of natural causes.

The File on Thelma Jordon (1950)

Thelma Jordon (Barbara Stanwyck) visits an assistant district attorney, Cleve Marshal (Wendell Corey), to complain about prowlers. The attorney is charmed by Thelma and, though he is married, he invites the woman out for drinks. Cleve gets drunk and tells Thelma that he loves her. The next day, Cleve apologizes to Thelma for his drunken rambling and invites her out to dinner. Cleve's wife and children have gone away to spend the summer at a beach house. This gives Cleve the opportunity to freely pursue an affair with Thelma. Thelma confesses to Cleve that she is also married, but says that her husband left her and she doesn't know where he is. She assumes that he is in some place where there's money, gambling and beautiful women.

Later that night, Thelma phones Cleve to tell him that she found her rich aunt shot dead in her home. Cleve believes that a burglar killed the aunt for her jewels, but he understands that suspicion will fall on Thelma.

Cleve is unable to stop his boss from charging Thelma with murder once the police recover the jewels and find Thelma's fingerprints on them. It is also learned that the aunt recently rewrote her will, leaving everything she owned to her niece. Thelma is further incriminated by her dark past, which involves gambling, blackmail and a criminal husband. Cleve arranges to prosecute Thelma and purposely antagonizes the jury in order to lose the case.

It turns out that Thelma's husband, Tony Laredo (Richard Rober), is still around. It was under his direction that Thelma murdered her aunt and staged the murder scene to make it look as if an intruder was responsible. Thelma has actually fallen in love with Cleve and wants nothing to do with Tony. Cleve catches Thelma and Tony together. Tony knocks Cleve unconscious and drives off with Thelma. Thelma, an unwilling passenger, struggles with Tony to cause the car to crash. Tony dies instantly. Thelma lives long enough to confess to murdering her aunt.

Thelma, as innocent as she may have seemed to Cleve, remains a suspicious character from the start. The situation is laid out too conveniently, suggesting that everything has been neatly planned. But Thelma never appears to be manipulating Cleve at any point. She comes across as genuinely distraught over her aunt's murder. And her feelings for Cleve seem very much real. As we learned in the end, Thelma did love Cleve and she was forced into the murder scheme by her ruthless husband.

In another film that was released the same year, a wealthy socialite finds an affair with a homicide investigator useful after she fatally shoots her husband. The film was The Man Who Cheated Himself (1950). That is our next film.

The Man Who Cheated Himself (1950)

A wealthy woman, Lois Fraser, has come to realize that her husband, Howard (Harlan Warde), only married her for her money. She has become exhausted by his many affairs and has recently embarked on her own affair with a homicide detective, Lt. Ed Cullen (Lee J. Cobb). She catches Howard packing his bags to leave her. But, after he's gone, she finds a receipt for the gun and assumes that he's coming back to shoot her. She calls Cullen and begs him to come over right away. Before he arrives, she finds the gun in a desk drawer. As soon as he greets her, Cullen can see that she is agitated and demands that she calm down. He steps out of the room to mix her a drink. Howard suddenly bursts through the balcony doors. Lois, panicked, raises the gun and shoots him. Cullen checks out Howard. "Two slugs in the chest," he announces. The man died instantly. Cullen works hard to cover up the murder. It helps greatly when he, himself, is assigned to investigate the shooting. But Cullen's kid brother, Andy, has recently been promoted from patrol officer to homicide detective and is assigned to assist his brother in the investigation. Andy becomes suspicious with the way that his brother is handling the case. He repeatedly catches his brother lying, dismissing important evidence and evading relevant questions.

Shadow on the Wall (1950)

Celia Starrling (Kristine Miller) cheats on her husband with her sister's fiancé. She's not too discreet about it. That is something that is particularly bothersome to her husband, David (Zachary Scott). He tells her:

I think you and Crane were incredibly stupid. . . You ought to have been more careful. . . Your first mistake was letting Crane park too near the apartment. I saw you and Crane, Celia.

The couple parked directly outside of the apartment building and kissed in plain view of numerous people coming in and out of the building. David had a perfect view of the kiss. But, if he hadn't come home early from his business trip, anyone else could have seen this. Maybe, the Starrling's housekeeper, or their doorman, or their superintendent, or their mailman.

David picked up an antique gun while on a business trip. He removes the gun from his suitcase to store it in a safe place, but his wife assumes that her cuckolded husband is about to shoot her and becomes hysterical. As David comes closer to calm her, Celia strikes him in the head with a hand mirror. The blow renders him unconscious. Moments later, Celia's sister Dell Faring (Ann Sothern) enters the room to confront her sister about the affair. Celia angers Dell with her nonchalant attitude. Dell snatches the gun from the floor and shoots her sister squarely in the stomach. When David regains consciousness, he finds his wife dead and assumes he accidentally fired the gun when he was hit in the head. David's young daughter, Susan (Gigi Perreau), secretly witnessed the murder and has gone into shock. Dr. Caroline Canford (Nancy Davis) is confident that she can cure Susan and get her to remember what she saw. Dell, terrified of being executed for her sister's death, sets out to murder the little girl.

Krisine Miller and Ann Sothern in *Shadow on the Wall* (1950)

Story of a Love Affair (1950)

A factory owner, Enrico Fontana (Massimo Girotti), is a jealous husband to the beautiful Paola (Lucia Bose). After he finds old photos of his wife with her boyfriend Guido (Massimo Girotti), he hires a private detective to look into his wife's romantic history. Guido becomes aware that the private detective is poking around and assumes his investigation has to do with the death of his former girlfriend, Giovanna, who died under mysterious circumstances only days before they were to marry. It is implied that Paola, who wanted to marry Guido, murdered Giovanna on a violent impulse and then realized it would arouse suspicion if she got together with Guido afterward. Guido visits Paola about the private detective and their meeting reignites their old passions. Paola hates her husband and dreams of killing him. She tells Guido, "Money is stupid. Between you and Enrico, it chose him. . . [Y]ou seem so strong but are so weak."

Fugitive Lady (1950)

The original Italian title: *La strada buia*

Barbara Clementi (Janis Paige) murders her wealthy husband, Ralph (Eduardo Ciannelli) so that she can be with her lover, Jim West (Massimo Serato). But West is appalled to learn of the murder. He sadly admits to being a corrupt man who will lie and steal to get what he wants. But, he assures her, he would never resort to murder. He leaves her home, walking out into a stormy night. Barbara frantically rushes after him with a rifle and shoots him. He falls onto the flooded street and dies.

The Late Edwina Blake (1951)

Dr. Septimus Prendergast (Harcourt Williams) is suspicious about the sudden death of Edwina Black and orders an autopsy. When arsenic is found in the body, the doctor summons Inspector Martin (Roland Culver) to investigate.

David Farrar and Geraldine Fitzgerald in *The Late Edwina Blake* (1951)

Edwina was a domineering and mean-spirited woman who intimidated her husband Gregory (David Farrar) and exploited her personal companion Elizabeth (Geraldine Fitzgerald). Her abuse created a strong bond between Gregory and Elizabeth, who became lovers.

Martin regards Gregory and Elizabeth as his prime suspects. The couple becomes unnerved by the homicide investigation and implicates each other in the murder. But, as it turns out, neither of them is guilty of murdering Edwina. Martin is able, by quietly and patiently poking around, to determine the truth. Edwina realized she was close to death and had her housekeeper Ellen (Jean Cadell) feed her arsenic so that the police would think her husband and his lover murdered her. Edwina was, as it turned out, cruel and vindictive to her bitter end.

The incident tested Gregory and Elizabeth's love and the couple has to accept that they failed the test. Elizabeth decides to leave, but she reaches the door and can hear Gregory calling out to his dead wife to acknowledge her victory. He collapses into a chair and hangs his head. Elizabeth walks over to him to offer comfort. She realizes now that they do love each other and they cannot let Edwina win.

The Truth of Our Marriage (1952)

The original French title: La Vérité sur Bébé Donge

François Donge (Jean Gabin) is dying in a hospital. He has been poisoned by his wife, Bébé (Danielle Darrieux), who could no longer tolerate his coldness and unfaithfulness.

We see through flashbacks how Bébé transforms from, in the words of IMDb's brogmiller, "joyous young bride to embittered wife."182 François doesn't care that his wife is unhappy with him. He tells her, "So now you know my tastes. I'm vulgar. So what? I'm sorry to spoil your girly dreams, but wake up. There comes a time to get real."

The author of The Self-Styled Siren blog wrote:

> Bébé is forced to visit her husband daily for appearances' sake. Decoin shoots Darrieux in the sick-room door looking like the angel of death, face alight, body in shadow, wearing a perfect black suit — graceful, chic, implacable.[183]

Their conversation in his hospital room is strained.

Bébé: They asked me not to stay long.

François: Oh. Then I'll get down to business. Come here. Straight to the heart of things. All the rest. . . The hardest part, you see, is. . . from the start, I had to look after everything. . . My guts had to empty, you see. And my kidneys start working again. The famous renal cell. All their junk, in other words. . . As far as that goes, Jalabert is right. First you need to live. And then I had to find out the truth and present it to you. To me, this is a game to be won, you see?

François realizes as he lays in the hospital bed and looks back on his marriage that he terribly mistreated his wife for years. But Bébé finds François' redemption to be pointless. She says:

> You want to do it all again, François, I know. It's impossible. You men love to decide that life is here or life is there. When you see you're on the wrong track and that you've cheated us, you simply ask us to start again from scratch. As if we could. Double our efforts!. . . Love isn't something to begin twice, François.

She insists, "I feel nothing anymore."

In the novel, Bébé is a dreamy 17-year-old girl marrying a cynical man significantly older than herself. Darrieux was 35 years old at the time she made the film. This changes the story significantly.

Plot details were lost as the story made its transition from novel to film. A sickly son, Jacques, plays a significant role in the novel, but he is reduced to a passing mention in the film.

Lola Walser, a Goodreads reviewer, wrote of the book:

> While François busies himself with his expanding businesses, exciting travel and numerous sexual adventures, Bébé sinks into almost total social isolation and listlessness. Not even the birth of a son, conceived only after she humbly asks for a child, helps to make them a real family.[184]

Bébé feels trapped in her home. She tells François that she would like to be a secretary at his office. But he demands that she remain at home. François bans Bébé's sassy best friend from their home, which isolates his wife further.

In the end, François dies and Bébé is taken into custody.

Derby Day (1952)

A housewife, Betty Molloy (Googie Withers), engages in an affair with a boarder, Tommy Dillon (John McCallum). The husband, Jim (Nigel Stock), becomes suspicious and comes home early one day. He finds Betty and Tommy in bed together and lunges at Tommy. Tommy kicks Jim down a flight of stairs, which causes Jim to break his neck. Betty and Tommy spend the rest of the film avoiding the police and trying to get out of the country.

Nigel Stock, John McCallum and Googie Withers in *Derby Day* (1952)

Heat Wave (1953)

A novelist, Mark Kendrick (Alex Nicol), rents a bungalow on a lake. He meets wealthy neighbors, Beverly and Carol Forrest (Sidney James and Hillary Brooke), who invite him to their lavish estate for a party. Mark considers it opportune for him to meet Beverly. He was dropped by his publisher earlier in the day and he could use a wealthy friend to loan him money. He has cocktails with Beverly. Beverly gets drunk and passes out, which gives Carol an opportunity to be alone with Mark. Carol is obviously trying to seduce Mark. He tells her, "You try too hard." She asks him, "What's a matter, don't you like women?"

Mark agrees to take a trip on the Forresters' boat. Beverly is injured when Mark swerves the boat suddenly to avoid colliding with a ferry. Carol gets the idea to throw Beverly off the boat and tell the police that her husband died in an accident. Mark is appalled by the plan and refuses to assist Carol, who coldly carries out the plan on her own. Mark changes his mind by the time that they arrive in port and corroborates Carol's story that Beverly's death was accidental. He expects to marry Carol, but she runs off to marry boyfriend that she's kept hidden away. He decides to set the situation right by confessing to the police about what really happened on the boat.

Blowing Wild (1953)

Jeff Dawson (Gary Cooper), an oil prospector, finds himself desperate for money after bandits destroy his latest oil well. He comes looking for work at Conway Petroleum Company, which is owned by his old friend Paco Conway (Anthony Quinn). But Paco has married Jeff's old girlfriend, Marina (Barbara Stanwyck), and the oil man doesn't believe that it would do well for his marriage to have Jeff around. He is absolutely correct. Marina is obsessed with Jeff and takes to stalking him. She assumes that Paco is the only thing that is keeping them apart and she simply needs to get rid of him to bring Jeff back to her. Stanwyck is much tougher than she was in *Double Indemnity*. This time, she doesn't need a man to help her to murder her husband. She murders Paco by shoving him down an oil derrick shaft. Jeff is appalled when he learns about the murder. What should be do? It doesn't matter. Erickson wrote: "A timely bandit attack solves everyone's problems. . ."[185] Marina wanders in a daze amid gunfire and explosions. A dynamited derrick topples and crushes her.

99 River Street (1953)

A diamond thief, Victor Rawlins (Brad Dexter), murders his married girlfriend Pauline Driscoll (Peggie Castle) and sets out to frame her hot-tempered husband, Ernie (John Payne), for the murder.

Therese Raquin (1953)

Thérèse (Simone Signoret), who feels miserable being married to Camille (Jacques Duby), falls in love with Camille's new friend, Laurent (Raf Vallone).

The film deviates significantly from the source novel. Thérèse's husband is a hypochondriac in the novel, but he is a frail mama's boy in the film. Laurent is a portrait painter in the novel, but he is a burly truck driver in the film.

Laurent carries Camille home one night when he has had too much to drink. Passed out in Laurent's arms, he looks like a small boy being to carried to bed by his father. Laurent later refers to the ease with which he was able to carry Camille, lamenting that this small man being all that stands in the way of Thérèse and him being together. "He weighs nothing," he says, "but he's there."

In the novel, Camille is described as follows: "Arrested in his growth, he remained short and delicate. His long, thin limbs moved slowly and wearily." This is in sharp contrast to how Laurent is described.

> [Therese] had never seen such a man before. Laurent, who was tall and robust, with a florid complexion, astonished her. It was with a feeling akin to admiration, that she contemplated his low forehead planted with coarse black hair, his full cheeks, his red lips, his regular features of sanguineous beauty. For an instant her eyes rested on his neck, a neck that was thick and short, fat and powerful. Then she became lost in the contemplation of his great hands which he kept spread out on his knees: the fingers were square; the clenched fist must be enormous and would fell an ox.

Laurent was . . . rather heavy in gait, with an arched back. . . One felt that his apparel concealed round and well-developed muscles, and a body of thick hard flesh. Therese examined him with curiosity, glancing from his fists to his face, and experienced little shivers when her eyes fell on his bull-like neck.

Camille's only passion in life is to play a board game with his mother and her friends every Thursday night. Thérèse's life is uneventful and joyless.

Laurent: Do you like to dance?

Thérèse: Dance? I never learned. I only know how to do sad things. To mend, look after people, count money.

Laurent: You're not made for doing sad things. You're strong and beautiful. Your body was made for dancing. . . for loving. You can't go on living like that, Therese, behind a cashier's counter or in a sick man's bed. It's worse than death.

Thérèse: You're right. It's worse than death. But I didn't know it.

Laurent: Still, she hesitates. She doesn't see it as possible to simply walk out on her husband.

Laurent concludes, "Gratitude, pity, they're chains, you know."

Thérèse and Laurent are determined to approach Camille calmly and civilly, but Camille refuses to accept the situation and is prepared to resort to "dirty tricks" (in Laurent's words) to stop his wife from leaving him. He asks his wife to spend three days with him in Paris. He tells her that she owes him that. When she hesitates, he threatens to drown himself. In truth, he plans to lock her up in his aunt's home. Laurent boards the train and confronts him. But Camille refuses to be calm and civil.

Camille: She's mine, and I'll keep her. It's my right!

Laurent: She doesn't love you anymore! She's never loved you!

Camille: Let her pretend! That's enough for me!

Laurent: Poor bum.

Camille: The law's on my side! I'll find you wherever you go, with the help of the police!

Laurent: Are you trying to push me over the edge?

Camille: You'll never have her!

Frustrated, Laurent becomes enraged and impulsively shoves Camille off the moving train.

The murder is planned in the novel, with Laurent drowning Camille during a boat trip. It is a difficult and traumatic task in the novel.

. . . [Camille] felt a rough hand seize him by the throat. With the instinct of an animal on the defensive, he rose to his knees, clutching the side of the boat, and struggled for a few seconds.

"Therese! Therese!" he called in a stifling, sibilant voice.

> The young woman looked at him, clinging with both hands to the seat. The skiff creaked and danced upon the river. She could not close her eyes, a frightful contraction kept them wide open riveted on the hideous struggle. She remained rigid and mute.
>
> "Therese! Therese!" again cried the unfortunate man who was in the throes of death.
>
> At this final appeal, Therese burst into sobs. Her nerves had given way. The attack she had been dreading, cast her to the bottom of the boat, where she remained doubled up in a swoon, and as if dead.

Laurent uses his powerful arms to tear Camille away from the side of the skiff. Camille, mad with rage and terror, twists around and buries his teeth into his Laurent's neck. Laurent lifts him into the air and flings him into the river. The book continues, "Camille fell into the water with a shriek. He returned to the surface two or three times, uttering cries that were more and more hollow."

Therese, this woman so sadly and quietly played by Simone, is one of the most sympathetic adulterers in film history.

The couple commits suicide together at the end of the novel. Great passions can often lead to murder, suicide, or insanity. But the film ends differently.

The filmmaker invents a blackmailer, a bitter ex-sailor named Michaud (Marcel André). Michaud turns up suddenly much like the blackmailer Kennedy (Alan Reed) turns up in *The Postman Always Rings Twice*. Michaud saw Thérèse and Laurent together the train, which contradicts their story to the police. He blackmails the couple for a substantial amount of money. He tells Therese, "Perfect love is worth a small sacrifice." To insure that his blackmail victims don't murder him, he writes up a statement for the police and instructs a hotel maid to mail this if he fails to return to his room. Thérèse and Laurent pay off the exorbitant blackmail fee, but Michaud is on his way to tear up his letter when he is struck by a lorry and dies. The last shot of the film is the maid mailing the letter.

Inferno (1953)

Donald Carson III (Robert Ryan), a crusty millionaire, breaks his leg during an excursion to the Mojave Desert with his wife Gerry (Rhonda Fleming) and his mining engineer Joe Duncan (William Ludigan).

Gerry and Joe hurry off to get help. But the couple, who have recently become lovers, realize that they would be better off if they leave Carson to die. They have to report the matter to the police, but they have the police searching the wrong area of the desert.

Carson's business manager, Dave Emory (Larry Keating), describes Carson as impatient and unreasonable. He tells the sheriff, "His fortune is inherited, you know. Mostly investments just now. He doesn't do much of anything really. Though he likes to think he does." Emory's comments suggest that Carson, who is ill-tempered despite his riches, is dissatisfied with his own uselessness.

Carson realizes that he has been abandoned by Gerry and Joe and draws strength from his desire for revenge. He becomes resourceful in his efforts to survive. He creates a splint for his leg, discovers water by digging a hole in a sandy basin, and shoots a deer for food. Eventually, his struggle to survive turns into a spiritual odyssey. He now has a purpose. Every achievement brings him greater pride. As he becomes satisfied with himself, the treachery of Gerry and Joe no longer matters to him.

Joe becomes worried if Carson has died according to plan. He returns to the desert and spies Carson hobbling towards town. He is about to shoot him when an old prospector, Sam Elby (Henry Hull), shows up in a car and gives him a ride. Joe follows the car to the prospector's shack. He sneaks up behind Elby and knocks him unconscious. He proceeds to go after Carson, but Carson catches him by surprise and strikes him with a wooden board. The two men battle, overturning a stove in the process. Flames from the stove spread throughout the shack. Elby awakens in time to drag Carson out of the fire, but the burning ceiling collapses on top of Joe and kills him instantly.

Joseph Cotton and Marilyn Monroe in *Niagara* (1953)

Niagara (1953)

Ray and Polly Cutler (Casey Adams and Jean Peters) travel to Niagara Falls for a long-delayed honeymoon. The Cutlers' marital bliss strongly contrasts the marital grief of another couple on vacation. George and Rose Loomis (Joseph Cotton and Marilyn Monroe) feel nothing but resentment and mistrust towards one another. George, who was recently treated at an army hospital for battle fatigue, requires constant care and attention. He often wavers between depression and irritability. George tells Polly that Rose was working as a barmaid when he first met her. He was a sheep rancher at the time and was able to offer Rose a better life, but his luck went bad with her. The next morning, while visiting the Falls, Polly sees Rose kissing a handsome young man, Patrick (Richard Allan). Rose is tired of her broken-down husband. She arranges for Patrick to ambush George in a tunnel beneath the Falls and murder him. But her simple plot doesn't go as planned. Her down-hearted husband finds the will to fight back and manages to kill Patrick. Rose assumes that George is dead. She pretends to be the worried wife when she reports George missing. The police summon Rose to identify the body they found in the tunnel. Rose faints when she sees Patrick's body on the morgue slab and has to be admitted into a hospital. Polly encounters George, who begs her not to tell the police. "Let me stay dead," he begs her. Rose, fearing that George will kill her, flees from the hospital and buys a bus ticket to the United States. But George catches up to her in a bell tower and strangles her to death. He becomes trapped inside the tower when the security guard locks the doors for the night. He spends the night with Rose's corpse, mournfully explaining to her that he did love her. He had to murder her to regain something that he had lost in the marriage. His dignity? His sanity? George figures to escape by stealing a boat. He selects a boat that happens to belong to Ray's boss, who plans on taking Ray and Polly fishing. Polly arrives early and catches George trying to hot-wire the engine. She pleads with him to surrender to the police. He pushes Polly away, causing her to fall and hit her head. He has no time to carry Polly off the boat as Ray and his boss are coming up the dock, so the desperate man speeds off in the boat. The boat runs out of gas and gets swept up in the current. George moves Polly safely onto a large rock before he plunges over the Falls.

Robert Cummings, Grace Kelly and Ray Milland in *Dial M for Murder* (1954)

Dial M for Murder (1954)

Dial M for Murder, delightfully directed by Alfred Hitchcock, was Hollywood's first (and last) 3-D adultery film. The plot involves a variety of unsavory characters, including an unfaithful wife, a hit man and a gigolo.

Toby Wendice (Ray Milland), a retired tennis star, is upset to find his wife, Margot (Grace Kelly), in possession of a love letter from her old friend Mark Halliday (Robert Cummings). Tony became suspicious when he noticed that his wife was receiving a mysterious letter every week. He says, "[The letters] usually arrived on Thursdays. She burnt all of them except one. That one she used to transfer from handbag to handbag. It was always with her. That letter became an obsession with me. I had to find out what was in it — and finally — I did. That letter made very interesting reading." It was, as he expected, a love letter from Mark. Rarely in films has a cheating wife been sloppier in keeping an affair secret. The incriminating letter was pivotal to other adultery films, including *Forbidden* (1932), *Evelyn Prentice* (1934), *The Letter* (1940), *Temptation* (1946) and *The Heart of the Matter* (1953).

Tony cannot divorce Margot without losing her money, which funds a lavish lifestyle for him. He comes up with a dastardly solution. He conspires with a small-time criminal, Charles Alexander Swann (Anthony Dawson), to murder Margot while he himself stands in plain view of witnesses at a party.

Tony tells Swann about Margot's affair. He was in the United States playing in a tournament when the affair began. He says:

> I soon realized that a lot had happened while I was away. For one thing, she wasn't in love with me anymore. There were phone calls which would end abruptly if I happened to walk in. . . One day we had a row. I wanted to play in the covered-court tournament and as usual, she didn't want me to go. I was in the bedroom. The phone rang. It all sounded pretty urgent. After that, she seemed keen that I play in the tournament after all. So I packed my kit into the car and drove off. I parked the car two streets away, walked back in my tracks. Ten minutes later, she came out of this house and took a taxi. I took another. Her old school friend lived in a studio in Chelsea. I could see them through the studio window as he cooked spaghetti over a gas ring. They didn't say much. They just looked very natural together. You know, it's funny how you can tell when people are in love. I went for a walk. I began to wonder what would happen if she left me. I'd have to find some way of earning a living to begin with. I suddenly realized how much I'd grown to depend on her. All these expensive tastes I'd acquired while I was at the top. And now big tennis had finished with me, and so apparently had my wife. I can't ever remember being so scared.

Tony is not entirely unsympathetic as he speaks of his wife cheating on him. Milland expresses more than a hint of grief, fear and humiliation in his performance. Is Tony hiding his ill feelings beneath his flashy smile? He says he was scared. Was he scared only about losing his comfortable lifestyle or was he also scared about losing a wife that he loved? Does he tell Swann about this to purge himself of great pain?

Swann is engaged in strangling Margot with a scarf when Margot grabs a pair of scissors and fatally plunges the sharp blades into his back. Chief Inspector Hubbard (John Williams) concludes based on the evidence available that Margot murdered Swann for blackmailing her.

Hubbard comes to have second thoughts about Swann's death. There was no evidence of forced entry, which suggests that Swann got into the residence with a key. But no key was found on Swann. The man didn't even have a key to get him into his own home. The inspector suspects that Tony left his personal key in a hiding place for Swann and Swann returned the key to the hiding place once he got the door open. Later, on his arrival home, Tony removed a key from Swann's pocket, thinking it was his hidden key when it was in fact the hit man's own house key. Hubbard stages an elaborate ruse with keys to trap Tony and prove that he collaborated with the hit man. It is proof of Hitchcock's great skill as a filmmaker that he could create a suspenseful third act out of this convoluted business about a key. Perhaps, as convoluted as this plot point is, it is equally as implausible. No self-respecting hit man should need to borrow a house key to get at his victim. You leave a house key for a dog sitter, not a hit man.

Paul Gordon, author of "Dial 'M' for Mother: A Freudian Hitchcock," wrote, ". . . [T]he oddity about *Dial M for Murder*. . . [is] the fact that Mark and Margot's adulterous affair is never condemned in the film, but actually becomes virtuous when compared to the husband's desire to kill Margot."[186]

Adultery plays a pivotal role in many of Hitchcock's classic films, including *The Lady Vanishes* (1938), *The Paradine Case* (1947), *Stage Fright* (1950), *Rear Window* (1954) and *Vertigo* (1958). In *Vertigo*, private detective Scottie Ferguson is hired to trail a friend's wife and ends up falling in love with the woman.

Human Desire (1954)

The film begins with two plot lines that eventually become fatally intertwined. Jeff Warren (Glenn Ford), a Korean War vet, gets a job as a train engineer with Central National railroad. Carl Buckley (Broderick Crawford), a brutish assistant yard supervisor, is in the habit of getting drunk and beating his beautiful and spirited young wife, Vicki (Gloria Grahame).

Carl becomes desperate when he loses his job. He knows that Vicki's childhood friend, John Owens (Grandon Rhodes), does extensive business with the railroad and can use his influence with the management to get him rehired. He pleads with Vikki to speak with Owens. Vicki goes to see Owen, who acts quickly to get Carl his job back. But Carl, being a jealous husband, comes to suspect that Vicki slept with Owens to seal the deal. He wallops his wife while she screams for mercy. But this does not satisfy his rage. He cannot let this supposed treachery by Owens go unpunished. He forces Vicki to write Owens a letter letting him know that she will visit him that night in his train compartment. He is in a deranged state when he breaks into Owen's compartment and attacks him with a knife. Owen does not survive the savage attack. Jeff sees Carl leaving the compartment and soon after encounters Vicki on the train. He can see that Vicki is in distress and feels bad for her. Later, after Owen's body is found, Jeff is worried that Vicki was involved in the murder and decides against reporting what he saw to the police.

Broderick Crawford, Gloria Grahame and Glenn Ford in *Human Desire* (1954)

Carl has retrieved Vicki's note to Owens and threatens to use it to implicate her in the murder if she talks to the police. Vicki explains the situation to Jeff. She tells him that she is frightened of Carl and shows him bruises that she received from Carl beating her. She pleads with Jeff to murder Carl. After losing his job again, Carl gets drunk and stumbles through the rail yard on his way home. Jeff creeps up behind Carl with a wrench, but a passing train prevents us from seeing what happens next. The implication is that Jeff bludgeoned Carl with the wrench, but Jeff meets with Vicki and tells her that he couldn't go through with it. He questions if Vicki really loves him and accuses her of manipulating him to get her out of a bad marriage. He was, however, able to retrieve her letter from Carl, who had passed out from his drinking. She is now free to leave Carl.

Vicki is on a train leaving town when Carl shows up. The two argue. Carl accuses Vicki of running off with Jeff, who is on board the train as the engineer. Vicki declares that she loves Jeff, but Jeff left her because she asked him to murder Carl. Carl, infuriated to hear this, strangles Vicki to death.

Diabolique (1955)

A headmaster, Michel Delassalle (Paul Meurisse), is cruel to his invalid wife, Christina (Vera Clouzot). By ridiculing her at every opportunity, he has managed to destroy her self-esteem. She says dolefully, "I'm not worth anything. I'm just a ruin, a little ruin. That's what he said." She tells him that she would rather die if it means that she didn't have to see him anymore. Michel replies, "Die, my sweet. Die quickly. We'll have a nice funeral for you, and we'll finally be rid of you. The school won't suffer." But the put-downs are not the worst of it. Michel beats her whenever she defies him. Christina owns the school and is not dependent on Michel. But she won't divorce him because, as a Catholic, she believes that divorce is a sin. She is willing to overlook Michel having an affair with a teacher, Nicole Horner (Simone Signoret). Nicole arrives at school one morning with a black eye. She claims that Michel has beat her and she can no longer cope with his abuse. A teacher who sees the two women together comments, "I may be a bit old-fashioned, but this is absolutely astounding. The legal wife consoling the mistress." Nicole convinces Christina that it would be better for both of them to murder Michel. Christina reacts with great reluctance, but she is desperate to be free of Michel and strangely sees murder as a more acceptable sin than divorce.

Vera Clouzot, Paul Meurisse and Simone Signoret in *Diabolique* (1955)

The women sedate Michel by slipping a drug into his drink and then drowning him in a bathtub. They dispose of the body in a swimming pool at the school, expecting the police to believe that Michel fell into the pool by accident and drowned. Nicole believes that the body will eventually float to the surface, but it has not appeared after several days. Christina has her maintenance man drain the pool, but she is shocked to discover that the pool is empty.

Christina visits the morgue to identify a body that turned up at a nearby river. She is sure based on the description in the newspaper that this must be Michel, but she is startled when she sees the body and realizes that it isn't Michel. She meets Alfred Fichet, a private detective, at the morgue. Fichet is confident that he can find her husband.

Moinet, a student, tells Christina and Nicole that he saw Michel earlier in the day. According to the boy, Michel ordered him to rake leaves as punishment for breaking a window with his slingshot. Christina disputes what he is saying, but Moinet insists that he's telling the truth. "I know it was him," he says. "I know it."

Later, Christina can see Michel eerily peeking out of a window in the background of a class portrait. She becomes frightened. The strain, more than her weak heart can take, causes her to faint. A doctor is concerned about Christina's condition and confines her to her bed. He is doubtful that Christina will recover. Christina confides in Fichet about the murder plot and the apparent reappearance of the murder victim.

Christina is awakened in the night by noises - footsteps, a door creaking, the clatter of Michel's typewriter. She wanders the dark hallways, feeling more and more distressed. She goes into the bathroom for a drink of water and is shocked to see Michel's corpse submerged in water in the bathtub. Michel suddenly rises out of the tub, causing Christina to panic and have a fatal heart attack. It turns out that Michel and Nicole conspired to frighten Christina to death. Fichet, who has been poking around the school, emerges from the shadows. He has overheard the couple discussing their scheme. He tells them that he will call in the police to have them arrested.

The school is closed and the teachers and student prepare to leave. Moinet breaks a window with his slingshot. He explains to a teacher that Christina gave him back his slingshot.

Fear (1954) both recalls *Gaslight* (1944) and anticipates *Diabolique*. Irene Wagner (Ingrid Bergman) is married to a pill manufacturer, Professor Albert Wagner (Mathias Wieman), but she is having a torrid relationship with Erich Baumann (Kurt Kreuger). Irene becomes distraught when Joanne (Renate Mannhardt), a woman who once dated Albert, blackmails her about the affair. But it turns out that Albert already knows about the affair and has orchestrated the blackmail plot to drive Irene into a suicidal panic.

Other films presented unfaithful husbands and mistresses devising creative ways to get rid of wives. Take, for instance, *Nightmare* (1964). Henry Baxter (David Knight) works out a plan with his mistress, Grace Maddox (Moira Redmond), to get rid of his wife so that he can inherit her fortune. They manipulate an emotionally unstable young woman, Janet (Jennie Linden), to believe that she is being stalked by a ghostly apparition - a mysterious shrouded woman who roams the corridors of her mansion at night. The woman is actually Grace, who wears a mask to look like Henry's wife. At the peak of her frenzy, Janet is introduced to Henry's wife at her birthday party. She is so terrified seeing this woman come forward to greet her that she grabs a knife and stabs her in front of several witnesses.

Another good example of this genre of film is *Scream of Fear* (1961). Jane Appleby (Ann Todd) has fallen in love with her chauffeur, Bob (Ronald Lewis), and the adulterous pair work together to kill her husband to get him out of the way and steal his fortune. But they must also get rid of Jane's stepdaughter, Penny, who is the sole beneficiary of the husband's will. When Penny (Susan Strasberg) arrives for a visit, the couple cleverly arranges for her to repeatedly come upon her father's lingering corpse to horrify her and make her look insane to the family doctor, Doctor Gerrard (Christopher Lee).

The murderous lovers that freely inhabited film noir were a source of comedy by the 1980s. A sleazy businessman, Sam Stone (Danny DeVito), conspires with his sexy mistress Carol (Anita Morris) to murder his obnoxious wife Barbara (Bette Midler) in the outrageously funny *Ruthless People* (1986).

The Big Bluff (1955)

Rick De Villa (John Bromfield) conspires with his mistress Fritzi Darvel (Rosemarie Stack) to murder his wealthy wife, Valerie (Martha Vickers).

The Girl in the Red Velvet Swing (1955)

The film is based on a true-life scandal. A playboy architect, Stanford White (Ray Milland), becomes obsessed with Broadway showgirl Evelyn Nesbit (Joan Collins). Evelyn's mother, Mrs. Nesbit (Glenda Farrell), is opposed to the relationship when she learns that White is married. Evelyn marries Harry Thaw (Farley Granger), the son of an American coal and railroad baron, but White cannot accept Evelyn being married and refuses to stay away. Thaw, who has a history of mental illness, becomes upset over White's continuing interest in his wife and fatally shoots him. The story was dramatized again in *Ragtime* (1981).

Please Murder Me! (1956)

Myra Leeds (Angela Lansbury) shoots her cheating husband Craig (Raymond Burr).

The Depraved (1957)

The filmmakers make poor use of plot elements from *Double Indemnity* and *The Postman Always Rings Twice*. Laura Wilton (Anne Heywood) is unhappily married to Basil Dignam (Tom Wilton), a bitter alcoholic who often beats her. She has an affair with an army captain, Robert Arden (Dave Dillon). She appears at first to be a demure housewife, but she harbors a dark desire to see her husband dead. She persuades Robert to murder Basil.

A Kiss for a Killer (1957)

A rich widow, Betty Farnwell (Isa Miranda), marries a handsome young gigolo, Philippe (Henri Vidal). But Philippe is soon seduced by Betty's shapely niece, Betty (Mylène Demongeot). The film, based on James Hadley Chase's 1954 pulp novel "The Sucker Punch," is an obvious retread of *The Postman Always Rings Twice*. melvelvit-1 of IMDb wrote, "The stunning Mylène Demongeot's lovely but lethal sex kitten is impossible to resist and it's easy to see how any man would kill for this seductive mix of Marilyn Monroe & Brigitte Bardot."[187]

The Unholy Wife (1957)

Phyllis Hochen (Diana Dors) is bored being married to a steady and responsible vineyard owner, Paul Hochen (Rod Steiger). IMDb aptly describes Phyllis as a "gold-digger floozy." Phyllis prefers to spend her time with a hardy rodeo rider, San Sanders (Tom Tryon). Phyllis wants to figure out a way to murder Paul. Phyllis' bedridden mother-in-law, Emma (Beulah Bondi), is easily frightened in her helpless state. She becomes unnerved hearing rattling shutters on a windy night. Her servant, Theresa (Argentina Brunetti), tries to allay her fears, but she will not calm down. "It's not silliness and it's not the wind, Theresa," she says. "There's somebody out there. There's someone trying to get in." Phyllis realizes that she can shoot Paul and pretend to have mistaken him for a prowler. She creeps around dark rooms with a gun. A door opens. She fires believing that it's Paul when it is, in fact, Paul's friend Gino Verdugo (Joe De Santis). Paul loves his stepson, Michael (Gary Hunley), and worries that it will devastate Michael to have his mother imprisoned for murder. So, he takes the blame for the shooting, expecting to be acquitted. Phyllis betrays Paul at his trial, assuring with her testimony that he is convicted of murder. Emma is aware of Phyllis' treachery. She takes an overdose of pills knowing that Phyllis will be blamed for her death. Phyllis is convicted of murdering Emma. She is also revealed to have shot Gino. Paul is released from prison and is reunited with Michael.

Chain of Evidence (1957)

Steve Nordstrom (Jimmy Lydon) is given a brief sentence in prison for punching a man who insulted his girlfriend. The victim of his assault, Carl Fowler (Timothy Carey), ambushes him in an alley and slams him over the head with a board. Steve survives his head injury, but he has no memory of his identity. A wealthy businessman, Morton Ramsey (Hugh Sanders), hires Steve as a handyman. Morton's wife, Claire (Tina Carver), sees that Steve is befuddled and hot-tempered. She plots with her boyfriend, Bob Bradfield (Bill Elliott), to murder her rich husband and have Steve take the blame. Bradfield kills Morton with Steve's hammer. But Steve regains his memory. He remembers seeing Bradfield at the Ramsey home on the night that Ramsey was murdered. Lt. Andy Doyle (Bill Elliott) discovers that Bradfield was Claire's lover. He interrogates Bradfield, who admits that Claire got him to kill Ramsey.

Witness for the Prosecution (1957)

A married man, Leonard Vole (Tyrone Power), seduces a rich widow to become the chief beneficiary in her will. Vole becomes the obvious suspect when the widow is discovered stabbed to death.

The Night Affair (1958)

When nightclub owner Albert Simoni (Roger Haninis) is murdered, the prime suspect is Simoni's drug addict girlfriend, Lucky Fridel (Nadja Tiller). But Inspector Vallois (Jean Gabin) takes a liking to Lucky and believes that she's innocent. Through a dogged investigation, he determines that Simoni was killed by a former girlfriend, Thérèse Marken (Danielle Darrieux). Marken, a married woman, had become obsessed with Simoni and couldn't bear him leaving her. Vallois spoke with her husband, Henri (Louis Ducreux), about the affair.

Henri: I knew she cheated on me. I can even understand why. She met him, she fell in love. . .

Vallois: Hardly!

Henri: Then why did she do it?

Vallois: Who knows why?

Jeanne Moreau in *Elevator to the Gallows* (1958)

Elevator to the Gallows (1958)

Florence Carala (Jeanne Moreau) and Julien Tavernier (Maurice Ronet) are deeply in love, but they are not free to be together as Florence is married to Simon (Jean Wall). The couple sees it as their best solution to kill Simon. Julien knows that Simon will be working alone in his office. He uses a rope to climb up to the office. Once inside, he confronts Simon with a gun. Simon reacts incredulously, but Julien offers no explanation before he fires a fatal shot. Julien arranges the scene to make it look like Simon shot himself. He is about to drive away when he sees that he left his rope hanging from the balcony. He recovers the rope and leaves by the elevator. A security guard gets ready to leave and shuts off the power, which causes the elevator to stop between floors. Julien accepts being trapped in the elevator for the night. Meanwhile, his car is stolen by Louis (Georges Poujouly), an emotionally disturbed young man. Louis becomes interested in Horst and Frieda Bencker (Iván Petrovich and Elga Andersen) because they own a flashy Mercedes. He acts friendly with the couple, joining them for drinks. He lets Frieda take photographs with a camera that he stole from Julien's car. Frieda drops off the roll of film at a photo lab in their hotel. Louis is interrupted by the Benckers as he is about to steal the Mercedes. He panics. He shoots them using a gun that he found in Julien's glove compartment. The fact that the gun belongs to Julien makes Julien the prime suspect in the Benckers' murder. Julien explains that he was stuck in an elevator all night. The roll of film is developed, putting Louis in the company of the Benckers on the night of their murder. This leads to Louis' arrest. But the police notice other photos on the roll. The detective shows Florence a blank sheet of photo paper lying in a chemical bath. An image gradually appears showing Florence and Julien in a loving embrace. This now casts suspicion on her and Julien for Simon's death. Strewn across the table are photos of the couple spending time together at a park. Florence touches the photos as if fondly remembering the day. She lovingly traces her fingers across Julien's face. She says, "We're together here. Together again, somewhere. You see, they can't keep us apart."

The Man Who Understood Women (1959)

A movie producer, Willie Bauche (Henry Fonda), has put great time and resources into turning his wife, Ann Garantier (Leslie Caron), into an internationally famous movie star. But Ann feels neglected by her work-obsessed husband. She meets a handsome soldier, Major Marco Ranieri (Cesare Danova), under a moonlit sky on the French Riviera. He explains that he is a fan and shows her a photo of her that he clipped out of a magazine. Time Magazine noted, "She bares her arid heart. They bolt to his clifftop villa."[188] Willie learns about the affair and hires a hit man, but he later worries that the the hit man might also kill his wife. Willie, who is dressed as a clown for a costume party, suddenly rushes across town to stop the hit man. In the end, Ann cannot bring herself to leave Willie.

Anatomy of a Murder (1959)

Army Lt. Manion (Ben Gazzara) murders a man who had sex with his wife, Laura (Lee Remick). Laura claims that she was raped, but it is doubtful that she is telling the truth. Manion's attorney, Paul Biegler (James Stewart), successfully defends Manion using a rare version of the insanity defense called irresistible impulse.

Midnight Lace (1960)

Midnight Lace has many influences, including *Gaslight*, *Diabolique* and *Dial M for Murder*.

Kit Preston (Doris Day) is being tormented by a mysterious stalker. She is chased by the stalker through a fog-shrouded park, she receives a series of threatening phone calls, and the stalker sneaks up behind her on a busy street and pushes her into traffic. Kit becomes unhinged. A police investigator, Inspector Byrnes (John Williams), suspects that Tony (Rex Harrison), Kit's philandering husband, is behind this relentless and systematic torment of Kit. The inspector manages by tapping Kit's phone to collect the evidence of Tony's guilt.

Portrait in Black (1960)

Shelia Cabot (Lana Turner), a glamorous socialite, has become distraught caring for her crippled husband Matthew (Lloyd Nolan), who is routinely cruel and controlling with her. She wants to rid herself of Matthew without losing the luxurious lifestyle that he has given her. She expresses her distress to her lover Dr. David Rivera (Anthony Quinn), who is also Matthew's personal physician. She plots with David to inject Matthew with something that will kill him. Matthew's assistant, Howard Mason (Richard Basehart), who loves Shelia himself, becomes suspicious when Matthew dies suddenly. Shelia receives an anonymous blackmail letter, the opening line of which reads, "Congratulations on the success of your murder." She tells David that the letter must have come from Howard. David ends up shooting Howard and has to get rid of the body. It turns out that Howard had nothing to do with the letter. Shelia sent the letter to herself to stop David from going away. David is devastated to learn this. Matthew's daughter, Cathy (Sandra Dee), quietly enters the house as Shelia and David are discussing their misdeeds. David chases after Cathy, who escapes him by climbing onto a window ledge. He goes after her, but he slips and falls to his death.

The Accident (1963)

The original French title: *L'Accident*

Julien Avène (Georges Rivière) is the principal of a small school located on a remote island off the western coast of France. He is desperately unhappy living with his alcoholic wife, Andrea (Magali Noël). But his mood is greatly uplifted with the arrival of a beautiful young teacher, Francoise (Danik Patisson). Julien says that he is so distressed being married to Andrea that he often feels like crying out for help. He asks Francoise, "If this hand came out of the water, would you reach for it?" He later says, "But, by God, you cannot ask a guy who is in the midst of falling from a cliff to stop his fall. But I'm falling!" Andrea learns that Julien and Francoise are having an affair and sets her mind to plotting a deadly revenge.

Station Six Sahara (1963)

Five men work in stressful conditions while isolated at an oil-pumping station in the Sahara. But then, one evening, a car crashes into their camp. The men remove a married couple from the wreckage. The beautiful young wife, Catherine (Carroll Baker), claims that her husband, Jimmy (Biff McGuire), fell into a jealous rage and crashed the car intending to end their lives. Jimmy, who was injured in the crash, remains bedridden while his overly friendly wife gets to know their hosts. AFI notes:

> Catherine's presence exacerbates the taut atmosphere as she sleeps first with Kramer and then with Martin. Unable to bear her seemingly flagrant infidelity, the crazed Jimmy stabs her to death and then kills himself. An ambulance removes the corpses, and the station returns to strained and bitter normality.[189]

The Soft Skin (1964)

Franca Lachenay (Nelly Benedetti) becomes unhinged when she finds photos of her husband Pierre (Jean Desailly) on a weekend getaway with a beautiful airline hostess, Nicole (Françoise Dorléac). She follows her husband to a restaurant. As he dines quietly at a table, she approaches him with a shotgun, throws the photos on the table, and shoots him dead.

Nightmare in the Sun (1965)

Marsha Wilson (Ursula Andress) picks up a handsome young man (John Derek) who is hitchhiking through the desert. She takes him back to her home and has sex with him. Her husband, Sam Wilson (Arthur O'Connell), arrives home unexpectedly and sees the hitchhiker leaving his home. He gets out a rifle and fatally shoots Martha. The Sheriff (Aldo Ray), who is one of Sam's friends, figures to protect Sam by blaming the murder on the hitchhiker.

Nightmare Castle (1965)

Stephen Arrowsmith (Paul Muller), a scientist, is enraged when he learns that his wife Muriel (Barbara Steele) is having an affair with the hunky gardener, David (Rik Battaglia). He savagely beats David with a hot poker and burns Muriel's face with acid. He keeps the pair chained to a bed while he taunts and tortures them. Finally, he sends a current of electricity through the metal bed frame, which electrocutes the couple. The ghosts of his victims return from their graves for revenge.

Thrilling (1965)

Thrilling is a three-part anthology film. The first story, "The Victim," involves an unfaithful husband who is terrified of his wife finding out about his affair. Nanni Galassi (Nino Manfredi) is spending a leisurely day at the beach with his wife, Frida (Alexandra Stewart). He goes farther out into the water than planned and, being a poor swimmer, finds himself struggling to stay afloat. He calls out to Frida, but she seems to ignore him. He nearly drowns before other swimmers carry him to the shore. He doesn't believe Frida when she says that her earplugs blocked his cries. He suspects that his wife knows about his mistress, Luciana (Magda Konopka), and wanted him to die. He thinks that she's disappointed that he didn't drown and will find another way to end his life. He is afraid to eat as she might try to poison him. He is afraid to sleep as she might smother him with a pillow. A psychoanalyst (Tino Buazzelli) tells him that his guilt over having a mistress has made him paranoid and he will only find peace if he ends the affair. He follows the doctor's advice, letting Luciana know that it's over between them. He arranges a romantic getaway with Frida in the hope of renewing their affections. The couple is enjoying a hilltop view when Frida walks toward him suddenly. He panics thinking that she is going to push him to his death. He backs away, stumbles, and rolls down the hill, nearly falling beneath a passing train. He finally confesses to Frida about his affair, although he never tells her who the woman was. Frida is upset at first, but she forgives Nanni. The next day, Nanni and Frida happen to meet Luciana and her husband Ernesto at the beach. The couples row out to sea in a boat. Frida and Ernesto swim back to shore, leaving Nanni and Luciana alone. Luciana jerks the oars to cause the boat to lurch. Nanni loses his balance and falls into the water. He flails and screams, unable to keep himself afloat. Lucianna rows away, coldly watching Nanni drown.

A Black Veil for Lisa (1968)

Police Inspector Franz Bulon (John Mills) hires a hit man, Max Lindt (Robert Hoffmann), to kill his unfaithful wife, Lisa (Luciana Paluzzi). But Lindt falls in love with his beautiful victim.

The Forbidden Photos of a Lady Above Suspicion (1970)

The original Spanish title: *Le foto proibite di una signora per bene*

Peter (Pier Paolo Capponi) is struggling to keep his business from going bankrupt. His unhappy wife, Minou (Dagmar Lassander), is addicted to alcohol and tranquilizers. She is approached by a strange man (Simón Andreu), who threatens to ruin her husband. He produces a tape recording of Peter talking about murdering a creditor. The brutish man forces Minou to have sex with him. Minou realizes that her best friend, Dominique (Nieves Navarro), has a connection with the blackmailer when she finds her with a pornographic photo of the man. A police inspector, Frank (Osvaldo Genazzani), is unable to find evidence to corroborate Minou's accusations. Minou, alone and desperate, takes an overdose of tranquilizers. But Frank arrives in time to save her life. He has found evidence that Peter set up the blackmail scheme. As turns out, Peter hoped to drive Minou to suicide so that he could collect on her life insurance policy and use the money to pay off his debts. Dominque, Frank's secret lover, was an accomplice.

Just Before Nightfall (1971)

Charles Masson (Michel Bouquet) is having an affair with his best friend's wife, Laura Tellier (Anna Douking). He accidentally kills Laura during a sadomasochist game.

Someone Behind the Door (1971)

Dr. Laurence Jeffries (Anthony Perkins), a neurosurgeon, manipulates an amnesiac patient (Charles Bronson) to murder his unfaithful wife Frances (Jill Ireland), This is similar to *The Hypnotist* (1957), in which a psychiatrist seeks to end his marriage by hypnotizing a patient to murder his wife.

A Woman for All Men (1975)

An ill-tempered and domineering millionaire, Walter McCoy (Keenan Wynn), marries the beautiful but deceitful Karen Petrie (Judith Brown). Walter's son, Steve (Andrew Robinson), falls in love with Karen. Woodyanders of IMDb wrote, "This provokes a tangled web of deception, infidelity, and even murder."[190]

Fire's Share (1978)

The original French title: *La part du feu*

Bob Hansen (Michel Piccoli), a shrewd real estate developer, catches his wife Catherine (Claudia Cardinale) in bed with his partner, Jacques (Jacques Perrin). He reacts nonchalantly. He needs his wife's money to finance his business and he needs his partner's help to close an important deal. So, he encourages their affair rather than losing both of them. He tells Jacques, "You like Catherine, congrats! I'd rather it be you." Catherine is disgusted to learn the truth - Bob and Jacques have conspired against her to close a crooked business deal. Hansen's cruel manipulations drive Catherine to commit suicide.

Magic (1978)

Peggy (Ann-Margret), unhappy in her marriage to Duke (Ed Lauter), has an affair with an amiable ven-
triloquist, Corky (Anthony Hopkins), without realizing that he is in fact a homicidal maniac.

Days of Heaven (1978)

Bill (Richard Gere), a steel worker, flees Chicago with his girlfriend Abby (Brooke Adams) and Abby's
sister Linda (Linda Manz) after he accidentally murders his boss in a fight. The three get jobs as harvest
hands on a large wheat farm in Texas Abby attracts the attention of the shy young farm owner (Sam Shep-
ard). When Bill learns that the farmer is ill and has little time to live, he persuades Abby to encourage the
farmer's attentions. She easily develops a relationship with the farmer. She introduces Bill and Linda to the
farmer as her brother and sister. The two are soon married in a solemn ceremony at a riverside. Abby comes
to love her husband, but she still maintains her relationship with Bill. One night, the couple sneaks off in the
fields and make love. Bill is pleased that his plan is working out so well.

Abby: You talk like it was all right?

Bill: He'll never have a chance to enjoy his money, anyway.

Abby: What makes you think we're talkin' about just a couple of months?

Bill: The man's got one foot on a banana peel, the other on a roller skate. We'll all be gone in a couple
of years. Who's gonna care that we acted perfect?

Abby: (resisting) I held out a long time. I had rich men pay me compliments. Have I ever said anything to make you. . .

Bill: You don't have to. I mean, I hate it, to see you stooped over out there, him lookin' at your ass like
you're a whore. I hate it.

When the farmer finds out the truth about Bill, he becomes incensed and goes after Bill with a gun. The
two fight and Bill fatally stabs him with a screwdriver. The police, led by a grieving farm foreman (Robert
Wilke), track down Bill and fatally shoot him when he tries to run away.

Deep Water (1981)

The original French title: *Eaux profondes*

The film is based on a Patricia Highsmith novel, also titled "Deep Water."
Vic Allen (Jean-Louis Trintignant), the owner of a perfume business, is unhappy in his marriage to his
younger wife Mélanie (Isabelle Huppert). Mélanie has no responsibilities. Not only does Vic bring in the
money, it appears that he takes care of their young daughter on his own.
Roy Stafford of The Case for Global Film wrote:

The marriage does not appear to be going well. Mélanie provokes her husband at every possible opportunity, flirting with a succession of young men at parties and inviting them to dinner, late night drinking and dancing, literally under her husband's nose. Vic appears to tolerate this behaviour and calmly tells the men that if he doesn't like them he may well 'bump them off.' They don't know whether to believe him. . .191

In the book, Vic has explicitly consented to Melinda having affairs as a way to save their failing marriage. When one of Melinda's lovers is murdered, Vic leads people to believe that he is the murderer, hoping to scare away potential lovers from his wife. But the real murderer is apprehended and Vic and Melinda's friends know now not to take Vic seriously. One night, at a neighbor's party, Vic finds himself alone in a pool with Melinda's latest lover, Charley. He suddenly leaps on top of Charley and drowns him. He is able to leave the pool area without anyone seeing him and acts surprised when the body is discovered. Emboldened, he goes on to shove his wife's next lover over a cliff. Don Wilson, a crime story writer who lives in the community, investigates the murders and finds evidence of Vic's guilt. Vic, knowing that the police are on their way to arrest him, strangles Melinda to death.

The film is the mostly faithful to the novel except for the ending. The film version of Melinda is titillated by the murders and helps her husband to evade arrest.

A second film adaptation of "Deep Water" was produced for German television in 1983. A third film adaptation starring Ben Affleck as Vic was produced in the United States in 2022.

Creepshow (1982)

Richard Vickers (Leslie Nielsen) has a sadistic desire for revenge when he learns that his wife, Becky (Gaylen Ross) has been having an affair with Harry (Ted Danson). He forces Becky and Harry at gunpoint to a secluded beach, where he buries them up to their necks on the sandy shoreline. He sets up a close-circuit camera so that he can watch the tide advance and drown them. But, after their deaths, Becky and Harry arrive at Richard's home as waterlogged zombies and enact revenge.

Confidentially Yours (1983)

Julien Vercel (Jean-Louis Trintignant), a mild-mannered real estate agent, learns that his wife, Marie-Christine (Caroline Sihol), was having an affair and her lover has just turned up murdered. Marie-Christine refuses to talk to Julien about the man. She says, "He's dead and so what? He was a bastard and a lousy lover." Julien tells her that they will need to divorce. She seductively opens her legs in an attempt to seduce him and get this notion of divorce out of his head. This is a unique way to handle an aggrieved husband. But then Marie-Christine turns up dead, too. Julien is suspected by the homicide detectives of murdering Marie-Christine and her lover. Barbara Becker (Fanny Ardant), Julien's faithful secretary, is sure of her boss' innocence and embarks on an investigation. She looks into Marie-Christine's past, which leads her into a dark underworld of gamblers and prostitutes. She manages through persistence and cleverness to discover that the unfaithful Marie-Christine had a second lover who became insanely jealous and committed the murders.

Blood Simple (1984)

Bar owner Julian Marty (Dan Hedaya) hires a sleazy private detective, Loren Visser (M. Emmet Walsh), to murder his unfaithful wife, Abby (Frances McDormand), and her lover, Ray (John Getz). But Visser figures to save himself work. He takes Marty's money and shoots Marty using a gun he stole from Abby. Visser is confident that Abby will be arrested for the murder until he realizes that he forgot his cigarette lighter at the murder scene.

Last Rites (1988)

Zena (Anne Twomey), a vicious mobster's wife, is incensed to learn that her husband has been cheating on her. She tracks down her husband and fatally shoots him. Angela (Daphne Zuniga), her husband's mistress, fears that she will be Zena's next victim. She begs Father Michael (Tom Berenger) to protect her from Zena. Father Michael feels a special responsibility as, it turns out, Zena is his sister.

Crimes and Misdemeanors (1989)

Judah (Martin Landau) has been distressed by threats from his mistress Dolores Paley (Anjelica Huston). Unless he marries her, she will expose their affair to his wife and report his criminal financial dealings to legal authorities. Judah hires a hit man to have Dolores murdered.

A Woman's Revenge (1990)

Cecile (Isabelle Huppert) remains in mourning a year after her husband Andre died in a car accident. It compounds her grief knowing that Andre was on his way to see his mistress, Suzy (Beatrice Dalle), when the accident occurred. Cecile has struggled to come to terms with her loss and, in the process, has come to blame Suzy for the tragedy. She visits Suzy to, she says, share their mutual grief. Suzy, lonely and troubled, accepts Celine's companionship and allows Celine to insinuate herself into her life. The two women manage, by maintaining a perverse love triangle with a dead man, to become inseparable. It becomes obvious after a while that Celine's sole purpose in befriending Suzy is to torment and punish her. She says bluntly, "You're bad luck to those who love you." In the end, she drives Suzy to commit suicide.

Enid is Sleeping (1990)

Harry (Judge Reinhold) is cheating on his wife Enid (Maureen Mueller) with his sister-in-law, Jane (Elizabeth Perkins). Enid catches the couple making love in her bed. Enraged, she brutally attacks Harry. She knows that Enid is not bluffing when she pulls out a gun and fires at Harry. She is familiar with her sister's sadistic nature (a flashback to 25 years earlier has already shown Enid shoving her little sister into an oven). Fortunately, the bullet hits a pillow, which bursts and releases feathers into the air. To save Harry, Jane strikes her sister in the head with a vase. Enid lays lifeless on the floor and doesn't respond to Harry's efforts to revive her. Harry and Jane, who fear being arrested for murder, try to make it look as if Enid died in a car accident.

Mouth to Mouth (1995)

The original Spanish title: *Boca a boca*

Víctor Ventura (Javier Bardem), an unemployed actor, takes a job as a phone-sex operator. A client, Amanda (Aitana Sanchez-Gijon), works her feminine wiles to entice Victor into murdering her husband, Bill (Josep Maria Flotats). The film spoofs film noir.

Faithful (1996)

Margaret Connor (Cher), a housewife, is devastated to learn that her husband Jack (Ryan O'Neal) is having an affair and contemplates killing herself. But then she receives a visit from Tony (Chazz Palminteri), a hit man hired by her husband, and she is no longer sure that she wants to die. Desson Howe of The Washington Post wrote, "[Margaret] bounces between begging for her life and imploring [Tony] to kill her, depending on her mood."[192]

Her Married Lover (1999)

Katie Griffin (Roxana Zal) suspects that her lover, Richard Mannhartm (Perry King), tampered with the brakes of his wife's car to cause his wife to crash.

Trust (2000)

Anne Travers (Caroline Goodall), a criminal defense attorney, defends her husband, Michael Mitcham (Mark Strong), who has been charged with murdering his mistress. But it turns out that Ann is the actual murderer.

What Lies Beneath (2000)

Claire Spencer (Michelle Pfeiffer) witnesses apparitions and poltergeist activity at her lake house. She informs her college professor husband, Norman (Harrison Ford), about what she has seen and he tells her that she is having hallucinations. Claire eventually figures out that she is being contacted from the hereafter by the ghost of Madison Frank (Amber Valletta), one of Norman's former students. The shocking truth is that Norman murdered Madison to prevent her from exposing their affair to the dean.

The Cat's Meow (2001)

Real-life film producer Thomas H. Ince died during a weekend cruise on the yacht of publishing magnate William Randolph Hearst. Ince's mysterious death has inspired great speculation over the last ten decades. *The Cat's Meow* proposes that Hearst (Edward Herrmann) flew into a jealous rage after finding love letters that comedian Charlie Chaplin (Eddie Izzard) sent to his mistress, Marion Davies (Kirsten Dunst). In the darkness of night, Hearst mistakes Ince (Cary Elwes) for Chaplin and shoots him.

Unfaithful (2002)

Connie Sumner (Diane Ladd) falls and scrapes her knee while shopping. She is helped up by Paul Martel (Olivier Martinez), who advises her to come to his apartment nearby so that he can clean and bandage her wound. She feels a sexual attraction for the handsome stranger and does not hesitate to follow him to his home. Before she leaves, Paul gives her a book to take with her. As it turns out, he has written his phone number on the opening page. Though Connie is married and has an eight-year-old son, she remains fascinated by Paul. She phones Paul and returns to his apartment. The two embark on a sexually passionate affair. She visits Paul frequently over the next several weeks. One day, Edward (Richard Gere) notices his wife putting an unusual amount of effort in getting ready. He asks her to meet him for lunch, but she tells him that she has a salon appointment. He becomes suspicious and phones the salon. He learns, as he expected, that she has no appointment. He hires a private investigator, who is able to provide photos of Connie with Paul. He goes to Paul's home to confront him. While talking to Paul, Edward is startled to see a snow globe that he gave his wife. Enraged, he grabs the snow globe and slams it into Paul's head. Paul, his skull fractured, dies. Unable to live with his guilt, Edward turns himself over to the police.

An affair starts in a similar way in *Citizen Kane* (1941). Charles Foster Kane (Orson Welles), a dignified publishing tycoon, is splashed with mud by a passing carriage. A young woman, Susan Alexander (Dorothy Comingore), cannot help but giggle seeing the mud-splattered gentlemen. She invites him to her nearby apartment to clean up. He expresses his gratitude by entertaining her with magic tricks. In *Unfaithful*, Paul performs a splendid sleight of hand by using his book to slip Connie his phone number.

Several adultery films failed at the box office during this period, but this film turned out to be a great success.

Match Point (2005)

Chris Wilson (Jonathan Rhys Meyers) gets his mistress, Nola Rice (Scarlett Johansson), pregnant. She refuses to get an abortion, insisting that he leave his wife Chloe (Emily Mortimer) so that they can raise the child together. Afraid she will tell his wife about their affair, Chris breaks into her apartment and murders her. He is interrupted by her neighbor, Mrs. Eastby (Margaret Tyzack), who he also has to kill. He stages the bloody scene to look like a burglary. To this end, he gathers up Mrs. Eastby's jewelry and throws it into a river. A ring bounces off a railing and lands on the pavement. A police detective finds Nola's diary, which details her affair with Chris. This makes Chris the chief suspect in the murder until Mrs. Eastby's missing ring is found in the pocket of a dead drug dealer. Chris can now safely resume his life with Chloe, who has just found out that she is pregnant.

Killer Babes (2007)

The original Dutch title: *Moordwijven* (which better translates into *Murderbitches*)

Three vain, dim-witted high-society wives, Kitty Kroonenberg (Bracha van Doesburgh), Estelle (Hadewych Minis) and Nicolette (Sanne Wallis de Vries), spend most of their time tanning at the pool or visiting their plastic surgeon for maintenance work. But the trio is roused to action when they read a book titled "Adultery: Top 50 Fifty Signs of Betrayal." The book convinces them that Kitty's husband, Evert-Jan (Hans Kesting), is cheating. The trio hires a deformed hit man, Cliff (Kees Boot), to murder Evert-Jan. Cliff is excited to learn that Evert-Jan owns a rare Cliff Richard record. He demands the record as part of his payment. Kitty is distressed to learn that Evert-Jan gave the record to Jan-Hein (Peer Mascini), a blind man in a wheelchair. Kitty breaks into Jan-Hein's home to steal the record. Jan-Hein attacks the intruder with a sword and accidentally jabs the sword through a jukebox, which causes him to be electrocuted. Cliff plans to run Evert-Jan's car off the road, but he is unaware that Nicotte's husband Ivo (Bart Klever) has borrowed the vehicle. Ivo is forced off the road. The car overturns and smashes into a tree. But, surprisingly, Ivo survives. Ivo's mistress, Laura (Dorien Rose Duinker), arrives at the hospital to visit Ivo. This enrages Nicotte, who attacks Laura. The brawling women knock Ivo out of bed and disconnect him from life support. He dies before the hospital staff can reconnect him. Evert-Jan arranges for Ivo's ashes to be scattered over a golf course. Estelle's husband Meindert (Bart Oomen) is naked in his office with Laura, who he met at Ivo's bedside. They look out the window to wave at the plane carrying Ivo's ashes. The plane suddenly crashes into the office, killing them. Evert-Jan managed to jump out of the plane before it crashed. Cliff flees police in a stolen truck. He accidentally drives the truck through a wall, which causes the death of Evert-Jan and his mistress Pamela (Jennifer de Jong). The final scene takes place a year later. The three ladies are traveling on a yacht with Cliff, who has gotten plastic surgery to make himself look handsome.

Married Life (2007)

Harry Allen (Chris Cooper), a middle-aged businessman, plans to poison his wife Pat (Patricia Clarkson) so that he can marry his mistress, Kay Nesbit (Rachel McAdams). He believes that he is being humane as Pat would be too hurt by a divorce to continue with her life. Harry confides his plans to his best friend, Richard Langley (Pierce Brosnan). Richard falls in love with Kay. He discovers soon after that Pat is carrying on an affair with John O'Brien (David Wenham). He takes on the daunting task of reconciling Harry and Pat so that he can prevent Pat's murder and win Kay for himself.

From the novel:

> I thought sadly how heavily the dice were loaded against the wife in any triangle of this kind. The other woman knows that the battle is on. The wife doesn't. The other woman is on her best behavior, trying to please, to charm, to flatter, and often, I suppose, to seduce. The wife, knowing nothing, is behaving like a natural person does: sometimes pleasant and amusing, sometimes dull, critical, or irritable. And silently watching her is her husband, noting her faults, comparing her with the allege paragon of all the virtues.[193]

Careful What You Wish For (2015)

Doug Martin (Nick Jonas), a young man, is spending the summer at his parents' lake house. Doug becomes enamored of Lena Harper (Isabel Lucas), a beautiful young woman who lives next door. Lena is married to a wealthy investment banker, Elliot Harper (Dermot Mulroney). She seduces Doug with the intent of framing him for Elliot's murder.

Chapter Six:
An Old Lover Returns

Filmmakers of the period maintained that the greatest threat to a marriage was an old flame. Cary Grant says in *Indiscreet* (1958), "I think an ex-suitor who doesn't realize he's an ex-suitor and doesn't stay ex'd is the most despicable kind of human being."

"Fallen Angels," a 1925 play by Noël Coward, involves two married women who learn that an old lover is coming to town and wants to see them. The women are so worried that they won't be able to resist the man's charms that they decide to pack their suitcases and get away.

Vidocq (George Sanders) encounters a former lover, Loretta de Richet (Carole Landis), in *A Scandal in Paris* (1946).

Vidocq: Rather like old times, isn't it?

Loretta: Except I'm married.

Vidocq: Oh, I'm so happy.

Loretta: Unhappily.

Vidocq: What?

Loretta: Married.

Vidocq: I'm so sorry.

Loretta: Oh, it's all right. All the more reason we should meet again.

The Great Gatsby (1926, 1949 and 1974)

Scott Fitzgerald's classic 1925 novel "The Great Gatsby" combines two adultery story tropes. First, we have the old lover who returns to town. Then, we have the wealthy married couple adrift in the emptiness and moral decay of their lofty class.

The novel was originally adapted into a film by Famous Players-Lasky in 1926. The film was quickly dismissed by critics for being a shallow interpretation of the novel. H. H. Niemeyer of St. Louis Post-Dispatch noted, ". . . [S]omewhere, in the translation into a mile of celluloid, the finer parts of the typed version have been lost."[194] Epes W. Sargent of Moving Picture World wrote, "Only the shell is transferred to the screen. None of the psychology of Gatsby's character, which is the reason for the story, is transferred to the screen. He might as well be a dramatized tailor's dummy for all the interest he arouses. . ."[195]

In the late 1940s, Richard Maibaum approached Paramount executives to produce a second film version of "Gatsby" with Alan Ladd. The studio had been holding onto the movie rights to the book for twenty years, but no executive was interested in producing a "Gatsby" film. Maibaum said that the executives hated the story as it involved "an unpunished murder, illicit sex, extramarital affairs, a low moral tone, and so on."[196] But they finally agreed at Maibaum's strong urging. Joseph I. Breen, the director of The Production Code

Administration, requested that Paramount "dismiss from further consideration. . . any thought of making [The Great Gatsby] into [a] screenplay."[197] Maibaum made changes to the story to appease Breen. An important change was that the writer made Gatsby's best friend, Nick Carraway (Macdonald Carey), into a powerful voice of morality. But, in the end, critics found that the film failed to capture the substance and nuance of the novel.

A third film version of Fitzgerald's novel came about more than twenty years later. It was the most faithful to the novel.

A wealthy couple, Tom and Daisy Buchanan (Bruce Dern and Mia Farrow), are mired in a loveless marriage. Tom's many affairs have caused great damage to their relationship. Tom's latest mistress, Myrtle Wilson (Karen Black), is married to George Wilson (Scott Wilson), a car mechanic who is negotiating to buy a car from Tom.

Mia Farrow and Robert Redford in *The Great Gatsby* (1974)

Daisy is reunited with an old lover, Jay Gatsby (Robert Redford). Gatsby has heartwarming memories of a brief affair that he had with Daisy five years earlier. The two separated when Gatsby went off to war. Gatsby wanted to marry Daisy after he ended his military service, but he knew that Daisy would not have him as he was. Being a poor farmer's son, he lacked the money that was needed to win the high-status Daisy. But he has now returned to her with great wealth. He is showy with his money, throwing lavish parties at his estate, for the sole purpose of impressing Daisy. His conspicuous lifestyle is best epitomized by his bright yellow Rolls-Royce. Confident that she still loves him, Gatsby expects Daisy to leave Tom for him. He has convinced himself that his old flame cannot possibly love her husband and must have only married him for his money.

Gatsby is foolish to believe that he can recapture the passion and intimacy that he once shared with Daisy. He has an idealized image of Daisy, which has driven him to obsess over a dream that has no substance. Daisy is obviously more excited by Gatsby's newfound wealth than she is excited by Gatsby himself. From the novel:

Almost five years! There must have been moments that afternoon when Daisy tumbled short of his dreams – not through her own fault, but because of the colossal vitality of his illusion. It had gone beyond her, beyond everything.[198]

But is Gatsby truly a romantic and does he really love Daisy? It is suggested that he sees Daisy as an object of status much like his Rolls-Royce. He tells Nick that "her voice is full of money."[199] Nick takes this to mean that Gatsby sees Daisy as a king's daughter living in a white palace or, more simply, "the golden girl."[200]

While at a hotel having drinks, Gatsby finally confronts Tom about his feelings for Daisy. He insists that Daisy doesn't love him and the two of them are going away together. Tom becomes angry and accuses Gatsby of being a swindler. He takes this opportunity to tell Daisy that Gatsby has earned his wealth by partnering with a gangster in the bootleg business. This upsets Daisy. Tom makes it clear to Gatsby that Daisy will never leave him. He understands that, despite their marital problems, he and Daisy have a strong bond. And he's right. In the end, Daisy is unwilling to leave Tom and run away with Gatsby. Gatsby is devastated.

After his failed confrontation with Tom, Gatsby agrees to accompany Daisy on her trip home. He lets Daisy drive his car.

George, who suspects Myrtle of having an affair, locks his wife in their bedroom. But Myrtle manages to escape and rushes out of their home. Tom had swapped cars with Gatsby earlier in the day and stopped for gas at George's garage. So, Myrtle had seen him in Gatsby's bright yellow Rolls-Royce and assumes when she sees the car now that Tom is driving it. She runs out into the middle of the road trying to wave down the car, but Daisy fails to see her in time and runs into her. Myrtle dies instantly. In a panic, Daisy drives away.

The next morning, Tom tells George that Gatsby was driving the car that killed his wife. George arrives at Gatsby's mansion with a gun. He finds Gatsby relaxing in his pool and fatally shoots him through the chest. He then shoots himself.

Nick arranges a funeral for Gatsby, which is only attended by himself and Gatsby's father. Elsewhere, Daisy and Tom continue in their loveless marriage just as before.

Betrayal (1929)

A Swiss peasant girl, Vroni (Esther Ralston), marries wealthy burgomeister Poldi Moser (Emil Jannings), but old lover Andre Frey (Gary Cooper) makes repeated visits to the couple over the next few years and persists in trying to get her to run off with him.

Private Lives (1931)

Private Lives is based on a play by Noël Coward.

The coincidences stack up in this story. Elyot Chase (Robert Montgomery) marries Sibyl (Una Merkel) the same week that his ex-wife, Amanda Prynne (Norma Shearer), marries Victor (Reginald Denny). Unintentionally, each couple arranges a honeymoon on the French Riviera and each couple books a suite in the same hotel. The next coincidence is inevitable. Amanda walks out on the terrace and spies Elyot lounging on the terrace of the neighboring suit. Adjacent divorcees. Adjacent marriages. Adjacent honeymoons. Adjacent suites. Suspending disbelief this much can tear a muscle. The balance of the plot is summarized by IMDb reviewer gftbiloxi[201]: "[Elyot and Amanda] suddenly desert their new spouses to resume their torrid love. Unfortunately, they both remain as eccentrically combative as ever, and it isn't long before the fur begins to fly."

Goodbye Again (1933)

The film is decidedly pre-Code. While on a book tour, author Kenneth Bixby (Warren William) is visited by a former college girlfriend, Julie Wilson (Genevieve Tobin). Julie assumes (wrongly) that she was the inspiration for the heroine in Bixby's latest novel. She tells Bixby that she still loves him and assumes from reading his book that he still loves her too. She begs forgiveness for not waiting for him and being "unfaithful" with her husband. Bixby is fascinated by Julie, who he sees as "a romantic, imaginative girl." Standing in the way of an affair are Julie's sister, her lawyer, her husband Harvey (Hugh Herbert), and Bixby's loyal (and loving) secretary Anne (Joan Blondell). But an affair occurs nonetheless. Ann is disappointed to learn Bixby has had sex with Julie. He falls back on trendy modern philosophy to justify his actions. "Ann," he says, "you've always been broadminded and tolerant and sophisticated."

Bixby becomes distressed when Julie insists that they get married. He finally reveals to her that she was not the model for the woman in his novel. She returns contritely to her husband, who agrees to take her back. Meanwhile, Bixby tells Anne that he loves her and begs for her forgiveness. So, the anarchy created by the return of the former lover is neatly resolved and everything is set right again. But can Harvey ever trust his wife again? Can Anne trust Bixby? Can Julie find happiness with Harvey? Maybe, this ending isn't as happy as the filmmakers want us to believe.

The film was remade as *Honeymoon for Three* (1941).

This Man Is Mine (1934)

Tony Dunlap (Irene Dunne) is happily married to Jim (Ralph Bellamy). But Jim's old flame, Fran Harper (Constance Cummings), returns to town after a divorce and has her mind set on winning back Jim. Tony is understandably shaken by the situation.

No one is more disgusted by Fran's shameless behavior than Fran's own brother, Jud McCrae (Charles Starrett). Jud and his wife Bee (Kay Johnson) offer steadfast moral support to Tony.

Tony: How can he put me through a thing like this? When I stop to think. . . I can't believe it.

Bee: Look here, Tony. You'd see Jim through pneumonia, typhoid or even something as loathsome as smallpox, wouldn't you?

Tony: Yes.

Bee: Well, Fran is a sort of cross between a tidal wave and a smallpox epidemic, but she'll pass.

Jim, though a dense fellow, comes to his senses and returns to his wife before the closing credits.

Change of Heart (1934)

Chris Thring (Charles Farrell) is heartbroken to be jilted by Madge Rountree (Ginger Rogers). He fails to see that Madge, who is vain, self-centered and fickle, would not make the dream wife that he imagines. Chris is stricken with one of those unnamed feverish movie illnesses. Catherine (Janet Gaynor), who has been in love with Chris since their college days, quickly sets out to cure him with three medical staples: a hot water bottle, clean linens, and milk. His condition stabilizes, but he requires additional care to pull through. A doctor arrives to conduct a complete examination. Ah, now we'll know what's wrong with him! The doctor's astute diagnosis: "You got a pretty sick man here." He prescribes one teaspoon every three hours of an unnamed syrupy mixture. Chris recognizes great virtue in Catherine as she nurses him back to health. Once he recovers, he asks her to marry him. The couple marries and sets out to begin their new life together. But, then, Catherine returns to take Chris back from Catherine. She has money now and is convinced that this will have a great influence on Chris.

Madge: Well, why can't I see Chris occasionally?

Catherine: Because he's my husband and I love him.

Madge: So do I. I wrote you that before you married him.

Catherine: I showed him your letter. You could have had him once. Why didn't you have him then?

Madge: Crazy, I guess.

Catherine: So I'm to step aside because you've changed your mind.

Madge: I could have had him. You nursed him and he turned to you. He was sick because he'd lost me.

Catherine: So that's the way you think I got him.

Madge: Please, Catherine, don't take that tone. I can't help it if I love him, can I? I want to do things for him. With all the money I have now I could help him in his profession. He oughtn't to be living in that slum.

Catherine: We're leaving this afternoon for the weekend. But I'm gonna tell you we'll miss that "slum". . . and be glad to be back to it. So you get him away from me if you can.

Madge: Is that a challenge?

Catherine: Yes.

Madge: Well, Chris is coming here to lunch. So, if he goes on that weekend, you win.

Chris is unmoved by Madge's pleas. Chris remains unwavering in his loyalty to his wife, not feeling he has the slightest obligation to his old flame.

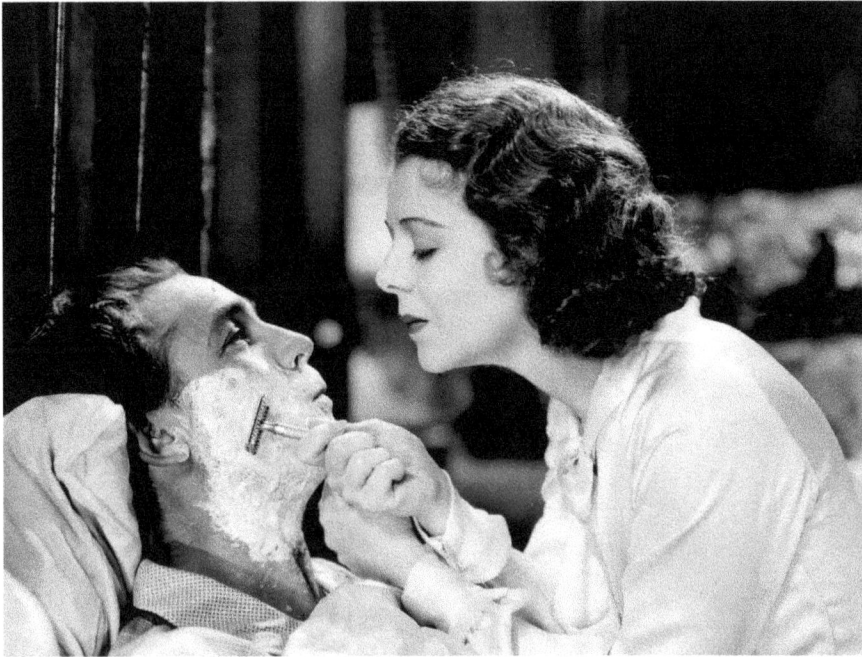

Charles Farrell and Janet Gaynor in *Change of Heart* (1934)

Come and Get It (1936)

The film was based on the 1935 novel "Come and Get It" by Edna Ferber.

The opening of the film is set in Wisconsin during the 1880s. Barney Glasgow (Edward Arnold), a lumberman, loves Lotta Morgan (Frances Farmer), a beautiful saloon singer. But he is an ambitious man and is willing to end their relationship to marry Emma Louise, the boss's daughter. Barney has great success as a partner in his father-in-law's lumber company, but he can never stop thinking about Lotta. Lotta marries Barney's friend, Swan Bostrom, and the couple has a daughter, also named Lotta. Twenty-three years later, Barney reunites with Swan. Lotta has died by now, but her daughter has grown to be the mirror image of her mother. Barney, enchanted by the young Lotta, becomes a generous benefactor, buying her fancy gifts, taking her out to elegant restaurants, putting her up in a fine suite, and paying for her education. It isn't an old lover who has come back into his life - the old lover, we know, is dead. But a lookalike has shown up and he has become obsessed with her. The film is, in this way, a forerunner to *Vertigo*. Barney's son, Richard (Joel McCrea), becomes embarrassed as his father's relationship with Lotta is stirring up gossip around town. He visits Lotta to ask her to stop seeing his father. Lotta assures him that nothing improper is going on between her and his father. Richard falls in love with the passionate and upstanding Lotta. Barney becomes irate when he learns that his son has become his rival for Lotta's affections. He is a possessive man. He is a man with large appetites. He wants to take control of Lotta as ruthlessly as he has taken control of entire forests in the operation of his lumber business. He will tolerate no competition. Blogger Melanie Novak wrote:

> He's infatuated with now-Lotta, confusing her with the woman he once knew. And confusing himself with the much younger man he once was. . . In the final moments of the film, father and son get into a physical altercation over Lotta. She breaks them apart, begging Richard to stop hitting his father, and calling Barney, "just an old man." The words land harder than any punch he's ever taken. He suddenly

sees himself through Lotta's eyes — not a legitimate rival for her affection, but a pathetic old pervert.[202]

The cause of Lotta's death is not revealed in the film. But Ferber was explicit in the novel on this point. Lotta is found brutally murdered in a gully. Her skull has been split open with an axe by an unknown assailant. This had been the fate of a real-life Lotta Morgan, who had been the inspiration for Ferber's enchanting saloon singer.

Walter Brennan, Edward Arnold and Frances Farmer in *Come and Get It* (1936)

Brief Ecstasy (1937)

Helen Bernardi (Linden Travers) and Jim Wyndham (Hugh Williams) fall in love after spending a night together. Jim must leave for business in India, but he becomes lovesick and cannot stop thinking about Helen. He sends her a cable with a marriage proposal, but a breeze from an open window blows the cable into a pile of trash being swept up by a cleaning woman.

Five years later, Jim returns to London and finds Helen married to a professor, Paul Bernardy (Paul Lukas). Sandra Brennan of AllMovie wrote: ". . . [W]hen Helen sees her old love, all her repressed passion rushes back. . . ."[203] Did a cruel fate cheat them? Is she the woman he was meant to be with? A viewer is likely to become as conflicted as the characters. The couple makes plans to run off together, but Jim comes to see that Paul is a good husband. He realizes that destroying this marriage that Paul and Helen built together would be wrong. So, he tells Helen goodbye and sadly leaves.

Second Honeymoon (1937)

Vicky (Loretta Young) has recently wed her second husband, Bob Benton (Lyle Talbot). The couple is enjoying a vacation in Miami Beach when Vicky walks out onto a ballroom terrace and is stunned to greet her former husband, Raoul McLiesh (Tyrone Power). Laura is excited to see Raoul at first. But she becomes more cautious after he tries to kiss her. Vicky invites Raoul to join Bob and their friends, Marcia (Claire Trevor) and Herbie (J. Edward Bromberg), for dinner. Raoul dominates the evening with his charm and tomfoolery. Laura later discusses her ex with Bob. Bob says, "He's the most amusing bird I've met in a long time. He's a nice guy, too. I can't see why you ever left him." This praise of the man she divorced upsets Laura. Bob responds, "I'm on vacation. There's room in my life for an egg like him." Laura insists that Raoul is a clown. She says:

He never does anything worthwhile. That's why I divorced him. He always made plans and always showed promise, but he never did anything. Just laughed and made jokes. Now, like tonight, we were all going along very nicely and quietly. Then Raoul appeared and suddenly everyone starting whooping and jumping around on one foot like suddenly they'd gone cuckoo.

Bob asks that they forget about him. Laura tells her husband:

Bob, I'm so glad you and I found each other. I despise living the way I did. He gave me no sense of security. I never knew where I stood from one second to the next. Everything was so uncertain. You have no idea the maddening life I had with him.

Bob is called away on business suddenly, which gives Vicky and Raoul an opportunity to spend time alone together. Despite what she told Bob, Vicky misses the excitement that Raoul brought into her life. She tells Raoul, "You're the only real thing that ever happened to me. Don't let me go this time, please don't!"

The film shares similarities with *Private Lives*, but it is a far more entertaining film.

Casablanca (1942)

Rick Blaine (Humphrey Bogart), a nightclub owner in Casablanca during World War II, is approached by a fugitive Resistance leader, Victor Laszlo (Paul Henreid), who needs to purchase stolen letters of transit to escape to America with his wife. Rick is shocked to learn that Laszlo's wife is Ilsa (Ingrid Bergman), a former flame who left him brokenhearted, confused and embittered a year and a half earlier. A flashback shows Rick and Ilsa enjoying a torrid love affair in Paris. Their time together abruptly ends when Paris is invaded by German troops. Ilsa gets news that Laszlo, who was believed to have died in a German concentration camp, is still alive and has escaped from the Gestapo. She is too ashamed to face Rick about her husband's sudden return and flees from Paris without explanation. The couple's reunion in Casablanca renews the love that they felt for one another in Paris. Ilsa no longer wants to leave for America with Laszlo. She wants to stay in Casablanca with Rick. But Rick realizes that losing Ilsa will destroy Laszlo and make it impossible for him to continue his vital mission as a freedom fighter. In a great act of self-sacrifice (one of the greatest in film history), Rick makes sure that Ilsa gets on the plane to America with Laszlo.

The Strange Love of Martha Ivers (1946)

Martha (Barbara Stanwyck), a young heiress who runs an expansive steel mill, is unhappily married to the town's district attorney, Walter O'Neil (Kirk Douglas). She is thrilled when her long-lost first love, Sam Masterson (Van Heflin), returns to town. She tells him that she was brokenhearted when he left and always wondered what happened to him. Sam is obviously happy to see his old childhood sweetheart, but his behavior is no more than friendly. Martha, in contrast, is seething with lust. She asks Sam to kiss her "for old times' sake." Sam kisses her but he is taken aback by the intensity of her kiss. She obviously wants to revive their old relationship, but he firmly resists her efforts. Martha admits that, for years, she dreamed of Sam returning. "And it came true," she says. "You're here." But he is quick to remind her: "So is Walter."

Barbara Stanwyck, Van Heflin and Kirk Douglas in *The Strange Love of Martha Ivers* (1946)

Walter understands the danger of having Martha's old lover show up. He tells her, "I've studied you all these years. A little girl in a cage waiting for someone to let her out." He quickly hires thugs to beat up Sam and drive him out of town. But Sam is defiant and won't let a few bruises and a bloody nose keep him away. He becomes more sympathetic of Martha when he learns that the heiress had to marry Walter to prevent Walter's father from exposing a dark secret from her past.

Again, two years after *Double Indemnity*, Stanwyck is playing a character with matricide on her mind. But Sam refuses to cooperate. He tells her, "Martha, you're sick... So sick that you don't even know the difference between right and wrong anymore."

If Winter Comes (1947)

The film is based on the 1921 novel "If Winter Comes" by Arthur Stuart-Menteth Hutchinson. The book was first adapted into a film in 1923.

Mark Sabre (Walter Pidgeon), a writer, is married to a cold, vicious woman, Mabel (Angela Lansbury). He is happy to learn that a former girlfriend, Nona Tybar (Deborah Kerr), is back in town. Their reunion, just as reunions do in films, resurrects old passions. Like Mark, Nona is unhappy in her own marriage.

Nona: Is it wrong for us to tell each other what's in our hearts?

Mark: Not if we keep it in our hearts and never let it hurt anyone.

Nona disagrees with Mark.

Nona: I've reached a point where I can't think of the rights of others anymore. I love you.

Mark: But you've got to face what it means. Once we take this step, there it is. . . for the rest of our lives. We'll have to live with the knowledge that we took our happiness at the expense of others. You know that.

Nona: Yes, I know that. I don't care what happens to the rest of my life as long I can spend it with you. They'll get over it, Mark, people do. You can't expect us to think more of what happens to them than to us. We're human.

An unmarried young woman, Effie Bright (Janet Leigh), is thrown out of her parents' home when her father learns that she has become pregnant. Mark takes her into his home, which begins gossip that he is the baby's father. The scandal causes him to be fired from a teaching job and leads Mabel to file for divorce, naming Effie as a co-respondent. Effie is reluctant to name the real father of her baby. She is distressed that she has not received a letter from the baby's father, who has gone into military service, and her involvement in the divorce scandal increases her distress even more. She commits suicide by drinking poison. Mark finds himself under attack at an inquest over Effie's death.

Upon his return home, Mark finds a letter that Effie left for him. In the letter, Effie reveals that the father of her baby was Harold Twyning. This is ironic as Harold's father was one of the self-righteous school officials who fired Mark. Mark cannot wait to show Mr. Twyning the letter, but he finds the man slumped over his desk sobbing. He looks up at Mark. "Killed. . .," he says, "my boy. . . my boy Harold." Mark immediately burns the letter in a fireplace.

In the final scene, Mark and Nona make plans for a new life together.

Singapore (1947)

A twist on the old lover returns premise can be found in *Singapore*. The film begins in Singapore during 1942. A marriage ceremony is suddenly interrupted by an attack by Japanese bombers. The groom, Matt Gordon (Fred MacMurray), rushes back to his hotel to retrieve a valuable stash of pearls while the bride, Linda Grahame (Ava Gardner), remains sheltered inside the chapel. Matt cannot find Linda when he returns. It turns out that Linda has been hospitalized for injuries suffered as the chapel collapsed around her. She awakens with amnesia, remembering nothing about her intended marriage. She meets Michael Van Leyden (Roland Culver), who has also been hospitalized for injuries. Linda and Michael fall in love and marry. In the meantime, Matt assumes that Linda died and leaves Singapore. He returns five years later and is shocked to find that Linda is alive and has no idea who he is. Matt is sure if Linda regains her memory she will realize that she belongs with him. Michael strenuously disagrees.

Michael: We were married. We built a whole new life. She's happy and I want her to remain that way.

Matt: How can she be happy if she doesn't remember the greater part of her life? Maybe the best part. What kind of happiness is that?

Michael: I don't think I made myself clear, Mr. Gordon. I don't care to know about my wife's past.

Matt: Well maybe you don't, but I do. I think it's up to her to decide what part of her life she wants to remember.

Matt treasures a very special ring that Linda gave him. The ring is inscribed, "One Life, One Love." Karen finds that she has feelings for Matt. Her memory suddenly comes back to her. She remembers everything about her relationship with Matt and wants to go away with him, but she believes that she has a duty to stay with Michael. Michael admits to Linda that he learned about Michael years earlier and kept this information from her. He also refused treatment that would likely have allowed her to regain her memory. He says, "I could have helped you, but I didn't." He believes that he did not act honorably as a husband and she is now under no obligation to respect their marital vows.

Michael is polite and friendly as he tells Karen of his deception. But let us not be fooled by his demeanor and take what he did lightly. He knew who wife was and refused to tell her. Kat Ellinger said in the Blu-ray commentary that he, in effect, "kept. . . ownership of [his wife's] identity."[204] Ellinger rightly called this "deeply sinister, deeply sinister."[205] Michael's confession frees Karen to walk out of her marriage and leave the country with her beloved Matt.

Amnesia played a similar role in *Random Harvest* (1942). A soldier, Charles Rainer (Ronald Colman), suffers amnesia from a war injury. He has no idea who he is or where he came from. He marries a beautiful and caring music hall singer, Paula (Greta Garson), who helps him to rebuild his life. But his old memories come back while he is on a business trip and he forgets everything about his marriage. He returns to the Rainer family estate and assumes control of the family business. He eventually becomes engaged to his sister's stepdaughter, Kitty (Susan Peters). But will he remember Paula before he walks down the aisle?

Cast Away (2000) shares plot elements with *Singapore*. A man presumed dead in a plane crash returns home after four years and finds that his onetime fianceé is now married and has a daughter. The couple is tempted to run off together, but think better of it and sadly part.

The Passionate Friends (1949)

Mary Justin (Ann Todd) is frightened by the passion that she feels for her boyfriend, Professor Steven Stratton (Trevor Howard). She rejects the idea that two people in love should feel as if they "belong to each other." She deeply fears the binding, all-consuming power of romantic passion.

Mary: I shall never love anyone as much as I love you.

Steven: Then why won't you marry me?

Mary: Oh, Steven. I don't quite know. Even if I did, I don't think you could possibly understand.

Steven: If two people really love each other, and want to be together, they want to belong to each other.

Mary: Steven, I want to belong to myself.

Steven: Then your life will be a failure.

It thunders suddenly outside. Mary sobs. She says, "Dearest Steven, don't be angry with me. I can't help myself. Why can't there be love without this clutching and this gripping? This. . ."

In the end, Mary sees passion and romance as too messy, too dangerous and too disorderly for her. She prefers to marry the mildly affectionate Howard Justin (Claude Rains), who offers her comfort, stability and security.

Ann Todd and Trevor Howard in *The Passionate Friends* (1949)

Years later, Mary and Steven meet again at a New Year's Eve party. They continue to see each other after the party. Mary does not bother to hide their meetings from Howard as, in her mind, she and Steven are no more than friends. At first, Howard pretends not to be upset by his wife socializing with Steven. But he is rightfully concerned that old feelings will reassert themselves. In time, just as Howard expects, these friendly meetings grow into something more. Mary commits herself to Steven. "I shall belong to you," she says. Howard's attitude changes when Mary pretends to go to the theatre with Steven and he finds that she left behind the theatre tickets. Steven tries to persuade Mary to leave Howard. He confronts Howard, asking that he let Mary divorce him so that the two of them can be together. Howard claims to know Mary better than Steven. He says that Mary is happy with the freedom and tranquility of their marriage and all Steven is doing by remaining in her life is creating turmoil for Mary.

Disgustipated of Letterboxd wrote:

On an interesting side note, the film goes to great lengths to contrast Howard and Steven. It begins right at the beginning with Howard sitting in the rarefied air of an isolated box seat as Steven is whirling about the chaos of the party-goers. At home, Howard is surrounded by bookshelves of tidy books in ordered volumes, whereas Steven is surrounded by a mess of books, some of them even owned by others. Howard is a banker dictating correspondence with clarity and precision. Steven is a biology professor up to the elbows in the messy, squidginess of life. The insistent apposite presentation of each competing lover ends up becoming quite amusing.[206]

Ann Todd, Claude Rains and Trevor Howard in *The Passionate Friends* (1949)

Mary and Steven do not see each other again until many years later during a holiday in the Swiss Alps. Howard arrives, having finished work at home, and sees the couple disembarking on a boat together. Assuming the two are having an affair, he becomes enraged and resolves to finally file for divorce. Mary insists that nothing happened with them at the Swiss hotel and he is wrong to be going through with the divorce. Howard is having none of it. He says:

I knew you didn't marry me because you loved me. But because you liked me. And the money and the position that went with me. I didn't mind that. Because I liked those things too and I thought we'd enjoy them together. I didn't expect love from you. Or even great affection. I'd have been well satisfied with kindness and loyalty. You gave me love and kindness and loyalty. But it was the love you'd give a dog. And the kindness you'd give a beggar. And the loyalty of a bad servant. Perhaps it's my fault. It probably is. I wanted this marriage, but now I don't. So I'm getting rid of it - with the rest of the things I don't want. You were my wife. And you made me hate and despise myself and I don't want you anymore. Do you understand? I don't want anything from you. I don't even want your gratitude. I just want to be left in peace. Now get out!

Distraught, Mary walks to the edge of a train platform with the intent of jumping in front of the oncoming train. Before she can step further, a man grabs her around the waist and pulls her away. It is Howard. Interestingly, Mary chose to kill herself in the same manner as Anna Karenina.

Prison Warden (1949)

Victor Burnell (Warner Baxter) is appointed by the governor to reform a troubled state prison. His wife Elisa (Anna Lee) is delighted to learn that one of the inmates is a former lover, Albert Gardner (Harlan Warde). She arranges for Gardner to be her personal chauffeur, which allows the couple to carry on an affair.

Untamed (1955)

IMDb: "In 1847, the Irish potato famine forces Katie O'Neill and her husband to emigrate to a troubled South Africa where Katie runs into an old flame."[207]

A Summer Place (1959)

Rotten Tomatoes: "[W]ealthy Ken Jorgenson (Richard Egan). . . brings his wife (Constance Ford) and teenage daughter, Molly (Sandra Dee), to the Maine vacation spot where he worked as a middle-class youth. When Ken reunites with his former flame, the now-married Sylvia (Dorothy McGuire), it sparks a passionate tryst."[208] The couple consummates their relationship in a boat house.

Dona Flor and Her Two Husbands (1976)

The film is based on a bestselling novel by Jorge Amado.

Flor (Sônia Braga) is in a troubled marriage with Vadinho (José Wilker). Vadinho is wicked husband. He refuses to work, beats Flor to get his way, and spends Flor's savings at casinos and brothels. Flor's friends and neighbors see Vadinho as a contemptible scoundrel. But Flor still loves him as she is thrilled by his licentious charm. Flor doesn't care that she has to live by his strict demands and irresponsible behavior. She desperately needs him. According to the novel, she cannot live without his "warmth, "gaiety" and "mad presence."[209]

Vadinho's dissolute life catches up to him. He dies from a heart attack while dancing wildly at a street festival.

Flor remarries. Her new husband, Teodoro (Mauro Mendonça), is a successful pharmacist. He is, in every way, the opposite of Vadinho. He is an elegant gentleman who treats Flor with great respect. But, unfortunately, he is dull in the bedroom.

Flor thinks of Vadinho during private contemplation in church. She prays to St. Clare for sexual fulfillment in her marital bed. On her return home, Flor is shocked to find a lively and naked Vadinho in her bed. He explains that she summoned his spirit from the afterlife. He is eager to have sex with Flor, but she refuses to break her marital vows to Teodoro. Regardless of her opposition, Vadinho continually attempts to seduce her. He tells her that her new husband will never be able to satisfy her. He sits cross-legged atop a wardrobe laughing demonically at Teodoro's slow and awkward lovemaking.

Vadinho is more mellow than he was in life. He is not dictatorial or violent. But he still has an ardent interest in the gaming rooms. He finds an old friend, Mirandão (Nelson Xavier), and uses his otherworldly influence to control Mirandão's betting at the casino. The casino owner is astounded by Mirandão's sudden run of luck.

Flor arranges for a witch to put Vadinho's soul to rest before she loses her resistance to his sexual advances. From the novel: "Vadinho was beleaguering the fortress which Dona Flor had assured him was invincible, undermining walls of dignity and modesty. In a relentless advance, in a stubborn assault, he was conquering the field hour by hour."[210] Supernatural forces amass against Vadinho, determined to put his rebellious spirit back into his grave. But Flor panics while Vadinho is fading from her grasp. She screams. It is a primal scream that rises from her soul. From the novel: "Her cry of love outdid Yansá's cry of death."[211] Vadinho returns and engages in erotic sex with Flor.

José Wilker, Sônia Braga and Mauro Mendonça in *Dona Flor and Her Two Husbands* (1976)

The film ends with a crowd leaving church after Sunday mass. Among the crowd is Flor, who holds Teodoro by one arm and Vadinho by the other arm. She has a blissful smile. Vandino is shamelessly naked as usual, but of course the other churchgoers cannot see him. He reaches behind Flor and grabs her ass, which is the final image of the film.

So, a married woman strays from her second husband to have sex with the ghost of her dead first husband. Is sex with a ghost adultery? But this really isn't a story about ghosts. In the 550-page novel, the ghost doesn't turn up until page 425. Similarly, the ghost doesn't appear until late in the film. The story is truly about the choice that some women have to make between sexual excitement and domestic security. It's much like *A Lost Lady*, in which Barbara Stanwyck had to chose between the rascally Ricardo Cortez and the gentlemanly Frank Morgan. The author emphasizes Vandino as a symbol of lust with his nakedness.

The Woman Next Door (1981)

The original French title: *La Femme d'à côté*

The film is François Truffaut's next to last film. Philippe and Mathilde Bauchard (Henri Garcin and Fanny Ardant) move into a new community. Mathilde is surprised that her neighbor is an old lover, Bernard

Coudray (Gérard Depardieu). Bernard has a stable marriage with Arlette (Michèle Baumgartner). But, despite their spouses, Bernard and Mathilde reignite their old passions. The pair soon become obsessed with each other. Mathilde finds it disturbing the way that Bernard wildly vacillates between wanting to be with her and wanting to remain faithful to his wife. She tries to keep away from him, but she finds that she needs him too much. When their relationship is exposed, Bernard chose to remain with his wife. He does everything he can to avoid Mathilde, which seriously upsets her. After collapsing at a tennis club, she is hospitalized for depression. Upon her release, she finds that Philippe has sold their home and moved to a new neighborhood. She returns to her old home that night. Bernard hears noises coming from the home and goes to investigate. He sees Mathilde in the shadows. The couple has sex. After they finish, Mathilde slips a gun out of her handbag and fires a single shot into Bernard's head. She then turns the gun on herself and fires. Truffaut wrote the part of Mathilde specifically for Ardant. He said that he saw in the actress "a taste of secrecy, a wild side, a touch of savagery and, above all, something vibrant."[212]

Gérard Depardieu and Fanny Ardant in *The Woman Next Door* (1981)

The Big Chill (1983)

A group of college friends reunite for a friend's funeral. Karen Bowens (JoBeth Williams), who is dissatisfied with her marriage, confesses to her old classmate Sam Weber (Tom Berenger) that she loves him. Sam hesitates to become involved with Karen, but the pair eventually have sex.

Violets Are Blue (1986)

Henry Squires (Kevin Kline) is thrilled when an old high school sweetheart, Gussie Sawyer (Sissy Spacek), returns to town. Gussie left their quiet seaside town to pursue a career as a globetrotting photojournalist while Henry remained in town to manage the local newspaper. Henry invites Gussie to his home for dinner. He introduces her to his wife, Ruth (Bonnie Bedelia), and son, Addy (Jim Standiford). Then, while Henry is walking Gussie home, they stop to passionately kiss. moonspinner55 of IMDb wrote, "The screenplay is a limp, squashy mess - a compendium of Woman's Picture clichés - and Kevin Kline doesn't have much to do but stare at others thoughtfully or look conflicted."[213] The overused premise had more appeal to Roger Ebert. Ebert wrote. "You meet the person you loved when you were 17, and now you are 33, and a lot of your life's history has been written. And yet, as your eyes meet, your last kiss is as clear as yesterday."[214]

The Glory and Misery of Human Life (1988)

The original Finnish title is *Ihmiselon ihanuus ja kurjuus*

Young lovers, Anna (Liisamaija Laaksonen) and Martti Hongisto (Lasse Pöysti), go their separate ways. Several decades later, Martti is married with five children. He copes with disappointment and frustration by drinking heavily and reminiscing about his youth. One day, he decides to find Anna, who is now a widow.

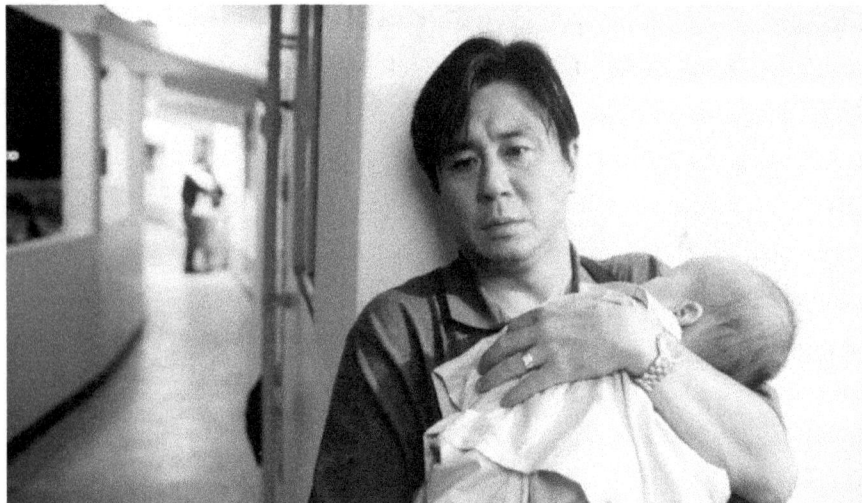

Choi Min-ski in *Happy End* (1999)

Happy End (1999)

The original South Korean title: *Haepi endeu*

Choi Bora (Jeon Do-yeon) has become frustrated with her husband, Seo Min-ki (Choi Min-ski), who lost his job and seems uninterested in finding a new one. She meets an old lover, Kim Il-beom (Joo Jin-mo), and they renew their past romance. Lying beside Il-beom, she says, "I love it when I come here. I feel so free." She is unaware that Min-ki has become suspicious and has been following her. Bora can see that Min-ki has become depressed and tries to comfort him. She likely senses that he knows about the affair. But, despite her concerns, she has a compulsion to keep seeing Il-beom. One day, she leaves her baby home alone as she rushes off to meet Bora. This neglect of their child is finally enough to unhinge Min-ki. He uses a knife he stole from Il-beom's apartment to stab her repeatedly. Il-beom is charged for Bora's murder. Min-ki doesn't care what happens to Il-beom. He focuses his attention on caring for his child, though he continues to feel grief remembering Bora. The final scene shows Bora standing on the balcony of her apartment. A yellow sky lantern, the type that mourners launch into the sky during a funeral procession, floats up to her. She reaches out to touch it, but it drifts away from her. Fans of the film have speculated about this ending. Is it a flashback that foresees Bora's death? Or, is Bora a ghost preparing to leave for the afterlife?

Forever Lulu (2000)

Ben Clifton (Patrick Swayze) is visited by an old girlfriend, Lulu McAfee (Melanie Griffith), who escaped from a mental health facility. He is ready to phone the authorities, but she tells him that she got pregnant before they broke up and they have a teenage son in Wisconsin. He doesn't know if she's telling the truth, but he joins her on her trip. Ben's wife, Claire Clifton (Penelope Ann Miller), doesn't trust her husband being on a road trip with his old girlfriend. She catches up with them and joins them on their journey. Though Lulu stirs up old feelings, Ben returns home with Claire in the end.

The Last Mistress (2007)

The original French title: *Une vieille maîtresse* (literally "An old mistress")

The Last Mistress involves yet another old lover who reappears and upends a marriage. It involves yet another obsessive love affair. The film is unique only in unfavorable ways. It indulges in cruelty, perversity and ugliness. In the end, it is mostly empty and unpleasant.

Funny People (2009)

George (Adam Sandler), who is dying from leukemia, seeks out an old girlfriend, Laura (Leslie Mann), who is now married. He enjoys being with Laura again. When he learns that his leukemia is in remission, he becomes determined to take Laura away from her husband, Clarke (Eric Bana). He visits Laura at her home while Clarke is away on business. His assistant, Ira Wright (Seth Rogen), keeps her daughters entertained while he sneaks off with Laura to have sex. Ira is a voice of morality. He is appalled that George would have sex with a mother and wife.

George: I can't leave her alone here. I have to save her.

Ira: Save her from her beautiful house and lovely husband and delightful kids? You said nothing was going on between you two. The dog could tell that you banged her. And I'm getting nauseous and sweaty. I can't. . .

Ira does not give up. He returns to the subject again. But George is now better prepared to defend himself. He says:

George: Ira, this is deep shit. People get divorced. They make mistakes, they change their lives. It's not that big of a deal. She's married to an asshole. I don't know what to tell you, man. Am I not allowed to be happy or something? I've been living alone and alone and alone. That's my life. This is the only girl I've ever loved and I'm not supposed to do anything about this? When am I supposed to be happy? Why does everyone else get to be happy?

Ira: Look, George, I'm just gonna tell you this, as a friend. From where I'm sitting it seems like your happiness might be coming at the cost of destroying this family.

Ira is right. George is a selfish jerk.

Clarke returns home and finds out that Laura was fooling around with George. Laura assures Clarke that they didn't have sex. She tells him, "He just went down on me." George becomes annoyed.

George: Tell him. Tell him. Is it me or him?

Laura: Him.

George: What? Come on! Are you serious?

Laura: He's my husband. We have a family. I love him.

Clark assumes that divine forces have punished him for having once gotten a hand job at a massage parlor.

Regrets (2009)

The original French title: *Les regrets*

Mathieu Liévan (Yvan Attal), a Paris architect, returns to his rural hometown to visit his dying mother. He is getting into his car when he notices Maya (Valeria Bruni Tedeshi), an old girlfriend that he hasn't seen for fifteen years. He is unable to move, having fallen into a rapturous stupor. Mathieu and Maya are both married now, but they seem to be brought together by a force they can't resist. Film critic Mick LaSalle wrote, "What follows is ninety minutes of on-screen agony and ecstasy. . . as the two decide to run off together (to Barcelona), then one backs off, and then years pass, they meet again, and the whole cycle threatens to repeat once more."[215]

Other filmmakers have played with the idea of old obsessions being triggered by a glimpse of a lost love. It took only a glimpse to persuade Jean Dujardin to chase after a former girlfriend without a thought of his marriage in *A View of Love* (2010). It took only a glimpse to persuade Vincent Cassel to neglect his fiancée in a wild pursuit of a former love in *The Apartment* (1996). (*A View of Love*'s wife and *The Apartment*'s fiancée are both curiously played by Sandrine Kiberlain).

Tamara Drewe (2010)

Tamara Drewe (Gemma Arterton) grows up in a small town located near a writer's colony. As a teenager, she is fascinated with the writers and develops a crush on Nicholas Hardiment (Roger Allam), a best-selling crime novelist who is the head of the colony. Hardiment bluntly rejects Tamara's advances. It isn't that Hardiment has ever been faithful to his wife, Beth (Tamsin Greig). He simply becomes fixated on Tamara's unpleasantly bulbous nose. Years later, Tamara returns to town to refurbish a home left to her by her recently deceased mother. She is now a beautiful young woman, largely due to a radical rhinoplasty that shaved away a large portion of cartilage. She has pursued her own writing career, having become a successful newspaper columnist. Hardiment is now eager to enter into an affair with Tamara. The couple quickly jumps into bed together. But Tamara eventually falls in love with Andy Cobb (Luke Evans), a workman at her home. It hurts Hardiment's ego to now be rebuffed by Tamara. Even worse, though, his own wife has lost interest in him. Hardiment becomes outraged to learn that Beth is having an affair with a fellow writer, Glen McCreavy (Bill Camp). He confronts Glen in an open field for a brawl, but he ends up being crushed to death in a cattle stampede.

Gemma Arterton in *Tamara Drewe* (2010)

The Red Thread (2016)

The original Argentina title: *El Hilo Rojo*

Manuel (Benjamín Vicuña) becomes enamored of a stewardess, Abril (China Suárez), during a flight. The young lovers split apart after a fling in Chile. They meet again seven years later. Though they both married now, Manuel and Abril maintain strong feelings for one another. The film promotes the idea that some lovers are destined to be together, with a great celestial matchmaker keeping the lovers attached with a magical red thread that no one can break.

Both Sides of the Blade (2022)

The original French title: *Avec amour et acharnement*

It's that same story yet again. A married woman is thrown into a tizzy by the reappearance of an old lover. Shelia O'Malley of RogerEbert.com wrote, "Sara [Juliette Binoche] is completely undone by this one glance. It opens up an abyss in her life, an abyss that didn't seem to exist only a day before."[216] The filmmaker offers nothing new on the subject. The film turns out, in the end, to be flat and meaningless. derek-duerden of

IMDb wrote, "What does this woman actually want?. . . Did Francois [Grégoire Colin] ever love her, or is he just welcoming the chance to get her back into bed??? I never really found out any of this and, frankly, by the end I decided I didn't care."[217]

Tonight You're Sleeping with Me (2023)

Nina (Roma Gasiorowska) is a journalist. She has two young daughters with her husband, Maciek (Wojciech Zielinski). Nina meets up again with an old boyfriend, Janek (Maciej Musial). The couple still has feelings for one another. Maciek picks a bad time to go hiking in Iceland. During his absence, Nina embarks on an affair with Janek. What does he have that her husband doesn't have? John Serba of Decider pointed out that Janek is impressive with his "tousled hair and rakish earring."[218] Nina comes across as immature. Her relationship with Janek is purely sexual. She wishes that they could build a cabin in the woods just for themselves. She says that they can live on sex and root vegetables. But she feels the strain of guilt while sneaking around with Janek. Serba wrote, "A real Sophie's Choice situation here. It's clear that Nina is one of the archetypal Women Who Wants To Have It All But Ends Up Struggling With All Of It, but that's the beginning and end of her character. She mopes and vacillates and stares into her manicured backyard. . ."[219] She ends the relationship, but she cannot stay away from Janek for long. She sobs to her mother (Ewa Wencel) about Janek. Her mother is quick to advise her to end the affair.

> Nina: Mom, I've fallen in love.
>
> Mother: Then you fall out of it!
>
> Nina: No.
>
> Mother: It won't work.
>
> Nina: I can't live without him.
>
> Mother: Then wait it out. You just have to wait this feeling out.

Nina fails to turn off her phone after speaking with Maciek. So, Maciek can hear her ecstatic moans as she returns to making love with Janek. Maciek sobs in deep anguish when he later talks on the phone with Nina. The intensity of his emotions terrifies her. It is while climbing down into a crevice to rescue a hiker that Maciek falls and suffers serious injuries. He is taken to a hospital, where he remains in a coma for days. Nina is wracked with guilt as she stays around the hospital waiting for the doctor's updates. Maciek finally reawakens and the couple reconciles.

Chapter Seven:
The Abusive Husband

Several films show that a husband who physically or emotionally abuses his wife can drive his wife into arms of a kinder man. Emotional abuse involves attempts to frighten, control, or isolate another person. This type of abuse doesn't involve physical violence, though it might involve threats of physical violence.

But emotional abuse can come in other forms, too. Let us take, for instance, *Things to Come* (2016). Nathalie Chazeaux (Isabelle Huppert) is blindsided when her husband, Heinz (André Marcon), tells her that he's leaving her for another woman.

Heinz: I must tell you. I met someone.

Nathalie: And why tell me? Couldn't keep it a secret?

Heinz: I'm moving in with her.

Nathalie: What? Are you sure?

Heinz: I'm sure.

Nathalie: Since when?

Heinz: A while.

Nathalie: A student? Who, then?

Heinz: You don't know her.

Nathalie: I thought you'd love me forever. I'm a goddamn idiot!

Heinz: I'll always love you. You know it.

Nathalie (*disgusted*): Come on.

The timing of this revelation couldn't be worse. Lately, Nathalie has lost a book deal and has had to cope with her mother becoming ill. It is cruel for Heinz to abandon his wife at this time.

The Breaking Point (1921)

Ruth Marshall (Bessie Barriscales) escapes poverty by marrying Richard Janeway (Walter McGrail), a drunken playboy who is obsessed with wild parties and wild women. Richard spends their honeymoon with an old girlfriend, Lucia Deeping (Ethel Grey Terry). Ruth gives birth while Richard is out carousing. One night, Ruth becomes infuriated when Richard brings their daughter down to a party to dance for his guests. Richard responds by ordering her to leave his house. Ruth loses control after Richard threatens to raise their daughter with Lucia. She attacks him and kills him. But a sympathetic family physician, Dr. Hillyer (Winter Hall), arranges the scene to make Richard's death look like a suicide.

Millie (1931)

A filmmaker has to be careful with an adultery story. He can, if he fears losing sympathy for his lovers, keep the wronged spouse in the shadows so that the viewers are unable to witness their suffering. But adultery does cause a great deal of suffering, which is front and center in films like *Millie*.

Stacey Laura Lloyd wrote in "The Real Reasons Why Men Cheat":

Cheating can be extremely detrimental and damaging to a relationship, as it can break down the trust, honesty, and respect that are at the core of any successful and long-term relationship.[220]

Esther Perel wrote in the article "Why Happy People Cheat":

In contemporary discourse in the United States, affairs are primarily described in terms of the damage caused. Generally, there is much concern for the agony suffered by the betrayed. And agony it is — infidelity today isn't just a violation of trust; it's a shattering of the grand ambition of romantic love. It is a shock that makes us question our past, our future, and even our very identity. Indeed, the maelstrom of emotions unleashed in the wake of an affair can be so overwhelming that many psychologists turn to the field of trauma to explain the symptoms: obsessive rumination, hypervigilance, numbness and dissociation, inexplicable rages, uncontrollable panic.[221]

The lead character of *Millie* is certainly caught in a maelstrom of emotions. Let's take a look at her story.

Millie (Helen Twelvetrees) is invited by an old friend, Angie Wickerstaff (Joan Blondell), to join her for drinks at a nightclub. Millie is shocked to discover her husband Jack (James Hall) at the club with another woman. She demands to know who this woman is. The woman defiantly confronts Millie. "Well," she says, "I'm his sweetheart. That's what I am. And you don't mean a thing to him." A divorce is inevitable.

Millie becomes bitter after the experience. Unable to trust men, she expects nothing but a good time from a lover and is willing to drift freely from one romance to another. But then she meets Tommy Rock (Robert Ames). She refuses to marry Tommy despite her great love for him. She says, "I tried it once and it didn't work out. Now I wouldn't marry the best man living. And you are that to me. But I'll stick to you, Tommy."

Millie works hard running a tobacco shop in a hotel lobby. She is eventually promoted by hotel management to concessions manager. This assures her independence. But men still believes that she needs a man in her life. She is relentlessly pursued by a lascivious banker, Jimmy Damier (John Haliday). As he tries to get Millie to come to his home, Jimmy tells her, "I want you to see my mandarin robes." She doesn't seriously consider the offer. She asks, "Don't you think you should put them in a museum for everyone to see?" He grins lasciviously. "No," he grins, "I keep those for people I like."

Millie is heartbroken to learn that Tommy has cheated on her. This sets her on a downward spiral as she avoids commitments with men and endeavors to dampen her pain with alcohol.

Years pass. Millie has physically deteriorated due to heavy drinking. She becomes upset to hear that Damier has taken her 16-year-old daughter Connie (Anita Louise) to the theatre. She warns Damier to stay away from her daughter.

Millie: If you hurt my baby, I'll. . . I'll stop at nothing.

Damier: Oh, what rot.

Millie: Oh, please, Jim, won't you do this for me? It's only for my peace of mind. It's not much I'm asking. Only to keep away from my little girl.

Damier: Sure, sure. If you're so wrought up about it, all right.

But Damier doesn't keep his word. Mike (Charles Delaney), Damier's chauffeur, tips off Millie that Damier has taken Connie to his lodge in the country. Millie arrives at the lodge to confront Damier. Damier insists that Connie is not with him and he grabs hold of Millie to force her outside. Her daughter, dressed in a mandarin robe, comes out of a bedroom to check out the commotion. Millie, distraught, pulls out a gun and shoots Damier.

Millie gets her daughter to leave before the police arrive. She goes to trial for first-degree murder, but she refuses to say the reason that she shot Daimer as it would mean getting her daughter involved in the scandal. Tommy, who still loves Millie, works with his friends to ferret out the truth and pass it on to Millie's attorney.

The defense attorney explains, "We mean, your honor, to prove that Millicent Blake went to the lodge that night and shot Jimmy Dammier not from jealousy, but to rescue her innocent 16-year-old daughter from this blackguard, who had lured her there under such circumstances." Millie is acquitted based on tearful testimony from Connie.

A woman embittered by her husband's affair also responds by sleeping around with lots of men in *The Divorcee* (1930). A woman embittered by her husband's affair approaches the situation with a great deal more reason, morality and self-respect in *An Unmarried Woman* (1978). *Mildred Pierce* (1945) highlights a woman's admirable efforts to rebuild her life after getting rid of a cheating husband. Mildred achieves self-sufficiency by opening a glitzy new restaurant. Other films, including *Something to Talk About* (1995) and *Meet Bill* (2007), examine a person's efforts to reclaim their life after leaving a two-timing spouse. We will explore those films later in this chapter.

Unfaithful (1931)

Fay (Ruth Chatterton) has been married to Ronald Killkerry (Paul Cavanagh), a well-regarded British nobleman, for a blissful four months. But her mood sours once she learns that her husband has a mistress hidden away. She pleads with Ronald to discuss the matter with her honestly, but he acts sly and cavalier and calls her "silly." His continued deceit is more than she can tolerate. She tells him, "Something that I believed in crashed. You won't know me, Ronnie, from now on." He taunts her wickedly when she threatens to divorce him. He reveals to her that his mistress is her brother's wife, Gemma (Juliette Compton). Her brother, Terry (Donald Cook), is known to be excitable. Fay is worried that Terry will become unbalanced and violent if the affair is revealed in the divorce proceedings. She remains married and she remains silent.

The next stage of the story is simply but ideally explained by Hafer:

. . . Fay decides to. . . live a gay lifestyle… with lots of men and excitement. Soon she meets an artist, Carl (Paul Lukas), and the two fall in love.[222]

Carl proposes that they marry, but she refuses. But it is at this point that fate intervenes. Ronald and Gemma, out on a date, get into a car crash. Ronald dies at the scene and Gemma is rushed to the hospital. Fay creates a story to cover up for Gemma. Gemma, according to Fay's story, was going with Ronald to get Fay away from Carl. So, in this fiction, Ronald becomes the wronged husband, Gemma becomes the caring sister-in-law, and Fay becomes the wayward wife. AFI notes: "The lie maintains society's finest opinion of Ronald and its worst opinion of Fay. . .."[223] But Fay is prepared to weather the scandal knowing that she can finally be with Carl.

The Impassive Footman (1932)

John Marwood (Allan Jeayes), a mean-spirited and jittery hypochondriac, has made life miserable for his wife, Grace (Betty Stockfeld). Grace accompanies John on a cruise in the hope that the rest will improve his health. She falls in love with the ship's handsome young medical officer, Dr. Bryan Daventry (Owen Nares). The couple maintains their relationship for several years while abstaining from sex. Marwood genuinely falls ill with a heart disorder and requires a delicate surgical procedure that only Daventry can perform. He is aware that Grace and Daventry are in love. He tells his footman, Simpson (George Curzon), that he wants him to present a letter to his attorney if he should die during the procedure. The letter makes it clear that Daventry is his wife's lover, which gives him a perfect motive to botch the surgery. In this way, the vindictive man can accuse the doctor of murder and bring about his downfall from beyond the grave. Marwood survives the surgery, but it turns out that Simpson has been concealing his true identity and harbors a fatal grudge against Marwood. He finally confronts Marwood and threatens to kill him, which causes his employer to have a heart attack and die. Simpson destroys Marwood's letter before he exits the home.

No Other Woman (1933)

Anna Stanley (Irene Dunne) encourages her steelworker husband Jim (Charles Bickford) to open a dyeworks, which becomes a great success. Anna has brought her husband to the top of the business world only to have him become arrogant and take a great interest in the gold diggers that now flock around him. One particular woman, Margot (Gwili Andre), holds his interest.

lbbrooks3 of IMDb wrote:

> In yet just one more of the several "weepies" she churned out under contract during the early phase of her film career, Irene Dunne still manages to shine as Charles Bickford's unappreciated, abandoned and ultimately besmirched spouse. [224]

The Prizefighter and The Lady (1933)

Big-headedness is a malady that can often bring on cheating.

Steve Morgan (Max Baer), a boxer, and Belle Mercer (Myrna Loy), a nightclub singer, meet in a sensational fashion. Steve is doing roadwork when Belle coming speeding down the road in her roadster and nearly knocks him down. Instead, she crashes her car into a ditch. Steve runs to wrecked car and carries her to safety. Can a near road fatality be classified as a "meet cute" scene? It isn't long before the couple falls in love and marries.

Women flock to the championship contender. A pretty socialite visits him every day to watch him train. She winks at him and says, "I like the scenery." She tells him that it gave her goosebumps to see him knock down his sparring partner. They set a date to swim together the next morning. Another socialite ogles him at the ringside. She tells her friend, "I wouldn't mind having him on a pedestal in my front yard." The temptations are more than he can handle. Belle becomes upset to find him dallying with other women. She warns him that she will leave him if he ever cheats on her again. Between bouts, Steve appears in a musical revue. Belle catches a woman hiding in his dressing room and resolves to divorce him.

Max Baer in *The Prizefighter and The Lady* (1933)

Steve is too busy going to parties to train properly. He becomes angry with his manager, The Professor (Walter Huston), for lecturing him. He slaps The Professor, who immediately quits. Belle is hired back as a nightclub singer by Willie Ryan (Otto Kruger), who was Belle's boyfriend before she met Steve. Ryan still loves Belle and is sad to see her devastated by the divorce. He uses his influence to get Steve a championship match, knowing that Steve is out of shape and is bound to be humiliated in front of a worldwide audience. Steve takes a bad beating in the early rounds, but Belle and The Professor feel sorry for him. His old manager climbs into his corner to coach him. He lets him know that Belle is "in back of [him] every minute." Steve rallies and is able to fight to a draw.

The Personality Kid (1934)

> *The Personality Kid* is similar to *The Prizefighter and The Lady*.
> Erickson wrote:

> . . . [A]rrogant prizefighter Ritzy (Pat O'Brien) is quite a piece of work, wearing a derby hat in the ring and dancing an Irish jig whenever he scores a knockout. Once he's risen to the top of his profession, Ritzy becomes even more insufferable, forsaking his faithful manager-wife Joan (Glenda Farrell) in favor of society artist Patricia (Claire Dodd).

Ritzy's champion status makes him arrogant. He now believes that someone as important as himself doesn't have to follow the rules that ordinary people have to follow. He now believes that he has a right to indulge his every whim, including the whim to stray from his marriage.

The Personality Kid is also similar to *The Big Timer* (1932), in which a boxer's manager girlfriend guides her man to success in the ring only to watch in shock as he becomes an egotistical and insensitive philanderer. The plot is the same but the profession is different in *What Every Woman Knows* (1934). A devoted wife advises and champions her husband throughout his rise in politics and her husband appallingly returns her devoted support by cheating on her with the lovely young niece of a countess.

Marriage in the world of professional sports is also the subject of *Easy Living* (1949), which presents a story of a sports star in decline. Pete Wilson (Victor Mature) must give up his position as a quarterback for the New York Chiefs due to a heart condition. His wife, Liza (Lizabeth Scott), has all of the qualities that a wife shouldn't have. She is shallow, selfish, greedy, ambitious and unfaithful. She has become romantically involved with Howard Vollmer (Art Baker), a wealthy businessman willing to sponsor her interior design business. Pete applies for a coaching job, but loses out on the job to his best friend Tim McCarr (Sonny Tufts) due to his wife's bad reputation.

The Everything Lucy website reports:

> A brief dalliance with team secretary Anne (an excellent performance from Lucille Ball) results in Anne's selfless efforts to help Wilson put his marriage - and his life - back together.[225]

The subject of the supportive wife brings up one other adultery film starring Mature. The film is *Affair with a Stranger* (1953). A playwright, William Blakeley (Mature), and his wife, Carolyn (Jean Simmons), are drawn apart after Carolyn suffers a miscarriage. William is also under great strain in his work. bkoganbing of IMDb wrote:

> Mature is a likable enough fellow who is an aspiring playwright on Broadway who likes to gamble and have a good time as well and Simmons is a girl who nurtures him until he gains success. But then being a Broadway success he falls prey to the usual temptations. A really big temptation comes his way in the form of his latest leading lady, husband collecting Monica Lewis.[226]

One More River (1934)

Clare Corven (Diana Wynyard) is emotionally and physically abused by her husband, Sir Gerald Corven (Colin Clive). We see this in a single scene. He sneers at her. He snarls at her. He grabs her roughly. Unable to bear his abuse any longer, she abandons her husband in Ceylon and boards a ship bound to her native England. During the journey, she becomes friendly with Tony Croom (Frank Lawton). A private detective hired by Sir Gerald secretly observes Clare and Tony, hoping to see something that can be used against Clare in court.

Suzy (1936)

Like *Unfaithful*, the film presents an unrepentant husband. The husband (Cary Grant) is defiant when his wife (Jean Harlow) catches him with his mistress (Benita Hume). He is annoyed with her for getting emotional and reprimands her for spying on him (even though she wasn't). "Suzy," he says, "I know I'm caught, darling. I don't like it and you don't like it. . . I should be flattered by all this attention."

Between Two Women (1937)

A student nurse, Claire Donahue, (Maureen O'Sullivan), is unhappy in her marriage to an alcoholic, but she feels guilty to leave him when he depends on her so much. Her husband Tom (Anthony Nace) strikes her across the face, which leaves her with a glaring black eye, but she still feels obligated to stand by him. Her dilemma becomes worse when she falls in love with a young surgeon, Allen Meighan (Franchot Tone). Allen is dismayed that Claire refuses to leave her husband and ends up marrying Patricia Sloan (Virginia Bruce), a patient who he saved with an emergency appendectomy. Tom is injured in an accident and dies during surgery. Patricia, a jealous wife, wrongly assumes that Allen is having an affair with the now-single Claire. She rashly leaves her husband for a society doctor, Dr. Tony Wolcott (Leonard Penn). Soon after, Patricia is injured in a train wreck and brought to Allen's hospital. Allen reconciles with Patricia during her recovery. The couple makes plans to take a long trip together, but Allen realizes that he and Patricia are not a good match and instead returns to Claire.

Doctor Glas (1942)

Helga Gregorius (Irma Christenson) brings an unusual complaint to Dr. Tyko Glas (Georg Rydeberg). She finds her clergyman husband, Pastor Gregorius (Rune Carlsten), to be coarse and unprincipled and can no longer bring herself to have sex with him. But Gregorius insists that a wife has a duty to have sex with her husband. He is willing to routinely ignore her protests and force himself on her for his own pleasure. Helga wants Glas to inform Gregorius that she has an illness that prevents her from having sex. Meanwhile, she has been freely having sex with a civil servant, Klas Recke (Gösta Grip). Glas falls in love with Helga and is willing to do anything he can to help her. He speaks to Gregorius, but the pastor refuses to give up his marital rights. Glas sees no other option except to murder Gregorius. In their next meeting, he slips poison into the pastor's coffee. The story is based on the 1905 novel by author Hjalmar Söderberg. A second film adaptation was produced in 1968.

Song of Surrender (1949)

Elisha Hunt (Claude Rains) is cruelly domineering with his young wife Abby (Wanda Hendrix). Elisha demands absolute obedience from Abby. He becomes infuriated when his wife purchases a gramophone. He considers it sinful for her to listen dreamy-eyed to music. She is fond of an exhilarating aria by Enrico Caruso, which she listens to again and again. He is prepared to smash the gramophone with an axe until Abby sobs and begs him to stop. Abby falls in love with Bruce Edridge (Macdonald Carey), who has moved into the community. She is ready to leave Elisha for Bruce when her husband falls ill. She cares for him dutifully until his passing soon after.

"ABIGAIL, DEAR HEART"
A Paramount Picture.

Wanda Hendrix and Claude Rains in *Song of Surrender* (1949)

From Here to Eternity (1953)

An army sergeant, Milton Warden (Burt Lancaster), begins an affair with his captain's wife, Karen Holmes (Deborah Kerr). This relationship involves a greater risk than the usual adulterous affair. Warden can receive a twenty-year prison sentence if he's found out by military authorities. Sergeant Maylon Stark (George Reeves) tells Warden about Karen's many previous affairs at Fort Bliss, including an affair that she had with him. He says, "There's something mighty strange about that woman." Karen explains the reason that she is gravely unhappy in her marriage. While she was pregnant, her husband would regularly spend the night out with other women and then come stumbling home drunk. One night, Karen pleaded with him to get home early from an officers' conference because she had not been feeling well. Instead, he went out drinking with a hatcheck girl. She explained:

> He was drunk when he came in at five a.m. I was lying on the floor. I begged him to go for the doctor, but he fell on the couch and passed out. The baby was born about an hour later. Of course it was dead. It was a boy. But they worked over me at the hospital. They fixed me up fine. They even took my appendix out. They threw that in free. . . And one more thing - no more children. Sure I went out with men after that. And if I'd ever found one that. . . I know. Until I met you, I didn't think it was possible either.

The Unfaithfuls (1953)

A wealthy businessman, Giovanni Azzali (Carlo Romano), has his wife Luisa (Irene Papas) followed by an investigator to establish grounds for separation. Azzali is anxious to obtain a divorce so that he can marry a model that he has been dating. But the agency can find no wrongdoing. He is appalled. He says, "You tell me, isn't she a pleasant woman? Then why? They all have a lover, why hasn't she? To spite me, that's why. After 10 years of marriage! It's impossible there's nothing!" He says that he and his wife haven't had sex in two years. He asks, "Can it be? A young woman, with all those young men around, courted like she is?"

A handsome young man, Osvaldo (Pierre Cressoy), works as an investigator, following around beautiful wives who are suspected of cheating by their rich husbands. He realizes after awhile that it is profitable to use the incriminating information he turns up to blackmail the wives. It is while mingling in the social circles of his rich clientele that he meets Liliana (May Britt), a former girlfriend now married to a wealthy industrialist. He seduces Liliana and steals an expensive necklace from her home. His theft of the necklace is blamed on a young maid, Cesarina (Anna Maria Ferrero), who loses her job and faces a prison sentence. Cesarina is so distraught that she commits suicide. Liliana, upset by Cesarina's death, reports Osvaldo to the police even though it means exposing their affair. When the police refuse to arrest him for lack of evidence, Liliana shoots Osvaldo down in the street.

So, both the husband and lover are horribly abusive. In the end, the unfaithful wife is the most righteous person in the story.

Valerie (1957)

John Garth (Sterling Hayden) is on trial for shooting his wife Valerie (Anita Ekberg) and her parents (John Wengraf and Iphigenie Castiglioni). Only his wife survived the shooting, but she has been confined to bed. Garth claims that he was driven to violence upon learning that Valerie was having an affair with Reverend Blake (Anthony Steele). But Valerie, who testifies from her hospital bed, tells a much different story. She insists that she was faithful to Garth, but he violated his marital vows of love and honor by treating her brutishly. Dr. Jackson (Stanley Adams) reveals burn marks as proof that Garth had been torturing Valerie. Garth leaps to his feet and draws his gun. He hopes to keep everyone at bay until he gets out of town. But, before he can get away, he is shot by Herb (Peter Walker), his estranged brother who loves Valerie.

Petulia (1968)

Petulia is a muddled film that has little to offer on the subject of adultery. A middle-aged orthopedic surgeon, Dr. Archie Bollen (George C. Scott), meets a nutty young woman, Petulia Danner (Julie Christie), at a charity party. Walt Mundkowsky of Traveling Boy blog wrote:

> The party bores Petulia ("Highway safety is so blah"), and she finds Archie interesting, so she propositions him rather awkwardly. ("I've been married six months and I've never had an affair.") Petulia is the very embodiment of chic – upswept blonde hair, white ostrich feathers, jewels, etc. – and Archie half-heartedly accepts.

> Archie admits to her that he is unhappy with his marriage.

> Petulia: What was it, Archie? The sex bit?

> Archie: What would you say if I told you that one day I just got very tired of being married?

Petulia is a British working-class girl who married a high society gentleman, David Danner (Richard Chamberlain). Except David is not really a gentleman. He is in a habit of getting drunk and angry and becoming violent with his wife. Petulia flees her abusive husband to begin an affair with Archie. In turn, Archie abruptly walks out on his wife and children, leaving his wife hurt and confused.

Julie Christie and George C. Scott in *Petulia* (1968)

A critical juncture is reached in the story when David finds Petulia and badly beats her. Surprisingly, Petulia returns to him without objection.

Adrian Danks of Senses of Cinema wrote, ". . . [A]t times in *Petulia* one wonders whether all this posturing is just a smokescreen for a rather conventional and ill-defined triangular love story (of the decidedly screwball kind)."[227] He called the film "confused and empty."[228]

Dennis Schwartz wrote:

Aside from the brilliant performances this surreal-styled film with its successful flashbacks but not so successful flash-forwards, was mostly a disorientated and emotionally cold film. It was impossible to warm up to these elusive and neurotic characters, each trapped by fate or indecision. By the film's end, the same problems that existed in the beginning were still present. Richard Chamberlain remains a jealous husband, unsure of his wife's commitment. Julie Christie is unable to know if she can love somebody. George C. Scott is still chasing something that he is not sure of.[229]

Mundkowsky wrote:

Its story simply fails to convince. "Petulia, you've turned me into something crazy," says Archie. And again at the film's close: "Did I change you, Archie?" – "You turned me into a nut." We are obviously supposed to believe that Petulia and Archie have switched positions at the end – that he has become a "kook" and she has become responsible. . . When the film ends, Archie seems no less tired, lonely or screwed up than he was at its start. And Petulia has not gotten more responsible . . ."[230]

He added: "The film's events seem too pat, too manipulated."[231] Agreed.

Diary of a Mad Housewife (1970)

Tina Balser (Carrie Snodgress) is constantly belittled by her husband. But then every man in the film is abusive to her. Her husband. Her lover. Even her psychiatrist. This trend peaks in the final moments, as described by Wikipedia:

> Tina reveals her story to her therapy group, who angrily criticize or belittle her. The final shot is of Tina's face, steadfast, as angry voices from the group are heard from off-screen.[232]

Not Now Darling (1973)

Gilbert Bodley (Leslie Phillips) has an affair with a mobster's wife, Janie McMichael (Julie Ege). It increases the stakes of an adultery film to give a woman a scary husband. In *The Big Town* (1987), a gambler (Matt Dillon) falls in love with the wife of a gangster (Tommy Lee Jones). In *Cat Chaser* (1989), a hotel owner has an affair with the wife of a cruel exiled general from the Dominican Republic.

Heartburn (1986)

A newspaper columnist, Mark Forman (Jack Nicholson), cheats on his wife Rachel Samstat (Meryl Streep) while she is pregnant.

Ju Dou (1990)

Jinshan (Li Wei), the wealthy owner of a textile mill, is cruel to his young wife, Ju Dou (Gong Li). He whips her. He ties her up and gags her. He holds her down while pouring water over her face. He employs a young nephew, Tianqing (Li Baotian), who he works hard for little pay. Ju Dou and Tianqing fall in love and sneak off regularly for sex. Ju Dou becomes pregnant as a result of the affair, but she pretends that Jinshan is the father. Ju Dou gives birth to a son, Tianbai. Tianbai is impressed by the cruelty of the powerful Jinshan and grows up to be, in the words of Roger Ebert, "a hateful strong-willed little monster."[233] Jinshan becomes ill and needs a wheelchair to get around. One day, he accidentally topples from his wheelchair and falls into a vat of red dye. Tianbai (Yi Zhang) laughs watching Jinshan drown. Jinshan's family takes Tianbai away for special tutoring. Ju Dou and Tianqing are free to be together for the next few years. But Tianbai (now played by Zheng Ji'an) returns more monstrous than before. He does not approve of Ju Dou's relationship with Tianqing. One day, he bludgeons Tianqing to death. In grief and rage, Ju Dou burns down the mill.

The Piano (1993)

Alliance Films provided the following plot summary at the time of the film's 2012 DVD release: "A mute woman is sent to 1850s New Zealand along with her young daughter and prized piano for an arranged marriage to a wealthy landowner, but is soon lusted after by a local worker on the plantation."[234]

Anna Paquin and Holly Hunter in The Piano (1993)

The Piano is a bizarre Gothic melodrama set in New Zealand during the 1850s. Ada McGrath (Holly Hunter), recently departed from her native Scotland, arrives in New Zealand as a mail-order bride for a grim and brutal homesteader, Alisdair Stewart (Sam Neill). As we understand it, her father arranged the marriage for a fee.

We never learn Ada's backstory. She has a young daughter, Flora (Anna Paquin). How did Ada come to be a mother? Where is Flora's father? Ada has refused to speak since she was six-years old. Why? It is surely an important part of the story that viewers want to know about. Ada is withdrawn, sullen and often angry. How has she come to be this way? Is she unhappy about being sent far from home to marry a strange man? Did she have agency in this marital arrangement? But Ada may be no more than a metaphor in this dreamlike story and a metaphor has no backstory.

Flora has invented a fanciful tale to explain to those who ask how her mother became mute:

One day, while my mother and father were singing together in the forest, a great storm blew up. But, so passionate was the singing that they didn't notice. They didn't stop as rain began to fall. And when their voices rose for the final bars of the duet, a great bold of lightning came out of the sky and struck my father, who lit up like a torch. At the same moment my father was struck dead my mother was struck dumb. She never spoke another word.

Ada has brought a piano from Scotland. She loves to play the piano, seeing its music as a powerful substitute for her voice. But Alisdair deems it as too large and heavy to be hauled to his home. He instructs his servants to abandon it on the beach. George Baines (Harvey Keitel), Alisdair's assistant, takes the piano to his hut and asks Ada for lessons. But Baines has a greater interest in engaging with Ada than engaging with her piano, though clearly the way to reach Ada is through the piano. In any case, the lessons prove to be erotic. The piano is a metaphor for communication and connection and, in the end, it lies at the core of a great sexual communion. In the meantime, Ada's marriage to Alisdair remains unconsummated.

The contrast between Alisdair and Baines is blatantly obvious. Alisdair is a colonist who stands cold and repressed above the Maori natives. Baines, spiritual and elemental, has assimilated into the native population, going as far as adopting their facial tattoos.

Suspicious, Alisdair walks to Baine's hut and peeks inside. He sees Baines having sex with Ada. He confronts Ada as she walks home through the forest and attempts to rape her.

Holly Hunter in *The Piano* (1993)

Undeterred, Ada instructs Flora to deliver to Baines a love note burnt onto a piano key. Flora, who does not approve of her mother's relationship with Baines, brings the piano key to Alisdair. Alisidair goes mad. He figures to stop his wife from cheating by eliminating her ability to play her piano. So, he grabs an axe and chops off Ada's index finger. Alisdair wraps the finger in a cloth and has Flora deliver it to Baines. A note that accompanies the finger makes it clear to Baines that, if he continues to see Ada, he will chop off more fingers. That night, Alisdair touches Ada while she sleeps and suddenly hears her voice in his head. He is so terrified by this that he agrees to let Ada leave New Zealand with Baines.

Film critics have focused on the piano, which serves as a strong metaphor. Joanna Di Mattia of Senses of Cinema wrote:

> [Ada] touches the piano like a lover, with tenderness, recognition, and the thrill of discovery. . . Ada removes some of the piano's packing material, like she's unbuttoning a shirt. . . The Piano turns on the complexity of meanings associated with touch – desire, control, liberation, risk, power, pleasure, and violence.[235]

Josh Larsen of the Larsen on Film blog wrote:

> [The piano] enters the screen from behind and over the camera, lowering into our field of vision like a holy artifact. . . [I]t becomes a voracious symbol, swallowing whatever meaning you care to give to it.[236]

Emma Bovary also carried on an affair while telling her husband that she was taking piano lessons.

This film was highly profitable.

Something to Talk About (1995)

Grace Bichon (Julia Roberts) glances into a restaurant window and sees her husband Eddie (Dennis Quaid) having a romantic dinner with another woman. She immediately gathers up the children and goes to stay with her family at their horse farm. Her father, Wyly King (Robert Duvall), encourages her to reconcile with Eddie. He tells her, "I'm not saying he hasn't done anything wrong. He knows he has. But he's a good father and a good provider. That's not so easy to come by. Now, look, child. People have survived worse tragedies than this. You're a grown woman with responsibilities, and you are too old to come running home. You can't work things out, that's one thing, but you haven't tried, and that I won't have." It turns out that he, himself, has cheated on his wife. But he argues, "I do not cheat! I may have fooled around, but I never cheated!" Grace goes on a date with a horse trainer, Jamie Johnson (Brett Cullen). They go back to his place for a nightcap. They kiss while sitting on the edge of his bed. She springs on top of him. But, as she is un-buttoning his shirt, she thinks of Eddie and cannot go through with it. Grace and Eddie reconcile in the end.

Town and Country (2001)

Porter Stoddard (Warren Beatty), an architect, has been married for 25 years to Ellie (Diane Keaton), an interior designer. He has never been faithful. Presently, he is jumping in and out of bed with three other women - beautiful young cellist Alex (Nastassja Kinski), his wife's best friend Ellie Stoddard (Goldie Hawn), and an heiress (Andie MacDowell). Beatty figured to play a bed-hopping Lothario much as he did 26 years earlier in *Shampoo*. But the actor, who was 38 years old when he made *Shampoo*, was now 64 years old. The situation wasn't the same. The film was, understandably, a bomb.

Happily Ever After (2004)

Gabrielle (Charlotte Gainsbourg), a Paris realtor, rightly suspects that her husband, Vincent (Yvan Attal), is cheating on her. But she manages to lift her spirits by daydreaming about a handsome man who she recent-ly met in a record shop.

Vincent's mistress is a licensed masseuse (Angie David). She is not a shallow, meaningless or unsympa-thetic character and yet the filmmakers fail to give her a name. She is fearful that Vincent, who is not forthcoming about his motives or plans, will eventually leave her. The mistress asks Vincent if he ever cheated on his wife before. He tells her that he hasn't. She says, "Pity. You could have told me how this will end."

Vincent learns from a friend that Gabrielle is aware of the affair. He loves his wife and is afraid to lose her. His mistress senses that he is about to leave her and sobs to her consoling mother.

Vincent and Gabrielle agree to move to the countryside. Vincent looks at Gabrielle packing and feels overwhelmed with emotion. He takes her in his arms and kisses her. Can we assume that the film has come to a resolution? Will Vincent be faithful? And will Gabrielle be faithful? In the final scene, she meets a cli-ent to show him an apartment. He happens to be the man that she met in the record store. The two have a friendly conversation while waiting for an elevator. As they ride the elevator, she imagines making love to him. What will happen once they are alone together in the apartment?

Meet Bill (2007)

Of course, a husband can be abused by an unfaithful wife. Bill Anderson (Aaron Eckhart) is married to a banker's daughter, Jess (Elizabeth Banks), and has a job at his father-in-law's bank. He hates his job and feels abused by his father-in-law. He finds a videotape showing his wife having sex with a local news anchor, Chip Johnson (Timothy Olyphant). He goes to his television studio and attacks Chip during a live broadcast. He leaves Jess following the incident. Once on his own, he reconsiders his life and works hard to improve himself. He manages through diet and exercise to get his body into shape. He earns respect from Jess and his father-in-law, Mr. Jacoby (Holmes Osborne). He resigns from the bank with plans to open a donut shop. Bill and Jess settle their difference and agree on an amicable divorce.

Waitress (2007)

Jenna Hunterson (Keri Russell), a waitress at Joe's Pie Diner, has been secretly saving money to flee from her abusive husband. Her plan is upset by a sudden pregnancy. The unhappy wife is soon engaged in an affair with her good-natured obstetrician, Dr. Jim Pomatter (Nathan Fillion). Jim explains to Jenna that he is usually nervous and neurotic around people, but he feels happy and calm with her. He is a married man, but he doesn't feel this great bliss with his wife. But that doesn't mean that he has a bad marriage. He never says a single negative word about his wife and never indicates that he and his wife are having problems.

Jenna is employed at Joe's Pie Diner. Joe (Andy Griffith), the grouchy old owner of the diner, doesn't personally manage the business, but he comes to the diner every day for a meal. He serves as the film's voice of morality.

Joe: How's the bad husband?

Jenna: Just awful.

Joe: And the lipstick smudger?

Jenna: The lipstick smudger?

Joe: The dog on the side. The affair.

Jenna: (*whispers*) Shh, Joe, I'm not having no affair.

Joe: Okay, you're not having no affair. (*reading the newspaper*) Want to hear your horoscope before I give you my order?

Jenna: No.

Joe: Too bad, here it is. "Aquarius. If, indeed, you're having an affair, it might be a good time to step back, look at your life and reassess things a bit."

Jenna: It don't say that in there.

Joe: Yes, it does. It says, "Even if you have a miserable, snake husband, you probably shouldn't be having no affair, cause it's beneath you and could make you seem like a common hussy. Not to mention the pain you could cause other people."

Jenna and Jim are about to run off together when her water breaks. That has never before happened in the history of the adultery film.

As she prepares for her baby's delivery, Jenna is greeted warmly by Jim's wife, Francine (Darby Stanchfield), who is a doctor at the hospital. This is not the bad wife that she expected. She tells Jenna, "Jim's told me so much about you. He thinks you're just a terrific woman." She turns to her husband affectionately and kisses him.

Jenna becomes enchanted to be holding her new baby girl. The anxiety and aversion that she has been feeling about the baby suddenly vanishes. She realizes at that moment that she wants her and her daughter to have a better life away from the abusive Earl.

Earl's greatest concern has been that, with the baby, Jenna will pay far less attention to him. Unlike Jenna, he remains unchanged upon seeing his baby for the first time.

Earl: Don't you go loving that baby too much.

Jenna: I don't love you, Earl. I haven't loved you for years. I want a divorce.

Earl: (*laughing*) That's not a funny joke. We got this new baby here. Shouldn't be making jokes like that.

Jenna: I want you the hell out of my life. You are never to touch me, ever again. I am done with you. If you ever come within six yards of me, I will flatten your sorry ass, and I will enjoy doing it.

It is another film first to have a marital breakup occur in a delivery room.

The next day, Jenna is wheeled out of the hospital by her friends, Dawn (Adrienne Shelly) and Becky (Cheryl Hines). She meets Jim on the way out. She thanks him for his help and support. He startles her by leaning forward to kiss her, but she quickly stops him before he makes it to her lips.

Jenna: I'm thinking your wife's around and you probably shouldn't kiss me. The way she looks at you, so much trust.

Jim: So that's it? It's over? I don't have any say in this?

Jenna: We could have a big drama here that gets drawn out for a couple years, makes everyone miserable. Or we could just end it right here, you know? No body count, just say bye-bye. I'm saying bye-bye.

She instructs Dawn to wheel her out. She ends up without her husband and without her lover and could not, from all appearances, be happier. It helps, of course, that Joe dies and bequeaths Jenna more than a quarter of a million dollars in his will. Jenna opens her own pie shop and achieves great success. It is the perfect feminist ending.

Jenna's pie shop, with its great big neon sign, is reminiscent of the chicken and waffle restaurant that Joan Crawford opens in *Mildred Pierce* (1945).

My Old Lady (2014)

The film examines the painful legacy of adultery.

Mathias Gold (Kevin Kline) arrives in Paris to claim a valuable home that he inherited from his father, but he finds an old woman Mathilde Girard (Maggie Smith) living in the home with her daughter Chloé (Kristin Scott Thomas). He asks the old woman to move out, but she informs him that she has a legal right to remain in the home until she dies. Mathias learns that his father purchased the home under a "viager" agreement, which prohibits the buyer from assuming possession of a property until the seller dies. So, he is unable to evict Mathilde and he is unable to sell the property. This is a problem as Mathias is in desperate need of cash. As he tries to figure out a loophole in the viager agreement, Mathias discovers that Mathilde was his father's mistress for many years.

Mrs. Girard: We were young. My husband was very successful in business, and your father was penniless. It just seemed the best plan. I . . .

Matthias: How is it at my age I can still be shocked?

Mrs. Girard: Well, I'm shocked that you're shocked. During three marriages, you never had a lover?

Matthias: I'm sorry to disappoint you, Madame G. Some people do the right thing.

Mrs. Girard: Well, why would you know the right thing and your father and I not know? What is so especially clever about you and your way of understanding life?

Matthias: Well, I know my pain. See, I know the pain that you brought into my life, and I don't like it.

Matthias clarifies the pain that the affair created. Distraught by his father's infidelity, his mother committed suicide. He, himself, cut his wrists in a failed suicide attempt.

Matthias learns that Chloé is involved in an affair with a married man.

Matthias: So, tell me. Who's the guy in the restaurant?

Chloé: What?

Matthias: The guy in the restaurant. He looked familiar. I think I saw him duck into a hotel with you the other day. But today he didn't seem quite so happy to see you, what with the wife and all, the kids. You know?

Chloé: How dare you?

Matthias: Oh, I dare! You give me all that holier-than-thou crap about family and tradition, and you're doing the hoopie with somebody's husband, some kid's dad?

Chloé talks to Matthias about their parents' affair. She says that her father knew about the affair, but he chose to suffer discreetly.

Chloé: That's the way French people do it.

Matthias: Yeah. *Vive la* French people! *Vive la* French people! Now, *that* is truly sad.

Chapter Eight:
Cheating Rich Folk

In early films, adultery is a rich person's game. Many early adultery films were premised on the idea that wealthy people are too selfish and frivolous to be faithful spouses. This was a world where men dressed in tuxedos and women ornamented with jewels enjoy an endless stream of cocktail parties. Betty Blythe is an unfaithful wife in *Tangled Lives* (1918). A Motography critic said that the film "mirror[ed] the moral laxness of the upper stratum." In *Forsaking All Others* (1934), a masseuse asks a socialite, "Say, how many times do you people need to marry before it takes?" The socialite replies, "Oh, we generally play best two out of three."

Marriage requires humility. It is more important to heed the interests of your marriage than to heed your own personal interests.

It could easily be argued that the gold digger, who is characterized by greed and materialism, is a product of capitalism. The rich folk films, as the vamp films, show how easily a marriage can be corrupted by the forces of consumerism. Capitalist greed is a key element in "Madame Bovary." Can a person preserve their natural goodness while being obsessed with accumulating wealth?

We can see this decadence in films as early as 1907, at which time the Austrian company Saturn produced the six-minute film *A Modern Eve*. Morals are blatantly lacking in the rich husband and wife depicted in this film. Artemis-9 of IMDb wrote:

> . . . [T]he Baron leaves to meet some lady of the night in the club's private room, with champagne and a sofa for two. At home, the Baroness gets bored, until she has an idea, soon put to practice. She sends a man a letter, signed Divine Lola, giving him rendezvous at a discreet pension. The modern Eve is not taking her husband's infidelities sitting down. She lays in her undershirt on a bed inviting her lover in, in a long embrace.[237]

Divorce and the Daughter (1916) is another money-is-the-root-all-evil story. A man (J. H. Gilmour) quits his job after suddenly inheriting a fortune. He moves his wife (Zenaide Williams) and three children to an artist colony, where he intends to explore his long-neglected creative urges. But a crafty widow, Mrs. Cameron (Kathryn Adams), becomes interested in the man's fortune and schemes to seduce him away from his wife.

Cecil B. DeMille's *We Can't Have Everything* (1918) involves rich folk entangled in moral dilemmas about marriage. A socialite, Charity Cheever (Kathlyn Williams), is determined to save her marriage despite her husband's infidelity. A former boyfriend, Jim Dyckman (Elliot Dexter), fails to persuade Charity that it's best to leave her rat of a husband for him. Later, after she finally abandons her marriage and is granted a divorce, Charity wants to reconnect with Jim, but Jim is now married to a scheming gold digger, Kedzie Thropp (Wanda Hawley).

What Do Men Want? (1921), directed by Lois Weber, is certainly anti-capitalism. Frank Boyd becomes rich when he invents a highly useful automotive part. He finds the business world exciting and sees his home life as dull by comparison. His financial success spoils his marriage.

Bruce Calvert of AllMovie wrote of Weber's *Too Wise Wives* (1921): "Director Weber shows how 'keeping up with the Joneses' can harm a marriage."[238] Sara Daly (Mona Lisa) is bored with her husband John

(Phillips Smalley), who she only married for his money. She looks to start an affair with a former boyfriend, who is now mired in his own unhappy marriage.

The disrespect of marriage in affluent circles is the basis of most adultery films in the 1930s. This film genre gained prominence in the 1920s with Erich von Stroheim's *Foolish Wives* (1922), Ernst Lubitsch's *The Marriage Circle* (1924) and D. W. Griffith's *The Battle of the Sexes* (1928). This is particularly true of *The Marriage Circle*, in which rich people treat marriage as frivolously as a game of musical chairs. Modern-day critics are fond of this particular film. Owen of Letterboxd wrote:

> Marie Prevost's vamp sets her sights on her best friend's husband and comes close to ruining their perfect marriage while her own husband, Adolph Menjou tries to gather enough information to divorce Provost. Prevost is superb, vibrant, funny and blatantly sexual.[239]

Isabella McNeill of Senses of Cinema wrote:

> Professor Stock hires a detective to follow his wandering wife, who has taken in interest in Dr. Braun; Charlotte too is suspect that her husband is having an affair, and encourages her friend Mizzi's attentions to Braun not realizing she is, in fact, "the other woman'; all the while, Dr. Braun's medical partner, Dr. Gustav Mueller (Creighton Hale), is secretly in love with Charlotte. A marriage circle indeed.[240]

Fortunately, the Brauns' marriage is not destroyed in the end.

A couple on the verge of divorce treats marriage as a game of one-upmanship in *The Coast of Folly* (1925). A marriage is bound to inspire a fierce competition when substantial assets are at stake. The plot takes place in two periods. Nadine Gathway (Gloria Swanson), a wild and reckless young woman, abandons her prudish husband and young daughter Joyce to have more fun in her life. She remains out of sight for twenty years until she learns that her husband has died and her daughter, who has become caught up in a divorce scandal, is about to be disinherited based on a morality clause in her father's will. Nadine is, according to AFI, "intent on helping the daughter she once deserted."[241] Nadine soon learns more about her daughter's situation. While enjoying a summer vacation in Palm Beach, Joyce (also Swanson) developed a friendship with Larry Fay (Anthony Jowitt), whose wife has recently left him and filed for divorce. Larry's wife, Constance (Dorothy Cumming), learned of their relationship and sued Joyce for alienation of affection. How can her daughter be rescued from scandal? Nadine invites Mrs. Fay to a wild party. As Nadine expected, Mrs. Fay gets herself into a compromising position at the party and Nadine is now able to blackmail her into withdrawing her suit.

Ed Lorusso of Silent Room wrote:

> The title derives from Joyce's grandfather's remark that she and her young friends are aimless, like "jellyfish washed up on the coast of folly" . . . She set out to prove her grandfather wrong and that her generation does not have a "compulsion of failure."[242]

The Right to Love (1920)

Sir Archibald Falkland (Holmes Herbert) feels no need to abide by stuffy British customs while living in Constantinople. He welcomes his mistress, Lady Edith (Alma Tell), to live in his home despite the strenuous objections of his wife, Lady Falkland (Mae Murray). Falkland hopes that his wife will consent to a divorce so that he can marry Lady Edith, but she stands her ground and demands that he get rid of his mistress. Falkland figures to force his wife's consent by framing her for adultery. He arranges to put Lady Falkland into a compromising situation with Prince Stanislaus Cerniwicz (Macey Harlam). But Lady Falkland's old boyfriend, Colonel Richard Loring (David Powell), learns of the situation and comes to Lady Falkland's defense.

Her Private Life (1929)

Lady Helen Haden (Billie Love) is unhappy being married to a coarse millionaire, Sir Bruce Haden (Montagu Love). Sir Haden divorces Lady Helen when he learns that she had an affair with a young American, Ned Thayer (Walter Pidgeon).

Sin Takes a Holiday (1930)

A prosperous attorney, Gaylord Stanton (Kenneth MacKenna), treats adultery lightly. Here is the IMDb summary:

> A plain secretary [Constance Bennett] works for a womanizing divorce lawyer [Kenneth MacKenna] who only dates married women. To avoid having to deal with the matrimonial pursuits of any of his potential romances, he offers her financial support if she marries him in name only.[243]

The pretend-to-be-married ploy was later used to much greater effect in *Indiscreet* (1958).

Fast and Loose (1930)

The Lenox family is wealthy and respectable. But the younger members of the family, Bertie (Henry Wadsworth) and Marion (Miriam Hopkins), don't see value in the family's respectable ways. Bertie can see that Marion is not happy about the upcoming marriage that her family has arranged for her. He tells his sister that she can't be happy if she's not in love.

> Marion: Maybe you're right. I don't suppose I ever will be. Got to get married sometime. I used to think that maybe the right man would come along someday. Well, I'll keep on waiting and looking.
>
> Bertie: Even after you're married to that fellow?
>
> Marion: Well, why not? He's only marrying me for the money anyway. And I'm only marrying him because. . . well, because. . . mother and uncle George want a title in the family. Well, here's to uncle George. May he slip on a banana peel and break his neck.

Honor Among Lovers (1931)

Julia Craig (Claudette Colbert) hosts party for her one-year wedding anniversary. But her marriage isn't something worth celebrating. In one corner of the party, her husband Philip (Monroe Owsley) quiets down a woman crying because he wants to cool their relationship. Another guest is Julia's old boss, Jerry Stafford (Fredric March), who is far too excited to see Julia again. After a while, he cannot resist taking his old secretary in his arms and kissing her. Later, Julia finds Philip in their bedroom crying. He admits that he lost their entire savings in a bad investment. Worse, he was so sure that the investment would pay off that he embezzled client's money to increase his shares. Julia is desperate. She offers herself to Jerry to get him to pay off Philip's debt.

The Rich Are Always with Us (1932)

Marriage is for serious people only. Simply, marriage is a patient, organized, sustained effort that shallow, selfish, capricious people cannot manage. Curtis Yarvin, author of the Gray Mirror blog, said that you can never expect a successful effort from a person so flighty that they "can lose a staring contest with a fruit-fly."[244]

The rich elite in this film show a flippant attitude towards marriage. Marriage is not something they see as a sacred vow, so they believe they can afford to be to cavalier about it. The characters treat marriage as a casual alliance that is maintained for property and status rather than affection and devotion. In the end, these characters flounder about with vague notions about marriage. But, to last, a marriage cannot be a vague notion.

"THE RICH ARE ALWAYS WITH US" starring RUTH CHATTERTON. A First National Vitaphone Production.

The Rich Are Always with Us is lighter than most others in this genre. The talk of love is at all times glib.

The film opens at a posh nightclub. Julian Tierney (George Brent) is working hard to persuade his married friend, Caroline Grannard (Ruth Chatterton), to have an affair with him. At one point, she no more than smiles while fending off a kiss from him. No shriek. No smack across the face. Just a happy little grin.

Caroline is standing near her husband, Greg (John Miljan), when she teases Julian that she will tell Greg that he has been proposing to her.

Julian: But Greg takes that for granted. Don't you, Greg?

Greg: Well.

When they are alone again, Julian continues his romantic pursuit.

Julian: What about that kiss? I told you I wasn't very well civilized.

Caroline: Now, Julian, it's all very well for us to play.

Julian: You may be playing. I'm not. I'm in love with you.

Caroline: You don't want to interfere with a happy marriage, do you?

Julian: Oh, don't be silly, I'm just a home-wrecker at heart.

Caroline: You may be a home-wrecker but you are out of practice. You're not getting anywhere.

Julian: Hmm. . . I wonder about that. Are you sure that you don't love me just a bit more today than you did yesterday?

Caroline: Now don't be ridiculous. Haven't you got any morals at all?

Julian: Well, they began to ache when I was sixteen. So I had them pulled out.

Greg has a mistress, Allison Adair (Adrienne Dore), who is pressuring him to leave his wife. At the club, Allison forces him to confront Caroline. Caroline's only concern is whether Greg loves Allison.

Greg: Yes, my dear. You know I must love her when I can drag you through a thing like this.

Caroline: Do you want to marry her?

Allison: Why shouldn't he if I can make him happy?

Greg: Yes.

Caroline: I agree of course to any arrangements you may wish to make.

Greg: Thank you, Caroline. I am sorry I have hurt you this way.

Caroline: Sometimes we just can't help hurting other people.

But a man has a duty not to hurt others with selfish and foolish actions. Morality gives a man substance. Rational thought gives a man substance. Emotions, not tempered by either morality or intellect, leave a man hollow at his core.

These rich folk films have an otherworldly element, much like fairy tales about princes and princesses. It took William Wellman's *Other Men's Women*, in which extramarital hanky-panky jeopardizes a working-class marriage, to expose the mucky reality of marital infidelity.

Adolphe Menjou and Barbara Stanwyck in *Forbidden* (1932)

Forbidden (1932)

With wealthy people, reputation was a major factor when it came to sorting out extramarital entanglements. This is evident in *Forbidden*.

The film was written by Broadway theatre writer, Jo Swerling. The script liberally borrows elements of Fannie Hurst's "Back Street" novel.

Lulu Smith (Barbara Stanwyck), a librarian, retreats from her drab existence in a small Midwestern town for an exotic cruise. Her glamorous transformation on the cruise is similar to Davis' later transformation in *Now, Voyager*. She meets an attorney, Bob Grover (Adolphe Menjou), and falls in love. Lulu leaves her job and moves to the big city to be near Bob. For the next few months, the couple enjoys a close and loving relationship. One night, Bob shows up wearing a Halloween mask. He mockingly acts out a melodramatic scene from *Strange Interlude*. Then, he playacts being a husband pleased with his wife's culinary efforts in the kitchen. He realizes in the midst of this sham domesticity that the time has come for him to tell Lulu the truth: he is married. He removes the mask for this moment of truth. But fear rises up in his body. He sinks into the sofa and, again, draws the mask down over his face. He is deathly afraid to reveal to Lulu his true self. But, after a few moments, he musters the courage to make his confession. He tells her that his wife is crippled and he cannot bring himself to abandon her. Crushed, Lulu promptly ends the relationship. She does not reveal to Bob that she is pregnant.

Bob has a private detective track down Lulu, who has disappeared since their breakup. The private detective is able to locate Lulu and finds that she has a baby girl. Bob visits Lulu and she confesses that the baby is his. Bob adopts the baby and hires Lulu as a governess, but Lulu becomes unhappy with the arrangement. It is too painful to watch another woman acting as a wife to Bob and mother to her daughter. She leaves her governess job to work as a columnist at a newspaper. Lulu is determined to keep her affair with Bob a secret since Bob is a rising politician and a scandal would destroy his career. In the following years, her daughter Roberta (Charlotte Henry) matures into a beautiful debutante.

Barbara Stanwyck and **Adolphe Menjou** in *Forbidden* (1932)

Bob receives a nomination for governor. He should be happy, but he is "disheartened and ashamed"[245] (Wikipedia) by his secret life with Lulu. He tells Lulu that he needs to stop lying to everyone and reveal the truth to the public.

Lulu has repeatedly spurned the affections of fellow news reporter Al Holland (Ralph Bellamy), who has now become her editor. Al finally realizes the reason that Lulu has avoided romantic entanglements when he intercepts a letter that Bob sent to her. Lulu tries to snatch the letter from him, but Al punches her with enough force to knock her across the room. He vows to expose Bob. Lulu slips into her bedroom and returns with a gun. Al approaches her demanding the gun, but she remains poised to fire. He realizes that she's not bluffing and attempts to flee, but she shoots him repeatedly. It is at this moment that a radio announcer declares Grover to be the state's new governor.

Bob finds out that he's dying and writes a will in which he confesses his affair and leaves half his estate to Lulu. He presents Lulu with the will when she visits him on his deathbed. But, not wanting to damage his reputation or create a scandal for her daughter, she tears up the will on her way out.

Adultery also places a political career at risk in *The Life of Vergie Winters* (1934) and *Ten North Frederick* (1958). In *Citizen Kane* (1941), Charles Foster Kane (Orson Welles) is defeated in his run for governor when his opponent Jim W. Gettys (Ray Collins) exposes his extramarital affair with an aspiring singer, Susan Alexander (Dorothy Comingore).

Adultery films were well populated with unhappily married husbands who, like Bob Grover, were too noble to abandon an invalid wife but not too noble to avoid fooling around with a side gal. We will return to this subject in Chapter Fourteen.

Lord of the Manor (1933)

Wikipedia: "During a party at a country house, a number of the guests switch their romantic partners."[246]

Constance Bennett in *Our Betters* (1933)

Our Betters (1933)

The film makes abundantly clear the lack of morality in the marriages of rich people. Hafer refers to this as "the wacky indiscretions of the upper-class."[247]

Everyone keeps a spouse for public get-togethers and a lover for private get-togethers. And they have no deep feeling for either their spouse or their lover.

Arthur Hausner of IMDb describes the set-up of the plot::

> American heiress Pearl Saunders [Constance Bennett] marries Lord George Grayston but later sees him embracing his lover on their wedding day. She has his title and he has her money; thereafter they are rarely seen together.[248]

Hanky-panky dominates a weekend get-together at Pearl's country estate. Duchess Minnie's lazy and dim-witted gigolo companion, Pepi D'Costa (Gilbert Roland), manages to regularly sneak off for sex with Pearl. Minnie spies them sneaking into a tea house together and, out of spite, asks Pearl's innocent young sister Bessie (Anita Louise) to retrieve her purse from the tea house. Bessie is disgusted to catch Pearl and Pepi in the act and rejects her sister's unsavory lifestyle.

Dinner at Eight (1933)

Kitty Packard (Jean Harlow) is married to a ruthless tycoon, Dan Packard (Wallace Beery). She complains that her brutish husband doesn't have class. But Kitty has little class herself. She is crass. She is immoral. Worse, she is lazy, lying in bed for most of the day. She becomes terribly bored with her useless existence. She finds it to be a delightful diversion to canoodle with her doctor, Dr. Wayne Talbot (Edmund Lowe). Dr. Talbot is ashamed of himself and confesses to his wife, Lucy Talbot (Karen Morley), about his philandering. She responds:

> Don't bother because I know all about it. . . Oh, Wayne, dear, I'm not going to make a scene. You know I never do, do I? Remember how nicely I behaved about the others? Mrs. Whiting and that Dalrymple girl and the Ferguson woman, Dolly. . . Now, dear, I knew just when it started. Now she's at the insistent stage. It's all just a great bore, isn't it, darling? Don't think I don't mind. But I can't let it tear me to pieces the way it did the first time. It was just before Wayne was born, remember? I thought the world had come to an end. The noble young physician was just a masher. Surely a little more than that. A great deal more. That's why it's so pathetic. You're two people, really. One's magnificent. . . and the other's so shoddy.

The Goose and the Gander (1935)

Rotten Tomatoes noted:

> Divorcée Georgiana (Kay Francis) learns that Betty Summer (Genevieve Tobin), the woman who "stole" and married her husband, Ralph (Ralph Forbes), is planning a rendezvous with yet another man, Bob McNear (George Brent). Determined to take revenge, Georgiana devises an elaborate scheme to lure Bob and Betty to a remote cabin, then bring Ralph there. The plan works well - until a couple of thieves snatch Betty's car for their robbery escape and end up at the cabin. . .

Betty is gleefully defiant in making the arrangements for her "fling" with Brent. Contrast this with the agony that the woman suffers over her infidelity in a more sensitive film like *Brief Encounter*. Betty insists: "I'm going to have my fling and I'm going to get away with it. Just for the satisfaction of doing it."

The Awful Truth (1937)

The first thing that we learn about Jerry Warriner (Cary Grant) is that he's an unfaithful husband. As far as his wife knows, he has spent the last two weeks in Florida. It is never made clear what the alleged reason was for his trip to Florida. Did he go there on business? Did he go there for his health? We just know that he never was really there. He hurries into the Gotham Athletic Club, where his friend Frank Randall (Robert Allen) comments on his lack of a tan. "What did you do there," he asks, "carry a parasol?" Jerry bristles at the question.

Jerry: Don't go spreading that around, Frank.

Frank: Pulling a fast one on the little wife?

Jerry: Frank, I'm surprised at you. I'm supposed to have been in Florida. Supposing one of Lucy's friends says to her: "Well, why isn't he tanned?" Lucy will be embarrassed. I'll tan and Lucy won't be embarrassed. What wives don't know won't hurt them. What you don't know won't hurt you. That's the trouble with marriages today. People are always imagining things. The road to Reno is paved with suspicions. First thing you know, they're in a divorce court.

Irene Dunne, Cary Grant and Esther Dale in *The Awful Truth* (1937)

Jerry understands that Lucy (Irene Dunne) is staying with her Aunt Patsy (Cecil Cunningham) at the aunt's cabin. But he runs into Aunt Patsy and she doesn't know where Lucy is. Lucy turns up with Armand Duvalle (Alexander D'Arcy), a suave and handsome voice teacher. She says that one of Armand's students invited them to a junior prom. Unfortunately, she says, their car broke down on the way home and they had to spend the night at the "nastiest inn."

Mrs. Barnsley: Jerry's a wonder. Now, if I stayed out all night and waltzed in with handsome Mr. Duvalle, and said the car broke down. . .

Lucy: It did. Why should Jerry be angry? I didn't build the car.

Jerry: You're perfectly right, dear.

Lucy: Of course I am. Can't have a happy married life if you're always suspicious.

Jerry has returned to Lucy with a gift from Florida - a sack of oranges that, Lucy notices, comes from California.

Cary Grant and Irene Dunne in *The Awful Truth* (1937)

This self-righteous husband and wife, who are so eager to boast about their trust for one another, divorce soon after.

Grant and Dunne were re-teamed for *My Favorite Wife* (1940), which also dealt with marital mistrust. Nick Arden (Grant) doubts that his wife Ellen (Dunne) remained faithful while marooned on a tropical island with virile Steve Burkett (Randolph Scott) for seven years.

The Shining Hour (1938)

Shallow marital partners are contrasted with sturdy, full-bodied partners in *The Shining Hour*.

Olivia Riley (Joan Crawford), a nightclub dancer, marries wealthy Henry Linden (Melvyn Douglas). Henry is excited to bring his new bride home to his family. But Henry's sister, Hannah (Fay Bainter), is disturbed to see Olivia showing an interest in Henry's younger brother, David (Robert Young). Hannah says, "A woman's love should go only one way, to one man. There are women whose love reaches out to every man, like the tongs of a fire that capture and consume."

Marriage is structure. Marriage is planning. Where will we live? How will we support ourselves? How will we make this relationship work in the long-term? The passion that drives cheating is hostile to planning and will never make concessions to it. Olivia is talking to David about a lakeside home that she and Henry are building. But this isn't what he wants to talk about.

Olivia: It will be white and colonial, with a big porch facing the lake for me to eat crackly pig on and grow fat. And a huge green lawn that slopes to the water's edge, with horseshoe pitching for me and a dainty little teahouse for Henry.

David: Stop talking about Henry and you and your rotten little house.

Unrestrained passion leads to moral abandon and moral abandon leads to a great amount of chaos and destruction.

David's wife, Judy (Margaret Sullavan), suspects that David is having an affair with Olivia and isn't sure that she should interfere. Maybe, she thinks, David and Olivia belong together. She tells Olivia:

You know the expression, "two people being made for each other"? Of course, it's used pretty indiscriminately. But do you believe that sometimes - very seldom, but sometimes - two people are made for each other and for no one else?. . . I should imagine it happens very seldom. But when it does, it's more important than people being hurt. It's more important than anything, isn't it?

The estate suddenly erupts in flames. Hannah is crazed when Henry finds her.

Hannah: You can't stop it now. . . It'll burn to ashes. If you'll let it, and the ashes will be carried away by the wind - away from here, away from the Lindens. Let it burn, Henry. It's got to burn.

Henry: You did this, Hannah. You set fire to the house!

Hannah: She set fire to ours - to David, to Judy, and you, and you can't put it out. It's the fires of hell, Henry, and you can't put it out! She did it, Henry! She did it! She did it!

Judy runs into the fire to kill herself so that David will be free to be with Olivia. Olivia runs in after her and saves her life, but not before Judy is badly burned by a falling beam.

The next morning, Olivia is ashamed of the harm that her bad behavior has caused.

Margaret Sullavan and Joan Crawford in *The Shining Hour* (1938)

Olivia: I don't know anything this morning, except that I'm not much of a person. And I'll never forget last night, and what I've done to Judy. . . Most people don't in their lifetime [know themself]. We found out last night. We're not very pleasant people, you and I. A world full of us wouldn't make one Judy - a love like that. I wouldn't have believed it if I'd read it in a book. But when she ran into that fire. I suddenly knew about us - how little we felt, how little we want what we think we do. And how little we know what we have already.

David: Oh, but Judy'd never want me now.

Olivia: You're wrong again, David. I wouldn't and you wouldn't, but she would. People who love like Judy and Henry. They love like that. Come on. She's waiting for you.

In Name Only (1939)

Alec Walker (Cary Grant) lives apart from his wife, Maida (Kay Francis). The estrangement began before the ink was dry on their marriage certificate. The difficulties center on a letter. Maida had a lover who shot himself because Maida abandoned him to marry Alec. The man's mother sent Alec a letter in which Maida admitted to her boy that she was only marrying Alec for money and social position. When confronted with the letter, Maida has no choice but to admit the truth. "I did love him," she says. "I was mad about him. What of it? I had a choice. I could take David and love and nothing else. Or I could take you and what went with you. I took you."

Alec would prefer to divorce Maida and have her completely out of his life, but he is trapped in a marital limbo as Maida refuses to grant him a divorce. After falling in love with a new neighbor, Julie Eden (Carole Lombard), he becomes desperate to dissolve his marriage in spite of Maida's obstinate opposition.

The film is unusual in that it depicts Alec's affair as more legitimate than his marriage. Adultery is generally a great betrayal of trust. But, in this case, it is the marriage that is a great betrayal of trust. Alec's relationship with Maida was from the start dead and meaningless. Without love and commitment, it is supported by nothing more than legalities. In contrast, Alec's relationship with Julie is something genuine and vibrant.

The Rules of the Game (1939)

Roland Toutain and Nora Gregor in *The Rules of the Game* (1939)

Christine (Nora Gregor) has been married to Robert (Marcel Dalio), a wealthy marquis, for three years. For most of that time, she has been having an affair with an aviator, André Jurieux (Roland Toutain). Robert has long been aware of the affair, but he can't complain as he himself is having an affair with Geneviève de Marras (Mila Parély). Robert's relationship with Geneviève pre-dates his marriage. Geneviève fondly remembers the days that she had Robert all to herself. She says, "I want to go back three years in time. When Christine didn't exist. Take me in your arms as you did then." But the situation has changed now. Robert struggles to tell Geneviève that he no longer loves her and wants to focus his attention on his marriage.

Geneviève: You've stopped loving me? Please give me an answer.

Robert: No, I don't love you anymore. I'm very fond of you, but. . .

Geneviève: But I bore you.

Robert: The words you come up with, my dear.

Geneviève: The right ones. I give up. You can fight hatred, but not boredom.

Robert organizes a weekend retreat at his country estate. He makes the daring decision to include André and Geneviève on his guest list. A friend, Octave (Jean Renoir), jokes that it would serve Robert's interests for Geneviève and André to fall in love during the retreat. But André and Christine spend the weekend making plans to run off together. Octave, despite being André's dearest friend, secretly loves Christine and is determined to take her away from André. Marceau (Julien Carette), a new servant, takes an interest in a maid, Lisette (Paulette Dubost). It doesn't matter to him that Lisette is married to the gamekeeper, Edouard Schumacher (Gaston Modot). Obviously, weak bonds join together the film's couples. Geneviève offers the following quote from 18th century aphorist Nicolas Chamfort: "Love as it exists in society is merely the mingling of two whims and the contact of two skins."

The film has serious undertones despite its frequent farcical interludes. Octave dresses in a bear suit to perform a musical number for the guests. André gets into a fistfight with Robert. The fight is comic and childish. A punch sends André tumbling over the back of a couch. Christine flirts with a random guest, Monsieur Saint-Aubin (Pierre Nay). This angers André, who gets into a fistfight with Saint-Aubin. Jealousy possesses Schumacher, who chases the wife-stealer through corridors with a hunting rifle. But, as the film nears its conclusion, it becomes darker. Mistakenly, Schumacher shoots and kills André. Robert tells Schumacher that he will report the killing to the authorities as an unfortunate accident.

Roland Toutain and Nora Gregor in *The Rules of the Game* (1939)

Marriage is designed to set up strong boundaries in society. But the characters in this film do not believe in those boundaries. Robert, in particular, indulges in a frivolous and hedonistic lifestyle. He advocates for a free expression of love. He states plainly, "I'm against barriers and walls." Christine is not frivolous. She expresses great sadness, desperation and guilt in her affair with André. Perhaps, her husband's errant ways required her to seek comfort and security outside of the marriage. She does not favor the free expression of love. She is on the verge of tears when she spies Robert and Geneviève together in the woods.

The film demonstrates the lack of marital fidelity creates chaos, conflict, and tragedy. Roger Ebert wrote, "Renoir's portrait of the French ruling class shows them as silly adulterous twits, with the working classes emulating them within their more limited means."[249]

Lucia Bosè and Alberto Closas in *Death of a Cyclist* (1955)

Death of a Cyclist (1955)

The original Spanish title: *Muerte de un ciclista*

Juan (Alberto Closas) is dating a married socialite, María José (Lucia Bosè). Maria is driving through the countryside with Juan when she becomes distracted and strikes a cyclist. The cyclist is still alive when they check on him. But María José is afraid that their relationship will be exposed if they contact the police. So, she insists that they leave the injured man to die. What sort of people would do this? We learn much about this couple as the story continues. María José is bored with her husband, Miguel Castro (Otello Toso), who often travels on business. She has enjoyed spending time with Juan. But, now, guilt and fear drive María José and Juan apart. Juan is sad and ashamed about the dead cyclist. He remembers the war. He says, "The war is very convenient. You can blame everything on it. All the death and destruction, all the guys like me left hollow inside who never believe in anything ever again. Not even the sweetheart who doesn't wait and marries a rich man." The sweetheart was María José, who married Miguel while he was at war. Rafael (Carlos Casaravilla), an art critic, suspects that the couple is having an affair. He hints to María José that he has damaging information that he can expose to Miguel if she doesn't pay him. She fears that he knows about the cyclist. But, as we eventually learn, he really knows nothing. María José is cold-hearted, concerned only about being exposed and suffering consequences for her actions. It disturbs Juan that she arranges for them to secretly meet at a church. The voice of a priest reciting sacred liturgy can be heard in the background while they discuss their great sins - murder, adultery and deceit. Later that day, Miguel confronts María José. He is aware of her affair, which disgusts him. He accuses his wife of being motivated by nothing other than selfishness and greed. He proposes an ultimatum. María José must be home the next evening so that they can leave the country together and have a fresh start in a new place. In the meantime, Juan has his own plans for the future. He is sure that he will regain dignity and joy by confessing to leaving the cyclist to die. "We have to purify ourselves," he says, "become clean and good again, and pay for a crime we committed." The final scene is chilling. Juan and María José visit the place where they left the cyclist. Juan reflects on his life and speaks of starting again. The whole time, María José sits tensely and grimly inside the car. We know what is about to happen, but the director keeps the audience in suspense. Then, when the tension of the scene builds to the maximum level, she turns the ignition key and runs the car into Juan. She drives home quickly so she can catch the plane with Miguel. She suddenly sees a cyclist pedaling toward her in the dark. She swerves to avoid him and drives off a bridge. The cyclist scrambles down to the wreck and finds María José dead.

The Opposite Sex (1956)

The Opposite Sex is a remake of *The Women* (1939). dougdoepke of IMDb wrote: "You may need a scorecard, however, to keep up with the rotating relationships among the high class types."[250]

Suzy Parker and Gary Cooper in *Ten North Frederick* (1958)

Ten North Frederick (1958)

A number of adultery films, including *The Power and Glory* (1933), *The Life of Vergie Winters* (1934), *Le bon Dieu sans confession* (1953) and *Ten North Frederick*, open on a stately funeral procession. In *Ten North Frederick*, the deceased man is prominent attorney Joe Chapin (Gary Cooper).

A pivotal element of the plot involves Joe's teenage daughter, Ann (Diane Varsi). Ann meets Charley Bongiorno (Stuart Whitman), a hard up trumpet player, at a fair. The two run off to marry without telling her parents. Edith (Geraldine Fitzgerald), Joe's ambitious wife, is worried that Ann's secret marriage to Charley will jeopardize Joe being elected lieutenant governor. She has her political henchmen threaten to charge Charley with statutory rape if he doesn't get the marriage annulled. Following the annulment, Ann learns that she's pregnant and suffers a miscarriage. She refuses to talk to her father when she learns he knew of the threats made to her husband and did nothing to stop them. Joe, racked with guilt, withdraws from the race.

Edith is enraged with Joe. She spites him by letting him know that she once had an affair with his friend Lloyd Williams (Philip Ober). She shouts at him, "I wasted my life! I wasted my life on a failure!"

Joe meets his daughter's roommate, Kate Drummond (Suzy Parker). Joe and Kate fall in love. Joe gives Kate a ruby, which is a family heirloom. But Joe, who is uncomfortable being so much older than Kate, soon breaks off their relationship. Kate meets another man and becomes engaged. Ann mentions the engagement to her father, who is happy to hear that Kate is in love. Ann admits that Kate has never gotten over a married man that she dated before meeting her fiancé. She says that Ann loves her fiancé, but she doesn't feel as deeply for him as she did for "the other one."

Depressed, Joe drinks a great deal. He dies soon after. Ann is helping Kate pack for her honeymoon when she comes across the ruby that Joe gave her. She recognizes the ruby and asks Kate if her father gave it to her. She admits that he did. Ann now understands that her father was the man that Kate loved so deeply.

Diane Varsi and Gary Cooper in *Ten North Frederick* (1958)

No Love for Johnnie (1961)

No Love for Johnnie includes some of the same key elements as *Ten North Frederick* - an ambitious wife who resents her husband for his career failures, a middle-aged man who finds joy in life when he falls in love with a young woman.

Alice Byrne (Rosalie Crutchley) has great ambitions for her husband, Johnnie Byrne (Peter Finch), who holds a seat in parliament. She leaves him when he is passed over for an appointment in a new administration. He has an affair with a young model, Pauline (Mary Peach). She soon breaks up with him because she believes their age difference would create too many obstacles in their relationship. Alice returns home and tells Johnny that she wants to resume their marriage. She leaves him her phone number and asks him to think about it. As soon as she leaves, he tears up the phone number.

Wives and Lovers (1963)

A 1960s middle-class couple prove to be as shallow as 1930s rich couple. Bill and Bertie Austin (Janet Leigh and Van Johnson), so terribly vain, shallow and dim-witted, are hardly suitable protagonists for a light marital comedy. The couple offers petty excuses for freely straying from their marriage. Bert's eye turns to his beautiful agent, Lucinda Ford (Martha Hyer), while Bertie's eye turns to Gar Aldrich (Jeremy Slate), an actor who is set to star in her husband's play. All it takes for this wife or husband to cheat on their spouse is a couple of cocktails. As soon as the cocktail of your choice has you feeling lightheaded, you can kiss whomever you like without letting the slightest bit of guilt or shame get in your way.

Julie Christie and Dirk Bogarde in *Darling* (1965)

Darling (1965)

The film centers on the worst examples of rich people - bored, childish, amoral, superficial and shallow.

Diana Scott (Julie Christie), a glamorous fashion model, becomes hooked on the swinging London life-style. She cheats on her husband Tony Bridges (T.B. Bowen) with a married television newsman, Robert Gold (Dirk Bogarde), who can advance her in her career.

Diana and Robert arrange to get a hotel room together to consummate their affair. Excuses are required so that their spouses don't question where they are. They cozy up together in a phone booth while they ring their respective mates to lie about their whereabouts. The whole time, they behave like gleeful children, struggling hopelessly to suppress their giggling. They have no shame about cheating on their spouses. There was a similar scene in *Saturday Night and Sunday Morning* (1960).

This unfaithful couple treats duty and commitment as something too ponderous and boring to consider. Diana says in voice-over:

The thought of breaking up a family was absolutely repellent to me. If anyone had told me that I was doing anything like that, I would have been horrified. I have always regarded families as. . . well. . . *unbustable*, you know?

In the images on screen, we see a joyful Diana, which belies her claim that she was horrified to be taking a married man away from his wife. She's not being at all honest and she's not really expecting anyone to take what she is saying seriously. *Unbustable?* She could hardly be serious using the tongue-in-cheek, made-up word *unbustable*. So, Robert leaves his wife and children to live with Diana.

IMDb reviewer jery-tillotson-1 found that Christie's "inner radiance"[251] made the character likable despite the repulsiveness of her "naked greed and amorality."[252] But can there be more to Diana? Despite her obvious selfishness and amorality, Diana acts genuinely pleased to learn she is pregnant with Robert's baby. And, later, she sobs uncontrollably after she suffers a miscarriage.

Julie Christie and Dirk Bogarde in *Darling* (1965)

Diana moves on to Miles Brand, a film producer who can give her work in films. The ambitious woman further advances her status when she marries Cesare, an Italian prince. But is this an ideal situation? Let Wikipedia provide the answer:

> Though waited on hand and foot by servants, she is almost immediately abandoned in the vast palazzo by Cesare, who has gone to Rome, presumably to visit a mistress.[253]

She realizes that her lifestyle has been vacuous and has left her wanting more out of life. She says, "If I could just feel complete."

Diana tries to return to Robert, but her old lover is unwilling to take her back (though he has sex with her before he tells her this).

Marriage means nothing in this empty world of wealth and hedonism.

Julie Christie in *Darling* (1965)

Lady Caroline Lamb (1972)

The film is set in London during the early 1800s. Lady Caroline Lamb (Sarah Miles) can find no passion in her marriage to Lord William (Jon Finch). She sleeps with multiple men outside of her marriage. She falls madly in love with Lord Byron (Richard Chamberlain). Caroline develops a reputation in her community for being morally corrupt and emotionally unstable.

A Little Romance (1979)

Richard King (Arthur Hill), a prosperous businessman, is fed up with his wife Kay (Sally Kellerman) cheating on him. He confronts his wife's lover, George de Marco (David Dukes).

Richard: If you don't mind, I don't think we're going to need to see any more of you from now on.

George: I think that's up to Kay, don't you?

Richard: I'd say it's up to Kay and me. I've been standing around too long watching this go on between you, being too civilized to fight for her. Maybe if I'd let her know how much I care about her, she wouldn't have had to find you.

George: Listen, Kay, you don't have to listen to this.

Richard: Oh, yes, she does. You're forgetting something. I've been in your shoes. I'm her third husband. I took her away from somebody myself. George, you came along when Kay needed a little excitement in her life, but I don't think it would last between you. Because I think all you're really interested in is seeing if you can take her away from me. Well, you can't.

Love and Money (1981)

Byron Levin (Ray Sharkey) has an affair with a wealthy banker's wife, Catherine Stockheinz (Ornella Muti).

White Mischief (1987)

The film is set in the early days of World War II. British men and women with wealth flee to safer spaces. One of the safer spaces exists in Kenya. An old millionaire, Sir John Henry Delves Broughton (Joss Ackland), arrives in Kenya with his beautiful young wife, Diana Broughton (Greta Scacchi). Decadence abounds in this wealthy colony. Ed Sutton of IMDb wrote, "They are busy swapping partners, doing drugs, and attending lavish parties and horse races."[254] Diana has an affair with an earl, Josslyn Hay (Charles Dance), who already has two other lovers among Kenya's affluent expatriates. Diana has an open marriage with her husband, so the affair is not something that should upset him. But the affair takes a more serious turn when Josslyn asks Diana to marry him. Josslyn is suddenly shot dead in his car. Is Sir John his murderer?

A Handful of Dust (1988)

Tony Last (James Wilby), an English lord, is married to trendy and shallow Brenda (Kristin Scott Thomas). Tony, who is more introverted than Brenda, doesn't share Brenda's fondness for parties. So, he allows Brenda to attend high-society parties with John Beaver (Rupert Graves), an insignificant and insipid social climber. Brenda and John become lovers. Brenda is unsettled by her son's death in a riding accident. She confesses to Tony about her affair. Tony agrees to divorce Brenda and provide her with financial support, but the greedy Beaver insists that she demands more money. Tony has offered as much money as he could afford and is unable to comply with Brenda's demands. He withdraws his original offer and dejectedly embarks on a scientific expedition to the Brazilian rainforest. Brenda, who has been left impoverished, is abandoned by Beaver. Tony becomes ill and must remain in camp while the other expedition members go on an excursion. Natives attack the expedition party and slaughter them. This leaves Tony on his own. Tony receives care from an eccentric settler, Mr. Todd (Alec Guinness). Mr. Todd is proud of his collection of Charles Dickens novels, but he has never learned to read and asks Tony to read the books to him. Tony's daily readings bring great pleasure to Mr. Todd. When a search party arrives to rescue Tony, Mr. Todd drugs Tony and hides him. He tells the rescue party that Tony was killed by the natives. He gives the search party Tony's watch to take back to his family. Mr. Todd is now assured that Tony will remain his guest indefinitely and continue their daily readings of Dickens. In England, Tony's cousins erect a statue in Tony's memory. pfgpowell-1 of IMDb wrote, ". . . [A] great many people, not least his 'modern' wife Brenda, treat [Tony] appallingly badly. He is loyal, values tradition, honest, accommodating and indulgent and in return loses everything. . . One reviewer here complained that 'nothing' happens in the film. Not a bit of it. A great deal happens but everyone is so polite and well-brought up that no one, not even Tony, questions the huge injustice of it all."[255]

The Ice Storm (1997)

The adultery films made during this period are relentlessly grim and degenerate.

The Ice Storm centers on two families in an upper-class suburb. Their affluence is no remedy to dissatisfaction and depression and, as it turns out, fails to ward off tragedy from their lives. A young boy is electrocuted by a broken power line, a teenage girl arrives home depressed from a party and curls up in bed without bothering to remove her party dress, a man breaks down and sobs uncontrollably. They seek happiness in empty, obsessive, immoral sex when they're not consuming drugs or alcohol. They have become burned out on the limited benefits of raw pleasure.

Roger Ebert wrote:

> Ben (Kevin Kline) is having an affair with a neighbor (Sigourney Weaver). His wife Elena (Joan Allen) is a shoplifter who is being hit on by a long-haired minister. . . the adults are attending a "key party" that turns into a sort of race: Can they swap their wives before they pass out?. . . Despite its mordant undertones, the film is often satirical and frequently very funny, and quietly observant in its performances, as when the Weaver character takes all she can of Kline's musings about his dislike of golf, and finally tells her lover: "You're boring me. I have a husband. I don't feel the need for another". . . What we sense after the film is that the natural sources of pleasure have been replaced with higher-octane substitutes, which have burnt out the ability to feel joy.[256]

Wikipedia notes:

> The novel explores the loss of innocence and moral compass in middle-upper class Americans. . . The rapidly changing sexual mores of the period are reflected in the lives of both families, whose members experiment with traditionally taboo sexual acts such as incest and adultery.[257]

The grim film lost money at the box office.

Your Friends and Neighbors (1998)

Wikipedia summarizes the film as follows: ". . . [T]wo urban, middle-class couples deal with their unhappy relationships by shamelessly lying and cheating in their quest for happiness."[258] The film in ways resembles a dark and perverse update of Ernst Lubitsch's *The Marriage Circle* (1924). Adolphe Menjou's Professor Josef Stock was a dastardly schemer, but this film has someone even worse than him. Cary (Jason Patric) is a sadistic womanizer. Wikipedia notes, "[Cary] seduces naïve and emotionally vulnerable young women, and quickly dumps them for his cruel pleasure of watching them cry."[259]

The perspective of the filmmaker is that a man's sexual prowess, and nothing else, determines the man's value as a husband. If we are to believe the film, a marriage is only a failure if the husband fails to satisfy his wife in bed. The film's final message, highlighted and underscored, is that sexual dissatisfaction is the root of all evil. Barry, whose poor lovemaking skills ruined his marriage, is shown to be even worse off in his final scene – he is unable to get an erection as he struggles desperately to masturbate. His sexual prowess has gotten to be so inadequate that he cannot even satisfy himself. This is a Grand Guignol ending in the tradition of *Freaks* and *Ethan Frome*.

The vulgar and grotesque characters are unlike anyone that you are liable to meet in real life. They are the grossly exaggerated creations of the filmmaker's evidently disturbed and degenerate mind. Nothing lifts these people out of their depression and neediness - not cheating, not divorce, not remarriage, not pregnancy. An extra in a bookshop delivers a refreshingly normal moment as she quietly peruses a book. That is all that she is doing, perusing a book. In that moment, though, she is more real and more interesting than the preening lead characters spouting their pretentious, overblown dialogue. Evidently, the sole purpose of the film is to play out the dark delusions of its filmmaker.

The film lost money at the box office.

Eyes Wide Shut (1999)

Dr. William Harford (Tom Cruise) becomes unnerved when his wife Alice (Nicole Kidman) confesses to having a sexual fantasy about a naval officer. Philip French of The Guardian describes the balance of the plot as follows:

> Suddenly, the phone interrupts their discussion, calling Bill to the home of an elderly patient who has just died. At this point an already edgy movie takes on a truly disturbing turn as Bill begins a journey to the end of the night that involves a succession of unconsummated sexual encounters - with the dead patient's grieving daughter, a beautiful prostitute, the nymphet daughter of a theatrical costumier, and at an upper-class orgy in a Long Island mansion to which he is led by the pianist Nightingale. Along the way he is tormented by black-and-white visions of his wife engaging in sex with the phantom naval officer.[260]

The Golden Bowl (2000)

Prince Amerigo (Jeremy Northam) has become impoverished and must take desperate measures to maintain his lavish lifestyle. He marries Maggie (Kate Beckinsale), the daughter of a billionaire, though he is in love with Maggie's beautiful best friend, Charlotte Stant (Uma Thurman). Charlotte marries Maggie's widowed father, Adam Verver (Nick Nolte), to remain close to Amerigo. Amerigo and Charlotte continue their love affair in the shadows for the next five years. But an affair cannot carry on for so long without others knowing about it. Maggie certainly knows about it and confronts Amerigo. Amerigo has come to deeply love his wife and their son. Maggie has come to mean much more to him than Charlotte. Despite her great affection for her father, Maggie realizes that she and her husband must move far away from Adam and Charlotte to save their marriage. Charlotte is distraught and desperate to learn that Amerigo is abandoning her. She has a tearful confrontation with him.

Charlotte: You and I. That's all there is for me. You and I. As if you've never married and I've never married and there are only those weeks we had together in Rome when you loved me.

Amerigo: Charlotte, that's all in the past. In the past.

Charlotte: In the past, is it? Buried and forgotten? That's how it is.

Maggie shows true compassion for Charlotte. She feels that she must find a way to comfort her.

Amerigo: What will you say to her?

Maggie: It will depend on what she will say to me, whatever she can find to save her pride. Anything to make her a little less unhappy. It's only one more lie.

Amerigo: Let it be the last, my dear.

Tempted (2001)

A wealthy businessman, Charlie Le Blanc (Burt Reynolds), is dying. He wants to leave his money to his young wife, Lilly (Saffron Burrows), but he feels that it is necessary to test her loyalty. He offers a handsome young man, Jimmy Mulate (Peter Facinelli), $40,000 to try to seduce Lily. Lily rebuffs Jimmy's advances, but she later learns about Charlie's seduction scheme from Charlie's secretary. Angry, Lilly meets with Jimmy and sleeps with him. Charlie has the rendezvous captured on a surveillance video.

Chloe (2009)

Catherine Stewart (Julianne Moore) suspects that her husband David (Liam Neeson) is cheating on her. She figures to test David's fidelity by hiring an escort, Chloe (Amanda Seyfried), to entice him. But her scheme doesn't work as planned. David turns out to be faithful, but Catherine is seduced by Chloe instead. Catherine immediately regrets the hookup. She quickly writes a check for Chloe and tells her that this payment ends their association. But Chloe, who has become obsessed with Catherine, resents being jilted. She gets revenge by seducing Catherine's son, Michael (Max Thieriot).

The Women on the 6th Floor (2010)

The original French title: *Les Femmes du 6e étage*

The plot isn't complex or original. A wife hires a pretty young maid, who eventually has sex with her husband. In the 1960s, Playboy illustrators were able to tell this story in a one-panel cartoon. But the film provides a story that is, in its heartfelt execution, tender, nuanced, profound and funny.

The film opens in Paris during 1962. We meet a prim and proper couple named the Jouberts. Jean-Louise (Fabrice Luchini), who owns and manages a brokerage firm, is trapped in a wretchedly monotonous routine. He inherited the firm from his father and has never enjoyed running it. He is an excessively orderly and fastidious man. He demands that his morning egg be boiled for precisely three and a half minutes. No more, no less. His wife, Suzanne (Sandrine Kiberlain), is haughty, spoiled, lazy, selfish and narrow-minded. Robert Temple of IMDb wrote, ". . . [Suzanne] is. . . ruthlessly climbing the social ladder. . . wallow[s] in spoilt self-pity [and] 'exhausts' herself every day having lunch with her friends and buying expensive dresses."[261] She is reminiscent of Florence in *The Constant Nymph* (1943), which we will examine in Chapter Nine.

Their maid, Germain Bronech (Michèle Gleizer), had a close and affectionate relationship with Jean-Louis' mother, but the mother is now dead and Germaine feels nothing but animosity towards Suzanne. We learn that the maid raised the Jouberts' two sons with no help from their mother. Germain cannot tolerate bossy, good-for-nothing Suzanne any longer and angrily quits a job that she has held for the last thirty years.

Suzanne is unable to do the slightest housekeeping. While she is looking for a new maid, Jean-Louis runs out of clean plates and clean shirts.

Francisco Franco's dictatorial rule of Spain, which brought about violence, unrest and economic strife, caused many Spaniards to flee their homes and seek refuge in France. This has created an underclass of Spanish workers in Paris. Jean-Louis serves as a landlord to a group of Spanish maids renting bedrooms on the sixth floor of his spacious home. One of the maids, Concepción Ramirez (Carmen Maura), introduces the Jouberts to her niece María Gonzalez (Natalia Verbeke), who has just arrived in town and is looking for work as a maid. Jean-Louis takes an instant liking to Maria, who is warm, vibrant and outspoken. She is hired on the spot to be the Jouberts' new maid.

Sandrine Kiberlain and Fabrice Luchini in *The Women on the 6th Floor* (2010)

Suzanne is jealous that Jean-Louis is spending time with the beautiful and wealthy Bettina de Brossolette (Audrey Fleurot), who has come to his brokerage firm to develop an investment portfolio. Suzanne insists, "She's a man-eater, fleeces married men, ruins them."

Jean-Louis enjoys socializing with the gregarious and vivacious maids. He has a terrific time at one of their parties. He attends Sunday church service with them. Suzanne abandons her sick husband to go to a charity sale, but the maids assemble in his bedroom to care for him. Temple wrote, "[Luchini] has at times the innocent puzzlement of silent comedian Harry Langdon come over his face, a kind of infantile bewilderment. . ."[262]

Suzanne does not approve of Jean-Louis' new friendship with the maids.

Suzanne: You care for those Spanish women, but not about what I did!

Jean-Louis: Is today Wednesday? At 11 AM you had your feet done, then to the dressmaker's, lunch with Marie-France, at 4 PM to Carette's to buy cakes, then off to play bridge with Colette and Nicole.

Jean-Louis experiences a poignant reawakening. He suddenly opens the shades of his firm's conference room. His staff is startled by the unfamiliar shafts of sunlight. His colleagues are dumbfounded by his generosity when he lends a vacant room to a maid who has fled from a violent husband.

Suzanne accuses Jean-Louis of having an affair with Bettina. She says, "For weeks you've had a smug smile on your face, you strut around! I know when something's going on!" She fails to realize that the smug smile really has to do with Maria. Jean-Louis has fallen in love with her. Suzanne demands that he leave their home at once. Jean-Louise quietly moves into a vacant room on the sixth floor. He is happy in the room. He says, "It's my first room of my own. First came boarding school, then the army, then marriage. I really feel free now."

Suzanne deeply regrets having thrown out her husband. She tells her friends, "Maybe Jean-Louis is right. He put some joy in his life. Those women up there are alive. Down here we're dead."

Suzanne wants Jean-Louis to return home, but he loves Maria and cannot go back to a wife who let him down for so many years. Maria spends one romantic night with Jean-Louis before returning to Spain to reu-

226 · ANTHONY BALDUCCI

nite with her son, who she put up for adoption years earlier. Three years later, a newly divorced Jean-Louis travels to Spain to find his lost love.

The Women on the 6th Floor is far more warm and tender than *In the Realm of the Senses*, a film about a husband who takes his affair with his maid to obscene and violent extremes, A husband's affair with the maid is treated in a light and silly manner in *Down and Out in Beverly Hills* (1986).

360 (2011)

Rose Daly (Rachel Weisz) has a rendezvous at a hotel with her extramarital lover, Rui (Juliano Cazarré). But she doesn't look like she's about to enjoy a romp. She strides into the hotel room in a sober mood. She tells Rui that their relationship must end. She makes it clear to him: "We don't have a future." He responds, "We have a beautiful present." She refuses to be distracted.

Rose: I want to talk to you. Can we talk?

Rui: Can I kiss you?

Rose: Can we talk first, please? I need to talk to you.

Rui: Why? What's wrong?

Rose: We - Will you stop? We can't. We have to stop this.

Rui: You're kidding, right?

Rose: No. Can you put some clothes on, please? Put your clothes on.

He removes his bath towel to expose his naked body and she becomes a giggly girl. So, they have sex. Afterward, she acts guilt-ridden. Is this reasonable? Rose works at a magazine and has been giving Rui photography jobs. He acts truly upset when she tells him that the magazine assignments must end as well. That night, Rose attends her daughter's play with her husband, Michael. Michael behaves in a loving manner toward Rose and their daughter. And Michael is played by the not-unattractive Jude Law. So, why did she cheat? It is never explained. Rose's story is one of many stories related in this film.

Some Kind of Beautiful (2014)

Richard Haig (Pierce Brosnan) has sexual compulsions that make him unwilling to marry, but he believes that he needs to change his ways when he gets his young girlfriend Kate (Jessica Alba) pregnant. He works hard to be a good husband and good father, but Kate has an affair with her friend Brian (Ben McKenzie). She explains that their marriage has always been wrong. She says, "I was really young. Okay? Really young. Not that you're not, of course. But I really thought that I loved you, but clearly I was working through Daddy issues. And then I got pregnant, and you were just trying to do the right thing. And you've always been a really good father, but let's face it, you never really loved me. But Brian does."

One Plus One (2015)

The original French title: *Un + Une*

We learn three simple facts about Antoine Abeilard (Jean Dujardin) in the first ten minutes of the film: he is a film score composer, he lives in Paris, and has a good-natured girlfriend named Alice Hansel (Alice Pol). Antoine travels to India to work on an Indian adaptation of "Romeo and Juliet." Samuel (Christopher Lambert), the French ambassador to India, invites Antoine to dinner. Antoine meets Samuel's wife, Anna Hamon (Elsa Zylberstein). Anna is preparing to make a pilgrimage to the holy city of Varanas. She has been unable to get pregnant and understands that people who visit the city can be cured of their ills. Antoine decides to accompany Anna to find a possible cure for his chronic headaches. Anna submits to a religious ritual upon her arrival in Varanas. She starts by purifying herself in the Ganges River. Next, she seeks strength and counsel from Amma, a beloved spiritual leader. During the trip, the couple has sex. They readily admit to each other that the sex was bad. They presume it was because they were feeling guilty. But they hardly look guilty. They are smiling from ear to ear. Anna takes no responsibility for climbing into bed with Antoine. She tells him, "It's your fault too, look at you! You're seductive, funny, free, everything! What am I to do with you?" But they agree in the end that they still have strong feelings for one another and it doesn't matter if the sex was bad. Anna and Antoine are met at the airport by Samuel as well as Alice, who has traveled from Paris. Samuel and Alice assume that Anna and Antoine have had sex because neither of them answered their phone the night before. Is this hard evidence? Anna and Antoine don't bother to argue the point. They admit to what they did and ask for forgiveness. Forgiveness is sharply denied by Samuel and Alice. Samuel says, "One thinks these things only happen to others. Or in the theatre." Pol steals the scene with her poignant portrayal of the heartbroken Alice. Anna tells Samuel, "You're a wonderful man and I screwed up everything." He acts cavalier about the situation. It isn't until everyone else leaves and he is alone that we can see the pain on his face. He answers a call on his cell phone and has to fight back tears as he talks. Years later, Antoine sees Anna at an airport with her rambunctious young son, Antoine (Olias Lelouch). It is an awkward meeting. Antoine is looking at this four-year-old with the same name as him and wondering if this could be his son. They go their separate ways. Antoine drives past Anna and her son on the rainy road. He sticks out a finger for an imaginary gunfight with the boy. Antoine and Anna look longingly at one another through rain-streaked windows. Antoine follows Anna to her home, a well-adorned barge owned by her parents. He gets out of his car, hesitates, then gets back into his car and drives off. Will this couple reunite? Antoine returns to the barge the next day. He knocks on the door. Anna opens the door and smiles. The film cuts back to India. Antoine is being hugged by Amma. Anna is being hugged by Amma. It is their wedding.

Obviously, Anna's pregnancy has more to do with Anna having sex with Antoine than Anna bathing in the Ganges River. But it could be that the mystical charm of Varanas acted to bring Antoine and Anna together for this important purpose? The film has a problem if we believe that Anna was simply attracted to Antoine's pretty face and easy sense of humor. This gives their affair a flippancy that threatens to remove any sympathy for the couple. Should we be quick to celebrate a marriage that destroyed two loving relationships?

Trust (2021)

Brooke Gatwick (Victoria Justice) is struggling to raise the profile of her art gallery. Her husband, Owen (Matthew Daddario), is a television news reporter who is busy with his own career responsibilities. The two have difficulty making time for one another. Brooke becomes attracted to Ansgar Doyle (Lucien Laviscount), a licentious painter who is exhibiting his work at her gallery. She travels with Ansgar to Paris, where he works his seductive charms on her. Back home, Owen (Matthew Daddario) is approached in a bar by an alluring young woman, Amy (Katherine McNamara). Amy recognizes Owen from television. She tells him that she is a journalism major. He is flattered by Amy's endearments and flirtations and takes her back to his home for sex. Afterward, Owen feels guilty and tells Amy that they can never see each other again. Days later, Brooke tells Owen that she was approached by Amy and learned from her of their illicit encounter. She angrily leaves Owen. Amy visits Owen to let him know that Brooke hired her to test Owen's faithfulness. Owen asks Brooke if she had sex with Ansgar in Paris. She refuses to answer. A flashback shows her alone in her hotel room with Ansgar. He embraces her and asks, "Do you think it matters to the universe if you kiss me or not?" She removes her dress and kisses him. But we are not shown if they actually had sex. It looks like the marriage is over. But then Owen shows Brooke plane tickets that he bought weeks before so that they could celebrate Christmas in Paris. He tells her that the flight leaves in three hours. She smiles. So, the two cheating spouses reconcile in the end. The film suggests that trust can easily be restored if a couple loves one another. And two tickets to Paris can help.

Chapter Nine:
Suspicion and Jealousy

The jealous husband was a stock character in early comedies. We see this in the plot of *A Taste of His Own Medicine* (1913). A jealous husband figures to prove his wife's infidelity by sending her a note enticing her to meet "an old admirer." But the wife is not at all pleased to receive the note. She submits the note to the police, who arrest the husband as a masher upon his arrival at the meeting place.

Filmmakers know that they can create sparks if they pair the pathologically unfaithful wife with the pathologically jealous husband. A good example of this is *Dear Murderer* (1947).

In *The End of the Affair* (1999), a private investigator says, "There's nothing discreditable about jealousy, Mr. Bendrix. I always salute it as a mark of true love." But is it?

Let us look at jealousy films in which adultery is sometimes or sometimes not imagined.

The Lady Who Lied (1925)

Fay Kennion (Virginia Valli) leaves her fiancé, Horace Pierpont (Lewis Stone) when she discovers a scantily clad woman in his hotel suite. She marries Dr. Alan Mortimer (Edward Earle) on the rebound. Horace follows the Mortimers to the Sahara to explain to Fay that the scantily clad woman had snuck into his hotel suite to blackmail him. Fay is glad to see Horace again. She admits to him that she has been unhappy in her new marriage due to her husband's frequent drunkenness. Horace invites the Mortimers to join him on a safari. During the safari, Alan becomes upset seeing his wife act affectionately towards her old lover and suspects that the two may have renewed their love affair behind his back. When Horace is bitten by a snake, Alan refuses to treat his rival. But Fay, despite being deeply in love with Horace, convinces Alan that she loves only him. Alan, no longer believing that his marriage is at risk, acts quickly to save Horace's life. The safari continues calmly on its trek through the desert, but bandits attack suddenly and kill Alan. With Alan dead, Fay and Horace are able to again look forward to a life together.

French Dressing (1927)

Philip Grey (H. B. Warner) is bored by his drab wife, Cynthia (Lois Wilson). He finds more excitement with Cynthia's friend, Peggy Nash (Lilyan Tashman). Cynthia finds out about Peggy and assumes (wrongly) that Philip is cheating with Peggy. She immediately travels to Paris for a divorce. Paris is new and exciting to Peggy. She wants to be new and exciting, too. So, she visits a fashion boutique to buy herself a stylish wardrobe. She meets Henri de Briac (Clive Brook), who offers to be her guide to the many attractions of Paris. Philip arrives in Paris to find Cynthia and straighten out their misunderstanding.

Merry Wives of Reno (1934)

Bunny (Glenda Farrell) invites a handsome young boat salesman, Frank (Donald Woods), up to her apartment allegedly to discuss buying a cruiser boat, but she really is interested in having sex with him. Frank becomes indignant. He exclaims, "I happen to be a married man!" Bunny responds coolly, "And I happen to be a married woman, so I'll forgive you if you forgive me." Frank rejects her advances and leaves, but he is so hasty in his retreat that he forgets his coat. Frank does a bad job explaining to his wife, Madge (Margaret Lindsay), why he has come home without his coat. Madge is not the most trusting wife. She decides that the missing coat is all the justification that she needs to travel to Reno for a divorce.

Jean Harlow and Myrna Loy in *Wife vs. Secretary* (1936)

Wife vs. Secretary (1936)

Linda Stanhope (Myrna Loy) is misled by gossip into believing her husband Van (Clark Gable) is having an affair with his secretary, Helen Wilson (Jean Harlow).

A person wrongly suspecting their spouse of adultery can have repercussions just serious as the repercussions that can come from a spouse actually committing adultery. Shakespeare made this clear with two classic plays, "The Winter's Tale" and "Othello." In "The Winter's Tale," King Leontes becomes obsessed with the ill-founded notion that his wife is having an affair with his childhood friend Polixenes. Spark Notes describes "Othello" as follows: "The story of an African general in the Venetian army who is tricked into suspecting his wife of adultery, Othello is a tragedy of sexual jealousy."[263] But comedy can also be derived from this sort of situation. Take, for example, *Do Not Disturb* (1965), in which a woman creates laughable problems in her marriage by wrongly assuming that her husband is having an affair with his secretary.

Wives Under Suspicion (1938)

The film is a lackluster remake of *A Kiss Before the Mirror* (1933). Amazon Prime notes:

District attorney Jim Stowell (Warren William) is convinced that every murder should be sentenced to the electric chair, regardless of motive or circumstances. He remains steadfast in this belief as he prosecutes an elderly professor (Ralph Morgan) for murdering his wife in a fit of jealous rage.[264]

Stowell becomes suspicious that his wife, Lucy (Gail Patrick), is having an affair with a young neighbor, Phil (William Lundigan). Stowell is overwhelmed with an urge to kill Lucy and Phil. But then he learns the truth - Phil loves another woman, who he intends to marry, and he had simply gone to Lucy for marital advice.

Poison Pen (1939)

Sam Hurrin (Robert Newton) receives an anonymous poison pen letter that falsely accuses his wife Sucal (Belle Chrystall) of having an affair with a local shopkeeper, Len Griffin (Edward Chapman). After having a few drinks, Hurrin shoots Griffin down in the street.

Primrose Path (1940)

Ellie May Adams (Ginger Rogers) runs away from her dysfunctional family. She meets Ed Wallace (Joel McCrea) at a beachside restaurant. The couple falls in love and marry. Ed is appalled when he finally meets his in-laws. He learns that his wife's mother and grandmother both made a living as prostitutes and he fears that Ellie May (Ginger Rogers) had at one time followed in their footsteps.

I Take This Woman (1940)

Georgi Gragore (Hedy Lamarr), a beautiful socialite, is gravely depressed over a failed romance with a married man. While traveling aboard a cruise ship, she attempts to jump over the railing to drown at sea. She is prevented from jumping by a kind-hearted young doctor, Karl Decker (Spencer Tracy). Upon her arrival in New York City, Georgi visits Karl at his clinic, which provides health care to a low-income community. She sees that Karl is doing good work and his patients adore him. It inspires her to want to help. Karl offers her a job as his assistant and she accepts. Karl and Georgi marry soon after, but it bothers Karl that he is unable to provide Georgi with the lifestyle to which she is accustomed. He takes a job at an upscale clinic to make more money, but he finds that most of his new patients are wealthy hypochondriacs.

As much as she loves Karl, Georgi can't stop thinking about her lost love, Phil Mayberry (Kent Taylor). Phil has arranged a divorce with his wife, Sandra (Mona Barrie), and he wants Georgi to come back to him. Georgi decides to visit Phil at his apartment to finally confront him about their relationship and see how she still feels about him. Phil doesn't care that Georgi now has a husband. He says, "I am sorry if we have to hurt him. But he knows, everyone knows we belonged to each other before he ever saw you." He insists that Georgi divorce Karl and marry him.

Spencer Tracy and Hedy Lamarr in *I Take This Woman* (1940)

Georgi: This is too important to decide impulsively.

Phil: Love *is* impulse.

Georgi: That is selfish.

Phil: Love *is* selfish.

Georgi: Not always.

Georgi is appalled by what Phil is saying. She realizes at that moment that Karl, the selfless healer, is a much better man than Phil.

Out of spite, Sandra tells Karl that she ran into Georgi at Phil's apartment. Karl blames himself for this situation. He says, "I saw something that didn't belong to me and I took it. But it turns out that finders isn't keepers." Believing that he needs to make drastic changes in his life, he decides to leave the clinic and leave his wife to work on a research project in China. But Georgi is determined to stop him from leaving. AFI notes: "Georgi rallies his old East Side patients to convince him to return to the clinic, and in so doing, finally convinces him of her love."[265] In the end, Georgi rejects wealth and status for love and kindness.

Misbehaving Husbands (1940)

One night, a department store owner puts a damaged mannequin into his car. Passersby believe the mannequin is a woman and assume that the married man is cheating on his wife. When his wife hears about this, she hires an unscrupulous divorce lawyer.

Twin Beds (1942)

Newlyweds Mike and Julie Abbott (George Brent and Joan Bennett) are finding it hard to be alone due to Julie's many convivial friends, who freely drop into the couple's apartment for visits. Abbotts have, in effect, an "open door" marriage. Mike becomes jealous that Julie is regularly visited by Nicolai Cherupin (Mischa Auer), a Russian opera tenor who has moved next door.

The Constant Nymph (1943)

Lewis Dodd (Charles Boyer), a young composer, visits his ailing mentor Albert Sanger (Montagu Love) at his farm in the Swiss Alps. Dodd is enchanted by Sanger's three musically gifted teenage daughters, particularly Tessa (Joan Fontaine). Tessa is secretly in love with Lewis. She dreams of helping him to reach his full potential as a composer. Sanger dies during Lewis' visit. Lewis contacts the girls' uncle, Charles Creighton (Charles Coburn), to fetch the girls. The uncle arrives accompanied by his beautiful daughter, Florence (Alexis Smith). Lewis and Florence find themselves attracted to one another and fall in love. The couple is married soon after. However, it soon becomes obvious that the marriage came about too quickly. Lewis disapproves of Florence's shallow obsession with social climbing. He is particularly bothered that, in hoping to elevate him as a composer, his wife has arranged for him to perform a musical recital for her influential friends. Meanwhile, the couple receives news that Sanger's bohemian daughters are not getting along well in boarding school. Lewis is happy to allow the daughters of his beloved mentor to live with him and his wife. Florence, though, is not so happy. In time, Lewis comes to feel an even greater animosity towards his wife. His list of grievances against her grows substantially. He resents her petty fixation on her social standing. He resents her snobbishness. He resents her controlling manner. He resents her constant mistreatment of her young cousins. He is particularly protective of Tessa, who has a heart condition. It becomes increasingly obvious to Florence that there is a romantic affections between her husband and Tessa.

Charles Boyer and Joan Fontaine in *The Constant Nymph* (1943)

Uncle Charles is the voice of reason in the film.

Florence: She'll get him. If she hasn't already!

Charles: My dear girl, what are you talking about? You know, Florence, I'm not quite such a fool that I don't see what's going on. It's obvious. A blind man could see it. I mean, what's going on with you, not with anyone else. You are the one that's heaping coals of fire. And let me tell you, if you care anything about this husband of yours, you'd better pull yourself together. Stop mooning about like a woman in a novel. You have little Tessa on the defensive for him. I heard it just now.

Florence: I dislike her intensely.

Charles: Yes, and you've made that quite obvious to all and sundry.

Florence: I saw my sister, Evelyn, get herself into just such a mess, and it killed her. Lewis has been very happy here, and so have I, until these wretched Sanger children came storming back. They're like a drug to him. There's some sort of language between them that only they themselves can understand. Oh, I feel like a stranger in my own house. He said quite casually to me today that he might go off, away, alone, after the concert. . . Lewis is the only man I ever truly cared for or I ever will care for. It's some sort of a strange, slow process of defeat. They're either very innocent... or very clever.

Charles: If you don't stop hammering away at it, you'll force them to make a bolt for it. You'll see. You don't want them to bolt, do you?

Florence: That's my nightmare. I'm so afraid of it. I couldn't stand it.

Charles: Poor little Florence. Come on. Get your chin up. You've always had your own way. You want everything you wanted all along the line. Now, if you have to be a loser, well. . .

Lewis has to spend much time and effort preparing for a major performance at a concert hall. He tells Tessa that, after the performance, he wants her to run away with him to Brussels. She recoils from his proposal. Florence suspects that the two have something planned and, on the night of the concert, she confronts Lewis about her suspicions. Lewis confesses to Florence that he loves Tessa. But he assures her that, because Tessa is unwilling to hurt Florence, she will not have him. Florence becomes furious. She refuses to believe that Tessa is concerned about her. She flies into a rage upon seeing her young cousin. She seizes her by the shoulders and shakes her.

Florence: I'm accusing you directly into your face. You flung yourself at my husband in this house, and you succeeded!

Tessa: I can't help it if I love Lewis! I did long before you came to Switzerland, and it's not a happy thing. It's brought nothing but sadness into my life, and yet, it's so much of me, I wouldn't want it to be different. But I have come to understand that he's your husband, and. . . I'm not going to see him anymore. That's the reason I want to go away. But, as for your thinking that we. . . or anything else. It's horrible, and it's shocking, and I wouldn't even lower myself to deny it. But I've told you that I love Lewis, and I can't help it.

Florence forces Tessa into her bedroom and locks the door. Smith was boosted above her 5'9" height by high heels, which made her appear as an intimidating adversary to 5'3" Fontaine.

In a 1933 film adaptation of the story, Tessa climbs out of the window and meets Lewis at the concert hall. The couple leaves by boat for Brussels, but Tessa falls ill during the journey. Lewis takes Tessa to a boarding house, where her condition worsens. He blames himself for putting Tessa into this situation. Tessa dies as he sobs at her bedside.

However, Tessa doesn't run off with Lewis in this version. She is unwilling to run off with her cousin's husband. She tells Lewis:

> She's my cousin. I've been living in her house. She's been very kind. And, anyway, you belong to her. But if it weren't for that, I'd rather go away with you than anything else in the world. But as things stand, I can't. I can't. They'd say we've been carrying on behind Florence's back. I'd be a traitor. I can't. One must do as one thinks right, mustn't one?

So, instead, she dies at Lewis and Florence's townhouse while listening to Lewis' performance on the radio. As she dies, Tessa dreams of meeting with Lewis back in the picturesque Swiss Alps. She tells him that she promised herself to him long ago. Not in words, but in her heart. Why didn't he wait for her to grow up? "But you belong to me," she says. "You always have, even before I was born. When you were a little boy, you must have longed inside of you for me - for me to take care of you. I was on my way to you then. I'm late, but I'm here."

Alexis Smith and Joan Fontaine in *The Constant Nymph* (1943)

The 1933 version of *The Constant Nymph* was fairly similar to the 1943 version.

Lewis asks Tessa if it matter to be good if being good means being unhappy. Tessa replies, "I don't believe we'd escape unhappiness being in one another's company."

This version's Florence, played by Leonora Corbett, is just as starchy, class-conscious and dementedly jealous as Alexis Smith's Florence. She confronts Lewis. She demands, "Is she your mistress?"

Tessa makes it clear to Florence that she has done her no harm, but she refuses to believe her and shoves her onto a couch.

Florence: You betrayed me. Under my own roof. In my own house.

Tessa: Well, let me get out of your house.

Florence: And whose house will you go to then?

Victoria Hopper, the 24-year-old actress cast as Tessa, had a small frame and a girlish face that made her believable as a sensitive 14-year-old schoolgirl. Corbett towers over Hopper just as Smith would later tower over Fontaine. But Hopper seems more physically vulnerable and childlike, which makes Corbett appear more monstrous.

Tessa's final words before she dies: "You know, Florence thinks I'm your fancy lady."

Claudia (1943)

Edmund Goulding directed *Claudia* and *The Constant Nymph* in the same year.

Claudia Naughton (Dorothy McGuire), a childlike newlywed, meets her roguish new neighbor, Jerry Seymour (Reginald Gardner). Jerry tells her, "I haven't a scruple. . . I have no hesitancy when it comes to other men's wives. . . I'm not a very nice person." But he comes to realize that Claudia is odd. He tells her on his way out, "Forget what I said about other men's wives. It doesn't go here." Claudia takes this to mean he doesn't find her physically attractive and she is greatly offended. The next day, Claudia is feeling glamorous in a new dress that her sister-in-law gave her. She flirts with Jerry to test if a man other than husband can find her desirable. She sees this as a harmless experiment, but David is furious when he catches Jerry kissing his wife.

The Story of Shirley Yorke (1948)

Lady Camber (Beatrix Thomson) dies during surgery. It comes out that the attending nurse Shirley Yorke (Dinah Sheridan) was once engaged to her husband, Lord Gerald Ryton (Derek Farr). Gossip leads to the nurse being accused of poisoning her patient to resume her relationship with the lord.

Unfaithfully Yours (1948)

A symphony conductor, Alfred de Carter (Rex Harrison), suspects his wife (Linda Darnell) of having an affair. He cannot get his suspicions out of his mind as he arrives at his latest concert. During the concert, he fantasizes about the various melodramatic ways that he can address the situation.

Wikipedia notes:

[H]e conducts three distinct pieces of classical music, envisioning revenge scenarios appropriate to each one: a complicated "perfect crime" scenario in which he murders his wife and frames Windborn (to the Overture to Rossini's Semiramide), nobly accepting the situation and giving Daphne a generous check and his blessing (to the Prelude to Wagner's Tannhäuser), and a game of Russian roulette with a blubbering Windborn, that ends in de Carter's suicide (to Tchaikovsky's Francesca da Rimini).[266]

Harriet Craig (1950)

Harriet Craig (Joan Crawford) is, as a wife, jealous, distrustful and possessive. She explains how she got this way in the film's denouement. She says:

> I wouldn't trust the love of any man after the things I've seen. I found out all about what you men call love the day my father left us. He always pretended to love my mother, and I worshiped him. And one day after school, I went to his office. I found him with a woman. A cheap, vulgar blonde. What a sight they were. And I saw him for what he really was, a fat old fool with liquor on his breath. He said he was ashamed, and tried to tell me it had nothing to do with his love for us. Well, maybe he could fool my mother, but he couldn't fool me. I told him I never wanted to see him again. I hated him, and I'd always hated him! That night, he didn't come home. He never came home. I watched my mother tramp the streets looking for a job. And at 14 I had to quit school and go to work. First in a factory, and then in a laundry. We almost starved! So don't talk to me about protection. Don't try to tell me anything about love.

Darling, How Could You! (1951)

Amy (Mona Freeman), an imaginative young teenager, sees a play about adultery and comes to the undue conclusion that her mother Alice (Joan Fontaine) is having an affair with a family friend.

My Wife's Best Friend (1952)

Virginia Mason (Anne Baxter) is furious to learn her husband George (MacDonald Carey) had a dalliance with her best friend, Jane Richards (Catherine McLeod).

Mandy (1952)

The saddest story in this category can be found in *Mandy*. Despite her husband's objections, Christine Garland (Phyllis Calvert) leaves home to enroll their young deaf daughter, Mandy, in a school for the deaf. The headmaster, Dick Searle (Jack Hawkins), takes a special interest in Mandy and provides special lessons for the girl outside of the school. Gossip spreads that Christine and Dick are having an affair. The gossip eventually reaches Christine's husband, Harry (Terrence Morgan), who hastily rushes off to confront his wife.

A Cuckoo in the Nest (1954)

Peter and Barbara Wickham (Brian Reese and June Thorburn) plan to travel by train to their country house in Somerset. However, Peter shows up late, after the train along with his wife have left without him. Peter meets an old friend, Carol Hankin (Kay Kendall), who has also missed the train. He suggests that they rent a car to get to Somerset on their own. Peter and Marguerite pretend to be husband and wife to get a room at an inn. Barbara comes to believe that Peter and Marguerite have run away together.

Never Say Goodbye (1956)

The film is a remake of *This Love of Ours* (1945).

Jealousy creates great suffering in *Never Say Goodbye*. Dr. Mike Parker (Rock Hudson) is having a drink at a nightclub when he is shocked to see his late wife, or at least a woman who resembles his late wife, playing a piano for patrons. Mike approaches the woman, but she becomes upset and flees into the street, where she is struck by a car. While the injured woman is treated at the hospital, Mike looks back at his marriage. Cue flashback. Mike meets Lisa Gosting (Cornell Borchers), a lovely nightclub entertainer, while working as a US Army doctor in Vienna in 1945. Mike and Lisa happily marry, but Mike's continual jealousy places a great strain on the marriage. After a particularly upsetting argument with Mike, Lisa visits her father in the Russian sector of Vienna. Before she can return home, the Russian military closes the border and she is not allowed to return home. Lisa is arrested when she tries to sneak across the border. She is accused of being a spy and sent to prison. A United States official, Colonel Washburn (Edward Earle), expresses great pessimism in his assessment of the situation to Mike. He admits that it can be difficult for a person to survive the brutal conditions of a Russian work camp. After awhile, Mike assumes that Lisa is dead. The flashback ends.

When Lisa is released from the hospital, Mike takes her to see their daughter Suzy (Shelley Fabares). Suzy is unwilling to believe that she is her mother. She becomes hysterical, thinking that her father is tricking her to accept a new wife. Suzy has only a vague memory of what her mother looked like. But, fortunately, there's a guest at their home who can help her with this. The guest, Victor (George Sanders), sketches portraits at a nightclub. Mike asks Suzy to describe to Victor what she remembers of her mother's appearance. Victor listens carefully as he prepares a portrait based on the girl's description. Wikipedia notes: "Lisa is about to leave when Suzy, having seen Victor's sketch, realizes who she is and calls out to Lisa to come back."[267]

Jubal (1956)

A bedraggled cowboy, Jubal Troop (Glenn Ford), is befriended by a genial rancher, Shep Horgan (Ernest Borgnine). Shep gladly gives Jubal a job as a ranch hand.

The newcomer wades into the various tensions - ranch hand Pinky (Rod Steiger) has a tense relationship with Shep, Shep has a tense relationship with his wife Mae (Valerie French), and Mae has a tense relationship with Pinky. Jubal manages, without intention, to provoke strong emotions to rise to the surface. Andrew Pragasam of The Spinning Image wrote, "Each of the principal characters fixate on Jubal Troop in their own particular way. Whether it is the almost paternal affection he inspires in the uncouth but affable Shep, the desperation and lust instilled in Mae or the seething resentment drawn from Pinky."[268]

The beautiful young Mae only married Shep because he had money. She tells Jubal that, before she met Shep, she had received nearly two dozen marriage proposals. But none of her prospective husbands interested her.

Mae: Then Shep came up to Calgary to buy cattle and everybody said he was a Wyoming cattle king. When I asked him was he really a cattle king he said sure, and would I be his cattle queen and come to his castle? And he laughed the way he does. His "castle." This is where he brought me - 10,000 acres of nothing.

Jubal: This is a fine ranch.

Mae: For men, horses and bulls. For a woman, it's 10,000 acres of lonesomeness.

Out of boredom, she had an affair with Pinky, but Pinky's volatile and controlling behavior caused her to quickly end their relationship.

Mae now becomes attracted to Jubal. Jubal is quick to fend off her advances. She kisses him, but he pulls away. He insists, "We're ending this before it starts." She is undeterred.

Mae: If you're talking about conscience, I haven't got any, not about him.

Jubal: He loves you, Mae.

Mae: Loves me? Shep? I'm no more than his pet filly, his heifer. You heard him. I'm livestock. With men, maybe he's great. With a woman, he's an animal.

Mae is afraid to leave Shep. She asks Jubal if she should go back home "with my tail between my legs" and "get laughed at."

Pinky dislikes Jubal for having displaced him as foreman. His brooding resentment leads to Othello-style treachery. The cowhands set up camp while on a cattle drive. As they are getting settled for the night, Pinky gets into an argument with Shep. Out of spite, he tells Shep that Mae and Jubal have been spending time together behind his back.

Shep rides home and is happy to find Mae sleeping alone in bed. But then she rolls over, half asleep, and calls out Jubal's name. Shep drags her out of bed and shakes her. He demands to know if Jubal was with her. Mae is fed up pretending that she loves Shep. She wants to get rid of him for good. She shouts:

Yes, he was. Here. Yes. You want to know why? 'Cause I'm sick of you. I'm sick to my stomach every time you kiss me. Let go of me! I hate you. I hate the way you look. I hate the way you look at me. I hate the way you feel. I hate every single thing about you. I love him. Do you hear? I love Jube!

Shep finds Jubal at a bar. He has his rifle in his hands and tells Jubal that he has come to kill him. He has no interest in hearing anything that Jubal has to say. Jubal has to act quickly to stop Shep. A cowhand, Reb Haislipp (Charles Bronson), tosses a revolver to Jubal, who shoots Shep square in the chest. Jubal kneels beside Shep and, with tears in his eyes, confirms that his friend is dead.

In the end, Mae is beaten to death by Pinky, Pinky is hung by the townsfolk, and Jubal rides off into the sunset with his true lady love (Felicia Farr).

Hell on Frisco Bay (1956)

Upon his release from prison, Steve Rollins (Alan Ladd) shuns his wife Marcia (Joanne Dru) for having briefly dated another man during his incarceration.

Home Before Dark (1958)

Charlotte Bronn (Jean Simmons) is discharged from a mental heath facility, where she has spent months recovering from a nervous breakdown. The doctor assesses the situation to her husband, Arnold (Dan O'Herlihy), as well as to us. He believes that her bitter relationship with her stepsister and stepmother has caused her a great amount of stress. She has long been resentful and jealous of her stepsister, Joan (Rhonda Fleming). But her feelings may not have been entirely irrational. It is possible that Joan once had a well-hidden affair with Arnold.

Stress Is Three (1968)

Fernando (Fernando Cebrián) drives to the beach with his wife Teresa (Geraldine Chaplin) and his best friend Antonio (Juan Luis Galiardo). Teresa is bored and finds pleasure in flirting with Antonio, but Fernando knows that he and Teresa have been having marital problems lately and he cannot help but be alarmed by the flirting. He comes to suspect that Teresa and Antonio are having an affair. Charlot47 of IMDb wrote, "By the end, when the three have reached a deserted beach, we are not sure how much of what we see is only in Antonio's tortured mind, which has turned to thoughts of murder."[269] Near the end of the film, Fernando sees Teresa and Antonio kissing behind a rock. But is this just another of his hallucinations? He imagines shooting Antonio in the chest with his speargun. But, afterward, the trio calmly pack and head home, speaking about returning to the beach at another time.

Cadillac Man (1990)

Larry (Tim Robbins) learns that his wife, Donna (Annabella Sciorra), is having sex with a co-worker at the car dealership where she works. In a jealous rage, he arms himself with a machine gun and takes everyone hostage at the dealership. He won't leave until he finds out who Donna's lover is.

Torment (1994)

The original French title: *L'Enfer*

Paul and Nelly Prieur (François Cluzet and Emmanuelle Béart) run a seaside hotel. Paul becomes jealous when he notices Nelly being friendly with a handsome guest, Martineau (Marc Lavoine). The next day, Paul secretly follows Nelly. Nelly takes a boat ride with Martineau to a nearby island. The couple remains on the island for nearly a half hour before they return to the hotel. Paul imagines them having sex on the island and cannot get the idea out of his head. His jealousy devolves into out-and-out madness. It is ambiguous if, in the end, he murders Nelly or he only imagines murdering her.

My Wife is an Actress (2001)

A man is jealous that his actress wife has to do a sexy bedroom scene with a handsome co-star.

Two (2002)

EdgarSTR of IMDb wrote: "[T]he film flows at a rapid pace, as the story advances and unravels the chain of misunderstandings that lead the titular couple to suspect each other of adultery."[270]

Unforgivable (2011)

A crime writer, Francis (André Dussollier), spends his summers on Sant'Erasmo Island. He becomes enthralled by a local realtor, Judith (Carole Bouquet), and is eager to marry her though she has a reputation on the island for being promiscuous. He becomes apprehensive when they return to the island the following summer. Surely, he thinks, she will be tempted to have sex with one of her old lovers. Francis hires Jérémie (Mauro Conte), a high-strung young man recently released from prison, to follow Judith. Francis, himself, is far from a trustworthy spouse. His first wife became so distressed by his chronic infidelity that she became addicted to sedatives. It was because the sedatives impaired her driving that she became involved in a fatal car crash. This has made Francis' daughter, Alice (Mélanie Thierry), resentful of her father. Alice is not a faithful spouse either. She leaves her husband Roger (Alexis Loret) and daughter Vicky (Zoé Duthion) to run off with a man. She says, "I can't say a word against Roger. He's a supportive husband, the perfect father. A bit too perfect, too supportive. I need to be unsettled." Judith notices Jérémie following her and angrily confronts him. It turns out that Judith recognizes Jérémie. When Jérémie was a boy, Judith and Jérémie's mother were lovers. Jérémie admits that he always saw Judith as a femme fatale. After they talk for awhile, he brazenly asks her for a kiss. The couple kisses and has sex. No character in this film is moral or rational, which makes it impossible to care what happens to anyone.

Chapter Ten:
The Kept Woman

The mistress sometimes became a victim, especially if she allowed herself to become a kept woman. A little-known film, *Dame Chance* (1926), presented an early portrayal of the kept woman. Between 1931 and 1933, Hollywood films were thick with kept women - Gloria Swanson in *The Trespasser* (1929), Greta Garbo in *Inspiration* (1931), Constance Bennett in *The Easiest Way* (1931), *The Common Law* (1931) and *Bed of Roses* (1933), Joan Crawford in *Possessed* (1931), Mae Clarke in *The Impatient Maiden* (1932), and Tallulah Bankhead in *Faithless* (1932).

A sugar daddy who sets up a woman with an apartment, money and clothes did not necessarily have to be married. The motives of an unmarried man funding a love nest was explicitly explained in *Possessed*. It's a romantic union without legal commitments or public scrutiny. Clark Gable, who has Crawford as his kept woman, says, "Losing a sweetheart is a private misfortune. Losing a wife is a public scandal."

We have already seen a kept woman in *Up for Murder*. But now let us examine the ultimate kept woman film.

John Boles and Irene Dunne in *Back Street* (1932)

Back Street (1932)

Back Street has no wild melodramatic twists. It is a serious, straightforward story.

The film opens in Cincinnati during the early 1900s. Ray Schmidt (Irene Dunne) is an exuberant, free-spirited young woman. She enjoys socializing with the traveling salesmen who come through town, but she has never had serious feelings about these men. But then she meets Walter Saxel (John Boles), who has come to town to attend a band concert with his mother. The couple instantly falls in love. Walter admits being engaged, but he indicates that his mother pushed him into this relationship. He believes that, if Ray comes to the band concert, he can introduce her to his mother and get his mother's approval for them to pursue a relationship.

Ray is delayed on her way to the concert by her sister Freda, who is threatening to throw herself out of window because her boyfriend Hugo has left her. She arrives at the band concert just as the crowd is breaking up. She wades through the crowd, desperately looking for Walter. She finally stops, knowing that she has missed him. She is heartbroken.

Walter is angry believing that Ray stood him up. He returns home to marry his fiancée as planned. Years later, Ray and Walter meet again in New York City. Walter is doing well as a financier on Wall Street. He is now married and has two children. He confesses that he is unhappy with his wife and still loves Ray. Now that they have found each other again, the couple is unwilling to go their separate ways. Walter says, "When I hold you in my arms like this, nothing else seems to matter. You're like a drug to me." But Walter has a busy and unforeseeable schedule due to his many work, family and social commitments. He cannot see how he could be free to see Ray unless she quits her job and lives on standby for his visits. She agrees with Walter and allows him to set her up in a low-cost apartment.

Irene Dunne in *Back Street* (1932)

Ray makes great sacrifices for the occasional bliss of true love. She is lonely most of the time, having to suffer long periods of separation from Walter. She wants to have a child, but this is not something that Walter will permit. The film depicts, according to John Flaus of Senses of Cinema, the couple's "rare satisfactions and ecstasies."[271]

Ray expresses her displeasure about this situation during one of Walter's visits.

Walter: Missed me?

Ray: You don't know how much! It's terrible!

Walter: Only three days have passed. . .

Ray: Only three days! It doesn't mean much to you, because you're always busy. Why, with me? I spend time hanging on the phone, or listening for your key in the door, always waiting, waiting. . . Oh, Walter, it's been terrible!

Ray pretends that it doesn't matter, but it doesn't take her long to return to the subject.

Walter: Didn't I write to you?

Ray: Darling, I had three postcards from you all summer.

Walter: Now, Ray, I know I wrote you more often than that. Some of them must have gone astray.

Ray: Well, it's possible.

Walter got done with his business in Europe four weeks early and decided to spend the extra time vacationing in Switzerland. When he finally got back home, he didn't get around to phoning Ray for two days.

Ray: You ought to know what my days are like. Playing solitaire, making over an old dress now and then, going to market. . . It's been fiendish at times, Walter. I gave up my job so that I could be free when you were here. Well, that was alright. But what I have got? Solitaire, waiting for the phone to ring, waiting for you to come, dying when you don't. I can't meet your friends, I can't make any of my own. You don't know how empty my life is.

Walter: Empty, darling? When do you have me?

Ray: That's just the point, darling, I don't always have you. I didn't have you this summer. You're going to be a busier man as the days go by. And there'll be other trips where Ray can't go along. I can't go on, Walter, waiting, hoping, empty-handed. Walter. . . give me a child!

Walter: Ray! Are you mad? I can't even imagine you suggesting such a thing! Aside from the moral issue involved, have you thought of the consequences? No, of course you haven't. Well, it would spell ruination. . . at least for me! Think of the possible scandal. What it might do to my future! It's unthinkable! After all, Ray, you're not my wife! Ray! I'm sorry, I didn't mean to say that!

Ray calmly accepts Walter's demands.

With his busy life, Walter isn't reliable in sending Ray the money that she needs to support herself. This makes it even harder for her to cope with their arrangement. She has a chance to escape from her hardships when she encounters Kurt Shendler (George Meeker), an old boyfriend from her hometown. Kurt has become rich from manufacturing automobiles. He has always loved Ray and asks her to marry him. She returns home to marry Kurt, but Walter comes after her and begs her not to leave him. She agrees, giving up a perfect chance to break free of Walter.

Walter: If you wanted to make me suffer, you succeeded. It's been terrible! I never knew I could need any human being as I've needed you. I have no right to ask anything of you. I'm a cad if you like. I can't offer you anything that you are about to enjoy - a home, respectability, children. I only know one thing. I need you! I love you! Come back to me, Ray. You're trying to run away from something, Ray, but you can't. We belong to each other.

Ray: But, Walter. . . if I do go back, where will it all end?

Walter becomes wealthy and travels internationally on business matters. He brings Ray along with him on his trips. Unfortunately, his traveling companion does not go unnoticed by Walter's friends, family and business associates. His children, now adult, hear the gossip and come to resent Ray. Walter's son, Dick, confronts Ray. But Walter walks into this scene and admonishes his son. That night, Walter suffers a stroke. While he lies dying in bed, he asks Dick to phone Ray so that he can hear her voice for one last time. Dick can now see how much his father loves this woman. After his father dies, he promises Ray that he will continue to support her. Ray is pleased by Dick's visit. After he leaves, she speaks lovingly to Walter's photo. She says, "Your son is going to take care of me. He was so nice. He might have been my son, our son. I wonder, Walter, what would have happened if I'd met your mother that day in the park." Tim Dirks wrote:

> [S]he retreated into fantasy and replayed in her mind that she had actually met his mother (Maude Turner Gordon) at a local band concert in the park, who greeted her warmly: "So you are Ray Schmidt. You are nice. My dear, you are all he said you were. And I hope you both will be very happy." In the film's final moments, . . she murmured: "I'm coming, Walter, I'm coming" and succumbed (by slowly bowing her head onto the table holding Walter's portrait).[272]

She collapses and dies.

Back Street provides a sympathetic perspective of the other woman. The carefree girl we meet at the start of the films becomes lonely, ashamed and anguished.

The film took adultery away from the gleaming Art Deco settings of other adultery films. The story's heroine is having an extramarital affair with a wealthy financier, but she herself lives in a meager and dimly lit apartment. It is inside this grim and airless place that much of the story is set.

Dunne made it her specialty to play the suffering heroine in adultery films, also including *If I Were Free* (1933) *No Other Woman* (1933), *The Age of Innocence* (1934), *This Man Is Mine* (1934) and *When Tomorrow Comes* (1939). Boles, too, continued in this genre. Both actors were reunited in *The Age of Innocence*.

The film was remade in 1941 with Charles Boyer and Margaret Sullavan. The remake was more substantial in the first two acts, effectively fleshing out the story, but it could not rise to the level of the original when it came to the tearjerker third act. It would have been difficult for any actress to improve on Dunne's poignant death scene.

Three Wise Girls (1932)

The film explores the love lives of three best friends, Cassie Barnes (Jean Harlow), Gladys (Mae Clarke) and Dot (Marie Prevost).

Gladys tells Cassie that she's having problems with her boyfriend, Arthur Phelps (Jameson Thomas). She says:

> I'm a sensible girl, Cassie. But where Arthur Phelps is concerned, I stop thinking. He's married, you know. . . And his wife won't give him a divorce. . . I went to [her]. I begged her to give him up. She threw me out. . . That's what love's done for me, Cassie. I can't give him up and I can't have him. I'm. . . . Well, I'm just up the creek without a paddle.

Cassie implores her to leave him. "I'd just as soon be dead," she says.

Cassie later finds out that her own boyfriend is married.

Gladys: Naturally. They're always married. And they're rich, and handsome, and you're in love with them.

Cassie: But he didn't tell me.

Gladys: Of course he didn't tell you. Why should he? They never do until you're so far gone you're tied up in a knot.

Cassie: What am I going to do, Gladys?

Gladys: Do? Nothing. Chalk it up to experience. Forget that he ever existed. You never met him, see? It was a bad dream.

Cassie: I can't give him up. Oh, I love him too much.

Gladys discusses Cassie's situation with Dot. She says:

Believe me, I've learned plenty. And if Cassie deliberately walks into the spot like I'm in, she ought to have her head examined. Why, you put yourself at the mercy of the man every time. He can walk out on you whenever he pleases and what can you do? Do you know what you become when you live the way I do? A panhandle. You have to bow, and scrape and beg for everything you get. And that goes for love as well as money. Their wives get everything. A home, security, respect, everything. And what do you get? Nothing. Nothing but grief.

Gladys attempts killing herself by drinking poison.

Constance Bennett in *Bed of Roses* (1933)

Bed of Roses (1933)

Lorry Evans (Constance Bennett) is a kept woman. She loves Dan (Joel McCrea), who operates a barge, but she is provided with a lavish lifestyle by wealthy publisher Stephen Paige (John Halliday). She must confront the conflict between her rational objectives (for comfort and security) and her emotional desires (for love and romance) when Dan asks her to marry him. Should she spend the rest of her life as the modest wife of a barge skipper or continue as the well-maintained mistress of a publishing magnate? Should she vacate a luxury suite for the sleeping quarters on a barge? Lorry is able to make a choice by kissing Dan. The kiss convinces her, without a doubt, that she will be better off with Dan. Marrying based on the power of a kiss is love at its hormonal best.

Bennett previously portrayed a kept woman in *The Easiest Way* (1931) and *The Common Law* (1931).

Up in Central Park (1948)

A wealthy married man (Vincent Price) tries to make a naïve young woman (Deanna Durbin) into a kept woman.

Shirley Booth and Robert Ryan in *About Mrs. Leslie* (1954)

About Mrs. Leslie (1954)

Vivien Keeler (Shirley Booth), a singer at a Greenwich Village club, meets George (Robert Ryan). He is a quiet man, but she can tell that there's great depth to him. The two get to know each other while strolling through Central Park. They find it easy to talk. Vivien is able to make her new friend laugh. George tells her that he is leaving for California to spend six weeks at a beach house. He explains that he has been working hard and needs a rest. He invites Vivien to be his "vacation companion." He offers to pay her. Vivien bristles at the offer at first. It sounds unsavory. But George explains that he is not interested in a sexual relationship. He just wants companionship.

George: We'll even be chaperoned.

Vivien: The last time I was chaperoned, she wound up with my date.

Much of their days at the beach house are spent swimming and fishing. Vivien observes George walking along the shore. She says in voice-over, "He was just a little boy, one of those poor little rich kids who didn't have anyone to play with." Their evenings are quiet, with George mostly reading books on the Civil War.

This film isn't *From Here to Eternity*. George and Vivien are never seen erotically outstretched on the shore. They possess a tranquil bliss, not the blind passion that allows a couple to embrace and kiss while the surge of a tide washes over them. George is a man intensely devoted to his job. He probably never felt an overwhelming passion for a woman. But George and Vivien are more than satisfied with the arrangement. A restful vacation at the beach becomes an annual ritual for them.

George gives Vivien money to help her out and she uses the money to open up a dress shop. She doesn't know anything about this highly introverted man until she sees him featured in a newsreel. He is a wealthy manufacturer and, more important to her, he is married. She later learns that the noted man died by way of a Times Square news ticker. She inherits enough money from his estate to buy a home, which she turns into a boarding house.

Fred MacMurray and Shirley MacLaine in *The Apartment* (1960)

The Apartment (1960)

The perfect mistress lament came from Shirley MacLaine's Fran Kubelik in *The Apartment*. She says to her married boyfriend Jeff Sheldrake (Fred MacMurray):

Look, Jeff, we had two wonderful months this summer, but that was it. Happens all the time. Wife and kids go away to the country, and the boss has a fling with his secretary or the manicurist or the elevator girl. Come September, the picnic's over. Goodbye. The kids go back to school, the boss goes back to the wife, and the girl. . .

Jeff tries to defend himself, but Fran doesn't want to hear what he has to say. She continues:

They got it on a long-playing record now, *Music to String Her Along By*: "My wife doesn't understand me. We haven't gotten along for years. You're the best thing that ever happened to me."

A lack of maturity is evident in the irresponsible way that Jeff and other married business executives carry on with young mistresses. Jeff tells his employee Bud Baxter (Jack Lemmon), "You see a girl a couple times a week, just for laughs, and right away they think you're going to divorce your wife. Now, I ask you, is that fair?" Baxter shoots back, "No, sir, it's very unfair. Especially to your wife."

The Mistress (1962)

The film explores the anguish of the other woman.

Bibi Andersson is The Girl. Max von Sydow is The Married Man. The meetings between them are cloak-and-dagger affairs. The Married Man shows up wearing the standard spy outfit - trench coat, floppy hat and thick eyeglasses. He is without expression. The clandestine phone calls they share consist mostly of breathy whispering.

Today when he arrives, she looks and behaves like a little girl excited that daddy has come home. The actress was 26 years old at the time, but she looked somewhat younger. She is small - 5' 4". Her face is sweet and angelic. von Sydow, at a height of 6' 4", towers over her.

The Girl: How long do we have?

The Married Man: Don't ask me that.

The Girl: I want to know.

The Married Man: Half an hour.

The Girl: Not more?

The Married Man: Twenty minutes really.

The Girl: Twenty minutes - my marriage with you.

She notices that his shirt is wrinkled.

The Girl: What will your wife say when you show up with your shirt like this?

The Married Man: She'll probably iron it.

The Girl: I'll iron it for you. Take off your shirt. You have enough time for that, right? Please let me.

Her friend (Per Myrberg), billed only as "The Boy," loves her, but she does not feel the same towards him. The Boy finds a secret letter that The Married Man wrote to The Girl. He now knows about the affair. The Girl accepts a temporary job as nanny in England so that she can get away from The Married Man. The Boy supports the move and helps her to pack for the trip. But The Married Man phones in the middle of their packing and demands to see her. She refuses him forcefully, but he persists and she cannot resist him for long. She says that he can come over. The Boy agrees to leave and come back later to finish the packing. When he returns, he finds his friend naked in bed. She's clutches her sheet to her bare chest, clearly ashamed. Obviously, The Married Man had been there while he was out. Not wanting to embarrass her, he ignores her awkward state and casually recommends that they get back to packing.

The next morning, The Girl is relieved to finally be aboard the train, unaware that The Married Man has slipped aboard as well. He operates as stealthily as an assassin. He is not happy about her leaving. He acts jealous and possessive. He intimidates her into spending the night with him in his compartment. A knock on the doctor startles them. Has someone found them out? It is just the conductor collecting tickets. The Girl breathes a sigh of relief. This confirms in her mind that this relationship is frightfully wrong.

The Married Man buys The Girl a train ticket under his wife's name. She says, "I borrow everything. Even your wife's name. I don't really exist. Feel! Pinch! Pinch hard! Can you feel that this is me?"

She is clear to him that she is not happy to see him.

The Girl: What do you want? What are you doing here? We've said goodbye.

The Married Man: No, we haven't said goodbye. Not in a proper manner.

He begs her to stay. He promises to finally divorce his wife.

The Married Man: Don't you love me anymore? No answer?

The Girl: I don't want to talk about this anymore.

The Married Man: But what have you decided?

The Girl: To never see you again.

He takes hold of her. She asks him not touch her because her skin is sunburned. She says, "It's tender. My skin is peeling. What animals shed their skin? Snakes, isn't it? I'm a snake. My old skin is peeling off."

In *Sunshine Cleaners* (2009), Rose (Amy Adams) musters the courage to end her relationship with a married man, Mac (Steve Zahn).

Rose: Look, this thing that we've been doing - it's not -

Mac: Let's not do that.

Rose: I don't want this anymore.

Mac: So that's it.

Rose: That's it then.

It can be that simple.

Any Wednesday (1966)

The executives in *The Apartment* relied on an employee's apartment for their illicit meetings. But John Cleves (Jason Robards) simply sets up his own love nest, which he lists in his accounting records as an executive suite. This way, he can write it off as a corporate expense. Installed at the executive suite is Cleves' beautiful young mistress, Ellen (Jane Fonda). He makes time in his schedule to visit her every Wednesday. Clever, eh? Maybe he should have used this same cleverness in selecting his new secretary. A client, Cass Henderson (Dean Jones), comes to town and is unable to find a hotel room. Cleves' new secretary, unaware that the executive suite is occupied by the boss' lady friend, refers Cass to the address. Cass is surprised to arrive at the suite and find it is occupied by Ellen. At first, he assumes that Ellen is a party girl that Cleves has hired to entertain him.

Cleves' wife, Dorothy (Rosemary Murphy), comes to see Cleves at his office. His secretary tells her that her husband had to stop off at the executive suite. This leads to Dorothy meeting Ellen and Cass at the suite and inviting them out to dinner with her and her husband. Before the end of the evening, Dorothy realizes that Ellen is her husband's mistress. She tells Cleves that she's leaving him and moving into the executive suite. He begs her to give him another chance. She says that he can come visit her on any Wednesday.

About Love (2017)

Nina (Anna Chipovskaya) loves her husband, Sasha (Aleksey Chadov), but their debts are putting a great strain on their marriage. Nina meets a bank president, Sergey (Dmitriy Pevtsov), who takes a liking to her. She is seduced by his wealth, enjoying lavish treatment whenever she sneaks off with him. It doesn't matter to her when she finds out that he's married. Sasha becomes furious when Nina tells him that she's sleeping with another man. He shoves her, tosses water into her face, and throws her out of their home.

Sergey and Nina are accompanied by bodyguards as they get into a limousine. Sasha, who has been hiding around a corner, comes rushing at Sergey with a knife. The bodyguards are about to shoot him when Nina intervenes. She slaps Sasha and demands that he calm down. "Sasha," she says. "It's too late. You can't change anything anymore." Once he is calm and listening to her, she speaks more gently to him. She convinces him to leave.

Years later, Nina encounters Sasha at a hotel. He is doing well in his career and is dating Nina's friend Lara (Mariya Mironova). He asks her if she loves Sergey. She says that she does, but she has accepted that Sergey doesn't love her. It hasn't brought them any closer having a child together. He had been clear to her that she didn't want the child, but she insisted on having the child anyway. Sasha and Nina get a hotel room and have sex. Sasha admits to her that he still loves her. Nina says, "Love is nonsense, Sasha. It's a sickness. I've become someone else, Sasha. I alone determine my life. I decide what's good, what's bad. I don't depend on anyone. It's my body. I do with it what I want. It's my soul. It will belong to no one else." She has given her body to an unaffectionate rich man in exchange for a fine lifestyle. Unlike Ray in *Back Street*, Nina has somehow found empowerment in being a kept woman. Is this possible?

Chapter Eleven:
Emotional Crisis

Bette Davis in *Beyond the Forest* (1949)

Forbidden passions can unleash a destructive force on one's life. The opening title card of *Beyond the Forest* reads in part: "Thus may we know how those who deliver themselves over to [evil] end up like the Scorpion, in a mad frenzy stinging themselves to eternal death."

Rick Reynolds of Affair Recovery wrote:

Dorothy Tennov coined the term "Limerence" in her 1979 book Love and Limerence: The Experience of Being in Love. The term was used to describe a condition she had witnessed in her interviews with over 500 people on the topic of love in the mid-1960s. Tennov described limerence as an intense romantic desire. It's a form of "crazy love" that consumes the thoughts of those so stricken. . . Limerence is an intense form of romantic love characterized by an emotional attachment or even an obsession with another person, which usually is involuntary, and which contains a strong desire for the reciprocation of those feelings. . . If they feel the other person doesn't return their "love" or if they feel the other party is moving away from them they can become despondent, depressed and even suicidal.[273]

Richard Taylor, the author of "Love Affairs: Marriage & Infidelity," wrote, "[Cupid's] arrow is a poisoned one which, upon finding its target, destroys all reason and intelligence, leaving the victim to stumble helplessly about in response to a kind of intoxication. . ."[274]

Husband's Holiday (1931)

Again, a film shows that a good marriage is not a safeguard against adultery. pitcairn89 of IMDb wrote, "[Boyd] can't make up his mind, between his wife (Vivienne Osborne) and girlfriend (Juliette Compton). He is the least likable character in the movie, as he dithers around, and tortures everyone around him."[275] AlsExGalR of IMDb wrote, "Mary won't give him [a divorce], assuming that he'll have his 'husband's holiday,' tire of the affair, and come back."[276] Mary finds out that her beloved sister, Cecily Reid (Dorothy Tree), is dallying with a married man. She now realizes that being the other woman doesn't necessarily make a woman an evil homewrecker. So, she finally agrees to the divorce. Boyd reacts with disappointment, realizing that he loves Mary and doesn't really want to leave her. Christine is devastated seeing that Boyd is still devoted to Mary. She fails at a suicide attempt, but she realizes afterward that she needs to start a new life. She writes Mary a letter to let her know that George never loved anyone but her. Then, she quietly leaves town. George returns to Mary, who happily accepts him back.

Merrily We Go to Hell (1932)

Jerry Corbett (Fredric March) tells his wife Joan (Sylvia Sydney) that he cannot stop himself from leaving their home to see his mistress. He pleads with her to lock the door so he cannot leave.

Robert Montgomery, Madge Evans and Walter Huston in *Hell Below* (1933)

Hell Below (1933)

In film history, interlopers have sometimes acted self-righteous about intruding into a marriage and stealing a spouse. Take, for example, Julie from *Jezebel* (1938). Julie is rattled when she learns that her beloved Press has married another woman.

Aunt Belle: (*consoling*) Julie, child, I'm so sorry.

Julie: For heaven's sake, don't be gentle with me now. Do you think I wanna be wept over? I've gotta think, to plan, to fight.

Aunt Belle: But you can't fight marriage!

Julie: Marriage, is it! To that washed-out little Yankee. Pres is mine! He's always been mine.

Another self-righteous homewrecker is Thomas Knowlton, the main character of *Hell Below*. Knowlton, played with fury and bluster by Robert Montgomery, is ruled by his emotions in a way that edges him closer and closer towards madness. He is a navy lieutenant, but he lacks the military discipline that an officer should have. Knowlton is determined to marry Joan (Madge Evans) even though it means taking her away from her paraplegic husband, Herbert Standish (Edwin Styles). He is a passionate lover. Too passionate. When he loves someone, no one and nothing else matters. The affair incurs the ire of Joan's father, T. J. Toler (Walter Huston), who holds great authority as Knowlton's commanding officer.

Is love and happiness more important than commitment and duty? This is addressed throughout the film.

Toler follows Joan to Knowlton's home. Knowlton doesn't act startled at Toler's appearance. He snidely offers the man a drink. Toler raises his glass for a toast. "To discipline," he says, "there's nothing like it. . . and nothing without it." Knowlton responds, "To discipline. . . it leaves almost nothing." The men proceed to get into an aggressive debate about marital fidelity.

Knowlton tells Toler that he has no intention of sneaking around with Joan. He promises to confront Joan's husband about their relationship. Toler warns, "You'll be careful, won't you, when he stands on both legs and fights for what he thinks is his."

Knowlton asserts that he and Joan didn't plan to fall in love. He says, "There's no book of regulations governing that."

Toler: There use to be a code of honor.

Knowlton: Code of honor? What's dishonorable about a man and woman falling in love and admitting it to the only person who has a right to know - her husband?

Toler: What's honorable about admitting an intention to steal and then going ahead with it? It's still theft, isn't it?

Knowlton tells Toler, "Life can't be lived on a sentimental basis, there isn't time." He insists that they love each other above and beyond old-fashioned rules and nothing is more important than making each other happy. He concludes, "We're going to get as far away from this red plush sense of honor and decency that you got as we can. . . Call it selfishness, call it rotten and low, call it anything you like. But it's love, too. The only thing we know and greater than anything."

Toler is unmoved by Knowlton's grand speech. He responds, "Get this, if she thinks she can sneak off in the dark with you - both of you riding roughshod over your obligations, slapping honor and decency in the face - if you two can find a happiness based on the misery of a shattered faith and a pair of withered legs, then I don't know anything about life."

Knowlton's love of a friend, just as fanatical as his love for Joan, causes him to defy orders and jeopardize the lives of other crew members. After their submarine torpedoes a German minelayer, Knowlton's friend

Brick (Robert Young) commands a boarding party to search the sinking vessel for code books. Brick's mission is suddenly interrupted by an attack from German planes. Knowlton receives an order from Toler to submerge the submarine before the planes have a chance to bomb them, too, but Knowlton madly fires a machine gun at the planes in a futile effort to save his friend. Another crew member has to knock him unconscious to stop him. In a later battle, Knowlton hallucinates seeing Brick alive on his rowboat. Contrary to Toler's orders, he forces his crew into an attack on German destroyers to initiate a rescue. His love of his best friend is so powerful that it causes him to abandon duty and logic during a life-threatening battle. His actions put the submarine into a perilous situation and lead to the death of eight crew members.

Knowlton has grave misgivings about his plans with Joan after he meets Herbert at a hospital. He pretends to be drunk and goes on a callous rant. He grumbles, "I'm sick of all this talk about what's right and what's wrong!" He repeatedly accuses Toler of being heartless and inhuman for talking to him about honor and decency. He calls him "a puritanical preacher." He tells him, "The first night [Joan and I] met, we fell into each other's arms and we liked it. That's all there is to that."

Toler understands that Knowlton's drunk act was designed to turn Joan away from him. He says, "You sent that girl back to her duty."

Navy commanders fear that German submarines are on their way to the Adriatic. There's only one channel that the submarine can use to get through. The Navy sends off a battleship loaded with explosives. Once at the channel, the captain is to make sure that the ship explodes so that the passage will be blocked by tons of rubble. Toler is in charge. He hopes to abandon the ship before it explodes. But Knowlton has snuck aboard. He pushes Toler over the side of the ship and stays on board to make sure that the ship reaches its destination. He is still on board when the ship explodes. He has sacrificed his life much like Jack did in *Other Men's Women*.

Kay Francis and Jean Muir in *Dr. Monica* (1934)

Dr. Monica (1934)

Dr. Monica Braden (Kay Francis) is an obstetrician. She has devoted her life to guiding women through pregnancy, but she wants more than anything to get pregnant herself and have her own baby. Unfortunately, her efforts to get pregnant with her husband John (Warren William) have been unsuccessful. Meanwhile, her husband is carrying on an affair with a young and beautiful aviatrix named Mary Hathaway (Jean Muir).

John has to go on a long business trip to Europe and figures that it's best to break off his relationship with Mary before he leaves. Mary is heartbroken, but she understands that their relationship couldn't last. She lets him know that their breakup doesn't change her feelings for him. "John," Mary says, "I love you so much. Right or wrong, nothing matters."

Mary finds that she's pregnant with John's child and approaches Monica to be her obstetrician. Monica regularly visits Monica's home to care for the expectant mother. One night, she overhears Mary becoming hysterical on the phone. "May I speak to Mr. Braden please," she cries out. "I've got to speak to him. You've got to tell me where I can get in touch with him. He's got to be here. John!" Mr. John Braden. Mary now knows the truth. AFI reported, "Although Monica is stunned at the news, her close friend Anna reminds her of her duty as a doctor, and Monica delivers Mary's baby."[277]

Mary leaves the baby with Monica and then commits suicide by flying her airplane into the ocean.

This film is unusual in that the cheating husband never has to confront his wife or his mistress. He never has to be punished for his bad behavior. Instead, the wife and mistress work out everything without involving him. He comes out in the end rather well off.

John Boles and Irene Dunne in The Age of Innocence (1934)

The Age of Innocence (1934)

Is it best for us to live by principles or desires?

Newland Archer (John Boles) is a prominent lawyer who works and socializes among the elite of New York City. He is looking ahead to a happy marriage with socialite May Welland (Julie Haydon). But he doubts his plans when he meets May's cousin, the beautiful and sophisticated Countess Ellen Olenska (Irene Dunne). Ellen has created a scandal for her family by abandoning her husband in Europe. Newland's law partner asks him to dissuade Ellen from getting a divorce to preserve her family's reputation. Newland and Ellen find themselves attracted to one another. It excites him the way that Ellen flouts convention. Newland tells Ellen that he wants to marry her, but Ellen refuses to hurt May by sneaking off with her fiancé. Ellen moves to Washington, D. C. to get away from Newland. Newland dejectedly marries May.

Ellen's husband, Count Olenska, asks her to return to him, but she is happy without him and refuses to resume their marriage. The count responds by cutting off her allowance. Her grandmother (Helen Westley) has also been providing Ellen with an allowance and she, feeling much like the count does, sees no good reason to continue financing her recalcitrant grandchild.

Newland remains obsessed with Ellen and, after a time, he seeks her out again. Ellen relents to reunite with him and the couple finally consummates their relationship. Ellen returns to New York to care for her sick grandmother. She sees Newland regularly. The two agree for Newland to divorce May so that they can be together. Newland tells her, "We can't go on like this - together, not together." But May become pregnant and he can no longer bear to abandon her.

The film advances twenty-six years. Newland, now a widower, has accompanied his son to New York. His son tells his father that he has arranged to visit his mother's cousin, Ellen, who has returned to New York and lives nearby in an apartment. Newland cannot bring himself to see Ellen again after these many years. He says, "I want to remember it all as it was." He sits outside the apartment building as his son goes inside alone. After a few moments, he stands and walks back to his hotel.

Newland and Ellen spend much of the film feeling horribly oppressed. The film features these two unhappy people dragging their feet through opulent sets. Ellen implies that she feels as dead and meaningless as a desiccated mummy on display at a museum. It is the least moral character in the film who thoroughly enjoys life. Mark Waltz of IMDb wrote, "Lionel Atwill plays a middle-aged high-society rascal who has led a scandalous life and has probably broken a lot of hearts."[278]

The Murder Man (1935)

Mary (Virginia Bruce), who writes an advice column, consults Steve Grey (Spencer Tracy) about one of her latest letters.

Mary: Since you're such a smart little boy, perhaps you can help me answer this one. "My wife has fallen in love with a musician. I still love her, but I fear the worst."

Steve: Tell him to buy a saxophone and enter a contest.

Mary: Idiotic as it sounds, it's vital to this poor, silly, little man. There is such a thing as love, you know?

Steve: Yeah, yeah, I know, I discovered that once myself.

Mary: Well, good, I'm glad to hear there's some real emotion under that hard-boiled exterior of yours.

Steve: Yeah, I know what love is and I know what hate is. And I know exactly what that poor sap is going through. He's in a hopeless muddle, that's why he writes to you. If I thought it'd help him any, I'd answer it for him myself. But, advice is no good. In a case like this, you're caught in the rapids. And you go exactly where it takes you.

In films, a lover is swept away in a grand passion. In *The Virtuous Sin* (1930), Marya says, "I think love is like a wave. If it comes on you unawares, nothing can stop it from sweeping over you."

I Married a Doctor (1936)

The film is based on the novel "Main Street: The Story of Carol Kennicott" by Sinclair Lewis (New York, 1920) and the play of the same name by Harriet Ford and Harvey O'Higgins (Indianapolis, July 18, 1921).

A small-town doctor, Dr. William P. Kennicott (Pat O'Brien), returns from Chicago with a new bride, Carol (Josephine Hutchinson). The townsfolk are wary of outsiders. One woman jeers, "As if there weren't plenty of eligible girls in our own city."

Carol comes to feel repressed in Gopher Prairie. The college-educated bride is appalled by the tedious small-town existence. But she finds a cause that excites her. She believes that the town's appearance could be greatly improved. Wikipedia notes: ". . .[S]he is filled with disdain for the town's physical ugliness. . ."[279] She imagines a beautifully redesigned version of the town, but she cannot find support for her ideas with the town council.

The subject of marital fidelity comes up between William and Carol. William believes that, in a good marriage, a husband and wife should be able to trust one another.

William: I have confidence in your goodness and decency.

Carol: What a horrid thing to say to a woman.

William: Don't you believe in goodness and decency?

Carol: Holding people together? No. I only believe in love. If that stops, they have nothing left, have they?

Carol develops a relationship with Erik Valborg (Ross Alexander), a tailor's apprentice who aspires to be a poet. Erik, like herself, is an outsider in town. Carol advises him to leave Gopher Prairie and attend college in the city. "You got to leave here," she insists. "You don't belong." Erik asks Carol to leave with him, but she tells him that he has misunderstood her feelings. She says, "I do love you. . . as a friend, my dearest friend."

Erik confronts William. He is determined to take Carol away from him. William tells him, "A man's happiness takes a lot of earning. A lot of earning. You go out and earn your's and don't try to spoil another man's happiness."

The rejected young man gets drunk to relieve his sorrow and is killed in a car crash. Most people in the community blame Carol for his death.

Robert Allerton Parker of The Independent and The Weekly Review wrote of the play:

. . . [O]ur sympathies are all on the side of Main Street and Dr. Will. That this is the intention of the playmakers is evident from their soundly built-up climax in the second act, when Carol is revealed embodied in Will all the bravery, courage and adventurous spirit she could not find elsewhere. More definitely in the play than in the novel, Carol emerges as a Puritan, prairie Emma Bovary, unable to face the realities of life and blaming her surroundings for her own fundamental emptiness."[280]

Max Holleran of Public Book is not too fond of Williams as he is portrayed in the novel. He wrote:

Dr. Kennicott is not an oaf or abusive; he is simply complacent and uninteresting. He loves his wife and his town but lets his marriage languish and accepts rural Minnesota parochialism with something like pride. When Carol organizes a smashingly successful Chinese-themed dinner party with paper costumes and exotic chow mein, he absorbs his friends' praise, bids them farewell, and then tells his wife to stick closer to the normal social script of telling a few corny jokes and serving meatloaf.[281]

Carol never consummates her infatuation with Erik in the book. It creates gossip that many people see Carol and Erik regularly walking together. One person observed that the pair is "quite chummy."[282] William gets her to break off her relationship with Erik before anything serious happens. This affair, which is a small part of the book, becomes the center of the film. The infatuation is made decidedly one-sided by the film. Cliff Aliperti of Immortal Ephemera wrote:

Carol's growing infatuation with Valborg that Lewis masterfully grows throughout the latter part of his novel is completely absent from I Married a Doctor. . . In I Married a Doctor any thought of romance resides solely with the intense young Valborg. . . This invention of the film leads to a more dramatic opportunity than originally offered by Lewis. . . Alexander comes off as a buffoon when he storms into the Kennicott home to declare, "You're free!" to Carol. Now had this happened in the novel, Carol may very well have jumped into Valborg's arms, but in the movie she's as put off. . . and provides a swift reality check to the moody youngster, who makes a far more immature decision and subsequent exit than the meeker Valborg of the page would ever imagine.[283]

Holleran wrote:

In the past, it's true, Americans did believe that their small towns were superior; indeed, the Jeffersonian tradition of democracy — built on the backs of yeoman farmers — regarded tight-knit, rural communities as the building blocks of American society. How exactly did Americans begin distrusting small towns? How did American small towns stop being great?[284]

He cites novelists' coming-of-age stories as the reason that Americans turned against the small town.

. . . [T]he city represents openness, with adolescents growing into adulthood among a multitude of interactions. Conversely, the small town — every bildungsroman reveals — is a dungeon, where the potential for personal development goes unfulfilled.

And of all the books to change this perception, of all the books that extolled cities and deplored small towns, one shines out: Sinclair Lewis's Main Street. First published in 1920 and a runaway best seller, Lewis's novel may have single-handedly, and radically, transformed American perceptions of life outside cities.[285]

Where is it that people get ridiculous ideas about life? Novels, novels, novels.

Carol is unwilling to get pregnant. From the novel:

How people lie! How these stories lie! They say the bride is always so blushing and proud and happy when she finds that out, but — I'd hate it! I'd be scared to death! Some day but — Please, dear nebulous Lord, not now! Bearded sniffy old men sitting and demanding that we bear children. If they had to bear them —! I wish they did have to! Not now![286]

Carol becomes frightened when she learns that she's pregnant. From the novel:

The baby was coming. Each morning she was nauseated, chilly, bedraggled, and certain that she would never again be attractive; each twilight she was afraid. She did not feel exalted, but unkempt and furious. The period of daily sickness crawled into an endless time of boredom. It became difficult for her to move about, and she raged that she, who had been slim and light-footed, should have to lean on a stick, and be heartily commented upon by street gossips. She was encircled by greasy eyes. Every matron hinted, "Now that you're going to be a mother, dearie, you'll get over all these ideas of yours and settle down." She felt that willy-nilly she was being initiated into the assembly of housekeepers; with the baby for hostage, she would never escape; presently she would be drinking coffee and rocking and talking about diapers.[287]

Carol flees to Washington D. C. with her child. A year later, she and Will have a brief reunion. She enjoys her time with Will, but she regrets their time together when she learns that Will has gotten her pregnant again. Mark Schorer of American Heritage wrote:

[The] pregnancy causes her to return [to Gopher Prairie], and with a second child to divert her, she relaxes, but not without continuing reservations, into the life of Gopher [Prairie].[288]

The story is obviously modeled on *Madame Bovary*. Emma Bovary, too, becomes bored with her marriage and disappointed with motherhood. She diverts her attention to a bright young law student, Léon Dupuis, who in some ways resembles Erik.

Mayerling (1936)

The Emperor Franz Josef of Austria-Hungary (Jean Dax) sees his son Rudolph (Charles Boyer) as a feckless young man. He arranges for him to marry a Belgian princess in the hope that marriage will make him more responsible. The story advances to the fifth anniversary of Rudolph's marriage. Rudolph is deeply unhappy with his life. But then he meets Baroness Marie Vetsera (Danielle Darrieux) and falls in love. She is more to him than life itself. He tells her, "You don't know what you mean to me, how good you are for me." But, as he is the heir to the Austrian throne, his life is not his own. His love for Maria is a forbidden love. Rudolph is so frustrated having his father control his life that he has a breakdown in front of Maria. But he is determined to end his agony and be with Maria. Rudolph tells Maria's brother, Georges (André Fouché):

No one in the world loves Maria more than I do. . . Before she came along - you couldn't understand all I'd have to say. She set me free with her gaiety, her youth, her love. Was I to refuse all that? Think about it. Nothing in this world is really mine, not even myself. Like everyone, you think I have everything I could desire. Or perhaps you think that being the emperor's son means I have no right to the woman I love. Be fair: What was I to do? Georges, Maria is my love, and soon all will know. As soon as I'm free, I'll marry her. She knows that.

The film is based on true events. The film builds steadily to the infamous suicide pact that ended the lives of Rudolph and Maria. The ClassixQuest blogger wrote:

> There was an ominous mood that accumulated throughout and any shred of positive emotion or romance was immediately stifled by a symbolic prop or line of dialogue that pointed toward the grave, such as the skull on Rudolph's desk, him firing a gun at his reflection in the mirror, his growing paranoia and mental anguish, a puppet show in which a character is punished for feelings of true love, and Maria wishing on her wedding ring that she dies before he does. . . Charles Boyer played the character completely drenched with grief throughout, leading to that out of control party scene that played more like a horror movie in that we do not know what deprave acts his depression will make possible. . . Death was obviously always going to be his escape hatch. He just had to find the right person with which to share that.[289]

It's Love I'm After (1937)

Basil Underwood (Leslie Howard), a conceited stage actor, is distressed by the persistent advances of a love-struck fan, Marcia West (Olivia de Havilland). He figures to dissuade Marcia by pretending to be married to his leading lady, Joyce Arden (Bette Davis).

Marcia: I forgive you. You can't help it that you met her before you met me.

Basil: Have you no shame?

Basil made the mistake of kissing Marcia, which convinced her that he has feelings for her. She tells him, "Oh, you're just being chivalrous about your wife. I admire you."
Marcia goes to confront "the wife."

Marcia: I'm terribly sorry for the heartache I've caused you, but it was something beyond the control of either Basil or myself. We were helpless to fight against it.

Joyce: Yes, yes, I understand. Love swept you along like leaves in the wind.

Marcia: Yes! Oh, I'm so glad you understand.

Joyce: Are you so desperately in love with him, my dear?

Marcia: I think he's wonderful. Basil, you married the most marvelous woman. She has such understanding.

In This Our Life (1942)

Rotten Tomatoes notes, "Stanley Timberlake (Bette Davis) is 24 hours away from marrying her lawyer fiancé, Craig Fleming (George Brent), when she absconds with Dr. Peter Kingsmill (Dennis Morgan), the husband of her sister Roy Timberlake (Olivia de Havilland)."[290]
Stanley expresses remorse to Roy for having had an affair with Peter. She says, "I didn't mean to hurt you. I don't know why it happened. I didn't know at the time. It's like lightning. Like being struck by lightning."

Stanley believes that she has a right to pursue her happiness. Her father, Asa (Frank Craven), tells Stanley, "In my day, we didn't talk about happiness. If it came, we were grateful for it. We were brought up in the belief that there were things more important." "What things?" asks Stanley. "Oh," he says, "old fogy, fantastic notions. . . such as duty and personal responsibility."

Those guilty of adultery can attribute their actions to a powerful force beyond them. In *Little Children* (2006), an adulterer sees her behavior being controlled by something even odder than lightning. "She didn't feel shame or guilt," says the narrator, "only a sense of profound disorientation, as if she had been kidnapped by aliens then released unharmed a few hours later."

Bette Davis and Olivia de Havilland in *In This Our Life* (1942)

Ossessione (1943)

The film is based on James Cain's "The Postman Always Rings Twice." Geoffrey Nowell-Smith, a Visconti biographer, wrote, "*Ossessione* is a film about the destructive power of sexual passion."[291]

Giovanna (Clara Calama) married overweight, middle-aged Giovanna Bragana (Juan de Landa) purely for the steady income provided by his roadside inn. Gino Costa (Massimo Girotti), a young and handsome drifter, arrives at the inn and stirs a passion in Giovanna. Gino asks Giovanna to join him on the road, but she has to refuse him. Giovanna is very different than Gino, who has been seduced by the open road. She prefers a stable and secure home life. The open road, with its endless possibilities and uncertainties, cannot offer her the security that she desires. The author of the Cinema Neorealismo website notes: ". . . [T]he force pulling him away from Giovanna is his fear of a traditional commitment."[292] He points out that, after the couple has sex the first time, "Giovanna shares with Gino all of her deepest problems while he listens to the sound of waves in a seashell.[293]

So, Gino leaves the roadside inn and resumes his nomad existence. On the road, he makes friends with another drifter, Spagnolo (Elio Marcuzzo). Spagnolo, according to Cinema Neorealismo, is a symbol of "liberated masculinity."[294] Giovanna encounters Gino again in a drunken, bleary-eyed state at a singing contest. This encounter brings them back together.

Massimo Girotti and Clara Calama in *Ossessione* (1943)

In time, the couple conspires to murder Bragana. They murder Bragana (off screen) and make it look as if he died in a car crash. The couple does not feel free after the murder. They feel a great weight pressing down upon them. They constantly sense the presence of the dead man at the inn. They murdered Bragana to end the guilt and deception that had taken over their lives. But the murder has brought them far more guilt and far more deception.

Cinema Neorealismo noted: "In one particularly memorable scene that anticipates a major theme of neorealism, *Ossessione*'s central female character enters her wildly messy kitchen, serves herself a bowl of soup and sits down with a newspaper, only to fall asleep, slumped over wearily in the midst of the confusion."[295]

The film achieves a realism lacking in (and arguably needed by) the glamorous and stylish Hollywood version.

After Giovanna becomes pregnant, Gino and Giovanna agree to start a new life somewhere else. The couple is driving off when they notice they are being trailed by the police. Determined to get away, Gino attempts to get around a truck, but he instead drives the car down an embankment. Giovanna dies as the car flips over and crashes into a river. Gino, devastated, surrenders to the police.

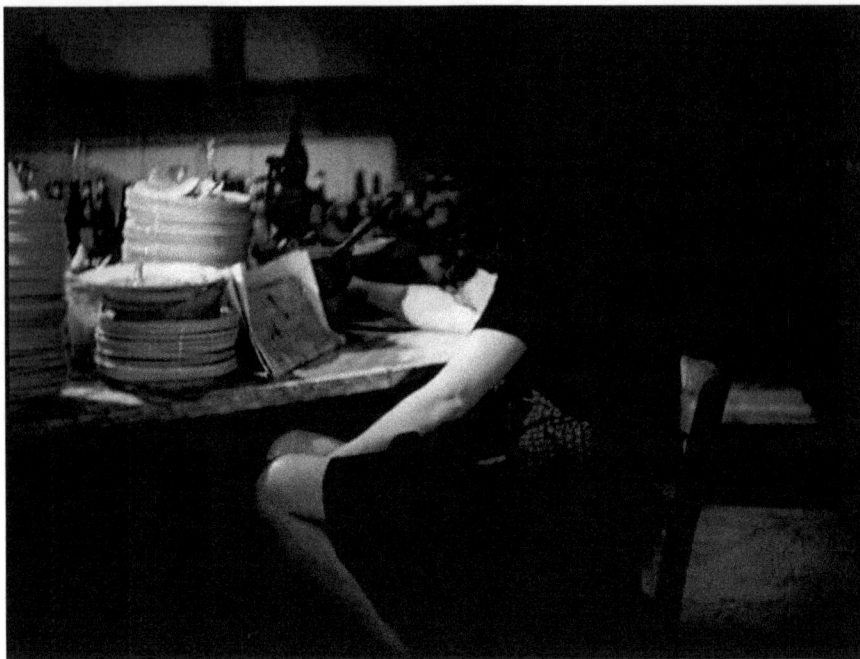

Clara Calama in *Ossessione* (1943)

Daisy Kenyon (1947)

Daisy cannot overcome her feelings for her married lover, Dan O'Mara (Dana Andrews), although she has to discreetly share him with his wife and two children.

Daisy dates a widowed war veteran, Peter Lapham (Henry Fonda). Paul falls in love with Daisy and asks her to marry him. Daisy is hesitant to accept. How can they possibly commit to one another? She can see that Paul is struggling with grief over the death of his wife. She, meanwhile, is still in love with Dan. But they marry anyway.

Surprisingly, Dan's wife asks for a divorce. Daisy has a poor choice: she can continue with a man who still loves his dead wife or continue with a man who loves only her but has unbreakable ties to a living wife. Peter is grateful for Daisy having been around when he needed her, but he is willing now to let her go off with Dan. Dan refuses to a settlement in the divorce suit even though it will mean that the details of his relationship with Daisy will come out in the trial. But it doesn't take long for him to see that the court proceedings are taking a toll on Daisy. He willingly signs a settlement to end his marriage. He can now marry Daisy as soon as she divorces Peter. But Daisy is not sure if that's what she wants to do. She goes off to her cottage in Cape Cod to think about it. On her arrival, she gets a call from Dan, who tells her that he and Peter are nearby. Dan says: "We're on our way to face this thing out. There's no use running away." Daisy drives off in a panic and crashes her car. She emerges from the wreck uninjured, but the wreck has shaken some good sense out of her and she now knows what she wants to do. When she arrives at the cottage, she is startled to greet Peter and Dan, who are anxious to plead their cases and have Daisy make a decision. She tells them, with no hesitation, that she wants to remain with Peter.

Dana Andrews, Joan Crawford and Henry Fonda in *Daisy Kenyon* (1947)

The Upturned Glass (1947)

Michael Joyce (James Mason), an eminent neurosurgeon, is separated from his wife and devotes his time and energy solely to his practice. One day, Emma Wright (Rosamund John) brings her young daughter Ann (Ann Stephens) to him. She is upset as her daughter is going blind. Emma relies heavily on Michael's emotional support as her husband is away on a business trip. Michael performs an intricate surgery that saves the girl's sight. Michael and Emma fall in love as the doctor supervises Ann's recovery. Once it becomes clear to them that they have fallen in love, the couple agrees to never see each other again. She says, "It could never be alright. Neither of us is free or likely to be free. There's nothing we can do about it."

Years later, Michael is stunned when he receives news that Emma toppled out of her bedroom window and died from a broken neck. He doubts that this could have been an accident. Could she have killed herself? He investigates the incident, going as far as romancing Emma's sister-in-law Kate Howard (Pamela Kellino) for information. He learns that Emma was in good spirits at the time of the incident. She was looking forward to her husband coming home. So, it doesn't appear to be suicide. He comes to believe that Kate pushed Emma out of the window out of a grudge. He has Kate trapped inside Emma's old bedroom. He shouts at her, "You tried to get money out of her because you thought she was being unfaithful. Then when that was no good you poisoned [her] child's mind against her. You might just as well have killed yourself. You're just as guilty this way." He acts deranged as he charges towards her. In a panic, she backs away and falls out of the window.

Letter from an Unknown Woman (1948)

James Naremore, who wrote a book about *Letter from An Unknown Woman* for BFI Film Classics, described the opening of the 1922 novella on which the film was based:

[A] carefree, successful, 41-year-old author, identified only as "R.,'. . . returns home to Vienna after a vacation in the mountains and finds in his mail a letter of roughly two-dozen pages in an unfamiliar handwriting. He relaxes in a chair, lights a cigar and reads a woman's words from the grave. "My child died yesterday", the letter begins. The woman is suffering from the same influenza that killed her child, and she, too, will soon be dead. She writes because "I have only you, who never knew me, and whom I have always loved."[296]

The novella's Austrian author, Stefan Zweig, achieved worldwide popularity for his prolific work in the 1920s and 1930s. Let us now move to the film.

Stefan Brand (Louis Jourdan) prepares to flee Vienna to avoid a duel. But, before he leaves, he receives a letter from a woman he cannot remember. The woman is Lisa Berndle (Joan Fontaine), who Stefan first met when she was a teenage girl living next door. He went on to meet her on two more fateful occasions. The second meeting proved to be the most fateful. While working as a dress model, Lisa regularly makes time in her day to wait for Stefan outside of his apartment. She finally meets him one night. He doesn't recognize her, but he asks her out to dinner. They enjoy a romantic evening, which ends in Stefan's bed.

The next day, Stefan leaves town for a concert and promises to contact her when he gets back. He never does. garykmcd of IMDb notes, "Brand has had many women in his life however and unaware that Lisa is genuinely in love with him, forgets all about her."[297] Meanwhile, Lisa finds out that Stefan got her pregnant. She has the baby and never lets Stefan know about it.

Joan Fontaine and Louis Jourdan in *Letter from an Unknown Woman* (1948)

Ten years later, Lisa is married to Johann Stauffer (Marcel Journet). Johann is aware of his wife's past relations with Stefan and thinks very poorly of the man. Lisa sees Stefan perform at an opera. He is no longer the star musician that he once was. She feels embarrassed for him and leaves the show early. Stefan, who has come off stage by this time, sees Lisa leaving the theatre and follows her outside. He is sure that he remembers her from someplace, but he can't figure out exactly who she is. Lisa is uncomfortable because she is expecting her husband to arrive to take her home. Johann does arrive and is unhappy to meet Stefan. Lisa later visits Stefan at his home. He still does not recognize who she is. Lisa knows now that he never really loved her and sadly departs.

The letter was forwarded to Brand from a hospital. It is announced in a card attached that Lisa and her son died of typhus. He asks his servant if he remembers Lisa. The servant nods solemnly. As he leaves his home, he sees a ghostly image of Lisa opening the door for him. He steps outside and gets into a waiting carriage. He has decided to accept his challenge to duel. His opponent is Lisa's husband, Johann.

Beyond the Forest (1949)

Rosa Moline (Bette Davis) is terribly bored with her weak-willed husband Lewis (Joseph Cotten) and embarks on an affair with a charming and wealthy industrialist, Neil Latimer (David Brian). Rosa's burning desire is represented by a raging blast furnace at the local mill.

Critics tend to react strongly to the film.

Erickson wrote, "A standard entry in most film historians' "Worst Movies" lists (even Davis herself hated it), *Beyond the Forest* is rather entertaining in its own schlocky fashion."

D for Doom describes the film as "one of the most awesomely camp extravaganzas in cinematic history." He wrote, "It's often listed as a film noir although it's perhaps better described as a noirish melodrama. The plot is not just pure melodrama. It's hyper-melodrama."[298]

The Time Out review reads:

Her personal rebellion takes the form of adultery, miscarriage and murder, in King Vidor's most demented film from his most frenzied period, immediately after *Duel in the Sun* and *The Fountainhead* and before *Ruby Gentry*. Davis, done up for all the world like Jennifer Jones, is too old for the part, but gives it her all. . . She's like a caricature of herself, and the movie, too, is soap gone into lather. Laugh it off, by all means, but American melodrama at this pitch of alienation is quite fascinating.[299]

Filmsite reports:

The actress Bette Davis (in her mid-career at the age of 40) was miscast in the film as the young, beautiful and dissatisfied sexpot, playing one of the baddest, no-good, trashiest, and most warped of all femme fatales as she schemed and murdered to escape her oppressive small-town roots and get out of her stultifying marriage. Her vicious portrayal often came close to being a caricature, with low-cut blouses, terrible makeup, and hip-moving swaggering.[300]

David Melville of The Senses of Cinema made an astute observation about the film. He wrote::

Given the tensions between the star and her role, it makes sense that Vidor should focus the film on Rosa's own problematic self-image. . . We spy her first – posed on a rock in a river, like some over-the-hill dime store Venus – gazing into a pocket mirror as she idly plucks her eyebrows. A few scenes later, a rich young beauty (Ruth Roman) arrives from Chicago and promptly sparks her envy. Davis, waiting until she is alone and unobserved, "borrows" her rival's mink coat and poses in front of a looking glass, tenderly and erotically caressing the fur. . . Finally, as the film grinds to its climax, an ailing Rosa (dying from a self-induced abortion) rises from her bed and makes one last-ditch effort to escape from Hicksville. She staggers to her bedroom mirror and smears herself, grotesquely, with lipstick and mascara. Her reflection leering out at her (and us) is an eerie flashforward to Davis in *What Ever Happened to Baby Jane?* (Robert Aldrich, 1962).[301]

Melville added:

> Perversely, it is the very wrongness of her casting that makes *Beyond the Forest* such a riveting experi-
> ence. . . Her desire to be all the things she so patently is not lends a poignancy to Davis as Rosa
> Moline. One that is wholly lacking in, say, Gene Tierney in *Leave Her to Heaven* (John M. Stahl,
> 1945) or Rita Hayworth in *The Lady From Shanghai* (Orson Welles, 1948) – two characters with
> whom she is often compared.[302]

Every one of these women is a murderous schemer. It is a fascinating rogues' gallery.

Gone to Earth (1950)

Hazel Woodus (Jennifer Jones), a young half-gypsy, has a wild side. She is, in this way, similar to *Wuthering Height*'s Heathcliff. She feels more of a kinship with her pet fox Foxy than any human being. She
found the cute but feisty creature while it was still a baby. It had been injured by hounds and near death. She
dedicated herself to caring for the fox, who she assumed was motherless like herself.

Jennifer Jones in *Gone to Earth* (1950)

In the novel, Hazel believes that the phantom hounds of a bad squire took her mother away from her. She
believes that Foxy, too, had his mother taken away by the squire's "death pack." From the novel:

> Hounds symbolized everything she hated, everything that was not young, wild and happy. She identi-
> fied herself with Foxy, and so with all things hunted and snared and destroyed.[303]

Hazel was discouraged by her mother from ever getting married. She remembered, "She said tears and
torment, tears and torment was a married lot. And she said 'Keep yourself to yourself. You were-na made for
marryin' any more nor me. Eat in company but sleep alone.'" But she does get married. She marries a Bap-

tist minister, Edward Marston (Cyril Cusack). Then, like Emma Bovary before her, she has an affair with a rakish landowner, Jack Reddin (David Farrar).

Jennifer Jones and David Farrar in *Gone to Earth* (1950)

Samm Deighan, associate editor of Diabolique Magazine, believes that *Gone to Earth* shares key similarities with *Wuthering Heights* (1939) and *Images* (1972). The three films, she says, have "supernatural and folk horror themes."[304] She said during her commentary for *Images*:

> [*Gone to Earth*] focuses on a woman. . . who's torn between a preacher trying to civilize her through Christian marriage and spiritual love and a hunter trying to claim her through sexual passion. And in *Wuthering Heights*, *Gone to Earth* and *Images*, there is this connection made between female sexuality and the natural world. All three female characters are driven to destructive ends by an inability to chose one particular man or reconcile these opposing internal forces.[305]

The novel provides insight on this subject. From the novel:

> She was fascinated by Reddin; she was drawn to confide in Edward; but she wanted neither of them. Whether or not in years to come she would find room in her heart for human passion, she had no room for it now. She had only room for the little creatures she befriended and for her eager, quickly growing self.[306]

Hazel is, much like a child, impetuous and superstitious. She takes no responsibility for her infidelity. First, she goes off with Reddin because he threatens to tell Marston about a torrid night they spent together in London. Then, she encounters a mystical sign that she believes is directing her to Reddin. Let us explore the novel further to better understand the mystical sign. From the Blu-ray marketing materials:

> When Hazel was fourteen [her mother] died, leaving her treasure — an old, dirty, partially illegible manuscript-book of spells and charms and other gipsy lore — to her daughter.

Hazel is instructed by the book to place a bracken flower beneath her pillow before she goes to sleep. The novel reads:

> . . . [W]hoso she dreamed of with that flower beneath her pillow must be her lover. She felt traitorous to Edward in doing this. She and Edward were handfasted. How, then, could she have any lover but Edward? Why should she work the charm? She puzzled over this during prayers, but no answer came to her questioning. . . [W]ith blue petal under her pillow, she lay down, she fell asleep in a moment. She dreamt of Reddin, for he had more control over her thoughts than Edward, who appealed to her emotions, while Reddin stirred her instincts.

The film is slightly different. Michael Barret of Pop Matters wrote,"Jack keeps ordering Hazel to come to him and telling her that she wants to obey. She's frightened, flattered, and intrigued all at once, and these contradictions are completely credible."[307]

The spell book left to Hazel by her mother includes specific instructions that the young woman is to follow. She is instructed to spread her shawl on the top of the mountain and, if she can hear fairy music, she has to walk in the direction opposite of the sun. She believes that she hears fairy music, but it is actually her father playing his harp in the distance. She walks in the direction opposite of the sun, which sets her in the direction of Reddin's estate. Reddin can see her approaching. He pulls her up onto his horse and rides off with her to his home. She doesn't protest, taking up residence in Reddin's estate.

Reddin provides Hazel with many material possessions and great physical comfort. In her bedroom, she has clothing strewn across the floor and scattered atop her bed. It is an orgy of clothing.

Marston storms into Reddin's home to retrieve his wife. Reddin is defiant in his confrontation with the aggrieved husband. He tells him, "She's mine, from head to foot. . . She needs a man, not a short-winded parson."

The scene is similar in the novel. Edward comes banging on Reddin's door. Hazel knows it's Edward outside and doesn't want Reddin to open the door. "I wouldna go," she says. "It's a tramp, likely." But Reddin throws open the door and greets Edward in a jovial manner. Edward calls out one word: "Beast!" Hazel is afraid of what Reddin might do to Edward. "Ed'ard! Ed'ard!" she calls out. "Dunna go for to miscall him! He'll hurt 'ee! He's stronger'n you. Do 'ee go back, Ed'ard!" But Edward refuses to leave without his wife. Reddin looks at Edward meanly and triumphantly. "Can't you see she's got my gown on her back?" he says. "She's mine. She was never yours." Edward tells Reddin to keep his foul mouth shut. From the novel: "Hazel wondered at [Edward]. His eyes darkened so upon Reddin, his face was so powerful, irradiated with love and anger."[308] Before leaving with Edward, Hazel insists, "I couldna help it, Ed'ard - the signs said go. . ."

In the final scene, Hazel rushes to rescue Foxy from a pack of hunting dogs. She has Foxy clasped to her chest as she flees from the frenzied pack. She is so desperate to keep ahead of the dogs that she fails to realize that she is running toward an abandoned quarry pit. From the novel:

> Then, as the pack, with a ferocity of triumph, was flinging itself upon her, she was gone. She was gone with Foxy into everlasting silence.[309]

Jones is a similarly wild woman in *Duel in the Sun* (1946).

Esmond Knight and Jennifer Jones in *Gone to Earth* (1950)

Where Danger Lives (1950)

Dr. Jeff Cameron (Robert Mitchum) is captivated by a dark-eyed beauty, Margo (Faith Domergue), who has been admitted to his hospital after a suicide attempt. He ignores his caring and good-natured girlfriend, Julie (Maureen O'Sullivan), to pursue a relationship with the emotionally unstable patient. Margo claims to live with a domineering father who restricts her activities. Jeff decides to confront the father to let him know that he loves Margo and wants to see more of her. But it turns out that Margo's "father" is actually her husband, Frederick Lannington (Claude Rains). Lannington beats Jeff over the head with a fireplace poker. Jeff knocks the man unconscious while warding off his blows. Jeff goes to the bathroom for a glass of water. When he returns, he finds that Lannington is dead. Jeff has suffered a concussion and isn't thinking clearly. Margo convinces him to flee with her to Mexico. While the couple is on the run from the police, Jeff learns that Margo is insane and smothered Lannington with a cushion.

September Affair (1950)

David Lawrence (Joseph Cotten), an engineer, has gotten weary of his marriage after 18 years. He asked his wife for a divorce, but she refused to give up on their marriage. He has traveled to Italy to spend time alone and ponder the situation. He meets Manina Stuart (Joan Fontaine), a concert pianist, and the two fall in love. The couple lingers too long in their excursion of Naples and misses their flight. During the course of the film, the filmmakers take us on a scenic tour of Italy - Naples, Pompeii, Capri and Florence.

Joseph Cotton and Joan Fontaine in *September Affair* (1950)

The plane crashes into the ocean and everyone on the passenger list, including David and Manina, is presumed dead. The couple realizes that, if they let people believe they are dead, they can start a new life together.

Manina's old piano teacher, Maria Salvatini (Françoise Rosay), lives nearby in Florence. David writes a large check for Salvatini to cash for them. He is careful to make the date on the check two days earlier than the date of the plane crash. Now, he and Manina have the money they need to fund their new life.

Maria is a voice of reason.

Maria: It's not a new life - it's a suicide pact! It won't work, Manina. What you're doing is selfish, cowardly and wrong. A poor foundation for happiness.

Manina: Cowardly because we have the courage to start again, or selfish because we don't want to hurt anyone, or wrong because we're happy?

It upsets Maria that Manina has given up her career. She tells Manina, "It's time you give up this ridiculous ghost life and take your place in the world. . . Oh, women, what fools we are!"

David's wife Catherine (Jessica Tandy) and son David Jr. (Robert Arthur) visit Salvatini to learn the reason for the mysterious check. Manina walks into Salvatini's home during their visit and David Jr. recognizes the concert pianist as one of the people who was supposed to have died in the plane crash. Catherine suddenly understands what happened. Manina figures that their lies have caught up to them and they can no longer hide from their past. She leaves David and returns to her work as a concert pianist. David is not willing to return to Catherine. He attends Manina's comeback concert. He meets with her afterward. She tells him, "Our love was built on deception. It had to end." Manina and David are heartbroken after agreeing to never see each other again.

The abrupt breakup makes no sense. Who benefits from it? Who could possibly want this? It isn't what David wanted, or Manina wanted, or Catherine wanted. It doesn't restore the family. But we know that it is at least what the Production Code wanted.

Bosley Crowther of The New York Times called the film "[a] rambling drama about the left-handed honeymoon of a middle-aged man and a lady pianist."[310]

Laura of Laura's Miscellaneous Musings found "an 'ick' factor" in David's decision to abandon his son.[311]

Joan Fontaine and Joseph Cotton in *September Affair* (1950)

Adultery films often take advantage of romantic settings in Italy. Take, for instance, *Enchanted April* (1935), *Dodsworth* (1936), *Anna Karenina* (1948), *If This Be Sin* (1949), *Indiscretion of an American Wife* (1953), *The Earrings of Madame de...* (1953), *Summertime* (1955), *A Certain Smile* (1958), *Eva* (1962), *Darling* (1965) and *Avanti!* (1972).

Forbidden Fruit (1952)

A married middle-aged doctor, Dr. Charles Pellegrin (Fernandel), falls in love with an exciting and unin-hibited young woman, Martine Englebert (Françoise Arnoul.) Martine sometimes goes out dancing and drinking while he has to remain at home with his family. Jealous of her spending time with young men at dance clubs, he becomes so furious that he slaps her. "Forgive me Martine," he pleads afterward. "I swear, I didn't mean it. I don't know what came over me. But I just suffer. When we are apart, I think, 'She is with Boquet.' And something gets tight here [*he points at his throat*], as if I am about to black out. Oh, Martine. I am so miserable." Unhappy with the situation, Martine packs up her few belongings and leaves town.

Carrie (1952)

Carrie works as a stitcher at a shoe factory. She desperately strains her eyes to operate a sewing machine under dim lighting. When the foreman shouts at her for working too slow, she tries to move more quickly, but she catches her finger in the machine and injures herself. The foreman, displeased that Carrie's bloody and mangled finger has disrupted production, acts promptly to fire her.

Carrie is courted by a cocky traveling salesman, Charles Drouet (Eddie Albert), who impresses her by tak-ing her shopping and buying her a jacket and shoes. Soon after, he is able to persuade the unemployed young woman to move into his apartment.

George Hurstwood (Laurence Olivier), the manager of the exclusive Fitzgerald and Moy's restaurant, is instantly taken with Carrie when she arrives at the restaurant to dine with Drouet. One evening, he takes Car-rie to the theatre. His feelings for the young woman are so strong that he is unable to think clearly. He wants to find happiness and he will risk every possible consequence to have it. He asks his wife, Julie (Miriam Hopkins), for a divorce.

CliffNotes reports: "Carrie, desiring marriage above all else, commits herself to Hurstwood on the very day that Drouet resolves to marry her. Hurstwood, promising marriage, is unaware of the danger that his wife is presently holding in store for him."[312]

Hurstwood meets up with Julie at a restaurant.

Hurstwood: Let me go free, Julie. I'll give you anything you want.

Julie: What have you got to give? Everything you own is in my name. You're in no bargaining posi-tion.

Hurstwood: Then why are you here?

Julie: To make sure that you behave yourself. If you see her one more time, I'll go to [your boss] Mr. Fitzgerald. Will you give her up?

Hurstwood: I'm not like you, Julie. I don't make threats, and I don't make promises.

Julie: Well, I make them. And I keep them.

Later, Hurstwood angrily confronts Julie at their home.

Hurstwood: You bled me for money. You schemed until everything I've got is in your name. That's all you wanted out of me.

Julie: You must be losing your mind. Now, get out of my room.

Hurstwood: You listen to me. I have found somebody who loves me, and I'm going to have that before I die.

Julie: Not if it harms me. I won't let you.

Hurstwood: You can't stop me. Nobody can.

Julie: The children, what are you going to tell them?

Hurstwood: Everything. They're grown up. They want to live and love just as I do. Get a divorce. You've got all the evidence and money you need. But this much happiness I'm going to have.

From the novel: "She gazed at him — a pythoness in humour."[313]

Hurstwood pursues the relationship without considering the inevitable fall-out. CliffNotes reports: "Hurstwood, determined to have 'Paradise, whatever might be the result,' forgets to reason carefully. He lies and throws himself into the sea of his selfish passion."[314]

Laurence Olivier and Jennifer Jones in *Carrie* (1952)

Everything comes to a head at the midpoint of the film, when Hurstwood must deal with three separate confrontations: one with Carrie, one with his wife, and one with Drouet. Wikipedia on novel: "The next day, the affair is uncovered: Drouet discovers he has been cuckolded, Carrie learns that Hurstwood is married, and Hurstwood's wife Julie learns from acquaintances that Hurstwood has been out driving with another woman. . ."[315] But George doesn't care. He doesn't want to think about it. The film is just the same.

Hurstwood: I love her.

Drouet: What right have you got to love her? What can you do for her? Lock her up some place while you sneak around town so your wife won't see?

Hurstwood: I'm gonna marry her. Tomorrow.

After counting the cash receipts for the day, Hurstwood goes to lock the money inside a safe. But, before he is able to put away the cash, he accidentally bumps the safe door, which slams shut and locks. The safe has a time lock, which prevents it from being open again until the next day. Hurstwood goes to deliver the money to his boss, Mr. Fitzgerald (Basil Ruysdael), but his boss explains that he just finished talking to Julie about his recent dalliance and believes that he is obligated to take action on the matter. He says that, for now, he will pay his salary directly to Julie. He is sure that, with him having no money to spend on his lady friend, she is sure to go away.

Hurstwood becomes desperate. He uses the restaurant's cash receipts to run away with Carrie. In the novel, Hurstwood marries Carrie under a fake name. Carrie marries Hurstwood without knowing if she really loves him. She is focused on the financial security that she believes the union will bring. The film version of Carrie is entirely different in that she has gone off with Hurstwood purely for love.

The happy newlyweds have great hope for their future together. Hurstwood left Mr. Fitzgerald an IOU, expecting him to trust that he'll pay back the money. Instead, the grumpy codger takes immediate legal action against Hurstwood. Hurstwood returns the unspent cash, but his reputation has already been ruined. He is unable to find employment, but he manages to buy a minority interest in a small saloon. It doesn't bring him much of an income, but he has enough money for food, rent and other essentials.

When Carrie finds out that she's pregnant, Hurstwood is more determined than ever to marry her. He offers to sign his share of his home to Julie if she will grant him a divorce. The greedy woman is glad to agree as it means that she will now possess all of their marital assets. But, unfortunately, Carrie loses the baby.

After a few years, Hurstwood's business partner terminates their relationship, causing the saloon to close and leaving him without an income. In the film, Carrie is unaffected when George tells her that he's broke. In the novel, Carrie is nearly as cold and mercenary as Mrs. Hurstwood. She believes that happiness is to be found in money.

Wikipedia notes about the novel:

> . . . Hurstwood abandons any pretense of fine manners toward Carrie, and she realizes that Hurstwood no longer is the suave, powerful manager of his Chicago days. Carrie's dissatisfaction only increases when she meets Robert Ames, a bright young scholar from Indiana and her neighbor's cousin, who introduces her to the idea that great art, rather than showy materialism, is worthy of admiration.[316]

The version of Carrie in the novel continues to show herself to be selfish and greedy. She is indignant when Hurstwood asks her to economize and she figures that she'd be better off earning her own money. She gets a job as a chorus girl and manages to work her way up to small speaking roles. Hurstwood gets a job driving a streetcar during a strike by streetcar operators. Carrie is disgusted that Hurstwood would work as a scab. She has had an offer by a girlfriend to live with her and she accepts. She encloses a twenty-dollar bill in her farewell note to Hurstwood. In the film, the kindlier Carrie separates from Hurstwood to give him a chance to reunite with his son, who is visiting New York with his new bride.

Twice, a job loss forces a key character to make a desperate decision. We can never trust our emotions - not love, not fear. Our emotions can work in devious ways to lead us to folly. The elegant and graceful man is reduced, through a slow and steady decline, to a beggar. It is an incredible, nightmarish tale written by a man clearly with a low opinion of his fellow man. From the novel:

> Lord, Lord, he thought, what had he got into? How could things have taken such a violent turn, and so quickly? He could hardly realize how it had all come about. It seemed a monstrous, unnatural, unwarranted condition which had suddenly descended upon him without his let or hindrance.[317]

Laurence Olivier in *Carrie* (1952)

Hurstwood went to his room, which the author describes as a "dingy affair — wooden, dusty, hard." His end is delivered in two paragraphs:

> Now he began leisurely to take off his clothes, but stopped first with his coat, and tucked it along the crack under the door. His vest he arranged in the same place. His old wet, cracked hat he laid softly upon the table. Then he pulled off his shoes and lay down.
>
> It seemed as if he thought a while, for now he arose and turned the gas out, standing calmly in the blackness, hidden from view. After a few moments, in which he reviewed nothing, but merely hesitated, he turned the gas on again, but applied no match. Even then he stood there, hidden wholly in that kindness which is night, while the uprising fumes filled the room. When the odour reached his nostrils, he quit his attitude and fumbled for the bed.[318]

As for Carrie:

Of Hurstwood's death she was not even aware. A slow, black boat setting out from the pier at Twenty-seventh Street upon its weekly errand bore, with many others, his nameless body to the Potter's Field.[319]

At one time, Hurstwood was important to her. He was a potent figure in his embodiment of earthly success.

[Men like Hurstwood] were the personal representatives of a state most blessed to attain — the titled ambassadors of comfort and peace, aglow with their credentials. It is but natural that when the world which they represented no longer allured her, its ambassadors should be discredited. Even had Hurstwood returned in his original beauty and glory, he could not now have allured her. She had learned that in his world, as in her own present state, was not happiness.[320]

The relentlessly downbeat film is not easy viewing. In his portrayal of Hurstwood, Olivier carries a doomed expression for much of the film. The audience must expect that the character will come to a bad end. And, of course, he does. He doesn't commit suicide as he does in the novel, but he toys with the knob on a gas burner. It is obvious that he has no hope for his future and suicide is on his mind. He wanders off after a brief reunion with Carrie, who has by now become a successful actress. He is hungry, ungroomed and sickly as the film ends.

"Sister Carrie" was highly critical of American capitalism. Dreiser was graphic in describing the poor working conditions in the shoe factory. Bad air. Bad lighting. Bad smells. The job was hellish for Carrie. From the novel: "Her hands began to ache at the wrists and then in the fingers, and towards the last she seemed one mass of dull, complaining muscles. . ."[321] Dreiser depicted Carrie's foreman as a heartless brute who freely exploits the factory's low-wage labor. It is certainly not humane for him to fire Carrie just after she has been bandaged up from a work injury. And then there is the immorality that comes from the main characters being obsessed with money. Paramount executives worried that the anti-American elements of Dreiser's story might not play well with an American public deeply concerned with Cold War issues. The film's release was delayed for two years while Paramount negotiated with the film's director, William Wyler, to recut the film to make it more palatable. Still, the film failed at the box office.

The old melodramas regularly showed that adultery was a road to ruin. Take, for example, the fate of August Schiller (Emil Jannings) in *The Way of All Flesh* (1927). Schiller, a bank clerk, takes a train to Chicago to deliver valuable securities. He meets a pretty young blonde woman (Phyllis Haver) on the train. She persuades him to take her to a saloon for drinks. The next morning, he wakes up in a hotel room without the securities. He finds the woman at the saloon and pleads with her to return the securities. The saloon owner, an accomplice in the theft, knocks him unconscious and drags him to a railroad track. He is removing Schiller's wallet when Schiller awakens suddenly. While struggling with the saloon owner, Schiller pushes the man in front of an oncoming train. He panics and flees the scene. Police later remove Schiller's wallet from the saloon owner's mangled body and assume that the dead man is Schiller. Schiller is so ashamed that he prefers to let his family believe that he's dead. The story advances twenty years. Here, IMDb describes the final scene:

Schiller is now aged, unkempt, and employed to pick up trash in a park. He sees his own family go to a cemetery and place a wreath on his grave. Following other scenes in a Christmas snowstorm, Schiller makes his way to his former home, where he sees that the son whom he had taught to play violin is now a successful musician. He walks away, carrying in his pocket a dollar that his son has given him, not recognizing that the old tramp was his father.[322]

Indiscretion of an American Wife (1953)

A married American woman, Mary Forbes (Jennifer Jones), has an affair with a young Italian professor, Giovanni Doria (Montgomery Clift), while vacationing in Italy. She breaks off the affair when the time comes for her to go home. But he will not accept this. He follows Mary around the train station, Rome's Stazione Termini, pressuring her to stay with him. Kelly referred to the film as "[a] neo-realist study of adulterous passion in the claustrophobic atmosphere of the Rome railway."[323]

The film trades in bigger-than-life emotions. These are emotions that are, at times, too big. The intensity of Cliff's performance is off-putting. At times, his character comes across as insane. This is a problem from the moment that Cliff appears on screen. He suddenly becomes enraged by Mary's fur-trimmed hat. "Take off that hat!" he demands. "It's a smug little hat." At one point, he is so desperate to get to Mary that he risks his life running past a speeding locomotive. Panicked railroad workers race across the tracks to stop him. Intercut into the action is a shot of a quartet of nuns shrieking in unison. Too big.

The Wayward Wife (1953)

The original Italian title: *La provinciale*

Gemma Vagnuzzi (Gina Lollobrigida) marries a professor, Franco Vagnuzzi (Gabriele Ferzetti), to escape poverty. She feels no love for Franco and resents that she had to marry a man she doesn't love. She befriends a dispossessed Romanian countess, Elvira Coceanu (Alda Mangini), who senses her dissatisfaction and realizes that she may be able to exploit it. The flamboyant countess is highly social, but her friendly and outgoing manner hides a dark and deceitful nature. Gemma meets an old friend, Luciano Vittoni (Renato Baldini). Elvira allows Gemma to take Luciano to her apartment. She gets her hands on a love letter that Gemma wrote to Luciano. She threatens to show the letter to Franco unless she does whatever she tells her to do. She extorts money out of Gemma. She moves into a spare room in Gemma's home. But she goes too far when she tries to pimp Gemma to a wealthy man. Gemma finally musters the courage to tell Franco about her affair. Franco promptly throws Elvira out into the street. Gemma has come to appreciate Franco through this crisis. She sees him as a strong and devoted husband and gratefully commits to their marriage.

The Sleeping Tiger (1954)

Frank Clemmens (Dirk Bogarde) attempts to rob Dr. Clive Esmond (Alexander Knox) at gunpoint, but Esmond uses his military training to quickly disarm him. Esmond is unfazed that Clemmens attempted to mug him. The doctor, a psychotherapist, simply sees an opportunity to prove his theories about criminals. He believes that it will be effective therapy to take the young criminal into his home and treat him like family. He tells his wife Glenda (Alexis Smith):

Look, Glenda, it's one thing to practice psychology in a prison ward, it's something else again to have your patient in ideal circumstances. The boy's young. . . he's intelligent. If I can find out what makes him tick, I may be able to straighten him out. The other way, well, it's a complete waste of a human being. If he goes to prison again, he's finished, I'm sure of that.

Glenda tells Frank, "I don't mind this experiment of Clive's, even though I think it's a waste of time. If it interests him at all, I'll help him all I can. Take you riding or teach you hymns. But this is my home too, and there's one thing I won't tolerate, and that's rudeness."

Glenda is instantly attracted to Frank, but she presents an icy facade in his presence. In time, she becomes more comfortable with Frank. She confides to him that she was raised in an unhappy home. She says, "My mother hated me. . . literally."

Glenda suddenly wants to have fun and asks Frank to take her to a dance club in Soho. Their time together at the dance club unleashes a great passion in her and allows her to fall freely into an affair with Frank.

Alexis Smith and Dirk Bogarde in *The Sleeping Tiger* (1954)

Clive's therapy isn't working. Frank is violent with the maid and Edmond needs to pay off the maid so that she doesn't report this to the police.

Next, Frank sneaks out to commit a robbery. Edmond lies to the police to give Frank an alibi. Frank finally opens up to Edmond about his troubled relationship with his father. Edmond and Frank suddenly develop a father-son relationship. Frank would now rather spend time with Edmond than spend time with Glenda. Glenda becomes jealous and tells Frank that they need to run away together. Frank refuses. He says that he needs to surrender himself to the police for the robbery. Glenda becomes hysterical. To stop Frank from leaving, she tells Edmond that he assaulted her. Edmond marches upstairs to see Frank. Glenda hears a gunshot. Edmond returns and tells her that he shot Frank and he's dead. She breaks down and confesses that she loved Frank. But Frank wasn't really shot. He climbed out of a window and is headed for the police station. Glenda jumps into her car and goes after him. She cajoles Frank to get into the car. As she drives off with Frank, she speeds recklessly down the road. She laughs madly as she tries to swerve in front of an oncoming truck, but Frank grabs the wheel and turns the car away from the truck. The car crashes through a billboard sign that depicts a pouncing tiger. She dies instantly. Frank survives.

IMDb reviewer bmacv wrote:

Comes the crunch as Knox, in a three-minute Freudian breakthrough reminiscent of Lee J. Cobb's instant rehabilitation of William Holden in *The Dark Past*, turns the lying, thieving, abusive Bogarde into a contrite milquetoast. When Bogarde then bids her farewell, Smith careens into dementia every bit as swiftly as Bogarde was healed and feigns an assault in hopes that Knox will defend her `honor' with that gun every therapist keeps in his desk drawer.[324]

The film's climax is campy fun.

Violent Saturday (1955)

Boyd Fairchild (Richard Egan), the manager of a local copper mine, is distressed by the extramarital activities of his wife, Emily (Margaret Hayes). Emily is disgusted with herself and is just as disgusted with her lover Gil Clayton (Brad Dexter). She tells him, "Oh, why don't you give up? Get a wife of your own and stop trying to make love to everybody else's."

Linda Sherman (Virginia Leith) finds Boyd drunk at a bar. She feels sorry for him and takes him home. She stays with him until Emily arrives home. Emily is anxious to have this strange woman get out of her home. Linda doesn't want to leave until she tells Emily what she thinks of her. She says that, if she was a decent wife, she wouldn't have spent the last ten years "kicking out his insides." Emily is shaken. She shouts that, if this woman doesn't leave, she will throw her out. Linda replies, "Why don't you get mad enough to try it? All I want is an excuse to pull that hair right out of your stupid head. Guess you don't have the guts. Better latch on to him, honey. Drunk or sober, he's the kind of guy I've dreamed about owning all my life."

Margaret Hayes and Richard Egan in *Violent Saturday* (1955)

Emily breaks down to Boyd. She says, "We can't change. Not us. You're an alcoholic and. . . I'm a tramp." She continues:

> After that girl left tonight, I went upstairs and I sat in the dark. You tell yourself the truth in the dark. I was remembering all the things I'm ashamed to remember in the light of day. Why have I done these things, Boyd? What's the matter with me? Am I sick? Do I belong in an institution? Well, I've read about people like me. They're sick people. They shouldn't associate with decent people.

Boyd and Emily make plans to go on a vacation, but Emily is killed during a robbery at a bank.

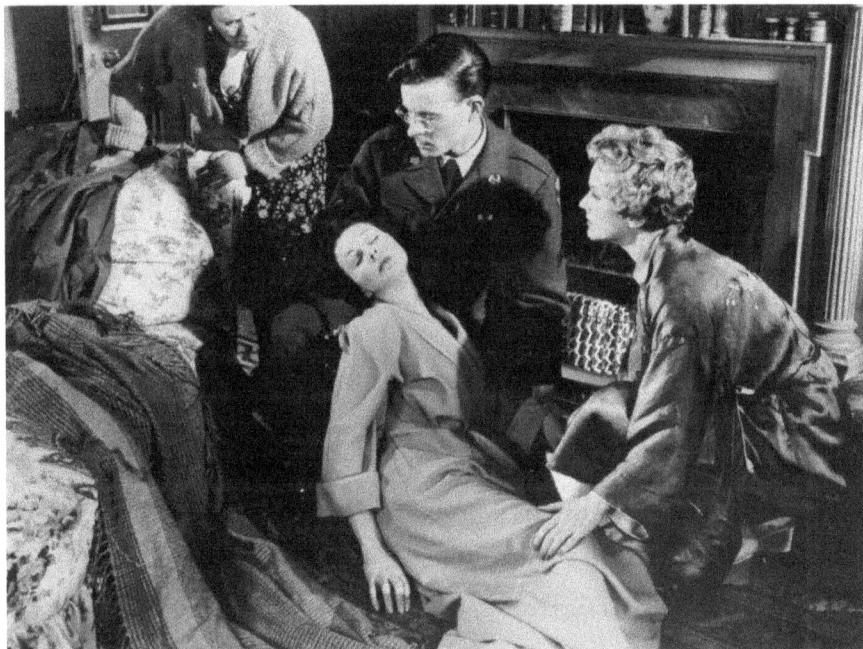

Vivien Leigh in *The Deep Blue Sea* (1955)

The Deep Blue Sea (1955)

The film is based on a British stage play by Terence Rattigan.

The film opens after Hester (Vivien Leigh), in a state of despair, has attempted suicide. Vanessa Keys of The Telegraph wrote: "Her marriage to a High Court judge is over and her tormented affair with a heavy-drinking former RAF pilot has left her emotionally stranded and desperate."[325]

Josephine Botting of BFI wrote:

> The verdict on Leigh's performance however was less than unanimous, some critics finding her a little "too prim, too elegant, too Mayfair," lacking in passion and credibility as a woman who could abandon affection and security in favour of lust and squalor. Yet these critics failed to perceive the subtlety and restraint of her performance, which so well suits the character of Hester, a woman emotionally exhausted after her dramatic rejection of convention and the respectability of marriage. At the key moments, Leigh's Hester lets her guard down and her desperation and desire, clearly at odds with her nature and upbringing, come to the surface.[326]

NowVoyager88 of Letterboxd wrote:

[Leigh's] every line and gesture is full of emotion, but only under a thick veneer of English will. That's what ranks this performance among her best; she is able to portray Hester's vulnerability and noble discipline. It is a fascinating combination of strength and fragility, and Leigh is the only actress of her generation who could have accomplished such a feat.[327]

But does she adequately portray vulnerability? Leigh fails to generate sufficient sympathy for the character. She refuses to apologize for her hurtful and irrational actions. We rarely see her express more than a stiff-lipped stubbornness and defiance.

The film introduces flashbacks to the earlier days of the affair. Freddie Page (Kenneth More) proudly tells a friend that he always steers clear of married women. But he breaks that rule when he makes a pass at Hester on the dance floor. She says, "I knew then, in that tiny moment, I had no power to resist him. No power at all." It is not a film about love or romance. It is a film about compulsion. Adultery is a compulsion for Hester just as it was for Emily in *Violent Saturday*.

Freddie sees her immoderate behavior as "damn idiotic." He says, "[She] marries the first man to ask her and falls in love with the first man to give her an eye." He admits that he doesn't love her as much as she loves him. He resents her great love because, as he sees it, it places unreasonable demands on him.

Miller (Eric Portman), her neighbor, believes that no one can judge her because no one feels what she feels. He says, "What right do they have to judge you? To judge you, they must have the capacity to feel as you feel. . . You, alone, know how you felt." Morals and logic must bow to personal feelings. You are entering a world of pure emotion.

At one point, Hester tells Freddie, "I just had to see you!" She says that she cannot stand being apart from him.

Sir William "Bill" Collyer (Emlyn Williams), the High Court judge to whom Hester was once married, has to provide jury instructions in a shoplifting case. Witnesses have testified that they saw a woman steal merchandise from the store. So, the criminal act is not in question. But the judge needs to advise the jury on the issue of impulse control.

The defense, therefore, rests solely on the question of the state of mind of the accused - on the question, as you might call it, of uncontrollable impulse. Now you've heard medical evidence which claims that this woman is suffering from what is virtually a disease of the mind - "kleptomania," as it is called. Now, as men and women of common sense, you will see how dangerous in law is this conception that crime may be excused by a plea of "uncontrollable impulse." Any criminal may make this excuse - "I don't know what came over me," "I never meant to do it," "Something happened that was stronger than my will." The law must guard itself against such pleas. And the law on this point is clear. Did this woman know what she was doing at the time that she did it? If she did, did she know it was wrong? Now, ladies and gentleman, those are the two questions you will have to decide. And they are so important that I think I shall repeat them: Did this woman know what she was doing at the time that she did it? If she did, did she know it was wrong?

Uncontrollable impulse is a category of mental illness.

The comparison of the compulsive adulterer and the kleptomaniac comes up when Bill comes to see her. But it is Hester who likens the two. She looks upon herself as a sort of criminal. She says, "I tried to be good and I failed. That's the excuse all criminals give, isn't it?" But she resents when Bill questions her. "I'm not in the witness box," she snaps back. "You'll never get me to confess I had any reason for trying to kill myself last night." She tells him that her mind was "temporarily disturbed." He asks her what it was that disturbed the balance of her mind. "Oh, dear, oh, dear," she says, "I don't know. A great tidal wave of illogical emotions." She admits to feeling anger at Page, hatred at herself, and "shame at being alive."

Hester says, "The fault lies with whichever of the gods had a good laugh up above by arranging for [Freddie and I] to meet." She sees their relationship as something inevitable. She tells Bill, "I believe it was fated for Freddie and I to meet." She adds, "It turns out to be a pretty evil fate." It is the lightning defense from *In This Our Life*. But Christian doctrine is clear that Hester could not blame God, or fate, or anything else for her relationship with Freddie. Christianity emphasizes that a man crafts his own life using free will.

Freddie's friend, Jackie Jackson (Arthur Hill), remembers being attracted to a young model with beautiful legs. "Gosh," he says, "she was something!. . . It was purely physical, I grant that now. At the time, it seemed it was all I could ever want from life." Jackie tells Hester, "It is the spiritual values that count in life, isn't it? I mean, the physical side is really unimportant, objectively speaking." He says that his father believed in "the importance of the spiritual values and the pettiness of the physical side."

Freddie is childish - irresponsible, selfish, narcissistic and immoral. In their first conversation, she calls him a "naughty schoolboy." She looks after him as if he was a little boy. She insists on being the one to polish his shoes. "Let me," she tells him. "Somehow you manage to get shoe polish all over your face, Lord knows how." It is important to her to know he needs her. She tells her husband, "I had more, far more to give you than you ever wanted." So, why didn't she just have a child with Bill?

Freddie certainly stirs the maternal instinct in Hester. The maternal instinct has drawn other women to bad boys in films, including *No More Ladies*, *Forsaking All Others*, *The Moment of Truth* and *Petulia*. Stacey Laura Lloyd wrote in the article "The real reasons why men cheat":

> One of the main reasons why men cheat is simply a matter of immaturity. When a man is immature, this unappealing attribute can impact a relationship in many different ways. For example, men who are immature often put themselves first in most situations, don't take into consideration their partner's feelings, insist on being right even when they're wrong, and are characteristically unreliable and irresponsible. To that end, being immature is also heavily related to acting impulsively, as most men who are immature tend to give in to their basic temptations and desires without a care or concern for the repercussions of their actions and the possible negative effects that their behavior can have on others.

> With this in mind, it's not too surprising that a man's low level of maturity is an underlying factor behind being unfaithful, since immature men often lack the sophistication, empathy, and sense of responsibility that would inhibit them from cheating on their partner.

We will further examine the man-child's role in the adultery narrative in a later chapter.

If we accept the film's view of love, then we must accept that love is madness. Film historian Michael D. Rinella wrote:

> An intensely personal piece of work, *The Deep Blue Sea* represented, as Rattigan confided to friend Laurence Olivier, "the phenomenon of love is inexplicable in terms of logic."[328]

Freddie tells Hester, "We're death to each other." Why invite death into your life?

Margaret Sullavan played Hester in a Broadway run of *The Deep Blue Sea* in 1952. The show was directed by Frith Banbury, who had directed the original London stage version of the play. Rinella wrote:

Banbury recalled that Sullavan "was this enchanting, tiny little thing." However, as rehearsals progressed, he felt she was unable to play the part as envisioned. Banbury found that Sullavan "could not capture the tragedy at the heart of Hester" as [Peggy] Ashcroft had so beautifully done [in the London stage play]. . . Sullavan did not deal well with Banbury's direction and "there were screams and shouts all the time" during rehearsals, recalled Banbury. Sullavan demanded a different director, preferably Joshua Logan, but Rattigan kept Banbury.[329]

Sullavan, who saw Hester as immature, played the character as if she was a little girl. The director, Frith Banbury, strongly opposed this interpretation of the character.

Rattigan felt Sullavan was miscast. He wrote:

She's not a good enough actress to play it. She has only two approaches to the part and both are inadequate. Either she plays it all out for "pathos," using her famous tearful voice (put on), in which case she is dull and self-pitying, and the play goes down the drain, or she plays it with her own voice and personality, in which case the play equally goes down the drain because the part becomes hard and matter of fact, and you lose patience with Hester, and can't see what all the fuss is about.[330]

But the script demands that an actress play the character with a hardness.

From Rinella's book:

Dorothy Kilgallen sniped, "The Deep Blue Sea is a major disappointment. [Sullavan] struggles valiantly with the dullest and most dilatory dialogue of the season, but all her sobbing, screaming, choking and emotional gymnastics fail to lift a single scene above the level of simple boredom." Despite his misgivings about Sullavan's performance, Rattigan wrote, "In spite of all this, I find I like her very much." However, Rattigan sensed she was incapable of playing the role honestly. As a result, she became "hysterical because she knows she can't."[331]

So, two Hollywood stars were arguably defeated by the role. Penelope Wilton received great acclaim for her performance as Hester in a 1993 revival of the stage play. Michael Billington of The Guardian wrote, "[P]art of Wilton's brilliance lay in showing Hester as a woman torn between two worlds. Visited by the husband she had abandoned, Wilton revealed a smiling warmth that suggested a faint nostalgia for the comforting routines of affluence. Yet in the presence of her lover, Freddie, Wilton was all rapturous ardour as she devoured him with kisses and artfully steered him towards the bedroom."[332] Wilton has a natural warmth that she was easily able to bring to the role. It is a wonderful warmth that she brings to every role that she plays. She made the character sympathetic despite the limitations of the script.

Hot Spell (1958)

Alma Duval (Shirley Booth) is devastated to learn that her husband, Jack (Anthony Quinn), is in love with another woman. His new love is a beautiful 19-year-old Ruby (Valerie Allen). Jack tells Alma, "Mama, Mama, she loves me. Honey, it's like I was twenty again. Like I was young the way I never was. The way you and me never knew love could be like." Jack packs his bags and runs off with Ruby. Ruby, reckless and carefree, demands that Jack drive faster. She presses her foot on the gas pedal while wildly kissing him. He is too late noticing a construction sign in his path. He cries out for Alma the moment before he crashes. Alma and her children attend his funeral. Alma talks of moving to Florida, where she hopes to find happiness.

Paul Newman and Ina Balin in *From the Terrace* (1960)

From the Terrace (1960)

Alfred Eaton (Paul Newman) is unable to spend much time with his wife Mary (Joanne Woodward) because of his frequent business trips. Left alone for months at a time, Mary becomes lonely, sad and resentful. It is Alfred's job to handle prospective acquisitions for his company. He is assigned to spend two months out of state to evaluate the value of a coal mine operation that belongs to Ralph Benziger (Ted de Corsia). Alfred feels lonely being away from home and finds himself attracted to Benziger's daughter, Natalie (Ina Balin).

> Alfred: A man walks around in a desert. All his life looking for water. All he ever finds is sand.
>
> Natalie: I didn't know you were lost in the desert.
>
> Alfred: I didn't know it either until last night. I walked into a house where there was warmth that didn't come from radiators. I saw your mother and father, and I saw you.
>
> Natalie: You're lonely. You're away from home, that's all.
>
> Alfred: No. In one evening, my whole life seemed to change. I know it sounds ridiculous, but you made me feel so I'd been cheated out of something all my life.

Alfred wants to divorce Mary and marry Natalie, but he works for a conservative employer who would not tolerate one of his executives getting a divorce. Mary suspects that Alfred cheated on her and responds by having an affair of her own. Alfred learns from his boss about the affair. Mary has been cheating with Dr. Jim Roper (Patrick O'Neal). The couple separates.

Alfred learns about a shady deal that a co-worker, Creighton Duffy (Howard Caine), has with Nassau Aircraft, a company that Alfred is evaluating. Duffy hires a detective to photograph Alfred in a hotel room with Natalie so that he can blackmail him to keep quiet.

MacHardie surprises Alfred when he announces that he is promoting Alfred to partner. Alfred, according to Wikipedia, "denounce[s] MacHardie's hypocrisy of placing success and social position above personal responsibility and happiness."[333] Alfred exposes Duffy's fraud before he walks out. Mary wants to reconcile with Alfred, but he has decided to start a new life with Natalie.

Characters express heightened emotions in melodrama. Characters express heightened emotions in parody, too. This leaves a fairly thin line between melodrama and parody. The characters in this melodrama never tire of being immoral. The film becomes its own *Mad* magazine parody. The characters cannot express the simplest word or act without being immoral about it. If a character sneezes, they have to sneeze on a baby.

Red Desert (1964)

The original Italian title: *Il deserto rosso*

Giuliana (Monica Vitti) is married to the manager of a petrochemical plant. She became despondent having to live in a bleak industrial area. She only recently was released from a hospital after a suicide attempt. She forms a relationship with Corrado Zeller (Richard Harris), a company employee who is visiting the plant. The two end up in a hotel room together, but she suddenly becomes distressed and leaves. Boyd van Hoeiji of Senses of Cinema wrote, "A more melodramatic narrative might have turned their encounters into an affair that helps Giuliana find her self-worth but. . . [the encounters] only underline Giuliana's sense of detachment."[334]

Belle de Jour (1967)

A beautiful young housewife, Séverine Serizy (Catherine Deneuve), is troubled remembering a time in her childhood when a man groped her. The incident has made her mistrustful of men and unable to be intimate with her husband, Pierre (Jean Sorel). A fascination with sadomasochistic sex prompts her to work as a prostitute at a high-class brothel. She develops a torrid relationship with a client, Marcel (Pierre Clémenti), who is a hot-tempered young criminal. Marcel becomes possessive with Séverine and can no longer bear her going home to her husband. He confronts Pierre outside of his home and shoots him. The shooting immediately attracts the attention of police officers, who shoot Marcel as he flees the scene. Pierre survives but is left blind and paralyzed.

Reflections in a Golden Eye (1967)

Leonora Penderton (Elizabeth Taylor) is unhappy in her marriage to Major Weldon Penderton (Marlon Brando). She has an affair with Weldon's best friend, Lt. Colonel Morris Langdon (Brian Keith). Langdon's wife, Alison (Julie Harris), had a nervous breakdown when her baby daughter died three years earlier. She cut off her nipples with garden shears. This has likely created a distance between her and her husband. Still, Alison is the one decent person in the film. She is aware of the affair. During a card game, she glimpses under the table and sees Leonora running her bare foot up and down Langdon's leg. She demands a divorce. But Langdon has her committed to a sanatorium. Langdon is broken up by the tragic news that Alison suddenly died from a heart attack.

In the Realm of the Senses (1976)

A married businessman, Kizicho (Tatsuya Fuji), develops an obsessive, intensely sexual relationship with his maid, Sada Abe (Eiko Matsuda). The relationship becomes more fervent after Kizicho abandons his wife, Ishida (Tatsuya Fuji), to devote more time to his new lover. Sada strangles Kizicho to death during a mad venture into sexual asphyxiation.

Bad Timing: A Sensual Obsession (1980)

Milena Flaherty (Theresa Russell) is admitted to a hospital after overdosing on pills. It is revealed through a series of flashbacks that the woman indulged in hard drugs and reckless affairs after she abandoned her husband, Stefan Vognic (Denholm Elliott). She has reached the end of her rope being involved in an abusive relationship with Alex Linden (Art Garfunkel).

It's My Turn (1980)

Ben Lewin (Michael Douglas), a former New York Yankee, has been confused and unhappy since an injury forced him into an early retirement. He becomes even more troubled when he learns that his wife is having an affair with his best friend. While out of town to attend a wedding, he becomes attracted to a mathematics professor, Kate Gunzinger (Jill Clayburgh). The couple ends up having sex in Kate's hotel room.

Kate is also uncertain about her life. She enjoys her job. She laughs a lot with her good-natured boyfriend, Homer (Charles Grodin). But she is not sure if this is enough. She is an independent woman who is not sure that she wants to be independent. She is considering a job that will give her more prestige and a greater income, but it will also give her less freedom to work on her research projects. Similarly, she has space in her relationship with Homer, but she complains that it's "too goddamn much space." The director, Claudia Weill, said, "Here's a woman who has too much 'space,' too much freedom. She finds that she wants a messy relationship."[335]

It is more difficult to understand Ben, who can be rascally in one scene and sensitive in the next. Roger Ebert wrote, "[H]e challenges [Kate] to trust her emotions. Yet when she does, he doesn't trust his."[336]

Kate wants them to leave their current partners and move in together. Ben is incredulous that she would make major changes in her life for "a guy you balled last night." He tells her:

> I felt more this weekend than I have in a hell of a long time. But the fact is, I've still got a daughter in Akron, and I don't wanna leave her alone. And I got a marriage. Seven years. . . I gotta resolve what's there. I'm not ready to jump into something new yet.

Kate accuses him of hiding behind a dead marriage.

Back at home, Kate criticizes Homer for being inattentive. Homer is happy with the relationship the way it is and doesn't want it to change. He doesn't want to have to stop and listen whenever Kate has something on her mind. He says, "Oh, God! No. I can't do that. That's like a full-time job. I can't. It would be exhausting to do that."

Kate persists in trying to win Homer to her point of view.

Kate: I just need to be more connected. I need to feel that my problems are your problems, and that your problems are mine, and that - that we nurture each other. It's not just you, it's me. I want to support you more too.

Homer: You mean, like we two as one?

Kate: Yes!

Homer: It sounds just like my marriage. It does. That sounds exactly like my marriage. . . Ah, no, this is not what we wanted. . . I'm sorry. I don't think I can do what you're describing. I - I - I really don't. I mean, I did that, and it really drove me crazy. . . I really don't wanna live through every moment of another person's life. I mean, not even yours.

In the end, Ben and Kate come together for a messy "we two as one" relationship.

Isabelle Adjani in *Possession* (1981)

Possession (1981)

Anna (Isabelle Adjani) tells her husband, Mark (Sam Neill) that she is leaving him for a self-improvement guru, Heinrich (Heinz Bennent). Later, Mark becomes distressed to find that Anna has left their child unattended. He visits Heinrich, believing that Anna is staying with him. But she is not there. Heinrich says that he hasn't seen her for days. Other films have shown the aggrieved husband confronting his wife's lover. But the confrontation has never been like this one. Heinrich reacts with a strange aloofness to Mark's protestations. He is a narcissist who regards Mark as insignificant. At one point, he seems to be making a sexual advance toward Mark. But his cool civility and creepy flirtations end when Mark grabs him and shouts into his face. Heinrich, who appears to be trained in martial arts, brutally beats Mark. Mark leaves Heinrich home with a bloody nose, a sundry of bruises, and a couple of loose teeth.

Mark argues again with Anna. She is volatile.

Anna: But it's difficult, don't you understand? It's difficult. I didn't want it to happen but it happened and now. . . Don't come any closer.

Mark: Anna, it's me.

Anna: Don't you understand? You disgust me. I can't stand you touching me. You make me. . . [*screams*]

Mark: You know, love isn't something you can just switch from channel to channel. I have your letters. "My love, trust me," you write and all the time you were fucking your arse off. You want me to believe you're a. . .

Anna: A whore! Yes! A monster, a whore. I fuck around with everybody. Whenever you turn around I fuck around with everybody on every corner. You will let me go. Anna: You can't stop me. I'll open the window and jump!

Mark: You need him that much?

Anna: Oh yes! Oh yes!

But Anna didn't leave Mark for Heinrich. The truth is that Anna left Mark to care for a multi-tentacled monster that she keeps hidden in a squalid downtown apartment.

It was a messy divorce that inspired Andrzej Zulawski to make *Possession*. The monster represents the terrible anguish and weird hysteria that often surrounds a divorce. Simon Abrams of Politico describes the monster as being "mired in filth and goop and sex and sin and confusion."[337]

Mrs. Soffel (1984)

A prison is obviously not a good environment for a marriage. It makes the sweltering rubber plantation in *The Letter* look warm and hospitable in comparison. The Biddle brothers, Jack (Matthew Modine) and Ed (Mel Gibson), are sent to death row for murdering a man during a robbery. Kate Soffel (Diane Keaton), the warden's wife, is bedridden with neurasthenic. She has nightmares in which she is suffocating. Paul Attanasio of The Washington Post believed that the audience is meant to see the nightmare-stricken Kate as a woman being stifled in her marriage. He wrote, "Worse, the overall setup is one big cliche' in which the sympathies are stacked. Behind his pince-nez and waxed moustache, Herrmann's warden is starchy and unappealing."[338] Attanasio added, "As she strolls through the prison, distributing Bibles to the inmates, [director Gillian] Armstrong photographs her through the bars (she's "imprisoned" too - get it?)."[339] Predictably, Kate falls in love with Ed. Ed has created public interest by writing letters to the newspaper. The press has turned the Biddles into celebrities. Women love the Biddles. Attanasio wrote, ". . . [W]omen everywhere, who [are] motivated by either a sense of injustice or Mel Gibson's irresistible blue eyes, besiege the hoosegow with cries of 'Free the Biddles' and gifts for the boys."[340] Kate reads the Bible to inmates. She claims to be motivated by Christian charity, but saving Ed's soul doesn't appear at all to be a concern. Pauline Kael wrote, "[Keaton] has a moment here that's freakishly inspired: Ed has been holding her against the bars and she's been speaking like a moral exemplar when suddenly, in mid-sentence, she lets out a dirty little giggle. We know then that Kate is living in a fever dream and doesn't want to wake up."[341] Kate commits to helping Ed and Jack to escape so that she can run off with them. She does no soul-searching about her desire to abandon her husband and children. Of course, she makes a mockery of the Bible by hiding hacksaws between its pages. Kael wrote, "What's daring in the way Gillian Armstrong presents this love story is that we don't quite trust the emotions of either Kate Soffel or Ed Biddle. She's sickly, frustrated, unstable; he's an opportunist, with only one opportunity - to make her love him so madly that she'll bring him and Jack the saws they need to get out."[342] A similar plot was devised thirty-five years earlier for *Prison Warden* (1949), which we examined in Chapter Six.

Fatal Attraction (1987)

Dan (Michael Douglas) cheats on his wife for a one-night affair with Alex (Glenn Close). Alex assumed that her evening with Dan was the beginning of a great and lasting romance. She may have read some of the same romance novels that Emma Bovary read. Alex terrorizes Dan and his family to make Dan aware of her pain and to force him to face up to his wrongdoing. Dan has to assume responsibility for his unfaithfulness while protecting his family from a homicidal maniac. This is brutal therapy.

Alex could have certainly identified with Emma Bovary, who provides her own furious rebuke to an untrustworthy lover at the climax of her story. But Emma drinks poison afterward. Alex, a feminist fantasy, never expresses her rage inwardly. She sees death as the only possible resolution to the situation, but the death is not to be her own.

Enemies A Love Story (1989)

The maddening chaos of infidelity is woefully showcased in *Enemies, A Love Story*. A plot that would be well-suited for an exaggerated and manic farce is crafted into a believable and tragic story.

Herman Broder (Ron Silver), a Jewish writer, lives in the Bronx with his wife Yadwiga (Margaret Sophie Stein). It has been four years since the end of World War II. Broder is troubled by memories of his life in Poland during the war. He escaped capture by the S. S. because Yadwiga, then his maid, hid him in a hayloft. Yadwiga is not his first wife. Soldiers took away his first wife, Tamara (Anjelica Huston), along with their two young children. He later received news that Tamara and the children were forced into a ditch and shot. He married Yadwiga out of gratitude when they emigrated together to America. Yadwiga is a sweet but dull wife. She takes good care of him, but she fails to inspire sexual passion in him. He finds great passion with a seamstress, Masha (Lena Olin), a Polish refugee who spent the war in a concentration camp with her mother. She purrs into Herman's ear, "Come home with me and I'll show you something your Yadwiga would blush at." But Masha doesn't always offer Herman pleasure. She is volatile, quarrelsome and suicidal. Herman's relationship with her is self-destructive. Hal Hinson of The Washington Post wrote, "Masha is a tempest of neurotic emotion. . . In their lovemaking, Masha and Herman go at one another passionately; they hold nothing back. Yet their ardor is mixed with desperation, as if they were trying through sex to reawaken themselves and climb back into life."[343]

Herman tells Masha that he can't divorce Yadwiga. She says, "You can't? When the King of England wanted to marry the woman he loved, he gave up his throne and you can't get rid of a stupid peasant?" Masha doesn't believe that Herman's marriage to Yadwiga is legitimate because he married her in a civil ceremony. She convinces him to marry her in a Jewish ceremony.

Tamara has in fact survived and has come to New York to reunite with her husband. Hinson wrote:

> Watching Herman's face as his towering, back-from-the-dead wife clomps toward him down a long hallway, you can see immediately that for him, this so-called miracle is yet another in a series of cosmic jokes of which he is merely the butt.[344]

So, now, Herman legally has three wives.

Herman tells Tamara about Yadwiga and Masha. Tamara feels compassion for Herman and becomes his confidant and advisor.

Masha is not happy with the arrival of this other woman. She says, "You have your shiksa and you have me, but some bitch from Europe shows up and you leave to run off to meet her." Herman is confused and distressed as he races between wives. He admits to Tamara that he is going crazy. She asks, "Were you always like this? Or did the war do it? I can't remember what kind of person you used to be." He says that he knows that Masha is insane, but he cannot live without her. Tamara responds, "You want three women, but you always go to the one who calls you the loudest and who is sickest. She's not your lover. She's your enemy."

Herman takes Masha to the Catskills for a rest. But she becomes enraged when he phones Yadwiga. She shouts, "We're here one night, and you go running to the phone to call your peasant. You lie to her. And you lie to me." Robert S. Leventhal, a professor at The University of Virginia, wrote, "Herman Broder's love is fractured, split, fragmented, as he himself is."[345]

Yadwiga tells Herman that she's pregnant. Masha claims to be pregnant, too, but her pregnancy turns out to be imaginary. Her mental condition is clearly deteriorating. She can no longer continue when her mother suddenly dies. She tells Herman, "I cannot leave my mother. I want a grave next to her's." She commits suicide. Afterward, a dejected Herman abandons Yadwiga.

Tamara cares for Yadwiga during her pregnancy. A close friendship develops between the women. After the birth, Tamara stays with Yadwiga to help her to raise her child.

Herman's unending torment fails to conceal the absurdity of the plot. The film is at times as absurd as *Love Finds Andy Hardy* (1938), in which Mickey Rooney mismanages his love life in his usual bad way and winds up with three dates for a high school dance. Fortunately, Judy Garland serves in the Tamara role and guides him out of his dilemma. In the end, a frazzled Rooney swears off polygamy.

Damage (1992)

Dr. Stephen Fleming (Jeremy Irons) is a prominent member of the English Parliament. He has a beautiful wife, two healthy children, and a fine home. Yet, he develops an overpowering attraction to his son's enigmatic girlfriend, Anna Barton (Juliette Binoche). Anna brings out in this staid man a passion that he has never felt before. He becomes frantic the first time they meet for sex. He kneels down before her. He demands, "Who are you? Who are you?" She warns him that she is a damaged person and he should stay away from her. "All damaged people are dangerous," she says, "Survival makes them so." She tells him about the death of her brother, Ashton, at the age of 16. She was close to her brother while they were growing up. But then she turned 15 and began to date boys, which made him insanely jealous. He wanted her all to himself and demanded that she have sex with him. When she locked him out of her bedroom, he pounded on the door for two hours. Finally exhausted, he got himself a razor and slit his wrists. In the novel, she conceded to have sex with him in the hope that it would soothe him. But it only made his condition worse. She blamed his suicide on "his pain, my foolishness, our confusion."[346]

Anna is twisted and damaged, but he is the same. Josephine Hart, who wrote the original novel, said that the story is about the destructive force of erotic obsession. But she clarified that erotic obsession is different than lust. She wrote, "Shakespeare is right. Lust is driven by the desire for pleasure, erotic obsession by the necessity of union."[347] theodarsey of IMDb wrote: "[Stephen and Anna] are not in it for the sheer physical sensation. . . Through sex with each other they appear to be working out their own individual pain, a sense of loss or longing for something they are unable to express any other way. . . This is why the sex comes off for the most part as passionless, futile, and far from pleasurable. These are not happy, normal people - they cannot experience much real pleasure the way the average person does."[348]

Stephen's son, Martyn (Rupert Graves), is shocked to catch Stephen and Anna in bed together and accidentally falls off a railing and dies. The incident receives massive press attention, which destroys Stephen's marriage and his career. Miranda Richardson, as Stephen's wife Ingrid, received critical acclaim for her wronged wife speech. The speech is appropriately anguished and angry. She tells him:

> Why didn't you kill yourself? You should have killed yourself when it began. Didn't you know? You thought you could go on? Every day into the future? Go on betraying us both every day? You are not an evil man. You should have killed yourself when you first realized and then I would have been able to mourn. It would have been hard, but I would have buried you. And I would have wept.

Hart said that the most common complaint of the novel was that the husband never repents. But, in her view, he could not regret behavior that he could not control.

A French Woman (1995)

The original French title: *Une femme française*

It's wartime Paris in 1940. Jeanne (Emmanuelle Béart) is visited at an evacuee shelter by Henri (Samuel Le Bihan), a soldier who befriended her husband Louis (Daniel Auteuil) in a prison camp. The couple goes into a back room to speak in private. Henri admits to an insolent and selfish reason for coming to visit Jeanne. He says, "[Louis]'d show me photos of you. I was so happy when your letters came. You were always on my mind. I'd fallen in love. Forgive me. . . I dreamed we made love." He talks with her briefly before he slips his hands beneath her skirt and strokes her thighs. Her sister, Helene (Laurence Masliah), is hidden in the shadows and witnesses the indecent act. A former POW employs a similar wife-stealing tactic in *Desire Me* (1947). One afternoon, Jeanne has noisy sex with Henri at her home while her young son is in the next room playing with toys. She is pregnant with twins by the time Louis returns home.

Jeanne and Louis are surrounded by sane and moral family members, but they themselves are outrageously corrupt and foolish.

Emmanuelle Béart in *A French Woman* (1995)

Derek Elley of Variety wrote, "Jeanne [is] driven by unknown demons. . ."[349] Is that true? She acknowledges her demons early in the story. She tells Louis, "There were days I thought you'd never come back. And on those days, I knew men were looking at me. Thinking I was pretty, desiring me. It gave me the strength to carry on. Keep me with you, by your side. Take me wherever you go. I have so much love to give you."

Jeanne's mother, Mathilde (Isabelle Guiard), talks about Jeanne's father dying in war while she was pregnant with Jeanne. She considered committing suicide, but she decided against it when she felt the baby kick for the first time. She wondered if the baby knew what she was about to do and kicked to let her know that she wanted them to live. She is sure that her father's death is the reason that her daughter has always acted wildly and irrationally. She certainly was irrational to marry Louis. The loss of her father makes her desperate to have a man around to love her. That man is not Louis, who is never around.

While pregnant again, Jeanne dances exuberantly on a dance floor with a strange soldier. Louis rushes to her and angrily pulls her away, nearly getting into a fight with the soldier.

Mathias Behrens (Gabriel Barylli), their landlord's son, arrives for a visit. He soon has his eye on Jeanne. When Jeanne goes into labor, he drives her to the hospital. This gives him an opportunity to get close to the lovely young lady. He ends his visit soon after, but he sends love letters to Jeanne. He arranges another visit so that he can secretly meet with her. She begs him to stop writing to her and never to see her again. He refuses to stay away. We learn nothing about Mathias except that he is embittered from his experience as a soldier.

Jeanne and Mathias make plans to flee with the children. Jeanne's mother is desperate to stop her. She tries her best to reason with her child. She tells her that she is being irrational and this decision will cause her to be followed by misery for the rest of her life.

Jeanne is restrained by her brother-in-law, Marc (Jean-Noel Broute), while his wife Helen (Jeanne's sister) puts her children in her car and drives off. Jeanne attacks Marc with ferocity, as if she is prepared to kill him. Marc is shocked by her violent reaction.

Louis returns home, but he is immediately preparing to leave again. He initially rejects the opportunity to be an attaché in Syria, which is a desk job that will allow him to settle down with his family. But, when he learns that Jeanne arranged the assignment with his superior, he accepts it. But it's too late to matter. Jeanne remains unhappy in Syria. While they are touring ancient ruins, she tells him, "I'm leaving. It's over. I did everything I could. I thought I could forget him. But I just can't. He has been here a week. I asked him to come." Mathias arrives to take her away and Louis attacks him. Jeanne panics seeing how savagely Louis is beating him. She picks up a rock and strikes Louis in the back with it. Both men lie bloody and inert as she sobs hysterically. Louis' spine is injured and he is unable to move. He is quickly transported by ambulance to a hospital. Medical experts are worried that he may be paralyzed for the rest of his life. But he recovers eventually. At a beach, a woman notices that he has a large ugly scar on his back. He tells her that it was a war injury. She tells him that he is a hero. Louis has in fact fought a war on two fronts. His war on the Jeanne front proved to be more dangerous.

Louis does not stop Jeanne from leaving with Mathias, but he denies her a divorce. She starts to drink heavily and neglect her children. Jeanne goes to confession at one point, but she finds no peace or direction in religion. Mathias gets fed up with her and leaves.

At this point, Jeanne amazingly reunites with Louis. An unknown and unseen narrator has the last word:

Life went on. Jeanne had other lovers, Louis fought in other wars. Then one Christmas, Jeanne became violently ill while reading the paper. She couldn't breathe. One month later, she was dead. She had slowly suffocated to death. This was all she had when she came in. The doctors couldn't save her. No cause of death was given.

While going through her purse, Louis finds a newspaper clipping reporting Mathias' death.

The film opened with a tragedy. While walking to a church for Marc's wedding, Louis' father Charles (Michel Etcheverry) suffered a heart attack at the foot of a statue. We were told that he died a few weeks later. In the final scene, Louis trudges past the same statue after having just learned of Jeanne's death. In a wild-eyed daze, he clutches his wife's purse and Mathias' obituary to his chest.

It is a pointless and unpleasant film, filled with despair and insanity from beginning to end. Elley wrote:

. . . [I]t's a painless slice of handsome moviemaking that offers goodly guilty pleasures: Emmanuelle Béart has never looked lovelier; Francois Catonne's lensing is a symphony of color, light and shade; Patrick Doyle's churning orchestral score is a further feather in his cap; the '40s/'50s costuming and production design are consistently eye-catching. Genevieve Winding's pinpoint editing brings the whole shebang in at a trim 97 minutes. . . However striking its individual sequences, though, the film still has a hollow center, a lack of any larger arc. . . Described by the helmer as a classic tragedy in five acts,. . . it's nothing of the sort, largely because of the script's lack of depth in the main characters.[350]

The English Patient (1996)

Two films elevated adultery to an epic scale: David Lean's *Ryan's Daughter* (1970) and the Lean-style *The English Patient*. In both films, a world war rages in the background. In both films, a traitorous act provides a pivotal plot twist.

The English Patient isn't, as some assume, history's longest adultery film. Strangely enough, the longest adultery film is *Ryan's Daughter* (at 206 minutes versus *English Patient*'s 162 minutes).

Count Laszlo de Almásy (Ralph Fiennes), a geographer, has an affair with a married woman, Katharine Clifton (Kristin Scott Thomas), in the sprawling, golden Sahara Desert. Geoffrey, who has been driven mad learning about the affair, tries to crash a plane into Almásy. Almásy survives the crash but Geoffrey dies. Katharine, revealed to be a passenger in Geoffrey's plane, has been seriously injured. Almásy carries her into a cave known as The Cave of Swimmers. She asks him, in the gentlest voice, to bury Geoffrey. He walks for days across the desert to get help for her. He discovers a Tiger Moth plane that was abandoned in the Libyan Desert by his best friend, Madox. He exchanges survey maps for fuel and takes flight to return to the cave. He is not surprised to find Katharine dead. He lays down beside her and gently strokes her hair. Katharine wrote him a letter while she still had strength left. She says in the letter that God wanted them to meet and be together. He carries her out of the cave sobbing and puts her into the plane. He intends to bring her body to Cairo for burial, but his plane is shot down by German forces. Bedouin tribesmen rescue Almásy from the remnants of the plane. Badly burned and near death, he is transported to Italy for medical treatment. A compassionate nurse, Hana (Juliette Binoche), cares for the dying man in a bombed out monastery. He relates the story of his love affair to David Caravaggio (Willem Dafoe), a former intelligence agent who has joined a refugee settlement in the area. In the end, Almásy compels Hana to overdose him with morphine so that he can die.

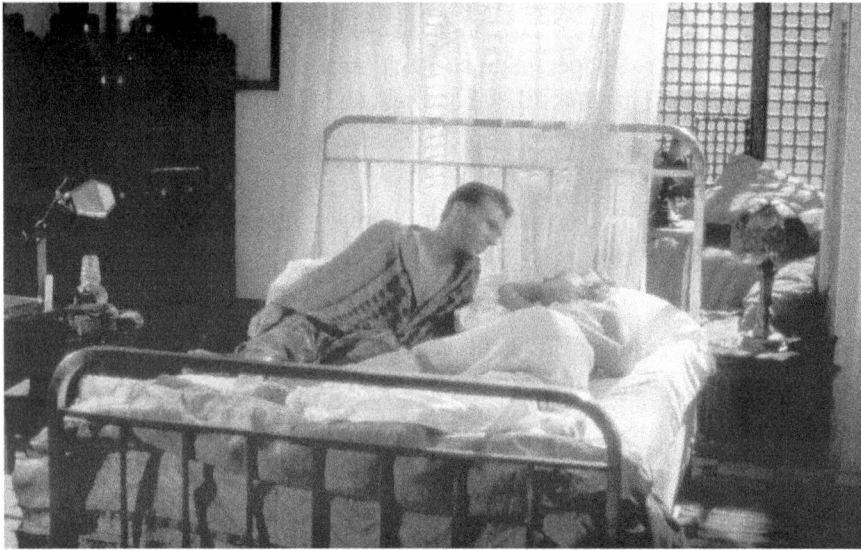

Ralph Fiennes and Kristin Scott Thomas in *The English Patient* (1996)

The film gains much of its power from the beauty of its cinematography. IMDb reviewer jhclues wrote:

Simply put, Minghella's film is genius realized; crafted and delivered with a poetic perfection, watching it is like watching a Monet come to life. From the opening frames, Minghella casts a hypnotic spell over his audience that is binding and transporting, with a story that has an emotional beauty that equals the engagingly stunning and vibrant images brought to life by John Seale's remarkable cinematography; images that virtually fill the screen as well as the soul of the viewer. In every sense, this is a film of rare eloquence, with a striking emotional capacity that facilitates an experience that is truly transcendental.[351]

It wasn't great love that had attracted Katharine to Geoffrey. Geoffrey tells a friend how he was able to persuade the lovely Katharine to marry him. He says, "She was always crying on my shoulder about somebody. I finally persuaded her to settle for my shoulder. A stroke of genius."

How does the affair begin?

Katharine makes drawings of cave paintings they have encountered and gives Almásy the drawings to paste into his scrapbook. But Almásy refuses the drawings and generally resists Katharine's efforts to become friendly with him.

Katharine: I thought you might like to paste them into your book.

Almásy: Well, we - we took photographs. There's no need.

Katharine: No, really. I'd like you to have them.

Almásy: Well, there's really no need. This is, um - This is just a scrapbook. They are too good.

Katharine is intrigued by his resistance. A married person should have a ready resistance to romantic entanglements outside of their marriage. A force field must be erected around the marital home and that force field must be steadfastly maintained to protect the home. There are doors in your heart that should be opened to no one but your spouse. There are doors in your head that should shut out fantasies of extramarital sex. A switch can be flicked in the human mind to shut off a blazing circuit of passion. Simply, a moral man must resist temptation. That's the oft told lesson of Adam and Eve. You never take a bite out of the apple.

This force field is addressed in other films.

In *Indiscreet* (1958), Philip Adams (Cary Grant) deters Anna Kalman (Ingrid Bergman) from getting any romantic ideas about him. He says, "I'm a married man, Miss Kalman. . . I must've sounded quite idiotic blurting it out like that." Anna asks him why he felt the need to warn her that he wasn't married. He replies, "Because those are the rules between grown-up men and women. Or should be."

This also comes up in *Man On Fire* (1957). Bryan Seward (Richard Eastham) has an affair with a friend's wife, Gwen (Mary Fickett). Gwen abandons her husband, Earl Carleton (Bing Crosby), and young son Ted (Macolm Brodrick) to marry Bryan. When she learns that she and Bryan are unable to have children, she embarks on a messy court battle with Earl to gain custody of Ted. Bryan blames Earl for making the court proceedings difficult. But Nina Wylie (Inger Stevens), an assistant of Earl's lawyer, reminds Bryan that this situation came out of Bryan stealing Earl's wife. Bryan bristles at this accusation.

Bryan: We fell in love.

Nina: You had no right to that, either one of you. It's that simple.

Bryan: I wish that I could develop such a lofty viewpoint.

In *Moonstruck* (1987), Loretta Castorini (Cher) impetuously has sex with her fiancé's younger brother, Ronny (Nicolas Cage). She immediately regrets it. She tells Ronny, "So maybe my nature does draw me to you. That don't mean I have to go with it. I can take hold of myself, and I can say yes to some things and no to other things that are gonna ruin everything. I can do that. Otherwise, you know, what - what good is this stupid life that God gave us?"

Self-control is the greatest enemy of adultery.

Hannah and Her Sisters (1986) opens at a dinner party at the home of Hannah (Mia Farrow) and Elliot (Michael Caine). Like *Brief Encounter* (1945) and *The Facts of Life* (1960), this introductory scene features a voice-over. The speaker is Elliot. He openly expresses his lust for his sister-in-law, Lee (Barbara Hershey):

> God, she's beautiful. She's got the prettiest eyes. She looks so sexy in that sweater. I just want to be alone with her and hold her and kiss her, and tell her how much I love her and take care of her. Stop it, you idiot! She's your wife's sister. I can't help it. I'm consumed by her. It's been months now. I dream about her, I think about her at the office. Oh, Lee. What am I gonna do? I hear myself mooning over you, and it's disgusting. Before, when she squeezed past me in the doorway and I smelt that perfume on the back of her neck. Jesus, I thought I was gonna swoon. Easy. You're a dignified financial advisor. It doesn't look good for you to swoon.

These are the sort of thoughts that a married man should never entertain. No mooning. No swooning. No squeezing past his sister-in-law in a doorway. No smelling the perfume on the back on her neck. No contemplating how sexy his sister-in-law looks in a sweater. His only thought should be "Stop it, you idiot!"

Kit Marlowe (Bette Davis) puts up a perfect resistance to the romantic overtures of her best friend's husband Preston Drake (John Loder) in *Old Acquaintance* (1943).

> Preston: Kit, you mean everything to me. The thought of you, the mention of your name. Kit, I am really in love with you, deeply in love with you. Look me straight me in the eyes and tell me you don't feel as I do. I'm never going back to Millie. So, don't let that make any difference in what you say, but tell me. Tell me the truth.
>
> Kit: Pres, I haven't let myself even think about it.
>
> Preston: Why not?
>
> Kit: Because there are things you just don't do. There are things that a woman just can't do and this is one of them.
>
> Preston: Kit, this is our chance for a happy life.
>
> Kit: That might be, Pres, if things were different.
>
> Preston: It's the only chance.
>
> Kit: There's no such thing as an only chance. Life goes on. Pres, Millie would always be between us, spoiling any chance of happiness that we might find. There are things that you just don't do if you want to live decently with yourself afterward.
>
> Preston: Do you mean to stand there and tell me that your friendship for Millie would mean more to you than your love for me?
>
> Kit: Pres, I know it's hard for a man to understand. All I know is that it's something I just couldn't do whether it was Millie, or any other woman who is a friend of mine. I guess it wasn't meant to be, Pres.

In the end, Preston finds another woman and runs off with her. The selfish person, Millie, and the selfless person, Kit, end in the same sad and lonely place. This puts into question whether or not morals have a practical purpose in our lives.

Now, back to *The English Patient*.

A sandstorm causes Katharine and Almásy to huddle for protection inside a truck. This forces them into an intimate situation.

Katharine feels even closer to Almásy when she secretly reads his notebook and sees that he has written affectionately about her. By peering inside his personal notebook, she has opened up a door that she should have left closed.

The couple returns to Cairo with many unresolved feelings. Katharine strides uninvited into Almásy bedroom, waking the man out of a sound and sweaty sleep. She resents him for having stirred such intense feelings in her. She strikes him repeatedly before falling into his arms and kissing him. He rips open her blouse, unable to control his passion for her any longer.

Katharine tells Almásy, "This a different world is what I tell myself. A different life. And here I'm a different wife." It's a poor excuse for the affair.

Almásy also doesn't take responsibility for the affair. He speaks about a Hungarian folk song in which a Hungarian count "falls under the spell of a mysterious English woman." He says that the woman was a "harpy" who beat the man and turned him into a slave.

Almásy becomes obsessed. His best friend, Madox (Julian Wadham), is a voice of reason.

Almásy: Um, Madox? That place - That place at the base of a woman's throat. You know, the hollow here. Does it have an official name?

Madox: For God's sake, man, pull yourself together.

The sweat is still fresh on Almásy's brow after a sexual encounter with Katherine when he meets Geoffrey, who has made a sudden visit home dressed as Santa Claus. Geoffrey embraces and kisses his wife, unaware that moments earlier she had been in the throes of sexual passion with Almásy.

Katharine is suddenly overwhelmed by feelings of guilt and realizes that she must end the affair. Upset by Katharine's decision, Almásy has a childish tantrum at a party.

The relationship is painful for the most part. Almásy says, "Every night I cut out my heart. But in the morning it was full again."

The story is an endless series of tragedies. Favorable reviews referred to the film as "multilayered." But having one subplot piled onto another subplot piled onto another subplot, with no obvious relationship from one to the other expect they all have something to do with love, is not multilayered. At a critical time in the third act, a minor character dies in a mine explosion and attention fully shifts to the effect that his death has on a friend. Why?

Caravaggio explains how he lost his thumbs. A German officer, Major Muller (Jurgen Prochnow), tortures him to get him to provide information. He muses:

What's the punishment for adultery? Let's leave it at that. You're married and you were fucking another woman, so that's, uh -- Is it the hands that are cut off? Or is that for stealing? Does anyone know? Well, you must know. You were brought up in Libya, yes?

In the end, the major chops off Caravaggio's thumbs.

Geoffrey trying to crash a plane into Almásy is mad. But *The Devil and The Deep* (1932) features a wronged husband with an more crazed solution to his wife's infidelity. Charles Sturm (Charles Laughton), a naval commander, crashes his submarine in an attempt to end his life and kill his wife and her lover, who are on board along with dozens of crew members.

The box office receipts of *The English Patient* totaled a lofty $232 million.

After Sex (1997)

Diane Clovier (Brigitte Roüan), a middle-aged book editor, is working with a young author, François (Nils Tavernier). While visting him at his apartment, she meets his handsome roommate, Emilio (Boris Terral). Roger Ebert wrote, "They seem almost immediately to fall into a mutual sexual trance, and are making love before they know each other."[352]

Diane is married with two children. But that doesn't matter to her. She is willing to jeopardize her marriage for a wildly impulsive affair. Ebert wrote:

> The first stage of their relationship is one of urgent risk-taking, as they meet whenever and wherever they can. She races across streets, crying out his name. Kissing, they fall onto the hood of a car in the middle of traffic, oblivious. Once they become so reckless that they are requested to leave a restaurant. Diane is amazed to feel so strongly and deeply; at one point, she is literally seen floating on air.[353]

Diane's attorney husband, Philippe (Patrick Chesnais), is defending a woman who fatally stabbed her husband in the neck because of his cheating. He prepares for her defense while suspecting that his wife might be cheating on him. This is similar to the plot of *The Kiss Before The Mirror*.

Emilio cools off on the relationship, perhaps unable to handle the intensity of Diana's feelings. Diane confronts Emilio at his workplace. The two get into an argument beside a coffee machine in the break room. While a co-worker awkwardly comes between them to use the machine, Emilio lets Diane know that he doesn't want to continue their relationship. She accuses him of being cold and unfeeling. "I hurt all over and you feel nothing," she says. She becomes furious and head-butts him in the face before storming out.

Diane suffers a breakdown in grand Madame Bovary style. She refuses to eat. She spends most of her time getting drunk and lying passed out on her sofa. Her husband and children, unable to cope, move out.

François takes Diane to the beach to recover. He gets her to laugh during lunch. But then she disappears on him. He finds her standing on a cliff high above the ocean. Just as he calls out to her, she leaps over the cliff. She falls a great distance and plunges into the water. After a few moments, she rises out of the briny depths and is relieved to be alive. She laughs in an expression of sheer joy. She has, evidently, been reborn.

The End of the Affair (1999)

The film is based on 1951 autobiographical novel by British author Graham Greene.

Putting Ralph Fiennes into another adultery film seems an obvious way to capitalize on the success of *The English Patient*. The tone of the two films is similar, too. Call it *The English Patient Part 2*.

The couple's meeting is an important part of the adultery film. It needs a build-up. It needs nuance. It needs depth. But none of that is evident when Maurice Bendrix (Fiennes) and Sarah Miles (Julianne Moore) meet at a party. Within seconds after meeting her, in the seclusion of a patio, Maurice leans forward to kiss Sarah. She leans forward as if eager to accept his kiss. Then the two are interrupted by her husband, Henry (Stephen Rea), and quickly pull back from one another. Similarly, a patio is an adulterers' haven in *The Road to Singapore*.

Sarah introduces Maurice to her eminent husband, who serves as the Minister of Home Security. Maurice tells Henry, "Your wife is charming." Henry responds, "She's a great help to me."

Maurice is an author. Speaking through this fictitious author, Greene let's us know the reason for an adultery story: "Goodness has so little fictional value." He adds, "Happiness is even harder to write than goodness." Sarah says that her husband prefers habit over happiness. Maurice's views on happy stories and happy characters was shared by Leo Tolstoy, who wrote in his novel "Anna Karenina": "Happy families are all alike; every unhappy family is unhappy in its own way."[354]

There's a scene where Maurice and Sarah are caught in the rain and Maurice throws his coat over their heads. Sarah turns unexpectedly and kisses him. It is a passionate kiss. With the coat draped over their heads, their illicit kiss is discreetly hidden from public view. Strangely, it turns out that the scene is simply something that Maurice imagined.

The 1955 film adaptation is far better. Moore's bare bosom and Fiennes' bare backside do nothing to enhance the story.

Suspicious River (2000)

Leila Murray (Molly Parker) is married to Rick Schmidt (Joel Bissonnette), but she has a compulsion to sleep with other men. She struggles futilely against these urges and is distressed to be unable to control herself. Rick is aware of her infidelity, but it is something that he sadly accepts. Leila, who has a job as a motel receptionist, begins to sleep with guests for money. She has an affair with a violently abusive man, Gary Jensen (Callum Keith Rennie). It is through this harrowing relationship that Leila recalls a suppressed memory of seeing her mother killed by a jealous boyfriend. A brief voice-over narration that Leila provides at the closing suggests that she has regained the will to live. It remains unknown if, by confronting the horrible memory of her mother's murder, she can now commit to being a faithful and loving wife.

The film shares plot elements with a 1967 French film, *Belle de Jour*.

He Loves Me, He Loves Me Not (2002)

The original French title: *À la folie... pas du tout*

The film opens with a young woman, Angélique (Audrey Tautou), sending a pink rose to her lover, Dr. Loïc Le Garrec (Samuel Le Bihan). She tells a friend, David (Clément Sibony), that Loïc is leaving his wife and they are going on vacation together. She goes to meet Loïc at the airport, but he never shows up. She sees on television that Loïc has been arrested for the murder of a patient. How did this happen? The film suddenly rewinds to the first scene. We now see the story from Loïc's perspective. Loïc receives the pink rose and has no idea who sent it. He becomes distraught when his pregnant wife, Rachel (Isabelle Carré), is run down by a woman on a moped. She is rushed to the hospital and learns that she has lost the baby. Loïc opens a package and finds a human heart inside. The doctor realizes that he has a stalker and suspects that it was the stalker who attacked Rachel. He assumes that the stalker is Sonia Jasmin (Nathalie Krebs), a patient who has made aggressive sexual advances toward him. He becomes angry with Sonia in his office. He grabs her, shakes her, and slaps her. She has him arrested for assault. Sonia is later found murdered and Loïc becomes the foremost suspect. As it turns out, Angélique is the stalker. She attacked Rachel and murdered Sonia. She has been house-sitting at a neighbor's home and met Loïc briefly. Rachel trusts that Loïc would never commit murder. She supports him fully. Angélique gets upset seeing Rachel lovingly kiss Loïc as the police take him away. She lets unlit gas jets run while she lies on the floor and prepares to die. Loïc is awakened by ambulance sirens and rushes next door to help revive Angélique. Loïc remembers a few small details that suggest Angélique is his stalker. He discovers an eerie shrine that she created for him in the neighbor's home. After Angélique is released from the hospital, Loïc has a confrontation with her at the neighbor's home. Angélique bashes him in the head with a brass figurine. Angélique is diagnosed as having a psychological disorder called erotomania. She is committed to a mental health hospital. The final scene takes place years later. Loïc is with Rachel and their young daughter in the backyard of their home. It is a remnant of his injury that he has to hobble about with a cane.

The Heart of Me (2002)

The story in set in London between 1934 and 1940. Rickie Masters (Paul Bettany) develops an obsessive relationship with his free-spirited sister-in-law, Dinah (Helena Bonham Carter). Rickie and Dinah suffer multiple emotional breakdowns as a result of their relationship. It is a relationship that drags along grand drama wherever it goes. Rickie gets Dinah pregnant, which is something that he must keep secret from his wife. Dinah suffers complications during the birth of the baby. Rickie crashes his car while speeding to the hospital in a snowstorm. The baby is stillborn. Dinah nearly dies from blood loss. Dinah has a breakdown after the loss of the baby and no longer wants to see Rickie. Rickie falls into despair at being unable to see Dinah. Bridie (Alison Reid), Dinah's friend, writes to Madeleine (Olivia Williams) about the affair. Madeleine is a grandly indignant wife. She calls Dinah "a devil." Dinah has a breakdown after unexpectedly encountering Rickie at a restaurant. Rickie, unable to stop her from sobbing, escorts her outside and hustles her into a carriage. As the carriage pulls away, she hangs out of the window and cries out, "I'm so alone. You love me. Help me." Rickie leaves Madeleine with the intention of running off with Dinah, but he suddenly collapses and has to be taken to the hospital. Madeleine and her mother, Mrs. Burkett (Eleanor Bron), are determined to keep Rickie and Dinah apart because of the bad effect that they have on one another. Mrs. Burkett lies to Rickie that Dinah moved to Paris. Rickie is on his way to pick up a bracelet that he had inscribed for Dinah. His errand is interrupted by a German bombing raid. He should quickly take shelter, but he wanders in a teary-eyed daze through fire and rubble. In the final scene, Madeleine and Dinah speak sadly of Rickie's death in the bombing and agree to set aside their past differences. The engraving on the bracelet reads, "And throughout all eternity, I forgive you and you forgive me."

House of Sand and Fog (2003)

Lester Burdon (Ron Eldard), a police officer, feels sorry for Kathy Nicolo (Jennifer Connelly) when he has to evict her. Despite being married, Lester goes on dates with Kathy. Kathy asks Lester where he lives.

Lester: In Millbrae. In a housing development called Palomino Meadows. You have to drive through it to get to the mall.

Kathy: Yeah, I know where that is. God, I've probably driven by it a dozen times. I've probably even seen your wife.

Lester: Carol.

Kathy: Yeah. Carol. What's your situation, Les?

Lester: I married my best friend. And for seven of the last nine years, I haven't wanted to give her more than a hug or a peck on the cheek. That's my situation.

Kathy: Do you still love her?

Lester: Look, it's just. . . it's not her. She's a good person. A good mother.

Kathy: Would this have happened anyway, even if you hadn't met me?

Lester: Yes.

Closer (2004)

The modern adultery film, like *Closer* and *Last Night* (2010), is cold, muddled and pretentious. *Closer* involves an emotionally confused woman who cheats on her husband. In *Beauty for Sale* (1933), a couple meets while huddled under a store awning during a rainstorm. Now, in the *Closer*, a couple meets in a cyber-sex chat room.

Longing (2006)

The original German title: *Sehnsucht*

Markus Koplin (Andreas Müller), a metalworker, is married to his childhood sweetheart, Ella (Ilka Welz). She is a beautiful and loving wife. But Markus suddenly falls in love with a waitress, Rose Kuchenbecker (Anett Dornbusch). He is confused to be in love with two women at the same time. He grows sullen and distant. Rose is sitting on a windowsill and smoking. Markus explains to her that they can longer see each other. She becomes upset, loses her balance, and falls out of the window. She is seriously injured and needs to be hospitalized. Markus is traumatized by the incident. Ella, who now knows about the affair, cannot bring herself to stay with Markus. He begs her not to leave him alone, but she leaves him anyway. He sits in his garage hugging his son's rabbit. Then he picks up a shotgun and shoots himself. The final scene, which takes place years later, features a group of neighborhood children talking about the shooting. It is an odd but effective epilogue that lasts for four minutes. The children debate if the man was dumb, or courageous, or romantic. It is revealed in the conversation that the man survived the shooting and one of the women took him back. Was it the wife? Was it the mistress? We aren't told.

The Heart Is a Dark Forest (2007)

The original German title: *Das Herz ist ein dunkler Wald*

Marie (Nina Hoss) learns that her husband, Thomas (Devid Striesow), has a second family in another part of town. This shocks her to her core. She becomes desperate to understand what caused Thomas to do this. Marie visits Thomas' other "wife," Anna (Franziska Petri). She asks, "Are you afraid I'll hit you?" But Anna isn't afraid. She greets Marie warmly. She is honest and sympathetic. She admits that she always knew that

Thomas was married. Marie visits her mother, Mietzi (Monica Bleibtreu). Mietzi's boyfriend, Helmut (Otto Sander), shows up unexpectedly. He is distraught because he believes that Mietzi has cheated on him. It is a tense situation, but Mietzi is able to convince him to leave. Thomas, a violinist, is performing at a night concert in an old castle. Marie attends the concert and confronts Thomas backstage. Thomas does not console her. He complains about her frequent tearful outbursts and tells her that it has been difficult living with her. She strikes him repeatedly. She threatens to kill their children ("They sleep and will never wake again"). Thomas is shocked by her behavior. Marie goes into the woods with a strange man and has sex with him. When the man leaves, she swims naked in a lake. After her swim, she discovers Helmut sitting on the shore with a gun. He stares at her with an anguished expression. He raises the gun to his head and fires. Marie does not react. After taking possession of the gun, she wanders naked to the street and boards a bus. She enters her home. Three shots can be heard coming from inside. Did she shoot her two children and herself? Did she shoot her children and her husband? Did she put three bullets into her husband? Did she just shoot up his violin? We are left to assume what happened. The film ends.

Revolutionary Road (2008)

Frank and April Wheeler (Leonardo DiCaprio and Kate Winslet) started out their marriage as a dynamic couple, but they have lost their spirit due to career frustrations. Frank is bored with his job as a regional sales manager for Knox Business Machines. April is upset at her failure to become an actress. Their life is not the great life that she imagined. She finds a confidante in a neighbor, Shep (David Harbour). "For years," she tells him, "I thought [Frank and I] shared this secret. That we would be wonderful in the world. I didn't exactly know how, but just the possibility kept me hoping." But now she has to accept this secret wasn't real. She says, "We were never special or destined or anything at all." The disappointment is more than she can bear. It has become something terrible that haunts her constantly. "I saw a whole other future," she says. "I can't stop seeing it." April stops having sex with Frank. Frank finds comfort and gratification having sex with his secretary, Maureen Grube (Zoe Kazan). One night, April has sex in a car with Shep. Frank resolves to work on his marriage. He confesses to April about his affair, but she doesn't understand the reason why he would tell her this.

April: Is it supposed to make me jealous or something? Is it supposed to make me fall in love with you, or get back into bed with you, or what? I mean, what would you like me to say, Frank?

Frank: Why don't you say what you feel, April?

April: I don't feel anything.

Frank: In other words, you don't care what I do or who I fuck or anything?

April: No, I guess that's right. I don't. Fuck who you like.

Frank: April, don't you understand that I want you to care?

April: I know. I know you do. And I suppose I would if I loved you. But I don't think I do anymore. And I only just figured that out.

April finds out that she is pregnant. She attempts to use a vacuum aspirator to abort the baby, but the procedure goes wrong and she bleeds to death.

April is unable to accept an ordinary life. She rejects conformity. She resists the constraints of marriage. But is this really a story of conformity and constraint? April never handles the situation in a calm or sensible manner. She suffers from an overwhelming depression, which is the real issue at the core of the story. Many people dream of being a great artist - an actor, or a musician, or a painter, or a dancer - but they find a way to get on with life if their dream doesn't come true. April lacks that ability, which proves to be a dangerous flaw.

Leonardo DiCaprio and Kate Winslet in *Revolutionary Road* (2008)

Nights in Rodanthe (2008)

Adrienne Willis (Diane Lane) leaves her cheating husband, Jack (Christopher Meloni). She accepts an offer to manage a friend's inn for the weekend. A storm traps Adrienne in the inn with another unhappy and troubled person, Dr. Paul Flanner (Richard Gere). Inevitably, Paul and Adrienne fall in love.

Come Undone (2010)

The original Italian title: *Cosa voglio di più*

Anna (Alba Rohrwacher) is satisfied with her life. She has a loving husband, Alessio (Giuseppe Battiston), and is fulfilled by her job at an insurance company. But then she meets Domenico (Pier Francesco Favino), a handsome waiter, and falls under a spell. They check into a sleazy motel. She is the aggressor, grabbing hold of him and passionately kissing him. They barely talk. Is this relationship entirely physical? Domenico breaks a date with Anna so that he can go to a pool with his wife Miriam (Teresa Saponangelo) and his daughter Agnese (Francesca Capelli). Anna becomes angry, which is unreasonable under the circumstances. At the pool, Domenico sees his daughter in the bleachers, then looks slightly to the right and sees Anna sitting in the bleachers as well. This worries Domenico as his wife already suspects that he is having an affair. Anna is brokenhearted when Domenico refuses to leave his wife and children for her.

Pier Francesco Favino and Alba Rohrwacher in *Come Undone* (2010)

Pure (2010)

The original Swedish title: *Till det som är vackert*

Katarina (Alicia Vikander), who was raised by an abusive alcoholic mother, is an unhappy young woman. She is uplifted by listening to Mozart's "Requiem" on YouTube. She gets a receptionist job at a concert hall. She is soon embroiled in an affair with a married conductor, Adam (Samuel Fröler). Adam eventually becomes bored with her and figures to give her the brush off. He says, "Katarina, we've had some really great days. I think you're lovely. But my family needs me and I need to concentrate on my job." She is living with a boyfriend, who finds out that she has been cheating and kicks her out. She begs Adam to take her back. She drops to her knees and performs fellatio on him. Can he fool her with pretty words? He says, "The love we've shared has to be free in order to breathe. Just like music. If you cling on to it, it'll die and wither like a rose in your hand." Katarina feels sad and desperate. She follows Adam and his wife to a bar. He tells her that his wife is suspicious and she needs to leave. He gets her fired the next day, but she refuses to leave and security guards have to drag her out. She returns again to beg for her job. He says that he'll let her have her job if she dances for him. She performs a sexy dance. But the dance is only meant to humiliate her. He calls her a nutcase and says that she will never work there again. In a blind rage, she shoves him out of a window. In the street, she watches paramedics spread a sheet over his still form. She visits her mother Birgitta (Josephine Bauer) in a hospital, where she is recovering from a suicide attempt. She sobs in her mother's arms. Katarina recovers from the experience and gets a manager position at the concert hall. She attends a performance at the hall. A new conductor has replaced Adam. The orchestra beautifully plays Mozart's "Requiem." She is transported away by the music as she had been at the start of the film. The camera comes in tightly on her face. She smiles. Vikander gives a sympathetic performance as the abused and anguished Katarina.

Plush (2013)

It's a simple story: emo rocker meets homicidal stalker. Hayley (Emily Browning), a young singer/songwriter, is married to Carter (Cam Gigandet) and has two small children. She balances her music career with being a wife and mother. She falls into deep despair when her brother/guitarist dies of a drug overdose. Her brother's replacement, Enzo (Xavier Samuel), collaborates with her on new songs and gradually seduces her. Hayley panics when she learns that she is pregnant. The baby must belong to Enzo as Carter had a vasectomy after their last child. She tries to break away from Enzo, but he is madly obsessed with her and refuses to go away. He kills Hayley's band manager, Annie (Dawn Olivieri), who plans to fire him. The film, according to Christy Lemire of RogerEbert.com, involves "the eye-linered Enzo's efforts to insinuate himself in Hayley's life while Hayley remains oblivious to just how deranged he truly is."[355]

Down by Love (2016)

Anna Amari (Adèle Exarchopoulos), a pretty teenage girl, arrives at a women's correctional facility. The facility's director, Jean Firmino (Guillaume Gallienne), is captivated by her. He is a middle-aged man with a wife and child. His wife, Elise (Stéphanie Cléau), is beautiful and affectionate. Yet, he reacts awkwardly when Elise greets him naked and tries to have sex with him. Why? We never learn. Jean finds Anna alone in the computer lab. He takes her in his arms and kisses her. He becomes obsessed with her. He believes that he is being discreet and that no one suspects. He could not be more wrong. Gossip about the affair becomes widespread. He is warned by his boss (Guillaume Marquet). His boss says "Your record is excellent. Don't ruin everything." Sue kicks him out of their home. She tells him, "You have a wife and daughter who love you. That's not enough? What more do you need? Some young girl to make you feel strong? You're pathetic." Sue is disgusted, but she is still willing to forgive him. She tells him, "Wake up, please. Wake up. I won't wait for you forever." She hugs him tenderly and sympathetically. Anna becomes pregnant. She doesn't want to tell the prison doctor because it would mean getting Jean in trouble. But Jean is arrested anyway. We never learn the reason that Anna is in prison. The film is based on a true story. Anna was modeled on Sorour Arbabzadeh, who was imprisoned for playing a key role in a gang murder.

From the Land of the Moon (2016)

A young woman, Gabrielle (Marion Cotillard), finds life on her parents' farm to be dull. She becomes infatuated with her married literature teacher, who introduces her to classic novels. Like Emma Bovary, she develops an understanding of love from romance stories. The teacher loans her his personal copy of "Wuthering Heights." She sees that he signed his name inside the book. She runs her fingers across the signature. She raises the book to her face so that she can smell it. Then, she licks it. Gabrielle confronts her teacher at an outdoor feast with a love letter that she wrote to him. He is shocked by the letter and tells her that she is mad. She doesn't understand. She wrote the letter in the style of the romance novels that he loaned her. Outraged, she shoves the teacher into a table and runs off screaming into the woods. She is later found collapsed and sobbing amid underbrush. Her pragmatic parents have managed through sensible business practices to establish a large and prosperous farm. They cannot relate to their delusional and hysterical daughter. Her mother, Adèle (Brigitte Roüan), offers José (Alex Brendemühl), an honest and hardworking bricklayer, a generous dowry to marry Gabrielle. She believes that he can be the solid husband that her daughter needs. Gabrielle refuses to meet with José, but her mother tells her that she either has to marry José or be sent to a mental institution. Gabrielle tells José, "You'll be unhappy. Why chose to be unhappy? I don't love you. I'll never love you." José's traumatic experiences as a soldier have made him withdrawn. He is handsome, loving and devoted as a husband, but he frustrates Gabrielle with his introverted manner. She can be outright cruel in her treatment of him. Gabrielle suffers a miscarriage due to kidney stones. She is sent for treatment to an exclusive clinic in the Alps. At the clinic, she meets André Sauvage (Louis Garrel), who lost a kidney as a result of a war injury. Gabrielle and André have a passionate love affair. Gabrielle wants to run away with André, but André dismisses the idea. "Right now," he says, "it's impossible." But he does give her hope that they will get together again at a later time. He gives her his home address in Lyon. She is discharged from the clinic on the next day. She regularly sends letters to André, but he never responds. One day, Jose shows Gabrielle her many letters to André, which have been returned unopened. She becomes enraged. She tells José to go away and throws sand at him. She learns that she is pregnant and believes that this is André's child. She finds peace after she gives birth to a son, Marc. Within the next few years, Gabrielle comes to recognize José as a good man and comes to love him. She accepts his introverted ways. She tells her sister matter-of-factly, "He's the private type. He never talks." That's it. It's no longer a problem. Marc (Victor Quilichini) demonstrates extraordinary talent as a pianist and qualifies to participate in a national competition in Lyon. Gabrielle visits André's old address in Lyon. She is greeted by a man who tells her that André is dead. He says that he remembers seeing Gabrielle the day before she left the spa. He says that André was transported to a hospital the same day and died hours later. Gabrielle insists that this cannot be true. She remembers André returning to the spa that night and making love to her. He says that this is not possible. It is revealed at this point that Gabrielle had become delusional during her stay at the spa. José describes his arrival at the spa the day before her discharge. But she has no memory of this. We see his visit in flashback. José met André while having a smoke on a patio. André looks shockingly shriveled and frail sitting in his wheelchair. This is not at all how André looked in previous scenes. André points to Gabrielle, who can be seen through the window of the dining room. He says that she is a beautiful woman and he would have taken an interest in her if he wasn't so sick. He admits to being unable to love a woman as he is impotent. José witnesses Gabrielle chasing the ambulance that takes André away. She collapses and needs to be helped back into the spa by attendants. It was José who made love to her that night, though Gabrielle imagined André to be her lover. This means that the son that she holds dear is, for sure, José's son. She apologizes to José. He tells her that he has bought a new home for them in Spain. She is pleased to have a new start.

Chapter Twelve:
Neglected Wives Get Bored

March's Child (1958) provides the neglected wife's statement of faith: "I felt lonely, too. I needed affection, some company. . . I was in desperation."

In a marriage, the husband plays an important role as protector. In *Enchanted April* (1991), elderly Mrs. Fisher (Joan Plowright) says, "In my day,. . . [h]usbands were taken seriously, as the only real obstacle to sin." A husband, as an obstacle to sin, should never neglect his wife.

The Evangelist (1916)

Christabel Nuneham (Gladys Hanson) feels neglected by her husband Philip (Ferdinand Tidmarsh). So, while her husband is busy with his work, she has an affair with a young army officer, Rex Allan (Jack Standing). Christabel regrets the affair after she is injured in a car accident. In the meantime, Philip learns of the affair and threatens to divorce her. Christabel receives spiritual enlightenment from an evangelist, Sylvanus Rebbings (George Soule Spencer), who works to reconcile the estranged couple.

Any Wife (1922)

Cyril Hill (Lawrence Johnson) catches his wife Myrtle (Pearl White) in the arms of his business assistant, Philip Gray (Holmes Herbert). Cyril divorces Myrtle, which frees her to marry Philip. But Myrtle is more unhappy than before with Philip and, out of desperation, drowns herself. But, wait, it was only a dream. Myrtle, who has been enlightened by her harrowing nightmare, recommits herself to being a good wife to Cyril.

The Office Wife (1930)

Larry Fellowes (Lewis Stone) works long hours at the office, which causes him to neglect his wife, Linda (Natalie Moorhead). Linda falls in love with a young gigolo (Brooks Benedict). Meanwhile, Larry falls in love with his secretary, Anne Murdock (Dorothy Mackaill). Wikipedia reports, "Linda returns to her husband. . . Anne watches as Larry goes to the bedroom with his wife and closes the door behind him."[356] The heartbroken secretary agrees to marry her long-time admirer, Ted O'Hara (Walter Merrill), after she submits her resignation. Linda ends up divorcing Larry despite their reconciliation. So, Anne gets a man who is her second choice and Larry ends up alone. It is not a happy ending.

Jewel Robbery (1932)

Wikipedia provides the following summary of the film's first act:

In Vienna, Baroness Teri von Horhenfels (Kay Francis) relieves the boredom of her marriage to her rich but dull husband (Henry Kolker) with love affairs. One day, at an exclusive jewel shop to purchase a diamond ring, her tedium is lifted by a suave, charming thief (William Powell) and his gang. In turn, he is entranced by her beauty. He locks her husband and her latest lover, Paul (Hardie Albright) (of whom she has already tired), in the vault. . .[357]

Later, Teri discovers that someone has broken into her home and forced open her safe. She looks into the safe and finds that her stolen ring has been returned. Teri later meets with The Robber for a romantic dinner at his home. He asks her to come away with him to Nice. The dinner is suddenly interrupted by a police raid.

Wikipedia, again: "He and his gang escape, leaving Teri tied up so as to divert suspicion. After she is 'rescued', she decides she needs a vacation away from Vienna to recover from the excitement. . . in Nice."[358]

Teri is an extreme version of the adultery film's bored wife. She is a thrill-seeker. She has a desperate need for constant excitement, forever craving something new and stimulating and willing to take unreasonable risks to get it. She is similar to Barbara in *The Wicked Lady*.

Norbert Lusk of Picture Play magazine was tickled by the way Francis pronounces "r" as "w." This was particularly evident in the line, "He sent those *woses*."[359]

Marlene Dietrich in *Angel* (1937)

Angel (1937)

Angel possesses the standard "neglected wife cheats" scenario. Sir Frederich Barker (Herbert Marshall) is a British diplomat busy attending peace conferences to prevent a world war. But his wife, Lady Maria Barker (Marlene Dietrich), cannot accept that her husband isn't paying attention to her.

In the original play by Melchior Lengyel, the husband consents to his wife having affairs just as she consents to him having affairs. But the wife becomes far more attached to her latest lover than she ever was to her previous lovers. But that's not what the film is about.

While visiting Paris, Maria figures to lift her spirits by having a fling with a playboy, Anthony Halton (Melvyn Douglas). Maria refuses to tell Anthony her name, so he gives her the nickname "Angel." Halton takes the tryst more seriously than she does. He meets her again in London. He asks her to leave her husband for him. He tells her, "All I know is that I love you, and I'll never let you out of my life."

The opening scene is set at an exclusive gambling casino in Paris. The casino is run by a displaced Russian royal, Grand Duchess Anna Dmitrievna (Laura Hope Crews). We soon learn that Dmitrievna also provides her visiting clientele with a special service outside of gambling. A leering Anthony says to her:

> You remember Willie Buckler. He always talked so much about you. And he told me, "If you want to have an amusing time in Paris, "go straight to the Grand Duchess." And here I am.

He is not leering about roulette. He asks Dmitrievna to arrange a dinner for two.

David Melville of Senses of Cinema doesn't see the duchess' establishment as a casino. He insisted in an article, "Voices from an Empty Room: Ernst Lubitsch and Angel (1937)," that the establishment is a brothel. Can he be correct? We see guests moving around chips at a roulette table. We see no lingerie-clad ladies running in and out of boudoirs. Does the dialogue give us the slightest clue of this? A patron refers to the place as a "delightful salon." A salon is, simply, an elegant establishment where prominent people gather. So, as far as we can see, it *is* a casino. Dmitrievna's hook-ups occur outside of the casino.

Maria arrives at the casino to visit Dmitrievna, who is an old friend. Melville's brothel interpretation went further at this point. He identified Maria as "one-time protégée of the madam"[360] and "once a high-class call-girl,"[361] but nothing in the dialogue implies that she is anything other than the duchess' friend. And yet the director, Lubitsch, includes a curious interaction during the scene. The arrival of Maria arouses the attention of an elegantly dressed man standing on the opposite side of the room. The camera is momentarily set up outside of the casino, capturing the scene through a series of windows. No sound can be heard. The man approaches Dmitrievna and whispers in her ear. Is the man simply asking who this enchanting woman is or is he, as his businesslike expression suggests, offering money to have sex with the woman?

Herbert Marshall, Marlene Dietrich and Melvyn Douglas in in *Angel* (1937)

Lubitsch may have imagined Dmitrievna's establishment as a brothel. He might have been influenced by Joseph Kessel's 1928 novel "Belle de Jour," which involves a wife secretly working at a brothel under the alias "Beauty of the Day" and pursuing a passionate affair with a client.

In London, Anthony tells Sir Frederick about this charming woman "Angel" who he met while visiting the grand duchess in Paris. Sir Frederick comes to suspect that Angel is his wife Maria.

Richard Brody of The New Yorker wrote, "[Lubitsch] contrasts Frederick's sexless gravity with Anthony's seductive frivolity. . ."[362]

Dreaming Lips (1937)

Gabrielle (Elizabeth Bergner), the wife of a famous violinist Peter Lawrence (Romney Brent), wants to leave her husband for another musician, Miguel de Vaye (Raymond Massey). Gabrielle tells Miguel that she has become drunk with happiness. From her perspective, a person who takes part in an extramarital affair is less immoral than a person who takes part in destroying their own happiness. But she cannot follow through with her plans when her husband falls seriously ill. Wikipedia notes: "Gabrielle dutifully remains by his side, never telling him of her indiscretion. Torn between two lovers, Gabrielle eventually decides to kill herself. . ."[363]

A 1986 remake, *Mélo*, suggests that the husband has mysteriously fallen ill because his wife has been poisoning his food.

The film is lackluster. Robert Temple, a stalwart IMDb reviewer, wrote: "The film falls entirely flat. Elizabeth Bergner is someone who lacks all screen presence. She comes across as vapid, vain, self-centered, and lacking in talent. To put it more bluntly, she cannot act, and she cannot compensate with any charm. . ."[364]

An allegedly superior 1953 German-language remake is unavailable. Not that everyone had a favorable reaction to this film. Richard W. Nason of The New York Times wrote of it:

> The old question of a young woman's ill-considered affair is not treated to any new insights, nor is it elevated to bittersweet romance. As a matter of fact, the husband never learns of the affair, so when the wife realizes her error and returns to him, nobody is the wiser, least of all the audience. Miss Schell flatly tells her lover, played by Frits von Dongen, "I lost my way. Peter's illness brought me back to my senses." Whatever this might have meant in human terms remains boxed up in her head. What is put on the screen by director Josef von Baky is confined to tedious apparencies.[365]

The Rains Came (1939)

A woman's lust sets the story into motion. Lady Edwina Esketh (Myrna Loy), the wife of Lord Esketh (Nigel Bruce), is not shy about taking in an eyeful of a handsome Indian doctor, Dr. Major Rama (Tyrone Power). "Who's the pale copper Apollo?" she asks. "Not bad. Not bad at all."

Her old friend, Tom Ransome (George Brent), is the voice of morality. He can see that Edwina is pursuing Rama. He accuses her of "philandering around missions."

Edwina: Don't be catty, Tom. I do believe you're jealous.

Tom: You know perfectly well I'm not jealous. If there ever was anything between us, we both know it's finished now – dead and gone.

Edwina: Then why do you come here and act drunk and dictatorial?

Tom: Because I see something happening I don't like.

Edwina: You are a beast, aren't you? Tom, we've double-crossed almost everyone in the world. Let's not start on each other.

Tom: I don't want to interfere really. But Rama's my friend, and I don't like it.

Edwina: If you only knew how wrong you are. He's the one man I've ever met I haven't been able to make an impression on.

Rama finds Edwina physically attractive from the start, but he has no real interest in her. He doesn't fall in love with her until she devotes herself to helping the sick and injured at the hospital.

Edwina and Rama never have sex. Also, Edwina's husband dies halfway through the film, which means that the second half of the film has nothing to do with marital fidelity at all. It is a 50% fidelity/50% infidelity film.

Skylark (1941)

Lydia Kenyon (Claudette Colbert) can no longer tolerate her husband, Tony (Ray Milland), a busy executive, putting his job ahead of their marriage. Lydia finally realizes her marriage is hopeless when Tony cancels their fifth-anniversary party to host a dinner party for a client. It makes matters worse when she learns that her anniversary present was picked out by her husband's friend, George Gorell (Walter Abel). Lydia becomes furious with the client's rude wife, Mrs. Myrtle Vantine (Binnie Barnes), and Tony makes the matter worse by demanding his wife apologize to the woman. Lydia leaves Tony and files for divorce. Tony is determined to win back his wife, but she is equally determined to terminate their marriage and start a new life. Tony must compete with a charming lawyer, Jim Blake (Brian Aherne), for Lydia's affections.

Four Mothers (1941)

The tamest marital infidelity can be found in *Four Mothers*. Adam Lemp (Claude Rains) has such great trust in the business acumen of his son-in-law Ben (Frank McHugh) that he invests his entire savings into Ben's real estate development in Florida. He even encourages friends and neighbors to invest. So, when a hurricane wipes out the development, Adam is put into a bad situation. Adam's family is determined to earn enough money to cover everyone's losses. Felix Deitz (Jeffrey Lynn), the husband of Adam's daughter Ann (Priscilla Lane), takes a job in Chicago. Adam's daughter Kay (Rosemary Lane) follows Felix to Chicago to find a job as a singer. One night, Felix and Kay go out dancing at a club. Felix impulsively kisses Kay, who puts up no resistance. Kay is distressed and confused afterward. "How could we?" she asks. The two agree that they are simply lonely and must remedy their loneliness by quickly moving back home. Felix confesses to Ann about the kiss as soon as he returns home. Kay, who is deeply ashamed, avoids Ann at first. But, at a family gathering, she finally tells her sister what happened. She admits that she wanted to kiss Felix. The sister smiles and says, "Alone with my Felix in the moonlight, I'd be insulted if you hadn't."

That Uncertain Feeling (1941)

The film is the fifth film adaptation of an 1880 French bedroom farce, "Divorçons."

Jill Baker (Merle Oberon) is married to a busy insurance executive, Bill (Melvyn Douglas). Jill is so greatly distressed by Bill's neglect that she suffers from nights of insomnia and comic bouts of hiccups. She visits a psychiatrist, Dr. Vengard (Alan Mowbray), and becomes friendly with one of Dr. Vengard's other patients, Alexander Sebastian (Burgess Meredith). Alexander, a concert pianist, is not a pleasant person. He is cynical, arrogant and temperamental. But Jill is enchanted by his musical skills, which amazingly stop her hiccups and insomnia. Jill doesn't resist when Alexander becomes randy and kisses her.

Bill is upset by Jill's sudden attachment to Alexander, but he is sure that their relationship will fail if they spend more time together. So, he moves out of his home and leaves Jill to Alexander. Jill and Alexander frequently quarrel just as Bill expected. Soon, Jill comes to Bill and pleads with him to take her back.

It is strange the nonchalant way that Bill lets another man take his place in the marital bed. The film was directed by Hollywood legend Ernst Lubitsch, but Lubitsch's mastery is not evident in the film. The director may have hoped to create sophisticated humor out of the situation, but the finished film is distasteful and unfunny. Not surprisingly, it failed at the box office.

William Powell, James Craig and Hedy Lamarr in *The Heavenly Body* (1944)

The Heavenly Body (1944)

An astronomer, William B. Whitley (William Powell), has locked himself inside his observatory to track a comet that he discovered. His wife, Vicky (Hedy Lamarr), resents her husband's preoccupation with his comet. The neglected wife turns to astrology, another form of sky-watching, for meaning and fulfillment. An astrologer predicts that, on a specific day, she will meet a handsome stranger and fall in love. A handsome stranger does enter her life that day. He is an air raid warden, Lloyd Hunter (James Craig), who shows

UNFAITHFUL: THE HISTORY OF THE ADULTERY FILM · 315

up at her front door. She humiliates her husband by flagrantly dating Hunter. She is enraptured by Hunter as he serenades her with a guitar. Hunter is unashamed to be canoodling with a married woman. He tells Whitley, "Sometimes, a man can't help himself." The stress of the situation turns Whitley into a wreck. The filmmakers strangely deny Whitley compassion. In the end, blame is laid squarely before him for neglecting his wife. It is made clear that she would not have had doubts about their marriage if he had only shown her that he cared.

Joan Crawford and John Garfield in *Humoresque* (1946)

Humoresque (1946)

Paul Boray (John Garfield), a violinist, has an affair with a wealthy sponsor, Helen Wright (Joan Crawford), who is married.

Egotistical and hot-tempered Paul is not a likable protagonist, but the filmmakers find a way around that problem. It is similar to the way that Tom Powers' loving mother was able to make the murderous Powers sympathetic in *Public Enemy* (1931). It is reflected sympathy. The viewer is likely to care about a bad guy if other more sympathetic characters care about him. You don't want Powers to fail because it would break his mother's heart.

Helen angrily confronts her meek husband about her dissatisfaction with their marriage. He delicately attempts to defend himself but, under her furious assault, he is bound to be defeated.

Helen: You say you've loved me, Victor. But what kind of a love has it been? I know you've always been courteous and always remembered my birthday. But is that the final sum and substance of our marriage? Courtesy and greetings?

Victor: I've never had the chance to love. You don't like emotions.

Helen: They're wearing. They make demands. They interfere with the pleasant life. So I've learned to hide away love and hate and everything strong in me. I've tucked them away where they wouldn't bother us. We've hung a sign on our lives, "Do Not Disturb."

Victor: You can have the divorce, Helen.

Paul's mother, Esther Boray (Ruth Nelson), is a fierce voice for reason and morality. She tells her son that he is letting his life get twisted by being involved with a married woman. It especially bothers her that he has turned his back on an old girlfriend, Gina (Joan Chandler), who she regards as a nice girl

The original short story did not involve adultery. A previous film adaptation, more faithful to the short story, was released in 1920.

Jennifer Jones and Van Heflin in *Madame Bovary* (1949)

Madame Bovary (1949)

The novel is mostly centered on a passionate affair between Emma Bovary, a doctor's wife, and Rodolphe, a rakish landowner. The relationship does not have a beautiful beginning. Rodolphe brings an ill servant to Dr. Charles Bovary's office. Emma assists Charles in bleeding the patient. Rodolphe is impressed that Emma does not become faint at the sight of blood. He leaves the office thinking:

> She is very pretty, this doctor's wife. Fine teeth, black eyes, a dainty foot, a figure like a Parisienne's. Where the devil does she come from? Wherever did that fat fellow pick her up?

He is sure that she must be bored with her husband. He thinks, "Poor little woman! She is gaping after love like a carp after water on a kitchen-table. With three words of gallantry she'd adore one, I'm sure of it. She'd be tender, charming." Finally, he bangs his cane on the ground and cries aloud, "Oh, I will have her!"

So, he sets out to seduce Emma. He asks her to go riding with him. Charles thinks that riding would be good for Emma's health and urges her to accept Rodolphe's invitation. Emma and Rodolphe begin an affair that will endure for the next four years. Emma, finally tired of sneaking around, insists that they run off together. Rodolphe pretends to agree, but he secretly prepares to leave town without her. He conceals a farewell letter inside a basket of apricots, which he instructs his ploughman to deliver once he is safely away. Emma falls ill upon reading the letter, leaving Charles to assume that something in the apricots has made her ill. Emma has a difficult time recovering from Rodolphe's abandonment. She becomes deeply depressed and spends much of her time in bed. But, once on her feet again, she begins an affair with an old friend, Léon. She pretends to be going to the city for piano lessons when she is really meeting Léon in a hotel room.

M-G-M's 1949 version of *Madame Bovary*, which was directed by Vincente Minnelli, is a terribly watered-down version of the story.

The immorality trial that the French government waged against the novel is dramatized as a framing device for the film. The prosecutor vehemently attacks the Emma Bovary character. He says:

> Emma Bovary, a woman who neglects her own child, a child that needs her, who scorns her own husband, a husband who loves her, who introduces adultery and ruin into her home, this is our heroine. This corrupt, loathsome, contemptible creature, this woman of insatiable passions, this monstrous creation of a degenerate imagination, this is the heroine we are asked to pity, to forgive, why, perhaps, to love. Gentlemen, nowhere in this entire work does Gustave Flaubert ask us to blame Emma Bovary and find her guilty of her crimes.

Emma is dissatisfied with her child just as much as she is dissatisfied with her husband. This makes her far less sympathetic than she would be if she was just an unfaithful wife.

Jennifer Jones and Henri Letondal in *Madame Bovary* (1949)

Kat Ellinger is unwilling to condemn Emma, as she made clear in her commentary for Arrow Video's Blu-ray edition of Claude Chabrol's 1991 *Madame Bovary*. She doesn't believe that Flaubert wanted the reader to be against the character. She says, "[J]ust when [Emma Bovary] wears out our patience, [Flaubert] flips and he turns and he manipulates his reader so that we are ultimately on her side."[366]

Roxanna Robinson, novelist and literature professor, has taught the novel to college students. She admits that, generally, her students look poorly upon Emma, but she has consistently defended the character to them. She wrote:

> [Emma's] vain and selfish, shallow, all those things, but she's also oddly innocent, a visionary. When Emma realizes that her romantic dream won't come true with the loyal, plodding Charles, she views her marriage as a failure and plunges into despair. But when she meets the handsome, aristocratic Rodolphe she sees another chance at passion. Tremulous, hopeful, vulnerable, she falls in love. Reckless, ecstatic, she meets him in her garden at night. She runs across the fields at dawn and arrives in his room breathless, and smelling like a spring morning. Her dewy skirts, her thin boots, muddy from the fields, her pounding heart and shining face: it's hard to think that Flaubert feels anything but tenderness for this Emma. . . I told my students that Flaubert asks us to accept a heroine who is deeply flawed; one who pursues an impossible quest and loses everything; one who is indefatigable and fearless.[367]

Too many literature scholars have devoted too much time and energy time defending Emma Bovary. True, the people with whom Mrs. Bovary associates in her daily life do not overflow with dazzling virtue. True, she is a forceful figure compared to the plodding people around her. But does that make her an admirable character? The other residents of her community are resigned to a practical understanding of life. They remain focused on their everyday duties, which they willingly fulfill in a faithful though perhaps unglamorous fashion.

Minnelli's Emma manages, in the end, to see the error of her ways. Rodolphe tells her that her desires are too great and threaten to destroy everyone who comes near her. Emma responds, "Oh, I asked for too much, I know it. I expected too much of you. . . Oh, I was childish. I confess it. We all have to grow up, you know."

But, in the novel, Emma never learns. She seeks a dramatic end to her life, imagining herself as a heroine of a romance novel. She poisons herself, expecting a quick and beautiful death. But her death is long and ugly.

Once she dies, a priest anoints her body with oil.

> First upon the eyes, that had so coveted all worldly pomp; then upon the nostrils, that had been greedy of the warm breeze and amorous odours; then upon the mouth, that had uttered lies, that had curled with pride and cried out in lewdness; then upon the hands that had delighted in sensual touches; and finally upon the soles of the feet, so swift of yore, when she was running to satisfy her desires, and that would now walk no more.

Our body, with its many sensations, needs and desires, often condemns us in our life on earth.

Madame Bovary (1991)

The ideal film adaptation of the novel was made in 1991 by Claude Chabrol. The film is far more faithful to the novel and far more compelling.

Emma seeks advice from a priest to relieve her depression, but the priest doesn't understand her problem. When she says that she's ill, he assumes that she is referring to a physical illness and surmises that she has already consulted with her doctor husband about it. He asks, "[D]oesn't he prescribe something for you?"

Isabelle Huppert and Jacques Dynam in *Madame Bovary* (1991)

Emma persists. She asks him if he can provide solace to a person in sorrow. He speaks to her of providing food and warmth for people in need. She says, "[I]t is no earthly remedy I need." The priest, who is distracted by other duties, is barely listening to what she has to say. In the end, he sends her off with no helpful advice.

Leon comes along at a time that she is depressed and he manages to lift her spirits. But Emma's passion for Leon fades in time. She never felt for him like she felt for Rodolphe. From the novel:

> They gradually came to talking more frequently of matters outside their love, and in the letters that Emma wrote him she spoke of flowers, verses, the moon and the stars, naive resources of a waning passion striving to keep itself alive by all external aids.[368]

Emma looks to find happiness in material things, adorning her body in elegant clothing and decorating her home with fine furnishings. She insists on living in a home with silk curtains, thick carpets and well-filled flower-stands. Unknown to her inattentive husband, her extravagant spending has burdened her family with overwhelming debt and the debt collectors are amassing to seize their belongings.

Emma is driven to suicide by the betrayal of her one true love Rodolfe, who refuses to pay off her debts. But is her illicit relationship with Rodolphe truly the cause of her downfall? Perhaps, this romantic dreamer was undone by materialism more than adultery.

Isabelle Huppert, Christophe Malavoy and Jean-François Balmer in Madame Bovary (1991)

Madame Bovary (2014)

This film version of "Madam Bovary" emphasizes the fact that, by her own admission, Emma lives in a fantasy world. "Well," she says, "I realized that before getting married, I was contemplating my coming life like a child in a theater. Sitting there in high spirits, and eagerly waiting for the play to begin."

Clash by Night (1952)

Clash by Night was directed by Fritz Lang, who was also the director of adultery-themed films *The Woman in the Window* (1944) and *Scarlet Street* (1945). The film is based on a Clifford Odets play.

Adultery is messy. This is never clearer than it is in *Clash by Night*. The story is set in a small fishing village where everyone lives in close proximity of one another and everyone knows one another too well. The town's canning factory, the main source of employment, is walking distance from the main characters' home. This is different than the big city adultery tales, where cheating partners are able to hide among the millions of faceless city dwellers. Jennifer Jones clearly recognizes this difference as she rebuffs the advances of a suitor in *Madame Bovary*. "This is not Paris," she says. "It's a small village." The affair in *Clash by Night* is raw and personal.

Mae (Barbara Stanwyck) returns home to Monterey, California, after a failed affair with a married politician. She has been exhausted by the hardships in her life. She is suffering a devastating depression much like her classic forebearers, Lady Chatterley and Emma Bovary.

Joe (Keith Andes), her younger brother, is more down-to-earth than Mae. He is not sympathetic to his sister's seamy situation.

Paul Douglas, Barbara Stanwyck and Robert Ryan in *Clash by Night* (1952)

Joe: The way you wrote, I thought you'd come back rich. Where's it parked?

Mae: What?

Joe: The car with the chauffeur and the rich husband.

Mae: There isn't any car. There isn't any husband, rich, poor, indifferent.

Joe: Ain't that what you left town for?

Mae: I left town because I. . . left town. What do you want, Joe, my life's history? Here it is in four words: Big ideas, small results.

Joe: And the guy you wrote Ma you were gonna marry.

Mae: I neglected to write that he was already married. Does it sound sordid? All right, it sounds sordid. He died, left me some money. But they took it to court. His wife, his brothers. I almost drowned in outraged relatives. Mae Doyle, 10 years later.

Mae misses her old lover. She tells Earl Pfeiffer (Robert Ryan):

He was a politician I knew. He died. I felt as if my own life had stopped. I didn't think I'd ever feel anything again. Where could I go? Home. But you forget. You even begin to hope again. One thing I know, he was a man who didn't tear a woman down. He made her feel confident. Sure of herself. More than she was, not less. He's the only man I ever knew who gave me that feeling.

She has not been happy with the men that she has met since his passing. She says, "Aren't there any more comfortable men? Now they're all little and nervous like sparrows or big and worried like sick bears. . . If I ever loved a man again, I'd bear anything. He could have my teeth for watch fobs."

Mae settles on marrying Jerry D'Amato (Paul Douglas), a guileless and bighearted fisherman. McElhaney describes Jerry having an "uncomplicated and somewhat childlike nature."[369] Earl makes advances towards Mae. Earl is married, but he is disgusted with his wife. We never see Earl's wife, but we understand that she is a vaudeville performer who is busy touring and cares little about her marriage.

Mae has a baby with Jerry and, as much as she loves the baby, she still feels bored and restless. She finally succumbs to Earl's relentless advances. Jerry's uncle Vince, who has a grudge against Mae, knows of the affair and tells his nephew, who doesn't believe him.

The truth eventually becomes obvious to Jerry.

Jerry: Why, Mae? Tell me why. I love you, the ground you walk on.

Mae: I tried, Jerry. God forgive me, I tried.

Jerry: Was I a bad husband? Did I say, Mae, don't do this, don't do that?

Mae: No.

Jerry: Did I go out and gamble? Did I get drunk? Did I eat, and you went hungry?

Mae: No.

Jerry: Well, why, Mae? My head's busting. What don't I understand?

Mae: I've got nothing to blame you for. It's me, me, something in me. A year. Was a year that long? You say to yourself, wait, be patient, things will change, you'll feel different. No good. Nothing changes. The days go by. Down to the grocery store, back to the house. Hang out the wash, take the dishes out of the closet. Go to bed, wake up. Wait, wait. Shut your mouth, close your eyes. This is the man you married. This is the life you've made. Expect nothing, hope for nothing. And every day a little older, a little duller, a little stupider. Love? It's superstition. Hope? Forget it. Forget how to laugh, forget how to cry. Tell yourself that's how everybody else lives, why should you be any different? Without love, there's. . . there's nothing. And tears. What good are tears?

Jerry turns to Earl.

Jerry: And I said come visit us. I asked you here. I. . . You. . .!

Earl: Jerry.

Jerry: What are you, animals? In a zoo, they keep them in a cage. They keep them apart, they keep them from hurting people, they. . . Animals. Animals. Animals.

The notion of people being associated with animals came up during Mae and Jerry's first date. Jerry mentions that he could imitate a duck. Moments later, he tells Mae that he likes her. "You don't know anything about me," she says. "What kind of animal am I? Do I have fangs, do I purr? What jungle am I from?"

The play had a violent ending - Jerry murders Earl while the men are locked together in a projection booth. Blogger William Ahearn believed it "gutted"[370] the story to remove the murder from the film. But it's not an original or profound idea to have an adultery story end in murder. A wronged husband murdering the man who seduced his wife is a melodrama trope. Lang's own *Scarlet Street*, with its own extramarital affair, climaxed with a murder. The story is more authentic and interesting in its new form. Jerry raises his hand to strike Mae and Earl, but he considers what he is about to do and he stops himself. If he reacts violently, he would be behaving like an animal, which would make him no better than them.

Megan Abbott, an Edgar Award-winning author and film noir specialist, asserted that "the fever that pulses through the movie is the same one that burns through most classic film noir: that constant, brooding fear of sexual betrayal and loss of power."[371]

Earl is hardly an appealing paramour. The New York Times accurately described him as "slick, morbid and self-pitying."[372] An interloper like Earl exposes his villainous nature with his relentless effort to conquer an unavailable and resistant woman.

Mae debates with Earl if they are doing the right thing.

Mae: How hard-boiled we are?

Earl: There isn't any other way. . . Love him or love me. You can't save us both. Somebody's throat has to be cut. If you can do it, cut mine. Leave me. Call it quits, here and now. You want to hide? Sneak away? Leave messages with bellboys? Baby, we have to. Love is rotten when it happens like this, the hard way. But if we want each other, this is the fire we walk through. Because this is forever, Mae. . . If you have a dream, live it. If you have a hope, chase it. . . What is it, do you feel guilty? That's the way they want you to feel.

Mae: They?

Earl: The world. All the people who haven't got guts enough to do what they wanna do. Listen, Mae, you walk out of this house now, and we're free.

Mae laments that she has always "walked away from things." Earl tells her that she shouldn't ever feel responsibility towards anything because responsibility is only a trap. What about the responsibility of Mae's baby? Earl admits that he isn't enthusiastic about taking the baby with them.

Mae: The baby would be a burden, wouldn't it? A drag.

Earl: All I said was go away for a while without her. Listen, Mae, don't make no mistake about kids. They grow up. They have their own lives to lead. They'll walk out on you.

Mae: Don't we owe a child some happiness?

Earl: It isn't a question of the kid's happiness. It's a question of yours.

Mae: And Jerry's.

Earl: I told you somebody's throat has to be cut.

Mae: But it's never ours, is it, Earl? It's always someone else's. Why? Because they're soft. And we're tough, we're hard. If someone suffers because of us, that's just too bad.

Earl: That's the way life is.

Mae: How many times have I told myself that? Nothing counted but me, my disappointments, my unhappiness. I married Jerry, moved into his house, used his money and had his child, and yet. . . yet I was never his wife. You're someone's wife when you belong to them. I never belonged to anybody.

She questions if it's love that brought her and Earl together. She thinks that she might have only become involved with him because she was lonely, or frightened, or bored. Earl snaps, "What was it with me, boredom? The lady of the house needed a little entertainment?"

This dialogue is similar to dialogue in *Therese Raquin* (1953).

Laurent: Thérèse, if you hesitate, everybody will be very unhappy. I've thought about it over and over, believe me. It would be better to leave at once, without a word of discussion.

Thérèse: To leave, without knowing where? Without a word, like thieves?

Laurent: That's the only way, Thérèse. We have to make a clean cut. That's the least painful. Are you afraid?

Thérèse: Afraid? Not at all. But I admire you. You're strong and free. You think only of yourself. What you want, you need at once without delay.

Laurent: Perhaps you prefer your security, your small life where nothing happens. It's funny. I thought you'd accept right away.

Thérèse admits that she is being held back by guilt.

Laurent: If a girl loves a man, if she trusts him, it's easy for her to leave with him.

Thérèse: Easy. My aunt took pity on me when my parents died.

Laurent: So much pity that she forced you to marry her son.

Thérèse: I lived in his house, I was already his cousin. I became his wife without it changing much.

Laurent: And you don't think it's monstrous?

Thérèse: I nursed Camille when he was ill. Why should I have saved his life if I kill him now by leaving?

Laurent: You prefer to ruin your life?

Back to *Clash by Night*.

Joe discusses Mae's affair with his wife, Peggy (Marilyn Monroe).

Joe: That ring on your finger. What did you put it there for, a decoration?

Peggy: She has the right to do what she wants, she's in love.

Joe: In love. Listen to me, blondie. The woman I marry, she don't take me on a wait-and-see basis. I ain't a dress she's brought home from the store to see if it fits and if not, back it goes. . . So if that little eye is gonna roam. . . if what you think is, "Joe's all right until something better comes along". . . honey, you'd better take another streetcar. Now, what's it gonna be?

Paul Douglas, Barbara Stanwyck and Robert Ryan in *Clash by Night* (1952)

Mae apologizes to Jerry and asks him to take her back. He hesitates at first, but he can see that she is sincere and agrees to keep the marriage together.

Joe McElhaney, Professor of Film Studies at Hunter College, compares the film to Raoul Walsh's *Manpower* (1941). He wrote, "Water and rain are also central. . ."[373] Patrick McGilligan, author of "Fritz Lang: The Nature of the Beast," complained that Lang's use of the crashing waves of the ocean to stand as a "metaphor for Mae's inner turbulence"[374] was "an old chestnut."[375] McElhaney wrote, "[T]he last image in the film is one of calm waters, order restored."[376] Does the final scene of the film signify defeat or renewal for Mae? It is, by every indication, renewal.

A stifling factory town is similarly present in *Beyond the Forest* (1949).

Yield To The Night (1956)

Mary Hilton (Diana Dors), a young salesgirl, is dissatisfied with her husband Fred (Harry Locke), whose job doesn't allow him to spend much time at home. But then she meets a handsome musician, Jim Lancaster (Michael Craig). The couple enjoys a torrid affair. Mary is shocked when Jim is drawn away from her by a wealthy older woman, Lucy Carpenter (Mercia Shaw), who is willing to finance a luxurious lifestyle for her new boy toy. Mary becomes crazed and sets out to murder her rival. She shoots the woman just as she returns home from shopping.

Lancaster is far more glamorous than Fred, but that is not particularly significant in the end. Mary should have learned a lesson from her best friend, Doris (Joyce Blair). Doris has married an older man who is neither handsome nor glamorous. But the man is loving, devoted, fun to be around, and provides well for Doris. Doris has no problem loving her unglamorous husband.

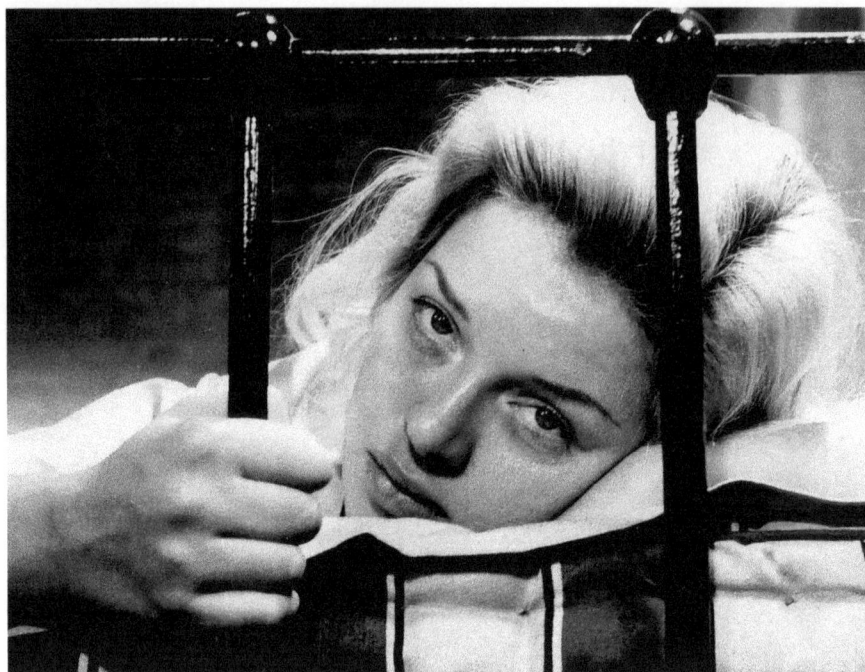

Diana Dors in *Yield To The Night* (1956)

Hilda Crane (1956)

Hilda Crane (Jean Simmons) has gone through two divorces in five years. Her mother (Judith Evelyn) is critical of her marital choices and advises her to marry Russell Burns (Guy Madison), a prosperous builder in town. A former lover, Jacques De Lisle (Jean-Pierre Aumont), resents Winona for having rejected him for her first husband, but he sees her return to town as an opportunity to resume their relationship. Hilda is not interested in reconnecting with Jacques, but Jacques is determined to change her mind and becomes aggressive in his advances.

Hilda has a neurotic urge to be married. She agonizes over which of two suitors she should choose, ignoring the obvious truth that both men are seriously flawed. But why does she need to marry either man? Why does she need to jump into a third marriage?

Still, taking her mother's advice, Hilda becomes engaged to Russell. She is warned by a friend that Russell's mother, Mrs. Burns (Evelyn Varden), is possessive of her son and is willing to feign health problems to draw her son's attention away from his love interests. On the day of the wedding, Mrs. Burns calls Hilda to her home to speak with her. She offers Hilda $50,000 to leave town immediately. Hilda refuses and, when Mrs. Burns suddenly slumps over in her chair, the bride takes this as a poor attempt to fool her. She ignores the woman and heads out to the church. But Mrs. Burns actually had a heart attack and died. Russell believes that his mother might have survived if Hilda had called for medical assistance. He starts out in his marriage as a glum and resentful husband. Hilda drinks often to cope with their troubled relationship. She eventually seeks solace with Jacques.

Hilda is confused, desperate and needy. The reviews on Internet Movie Database suggest that viewers find it difficult to muster the sympathy for the character that the filmmaker demands.

Strangers When We Meet (1960)

Screenwriter Sam Hamm has called *Strangers When We Meet* "the best story of adultery ever filmed by Hollywood."[377]

Larry Coe (Kirk Douglas), an architect, is at odds with his wife, Eve (Barbara Rush). He wants to be imaginative in his architect designs, but Eve knows that he can make great money designing conventional buildings. Jacqueline T. Lynch of Another Old Movie Blog wrote, "She appears to quash her husband's artistic side for the more commercial aspects of his work, regretting his decision to go freelance, and badgering him to accept a safe and dull job with a firm he does not want."[378]

Larry often acts impulsive and justifies his behavior by claiming that he, as an artist, must be guided by his impulses. Eve must counter her husband's impulsiveness by being practical, organized and controlled. It does not comes across as a natural role for her, only a role she must play for the sake of the marriage.

Larry meets a pretty new neighbor, Maggie Gault (Kim Novak). Maggie expresses a genuine interest in his home designs. It greatly pleases Larry that she goes to the library to read about his work in Homes and Gardens magazine.

Larry next meets Roger Altar (Ernie Kovacs), an author who wants Larry to build a home for him. Larry lets Roger know that he likes to experiment in his work. He says, "I can't afford to have a dull house go up with my name on it." Roger tells him that he is free to experiment as long as the cost of the house doesn't exceed his budget. Jacqueline T. Lynch of Another Old Movie Blog wrote:

> Kovacs, egotistical, emotionally brittle, and skirt chasing, is at a crossroads in his career. He fears failing, but also fears churning out the same material to play it safe.[379]

Larry challenges Roger to take chances with his new book.

> Larry: Boy, I'd love to see what would happen if you really broke loose.
>
> Roger: Don't you think that's what I want to do?
>
> Larry: Then do it. Write a book that you like, and to hell with the critics.
>
> Roger: You don't know.
>
> Larry: Rog, I know one thing. You've got to find out what's important to you.

Maggie's husband shows no interest in sex. At a party, he admits that his job takes a lot out of him and he comes home at night feeling hopelessly tired. Lynch wrote:

> Her husband, dull and preoccupied, seems unresponsive and utterly lacking in passion for her. In one melancholy scene, an anxious Novak greets him half dressed, lights dim, their son sleeping over at a neighbor's, trying to seduce her husband, pleading him to make love to her. His awkward brush-off is as baffling as it is heartbreaking. We are not given explanations as to his indifference, because we never really get to see his side of their marriage, but it would have been a different movie if this has been explored.[380]

Cammmalot of Letterboxd wrote:

There's a heartbreaking scene early on when Novak practically confesses to her husband what she's about to do and begs him not to let her go, but of course he's completely complacent and oblivious: "You go on and have a good time, okay?"[381]

Maggie puts up resistance to Larry's advances, but he is persistent and she is unable to resist him for long.

Maggie reveals to Larry that she was once raped by a man who had previously made advances on her. Her story suggests that she invited the rape by leaving her door open to the man and taking sleeping pills to make it that she couldn't put up a fight. Presumably, she wanted to have sex with the man without taking responsibility for it.

Lynch wrote:

Played by Virginia Bruce, mother once had an affair that hurt her marriage and destroyed her daughter's affection for her. When her mother catches on to Novak's affair with Douglas, there is a knowing look exchanged between them. We imagine that Novak has begun to understand that mother is a human being, just as we all must come to terms with our parents being human and messing up.[382]

Maggie admits to Larry that she is curious about his marriage.

Larry: Look, Maggie, you know people aren't born married. They meet, date, go steady, get engaged. . . the whole natural progression that you and Ken. . . Why are we talking about this?

Maggie: You love her very much, don't you?

Larry: Come on, Maggie.

Maggie: Is it painful for you to talk about her?

Larry: No, but I don't see why we keep on.

Maggie: Is she very bright, Larry?

Larry: Yes, she is.

Maggie: Do you think she's pretty?

Larry: What's the next question? "Is she better than me?" Go ahead, ask it.

Maggie: I'd never ask that.

Larry: Why not? You've asked everything else.

Maggie: I guess I'm afraid of the answer.

Maggie obviously suffers intense insecurity.

Maggie tenses up when she answers her phone and hears Eve's voice at the other end. Eve is only calling to invite her to a party at her home. Maggie becomes even more tense at the party. She recoils when Larry comes up behind her and touches her bare back. "Larry. . . please!" she exclaims.

Larry's snoopy neighbor, Felix Anders (Walter Matthau), finds out about their affair. Felix and Roger represent different parts of Larry's psyche. Roger mirrors the man's artistic spirit. Felix embodies the tawdry and rampant lust that now possesses him. Lynch wrote:

We learn that Matthau lives a double life, and has affairs with other women. Pleased that Douglas has joined the club of unfaithful husbands, he gleefully needles him. Matthau tells him his wife already suspects, and Douglas is paralyzed by that thought.[383]

Felix is happy to have a chance to pontificate on the subject.

Felix: There's nothing romantic about the slob they see shaving in his pajamas. You and me, Larry, we're furniture in our own homes. But if we go next door. . . Next door, we're heroes. A guy like you, works at home, you got plenty of opportunity for going next door.

Larry: Sure. I go next door all the time. A lovely lady of 60 lives there.

Larry becomes irritated with Felix.

Felix: Outraged innocence is always a good gimmick, Larry, but the amateur tends to overplay it. The pro, Larry, is a guy who establishes a definite behavior pattern at home and never deviates from it, but never. No sly secret glances when your wife's at the same party. No trips to the kitchen for a quick kiss. Kid stuff. The pro doesn't take any real chances.

Larry: You're taking a real chance right now, Felix. I'm liable to bust you right in the mouth.

Felix: Are you? I doubt it. Then you'd have to tell Eve that we were discussing your blonde, wouldn't you? And Eve's pretty close to smelling something in the wind, anyway. I spotted that worried-wife look on her face when I came in. That's why she threw this little shindig, Larry. To draw the straying male back to hearth and home.

The next day, Felix enters the Coe home uninvited while Eve is preparing to take a shower. Eve hastily puts on a bathrobe. She is clearly annoyed. Felix pretends to want gardening advice from her. She responds, "If you'll forgive me, Felix, I'm just not in the mood right now for talking." But Felix is not deterred. He is leering, which makes it obvious that something else is on his mind. He suddenly changes the conversation, telling Eve that her hair looks different. He remarks, "Why don't you let your hair fall free around your face, Eve? You have such a lovely face." Eve gets angry. "Listen, Felix," she snaps, "I don't have time for this kind of foolishness." He brazenly removes her hair ribbon. "Get out!" Eve screams. She becomes hysterical. This gets her unwanted visitor to finally depart. Larry comes home just as Felix is leaving. He finds Eve crying and assumes that their sleazy neighbor has done something inappropriate to her. He chases after him. Felix is defiant when confronted by Larry. "Tell me, architect," he asks, "how am I any different from you?" Larry returns to Eve. She tells Larry, "I've been sitting here wondering. What gave Felix the peculiar notion that I'd be an easy mark? Do you know why, Larry? It seems so simple. It explains so many things. So simple." Larry is stunned that Eve knows about his affair. She tells him:

I guess I've known all along. . . I want you to leave the house, Larry. I don't want you near the children. I don't want to see you. I want to forget that I ever loved you or knew you. I just want you to go. Go wherever you want to go. Do whatever you want to. Go with her. Go to hell. Just get out of my sight.

She pauses. Then, with a softer voice, she asks him:

330 · ANTHONY BALDUCCI

Can't you be happy here? Is it me? Because if it is me, Larry, I want you to tell me where I was wrong. I can change. It's just that I don't. . . . it's just that I don't know what I should do.

She cries.

Larry: Please don't cry, Eve.

Eve: I can't help it. Larry, I want us to be the way we used to be. I don't understand what's happened. I don't know us anymore. Where are we?

Larry: I don't know, Eve.

Eve: Larry, please help me. You see, I don't think I could live without you. Please, Larry. Don't leave me.

Larry accepts a new job in Hawaii. He will be busy for the next five years building a city. He has completed Altar's home and wants Maggie to see it before he leaves. It is a bittersweet farewell. Wikipedia notes:

Larry wishes he and Maggie could live in the house and if they did, he would dig a moat around it and never leave it. Maggie says she loves him. The contractor for the house shows up and thinks Maggie is Larry's wife. They both take a moment to savor the irony of his remark and Maggie drives away.[384]

SOMEONE ELSE'S
HUSBAND AND
SOMEONE ELSE'S
WIFE...!
How does such a thing happen, and
why? Where does it take place, and
when? What does it lead to, and to
whom? From the outspoken bestseller on marital infidelity!

COLUMBIA PICTURES presents

KIRK DOUGLAS | KIM NOVAK
ERNIE KOVACS | BARBARA RUSH

Strangers
When
We Meet

Mad
for each
other...
married,
but not
to each
other!

co-starring
WALTER MATTHAU
VIRGINIA BRUCE · KENT SMITH · HELEN GALLAGHER A BRYNA-QUINE Production
Screenplay by EVAN HUNTER, based on his own novel · Produced and Directed by RICHARD QUINE   CinemaScope EASTMAN COLOR

Love and the Frenchwoman (1960)

Nicole Perret (Dany Robin) has become unhappy with her husband, Jean-Claude (Paul Meurisse), after ten years of marriage. She is easily drawn into an affair with Gilles (Jean-Paul Belmondo), who flirts with her at a dinner party. Jean-Claude suspects that something is going on between Nicole and Gilles. He brings up the subject of unfaithful wives to Nicole. Nicole claims that the unfaithful wife is misunderstood. She surmises that this sort of woman is desperately unsatisfied, which surely makes her a victim. Jean-Claude insists that these dishonest women are no more than sluts. In a meeting with Gilles, Jean-Claude makes false gesture to step aside so that Gilles can marry Nicole. Just as Jean-Claude expected, this is sufficient to scare off the lover boy, who has no wish to make a serious commitment to Nicole. A twist is that the high-minded and smug Jean-Claude, who accused cheating wives of being sluts, is himself having an affair.

Shadows of Adultery (1961)

Anna (Annie Girardon) feels that she has no freedom being a housewife. Her wealthy husband, Eric (Daniel Gelin), buys her an art gallery to run, hoping that this will give her the sense of independence that she so desperately needs. But she remains as restless and confused as a caged lion. She has an affair with a record producer, Bruno (Christian Marquand). Eric learns of the affair and chooses to leave Anna for another woman. She rushes to the airport to stop Eric from leaving her, but her efforts are hopeless. She is gravely upset and takes her frustration out on Bruno, who has accompanied her to the airport. She shouts at him,"You took me, but couldn't keep me. You're not strong enough for me." She can barely be heard over the roar of the jet engines. She looks lonely as she drives off without Bruno.

Gertrud (1964)

Gertrud (Nina Pens Rode), a former opera singer, is neglected by her busy politician husband, Gustav Kanning (Bendt Rothe). She leaves Gustav with the intention of running off with Erland Jansson (Baard Owe), but Jansson has a girlfriend who is expecting his child and he has no interest in running off with another woman. Kanning pleads with Gertrud to stay with him. He tells her that he will not interfere if she still wants to see Jansson. She refuses and, instead, moves to Paris to study psychology. She is still alone in Paris thirty years later, but she says that she has no regrets. The film is too dry to be interesting.

Intentions of Murder (1964)

The original Japanese title: *Akai satsui*

A housewife, Sadako Takahashi (Masumi Harukawa), is oppressed by her unkind, domineering and neglectful husband, Koichi (Kō Nishimura). Koichi might be showing little interest in Sadako as he is having an affair with his adoring secretary, Yoshiko Masuda (Yūko Kusunoki). Hiraoka (Shigeru Tsuyuguchi) is in desperate need of money for heart medication. He burglarizes Sadako's home and, while attempting to subdue Sadako, suddenly rapes her. Sadako and Hiraoka develop a strange bond. Hiraoka has fallen in love with the unhappy housewife and convinces her run off with him. Her feelings for him are more doubtful. At one point, she plots to poison him, which does not suggest that she has warm feelings for the man. Hiraoka dies from a heart attack. Sadako returns home a stronger woman and is now determined to stand up to her husband.

Life At The Top (1965)

The film is a sequel to *Room at The Top*.

Joe Lampton (Laurence Harvey) returns home early from a business trip. As a joke, he figures to surprise his family by wearing a Huckleberry Hound mask. But he is the one surprised when he catches his wife Susan (Jean Simmons) in bed with his best friend, Mark (Michael Craig). Joe becomes distraught. He asks Susan why she cheated on him.

> Joe: Is he better in bed than I am?
>
> Susan: You think that's the answer to everything.
>
> Joe: I want to know why you went with him.
>
> Susan: I don't know. Maybe it was raining, or there was nothing on the telly, or Barbara was sick on the floor, or you weren't here. What's the bloody difference?!

So, Susan is the bored, neglected wife who strayed impulsively from her marriage. Joe would have known that if he had watched more adultery films. But he is not happy with her answer and demands a clearer explanation. She becomes flustered.

> Susan: Because - that's why. Because. Because.
>
> Joe: Oh, you're a bloody child.
>
> Susan: You mean I don't have an ulterior motive for everything I do, like you do, well, then I am a child, and glad of it.

Joe dates Norah Hauxley (Honor Blackman), a news anchor. He feels relaxed around Norah and opens up to her about his childhood. She is charmed by his frankness. Joe leaves Susan to live with Norah, but the relationship doesn't go well. Norah is disappointed with Joe for failing to "get [his] bearings." She believes that he still feels attached to Susan. She says, "You want to use me as a stick to beat your wife with." She harshly criticizes him for his diffidence.

> Joe: I will say this much for Susan, she never patronized me.
>
> Norah: Oh, you loathed her!
>
> Joe: I was never a project to her, an underdeveloped person!

Susan visits Joe to ask for his forgiveness. She insists, "What happened to us is commonplace." Joe agrees with Susan to get back together and work on their marriage.

The Sandpiper (1965)

The Sandpiper, a contrived film, is boring and unconvincing.

James Hitchcock of IMDb wrote: "Edward. . . finds himself increasingly drawn towards Laura, possibly because she is so different both from him and from his wife Claire. Claire is attractive and supportive of her husband but rather staid and conventional compared to the bohemian Laura."[385]

A Fine Madness (1966)

Samson Shillitoe (Sean Connery) is a noted poet with writer's block. His wife, Rhoda Shillitoe (Joanne Woodward), is worried that Samson might commit suicide and seeks help from a psychotherapist, Dr. Oliver West (Patrick O'Neal). Dr. West's wife, Lydia (Jean Seberg), feels neglected and takes an interest in Samson. Dr. West becomes dismayed when he sees Lydia romping with Samson in a hospital hot tub. The doctor, eager to eliminate his new rival, recommends that Samson undergo a new experimental form of lobotomy to reduce his aggression. This could have been a Grand Guignol ending, but Samson comes through the surgery intact.

Moment to Moment (1966)

Kay Stanton (Jean Seberg), the wife of naval officer Neil (Arthur Hill), has an affair with a naval ensign, Mark Dominic (Sean Garrison). But she feels guilty and wants to end the affair. She tells Mark, "It was some sort of animal hunger, with no thought of Neil or my life with him. I am so ashamed. Please forgive me." Mark becomes crazed. He brings out a gun. Kay is struggling to take a gun away from him when the gun goes off accidentally and fires a bullet into Mark. Believing that Mark is dead, Kay panics and dumps his body in a ravine. Mark turns up alive, but he is suffering from amnesia.

The April Fools (1969)

A Wall Street broker, Howard Brubaker (Jack Lemmon), has an affair with his boss's wife, Catherine Gunther (Catherine Deneuve). In the end, the couple runs off to Paris to start a new life together.

Ryan's Daughter (1970)

Audiences responded poorly to the film. Many critics found the scale of the film to be excessive. Charles Champlin of the Los Angeles Times wrote, "The original love story which Robert Bolt has set in these desolate seascapes seems both too frail and too banal to sustain the crushing weight of 3 hours and 18 minutes of Super Panavision."[386]

The film is loosely based on *Madame Bovary*. Rose Shaughnessy (Sarah Miles) and Randolph Doryan (Christopher Jones) enjoy clandestine meetings in fields much like lovers Emma Bovary and Rodolphe Boulanger did.

Jack Lemmon and Catherine Deneuve in *The April Fools* (1969)

Rose Ryan, the daughter of pub owner Thomas Ryan (Leo McKern), marries an older widower, Charles Shaughnessy (Robert Mitchum), who works in the village as a teacher. But marriage turns out disappointing for her. Charles is not exciting in any way. The man's dullness is no secret in the community. At the pub, Thomas openly discusses the topic with Mr. McCardle (Arthur O'Sullivan).

McCardle: It's working with children, makes a man childish.

Ryan: No, it was that wife of his, knocked all the spirit out of him.

"There must be more!" Rose tells the village priest, Father Hugh Collins (Trevor Howard). "Be careful what you ask for Rose," the priest tells her. "Because as sure as hell you'll get it."

Rose meets a handsome soldier, Major Randolph Doryan, at the pub. She stares longingly at him as he stands in his uniform at the bar. Doryan has been awarded the Victoria Cross for his fighting on the Western Front. But he feels no pride for his war efforts. He is a damaged man. He limps due to a leg injury and is prone to panic attacks due to shell shock.

Doryan has a sudden flashback of a massive battle and experiences a panic attack. The only person present other than Rose is the dim-witted Michael (John Mills). Michael becomes frightened as Doryan shudders and sweats. Rose quickly pushes Michael out of the pub. Doryan, who imagines the sounds of bombs, ducks beneath a table for safety. Rose crawls under the table and sees that he is paralyzed with fear. Seeking to comfort him, she slowly reaches towards him and takes hold of his hand. This small intimate contact erupts a passion in both of them. They embrace and kiss. This begins a torrid love affair.

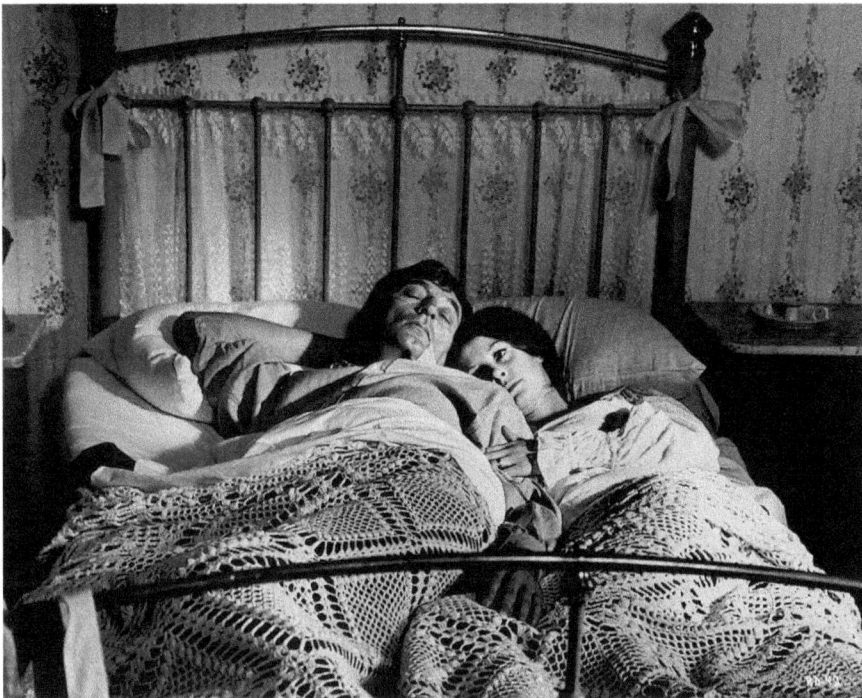

Robert Mitchum and Sarah Miles in *Ryan's Daughter* (1970)

Charles learns of their affair when he notices their footprints running across the sand on the beach. The footprints lead directly to a secluded cave.

Christopher Jones and Sarah Miles were, in real life, adulterers. Jones had an affair with Sharon Tate in 1969. At the time, Tate had been married to Roman Polanski for a year and was six months pregnant. Jones waited 38 years to speak about the affair. He said, "I loved Sharon and she loved me. . . I knew that she was married to Roman and I had no intention of splitting them up. I don't feel guilty."[387] Miles had an affair with legendary actor Laurence Olivier while Olivier was married to his third wife, Joan Plowright. At first, they met regularly in a basement apartment that Olivier rented specifically for their assignations. "It was such fun, she said. "He was such a funny man. Everyone. . . think[s] he was obsessed with his career and acting, but most of the time we just laughed."[388] She boasted about her massage skills. "He loved my touch," she said. "Oh what fun we had!" She also had an affair with long-married actor Robert Mitchum. She said that they got very close during the making of *Ryan's Daughter*. She spent much time in the actor's caravan during breaks in shooting. "But we weren't doing it," she insisted. "People always assume you are doing it and we both knew what everybody was thinking and I find that a bit tacky." She claimed that it wasn't until years later, after she divorced Bolt, that her and Mitchum consummated their relationship. She was out of her marriage by the time, but Mitchum wasn't out of his.

Lean, an incorrigible womanizer, had trouble achieving marital bliss. The director was married six times. Oddly, he came to specialize in directing adultery films - *Brief Encounter* (1945), *The Passionate Friends* (1949), *Summertime* (1955), *Doctor Zhivago* (1965) and, finally, *Ryan's Daughter*.

At the time that he made *The Passionate Friends*, Lean was married to Kay Walsh, an actress who appeared in Lean's *In Which We Serve* (1942) and *This Happy Breed* (1944). But his marital vows didn't stop him from seducing his latest leading lady, Ann Todd, who was married at the time to his aviator cousin Nigel Tangye. Geoffrey MacNab of Independent wrote, "[Todd's] autobiography contains a comic account of

Tangye. . . swooping down in vengeful mood in a small plane and terrifying Lean and his crew when they were shooting his next feature. . ."[389] It sounds like the plane attack scene from *The English Patient*.

Lean later wrote about his marriage to Todd, "She treated me so horribly that I think I was far more hurt than I have ever acknowledged."[390]

Geoffrey Macnab of The Independent wrote:

What is surprising is the sympathy [*The Passionate Friends*] shows for the jealous husband, who is terrified that his wife will leave him for her former sweetheart. At times Rains' character is made to seem absurd – he's too stiff to dance and too pedantic to speak in anything other than a banker's dry discourse. Yet Lean – despite his own reputation for breaking up relationships – treats the character with sensitivity; we are always aware of his suffering.[391]

Ryan's Daughter also shows sympathy for the husband. Charles finally confronts Rose about her affair. He admits that he should have spoken to her sooner. He says, "It was easier not to, I suppose. I didn't want to know, you know. And then I thought, if I let you burn it out, the pair of you. . . you'd perhaps come back to me." But his thoughts on the matter changed. He says, "Rose, I thought I could stand by and let you two burn it out, like I said. But I find I can't. I'm not sure I ought to have tried, but anyway, I can't. So I'm going to leave you."

Rose assures him that the affair is over. But she awakens in the middle of the night and goes to meet Doryan. Charles, distraught to wake alone in bed, wanders in his nightshirt on the beach.

Father Collins goes looking for Charles. Someone sees the priest and asks him who he is trying to find. He says,"A man whose wife went off two nights back with her fancy fellow. And a man I've been looking for since dawn today. A man who must be half out of his mind to have gone off as he did, barefoot."

Miles makes Rose sympathetic. The actress was good at playing sad, emotionally fragile women.

The film includes a subplot involving the Irish Republican Brotherhood, a political organization mounting a violent rebellion to end British rule in Ireland. The villagers come to believe that Rose informed the British military of an arms shipment to the Irish Republican Brotherhood. A mob seizes Rose from her home. They cut off her hair and strip off her clothes. The villagers are aware of Rose's affair with Doryan. Could it be that she is really being punished for this?

Doryan commits suicide by detonating explosives included in the arms shipment.

Anthony Hopkins and Gregory Peck were considered for the role of Charles. But the screenwriter, Robert Bolt, got the idea to cast Mitchum in the role. He said:

Was speaking to someone who'd seen him with his wife on telly, doing an interview, and was amazed by the dignity and mildness of the actor against his swaggering tough-guy image.[392]

David liked the idea. He said:

[Charles'] a jolly good, dull character. Now, if you get a jolly good, dull actor and play him in that part, the audience will be yawning their heads off in five minutes flat. So we decided to cast against type. I remember thinking of all the times that Hitchcock cast against type - the most amiable people playing absolutely horrible villains. We went through what we thought were really good actors and ended up with Mitchum.[393]

The film's producer, Anthony Havelock-Allan, was against casting Mitchum. He said:

I thought Mitchum absolutely wrong for the part. I said that I didn't think any audience in the world would believe that Mitchum would stand by for one second and allow somebody else to pinch his girl from under his nose without making a protest. He's not that kind of man. You're playing him as a weak man and he quite patently isn't. He's a tough guy, a reactor, and a violent one at that. And I don't believe in him in his nightdress looking out of the window and watching his wife go to meet a man whom he'd half kill in real life.[394]

It turned out that Havelock-Allan was right. Jack Beatty of The Atlantic wrote:

Lean agreed to sit in at a meeting of the New York Film Critics to discuss the film. One asked him, "Can you please explain how the man who directed *Brief Encounter* can have directed this load of shit you call *Ryan's Daughter*?" Outraged at Lean's casting of Robert Mitchum as a sedate schoolmaster unable to satisfy his new young wife, Pauline Kael got down to cases. "Are you trying to tell me that Robert Mitchum is a lousy lay?"[395]

It was hard to believe that Mitchum could steal a woman from Cary Grant in *The Grass is Greener* (1960) (which we will examine in Chapter Twenty). It was now hard to believe that Christopher Jones could steal a woman from Mitchum.

Robert Mitchum and Sarah Miles in *Ryan's Daughter* (1970)

Doctors' Wives (1971)

A group of doctors' wives find that it is hard to share their husbands with their demanding careers. Lorrie Dellman (Dyan Cannon) is desperately bored being married to Dr. Mort Dellman (John Colicos) and finds bed-hoping to be a happy diversion. During a card game with the other wives, she boasts that she has slept with most of their husbands. They are not sure if she is joking. Dellman catches Lorrie in bed with a randy dermatologist, Paul McGill (George Gaynes). He fires a fatal shot into Lorrie's back and a second shot into McGill's chest. McGill is rushed to the hospital for heart surgery. The wives hear about the shooting, but they do not know which of their husbands was shot. *Doctors' Wives* is *Letter to Three Wives* with a corpse. Affairs are an epidemic at the hospital. Dr. McGill's wife, Elaine (Marian McCargo) has a disappointing affair with a young intern, Mike Traynor (Anthony Costello). Dr. Peter Brennan (Richard Crenna), a popular surgeon, is unhappy with his wife Amy (Janice Rule), who is a morphine addict. He has found comfort with his nurse, Helen Struaghn (Diana Sands). But Helen feels insecure in their relationship.

Peter: I rely on you, Helen.

Helen: That's a man saying goodbye to his mistress. . . You go on, Pete. You finish your beer, and then you shove off. Godspeed. Wait a minute. Let me tell you something. I've been kidding myself all along. For years, I had this nutty idea that someday [Amy] would push you too far. . . Every husband, including you, is going back to his wife. Heh, for a while. . . I knew it this morning. There was something in you. Something. . . And I don't care for this to be a place for you to think. You think with her. I've had affairs before you, and I'll have affairs after you.

Peter: Jezebel? Isn't that a little outdated?

Helen: Yeah, well, she was a determined dame too. And I'm determined, Pete. I'm quitting. I'm going away somewhere. I don't know where. I don't know what the hell I'm gonna do. I'd like to get married again to someone who isn't married.

Helen is unable to quit Peter. She is defiant when Amy confronts her at the hospital. She insists that she loves Peter and will always stay with him. She says, "I'll be his girl. Or his shoulder. Whatever he wants me to be." Amy says, "You won't be his wife."

Glass Houses (1972)

Victor (Bernard Barrow) neglects his wife Adele (Ann Summers) while he is having an affair with a beautiful young woman, Jean (Jennifer O'Neill). His daughter, Kim (Deirdre Lenihan), becomes suspicious seeing her dad coming home late most nights. She warns her mother, but her mother can't bear to consider Victor cheating. Adele occupies her spare time attending civic meetings. A civic meeting brings her together with a neighbor, Les Turner (Clarke Gordon), and the two begin an affair.

Effi Briest (1974)

The film is set on the Baltic Coast of Germany during the 19th century. Effi (Hanna Schygulla) is young and immature when she marries Baron Geert von Instetten (Wolfgang Schenck). Instetten, who is a much older man, is unable to understand his young wife's needs and desires. He is often away on business, which causes Effi to feel alone and neglected. Effi is seduced by the unscrupulous Major Crampas (Ulli Lommel). Effi is intrigued by Crampas, who is earnest and interesting. Effi and Crampas go on excursions into the woods and picnic on the beach. Crampas tells Effi a story about a cuckolded king who orders for his wife's lover to be beheaded. The lover's dog stands faithfully beside his master as the axeman attends to his work. Afterward, the dog snatches up his master's head and delivers it to the king's dining room, where it sits on the table and stares accusingly at the king while he eats. Innstetten dislikes Crampas, who he sees as a rake. Crampas asserts that laws in general are boring. Instetten insists that civilization could not survive without law and order. When Innstetten finds Effi with love letters from Crampas, he disowns her and takes their young daughter away with him. He later kills Crampas in a duel. Effi sees her husband as cruel and calculating. She insists that virtue can be more disgusting than infidelity. She tells her mother, Frau von Briest (Lilo Pempeit), that it was sad and pointless for Instetten to have murdered Crampas as he was someone she never loved. A minister's wife persuades Instetten to let Effi see her daughter, but Instetten has obviously turned her daughter against her. This pains Effi more than anything. Effi's mother declares that Effi is "pining away." Effi is visited by Pastor Niemeyer (Theo Tecklenburg), who has known her since she was a little girl. He shows a definite fondness for her. She asks him if he can still get into heaven. He assures her that heaven remains open to her. Thereafter, she expresses a longing to return to her heavenly home. She is happy as she lays in bed dying. She expresses remorse for her unfaithfulness and says that she now accepts that Innstetten's response to her infidelity was correct and unavoidable. The film is based on a well-known 1894 novel by Theodor Fontane. This is the best of five film adaptations. The other four adaptations are *The False Step* (1939), *Roses in Autumn* (1955), *Effi Briest* (1968) and *Effi Briest* (2009).

Hanna Schygulla in *Effi Briest* (1974)

Cousin cousine (1975)

At a wedding, Marthe (Marie-Christine Barrault) and Ludovic (Victor Lanoux) are abandoned by their spouses, who have gone off together to have sex. The couple seems relieved to not have their spouses around and thoroughly enjoy each other's company. They become engrossed in conversation, but eventually take to the dance floor for a waltz. Their spouses, Pascal (Guy Marchand) and Karine (Marie-France Pisier), are suspiciously disheveled on their return.

Marthe and Ludovic are authentic and sympathetic characters, which makes them far superior to their fairly cartoonish and despicable spouses. Pascal is a sleazy womanizer. Karine is a loopy basket case.

Ludovic meets Marthe for lunch to tell her that he found a letter that Karine addressed to Pascal. Marthe is unconcerned about the letter. She borrows a lighter from Ludovic and happily sets the letter on fire. Why should it matter to them when they have found each other?

They continue to spend time together. One day, they buy bathing suits and go swimming at a public pool. They are comfortable and happy being together. But they agree to keep their relationship platonic. Ludovic says:

> We'll see each other for the sake of being together. But we'll have nothing to be ashamed of. Then years will go by, we'll become this amazing couple. [People will say,] "Apparently it's been 20 years and they don't even sleep together."

Karine becomes desperate to win back her husband, but he is no longer interested in her. Similarly, Pascal promises to reform, but Marthe doubts that he has the willpower to stay away from other women.

After a while, Marthe and Ludovic no longer see any value in keeping their relationship platonic. They rent a hotel room for two days. Although they have a great deal of sex, this isn't all that they do in the room - Marthe cuts Ludovic's toenails, Marthe gives Ludovic a recipe for lemon rabbit, and Marthe and Ludovic take time to draw pictures on each other. On her return home, Marthe defiantly confronts her waiting husband. She tells him, "One word and I'll leave. You'll never see me again."

Marthe and Ludovic's love for one another grows stronger. At a family gathering for Christmas, the couple openly kisses on the dance floor.

Wikipedia reports the film's ending as follows:

> Marthe and Ludovic lock themselves in a bedroom and make love throughout the evening while their families eat, drink, watch Midnight Mass, and exchange gifts. The couple finally emerges from the bedroom, say goodbye to their crazy families, and ride off into the night together.[396]

The World is Filled with Married Men (1979)

Linda Cooper (Carroll Baker) learns that her husband David (Anthony Franciosa) has cheated on her with a model, Claudia Parker (Sherrie Lee Cronn). She is determined to punish him by having an affair with a rock singer, Gem Gemini (Paul Nicholas).

Loving Couples (1980)

Dr. Evelyn Lucas Kirby (Shirley MacLaine) resents her inattentive husband, Walter (James Coburn). This makes her vulnerable to the flirtations of a handsome patient, Greg Plunkett (Stephen Collins). Greg has a girlfriend, Stephanie Beck (Susan Sarandon), who learns of the affair. She approaches Walter in the hope that he will talk to Evelyn and convince her to break up with Greg. But, instead, Walter and Stephanie start an affair of their own. The two couples happen to arrive at the same Acapulco resort on the same weekend. They nearly collide while swimming underwater in the hotel pool. Everyone acts fairly good-natured about the situation. Evelyn and Greg move in together. Evelyn is happy until she learns that Greg is having sex with a client, Mrs. Liggett (Sally Kellerman). Stephanie doesn't feel that Walter loves her and breaks up with him. She misses Greg, but she is reluctant to go back to him. Walter figures to woo back Evelyn with a romantic gesture. Dressed up as a cowboy, he rides a horse up to her car on the expressway. She laughs joyfully, which suggests that the romantic gesture has worked.

The idea of couples becoming entangled and swapping partners would be treated more seriously in *Afterglow* and *We Don't Live Here Anymore*.

Separate Ways (1981)

Valentine Colby (Karen Black), a bored housewife, attends an art class. A young art student, Jerry Lansing (David Naughton), asks her on a date and she accepts. The couple spends the afternoon rollerskating in a park. Afterward, they go to his apartment and roll around his bed kissing. But Valentine will not allow it to go further. She thanks Jerry for "a lovely afternoon" and leaves. In the end, her husband Ken (Tony Lo Bianco) opens up to her about his deep love for her, which brings her closer to him.

A Night in Heaven (1983)

Faye Hanlon (Lesley Ann Warren), a married college professor, has been feeling depressed. Her younger sister, Patsy (Deborah Rush), looks to cheer her up by taking her to a strip club. Faye is surprised that a student, Rick Monroe (Christopher Atkins), is working at the club as a stripper. Rick, who needs Faye to let him retake his final exam, gives the professor a spirited lap dance. His efforts are obviously effective as Faye gasps, moans and cries out. After the strip show, Faye and Rick check into a hotel room for sex. After Faye leaves, Rick invites his girlfriend Slick (Sandra Beall) to the room. Faye returns unexpectedly and catches Ricky and Slick taking a shower together. She feels humiliated and rushes out of the room. Faye's husband, Whitney (Robert Logan), learns about Faye's ill-fated liaison with Rick. He confronts Rick at a dock. He forces the young man at gunpoint to stand on a skiff and remove all of his clothing. While Rick sobs and begs for his life, Whitney shoots holes in the skiff to make it sink. Whitney returns home to reconcile with Faye. The film ends with a repentant wife and a forgiving husband.

Sudden Love (1984)

The original Greek title: *Xafnikos erotas*

Eleni (Betty Livanou), an unsatisfied housewife, embarks on a romance with an economist, Grigoris (Antonis Theodorakopoulos).

Thief of Hearts (1984)

Mickey Davis (Barbara Williams) feels neglected by her husband, Ray (John Getz), and uses her diary to explore her sexual fantasies. A burglar, Scott Muller (Steven Bauer), breaks into the Davis home. He is excited by Mickey's diary and plots to seduce the sexually frustrated wife.

The American Bride (1986)

The original Italian title: *La sposa americana*

Edoardo (Thommy Berggren), a young literature professor, has an affair with his sister-in-law, Anna (Stefania Sandrelli), who has been unhappy since learning that her husband Sacha (Harvey Keitel) is homosexual.

Sex, Lies, and Videotape (1989)

John Mullany (Peter Gallagher) is frustrated that his wife Ann (Andie MacDowell) never wants to have sex. His frustration causes him to embark on an affair with his wife's sister, Cynthia Bishop (Laura San Giacomo).

Sibling Rivalry (1990)

Marjorie Turner (Kirstie Alley), a neglected wife, is unhappy and frustrated. She gets upset at a supermarket checkout. A handsome stranger, Charles (Sam Elliott), manages with his cheerful and charming demeanor to calm her down. She agrees to go out for a drink with him. Afterward, the couple goes to a hotel for a romantic afternoon. Unfortunately, Charles suffers a fatal heart attack during sex.

The Paint Job (1992)

A shy wife, Margaret (Bebe Neuwirth), falls in love with Wesley (Will Patton), a house painter who works for her husband Willie (Robert Pastorelli). Wesley finds Willie to be acting suspiciously and follows him to see what he's doing. He is shocked to learn that Willie is a serial killer.

Josefin Nilsson and Jacob Ericksson in *Adam & Eva* (1997)

Adam & Eva (1997)

Adam (Björn Kjellman) and Eva (Josefin Nilsson) have become bored with their marriage after four years. Eva wants to buy a house and have a baby, but Adam doesn't want the responsibility. In an act of reckless stupidity, Adam has an affair with his brother's young babysitter, Jackie (Dubrilla Ekerlund). Eve learns of Adam's cheating and leaves him. Adam desperately wants her back, but she refuses to forgive him and files for divorce. Eve marries a stand-up comedian, Åke Braun (Jacob Ericksson). She rushes to have a child with Åke, but their marriage ends after six months. Adam and Eve meet by chance in a store. Adam expresses regret and remorse about their marriage. Eve can see that he has changed. The couple remarries and has a baby.

Playing by Heart (1998)

Gracie (Madeleine Stowe) is unfulfilled in her marriage to a neurotic and distant husband, Hugh (Dennis Quaid). She regularly meets Roger (Anthony Edwards) in hotel rooms to have sex. Grace tells Roger, "I want it to be what it is: two very sexually compatible people enjoying each other with no obligations, no complications, no individual history, no mutual history, and no guilt."

American Beauty (1999)

Carolyn Burnham (Annette Bening) has become a stuffy and materialistic wife. She has achieved success as a realtor and gets great satisfaction from her high sales figures. She is disgusted with her unambitious husband, Lester (Kevin Spacey), who has been laid off from his job. She is excited by Buddy Kane (Peter Gallagher), who is the top realtor in town. She ends up having an affair with the success-driven Buddy. During sex, Buddy shouts, "You like being nailed by the king?" Carolyn squeals, "Yes, your Majesty!" Lester has secretly gotten a job working at the drive-thru window of a fast-food restaurant. He catches Carolyn and Buddy passionately kissing while waiting for their drive-thru order. Buddy, who is married, explains that he values his image in the community and needs to break up with her. Lester is fatally shot by a neighbor. When she learns of Lester's death, Carolyn throws open his clothes closet, embraces his clothing, and sobs uncontrollably. This is another film that blames capitalism for ruining a marriage.

A Walk on the Moon (1999)

This is a far more conventional adultery film than *Eyes Wide Shut*, which came out the same year. The Kantrowitz family, including husband Marty (Liev Schreiber), wife Pearl (Diane Lane), teenage daughter Alison (Anna Paquin), young son Danny (Bobby Boriello) and Marty's mother Lillian (Tovah Feldshuh), are guests at a summer camp retreat. Marty can only spend the weekends at the camp because of his job as a television repairman. While her husband is away, Pearl begins a relationship with Walker Jerome (Viggo Mortensen), who sells blouses out of a market stall.

Marty's mother Lillian (Tovah Feldshuh) is the voice of morality. She reminds Pearl that Marty has always been good to her. She speaks of his compassion, his generosity and his self-sacrifice.

Pearl breaks it off with Walker, but she can't stay away for long. Walker asks Pearl to run away with him. He says, "You ever been out West, Pearl? You want to go with me? We don't have to wait. We can just pack up the bus. Um, we'll just. . . we'll just camp out all the way across the country, and we'll sleep under the stars every night."

Marty confronts Pearl and asks what her plans are. Tears well up in her eyes. She looks at him helplessly. She finally answers, "I don't know." "What the hell is that supposed to mean, Pearl?" he asks.

Pearl got pregnant at 17 and she and Marty had to marry quickly. Now, she resents having had to surrender her youth to be a wife and mother.

Pearl: It wasn't you, Marty. It was me. There were things I wanted to do with my life. I don't even remember what some of them were. Somewhere along the line, I disappeared. I stopped being the person you fell in love with. And I wanted - I wanted to be that way again with you. But I couldn't.

Marty: I wanted things too, Pearl. Think I like fixin' TVs? Think I said, "Gee, that's what I want to be when I grow up?" I mean, who knows what I could've been if I had a chance to go to college. But I didn't. And you know what? I was okay. Because I figured no matter what I screwed up in my life, no matter what I felt gypped out of, I had the most important thing right. I had you. Now, I don't. But I still have one question, Pearl. Who stopped you? Who stopped you from doing these things? Did I stop you? I mean, did - did - did you ever once come to me and say, "Marty, I want to make a change in my life?" And did I say, "No, Pearl, you can't"?

Pearl: Marty, it's not that simple. I tried. I couldn't always find the right words, you know, but I - Y- You - You didn't hear me. You make jokes.

Marty: It's true. I'm a bad listener. Not such a good talker, either. And I make jokes. But who stopped you, Pearl?

In the end, though, Pearl decides to forego the stars and stay with Marty. She tells her daughter that the affair was an accident.

The film lost money at the box office.

Mademoiselle (2001)

Claire (Sandrine Bonnaire), a pharmaceutical rep, is a married woman with two small children. She leaves her family behind in Lyon to attend an annual convention. At the convention, she enjoys a trio of actors who improvise a routine as comic waiters. She is attracted to one of the actors, Pierre (Jacques Gamblin). Rather than return to Lyon on a bus with her co-workers, she gets a ride with Pierre and his friends. She experiences a unique and varied emotional journey as she tags along with the acting troupe. She is sometimes bemused, sometimes excited, and ultimately joyful. Claire and Pierre have sex (off screen) in a hotel room. But perhaps the best part of the experience isn't the sex but, instead, the two of them riding through a city on a borrowed motorcycle.

Claire has run off for a fling, nothing more. She has spent a happy day with her illicit lover and now she is ready to return with fond memories to her normal routine as a wife and mother. But, in the final shot, the camera holds on her face, which goes from a brief smile to a wistful and perhaps pained expression. It's as if she has remembered the joy of her excursion and also remembered that she may never feel that joy again.

Mademoiselle questions the validity of marriage. The clear message was that, regardless how cute a woman's children are and how supportive or good-natured her husband is, marriage is unfulfilling for a woman, who needs sexual adventure and romantic motorcycle rides to be happy and gratified. This was a trend in adultery films at the time.

The portrayal of adultery was bound to change with the rise of feminist voices. Feminist filmmakers, including Jane Campion, Gillian Armstrong, Adrienne Shelly and Brigitte Roüan, brought forth a new perspective on the subject. In their view, marital fidelity stood in the way of a woman leading a free and satisfying existence.

The Good Girl (2002)

Justine Last (Jennifer Aniston) is a morose 30-year-old cashier at a discount store. She feels neglected by her dim-witted husband, Phil (John C. Reilly). She takes an interest in a shy and sensitive new cashier, Holden (Jake Gyllenhaal). Justine and Holden get to know each other during work breaks. Justine believes that Holden understands her. One day, the couple goes to a motel after work to have sex. Justine enjoys the affair at first, but she becomes frightened when Holden becomes obsessed with her and offers to murder Phil. Holden steals $15,000 from work so that he and Justine can run off together. But the store manager, Jack Field (John Carroll Lynch), knows that Holden stole the money and calls the police. Holden is distraught that Justine fails to meet him at the hotel. Instead, she lets Jack know where Holden is. When the police come to arrest Holden, he shoots himself in the head and dies.

The script sets the story in a small town in Texas, but the film fails to convey its setting in an authentic way. It is doubtful that the actors, with their exaggerated Texas accents, have ever had a front-row seat at a rodeo, eaten a Frito pie, or shook red clay off their shoes. What did anyone involved in the film know about life in a small Texas town? The film's principals, Aniston, Gyllenhaal, Zooey Deschanel and Mike White, grew up in wealthy neighborhoods in Los Angeles. The shooting locations weren't even authentic. The film was shot in Santa Clarita, a prosperous community in northwestern Los Angeles County.

We Don't Live Here Anymore (2004)

Jack Linden (Mark Ruffalo) and Hank Evans (Peter Krause) are fellow literature professors at the local university. The men and their wives, Terry Linden (Laura Dern) and Edith Evans (Naomi Watts), are close friends and frequently meet for dinner. The two couples are grossly dysfunctional. Terry and Edith both complain that intimacy and affection is lacking in their marriage. Hank is depressed because he is unable to finish a book that he has been writing. Jack is mostly bored. No one is able to communicate. Everyone is needy and insecure. The entanglement of these unhappy people blurs marital boundaries and creates reckless shifts in their relationships. So, not surprisingly, the couples secretly exchange partners. Edith muses to Jack, "I wonder how we'll get caught." She believes that Terry will be the one to catch them. Jack asks, "What? Don't you think Hank is gonna notice?" She replies, "Well, if he does, it'll be a miracle. Oh, come on, Jack. You're talking like he's Charlie Chan or something. Like he gives a shit." Jack notices that Hank and Terry have gotten close and is convinced that they are having an affair. He is appalled though he, himself, has been unfaithful.

Jack: Your husband is making passes at my wife. How do you feel about that?

Edith: Well, everybody deserves to be happy, right?

Jack confronts Terry. It is important to Terry that Jack understands the reason that she cheated on him. She tells him:

> You don't make love to me anymore. You fuck me. I sat on those steps with Hank and he held my hand and he listened to me. He listened to me while I talked about this shitty marriage. And he told me he felt close to me. And I was happy when he said it. And I was happy when I made love to him. I was so goddamn happy for a minute, and then I thought of you. I just wanted to be here with you and get us back. And be in this fucking bed, in this house, with my husband and my kids where I belong.

The affairs have been therapeutic for Hank and Terry. Terry has found strength and clarity. Hank, who hasn't had Edith complaining and demanding his attention, has been cured of his writer's block. He says, "It's much easier living with a woman who feels loved." But Jack and Edith have not found the same satisfaction. Edith pursues happiness by leaving Hank.

Keeping Mum (2005)

Gloria Goodfellow (Kristin Scott Thomas) feels neglected by her busy vicar husband, Walter (Rowan Atkinson). This leads her to have an affair with her handsome golf instructor, Lance (Patrick Swayze). The Goodfellows hire a new housekeeper, Grace Hawkins (Maggie Smith), without knowing that she is a psychopathic serial killer. Miss Hawkins kills Lance with a clothes iron when she catches him outside their home videotaping the Goodfellows' teenage daughter, Holly (Tamsin Egerton), undressing in her bedroom.

Gabrielle (2005)

Gabrielle Hervey (Isabelle Huppert) is unhappy with her distant and hard-hearted husband, Jean (Pascal Greggory). He comes home one night and finds a letter from her. She explains in the letter that she has left him for another man. IMDb's writers_reign wrote, ". . . [H]ardly has the ink had time to dry on the letter than she is back again. . ."[397] Her return remains ambiguous. The couple reflects on their marriage, but Gabrielle is infuriatingly cryptic in what she has to tell her husband. He is worried that they are going to live as enemies now. She says, "I can easily live here with you. You won't be my enemy or hurt me. I couldn't have come back otherwise."

Gabrielle assures Jean that she doesn't regret their marriage. She says:

> It led me to him. Without you, he doesn't exist. My life with you pointed me to him. It occurred to me he might be under your orders. I even imagined you had chosen him.

Gabrielle is prepared to live with Jean in a loveless marriage. When she removes her clothing and offers her lifeless body to him, he becomes horrified and flees the room.

Gabrielle perhaps needed a stronger husband, like the husband that Jean Gabin played in *The Moment of Truth*. Gabin was able to give pushback to his wife's tsunami of "I must follow my heart" emotion and argue against her shabby and pretentious arguments for infidelity.

The cheating wives played by Huppert tended to be less sympathetic than the other cheating wives of the period - Diane of *After Sex* (1997), Claire of *Mademoiselle* (2001), Emma of *I Am Love* (2009), Véronique of *Mademoiselle Chambon* (2009), and Suzanne of *Leaving* (2009). LaSalle wrote:

> In *Madame Bovary, Story of Women, Gabrielle* and other films, Huppert acts mainly out of boredom and contempt. *Gabrielle* contains a classic Huppert moment, in which she sits, expressionless (of course), listening to her husband (Pascal Greggory) lecture her about her affair. When, with great ostentation, he arrives at his conclusion - "I forgive you" - she explodes into laughter, and what a wonderful laugh it is, one of childlike delight and infinite amusement. That moment could be transposed, without much difficulty, into a half-dozen other Huppert films.[398]

The Duchess (2008)

The film is set in 1774. William Cavendish (Ralph Fiennes), the Duke of Devonshire, marries Georgiana Spencer (Keira Knightley) with the hope that she will bear him an heir. William is not an ideal husband. He is aloof. He is unfaithful. Georgiana finds out almost immediately that he is having an affair with Lady Bess (Hayley Atwell). Georgiana withdraws from William and falls in love with a young politician, Charles Grey (Dominic Cooper). The couple's passionate relationship becomes a badly kept secret. William cannot allow this to continue. The issue is Georgiana's indiscretion, not her infidelity. He tells Georgiana that he will take her children from her unless she ends the affair.

> Georgiana: My life for theirs.
>
> William: That's one way of putting it. Your mother called it "common decency before personal gratification," or some such thing. The exact words escape me.
>
> Georgiana: How about "imprisoned in my own house?"
>
> William: No. That's not how she put it. I would have remembered that.

He tells Georgiana that he loves her. "In the way I understand love," he says. He accuses her of having romantic delusions of love. He tells her, "Grey is a dreamer like yourself, and you both dream of another world that does not exist and it never will."

Georgiana tells William that she bears Grey's child. William demands that Georgina remain hidden at a country estate during her pregnancy and, once she gives birth, turn over the baby to the Grey family. Lady Bess is sympathetic to the grieving duchess. She insists on going to the country estate to care for Georgiana.

Tilda Swinton in *I Am Love* (2009)

I Am Love (2009)

The members of the Recchi family are rich Italian aristocrats that operate textile mills in Milan. Tancredi Recchi (Pippo Delbono) has recently had to take control of the business due to his father's death. Tancredi's quiet wife, Emma (Tilda Swinton), is out of place among this high-powered group.

Tancredi and Emma's son, Edoardo Jr. (Flavio Parenti), has no interest in the textile business. He has studied in school to be a chef and is now working with a classmate, Antonio (Edoardo Gabbriellini), to reno-vate a restaurant in San Remo, a coastal town known for its picturesque greenery. Edorardo Jr. introduces Antonio to Emma, who is immediately attracted to the young man.

Emma passes through San Remo on her way to visit her daughter Betta in Nice. She is wandering through the streets when she spots Antonio. He happily takes her to see the restaurant. Emma is enchanted by the lush green fields that surround the restaurant. The environment excites something in her. She lays in the tall grass and soaks in the bright sunshine. The visit is brief. But she returns on another day to speak to Antonio about preparing a menu for an upcoming party. They meet inside a dimly lit cafe. Antonio senses that Emma has feelings for him and doubts that she is really interested in planning a menu. His hand nervously taps the table. She lays her hand over his to relax him. This is all that it takes to bring them together. They hurry off to his restaurant to, in the words of Marvin Gaye, *get it on*.

Afterward, they cook dinner together. Emma shows Antonio how to make a Russian fish soup called *ukha*. This is a special family recipe that was passed down to her from her mother. She has only ever made the soup for Edoardo Jr., who is very fond of it. Antonio cuts Emma's hair on the terrace. They make love again, this time in a flowery field. For this special day, they have abandoned themselves to their sexual pas-sions.

Edoardo Jr. becomes suspicious when he finds a lock of his mother's hair on the terrace floor. He is even more suspicious when he attends Emma's dinner and sees Antonio preparing *ukha*. He becomes furious with his mother. Emma follows him outside. She reaches out to him, but he pulls away, loses his balance, and falls into a pool. He strikes his head on the edge of the pool, which causes him to sustain a cerebral hemor-rhage. He dies at the hospital.

After Edorardo Jr.'s funeral, Tancredi is attempting to console his tearful wife when she suddenly tells him that she is in love with Antonio. He is appalled. He tells her, "You don't exist."

Emma rushes home to pack up her belongings and leave. Wikipedia reports, "When the family members look back into the foyer where Emma was standing, she is gone."[399]

A film critic wrote about two old women who sat behind him during the film. When the film ended, they complained that they didn't understand it. He wrote:

> What exactly happened? The son dies, Tilda Swinton tells her husband that she's been unfaithful and in love with the handsome cook, the women [Emma and her maid] all start to cry, and then she runs out of the luscious Milan house. . . and. . . well, you have a musical crescendo, and then. . . hmmm.[400]

After the end credits, there is a quick and uncertain image of a couple lying together in a cave. Presumably, this is Emma and Antonio. But what does it mean? The critic found the image to be beautiful even though he didn't know what it meant (he referred to it as "unresolved" and "non-explanatory").

YouTube commentator Be Kind Rewind sees *I Am Love* as a film about longing and identity. She praises Swinton for her deep reactions to "small moments." She noted, "Something as simple as [eating] a prawn becomes a turning point, a haircut is a revolution."[401]

Kristin Scott Thomas and Sergi Lopez in *Leaving* (2009)

Leaving (2009)

Suzanne (Kristin Scott Thomas) has lost interest in her doctor husband, Samuel (Yvan Attal), and is bored with her comfortable lifestyle. She prepares to return to work as a physiotherapist after having spent the past fifteen years raising her two children. She hopes that this will make her life satisfying again.

Suzanne is fascinated by Ivan (Sergi Lopez), a builder hired by Samuel to convert their garage into her new office. Suzanne goes to bring Ivan a payment, but she is so excited to see him that she neglects to lock the brake on her car. When the car rolls down the sloping street, Ivan hurries to stop it, but manages in the process to get his foot smashed under the wheel. Suzanne rushes him to the hospital. For the next few days, she feels obligated to care for the injured man. Her loving and tender nursing inspires an intimacy between them. Soon, they fall into each other's arms. The IMDb plot summary reads, "Her first tryst with Ivan is accomplished through an almost paralytic clinging, as if she is a dead battery charging itself."[402]

Film critics drew a connection between the film and Thomas' affair with actor Tobias Menzies, which allegedly broke up her eighteen-year marriage to Dr. François Olivennes.

Without hesitation, Suzanne tells Samuel that she plans to leave her family to be with Ivan. She is startled when her normally aloof husband breaks down in tears. She is quick to comfort him, assuring him that she will end the affair. The woman drawn to a man after smashing his foot is now drawn back to her husband after smashing his feelings. But she cannot keep away from Ivan. She tells him, "I enjoy everything when I'm with you." She gets a call from Ivan while having dinner with her family. She completely forgets about the dinner and tries to sneak off to be with her lover, but her husband catches her. He drags her up to the bedroom as his stunned children and parents watch and locks her inside, but she desperately clambers out of a window. The next day, she collects her belongings from her home. Suzanne tells Samuel that she is leaving him and getting a divorce. He becomes furious and vows to stop her. Suzanne storms out of the house.

Suzanne is happy to move into Ivan's modest apartment. She is not prepared for the lengths that Samuel will go to get her back. Her betrayal has unleashed a cruel determination in him. She opens an office for her physiotherapy practice, but Samuel purchases the building and has her evicted. Samuel then uses his high-powered connections to get Ivan fired from his job. Suzanne tries to withdraw money from the bank, but she learns that her husband has blocked the account. Suzanne and Ivan are left without an income and become desperate.

Suzanne and Ivan take a road trip with Suzanne's son and Ivan's young daughter, but they run out of money and Suzanne has to sell her watch to buy gas. The next day, Suzanne visits Samuel to demand money from him. When he refuses, she snatches his wallet from a table and rummages through it for cash. He remarks, "What, are you a pickpocket as well, now?"

The doctor's wife gets a job as a fruit packer to at least earn money for food. Divorce laws are set up to prevent a situation like this, but let us accept this implausible situation for the purposes of the story.

With Ivan's help, Suzanne breaks into her former home to steal expensive paintings that she believes belong to her. Samuel has Ivan arrested. The fact that Ivan has a criminal record and spent time in prison weighs heavily against him. Samuel is only willing to drop the charges if Suzanne comes back to him. She agrees although she is distraught by the arrangement.

Samuel ignores his wife's mental state. In his view, she is simply not thinking clearly. After all, he has provided well for his family and has never transgressed in any way. Unlike Ivan, he has at least managed to keep himself out of prison. He can see no logic in Suzanne leaving him for an ex-convict. He has, based on this reasoning, convinced himself that the affair was a simple lapse in judgment and everything will eventually return to normal. But he is wrong. Fatally wrong.

Suzanne has suffered a breakdown and descends further and further into despair. Samuel has sex with her as if he expects it to renew their marital bond. But, unlike Isabelle Huppert's Gabrielle, Suzanne has returned to her husband without resigning herself to unwanted sexual relations. Samuel initiates sex with her nearly paralytic body, which is rape rather than the lovemaking that he imagines it to be. Afterward, she gets a gun out of the closet and shoots him while he sleeps. She knows that she will be arrested, but she has to see Ivan first. She quickly leaves the house to meet Ivan in the countryside for a desperate and tearful farewell.

The film starts out as *Lady Chatterley's Lover* (an upper class woman is attracted to a workman on her property), enters *Anna Karenina* territory (she vows to her husband to end the relationship, but she cannot resist going to her lover), and veers into clear *Madame Bovary* influences (she becomes gravely ill being away from her lover). But the violence that erupts in the final ten minutes of the film is all its own.

The film is similar in ways to *Lady of the Tropics* (1939) - cruel and intricate coercion by a romantic rival, a woman willing to sacrifice herself to save her lover.

A series of films made during this period treated cheating women sympathetically. LaSalle points out that, in contrast, a cheating husband was treated as a louse. He wrote, ". . . [I]n *Le grand alibi*, for example, the serial philanderer, played by Lambert Wilson, is murdered, and there is no sense of a blessed spirit leaving the universe."[403] Filmmakers, he found, almost always gave the woman a compelling reason to cheat. In the case of *Leaving*, they also gave a wife a compelling reason to murder her husband.

Gemma Bovery (2014)

Martin (Fabrice Luchini), a baker in a small village, is an ardent admirer of Flaubert's "Madame Bovary." He is fascinated when he meets new neighbors named Gemma and Charles Bovery (Gemma Arterton and Jason Flemyng). Like Emma, Gemma is desperately bored and enters into an extramarital affair. Martin is convinced that Gemma is heading toward the same tragic end as Emma. He tries to warn her by sending her an anonymous letter with pages from the Flaubert novel. But this has no effect. He finally confronts her. He tells her, "Whatever happens to Madame Bovary happens to you. . . I know it seems stupid. But believe me, Gemma, there's a moment when life imitates art." The police find Gemma dead. Martin insists that the police check her body for arsenic. Truth, though, is that Gemma choked on a bite of the baker's bread.

No Thank You (2014)

The original Finnish title: *Ei kiitos*

Heli (Anu Sinisalo), an art teacher, is bored with her marriage. Her husband, Matti (Ville Virtanen), prefers to play video games rather than have sex with her. She has tried using Valium and brandy to cope, but this hasn't been enough. She has an affair with a young student, Jarno (Kai Vaine).

Marriage Story (2019)

Nicole Barber (Scarlett Johansson) is angry at her husband Charlie (Adam Driver), who she sees as a neglectful and unsupportive partner. She forces him out of the marital bed. The couple sees a marriage counselor. But Nicole is hostile during their counseling session, believing that the counselor favors Charlie over her. "Well," she snaps, "I think I'm gonna go if you two are gonna just sit around and suck each other's dicks." This leaves the marriage in limbo and leaves Charlie sleeping on the couch. Charlie drifts into an affair with a co-worker, Mary Ann (Brooke Bloom). Nicole hacks into his computer and finds emails that he has exchanged with Mary Ann. This convinces her to file for divorce. Nicole is a maelstrom of emotions and is monstrous in the way that she lets her emotions dominate her marriage.

Alexander Skarsgård and Keira Knightley in *Aftermath* (2019)

The Aftermath (2019)

In past films, marriages became strained when transplanted to an inhospitable place. But none of those places were as bad as the bombed-out ruins of post-war Hamburg. Lewis Morgan (Jason Clarke), a British colonel, is put in charge of rebuilding Hamburg. Lewis's wife, Rachael (Keira Knightley) is displeased with Lewis' grim new assignment. But she doesn't say much about it to him. The couple has grown distant since their young son, Michael, was killed in a German bombing. The British occupation forces requisition the house of a German architect, Stefan Lubert (Alexander Skarsgård), to house the Morgans. Lewis cannot bring himself to force Stefan and his teenage daughter, Freda (Flora Thiemann), out of their home. But Rachael has a hatred of the Germans that prevents her from being cordial to her hosts. Rachael softens toward Stefan when she learns that his wife was killed by Allied bombing. Stefan is enchanted to hear Rachael play his wife's piano. It is almost as if, at that moment, his wife has returned to him. Rachael and Stefan grow closer. Rachael tells Lewis that she is going away with Stefan. She says that their marriage died when Michael died. "You left me," she says. Lewis speaks of the grief that he has felt over Michael's death. He tells her that he kept away from her because she was a painful reminder of their son. "I could smell him on your skin," he says. She hugs him and says goodbye. She is at the train station with Stefan and Freda when she suddenly realizes that she cannot leave Lewis.

Chapter Thirteen:
A Sensitive Perspective

In the sensitive adultery film, the protagonist sees it as their duty to struggle with the moral issues raised by an extramarital affair. They care deeply that no one is hurt by their actions. In this genre of the adultery story, the dramatist is able to deeply explore human frailties and fallibility.

Street of Women (1932)

Larry Baldwin (Alan Dinehart), who remains in a loveless marriage for the sake of his daughter, has an affair with dress designer Natalie Upton (Kay Francis). She, unlike his wife, is caring and supportive. She is essentially a mistress with a heart of gold. Years have passed. Larry believes that his daughter is old enough now to handle her parents breaking up. He plans to tell his wife that he wants to leave her to marry Natalie. Meanwhile, Natalie invites her brother Clarke to stay with her while he's in town. With Clarke around, she is not able to spend time with Larry. Larry's daughter, Doris (Gloria Stuart), meets Clarke and the couple falls in love. Clarke proposes marriage to Doris, who accepts. Now that Clarke and Doris are engaged, Larry and Natalie must rethink their plans. Fearful that the divorce could cause a scandal for the young couple, they agree to end their relationship. In a number of adultery films, a single message was made clear: consider the children. Link Gibson (Roland Young), who loves Natalie, sees this as an opportunity to marry Natalie. But it becomes obvious to him that Natalie is brokenhearted about losing Larry. Link visits Larry's wife, Lois (Marjorie Gateson), and persuades her to allow her husband an amicable divorce.

Irene Dunne and Walter Huston in *Ann Vickers* (1933)

Ann Vickers (1933)

Ann Vickers (Irene Dunne), a social worker, embarks on a crusade to improve conditions in a women's prison. She meets a judge, Barney Dolphin (Walter Huston), at a party. Dolphin is sympathetic to her views on reform and is intrigued by the changes that she recommends. Dolphin is married, but this doesn't stop the couple from dating and falling in love. Dolphin is put on trial for bribery. He asks his wife, Mona (Gertrude Michael), to return the bribe money, though it would likely bankrupt them. She prefers her husband's imprisonment over financial ruin and chooses to hold onto the money. She abandons her husband upon his conviction. Ann learns that she is pregnant with Dolphin's child. She stands by Dolphin while he serves his sentence and reunites with him upon his release. The film shows that a mistress can be more faithful than a wife.

Richard Taylor, the author of "Love Affairs: Marriage & Infidelity," recognizes a possible advantage to the extramarital affair. A husband and wife, who share possessions, ambitions and position, have a reason to care for one another. But, Taylor believes, partners in a love affair have nothing to hold them together other than the feelings that they have for one another.[404]

The Stranger's Return (1933)

During a visit to her grandfather's Iowa farm, Louise Storr (Miriam Hopkins) meets a cultured and personable young farmer, Guy Crane (Franchot Tone). Louise is attracted Guy, but she must keep her distance from him as he is married. Louise is invited to lunch by Guy's wife, Nettie (Irene Hervey). Louise is taken by Nettie's warm hospitality, but she cannot see how a woman as plain and simple as Nettie could be married to Guy. Grandpa Storr (Lionel Barrymore) explains, "It's a common thing around here. Childhood sweethearts. He went up to college and she didn't. Afterward, they didn't stop to find out if they still liked each other." Nettie is pleased that Guy and Louise get along well. She tells Louise that she isn't able to talk to Guy about the things that he likes to talk about. She says that Guy gets lonely at times and could use a friend like Louise. Is she naive about the threat posed by Louise or does she believe that Guy's happiness is more important than his fidelity? While driving Louise home, Guy admits to feeling foolish around her. He abruptly stops the car and kisses her. Guy and Louise are too fond of Nettie to let their relationship go further. Grandpa dies and leaves the farm to Louise. Louise is afraid to take over the farm as it would mean living near Guy and having to endlessly struggle with her feelings for him. Guy solves the problem by accepting a job to teach agriculture at Cornell University in New York.

If I Were Free (1933)

A couple, Gordon Evers (Clive Brook) and Sarah Cazenove (Irene Dunne), wish to end their bad marriages to be together. But Gordon's wife, Catherine (Lorraine MacLean), refuses to consent to a divorce. Sarah's husband, Tono, is not around to grant consent, having run off with another woman. Sarah remains traumatized by her memory of Tono. Before he left, he threatened Sarah at gunpoint because she refused to pay the debts that he had incurred through his extravagant spending. He soon turns up again, but he now wants money to agree to a divorce. She refuses him. But Sarah realizes that it could hurt Gordon's career as a judge if it becomes public that he is dating a married woman. So, she ends their relationship. Soon after, Gordon learns that he has less than a year to live due to a bullet that became lodged near his heart during the war. He agrees to undergo a risky surgery to remove the bullet. Gordon's mother (Laura Hope Crews) comes to Sarah and tells her that Gordon needs her. It is unique in a film for a mother to support her son's affair. Sarah sits at Gordon's bedside after the surgery. He is extremely weak and knows that he is dying. He reminisces about a rowboat ride he took with Sarah in Paris. Sarah sings to him as she once sang to him in the rowboat. He is imagining the rowboat ride as he takes his final breaths. Is Gordon now free to be with Sarah in the afterlife?

Marriage is not for fools. Yet, films show us the sad fate that fools face in marriage. Let's be honest, fools face a sad fate in most everything they do. I say this as someone who has, at times, been a fool.

The biggest fool is someone who marries someone they never should have married in the first place. We see that often in films. A man who knows he's in a marriage with the wrong person can be a miserable wretch. And what should that man do if he suddenly meets the exact sort of person he *should* have married? Does he shrug his shoulders and walk past the person? It can feel like you're drowning in an ocean and suddenly an angel appears, smiling and aglow, and tosses you a rope. You grab the rope, right?

Filmmakers have seen this as the great adulterer's loophole and have exploited this as often as they can. But this is shamefully dishonest. These desperate situations, though they create good drama, are not common and certainly shouldn't be used to make adultery acceptable. Filmmakers have been able to carefully and perfectly construct these scenarios in a way that life rarely does. Adultery is far more often a shallow, frivolous and self-indulgent act.

Nonetheless, fair or not, films in this category have succeeded in presenting a persuasive argument for adultery.

Clive Brook and Irene Dunne in *If I Were Free* (1933)

Beauty for Sale (1933)

The film opens at an upscale beauty salon. The favorite topic at the salon is adultery. The patrons gleefully gossip about who's cheating with who. Adultery is an epidemic in this universe.

A manicurist, Letty Lawson (Madge Evans), makes a house call to Mrs. Sherwood (Alice Brady). Mrs. Sherwood is not much of a wife. She lays in bed all day chattering about numerology. Letty gets upset when the woman's ornery Pekingese chews up her hat. Mr. Sherwood (Otto Kruger) feels bad about this and immediately takes her out to buy an expensive new hat. Letty meets Mr. Sherwood again while sheltered under a store awning during a rainstorm. Frightened by the lightning, she falls back into his arms. Feeling this lovely young woman in his arms delights him. This is the beginning of a beautiful relationship. Letty and Sherwood go out together often, but they keep their relationship platonic. She tells her friend Carol (Una Merkel) that they have nothing more than a "pleasant friendship." Sherwood asks his wife for a divorce so that he and Letty can have more than a friendship, but she refuses to grant her consent.

Kerby Anderson of Probe Ministries wrote:

Sex may not be involved in some affairs. The relationship may be merely an emotional liaison. Counselor Bonnie Weil warns that these so-called "affairs of the heart can be even more treacherous than the purely physical kind. Women, particularly, are inclined to leave their husbands when they feel a strong emotional bond with another man."[405]

Una Merkel and Madge Evans in *Beauty for Sale* (1933)

Carol tells Letty that she had a bad experience with a married man and this is a reason that she's become so mercenary. She advises her friend to "run like a rabbit" from a married man. Her friend Jane (Florine McKinney) is abandoned by her mama's boy lover when she gets pregnant. After Jane kills herself by leaping out of her bedroom window, Letty realizes that she is on a fatal course with Sherwood. "I can't do it, " she tells him. "I thought everything over and it's not good enough." She says that she learned an awful lesson from "two girls [who] loved men they couldn't marry." She believes that, without the commitment of marriage, it is easy for a man to get tired of a woman and leave her. "Well," she says, "one of the girls is dead and the other is hard and bitter and unhappy." Although she has strong feelings for Sherwood, Letty is unwilling to continue their relationship. Instead, she reluctantly agrees to marry obnoxious Bill Merrick (Edward J. Nugent). Sherwood is devastated to learn of Letty's impending marriage. Letty decides at the last moment that she cannot go through with the wedding. She begins to hyperventilate outside of the church.

Once she regains her composure, she turns away from the church and races off down the street. Carol and her fiancé, Freddie Gordon (Charley Grapewin), are out house hunting when they learn the Sherwoods' newly constructed country mansion is for sale. It turns out that Mrs. Sherwood left her husband to marry the architect who designed the mansion. Carol passes the news to Letty, who cheerfully rushes off to be reunited with Sherwood.

Christopher Strong (1933)

Christopher Rawlinson (Colin Clive) is introduced to a lovely young aviatrix, Cynthia Darrington (Katherine Hepburn), by his daughter, Monica (Helen Chandler). A friendship begins between Christopher and Cynthia, but it quickly develops into something more. His wife, Lady Elaine (Billie Burke), becomes suspicious of the pair spending so much time together. Cynthia wants Christopher to tell Elaine about them. "I don't want to cheat and lie," she says. But he is worried about hurting his wife. She tells him that he is cautious, which makes him very different than her. She says, "I've wanted so few things in my life. I've never wanted love before, and now it seems right to me to have it at last. But being in love with a reckless person like me wouldn't suit you at all, so I'm going to tell you I'll never see you again and say goodbye tonight."

Chris and Cynthia meet again unexpectedly and can no longer resist their feelings for one another. Cynthia becomes pregnant, but she keeps the pregnancy secret from Christopher because she knows that this would force him to divorce his wife.

Cynthia sets out to break the world altitude record. But she also has a fatal ambition. She writes Christopher a farewell note before her flight. She states in the note: "Courage can conquer even love." Wikipedia reports, "As the plane climbs, flashbacks over the altimeter show her memories"[406] Once she has broken the record, Cynthia takes off her oxygen mask and quickly loses consciousness. The unmanned plane goes into a nosedive and is destroyed in a fiery crash. This is much like the ending of *Dr. Monica* (1934).

The Life of Vergie Winters (1934)

The film follows the "mistress suffers bravely" formula of *Back Street*. The story opens with a funeral procession for John Shadwell. A flashback follows. John (John Boles) and Vergie (Ann Harding) are in love, but Vergie's father Jim Winters (Edward Van Sloan) tells John that Vergie has been seeing another man and has gotten pregnant. He says that it would be best if his daughter marries the father of her child. But Mr. Winters is lying. He's been paid off by a man who wants the affluent John to abandon Vergie and marry his own daughter, Laura (Helen Vinson). John doesn't realize that he has been duped until after he marries Laura. He reunites with Vergie, determined to continue their relationship. The danger of their affair becomes even greater when John campaigns for Congress. Knowing that a scandal would ruin his political career, Vergie breaks off the affair. John is elected to Congress and moves to Washington, D.C. with Laura. Meanwhile, Vergie gives birth to a daughter, Joan. John adopts Joan, pretending that she is the child of a destitute friend. He eventually resumes his affair with Vergie. Gossip about their illicit relationship leads to a boycott of her millinery shop. The story advances several years. Vergie watches her daughter, now a young adult, horseback riding with her fiancé, Ranny Truesdale (Frank Albertson).

Bonita Granville and Ann Harding in *The Life of Vergie Winters* (1934)

John tells Laura that he wants a divorce to marry Vergie. Enraged, Laura follows John to Vergie's home and shoots him. Vergie drops to her knees beside him and sees that he is dead. Vergie refuses to implicate Laura. The police, left to assume that Vergie fired the fatal shot, arrest her. Vergie is convicted of murder and sent to prison. A year later, Laura makes a deathbed confession of the murder. Joan and Ranny secure a pardon for Vergie and welcome her to live in their home.

Harding perfectly conveys Vergie's suffering. This was the only film in which Harding played the other woman. She was the wronged wife in three other adultery films, *The Lady Consents*, *When Ladies Meet* and *Enchanted April*.

To satisfy the Production Code, elements of the original script that justified their affair had to be removed before the film went into production. The film was nonetheless condemned by the Roman Catholic Archdiocese of Chicago as "immoral and indecent."[407]

Chained (1934)

Diane Lovering (Joan Crawford), the mistress of shipping magnate Richard Field, is devastated when she learns that Richard's wife will not grant her husband a divorce. Diane tries to lift her spirits by taking an ocean voyage to South America. She meets Mike Bradley (Clark Gable) on the trip. Diane and Mark fall in love after a short period of bickering. By the time they reach Mike's ranch in Argentina, the couple has agreed to get married. Diane returns to New York to tell Richard, but Richard surprises her with a wedding ring. Richard explains that his wife finally agreed to divorce him if he paid her a large monetary settlement and gave away his right to see his sons. He already signed papers and he can't change his mind. Diane cannot turn down his marriage proposal under the circumstances. She writes a letter to Mike calling off their wedding. She realizes that, if she tells him the truth about her decision, he will not accept it and will come after her. So, she tells him that she has decided to marry Richard for his wealth. A year later, Diane and Mike run into one another at a gun shop. The couple agrees to have dinner together. Mike figures out the situation and resolves to confront Richard. The problem is that Richard turns out to be a good fellow. So, Mike sadly leaves his home. Richard is such a good fellow that he offers to divorce Diane so that she can marry Mike and settle down on his Argentine ranch.

Never has an adultery film featured so many nice people. It may be that the filmmakers were eager to comply with the newly established Code rules.

Anna Sten and Gary Cooper in *The Wedding Night* (1935)

The Wedding Night (1935)

Novelist Tony Barrett (Gary Cooper) find finds himself in a crisis. He has married a woman who enjoys a fast and affluent lifestyle. He describes his life with his wife, Dora (Helen Vinson), in one plain word: "madness." He has become exhausted in this demanding and unfulfilling relationship. At a time that Dora's extravagant lifestyle has gotten him into debt, his publisher has turned down his latest book. He has come to believe that he is washed up as a writer.

Tony and Dora can no longer afford the rent on their apartment, but Tony owns the farm where he was born and raised. The farm, which has gotten run down since his parents died, doesn't appeal to Dora. She insists, "I won't go to that awful place." But they have no choice.

Tony makes money selling off much of his land. With money to spend, Dora heads back to New York, leaving Tony to work on his novel. Manya Novak (Anna Sten), the daughter of farmer Jan Novak (Sig Ruman), helps out at Tony's farm. She visits Tony every day, without fail, to cook and clean for him. Manya, who is loving and full of life, inspires a passion in Tony that he has never felt before. As he spends time in her company, he becomes reinvigorated as a writer and falls deeply in love. Novak can tell that his daughter has feelings for Tony. He forbids her from seeing this man anymore, but she ignores him and continues to visit Tony anyway. A snowstorm prevents Manya from returning home one night. Novak is enraged that his daughter spent the night with Tony and demands that she immediately marry Fredrik (Ralph Bellamy), a young farmer who has long desired to have Manya as his wife.

On her return, Dora reads Tony's manuscript, which details a deeply emotional love affair. She suspects that her husband modeled the affair on his own relationship with Manya, with whom he has become closely attached during her absence. Dora confronts Manya about the novel. She insists that the novel's wife would never give up her husband. She tries a similar roundabout tactic with Tony. She says, "I can help with the ending at least. I may not give you the one you've been looking for, but I know the wisest one." She insists that the husband and wife remain together. "It's the only ending there is, Tony," she says. "They've had too much together." Tony disagrees. He says, "They let each other down. What they had is gone." Dora will not accept this. "I know he thinks it is," she says. "But it can't be over. They'll come to life again."

Manya does go through with the marriage ceremony, but she shows her husband no passion on their wedding night. Enraged, Fredrik storms out of the house to find Tony and take out his frustration on him. Manya chases after him. She tries to stop him from attacking Tony, but he shoves her away and she falls down a flight of stairs. Tony rushes to her and carries her to the couch. He can see that she has been seriously injured. He tells her that he loves her before she dies. Tony is heartbroken. Days later, he is thinking about Manya when he looks out a window and imagines her in ghostly form waving at him.

Break of Hearts (1935)

Constance Dane (Katherine Hepburn), a music composer, marries Franz Roberti (Charles Boyer), a famous orchestra conductor with a reputation for being a womanizer. It shouldn't surprise her when, one night, she catches him having dinner with another woman. Constance divorces Franz and becomes engaged to an old friend, Johnny Lawrence (John Beal). Constance learns from a mutual friend that Franz, in despair over losing her, has been drinking heavily. AFI reports: "Finding him haggard and drunk in a cafe, Constance plays the piano piece she had written as a tribute to their love and inspires him for a moment before he collapses." Constance breaks off her engagement to Johnny to commit herself to restoring Franz to his past glory. The wronged wife is presented as grand and noble for forgiving her philandering husband.

Dodsworth (1936)

Fran Dodsworth (Ruth Chatterton) is mired in a selfish midlife crisis. She has fulfilled her duties as a wife for twenty years. Her husband, Sam Dodsworth (Walter Huston), has had no complaints, having regarded her as ideal in the way that she has run their home. It would have been easy to portray Fran as superficial and silly. But this film is looking for something more profound and more realistic than that.

During her travels through Europe, Fran grows increasingly grotesque in her narcissistic pursuits. Sonya Roberts of IMDb notes, "Increasingly obsessed with maintaining an appearance of youth, she falls in with a crowd of frivolous socialites. . ."[408] Mark Deming of All Movie Guide wrote, "Fran has begun to think of herself as a cosmopolitan sophisticate and thinks of Sam as dull and unadventurous."[409] She says that she is happier in her newfound freedom, but she only seems more desperate and more unnerved. If we fail to temper our worst impulses, we can become something abominable.

Meanwhile, Dodsworth falls in love with a widow, Edith Cortright (Mary Astor). According Roberts, Edith is "everything [Fran] is not: self-assured, self-confident, and able to take care of herself."[410]

Walter Huston and Mary Astor in *Dodsworth* (1936)

After being out drinking and dancing for most of the night, Fran is escorted to her hotel suite by a handsome young nobleman, Kurt von Obersdorf (Gregory Gaye). The couple embraces and kisses in the doorway before Kurt leaves. Dodsworth, who has been awakened hearing his wife come in, sleepily shuffles out of his bedroom. He tells Fran that he wants to talk with her, but she is unwilling to talk. The two end up arguing. Fran accuses Dodsworth of spying on her. She tells him:

> Well, I love Kurt, and Kurt loves me and I'm going to marry him. He asked me tonight. I decided it just now this minute when I found you here hiding behind doors. The Great Dodsworth. Great prowling elephant. You can't play the injured innocent with me! You've never known me, you've never known anything about me. Not what I had on or what I thought or the sacrifices I've made. . . I'll be happy with Kurt. I'm fighting for life! You can't drag me back!

Fran intends to marry Kurt, but Kurt's mother will not give her consent for the marriage. Fran, now on her own, seeks a reconciliation with Dodsworth. Dodsworth feels sorry for her and agrees to travel back to the United States with her. But Fran does not recognize the sacrifice that her husband is making for her. She is mostly concerned with preserving her own dignity. She says, "After all, as I look back, I don't blame myself.

I can't, really. You know, you were a good deal at fault, too." The camera cuts to a close-up of Dodsworth. He's glaring at his wife, disgusted by what she has just said. She is not truly repentant at all. She really wants him to shoulder the blame for her cheating and look upon the experience as a happy life lesson. This is a road too far to travel for him. He decides at this moment that he longer wants to waste another moment with her. He rises from the table. He announces loudly and clearly, "I'm not sailing with you. . . No use trying to put it tactfully. You and I can't make a go of things any longer." She is flabbergasted. Words sputter out her mouth. "You haven't learned a thing," she shouts. "you haven't learned a single thing from all our sorrows, and I flattered myself you really wanted to come back to me. I tried, didn't I? I might've known you'd be just the same. I did know it, yet I gave you another chance." He replies, "I'm not takin' another chance, because I'm through, finished. And that's flat." He joyfully returns to Edith.

ZaZa (1938)

A cabaret singer, Zaza (Claudette Colbert), falls in love with a wealthy patron, Dufresne (Herbert Marshall). Zaza ends her career to run off with Dufresne, but she learns to her chagrin that her lover is married. She goes to Paris to confront Dufresne's wife and demand that she consent to a divorce. But, before she can see the wife, she meets Dufresne's young daughter, Toto (Ann E. Todd). The little girl's cuteness proves to be more powerful than the grand love that she feels for Dufresne. She later tells a friend that the wife is not the issue. She says, "I can fight against *her*, but not the child. Not *that* child." She makes a widely heralded return to the stage, where she sings a farewell song to Dufresne.

Intermezzo (1939)

A concert violinist, Holger Brandt (Leslie Howard), is so enchanted by his daughter's brilliant and beautiful piano teacher, Anita Hoffman (Ingrid Bergman), that he leaves his wife Margit (Edna Best) to be with her. But, after a time, Holger greatly misses his children.

He goes to visit his daughter, Ann Marie (Ann E. Todd). Excited to see him, she rushes across the street towards him and steps out in front of a moving car. At the hospital, Holger learns that his daughter will recover, but he feels guilty that he hasn't been looking after his family. Margit forgives him and tells him that he can come home. He accepts her offer, putting an end to the affair.

IMDb reviewer ccthemovieman-1 wrote:

> There IS a good message here: that a married person having a fling with a pretty young woman might be an exciting prospect but in the end, "you reap what you sow" and if either of the two parties has a conscience, the illicit romance will be doomed, especially if there are kids involved.[411]

Now, Voyager (1942)

IMDb: "A frumpy spinster blossoms under therapy and becomes an elegant, independent woman."[412]

Charlotte Vale (Bette Davis) is treated at a sanitarium for anxiety and depression. Upon her release, her psychiatrist Dr. Jaquith (Claude Rains) encourages her to go on a cruise. In the novel, Dr. Jaquith tells her:

Paul Henreid and Bette Davis in *Now, Voyager* (1942)

We've taught you the proper technique. Now go ahead and practice it on the cruise. Respond! Take part! Contribute! Be interested in everything and everybody. Forget you're a hidebound New Englander and unbend. Loosen up. Be nice to every human being who crosses your path.[413]

Charlotte, though normally shy, enjoys a romantic adventure with debonair Jerry Duvaux (Paul Henreid) during a cruise to Rio de Janeiro. Jerry admits to being in an unhappy marriage, which he keeps together for the sake of his young daughter Tina. Tina is a hopelessly despondent child. Jerry shows Charlotte a photo of her. He explains that he couldn't get her to smile. "She's convinced she's an ugly duckling," he says. Jerry's friend, Deb McIntyre (Lee Patrick), later tells Charlotte that Jerry's wife Isobel is jealous of Tina. He says, "[She's] the child she never wanted. Did you know that before Tina was born, Isobel actually went to a doctor and tried to get him to say her health wouldn't permit her to have a child." At the end of the cruise, Charlotte and Jerry end their relationship so that Jerry can continue to look after Tina.

Once home, Charlotte clashes with her tyrannical mother to maintain the independence that she achieved during her time away. The stress brought about by their conflict is taxing for both of them. Charlotte blames herself when her mother suffers a fatal heart attack. She reenters the sanitarium to cope with her guilt. Here, she meets a troubled young girl, who turns out to be Jerry's daughter Tina (Janis Wilson). The girl's admission was arranged by her father, who remembered Charlotte speaking of the helpful treatment that she received under Dr. Jaquith's care. Charlotte and Tina become close and, eventually, Dr. Jaquith allows Charlotte to take Tina to live with her. But the doctor has a strict condition: Charlotte and Jerry cannot resume their affair, which could create problems for the child.

Charlotte finds happiness and fulfillment as Tina's guardian. She tells Jerry, "When Tina said she wanted to stay with me, it was like a miracle happening. Like having your child. A part of you. I even allowed myself to indulge in the fantasy that both of us loving her, doing what was best for her together, would make her seem like our child after a while." Jerry questions if Charlotte can remain happy under this arrangement. Charlotte replies, "Oh, Jerry, don't let's ask for the moon. We have the stars."

Past films, including *Forbidden*, *The Life of Vergie Winters*, *Dr. Monica* and *Give Me Your Heart*, involved a wife caring for the child of her husband's mistress. This time, the mistress cares for the wife's child. We never get to meet Isobel. She remains a scary beast lurking in the shadows.

Celia Johnson and Trevor Howard in *Brief Encounter* (1945)

Brief Encounter (1945)

The film is based on Noël Coward's 1936 play "Still Life." Emma Rice directed a London stage revival of "Still Life" in 2018. She wrote, "In 'Still Life'. . . Noël Coward wrote a play about an affair. Not a sordid affair but a love affair between two married people. An impossible affair, a painful affair, an unacceptable affair. It is written with such empathy, such observation and such tender agony."[414]

It is not a love-at-first-sight story for Laura Jesson (Celia Johnson) and Alec Harvey (Trevor Howard). The couple first meets inside a cafe at the train station. Alec removes a bit of grit from Laura's eye. Laura thinks that Alec has a "nice face" and promptly forgets him. But they have other encounters. Alec comes into a restaurant for lunch and cannot find a seat. He asks Laura if she would mind him joining her at her table. She agrees. The couple enjoys having lunch together. They talk a lot. They laugh a lot. Laura says in a voice-over, "It seemed so natural and innocent." He takes a liking to her, complimenting her for being "sane and uncomplicated."

Laura has not had sex with Alec. Surely, she thinks, their time together has been harmless. Surely, she has not been cheating on her husband. But she knows that this is not true. She says in her voice-over:

Celia Johnson and Trevor Howard in *Brief Encounter* (1945)

I imagined him. . . letting himself into his house with his latchkey. His wife - Madeleine - would probably be in the hall to meet him. Or perhaps upstairs in her room. . . I wondered if he'd say, "I met such a nice woman at the Kardomah. We had lunch and went to the pictures." Then suddenly, I knew that he wouldn't. I knew beyond a shadow of doubt that he wouldn't say a word. At that moment, the first awful feeling of danger swept over me. . . I wanted to get home as quickly as possible. I looked hurriedly round the carriage to see if anyone was looking at me. . . as if they could read my secret thoughts. No one was, except a clergyman in the opposite corner. I felt myself blushing and opened my library book and pretended to read. By the time I'd got to Ketchworth, I'd made up my mind definitely that I wasn't going to see Alec anymore.

In the play, Alec dismisses Laura's misgivings. He says, "We haven't done anything wrong. An accidental meeting - then another accidental meeting - then a little lunch - then the movies - what could be more ordinary?"

In the film, as in the play, Laura engages in an emotional struggle.

Laura: No, please, we must be sensible. Please help me to be sensible. We mustn't behave like this. We must forget that we've said what we've said.

Alec: Not yet, not quite yet.

Laura: But we must. Don't you see?

Alec: Listen, it's too late now to be as sensible as all that. It's too late to forget what we've said. . . I love you. You love me too. It's no use pretending it hasn't happened, because it has.

Laura: Yes, it has. I don't want to pretend anything either to you or to anyone else. . . but from now on, I shall have to. That's what's wrong, don't you see? That's what spoils everything. That's why we must stop here and not talk like this. We're neither of us free to love each other. There's too much in the way. There's still time if we control ourselves and behave like sensible human beings. There's still time.

A turning point occurs when Alex's friend Steven goes out of town on business. Alec agrees to park his friend Steven's car in a garage and then bring the key back to the friend's flat. He asks Laura to come along with him to the flat. She refuses the invitation, obviously fearful of what this could lead to, and returns to the train station. But, just as she steps onto her train, she changes her mind and gets off. She anxiously hurries to the flat. Alec gladly lets her inside and they sit together on a sofa. Alec grabs her and kisses her, but she insists that she can't stay. Just then, Steven (Valentine Dyall) arrives home early, causing Laura to leap up and run off down a back staircase. Steven finds a scarf that Laura left behind. He admits to having heard "undignified scuffling" as he came in. He is snide and sarcastic with Alec. He admits that he is disappointed with his old friend. Lean said:

> The Valentine Dyall character is not sympathetic at all. That flat is really a hostile place, uncosy, unwelcoming. It's all to do with guilt. If the flat had been different, it would have taken away a whole colour. I don't think the audience should have thought, "Well, come on. Now you're alone." They're not alone. Laura's husband is there as far as she's concerned. And guilt is all over the place.[415]

Meanwhile, Laura runs in the rain, not sure of where she's going. She says in voice-over, "I was so utterly humiliated and defeated and so dreadfully, dreadfully ashamed." Alec finds her highly agitated when he catches up to her. She is tired of the lying and sneaking around. She says, "It's awfully easy to lie when you know that you're trusted implicitly - so very easy and so very degrading." But Alec doesn't agree.

Alec: We know we love each other. That's all that really matters.

Laura: It's not all that really matters. Other things matter too, self-respect matters, and decency. I can't go on any longer.

Alec: Could you really say goodbye, never see me again?

Laura: Yes, if you'd help me.

Alec: I love you, Laura. I shall love you always until the end of my life. I can't look at you now because I know something. I know that this is the beginning of the end - not the end of my loving you, but the end of our being together.

Laura: But not quite yet, darling. Please, not quite yet.

Alec: Very well. Not quite yet. I know what you feel about this evening - I mean about the sordidness of it. I know about the strain of our different lives, our lives apart from each other. The feeling of guilt, doing wrong is too strong, isn't it? Too great a price to pay for the happiness we have together.

The film has a boat scene similar to a scene in *Cynara*. Kelly wrote, "In *Brief Encounter*, . . . Laura and Alec go boating, but he turns out to be a poor oarsman and they get caught up with the bridge fencing, at which point Alec is obliged to suffer the indignity of stepping out of the boat into the shallow water to redirect it."[416]

Celia Johnson in *Brief Encounter* (1945)

It is interesting to see how their relationship develops. There is a great deal of misery in the sensitive adultery film. The characters in these films often spend the first half of the film rising to great ecstasy. But then everything changes. The characters must spend the second half of the film plummeting to the greatest of despair. This happens very clearly in *Brief Encounter*. Laura repeatedly speaks of being happy. She says, "I felt gay and happy and sort of released." She says that she feels "perfectly happy" and never wants this relationship to end. She says, "I should have been utterly wretched and ashamed. I know I should, but I wasn't. I felt suddenly quite wildly happy. . . like a romantic schoolgirl, like a romantic fool." She later notes in hindsight, "I was happy then." For, recently, her feelings have changed. Alec asks her at one point if she's happy. She replies, "Happy? No, not really." She reaches the point that she wants to die. She says, "I had no thoughts at all. Only an overwhelming desire not to feel anything ever again. Not to be unhappy anymore." In the final moments of the film, when the affair is over and done with, she sobs uncontrollably. She nearly jumps in front of a train to kill herself. Kelly wrote, "It all adds up to a state of wretchedness. . ."[417]

The play opens with Laura saying:

I'm a happily married woman. Or rather I was until a few weeks ago. This is my whole world and it's enough, or rather it was until a few weeks ago. Your heart dances. The world seems strange and new. You want to laugh and skip and fall forever. You are in love. You are in love with the wrong person.

The same happens in *The English Patient*.

Almásy: When were you most happy?

Katharine: Now.

Almásy: And when were you least happy?

Katharine: Now.

Almásy: What do you love?

She says that she loves water, fish, hedgehogs, baths. . . and her husband.

Almásy: And what do you hate most?

Katharine: A lie.

Brief Encounter ends like the play did. Wikipedia notes of the play:

Alec and Laura enter. He is leaving to take up his new post in South Africa, and she has come to see him off. They are prevented from having the passionate farewell they both yearn for when Dolly, a talkative friend of hers intrudes into their last moments together, and their final goodbye is cruelly limited to a formal handshake. He leaves, and Laura remains, while Dolly talks on. Suddenly, as the sound of the approaching express train is heard, Laura suddenly rushes out to the platform. She returns "looking very white and shaky." Dolly persuades Myrtle to pour some brandy for Laura, who sips it. The sound of their train is heard, and Dolly gathers up her parcels as the curtain falls.[418]

Celia Johnson and Trevor Howard in *Brief Encounter* (1945)

A television remake was produced in 1974 with Sophia Loren as Laura and Richard Burton as Alec. Brian McFarlane, professor at the Swinburne University of Technology, wrote:

There may be other films more disastrously conceived and executed than this, but they don't come readily to mind. . . If you want to make a touching drama about love and renunciation in a quiet English setting, you'd perhaps think twice about casting as the leads an international sex symbol and a noted lothario: "gloriously miscast" as they were described in the obituary of Rosemary Leach who had a supporting role in the telefilm.[419]

Burton's Alec is less oblique about his motive for getting Laura up to his friend's flat. He sees it as a perfect opportunity for them to express their love in more than a platonic way. Loren's Laura is outraged when Alec's friend Steven arrives home suddenly and catches them about to have sex. She later tells Alec, "It all seemed so innocent to start with. Meeting by the cathedral, having lunch. It was so innocent, it couldn't be dirty or furtive. It was like a dream of love. We know the reality now. It is degrading."

Other illicit train station couplings occurred in films as varied as *Anna Karenina* (1948) and *A Cuckoo in the Nest* (1954). But *Brief Encounter* began a new genre of film.

Another forbidden romance begins on a commuter train in *Say Hello to Yesterday* (1971). A middle-aged housewife (Jean Simmons) lives with stockbroker husband and two small children. Little is revealed about her home life. She is obviously angry with her husband when she leaves her home for the day. But the reason for the disagreement is not divulged. Was it serious? Did it matter? She is traveling by train to London to shop when she meets a young man (Leonard Whiting). Instantly, the young man is attracted to her and engages in a dogged effort to seduce her. She succumbs to his charms and agrees to spend the day with him. The couple climbs monkey bars in a park, they visit a planetarium, and they stroll through London. At the end of the day, they get a hotel room and have sex. Afterward, he suggests that they meet for sex every other Thursday. But she just wants this to be a one-night stand. She tells him, "I've made my choice. You pays your money and you lives in Cobham." This makes him angry. He tells her, "Every time that old man in Cobham touches you, you'll remember today. You will think of me and you will long for me." She glares at him, offended by him insulting her husband. She replies, "George is better in bed than you will ever be." He regrets becoming angry and sees off his lovely companion at the train station. Our heroine is no Laura. Extramarital sex is a lark to her.

Imagine if *Brief Encounter*'s Laura was a femme fatale. That is the idea proposed by *Derailed* (2005). Charles Schine (Clive Owen), an advertising executive, works hard to support his wife Deanna (Melissa George) and his teenage daughter, Amy (Addison Timlin). He could use a bit of stress relief. One morning, while riding a commuter train to the office, he become friendly with Lucinda Harris (Jennifer Aniston). Except the lady is not who she says she is. She is working with her boyfriend, Philippe LaRoche (Vincent Cassel), to lure Charles into a blackmail scheme. The couple goes to a motel for sex. But they have barely gotten started when LaRoche, in the guise of a robber, breaks into the room and attacks Charles. LaRoche, who is brandishing a gun, has a major advantage. Once Charles is subdued, LaRoche pretends to rape Lucinda. LaRoche tells Charles, "You upper-crust motherfucker. Huh? You got it all, and yet you're ready to fuck it up for just a bit of pussy?" It is a question that should be posed to many protagonists of adultery films. Lucinda insists that they keep quiet about the attack so that their spouses don't learn about their dalliance. It doesn't matter to her that they never had sex. She says, "Because we didn't fuck doesn't mean we didn't cross the line. We went to the hotel. We started to do it. And we didn't stop out of the conscience of our hearts." They agree to never see each other again. Soon, though, Charles is contacted by LaRoche, who demands $100,000 not to go to Charles' wife Deanna (Melissa George) about his infidelity. He pays the money, but LaRoche contacts him again for even more money. Charles confides in an ex-convict friend, Winston Boyko (RZA). Winston is confident that he can scare off LaRoche. But LaRoche murders Winston. Charles realizes that LaRoche could murder him just as easily. He needs to fight back with cleverness and brutality if he wants to survive. The film is, in the end, an empty and lurid thriller.

The Fallen Idol (1948)

The idol of the film is Baines (Ralph Richardson), the kind-hearted butler to a diplomat. The diplomat's son Philippe (Bobby Henrey) adores Baines, who amuses him by making up stories that depict himself as a daring lion hunter in Africa. Baines has a unhappy relationship with his mean-spirited, domineering wife, Mrs. Baines (Sonia Dresdel).

One morning, Philippe trails after Baines and discovers him at a tea shop with a young woman, Julie (Michèle Morgan). Julie is his mistress, but Baines introduces her to the boy as his niece. It is an awkward scene. Julie has met with Baines today to break off their relationship. She doesn't believe that he will ever leave his wife and has decided to avoid further suffering by moving away. This is a difficult topic to discuss, but it is especially difficult as the couple has to whisper and speak in code to conceal their heartbreaking situation from the boy. Despite their nervousness over Philippe's presence, Philippe clearly finds Baines' pastry more interesting than his mistress. It becomes obvious in the scene that Julie and Baines' relationship is tender and loving but terribly anguished.

Later, Philippe sees Baines tussling with his wife near a staircase, but he flees outside before the argument reaches a conclusion. When he learns that Mrs. Baines died from falling down the staircase, he assumes that Baines pushed her. He figures to lie to the police to protect Baines, but his nervous and inconsistent lies only serve to throw suspicion on Baines.

Richardson is as achingly sympathetic as Laughton was in *The Suspect*. The film's one flaw is Henrey, who comes across as somewhat obnoxious.

No Sad Songs for Me (1950)

Brad Scott (Wendell Corey) expresses great shame as he confesses to his wife, Mary (Margaret Sullavan), that he had an affair with his assistant, Chris Radna (Viveca Lindfors). He says:

> I don't know how it started. I suppose being with her most of the time, getting to depend on her, you get involved without knowing how. First, you tell yourself, 'Nothing's changed.' Tell yourself that ten times a day. But, deep down in your heart, you know that you're walking a tightrope. Either you get off the tightrope or fall off. So, tonight, we talked it over and decided to call it quits. She's going away.

But Mary reveals to Brad that she is dying. She wants Brad and Chris to be together when she's gone.

Perfect Strangers (1950)

David Campbell (Dennis Morgan) and Terry Scott (Ginger Rogers) embark on a romance while the two are serving together on a jury. For David, who is married and has two kids, this is a perilous situation. The immorality of adultery is a pressing issue as the trial involves an unfaithful man accused of murdering his wife.

One of the other jurors, Arthur Timkin (Howard Freeman), catches David and Terry having a clandestine meeting on a hotel rooftop. He later confronts them in the jury room about their relationship. Terry, though embarrassed, responds frankly:

> I didn't set out to steal another woman's husband. That's something you think you'll never do. But then when you find out, that's what you've done and you admit to yourself that you're the other woman. Then you realize that all your happy moments kind of belong to somebody else. And soon you don't

have any more happy moments. I did fall in love with him just as you suspected. It happened. It didn't ask us whether we were married or not. It just hit. I love him.

The other jurors admire Terry for her honesty and tell Timkin to mind his own business.

Dennis Morgan and Ginger Rogers in *Perfect Strangers* (1950)

Once the trial is over, Terry is doubtful that they can continue their relationship.

Terry: David, you know, I can be just as selfish as anybody. I want you to take me away with you right now. . . But then I start thinking of your wife and your children. They love you. I don't want them to hate us as much as they'd have a right to.

David: You're not selfish. If you were, I probably wouldn't feel the way I do. What about me? Can I go home now and say what an interesting experience [I had] and close the door on it just like that and forget it?

In the end, Terry and David agree that pursuing their affair would make them bad people. To assure they stay apart, Terry makes the decision to move to another state.

Young Man with Ideas (1952)

Max Webster (Glenn Ford), a young lawyer struggling to build a practice in Montana, is convinced by his wife Julie (Ruth Roman) to pursue more lucrative career opportunities in Los Angeles. The couple and their daughter Caroline (Donna Corcoran) struggle financially as Max prepares for the California bar exam. The stress of the situation puts Max and Julie at odds. Max comes to believe that Julie has lost faith in him and develops feelings for a beautiful and caring study partner, Joyce Laramie (Nina Foch). Joyce finds Max to be ideal in many ways. One night, she dresses in a slinky off-shoulder dress in hope of arousing his interest. But the couple, whose thoughts are preoccupied by age-old legal principles, is too high-minded to let their feelings go beyond a single kiss.

The End of the Affair (1955)

The film is based on a 1951 autobiographical novel by British author Graham Greene.
The story begins with a voice-over from Maurice Bendrix (Van Johnson):

It began in London during the war. I had been wounded and discharged out of the Army. But I stayed on in London, for I was a writer, and had become interested in another group fighting the battle for England's survival, the men on the home front, the civil servants. A week earlier I had been introduced to one of these, Henry Miles, and he had asked me to a sherry party he and his wife were giving.

Van Johnson and Deborah Kerr in *The End of the Affair* (1955)

Maurice is excited to make the acquaintance of Henry's delightful wife, Sarah Miles (Deborah Kerr). Maurice and Sarah embark on an affair. The couple is getting cozy together at his apartment when an air raid occurs. A bomb decimates the building. The two survive the bombing, although they are understandably shaken. Afterward, Sarah abruptly breaks up with Maurice. She offers no explanation. Maurice is devastated by what he sees as a betrayal.

After the war, Maurice runs into Henry (Peter Cushing), who takes him back to his home for a drink. Henry confides in Maurice that Sarah has been sneaking off much of the time and he believes that she is having an affair. By the next morning, Maurice is overwhelmed with jealousy. He hires a private investigator,

Albert Parkis (John Mills), to follow Sarah. Parkis poses as a guest at another of the Miles' sherry parties and steals Sarah's diary from her bedroom. The diary reveals that, following the bombing of Maurice's apartment building, Sarah found Maurice lying lifelessly underneath a heavy door that collapsed on him. She got down on her knees and prayed. She wrote out her prayer in the diary:

> I love him, I'll do anything, only just let him be alive. I'll never quarrel with him again or make him unhappy. I'll be sweet and kind and good. I will be good. I'll live as you would want me to live. I'll give Maurice up forever, only just let him be alive! Just let him be alive!

She suddenly heard Maurice calling out her name. He had somehow regained consciousness and crawled out from beneath the door. It seemed like a miracle. She was willing to keep her word to God and, as much as it broke her heart, gave up Maurice. It turns out that, during her mysterious absences, Sarah has been spending time helping out at a church.

Sarah remains with Henry in the end. Henry is impotent in the source novel, but this plot point was left out of the film. Cushing's portrayal of Henry makes the character more interesting and sympathetic than he is in the novel. It is Sarah's sad fate in the original story to die from a lung infection.

A man is turned away from an affair by his Catholic faith in *The Heart of the Matter* (1953), which is also based on a Graham Greene story.

Deborah Kerr in The End of the Affair (1955)

Room at The Top (1959)

Joe Lampton (Laurence Harvey), an ambitious young accountant, seeks to advance up the corporate ladder by pursuing Susan Brown (Heather Sears), the daughter of a wealthy mill owner. Susan's father, Abe (Donald Wolfit), hopes to end his daughter's budding romance with this social climber by sending her abroad. Joe meanwhile embarks on a relationship with a moody and older married woman, Alice Aisgill (Simone Signoret). Alice is terribly unhappy in her marriage. Her husband, George (Allan Cuthbertson), is a cruel and arrogant man who is having an affair with his secretary. Joe and Alice's relationship becomes tempestuous. After an argument, Joe leaves Alice and returns to Susan. But he misses Alice and reunites with her for a romantic getaway. The two plan to marry, but George is unwilling to let Alice divorce him. Mr. Brown visits Joe to let him know that Susan is pregnant. He tells Joe that, if he leaves Alice and marries his daughter, he can have a high-paying job at his mill. Joe sees his relationship with Alice as hopeless and understands that he has an obligation to Susan. So, he accepts Mr. Brown's proposal. Upon hearing the news, Alice gets drunk and drives her car off a cliff. Joe is grief-stricken to learn of Alice's death. His wedding day should be a happy day for him. After all, he now has the wealth and status that he always wanted. But Alice remains on his mind throughout the day. While he and Susan drive away from the church, Susan notices that he is crying and assumes that he is being sentimental about their wedding.

The Facts of Life (1960)

The film opens with a voice-over from Kitty Weaver (Lucille Ball), who we see sitting in an airport lounge.

> Am I really doing this? Me? Kitty Weaver? Pasadena housewife? Secretary of the PTA, den mother of the Cub Scouts? Have I really come to Monterey to spend the weekend with my best friend's husband?

Three couples arrange a six-day vacation together in Acapulco to cut down on expenses. Larry Gilbert (Bob Hope) is unhappy about it. He asks his wife why they can't go on vacation alone. "Why is it always the six of us?" he complains, "I want a vacation, not group therapy." A series of contrivances (a sick child, a business emergency, a double header of Montezuma's revenge) winnows the half dozen in the group down two: Larry and Kitty. The situation leaves them alone to enjoy various tourist activities, including fishing, boating, swimming, picnicking, and shopping. It suddenly becomes a romantic holiday for a couple who, like a pair of honeymooners, are excited to establish new bonds. Fate has brought them alone together for a back-door honeymoon. In an adultery film, a couple can be thrown together with far less effort. Nothing as elaborate as intestinal bacteria or feverish children is required to set the plot into motion.
Kitty says in voice-over:

> Both Jack and Mary called to say they couldn't get down at all. Poor Doc and Connie remained under the weather, and Larry and I were left alone. Alone to be in love, comfortably, wonderfully, happily in love, and loving every moment of it. We were relaxed and easy with each other. I read, he painted and even occasionally wanted my critical judgment. We swam and had wonderful picnic lunches on the beach and we talked endlessly about everything, even the problems of raising children.

The affair doesn't end after Acapulco. Kitty says in voice-over:

> If we could have just said goodbye, and never seen each other again, it might have been easy. But no, no such luck. Not for us. Weekly bridge games at each other's homes. Winter concerts at the Phil-

harmonic. Season tickets to the Rams. Weeks of being constantly thrown together, and never being given a chance to forget.

The affair is resumed at a Saturday night dance at their club. Larry and Kitty dance together and their feelings for one another come flooding back. They no longer want to keep away from each other. But every effort they make to enjoy a romantic get-together goes wrong.

A strong and faithful marriage brings order, stability and dignity to the home. The affair has torn away everything that has protected them. The image of the couple hunkered down miserably inside a cabin under a leaky roof symbolizes the perilous situation that these homewreckers have placed themselves into.

Lucille Ball and Bob Hope in *The Facts of Life* (1960)

Basinger wrote:

[T]he answer to the question "Am I really an adulteress?" will be the usual "Yes, but not really". . . It, too, is an "almost adultery" story about settled people who accidentally, against all expectations and intentions, end up falling in love with each other. . . They look and act like what they are: two no-longer-young people who are lonely and a bit sad, and who begin to find another human who's interested in what they have to say, who will pay attention to them, who'll appreciate their special qualities. . . [The film] ultimately resolv[es] itself with a no-harm-done coda. . . Audiences liked infidelity stories that came close, but didn't deliver.[420]

Erickson wrote: "Though the affair is never consummated, Hope and Ball are prepared to run off together, but in the end they decide that adultery at their age just isn't worth the trouble."[421]

The Lady with the Dog (1960)

The original Russian title: *Dama s sobachkoy*

   Dmitri Dmitritch Gurov (Aleksey Batalov), an unhappily married banker, is vacationing alone at a seaside resort when he sees a fascinating young woman walking her Pomeranian along the beach. He talks to the woman, named Anna Sergeyevna (Iya Savvina). She tells him that her husband has been delayed in joining her due to medical treatment that he's receiving for his eyes.

   Dmitri does not generally take women seriously. Not his wife. Not his many mistresses. But Anna is different. Anna and Dmitri soon engage in an affair.

   Kamlesh Tripathi wrote on her blog: "The story beautifully captures the quiet desperation of the two protagonists, their dissatisfaction with their meaningless lives and loveless marriages, and their craving for something better. Their deep love for each other fills that void and radically transforms their outlook on life."[422]

   Robert Fulford, a Canadian journalist, offers a similar interpretation of the story: "Under the pressure of love, Gurov looks inside himself and sees someone he has not known before, someone capable of feelings that he barely knew existed."[423] Love causes a person to see the world differently and see themselves differently.

   Anna's notions about love are similar to the notions about love that Tessa expresses in *The Constant Nymph*. She says, "It has always seemed to me that we didn't just meet in Yalta by chance. It is just that we've found each other after a long parting. . . We're like two migrating birds, male and female, who had been caught and forced to live in separate cages. And they're going to die of grief."

   She desperately wants out of her cage. She says, "What are we to do? What are we to do to get rid of the necessity of pretending, telling lies, hiding, living in different cities, not seeing one another for so long? How are we to free ourselves from our intolerable chains? How?"

   The film ends without Anna and Dmitri having found answers to these questions.

All the Right Noises (1970)

   Tom Bell (Len Lewin), a theatre lighting technician, is happily married with two small children. Yet, he has an affair with a teenage actress, Val (Olivia Hussey). This is an adultery story that bypasses the usual drama. The film presents a conflict-free adultery story. Bell's marriage is without problems. He mentions at one point that his wife Joy (Judy Carne) is sometimes too busy to spend time with him, but this doesn't seem to be a serious issue. Vera accepts at the start that their relationship can only be temporary. She makes no unreasonable demands on Bell. Joy never finds out about Val. The man loves his wife, he loves his children, and he loves his girlfriend. He is careful not to hurt anyone. At one point, Val thinks that she might be pregnant. But they figure that she needs to see a doctor and they shouldn't worry about it in the meantime. She sees a doctor, she isn't pregnant, and all is well in the world. In the final moments of the film, Joy sees her daughter playing with a hair band that Vera left behind during a visit. Does she now suspect that another woman was in her home? Will she confront her husband? Will will finally see conflict and drama? No, she shrugs and the film ends. The film has a natural quality. The characters are likable. So, despite its lack of drama, the film is engaging and strangely endearing.

The hopeless sad sack at the center of *Autumn Marathon*, a 1979 Russian drama, is far different from the easygoing Tom Bell. Let us look at the plot. Andrey Buzykin (Oleg Basilashvili), a married schoolteacher, has an affair with Alla Yermakova (Marina Neyolova). The affair is already underway when the film starts. Alla's Uncle Kolya (Nikolai Kryuchkov) tells Andrey that he must make a commitment to his niece, regardless of how difficult it might be to leave his wife Nina (Natalya Gundareva). A mutual friend, Varvara Nikitichna (Galina Volchek), knows Andrey's wife. She tells Alla that Andrey has a strong marriage and he will never leave his wife. This greatly upsets her. Alla is proud of the stylish coat that she made for Andrey. But he has to explain to her that it would be best for him to leave the coat with her. How would he explain the coat to his wife? Alla is hurt. This little sort of problem must be common in their relationship. He has to keep a strict schedule to satisfy his responsibilities to his wife, his mistress, and his work. So, he is always setting an alarm on his watch. Alla becomes upset whenever the alarm goes off and eventually demands that he get rid of the watch. Nina has become suspicious because Alla sometimes calls their home and quickly hangs up if Nina answers. This once happens while the couple is entertaining a dinner guest, Bill Hansen (Norbert Kuchinke). Bill, who is engrossed in talking about his efforts to translate Dostoyevsky, is amusingly oblivious to the seething conflict between his hosts. Andrey is a harried man who never appears happy in his double life. His desperate efforts to satisfy Nina and Alla drain the life out of him and, in the end, satisfy no one. He is a broken man by the time he finally ends the affair.

A Touch of Class (1973)

Melvin Frank, who directed and co-wrote *The Facts of Life*, returned to the subject of adultery with *A Touch of Class*.

Steve Blackburn (George Segal), a married insurance executive, meets Vicki Allessio (Glenda Jackson), a divorced fashion designer, while playing baseball with his friends in London's Hyde Park. It isn't a pleasant meeting as Steve tramples Vickie's young son while racing to catch a fly ball. The two meet again when they agree to share a cab to get out of the rain. Steve casually informs Vickie that he is married, but he is ready and eager to have meaningless sex with her. He is even more shameless in his sleaziness than George Brent was in *The Rich Are Always with Us*. But he doesn't see himself as a sleaze. He is simply, in his view, a "sweet sex-crazed typical American."

The problem is that breezy immorality is not always conducive to something as complicated as an affair. Adultery, especially adultery in films, can require care and cleverness to assure that both parties enjoy the experience and the spouse or spouses never find out. Like in *The Facts of Life,* many comic obstacles fall into the couple's path on their way to their top-secret sex romp. Erickson wrote, ". . . [N]othing, absolutely nothing, goes as planned."[424]

Steve succeeds as planned in bringing Vicki to a "discreet, out of the way hotel," but the shabbiness of the hotel causes Vicki to quickly lose interest. She tells him:

> In the past two days, you have picked me up in the rain, given me tea, bought me lunch, and lured me to this hideaway with the intention of getting me into bed for what you Americans so charmingly call a quickie. Well, I'll be honest with you, I'm a divorced woman, I'm under a lot of strain, I am not sleeping too well, and I could do with some good healthy uninvolved sex with someone who loves his wife

and isn't going to be a pain in the ass when it's over. But not in this overworked little joy station where the sheets haven't been changed in a week. If you would like to arrange a nice weekend somewhere, away from London, preferably in the sun and where the sheets are changed every day, please do.

So, Vicki is as agreeable to meaningless sex as Steve is. But the meaningless sex must have a touch of class.

Steve arranges to take Vicki away to Marbella, Spain. But, when he tells his wife Gloria (Hildegard Neil) that he's going to Spain on business, she insists on coming along with him. He convinces her that it isn't a good idea to leave the kids, but her solution to the problem is to bring the kids to Spain with them. It takes a great deal of farcical maneuvering to get Steve out of this predicament. Frank makes sure that the audience doesn't care about wifey Gloria by making the character more stone-faced than Buster Keaton. There's so little substance to Mrs. Blackburn that the actress playing the character could have easily been substituted with a cardboard cut-out. The ticket counter agent at the airport is given more of a personality.

An airport scene in which an old friend suddenly shows up and interferes with the couple's flight plans is lifted nearly intact from *The Facts of Life*.

Steve and Vicki bicker a lot when they arrive in Spain. Steve is sensitive and Vicki is fussy. Neither trait is suited to a couple engaging in the fine art of casual sex. The pair cannot even agree on who should lie on which side of the bed. Vicki comes to find Steve's sensitivity intolerable. She says, "I've never known a grown man whose feelings could be hurt so easily." She is also irritated by his need to appease his male ego. "This isn't a romantic holiday," she says. "It's a proving ground." He reaches a boiling point with her criticisms. He tells her, "Boy, I've had a bellyful of your chickenshit innuendos, your snotty insults, and your smartass needling." But, somehow, their anger builds up into some much needed passion. The getaway surprisingly turns out to be ideal.

On their return to London, the couple rents an apartment near both their homes and meet there whenever they can. One time, Steve is on his way out the door to meet Vicki when his wife insists that he walk their dog Dilly. He has no choice but to transport his little pal to his love nest. But he ends up rushing off after sex without remembering to take Dilly with him. It creates an awkward situation when he arrives home dogless.

The first half of the film is witty, clever and funny. The second half is mostly sentimental, maybe at times sappy. The witty dialogue is abruptly replaced by tears. The gags are replaced by apologies. A common complaint is that the film fails to blend its comedy and pathos well.

Steve and Vicki cry together watching *Brief Encounter*. Are these the same two people we met at the beginning of the film? IMDb's dglink wrote, ". . . [T]he scene further dampens the film and pushes the characters into a soul-searching phase that leads to the inevitable [sullen] fadeout."[425]

Vicki resembles a kept woman in the way she cleans and decorates the couple's hideaway, cooks meals for their assignations, and spends a great deal of time waiting for Steve to show up. So, does this film fall into the kept woman category? Steve and Vicki fall into an upper-income bracket. Steve can afford a steady diet of plays and concerts, he can afford a casual and impromptu week-long getaway to a resort in Spain, and he can afford a cozy love nest. So, does this film fall into the rich folk category? Everything considered, a film in which the cheating couple cry over *Brief Encounter* has to be slotted into the sensitive perspective category.

Terms of Endearment (1983)

Emma (Debra Winger) leaves her English professor husband, Flap (Jeff Daniels), when she learns that he's having an affair with one of his students.

Man, Woman and Child (1983)

Robert Beckwith (Martin Sheen) had an extramarital affair while visiting France ten years earlier. He now learns that the affair produced a son, Jean-Claude Guerin (Sebastian Dungan), who recently lost his mother in a car accident.

Falling in Love (1984)

Meryl Streep and Robert De Niro in *Falling in Love* (1984)

Falling in Love was a high-profile 1980s update of *Brief Encounter*. An extramarital romance blooms between Frank Raftis (Robert De Niro) and Molly Gilmore (Meryl Streep) on New York's Metro-North Hudson Line. Molly tells her best friend, Isabelle (Dianne Wiest), that she likes Frank and he makes her feel good. Isabelle is cheating on her husband. Frank's best friend, Ed Lasky (Harvey Keitel), is cheating on his wife. Marriage has little weight in this universe. So, if a woman likes a man and he makes her feel good, this is a sufficient reason for her to stray from her marital vows. Frank and Molly meet regularly after their first meeting. Like Alec, Frank takes his lady love to a friend's apartment. Like Laura, Molly cannot bring herself to have sex. Frank is offered a job that requires him to move out of state. Improbable as it is, he needs to pack up and leave within a few days. He calls Molly to say goodbye. Her husband, Brian (David Clennon), overhears the call. She desperately explains to Brian that she must see Frank before he leaves. He says, "Why are you doing this? I don't understand. He's going away. That's the end of it, isn't it? That's the end of it." She pleads with Brian, but he can only react with frustration and bewilderment. She finally decides that his wishes do not matter. She must get to Frank. She races out into a rainy evening and recklessly drives her car through busy traffic on a freeway. She nearly crashes trying to get around a truck. She barrels toward a train crossing with the intent to outrace a train. At the last moment, she thinks better of it and steps on the brakes. She never reaches Frank before he leaves. The film advances a few years. Frank has moved back to New York without Ann, who left him because of his affair. Similarly, Brian left Molly after her soggy night scramble to meet Frank. This affair that was treated so lightly in the film has destroyed two marriages. Frank and Molly meet by chance in a bookstore. Frank remains resentful that Molly didn't see him on the night that he left New York. He doesn't seem to understand that the woman had a husband and might not be able to suddenly run off on a stormy night to meet her lover. They speak briefly. It is an awkward conversation. It is with a distinct chill that they say goodbye. But then Frank chases after Molly and they reunite on the Metro-North Hudson Line. They tenderly kiss and embrace.

The film, though it featured two of the biggest stars at the time, was a failure at the box office. Why? The film is lifeless. It lacks lacks the tension and moral core of *Brief Encounter*. Frank and Molly are far too casual about engaging in adultery. We never see the angst that dominates *Brief Encounter*. Frank shows more emotional turmoil ordering a beer. He tells the waitress, "Okay, Miller, Miller lite. No, I'm sorry. Schlitz." Molly asks him how old his children are. Frank delivers his answer as if he is delivering a soliloquy from "Hamlet." He says, "Mike's 6. Joe is. . . 4. . . No. . . No, no. He's 5. What am I talking about? 5 last January. We went to the city for his birthday. The circus was in town." He offers long pauses and faraway glances. De Niro presumably acts low-key in a bid for authenticity. But he comes across as alternately foggy, bland, and blindly casual. An actor trying hard to be authentic will inevitably be inauthentic. Streep has the opposite problem. She overacts at times. The film has two solid dramatic scenes - the scene where Molly is confronted by Brian and the scene where Frank is confronted by his wife, Ann (Jane Kaczmarek). Clennon and Kaczmarek bring true emotion to their performances.

Crooked Hearts (1991)

Edward Warren (Peter Coyote), has always presented himself as the perfect family man. It destroys that well-kept image and devastates his family when his son Charley (Vincent D'Onofrio) discovers love letters written to his father by a young waitress, Jennetta (Marg Helgenberger).

The Scarlet Letter (1995)

It would be hard to find a worst bastardization of a classic novel. The story begins in 1642. Hester Prynne (Demi Moore) lives alone in a Puritan settlement in Massachusetts Bay. She expected to be joined by her husband, Roger Prynne, who had to delay his trip to finish business in England. Hester receives news that Indians attacked Roger's ship and slaughtered the passengers. It is at this time that we are introduced to Arthur Dimmesdale (Gary Oldman), an Oxford-educated young minister. Arthur first meets Hester on a road, where he helps her to pull her wagon wheel out of the mud. Hester is drawn to Arthur immediately. The couple becomes lovers. They are able to keep their relationship a secret until Hester becomes pregnant. Because she will not identify the baby's father, Hester is imprisoned by the town fathers for immorality. Arthur is fearful of coming forward in Hester's defense. Hester is brought to the town square before an agitated mob. She is forced to wear a scarlet "A" so that people can be reminded that she is an adulteress. Her husband,

Roger (Robert Duvall), secretly returns and is determined to murder his wife's lover and make it seem that he was killed by Indians. Roger kills the wrong man and sets off a war with the Indians. Roger, distraught by the bloody consequences of his action, hangs himself. Arthur, consumed by guilt, has gone into a shocking physical decline. He stands on the scaffold before the townsfolk and confesses that he is the father of Hester's daughter, Pearl (Scout Willis). Arthur is about to be hung when the Indians attack the town. Wikipedia summarizes the ending as follows: ". . . [Hester] finally abandons her scarlet letter and departs with Dimmesdale for Carolina."[426]

Demi Moore in *The Scarlet Letter* (1995)

The novel is vastly different. To start, it doesn't showcase the passion of the lovers. Their affair came to an end before the story begins. We never read of their first meeting, or their early stirrings of love, or their surrender to the irresistible ardor that overtakes them. We only get bad stuff - the guilt, the remorse, the fear, the punishment. The guilt and remorse are exclusive to Arthur. Hester wears the scarlet letter with pride. She treasures the love that she shares with Arthur and feels nothing but joy for the beautiful daughter that they produced together. Hester understands that Roger was lost at sea. The fact that she reasonably believes that her husband is dead hardly makes this a case of wanton adultery. A townsman defends Hester on this point. He says plainly, "Her husband may be at the bottom of the sea."[427] He sees it as understandable for this youthful and fair woman to be "strongly tempted to her fall."[428] But many of the townsfolk are likely more outraged that she is an unwed mother. Roger arrives soon after. He mentions having met with "grievous mishaps by sea and land." But he is not specific about what happened to him. At some point, he was taken captive by Indians, who hoped that his Puritan brethren would pay a ransom for his return. The Indians presumably lost interest in him and let him go free. Hester pleads with Arthur to start a new life with her in Europe. Indians play a minor role in the novel. Most important, they do not wage a fiery attack on the town. In the climactic scene, Arthur ascends the scaffold to confess to fathering Hester's daughter. Then, he pulls open his shirt to reveal a scarlet "A" seared onto his chest. Arthur, relieved to have confessed his sin, dies peacefully in Hester's arms. Hester establishes a new life in another town. Many years later, she returns to her old seaside cottage in Massachusetts Bay. By then, her daughter has grown and started her own family. Hester defiantly resumes wearing the scarlet letter. She makes arrangements to be buried beside Arthur upon her death. Their graves share a single headstone engraved with a scarlet letter "A."

The film had a $43 million budget, which made it the most expensive film adaptation of "The Scarlet Letter." The intimate story of Hester Prynne was transformed into a loud, bloody action film. Of eleven film adaptations, this adaptation is the least faithful.

The Silence of Adultery (1995)

Michael Harvott (Robert Desiderio) takes his autistic child to a therapy center. The center's director, Dr. Rachel Lindsey (Kate Jackson), is a sympathetic woman. She listens attentively as Michael expresses his sadness over his son's condition. The two have other conversations. Michael tells Rachel about his wife leaving him and admits to having regrets about his marriage. Rachel admires Michael for his openness. She has doubts about her own marriage to Paul (Art Hindle). The couple soon embarks on an affair. Rachel tells Michael that, every time they meet, she feels like she's escaping into a fantasy world. This may be the reason that she often looks to be sleepwalking. In the end, Rachel chooses to leave Michael to work on her marriage.

You Can Count on Me (2000)

Sammy Prescott (Laura Linney) has a strong bond with her brother, Terry Prescott (Mark Ruffalo). The siblings became close as children after their parents died in a car accident. Sammy presents herself as a responsible person and is disdainful of Terry for being foolish and undependable. But maybe she is not as responsible as she thinks she is. She puts off her good-natured boyfriend, Bob (Jon Tenney), when he asks her to marry him. Why? She struggles at work with her demanding new boss, Brian (Matthew Broderick), and finds herself detesting him more every day. But then she sees a vulnerable side to him and asks him out for a drink. He complains that his pregnant wife has been in a bad mood. She surmises that her bad mood is just hormones. "Well, no," he says, "it isn't. But never mind." After they finish their drinks, they have sex in his car. She rebuffed a good man who wants to marry her to have sex with her detestable married boss in the backseat of a car. This is certainly bad judgement on her part.

In the Mood for Love (2000)

Chow Mo-wan (Tony Leung), a journalist, moves into an apartment building on the same day that Su Li-zhen (Maggie Cheung), a secretary, moves in. Chow and Su are both married, but their spouses are often absent due to their jobs. Chow expresses concern that his spouse is being unfaithful. Sue admits to a similar fear. Chow and Su bond over their mutual loneliness. Chow asks Su to help him write a serial for a newspaper. Though they develop deep feelings for one another, they commit to keeping their relationship platonic. But, after a time, Chow admits to Su that he loves her. He tells her that he's leaving Hong Kong for a job and wants her to come with him. She hesitates in meeting up with him at his hotel room. But then she realizes that she can't live without him. By the time she arrives at the hotel, he has left to catch his plane. He sadly leaves for Hong Kong without her. In the final scene, which takes place years later, Chow is motivated by nostalgia to visit his old apartment building. He leaves without realizing that Su has recently moved back to the building.

Joki (2001)

Ilpo (Heikki Rantanen) comes home early from the paper mill and finds a strange man in bed with his wife. The wife is more concerned about how her lover feels to be brusquely ejected from her home than she feels about her husband catching her having sex with another man. He painfully watches through a window as his wife comforts the man and hugs him. Ilpo is upset that she left their daughters in the backyard while she was having sex. He found one of the daughters sitting on the roof. He is suddenly overtaken by anger. He grabs her by the hair and drags her across the room while he demands that she change the bed sheets. He quickly regains his composure and apologizes.

> Ilpo: Are you sure about him?
>
> Wife: What do you mean?
>
> Ilpo: That he'll get along with the girls.
>
> Wife: I don't know
>
> Ilpo: You'd better ask him. Maybe he's only interested in fucking you.

She bristles with anger at Ilpo's suggestion that her lover has no true feelings for her.

> Wife: I love him and he loves me. And he tells it to me. You never speak to me at all. Did you ever even love me?
>
> Ilpo: It's better for all of us if you move out right away.

She admits that he and her lover had been together for six months and had never taken the time to consider where they were going with their relationship. The *Joki* scene underscores the tragedy of marital infidelity. It is a powerful scene. Compare this tragic scene to the silly scene in *Along Came Polly*. The husband, played by Ben Stiller, catches his wife having sex with her scuba diver instructor. His wife is still wearing her scuba flippers as she has sex. Her legs are spread outwards in the air with her flippers flopping about. It hardly makes sense to contrive laughter from this sort of scene.

Possession (2002)

A scholar, Roland Michell (Aaron Eckhart), visits the British Museum to conduct research on a Victorian-era poet, Randolph Henry Ash (Jeremy Northam). He discovers a love letter enclosed inside the pages of an old book. The letter is startling as Ash, who was known to be a devoted husband, crafted the letter's passionate missives to a woman he often saw in secret during his marriage. Roland is joined in his research efforts by a fellow scholar, Maud Bailey (Gwyneth Paltrow). The Victorian poet proves to be less repressed than Roland and Maud, who struggle with their affection for one another.

Ira & Abby (2006)

Ira Black (Chris Messina) is shocked to learn that his newlywed bride, Abby (Jennifer Westfeldt), was married twice before. Abby has tended to marry hastily. But her latest marriage, though just as hasty as the others, means something more to her. The couple goes to a marriage counselor to work on their problems. Ira becomes upset when he sees Abby in a restaurant with her good-looking ex-husband, Ronnie (Jon Hamm). He doesn't realize that Abby is counseling Ronnie about his struggles with drug rehab. Ira meets an ex-girlfriend, Lea (Maddie Corman), and accepts her invitation to share a bottle of wine at her apartment. He is so angry at Abby that he is willing to have sex with Lea. But he stops after the two of them kiss. The filmmakers depict adultery as something commonplace. Ira's father and mother admit that they both cheated. Abby's father admits that he cheated. Modern filmmakers work hard to normalize adultery.

Little Children (2006)

A married mother, Sarah Pierce (Kate Winslet), starts a friendly conversation with a married stay-at-home dad, Brad Adamson (Patrick Wilson), at the local playground. Sarah tells Brad that the other mothers at the playground fantasize about him and have nicknamed him "The Prom King." One of the mothers, she says, bet her five dollars that she wouldn't dare to approach him and get his phone number. He happily writes out his phone number for her. "Do you really want to freak them out?" she asks. He looks into her eyes and he knows exactly what she wants. The two move closer and kiss. At this point, their congeniality gives way to unadulterated, undisguised passion.

Neither one is looking to have an affair. But both of them are lonely. Their marriages have grown cold. Sarah's husband has developed an addiction to internet porn. The film is heavily populated by little children, but it is adults like Sarah and Brad who are the real little children of the title. A passage from the book makes this clear:

> After all, what was adult life but one moment of weakness piled on top of another? Most people just fell in line like obedient little children, doing exactly what society expected of them at any given moment, all the while pretending that they'd actually made some sort of choice.

Sarah and Brad plan to run away together. A sense of anxiety dominates the film. Carina Chocano of The Los Angeles Times found at the film's core "[a] sheer, white-knuckled terror."[429] On his way to meet Sarah, Brad sees a group of teenagers skateboarding. He easily falls in with the teenagers, who urge him to perform a jump with a skateboard. Brad falls doing the jump and is knocked unconscious. When the paramedics arrive, he asks them to contact his wife.

This film lacks the sensitivity of *Brief Encounter*. The filmmakers are not kind to Sarah and Brad. Every character is, in one way or another, shown in a harsh light. Every inch of every person is bad. Every child is a brat. Every mother is a bitch. Every father is a jerk. Nothing about these unpleasant characters feels real. The filmmakers make no particular judgment about adultery. They express scorn for everything just about equally. The director appears to have greater disdain for Brad being away from his family to play football with his friends. Brad is portrayed as cowardly and childish for not running away with his lover. The film's one sympathetic character is a child molester, Ronnie J. McGorvey (Jackie Earle).

Mademoiselle Chambon (2009)

Two reserved and gentle people become lovers in an extraordinarily tender story about infidelity.

Jean (Vincent Lindon), a quiet construction worker, falls in love with his young son's delicate and warm-hearted teacher, Véronique Chambon (Sandrine Kiberlain). Jean is awkward and inarticulate, but Véronique is drawn to him nonetheless.

Véronique asks Jean to speak to her class about his work as a builder. The students are fascinated listening to him explain his job. He does well answering their questions and feels proud of himself afterward.

Véronique asks Jean to repair a window in her home. Eager to help, Jean arrives at her apartment the next day with a full array of tools. Véronique dozes off while Jean is working on the window. He finishes his work and looks at the personal effects that she keeps around her home. He is, by doing this, entering her intimate space. It is similar to Katharine reading Almásy's diary in *The English Patient*. He is struck by a photo of her gracefully playing a violin, which is likely the moment that he falls in love with her.

It is obvious that Véronique and Jean are attracted to one another, but they are fearful of acting on their feelings. At one point, Jean impulsively kisses Véronique. But he quickly panics and leaves.

Jean becomes tormented by the feelings that he has for Véronique. He often becomes short-tempered with his co-workers and his wife, Anne-Marie (Aure Atika). He becomes quiet and gloomy at other times.

Sandrine Kiberlain in *Mademoiselle Chambon* (2009)

Jean invites Véronique to play the violin at his father's birthday party. Anne-Marie has been concerned about her husband's strange behavior lately. She can tell by how he looks at Véronique playing her violin that he is in love with her.

Jean drives Véronique home after the party. It is at this point that they finally make love. Véronique tells Jean that she has accepted a job in another town and is leaving in the morning. The couple makes plans to leave together. Véronique waits for Jean on the train platform as planned, but he arrives at the station and is unable to bring himself to go inside. She boards the train and leaves alone.

Someone I Loved (2009)

The original French title: *Je L'Aimais*

Pierre (Daniel Auteuil) reacts with great sympathy upon learning that his daughter-in-law, Chloé (Florence Loiret Caille), and his grandchildren have been abandoned by his son, who has run off with another woman. He hurriedly gathers up his anguished daughter-in-law and the children and takes them to a remote chalet, where Chloé can hopefully find peace and sort out her thoughts.

Chloe tells Pierre, "I never saw it coming." At first, she resists Pierre comforting her.

Chloe: You all hurt me in this family! You all hurt me. . .

Pierre: He's unhappy.

Chloe: He told you that?

Pierre tries to assume his son's perspective. Chloe is angered by this. She says, "You're cleaning up after your son. It looks bad."

Chloe laments, "I let him go without yelling. I closed the door quietly because you don't slam doors. And now I'm here with you, with my little girls." In these moments, the film emphasizes the devastating effects that adultery has on the wronged spouse.

Daniel Auteuil and Marie-Josée Croze in *Someone I Loved* (2009)

Jean admits to Chloe that he once had an affair. He fell in love with a translator, Mathilde (Marie-Josée Croze), during a business trip to Hong Kong. At the time, Pierre was unhappy with his home life, having to regularly come home to a nagging wife and argumentative children. Phoenix Cinema reports:

> We know that Pierre didn't leave his wife – that is evident in the film's very first scene. . . While Pierre's story of the affair consumes most of the film, there's also Chloe's reaction. As a woman on the losing end of an affair, will she have sympathy for Pierre? How will she feel about Pierre's decision to remain with his family? As the wounded party in her marriage, she makes a unique audience for Pierre, and his story gives her incredible insight into the other half of adultery.[430]

The film presents an interesting "meet cute" scene. Pierre is introduced to Mathilde prior to an important meeting with Hong Kong clients. She sees that Pierre is nervous and helps him throughout his presentation, going as far as suggesting an answer to a client question that has him stumped. One of the clients expresses his disapproval of Pierre.

Mathilde: He says you're not concentrating.

Pierre: I am! I am concentrating.

Mathilde: He says you're falling in love. Dealing with a Frenchman in love is too dangerous.

Pierre: No, it's all right.

Pierre tells Chloe, "I loved her more than anything. More than anything. I never knew you could love someone like that. I mean, I didn't think I was programmed to love like that. And I loved a woman. I fell in love the way you fall ill, without meaning to. And I lost her the same way." He says at one point, "Mathilde taught me to live."

Illicit affairs are a heady business. He tells Mathilde about a conversation that he had with a neighbor, Mr. Xing. He told him:

> I'm going to live with Mathilde. Because, you see, I can't live without her. I need her. She gives me life. I know who I am at last. Do you realize? I'm in love at last. Understand, Mr Xing?

Pierre is told by his secretary that she needs to go on sick leave. She explains that, two months earlier, her husband left her for another woman. She became so distraught that her doctor had to put her on pills. She is still having a hard time functioning on her job. Pierre can see the woman is distraught talking about the infidelity. He feels guilty thinking how he's doing the same thing to his own wife.

Mathilde meets Pierre at a cafe in Paris. She is so excited to see him that she reaches across the table and snatches his hand. But he is so worried that someone he knows might see them together that he quickly pulls his hand away. This sharp rejection catches her by surprise and upsets her. Pierre still has the cigarette lighter that she loaned her on their first meeting. When he brings out the lighter to light his cigarette, he cannot get it to work. "Is it a sign?" Mathilde asks.

When Mathilde realizes that he won't leave his wife for her, she tells him that their relationship has become nothing more than a game and they need to treat it like a game. She now imposes strict rules on their get-togethers. The main rule is that she no longer wants him to speak of love. She is interested in having no more than playful trysts. The film's third act depicts a painful slow-motion breakup. Mathilde, lying in bed, tells Pierre, "I'll try to live without you. I hope I'll be able to."

Pierre reacts grimly when Mathilde tells him that she's pregnant. This is more than Mathilde can bear. She says, "I'm tired, Pierre. You've no idea how tired. I can't go on. Keep away. You have to let me go now. Will you let me go? Will you let me go? You have to let me go. You know I love you, don't you?" That is the end of their relationship.

Pierre's wife, Suzanne (Christiane Millet), doesn't talk to him about the affair until it is already over. She is angry. She says, "I thought, 'It'll be okay. I don't have time, but I trust him.'" Then you got ill and I turned a blind eye. But now, I can't take it anymore. All of it. Your selfishness, your contempt, the way you. . ." She is interrupted by a waiter. But the conversation quickly resumes. Suzanne says:

> I didn't see a lawyer. I didn't have the nerve. I couldn't leave you. I love my life, my family, my children, our home, our neighbourhood. You can do whatever you want. Keep on screwing her. I won't leave. I've built things up. We haven't even slept in the house by the sea yet. And our friends, the people we know. I can't. Besides, I'm told it's common. A lot of men cheat on their wives. It's a male thing. I want to keep bearing your name and stay Mrs. Pierre Houdard. I don't exist without you.

Pierre lives with great remorse. He says to Chloe , "I lost the love of my life and stayed with a woman I permanently damaged."

Chloe is brought to tears by the story. "It's beautiful," she says. "And that pisses me off. "

Pierre briefly sees Mathilde again years later. She is with a cute young son. She denies that this is Pierre's child, but she is obviously lying.

Stricken (2009)

The original Dutch title: *Komt een vrouw bij de dokter*

Stijn (Barry Atsma), a rich and good-looking advertising executive, is unable to remain faithful to his wife Carmen (Carice van Houten) when so many women are willing to welcome him into their beds. He has a particularly passionate relationship with his latest mistress, Roos (Anna Drijver). But then he learns that Carmen has breast cancer and feels that he needs to be faithful and supportive as a husband. At first, he struggles to tear himself away from Roos. But, in the end, he gives himself wholeheartedly to his dying wife.

The 7.39 (2014)

The author, David Nicholls, told The Independent, "Obviously it's impossible to ignore *Brief Encounter*, but we definitely set out to go in a different direction, to deal as much with the aftermath of the affair. *Brief Encounter* is a brilliant film but you feel rather as if the cards are stacked against their home life where the kids are always screaming and the husband is always behind a newspaper. I mean I wonder how *Brief Encounter* would be if you saw Trevor Howard's wife and she was terrific."[431] For the record, *Brief Encounter* has no screaming kids. And the husband, despite his fondness for newspaper crossword puzzles, is not cold and inattentive.

The story is set into motion when Carl Matthews (David Morrissey) argues with Sally Thorn (Sheridan Smith), who he believes took his seat on a commuter train. The next day, Carl humbly apologizes to Sally. He says, "It's this journey, you know, it makes people tense. Especially me on a Monday morning. Veins popping out of my head, tingle down my left arm."

The two continue to talk. A relationship quickly develops. Carl looks to spend time with Sally by joining the health club where she works. One evening, when the train is not running, they spend the night together at a hotel.

Carl has an exemplary wife, Maggie (Olivia Colman), and two well-adjusted teenage children. Sally's situation is less ideal. She has cooled on the idea of marrying her dull fiancé, Ryan Cole (Sean Maguire).

Carl has this terrible fantasy where he encounters a catastrophe at his home. "There'll be a low rumble," he says, "and the whole house falls down." This same idea came into play with *Facts of Life*. A scene with a home falling down becomes a metaphor for an affair destroying the marital home.

Sally is confused and anguished.

Sally: God, I want to cry. . . Sometimes I feel like I can't do this. You know, it doesn't seem natural for every day to do exactly the same thing. I don't feel like I've done enough! And then I think, "Well, what are you expecting to happen?" You know? Ryan. . . He's a nice man. He's nice. He's nice. . .

Carl: We all grow up and settle down eventually, don't we?

Sally: It's not the growing up, it's the settling down. I try and see my face in that picture and I just. . . I can't do it.

Carl: I think if you love each other, and you're happy, I mean generally, you know, most of the time then. . . That's enough, isn't it?

Sally: Is it?

Carl: Christ, I bloody hope so.

Maggie is far from pleased to learn of the affair. Carl struggles to explain.

Carl: We never talked about you. It's got nothing to do with you. Oh, I think it's got something to do with me. But it's not because of you. I've always been happy here, there's never been anything missing here. I've always loved it here. I've always loved you.

Maggie: So why? Is she younger?

Carl: No. Yeah, a little bit but. . . you know, in many ways you're similar.

Maggie: Well that's flattering, that she reminds you of me.

Carl: That's not what I. . . I'm just trying to explain.

Maggie: I don't want to hear it! What could you possibly say? That you were stuck in a rut? Me too! That you felt invisible, under-appreciated, not special anymore? Me too! That you sometimes wanted more sex or different sex? Or you felt old and tired and ugly and dull and you just wanted to know what it felt like to be fancied again?! There is nothing - NOTHING - that you don't feel that I don't feel just as much and maybe more! But I don't do anything about it because I have a family that I love and I would not betray them!

Carl: I met someone. And I felt something for her and she felt something for me. All right? We never looked for it. If I'd sat on a different seat or got on a different train, this might never have happened. And I know you don't want to hear this but we couldn't help ourselves, okay?

She asks him if he loves her.

Carl: I think I possibly might, yeah. But I love you too and, I mean, I love you both.

Maggie: Doesn't work like that. The new one pushes the old one out.

She tells him to pack up and leave.

Sally takes Carl to the hospital after Ryan beats him up. Maggie also shows up at the hospital and gets to meet Sally. Sally explains to Maggie that her husband was feeling a bit lost and she just happened to be there for him. She says, "I don't think we're bad people." Maggie replies, "Bad people never do." After setting aside her anger, Maggie says, "We were a team, a really good team. . . I thought so anyway. This has destroyed us."

Sally and Carl don't plan to see each other again, but then Sally finds out that she's pregnant. The couple gets back together intending to raise the child together, but their reunion doesn't last long. Sally doesn't believe that it would work out for Carl to leave Maggie for her. She tells him, "We were better on the train. We were better there - it was just us two. Out in the world, we'd just. . . It wouldn't work. I know what you want and it's fine. We had a fine time for a while, didn't we?"

Carl reconciles with Maggie.

Years later, Carl sees Sally at a train station with her child and a husband. She looks very happy. He's glad for her. He smiles.

Carl, depicted by Morrissey as weary and beleaguered, is sympathetic despite his errors in judgment. Smith provides a heart-wrenching performance as the anguished and confused Sally. The always reliable Colman provides depth to Maggie.

David Morrissey and Sheridan Smith in *The 7.39* (2014)

Chapter Fourteen:
Illness

In the adultery film, illness often drives a spouse into an affair. The invalid spouse trope hearkens back to *Lady Chatterley's Lover*. This can be a problem in real life, too.

Paula Dumas of Migraine Again wrote:

Physical illness creates a risk for divorce. It can be overwhelming to be the caregiver to a sick spouse. Frustration and resentment can lead to abandonment. Many migraine sufferers wrote to the Migrane Again website about losing a spouse over their chronic migraines. Nikki wrote, "I was alone in my marriage when it came to my chronic migraines. He would keep the kids occupied but the sympathy ended years ago. I think this played a part in him having an affair and leaving."[432]

Karen Bruno of WebMD wrote:

Having a chronic illness such as diabetes, arthritis, or multiple sclerosis can take a toll on even the best relationship. The partner who's sick may not feel the way they did before the illness. And the person who's not sick may not know how to handle the changes. The strain may push both people's understanding of "in sickness and in health" to its breaking point. . . Clinical psychologist Rosalind Kalb, vice president of the professional resource center at the National Multiple Sclerosis Society, says, "Even in the best marriages, it's hard. You feel trapped, out of control, and helpless."[433]

Judith Graham of KHN wrote:

For a dozen years, Larry Bocchiere, 68, didn't find it especially difficult to care for his wife, Deborah, who struggled with breathing problems. But as her illness took a downward turn, he became overwhelmed by stress.

"I was constantly on guard for any change in her breathing. If she moved during the night, I'd jump up and see if something was wrong," he said recently in a phone conversation. "It's the kind of alertness to threat that a combat soldier feels. I don't think I got a good night's sleep for five years. I gained 150 pounds."

Marriages are often shaken to the core when one spouse becomes sick or disabled and the other takes on new responsibilities.[434]

Strange Interlude (1932)

The film is based on a play by Eugene O'Neill.

Four different men are in love with Nina (Norma Shearer). She realizes that she loves only Gordon, a fighter pilot, but her father opposes the couple getting married. Devastated when Gordon dies in battle, she marries one of her other suitors, Sam Evans (Alexander Kirkland).

Nina is shocked to learn that insanity runs in Sam's family. She is speaking to her mother-in-law, Mrs. Evans (May Robson), when she hears a mad cackle coming from upstairs. Mrs. Evans explains, "That's my husband's sister, Sammy's aunt Bessie. She's out of her mind. Hasn't been out of her room in years. I've taken care of her. . . My husband's mother died in an asylum. Her father before her. It's gone on and on for heaven knows how long. It's the curse on the Evanses."

Mrs. Evans' speech is a bit different in the play. She says of Aunt Bessie, "She just sits, doesn't say a word, but she's happy, she laughs to herself a lot, she hasn't a care in the world." The play is without the mad cackle, which is an overstated embellishment of the filmmakers.

Nina insists, "I won't believe it. You wouldn't have dared have Sam." Mrs. Evans responds:

> That's just it. I did have Sammy and, if I hadn't, I am sure that my husband would have kept his mind with the help of my love. After Sammy came, we lived in fear, thinking any minute the curse might get him every time he was sick. When Sammy was eight years old, his father couldn't stand it any longer. His mind snapped. Living like that with that fear is awful torment, I know that. I went through it by his side. It nearly drove me crazy too. But I didn't have it in my blood.

They worried that Sammy's father might go mad at any time. And then she became pregnant. Mrs. Evans says:

> I prayed Sammy'd be born dead, and Sammy's father prayed, but Sammy was born healthy and smiling, and we just had to love him, and live in fear. He doubled the torment of fear we lived in. And that's what you'd be in for. And Sammy, he'd go the way his father went. And your baby, you'd be bringing it into torment. (*a bit violently*) I tell you it'd be a crime - a crime worse than murder! (*then recovering - commiseratingly*) So you just can't, Nina!

Still wanting a baby, Nina conceives a child with Dr. Ned Darrell (Clark Gable) and lets Sam believe that the child is his.

Thunder Below (1932)

Susan (Tallulah Bankhead) is planning to leave her husband, Walt (Charles Bickford), for his best friend Ken (Paul Lukas) when Walt suddenly learns that he's going blind. Susan cares for Walt as he loses his vision, but she still expects to run off with Ken eventually. In the end, Ken cannot bring himself to hurt his friend by stealing his wife. Susan is devastated by his decision. AFI describes the ending succinctly: "[Susan] writes a goodbye note to Ken and jumps to her death into the sea."[435]

Whirlpool (1935)

The original French title: *Remous*

Newlyweds Henry and Jeannie Saint-Clair (Jean Galland and Jeanne Boitel) are driving down a narrow country road when a car comes speeding around a bend and smashes head-on into their vehicle. Henry, left crippled from the accident, is no longer able to have sex with his wife. Jeannie still loves him, but she is eventually drawn into an affair with handsome and athletic Robert Vanier (Maurice Maillot). Upon learning of the affair, Henry commits suicide. Jeannie, distraught over her husband's death, ends her relationship with Robert.

Vanessa, Her Love Story (1935)

Benjamin (Robert Montgomery) describes himself as a "heathen and a vagabond." Nonetheless, he falls in love with Vanessa (Helen Hayes) and asks her to marry him. As he prepares for the wedding, Vanessa's father has a heart attack and knocks over a candle. The man futilely attempts to stamp out the flames while, at the same time, grappling with the heart attack. The flame spreads through the entire home. Benjamin braves the flames to rescue Vanessa and her father. He finds the father dead and focuses his attention on getting Vanessa to safety. Once they are outside, he decides it's better to keep her calm and tell her that her father has been rescued. She later comes to resent him for lying to her. She tells him that she never wants to see him again.

People sometimes choose bad marriage partners, which is definitely a theme of this film. Vanessa marries Ellis Herries (Otto Kruger), a baron, without realizing that he is insanely paranoid. Meanwhile, Benjamin has discovered that the woman he married is cheating on him.

Hafer wrote:

> [Vanessa] is miserable, Benjamin is miserable and Ellis constantly assumes his wife is cheating and plots to kill her... [T]he plot is hopelessly convoluted and bizarre...[436]

Give Me Your Heart (1936)

Belinda Warren (Kay Francis) becomes pregnant while having an affair with a British aristocrat, Robert Melford (Patrick Knowles). Robert is a married man, but his marriage is far from ideal. His wife, Rosamond (Freida Inescourt), is an invalid who is unable to have children.

Belinda's writer friend, Tubbs (Roland Young), tries in a roundabout way to give Belinda advice. Tubb is a voice of reason, which we have often seen turn up in these stories.

> Tubbs: If I were writing for the cheap magazines, I'd fill [my story] full of jealousy and excitement and whoop-de-doo, but unfortunately these people are ladies and gentlemen. It's the girl I'm worried about. I don't know how to handle her.
>
> Belinda: What kind of a girl is she? I mean, does she love the man, or... or do you think she's just an adventuress?
>
> Tubbs: Oh, no. She's a grand person. Grand. Whether she loves the man or not, I haven't been able to decide.
>
> Belinda: I should think if she was the sort of person you said she was, she must love the man very much.
>
> Tubbs: Yes, of course. Yes, she must. Yes. There are several roads the story could take. Of course, the man could leave his wife and run away with the girl. But in that case, I'm afraid, the broken-hearted shadow of the wife would always be between them and they'd never be happy.
>
> Belinda: Tubbs, I don't want to talk about your story. Let's -
>
> Tubbs: And on the other hand, of course, the girl might break with the man and go away. It'd be tough on her and tough on the man... And on the wife if the man was too miserable. I don't see any solution, but I hate to see three characters I love in a situation like this.

Belinda: Oh, let's forget it. I've got an idea. Why don't you write a story that can have a happy ending?

Tubbs: No, it's started, and it's got to finish.

Belinda speaks to Robert's father, Lord Farrington (Henry Stephenson). Like Tubbs, Lord Farrington tries to explain the importance of morality.

Lord Farrington: There are certain moral codes that hold our civilization together - decencies that must be preserved if marriage and family and all the rest of our civilized ideals are not to come tumbling about our ears.

Belinda: Codes, decencies, ideals - a pack of words - superior, intolerant words! What have they got to do with anything that's real, with feelings?

She stops herself. She calms down. "No," she says. "No. You're right, Lord Farrington. I know that you're a fine man. If you say these things are true, then they must be." She brings up her father, Oliver, saying that he would agree with what he's saying.

Belinda allows Robert and Rosamond to adopt the baby. Afterward, she travels to the United States to forget Robert and the baby.

In the United States, Belinda meets a businessman, Jim Baker (George Brent). Jim falls in love with her and asks her to marry him. Belinda agrees, though she remains secretive about her past. Jim is bewildered that his new wife is often angry and distant. He loses patience with her and secretly considers divorce. Tubbs understands that Belinda is heartbroken and will remain that way unless she can stop worrying about her son. He contrives for Belinda and Jim to have dinner with Bob and Rosamond, who happen to be staying at a nearby hotel.

Rosamond brings out a photo of her son, Edward. Belinda is unwilling to look at the photo. But Tubbs urges her to look and she finally does. She immediately cries, which everyone notices. Rosamond can figure out the situation by her reaction to the photo and Bob's obvious embarrassment. She takes Belinda upstairs to her hotel room to see Edward sleeping. AFI notes: "When Belinda sees how deeply Rosamond loves her son Edward, she is freed from her years of guilt." She also realizes that Jim deeply loves her and she needs to be a better wife to him.

When Tomorrow Comes (1939)

The film was adapted from "The Root of His Evil" by James Cain.

Helen Lawrence (Irene Dunne) is swept off her feet by Philip Chagal (Charles Boyer). She arrives home from their first date in a daze. She says, "I just feel sort of numb in here." Her roommate says, "You sound as if you've been away for twenty years like Rip Van Winkle." She admits that this is exactly how she feels. An adultery film can be dreamlike, its characters lost in a netherworld where time and place have no meaning and emotion is the only thing that matters. Nathaniel Hawthorne wrote in the classic novel of adultery, "The Scarlet Letter," about "a neutral territory, somewhere between the real world and fairy-land, where the Actual and the Imaginary may meet, and each imbues itself with nature of the other."

Charles Boyer and Irene Dunne in *When Tomorrow Comes* (1939)

It isn't long before Helen learns that Philip is married. Philip tells Helen that his wife, Madeline (Barbara O'Neil), suffers psychotic episodes, which makes their life together miserable.

Helen: How long has she been this way?

Philip: About five years. A baby came. It was born dead. She never got over it.

Philip asks Helen to come to Paris with him. She tearfully refuses. She says, "If I came to Paris, I would be living in the shadows of your life. I couldn't do that, Philip. Not even for you. I would come to hate myself in time."

Stormy Waters (1941)

Laurent (Jean Gabin), a salvage-boat captain, rescues a merchant vessel that got caught out in a storm. The vessel's captain (Jean Marchat) runs off rather than pay the salvage bill. He leaves behind his injured wife, Catherine (Michele Morgan). Laurent cares for the woman and, in the process, falls in love. The problem is that Laurent has a gravely ill wife, Yvonne (Madeleine Renaud), who is waiting for him on shore.

Laurent is extremely uneasy about being unfaithful to his wife. He says, "What am I doing here with you? It's mad! Look at me. Do I look like a womanizer?"

The climax of the film is described in my book "I Won't Grow Up! ":

The moment he announces to Catherine that he is leaving his wife, a crewman visits to tell him that Yvonne has suddenly taken ill and is close to death. Lightning flashes outside the window as if this news has arrived by way of cosmic forces. Laurent rushes to Catherine's bedside in time to see her die before his eyes. Laurent is, as one critic described him, "distraught" and "incredulous." Fate punished him for his infidelity, leaving him to deal with shame, confusion and remorse. The film ends hauntingly with Laurent, in stony silence, steering his tugboat out onto dark and stormy seas to answer a distress call. He must accept his loss and carry on with his work. This is, after all, the nature of a man's life.

The Woman on the Beach (1947)

Scott Burnett (Robert Ryan), a Coast Guard lieutenant, is haunted by his battle experiences in World War II. He becomes infatuated with Peggy Butler (Joan Bennett), an enchanting woman he meets on a deserted beach. Peggy is married to Tod (Charles Bickford), who was a celebrated painter before going blind. Tod is bitter that he had to quit his career. Out of frustration, he is often unkind to Peggy. Scott comes to care about Peggy's happiness and well-being. One morning, he reveals his feelings to Peggy while the couple are secluded inside of a shipwreck. He takes Peggy in his arms and kisses her. He asks her to run away with him, but she refuses to abandon her sick husband. Scott figures to free Peggy from Tod by murdering Tod during a fishing trip. Peggy panics when the weather gets stormy and phones the Coast Guard to search for Tod and Scott. Tod and Scott are oblivious to the storm as they confront one another over Peggy. The men fight. Tod punches Scott, knocking him overboard. The Coast Guard arrives in time to rescue the men. Scott sees how happy Peggy is to find Tod is alive. He realizes then that it would be wrong to split apart the couple.

Charles Bickford and Joan Bennett in *The Woman on the Beach* (1947)

Blind husbands have had to deal with cheating wives in other films. We can trace this as far back as a 1912 film fittingly titled *Blind Man's Unfaithful Wife*. A blind man discovers that his wife is carrying on an affair with his friend. He leaps upon the man and strangles him to death. Distraught, his wife commits suicide by drinking poison. This speedily occurs in a span of nine minutes. The same situation is explored at greater length in *Man in the Dark* (1964). A blind husband prepares to remove his deceitful wife from his will, but his wife concocts a scheme with her lover to murder the husband before the will can be changed. The husband becomes aware of the plot and manages to outwit the murderous pair.

Whiplash (1948)

Mike (Dane Clark) falls in love with a woman (Alexis Smith) without realizing she's married. She is afraid to tell him the truth and suddenly disappears. Mike encounters her again at a nightclub in New York City. She pretends not to know him. He tells her, "You know, I should have had you pegged from the start. A phantom lady. No questions. A quick slip when things begin to get out of hand. Oh, very neat." It turns out that she is the wife of the nightclub owner, Rex Durant (Zachary Scott). One of Durant's thugs, Costello (Douglas Kennedy), cracks Mike in the head with the butt of a gun. Mike fights back and gets the better of Durant's men. Durant is favorably impressed by how well Mike fights. He arranges to promote him as a boxer.

Zachary Scott, Alexis Smith and Dane Clark in *Whiplash* (1948)

Durant is a menacing character. Laurie's brother Dr. Arnold Vincent (Jeffrey Lynn) tells Mike, "Rex Durant is a special kind of husband. Likes to stick pins into people. Laurie, for instance." Mike learns that he received a concussion from Costello's blow to his head and the punches that he would receive in the ring are liable to aggravate the injury and cause his death. Durant, who realizes that Laurie is in love with Mike, pressures the boxer to fight in an upcoming bout in the hope that he will be killed in the ring.

A Durant henchmen holds Dr. Vincent captive in a hotel room so that he cannot reveal Mike's concussion to boxing authorities. The doctor cleverly manages to escape and hurries to the boxing arena. He confronts Durant as he exits the arena through a darkly lit delivery entrance. He threatens to turn his X-ray plates over to the police. Just then, Costello arrives and shoots him. As he lies dying, Dr. Vincent fires a shot at Costello, who lets loose of the wheelchair. In a moment perhaps more comic than intended, Durant rolls down the ramp in his wheelchair and barrels into a busy street, where he is struck by a truck. A curious crowd gathers around Durant's lifeless body.

Mike emerges victorious from a brutal match, but he is dazed and has to be taken to a hospital. The film ends with Mike and Laurie kissing on a sunny beach.

If This Be Sin (1949)

An overworked barrister, Sir Brian Brooke (Roger Livesey), faints during a trial and finds after he is revived that he has become temporarily blind. His wife, Lady Cathy Brooke (Myrna Loy), takes him to their retreat in Italy. During his efforts at recovery, he comes to suspect that Cathy is having an affair with his assistant, Michael Barcleigh (Richard Greene). Cathy is in fact having an affair, but she has no intention of admitting it. She assures Sir Brian that the assistant is in love with his daughter, Monica (Peggy Cummins). To uphold the ruse, she encourages Michael to court Monica.

The melodramatic *If This Be Sin* has the same basic plot as the silly 1932 comedy *This is the Night*.

The Rossiter Case (1950)

A husband, Peter Rossiter (Clement McCallin), cheats on his paralyzed wife, Liz (Helen Shingler), with her sister, Honor (Sheila Burrell). Honor is shot dead with a gun that belongs to Peter. The police are about to arrest Peter when Liz, who has secretly regained the ability to walk, confesses to the crime.

Louis Calhern, Lana Turner and Margaret Phillips in *A Life of Her Own* (1950)

A Life of Her Own (1950)

Steve (Ray Milland) and Lily (Lana Turner) have been dating for weeks before Steve confesses that he is married. His wife, Nora (Margaret Phillips), became a paraplegic after suffering injuries in an automobile accident. Steve feels guilty as he was the driver. He has come to accept that his unhappy life is punishment for the accident. Lily arranges a big party to celebrate Steve's birthday. But Steve is called away by Nora, who happily awaits him with a birthday cake. She is proud to show him that she has made progress walking with crutches.

Lily is frustrated to have her birthday plans spoiled. She sees no way for her to resolve this matter without confronting Nora. Her friend Jim (Louis Calhern), acting as the voice of morality, tries to change her mind.

Jim: He was alright with her before he met you.

Lily: Oh, no. No he wasn't. He had made himself forget what it was like to be happy. I thought he could go back to her, but I was wrong. He can't make everything stop for him again. He can't make himself an invalid because she is. It's too late now. . . He's tearing himself to pieces over this, and I'm not going to let him. I can't, I can't!. . . It's killing him, isn't it? Why is her suffering all that matters? Why isn't his life as important as hers?

Jim: And you're doing this just for him, not for yourself?

Lily: Alright. Why isn't my life as important as hers? Look, Jim. She doesn't have him. Not the way I do. She can't. Maybe she doesn't really love him. Maybe she just depends on him.

Jim: No, no, Lily. . . She loves him.

Lily: Does she? I'm sorry. . . But if she loves him, she can't want him to be this unhappy. If I go and talk to her, if I explain it to her, then. . . Well this way all three of us are miserable.

Jim: And your way, only one of you will be miserable. Nora, is that the way you figure?

Lily: Well, it's fairer that way. It's fairer.

Jim: I don't believe you can work it out that mathematically, Lily. Neither do you, or you wouldn't be trying so hard to convince yourself that what you want to do is intelligent, sane, and sensible. . . When you're dealing with other people's lives, you have to think morally what's right and what's wrong. . . [G]oing to any woman and smashing everything she lives for - that's wrong. . . Do you think you'd ever be happy again if you did this? You know you wouldn't. Nobody could. The real truth is, Lily, that what you call your happiness is founded on a wrong thing, a bad thing, and that's why I don't believe any good can come out of your going there. You know, this is the kind of thing. . . Well if you did this, you could never believe yourself decent again.

Lily: Don't talk to me about being decent. Steve's my chance. The only chance I've ever had. The only man who ever loved me that I could love, too. Before him there was no one, just men. I've had men buzzing around me since I was 14. And I didn't want it that way. I never wanted it that way. I had to kid myself that there was a reason for staying alive. Well, I kidded myself. I told myself if I had money, if I was important, people knew my name and who I was, then I'd be happy. Then it would be worth it. But it was never true. It was never true. I don't know what'll happen to me if I lose Steve. I don't know how I'll get through, but I'm not going to lose him. For my sake and his. He's my first chance and maybe I'm his last chance. And he's going to have it and I'm going to have it. Are you coming with me?

Lily is simply resolved to do this. But she meets the good-natured Nora and is unable to go through with her plans. She encounters Steve at the elevator and tells him that their relationship is over.

Lily considers committing suicide, but the idea quickly passes.

Edmund Gwenn and Edmond O'Brien in *The Bigamist* (1953)

The Bigamist (1953)

An adoption agent, Mr. Jordan (Edmund Gwenn), investigates a pair of eager applicants, Harry and Eve Graham (Edmond O'Brien and Joan Fontaine), to determine their fitness as parents. The couple tried to have a child on their own, but they learned that Eve is infertile. Jordan, who is thorough in his job, becomes suspicious by information that he has uncovered. Eventually, he learns that Harry is living under an assumed name in another city. When he visits Harry's second home, he is shocked to find Harry residing there with a different wife (Ida Lupino) and a small child. Jordan lets Harry know that he will need to inform the police that he is a bigamist. Harry explains how he got into this situation. Originally when his wife Eve learned that she was infertile, he gave her a job in his business to occupy her time. She focused her energies on the business and paid little attention to him or anything else. Harry became lonely and, while on a business trip, he became interested in this other woman, Phyllis. Harry continued to see Phyllis during his regular business trips to her town. When Phyllis became pregnant, Harry was prepared to tell Eve and file for a divorce, but he found Eve distraught from having just learned that her father died. Then, suddenly, Eve told him that she wanted to adopt a child. Harry went through with the adoption process because he knew that Eve was desperate to have a child. The film climaxes with a trial.

The bigamist turned up in many early Hollywood films. Typically, a discontented husband deserts his wife and goes on to marry another woman under an assumed name. This was the case with *A Mother's Heart* (1914), *The Flower of No Man's Land* (1916), *A Woman's Daring* (1916), *Mayblossom* (1917), *The Claim* (1918), *The Song of the Soul* (1918), *Without Honor* (1918) and *Locked Lips* (1920). In *The Light at Dusk* (1916), a Russian man leaves his wife and infant daughter to immigrate to the United States. While establishing himself in his new homeland, he loses sight of his family and remarries. Sometimes, the husband faked his death. This happened in *Love's Wilderness* (1924) and *The Living Corpse* (1929). In *Meet the Wife*

(1931), a husband vanishes after an earthquake hoping that his wife will assume he was one of the earthquake's fatalities.

Wives were willing to presume their husband died despite the lack of a corpse or an official decree. In *Wolves of the Night* (1919), a woman believes that her husband died in a mining accident in Chile. In *Civilian Clothes* (1920), a wife believes that her husband died in war. In *What Would You Do?* (1920), a wife believes that her husband committed suicide in South America after his partner's fake oil stocks put him at risk of prison. In *The Combat* (1916), a wife assumes that her husband is dead after he escapes from prison and disappears into a treacherous mountain range. So, it is a surprise when the husband returns after the woman has remarried.

Filmmakers were more sympathetic in showing a wife deserting a marriage. In *Almost Married* (1932), a woman desperately flees from an insane husband on their wedding night.

Other stories featured a husband who suffered amnesia and innocently drifted into a new marriage. This was the plot of *Wolves of the Night, Where Am I?* (1923), *The Opening Night* (1927), *The Matrimonial Bed* (1930), *Kisses for Breakfast* (1941) and *The Constant Husband* (1955). *The Price of Power* (1916) is unique in that a man deserts his first wife out of boredom and deserts his second wife due to amnesia.

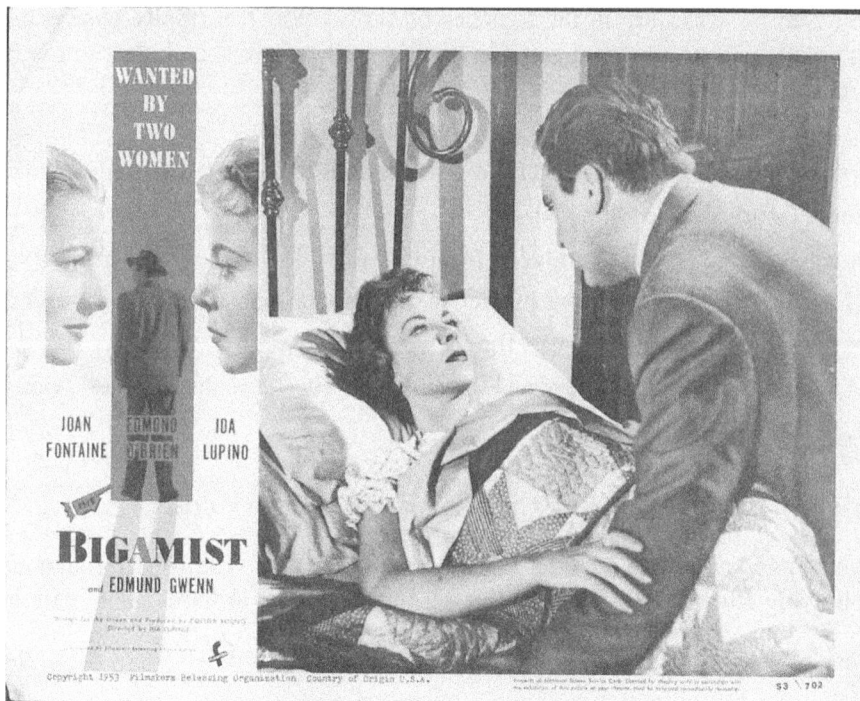

The Bigamist was different. Harry never deserts his wife. He never hits his head and loses his memory. He knowingly becomes involved in an illicit affair, which eventually turns into an illicit marriage. Other films had similar storylines, but the situation was usually played for laughs. This can be seen with *Don Juan Quilligan* (1945), *The Captain's Paradise* (1953), *The Constant Husband* (1955), *The Remarkable Mr. Pennypacker* (1959) and *Micki & Maude* (1984). *The Remarkable Mr. Pennypacker* is absent of guilt and criminal charges. The film's bigamist, Horace Pennypacker (Clifton Webb), is proud of himself for having successfully established two large and happy families.

The Shadow (1954)

The original Italian title: *L'ombra*

Gerardo Landi (Pierre Cressoy) becomes despondent from having to care for his paralyzed wife, Alberta (Märta Torén). He finds joy again in an affair with Alberta's friend, Elena (Gianna Maria Canale). Alberta divorces Gerardo over the affair. Gerardo and Elena are happy together, especially after they have a child. But then Elena dies in an accident. Alberta, who has regained her ability to walk, comes to see Gerardo. She forgives him for his infidelity and agrees to raise his child with him.

L'Amant de lady Chatterley (1955)

GrandeMarguerite of IMDb wrote:

"Lady Chatterley" is probably the most famous adultery in literature (all right, all right, so I have heard about "Anna Karenina" and "Madame Bovary"!). To sum it up: Sir Clifford Chatterley, an impotent landowner, embittered by his injury in the trenches of World War I, virtually pushes his wife into an affair, but doesn't realize it's not with someone belonging to the same social class but with his common gamekeeper.[437]

The film was banned in the United States on the grounds that it promoted adultery, but it was released in 1959 after the Supreme Court reversed that decision.

Sir Clifford Chatterley (Leo Genn) is paralyzed from the waist down due to a war injury. Constance rides her horse recklessly around the estate to work off her sexual frustration. Clifford suggests that his wife have a child with another man, but she quickly rejects the idea.

The film is not the best adaptation of the novel, but it has a few interesting scenes. Constance and Oliver often speak of love.

Constance: I can't love you. I want to love you, but I cannot. It's too horrid.

Mellors: It happens, you know. No need to make a drama out of it. The life of a man and a woman is made of days following other days, patiently. Love is humble. And arduous. And patient.

Constance: If I can't love you, then it's too horrid.

Mellors: Don't think! If you think, you frustrate the part of you that wants to love me.

Mellors adds, "All you [women] want is a sensual adventure or a romance, like in the magazines. But you won't give anything true. Nothing of yourselves. Never."

Constance brazenly kisses the gamekeeper, Oliver Mellors (Erno Crisa), behind her husband's back after they have jostled his wheelchair out of the mud. Similar lusty defiance can be found in *All Night Long* (1981). George (Gene Hackman) grabs Cheryl Gibbons (Barbra Streisand) by the ass while her husband, Bobby (Kevin Dobson), briefly has his back turned.

L'Amant de lady Chatterley has an odd scene fabricated by the scriptwriter, Marc Allégret. Mellors is leaving his job and cannot take his dog with him. Rather than give away the dog to someone else, he takes the dog in the woods and shoots him. He tells Constance, "One loves as one is able."

Constance becomes determined to leave Clifford for Oliver.

Constance: Soon, I'd want to come here and live with you forever. Here or elsewhere.

Mellors: You think they'll allow it?

Constance: I will allow it.

Clifford is angry to learn of her intentions. He tells her, "You're nothing but instinct, darkness, disorder as all women are." But, regardless of his indignation, she leaves him shamelessly and fearlessly.

Interlude (1957)

The film is a remake of *When Tomorrow Comes* (1939).

An American tourist, Helen Banning (June Allyson), arrives in Germany to see the sights. A symphony conductor, Tony Fischer (Rossano Brazzi), invites Helen to spend the day with him touring the beautiful city of Salzburg. She enjoys their time together, but she becomes upset afterward when she learns that Tony is married. Tony explains that his wife, Reni Fischer (Marianne Koch), is mentally ill and he can find no joy in being married to her. Tony admits that he may have been selfish. He says:

Yes, I am married. She's my wife. I know that's damning with you. It means everything. I only wish things were as simple as that. What do you expect of me? I am not a saint! Is it so bad for a man to reach out, to grab? At last there's someone who makes him want to live.

Helen is told by a close friend, Dr. Morley Dwyer (Keith Andes), that what she is experiencing with Tony is "a delusion, a dream, a lovely nightmare."

Reni is paranoid and excitable. She begs Helen not to take Tony away from her. Helen rescues Reni when she tries to drown herself in a lake. She sees now that Reni needs Tony and, despite the great love she feels for Tony, she believes that it is best to end her relationship with him.

The "in sickness and in health" vow is the message that prevails here.

A Novel Affair (1957)

The original British title: *The Passionate Stranger*

Judith Wynter (Margaret Leighton) is married to Roger (Ralph Richardson), who is confined to a wheel-chair due to polio. The couple has a strong marriage and deeply loves one another. Judith is a popular novelist who tends to incorporate elements of her real life into her work. She gets an idea for her new book when Roger hires handsome Carlo (Carlo Giustini) as a chauffeur. She writes her latest book about a wealthy married woman who falls in love with her chauffeur. But the woman, unlike herself, is bored and unsatisfied. Her wheelchair-bound husband, unlike Roger, is pompous and mean-spirited. Carlo reads the manuscript, which she has left behind in her car, and assumes that she is madly in love with him. The film is divided into real-life scenes (in black and white) and the novel's more extravagant make-believe scenes (in color). The latter scenes spoof the cliches of the melodramatic adultery film.

Maigret Sets a Trap (1958)

Architect and decorator Marcel Maurin (Jean Desailly), an impotent man-child, is unable to satisfy the sexual needs of his wife, Yvonne (Annie Girardot). He is enraged to learn that Yvonne had an affair with Georges Vacher (Gerard Sety). It is not her first affair, as he well knows, but she vowed to him after the last one that she would never again be unfaithful.

Marcel: With what kind of thug? Picked up where? Admit it, you little skank! So you're back at it again. You had to start again! You like them, those brutes, those roughnecks. You like those apes! So say it, you little slut! Say it! Do you want me to slap you? Tell me, do you want a slap? Do you admit you deserve it?

Yvonne: Yes. I said, yes!

Marcel: Slut! Slut! Slut!

Jean Gabin and Annie Girardot in *Maigret Sets a Trap* (1958)

Yvonne explains her affair to Inspector Maigret (Jean Gabin). She says:

He'd been cheating on me for years. I put up with it for as long as I could. I know very well my husband's good and bad qualities. At 12, I was already in love with him. He always was much brighter, much more brilliant than I. Women notice. To them, he's the artist. And I'm the little bourgeoisie hanging on. But you get tired of hanging on. It eventually becomes exhausting. . . humiliating, especially. And one day, an affair lasted longer than the others. I learned that my friends knew about it. I was filled with an idiotic fury, and I wanted to take revenge. Pay him back in kind. You probably don't understand. I wanted to betray him with anyone, it didn't matter. But I betrayed myself, dismally.

Marcel, unhinged by his wife's affair, relieves his rage by stalking the streets at night and murdering women. Farley Granger played a homicidal man-child similar to Maurin in *Edge of Doom* (1950).

The female equivalent of the impotent husband was the infertile wife or the frigid wife. An infertile wife plays a pivotal role in *The Bigamist* and a frigid wife incites her husband's infidelity in *The Way West* (1967).

The Fugitive Kind (1960)

Lady Torrance (Anna Magnani) runs a general store alone while her husband, Jabe Torrance (Victor Jory), lies dying of cancer upstairs. She takes an interest in a drifter, Valentine Xavier (Marlon Brando). Lady's affair with Valentine produces a pregnancy. Jabe is enraged to learn of his wife's affair. He sets the building on fire and, as flames rise up around him, shouts out of the window, "The clerk is robbing the store! He's burning it!" Lady is trying to stop him when he takes out a gun and fatally shoots her. Sheriff Jordan Talbot (R. G. Armstrong) is aware that Val has been having an affair with Lady. He has been waiting for an excuse to hurt the man. So, when he arrives, he turns a hose on Val, which pushes him back into a burning gazebo. The gazebo collapses on Val, causing his immediate death.

By Love Possessed (1961)

Arthur Winner (Efrem Zimbalist Jr.), a prominent attorney, has an affair with the alcoholic wife (Lana Turner) of his impotent business partner, Julius Penrose (Jason Robards Jr.).

The Way West (1967)

This western set in 1883 involves settlers traveling by wagon train to Oregon. A frigid wife, Amanda Mack (Katherine Justice), rejects her husband's amorous attentions, compelling him to get drunk and satisfy his urges with a young and willing Mercy McBee (Sally Field).

The Adulteress (1973)

Hank Baron (Eric Braeden) helps a drunk stranger, Carl Steiner (Gregory Morton), to get home safely. Carl's young wife, Inez (Tyne Daly) is grateful and asks Hank to spend the night. The next morning, Carl offers Hank a job as a handyman on his farm. Carl feels responsible for his son dying in an accident. His guilt has caused him to become impotent. He welcomes Hank to satisfy Inez in bed, hoping he will get a son out of their lovemaking. ccmiller1492 of IMDb wrote, "A kind of sexual healing is intended, but as the affair progresses it brings out the worst in all three, eventually erupting in seething resentments and murderous rage."[438] Carl asks Hank to leave once Inez becomes pregnant. But he suddenly panics that Hank might convince Inez to leave with him. He attacks Hank with a scythe, but he accidentally strikes Inez in the stomach.

Wedding in Blood (1973)

The original French title: *Les noches rouges*

Pierre Maury (Michel Piccoli) has a sickly wife. Lucienne Delamare (Stéphane Audran) has a husband who is always away on business. We know by now from past films that adultery is inevitable.

Madeline, Study of a Nightmare (1974)

IMDb: "A young woman is tormented by nightmares of her miscarriage. She becomes unfaithful to her husband and meets various lovers. Eventually, reality begins to unfurl around her."[439]

Maria's Lovers (1984)

Ivan Bibic (John Savage), a man haunted by his experiences in a Japanese POW camp, finds himself unable to have sex with his new wife, Maria (Nastassja Kinski). Clarence Butts (Keith Carradine), a slick musician, arrives in town and easily seduces the sexually unfulfilled Maria.

Story of Women (1988)

The original French title: *Une affaire de femme*

The film's adulteress, who is appallingly selfish and callous, is more depraved than most of the adulteresses that preceded her on screen.

The film opens in 1942. The setting is Cherbourg, France, which is occupied at present by the German army.

Marie (Isabelle Huppert), a housewife with two small children, is living in impoverished conditions while her husband is being held in a prisoner-of-war camp. She doesn't start out in the film as a cold-hearted person. She is loving to her children. She cries when her Jewish friend Rachel (Myriam David) is dragged off to a concentration camp. But she goes astray while coping with the various wartime hardships and atrocities.

Her husband, Paul (François Cluzet), makes a surprise return home. The Germans released him under a prisoner exchange program. But Marie is no longer attracted to the man, who has been physically and mentally broken by the war. She ignores him as much as she can and, when she can't ignore him, she glares at him with the greatest contempt.

Marie assists a neighbor to abort a baby. She sees that a demand for abortions exists and figures to make money by offering her services to other women. She is undeterred when a woman dies during the procedure and the woman's husband, devastated by her loss, commits suicide. She doesn't act without morals because she has an evil soul. It is her immature intellect, which fails to recognize the consequences of her actions, that has set her on this dark path. Roger Ebert wrote, "[Marie] stumbles into being an abortionist for two reasons: There is a demand, and she can use the money. She moves into a better apartment. There is more food for her children. As nearly as we can tell, she never gives a moment's thought to whether what she is doing is right or wrong."[440]

Marie becomes obsessed with the money that she earns and the luxury that it brings. She rents out the bedrooms to her spacious new apartment to prostitutes. She finds sexual fulfillment with a Nazi collaborator, Lucien (Nils Tavernier). She pays her maid to have sex with Paul so that she won't need to bother with him. Paul, who has become disgusted with his dissolute wife, reports her abortion activities to the police.

Marie is brought to Paris for trial. She fears that she might have to spend as long as ten years in prison. She has no idea that the prosecutor intends to demand the death penalty for her. Her defense attorney, Fillon (Vincent Gauthier), visits her in prison. He can see that she is naive and uneducated. She behaves childlike during their conference. She speaks of her dream to become a cabaret singer. She asks Fillon to get her a postcard of the Eiffel Tower so that she can send it to her children. At trial, she is shocked to tears when the judge sentences her to be executed by guillotine.

The final scene offers contemporary narration from Marie's son, Pierrot, who is now a middle-aged man and has only sad and distant memories of his mother. As we watch Marie being led to the guillotine, Pierrot offers a final word: "She was sometimes so lighthearted. And she liked to sing so much."

Isabelle Huppert in *Story of Women* (1988)

Stork Staring Mad (1994)

The original Norwegian title: *Over stork og stein*

Erling (Johannes Joner) is unable to get his wife Liv (Anneke von der Lippe) pregnant. The couple hopes to find a man who closely resembles Erling. They find a cafe poet, Torfinn Kleber (Dennis Storhøi). Erling pretends to be Liv's brother while Liv gets to work seducing Torfinn. Erling becomes consumed with jealousy. To bolster his ego, he picks up a young woman at a party.

Lady Chatterley's Lover (2006)

The best film version of "Lady Chatterley's Lover" was produced by Pascale Ferran in 2006.

The story begins with Constance Chatterley in a terribly depressed state. But we soon see a change in her mood. She happily bonds with Mellors while the two watch broody hens sitting on eggs. From the novel:

> And, one day when she came, she found two brown hens sitting alert and fierce in the coops, sitting on pheasants' eggs, and fluffed out so proud and deep in all the heat of the pondering female blood. This almost broke Connie's heart. She, herself was so forlorn and unused, not a female at all, just a mere thing of terrors.

> Then all the live coops were occupied by hens, three brown and a grey and a black. All alike, they clustered themselves down on the eggs in the soft nestling ponderosity of the female urge, the female nature, fluffing out their feathers. And with brilliant eyes they watched Connie, as she crouched before them, and they gave short sharp clucks of anger and alarm, but chiefly of female anger at being approached.[441]

Mellors tells her, "There's no self in a sitting hen." Constance sobs while holding a chick.

Wikipedia notes of the novel: "The contrast between mind and body can be seen in the dissatisfaction each has with their previous relationships."[442] Constance laments the lack of physical intimacy in her marriage. Mellors speaks of leaving his wife, Bertha, for her brutish sexual habits. Bertha was far too aggressive for him. Spark Notes reports, "Their marriage faltered because of their sexual incompatibility: she was too rapacious, not tender enough."[443] Here is an excerpt from the novel:

> She wanted me, and made no bones about it. And I was as pleased as punch. That was what I wanted: a woman who wanted me to fuck her. So I fucked her like a good un.[444]

But it went wrong. The more they had sex, the harder it was to bring her to orgasm. After a while, she needed to masturbate herself furiously to reach an orgasm.

> Self! Self! Self! All self! Tearing and shouting! . . . Like an old trull! And she couldn't help it. . . She had to work the thing herself, grind her own coffee. And it came back on her like a raving necessity, she had to let herself go, and tear, tear, tear. . . That's how old whores used to be, so men used to say. It was. . . a raving sort of self-will: like in a woman who drinks. Well in the end I couldn't stand it.[445]

Ivy Bolton, Clifford's nurse and caretaker, is an important character in the novel. From the novel:

> [Mrs. Bolton] knew what she was up against: male hysteria. She had not nursed soldiers without learning something about that very unpleasant disease.

> His wife was obviously in love with another man and is intent on leaving him, but he remains in deep denial.

> She was a little impatient of Sir Clifford. . . If he would have admitted it, and prepared himself for it: or if he would have admitted it, and actively struggled with his wife against it: that would have been acting like a man. But no! he knew it, and all the time tried to kid himself it wasn't so. He felt the devil twisting his tail, and pretended it was the angels smiling on him.[446]

Mrs. Bolton cried openly to compel him to cry. Her thought in the book was: "The only thing was to release his self-pity. Like the lady in Tennyson, he must weep or he must die." This "wallowing in private emotion," as the book described it, freed him to be cold in his business dealings.

What should we think about adultery? "These things happen," Mellors says, matter-of-factly.

This is, perhaps, the happiest, most tender, most beautiful adultery film ever made. Adultery films often have a grim ending. No person could have a worst fate than the adulterers in *The Toy Wife* (1938) or *Carrie* (1952). But it's different with *Lady Chatterley's Lover*. Adultery wins out over marriage in the end.

Never Forever (2007)

Sophie Lee (Vera Farmiga) is married to a Korean-American, Andrew (David Lee McInnis). The couple is having difficulty trying to have a baby. Andrew is devastated to learn that he is sterile. He is so ashamed that he tries to kill himself. Sophie is determined to find another way to get pregnant without Andrew knowing. She visits a sperm bank, but the sperm bank will not assist a married woman without the consent of her husband. Sophie meets an Asian man, Jihah Kim (Ha Jung-woo), who works at a dry cleaners. She offers Jihah money to get her pregnant. He agrees. Not surprisingly, their sexual relations cause the couple to develop an intimate bond. Sophie is ecstatic to finally become pregnant. But her joy is short-lived. The police arrest Jinah for being in the country illegally. Andrew learns about Jinah and threatens to leave Sophie unless she aborts the baby. Sophie refuses, which enrages Andrew and causes him to become violent. The film advances a few years. Sophie is on a beach with her young son. It is obvious from her well-rounded belly that she is pregnant again. But who is the father? Who knows and who cares? Sophie is a screwy character who never knows what she wants. The film is pretentious and empty.

A Royal Affair (2012)

The original Danish title: *En kongelig affære*

The story is set in Denmark during the 18th century. Queen Caroline (Alicia Vikander) grows distant from her mentally disturbed husband, King Christian (Mikkel Følsgaard). She has an affair with the king's personal physician, Johann Friedrich Struensee (Mads Mikkelsen). Struensee becomes a close confidante of King Christian and persuades the monarch to undertake extensive government reforms. Ove Høegh-Guldberg (David Dencik), a powerful politician, resents that the foreign-born Struensee is exerting a great influence over Denmark politics. He stages a coup and has Struensee beheaded.

A Promise (2013)

Karl Hofstadter (Alan Rickman), the owner of a steelworks, is pleased with the work of a young engineer, Friedrich Zeitz (Richard Madden). Ill health prevents him from working at the steelworks, so he uses Friedrich as his proxy. Friedrich falls in love with Hoffmeister's younger wife, Charlotte (Rebecca Hall). Charlotte shares his feelings, but she can never betray Karl. She and Friedrich do no more than hold hands. Still, their innocent relationship disturbs Karl. It pains Karl to be lying helplessly in bed as he hears them laughing together downstairs. This remains an issue as Charlotte often laughs in Friedrich's company. Hofstadter gets rid of Friedrich by transferring him to a mining operation in Mexico. Charlotte cries often once Friedrich is gone. It makes it worse that the separated lovers are unable to pass letters through a military blockade. Karl, who learns that he is dying, tells Charlotte that he was wrong to keep her and Friedrich apart. Karl dies soon after. Charlotte and Friedrich are reunited after the war.

Chapter Fifteen:
The Fiancé

Filmmakers had to follow rules when it came to a character cheating on a spouse, but those same rules vanished when a character was cheating on a fiancé. It is possible the person had been together with their betrothed for years. It was eight years in the case of *Where There's Life* (1947). The couple could have developed a solid commitment and deep trust, no different than what a married couple has. They could share dreams much like a married couple. An unfaithful fiancé creates serious complications in George Eliot's 1860 novel "The Mill on the Floss." Brian McFarlane wrote: ". . . [T]he heroine, Maggie Tulliver, comes to accept that she cannot make her happiness out of the unhappiness of others when she falls in love with her cousin's fiancé." But the Production Code did not concern itself with the standing of a fiancé. Unfaithfulness to a fiancé, no matter how long the couple has been together or how deeply either person has felt for the other, was not a matter of great importance. This fiancé cheating became no-holds-barred cheating in Hollywood films.

Audiences weren't bothered. A lead character did not risk losing the audience's sympathy if they conveniently forgot they were set to marry to one person while getting romantically entangled with someone else. It was fair game to cheat on a fiancé or fiancée. This situation was something that developed often in comedies. Take, for instance, *The Awful Truth* (1937), *Personal Property* (1937), *Vivacious Lady* (1938), *Bringing Up Baby* (1938), *Blond Cheat* (1938), *Paris Honeymoon* (1939), *The Philadelphia Story* (1940), *His Girl Friday* (1940), *The More the Merrier* (1943), *Christmas in Connecticut* (1945), *Welcome Stranger* (1947), *Holiday Affair* (1949), *A Millionaire for Christy* (1951), *Half Angel* (1951), *Pat and Mike* (1952), *Sabrina* (1954), *Bell, Book and Candle* (1958), *All In a Night's Work* (1961), *Walk, Don't Run* (1966) and *Sideways* (2004). It happened too in drama, whether melodramas like *Dangerous* (1935), *Leave Her to Heaven* (1945), *The Great Sinner* (1949), *The Second Woman* (1950) and *The Turning Point* (1952) or sensitive dramas like *Cheers for Miss Bishop* (1941) and *Dear Heart* (1964).

We have two pending nuptials in *An Affair To Remember* (1957). Terry McKay (Deborah Kerr) is engaged to Kenneth Bradley (Richard Denning). Nickie Ferrante (Cary Grant) is engaged to Lois Clark (Neva Patterson). But, after falling in love during an ocean cruise, Terry and Nickie resolve to abandon their marriage plans to be together. Kenneth and Lois have every right to complain, but they could not be more supportive. In this romantic dream world, a person is obligated to graciously step aside for grand love.

Triviality of an engagement is made clear in *Three Smart Girls Grow Up* (1939). Penny Craig (Deanna Durbin) tries to undo her sister's ill-advised engagement by matching her sister with an up-and-coming concert pianist, Harry Loren (Robert Cummings). Harry is puzzled. "I thought you told me [your sister] was engaged?" he asks. Penny responds, "Engaged. Oh now, Harry, you know very well that an engagement doesn't mean a thing. My cousin Caroline's been engaged six times and she still isn't married." A situation in which a person cheats on their fiancé is treated with barely any gravity.

It don't mean a thing if it ain't got that ring. *Moonstruck* (1987) shows us, in great comic fashion, that a woman can simply end an engagement by flinging an engagement ring at her fiancé. The fiancé's brother takes the ring and offers it to the woman. She takes it. The engagement has transferred that easily.

Jeanine Basinger noted in her analysis of *The Philadelphia Story* (1940) that most viewers are glad that socialite Tracy Lord (Katharine Hepburn), dumps her fiancé because, very clearly, he is the "wrong man."[447]

The interloper, in this context, serves as a champion of the sustainable marriage. He deserves to be hailed as a hero for stopping the heroine from marrying the wrong man.

Dennis Morgan behaves appallingly in the casual way he steals his friend's fiancée in *Two Guys from Milwaukee* (1946). He simply explains to his friend, "Buzz, I'm sorry, really I am. The moment I met Connie, something exploded between us."

Presumably, it was an explosion of dopamine. But what is the real value of dopamine? Robyn, a popular Twitter commentator, wrote, "More than we should want a man who makes us feel good (just fleeting dopamine) we should want a man who is a provider and a protector."

Shakespeare explored the subject of fiance fidelity in "Cymbeline." Posthumus praises his intended bride, Imogen, for her chastity. Iachimo, a mischievous and resentful villain, challenges Posthumus' boast. He bets Posthumus that he can, if allowed the opportunity, seduce Imogen. Posthumus confidently accepts the bet. Imogen rejects Iachimo despite his aggressive efforts at seduction. But he remains determined to win his bet. He hides in Imogen's bedroom and waits for the princess to fall asleep. He quietly spies upon Imogen's partly naked body and spots a mole underneath her breast. He can now, by describing the mole, trick Posthumus into believing that he has bedded his bride. Posthumus instructs his servant Pisanio to murder Imogen, but Pisanio is fond of Imogen and has her disguise herself as a boy to escape. In her new guise, Imogen adopts the name "Fidele," which means "faithful."

Two Seconds (1932)

John Allen (Edward G. Robinson) doesn't believe that it's right for his friend, Bud Clark (Preston Foster), to pick up a young woman while he is engaged to be married. He cries out, "You're engaged!" Bud responds, "That don't tie me down yet. Til the preacher makes me say 'love, honor and obey,' I can still have a little fun."

They Call It Sin (1932)

Marion Cullen (Loretta Young) is a church organist in a small town. Her parents value marriage and family. We see that as her family sits down for dinner and her father, Mr. Cullen (Erville Alderson), says grace.

Dear Lord, our Father. We thank thee for this day in which we may pause to contemplate thy blessings. We thank thee, dear Lord. For this loving family. And for this home. And this food. And all the happiness that thou has sent us. Amen.

Marion goes on a date with Jimmy Decker (David Manners), a businessman visiting from New York City. The two fall in love, but Jimmy has to get back home to marry the boss' daughter Enid Hollister (Helen Vinson). Jimmy finds that he can't stop thinking about Marian and seeks advice from his best man, Dr. Travers (George Brent).

Loretta Young and Una Merkel in *They Call It Sin* (1932)

Dr. Travers: Just leave [the beautiful women] for unattached bachelors like myself.

Jimmy: What do you suppose is wrong with a fellow who is engaged to one girl . . . and is continually thinking about another?

Dr. Travers: Oh well, don't worry about it, old man. After all, in a few weeks you'll be married.

Jimmy: I guess you're right. I'll probably not see her again anyway. Still, I have a guilty feeling about it.

Marion travels to New York City in search of Jimmy. When she learns that Jimmy is married, she gives up her romantic aspirations and instead pursues a career as a showgirl on Broadway. Jimmy encounters Marion at a party. He tells her that he loves her and wants them to get back together, but she refuses to break up his marriage. In the end, Marion finds love with Travers and happily accepts his marriage proposal.

Love Before Breakfast (1936)

Kay Colby (Carole Lombard) has two men vying for her affections. Kay prefers Bill Wadsworth (Cesar Romero) and agrees to marry him. But Bill's rival, Scott Miller (Preston Foster), intends to use his wealth to alter the situation to his advantage. He purchases the company where Bill works and has Bill transferred to Japan. But this strategy only angers Kay. Kay looks more favorably on Scott when Bill suddenly stops writing to her. She agrees to marry Scott, but lets him know that she doesn't love him. Scott doesn't want to marry a woman who doesn't love him, so he brings Bill back from Japan. Kay finds that she is not happy to have Bill back and misses Scott. She decides in the end that she loves Scott and wants to marry him.

Loretta Young and Una Merkel in *They Call It Sin* (1932)

The Bride Wore Red (1937)

A wealthy young man, Rudi Pal (Robert Young), is staying at an exclusive Swiss resort with his fiancée Maddalena Monti (Lynne Carver), Maddalena's father Admiral Monti (Reginald Owen) and the Contessa di Meina (Billie Burke). Rudi is suddenly distracted from his fiancée by a cafe singer, Anni Pavlovitch (Joan Crawford), who he mistakes for a socialite. Anni is in love with a humble postman, Guilio (Franchot Tone), but she cannot resist the opportunity to date a wealthy man.

The rich hotel guests dress as peasants for a costume party. At one point, Anni and Rudi sneak off together. Anni is upset by Rudi's suggestion that she become his mistress ("Anne, why should my marrying Maddelena be a problem to us?"). Anni lets Rudi know exactly where she stands. She says, "Maybe I want what Maddelena wants. To wear my love in the open. To be proud and happy with you." Rudi, afraid of losing Anni, asks her to marry him. She accepts. Maddalena is gracious when Rudi breaks the news of his engagement to Anni.

The countess receives a telegram that exposes Anni as a cabaret singer. AFI reports:

> Maddalena is genuinely sympathetic, and Anni tells Rudi that he should marry his childhood sweetheart because she really is a lady. . . [Anni] leaves the hotel after the manager demands payment of her bill. When she leaves, taking only her peasant costume from the ball, Giulio is happily waiting for her.

Breakfast for Two (1937)

Valentine Ransome (Barbara Stanwyck), a heiress, sets out to reform an ineffectual playboy, Jonathan Blair (Herbert Marshall), by becoming a majority shareholder in his failing shipping company and challenging him to stand up to her. She also makes it her objective to sabotage his relationship with an obnoxious fiancée, Carol Wallace (Glenda Farrell).

Joan Crawford in *The Bride Wore Red* (1937)

I Know Where I'm Going! (1945)

Joan Webster (Wendy Hiller), a highly ambitious and coldly calculated woman, has arranged to marry a wealthy businessman, who lives on a remote private island in Scotland. She sets out on a difficult journey to the island. A storm strands her on the island of Mull, where she meets charming naval officer Torquil McNeil (Roger Livesey).

Joan, normally willful and headstrong, finds herself quickly losing control as she falls in love with MacNeil. She becomes desperate to reach the island. "I'm not safe here!" she cries out. "I'm on the brink of losing everything!" Now that she's in love, the determined woman with her firm plans no longer knows what to do.

It is a sign that fate has thwarted her marriage plans when her boat gets caught in a storm and her wedding dress is blown overboard, where it is lost to a whirlpool.

Joan speaks to Robert over a radio link at the Coastguard station. But, strangely, she doesn't recognize his voice.

Joan: Is there anything the matter with your voice? Have you got a cold? Over.

Robert: Oh, no, I haven't got a cold. Do I sound as if I had?

It's an odd exchange. Robert sounds much older than Joan. He sounds much older than MacNeil. Is that the issue? She may suddenly be struck by how gruff his mature voice sounds.

Joan is captivated by a happy and loving old couple celebrating their diamond wedding anniversary. She sees value in marrying a man you love and a man with whom you can grow old.

MacNeil tells Joan tales about faithless women. He first tells an old folk tale about a prince who had to travel across the loch. He was worried that his boat would be dragged down into its notorious whirlpool. MacNeil says:

> They told him to take three anchor ropes, one of hemp, one of flax. The third rope was made of the hair of maidens who were faithful to their lovers. The maidens willingly gave their tresses, and Prince Vreckan sailed for the Hebrides. The first night, the hemp rope broke. The second night, the rope of flax broke. The third rope held. . . until the tide turned. Nothing is stronger than love. . . But one maiden was untrue to her lover. Only one. And when that strand broke, the whole rope broke with it.

He later tells her about MacNeil of Kiloran, who took a beautiful wife from the mainland. The problem was that she was in love with a cousin, a MacLaine who lived in Moy Castle. He says:

> After a year and a day, when her husband was away ravaging the mainland, she escaped from Kiloran and took refuge in Moy Castle with her lover. One black night, Kiloran came. He besieged and took the castle and killed every soul except the two lovers. There's a deep dungeon just off the back of the great hall. It's a well with nine feet of water in it and a rounded stone just big enough for a man to stand upon or drown. Kiloran stripped the two lovers, chained them together and threw them into the dungeon. He sat in the great hall feasting while they held one another above the water till their strength failed and they dragged one another down. Before she died, the woman cursed Kiloran and every future MacNeil of Kiloran if they should ever cross the threshold of the castle. There's the curse carved in stone on the ramparts. There to this day. It's a terrible strong curse.

The curse, as it turns out, is: "Never shall he leave it a free man. He shall be chained to a woman till the end of his days and he shall die in his chains." The chains of marital devotion are appealing to Joan and MacNeil.

Roger Livesey and Wendy Hiller in *I Know Where I'm Going!* (1945)

The film brings to mind the ancient story of Tristan. Tristan is tasked with escorting Iseult from Ireland to Cornwall to marry his uncle, King Mark. Iseult's mother slips her daughter a love potion to assure that she will bond with her new husband, but Tristan and Iseult mistakenly drink the potion during their journey. This stirs up a love affair between them. They struggle hard to remain true to their commitments, but their passion for each other is overpowering and it eventually drives them to their deaths. The Tristan story is the basis of a classic French film, *L'éternel retour* (1943).

Dennis Morgan and Barbara Stanwyck in *Christmas in Connecticut* (1945)

Christmas in Connecticut (1945)

Elizabeth Lane (Barbara Stanwyck), a food writer, has attracted millions of fans to her magazine column by pretending to be a traditional wife and mother who lives in a picturesque country home. Not even her publisher, Alexander Yardley (Sydney Greenstreet), knows the truth. Yardley figures to gain publicity by having a returning war hero, Jefferson Jones (Dennis Morgan), come to Lane's home for Christmas dinner. Lane contends with many problems in trying to keep up her charade. The situation becomes even more complicated when she and Jones fall in love. Jones is confused because he doesn't get the sense from the way Elizabeth acts that she's married. She is in fact nearly married. She has arranged to secretly marry a longtime suitor, John Sloan (Reginald Gardiner), during the holiday weekend. But, as soon as she met Jefferson, she lost interest in this idea.

Elizabeth: Jefferson Jones, are you flirting with me?

Jefferson: Oh, no, I wouldn't dare.

Elizabeth: Oh, don't apologize. I'm flattered. It's intriguing to a married woman to find she's still attractive to the opposite sex.

Jefferson: But I. . .

Elizabeth: Do I attract you?

Jefferson: Yes. But you see, you were so different from what I expected. I was. . .

Elizabeth: Knocked for a loop?

Jefferson: You said it.

Elizabeth: Oh, how nice.

Jefferson: But I. . . I shouldn't have told you. Your being married and all that, I. . . But, you know, I find it hard to believe you are married.

Elizabeth: I find it pretty difficult myself.

Jefferson: You don't act as if you were married.

Elizabeth: I don't feel as if I was married.

Jefferson: Really?

Elizabeth: Must be the moonlight and the snow.

Elizabeth asks Jefferson if he has ever kissed a married woman.

Jefferson: No.

Elizabeth: No?

Jefferson: No.

Elizabeth: No, you're not the type.

Jefferson: I. . . I wish I was.

Elizabeth: Oh, me too. Well, and that's that.

Jefferson: Yeah. I guess it is.

Paris Frills (1945)

Les Adams of IMDb wrote: "A philandering young dress designer plays fast and loose with the hearts of all the fair maidens he encounters, and leaves them in a Paris lurch. But when he meets the fiancée of his best friend, he falls deeply and truly in love with her. The girl is soon faced with two choices; marry the reliable fiancée whom she doesn't love, or run off with the dress designer with whom she is infatuated. She sees that she also has a third option and makes the wise choice…she rejects both."[448]

Johnny Frenchman (1945)

Sue Pomeroy (Patricia Roc) has been dating no one but Bob Tremayne (Ralph Michael) for years. This is known in their Cornish fishing village as "walking out." A couple in these circumstances is expected to marry. Bob, who is about to enter military service, proposes to marry Sue during his first leave. But Sue isn't ready to make that commitment. Bob is hurt and confused. She tells him, "I know I've kept you hanging about, but it's not because I don't care for you."

While Bob is away, Sue falls in love with a French fisherman, Yan Kervarec (Paul Dupuis). Bob indirectly responsible for bringing the couple together. He injured Yan during a playful wrestling match, which caused the young man to be disqualified from military service and left him hanging around the village with Sue.

Sue and Yan become anxious to marry. Sue's father, Nat (Tom Walls), strongly disapproves.

Nat: What about Bob? You've been walking out with him.

Sue: I know, but that was before I met Yan. Oh, I'm still very fond of Bob, but this is. . . Well, I feel quite different.

Nat: Bob's your boy! And he's away fighting. Look nice, wouldn't it, if you were to chuck him over for a foreigner.

Escape Me Never (1947)

Sebastian Dunbrok (Errol Flynn), a struggling composer, takes in Gemma Smith (Ida Lupino), an unwed mother abandoned by his brother Caryl (Gig Young). Caryl plans to marry an heiress, Fennella McLean (Eleanor Parker), but she hears gossip that a woman and child are living with her betrothed. The person spreading the gossip has gotten the brothers confused. Both men are named Dunbrok, both men are composers, and both men fit the same general physical description. Fennella breaks off her engagement to Caryl before leaving on vacation with her family. Sebastian, Caryl, Gemma and the baby head out on a road trip to find Fennella and explain the error. Oddly, they don't plan to mention that Caryl is the father of Emma's baby. Sebastian ends up falling in love with Fennella, but he sees it as his duty to marry Gemma.

Fennella is determined to stop this altruistic marriage. She confronts Gemma.

Fennella: Gemma, give him up.

Gemma: So that you can have him?

Fennella: Yes. There's so much I could do for him. Just as I've already helped him.

Gemma: Oh, have you?

Fennella: Yes. I gave this party so that he could meet Steinach. I persuaded Heinrich to conduct his ballet. I even inspired Sebastian to write the ballet in the beginning. He got the idea for it in Orzano the night we met. So, you see, if you were to give him up, I. . .

Gemma: Don't say that again.

Fennella: Very well. But you must realize that no woman can hold a man like Sebastian if he doesn't want to be held.

Sebastian is tempted to leave Gemma for Fennella, but it comes to realize that this would be a bad idea.

Sebastian: Look at me. Even the most selfish pig may have something he won't face, even though it's the only decent thing that ever happened to him. I was afraid, that's it. I was afraid to admit what Gemma meant to me because, I suppose, I wanted to go on being a selfish pig.

Fennella: Sebastian, you mean you brought me down here. . .

Sebastian: And that's the luckiest thing that ever happened to you, because I'm taking you back to Caryl. Caryl, he's your kind of man. And Gemma, Gemma's my kind of woman. Look, Fenella, you're a sensible girl. What you want is a nice marriage, a nice husband.

Holiday Affair (1949)

In *Holiday Affair*, the other man makes it clear that a woman is still fair game even if she has a fiancé. Steve Mason (Robert Mitchum) wants to marry Connie Ennis (Janet Leigh) although she is already engaged to Carl Davis (Wendell Corey).

Steve: Connie, I think Carl is just about one of the nicest fellows I could ever hope to meet. But I think you ought to marry *me*. . . Maybe you think it's wrong of me to speak this way in front of Timmy. I don't see how it can do a boy any harm to know that two men like his mother. Maybe it's bad taste to speak in front of Carl. But would it be better if I sneaked around and tried to get Connie behind the kitchen stove? I don't think so. If you think this is biting the hand that's fed me, then look at my problem. I've walked out of Connie's life a couple of times now and each time something brings me back. Lost packages. A train. A cop. Accidents. I'm afraid I can't keep counting on accidents. If I walk out now, I'm sunk. I'll never see her again. The way I figure it when a man's in love with a girl, he's got a right to ask her to marry him. Any girl. Anybody's girl. What do you say, Connie?

Connie: I think you better get your hat and coat.

Steve: That's a fair answer to a fair question. I wish you all a very merry Christmas.

Janet Leigh and Robert Mitchum in *Holiday Affair* (1949)

Carl comes to realize that he is not meant to marry Connie. He tells her:

I know that as my wife you'd be thoughtful, considerate and competent about everything. About our home, my health and my career. But I have a sneaking suspicion I ought to see if somewhere there isn't a girl who might be in love with me. Even if she's a dumb, frowzy blond who slops up the house and feeds me on canned beans.

Your spouse should be a loving and devoted mate.

Marie of the Port (1950)

The original French title: *La Marie du port*

José Arroyo of Notes on Film wrote:

. . . Henri Châtelard (Jean Gabin), a well-to-do owner of a restaurant and cinema in Cherbourg, . . . accompanies his mistress Odile (Blanchette Brunoy) to her father's funeral in the small village of Port-en-Bessin in Normandy, only to fall in love with her sister, Marie (Nicole Courcel). There are several obstacles to the union of Châtelard and Marie: Marie is seeing a young local boy Marcel (Claude Romain), crazy in love with her and threatening suicide; she's Odile's sister; there's a considerable difference in age. . . Marie doesn't want to be a mistress like her sister, living the good life but shunned by "respectable" people — she wants a ring.[449]

Odile, his fiancée, is glamorous but lazy, shallow and easily bored. But Marie, unlike her older sister, is serious, hard-working and conscientious.

Henri watches a film about life in Tahiti. He envies the freedom that the natives have. "They wear pretty blouses too [referring to Marie's pretty new blouse]. And no conditions for taking them off - marriage, a ring."

Marie tells Marcel that she is in love with Henri. He becomes agitated. He shouts, "I don't want to hear about love. Sure, everybody's in love. It's all they think about. I love you. You love me. He loves me. Then they're unfaithful and they break up." She speaks of her plan to go to Cherbourg with Henri. But, then, she suggests that she will one day return to her boyfriend to marry. He finds her plan to be confusing. He says, "Women are all the same. I love him. He loves me. A lot, a little, passionately."

Half Angel (1951)

Nora Gilpin (Loretta Young), an uptight nurse, has a sudden passion awakened in her upon seeing a wealthy lawyer, John Raymond, Jr. (Joseph Cotten), attend a board meeting at her hospital. She fights fiercely against her attraction to the man, who has a reputation for being an arrogant playboy. She figures to get over her silly infatuation by finally consenting to marry her longtime suitor, Tim McCarey (John Ridgely). She is busy arranging the wedding when she suddenly develops a psychological disorder - sleepwalking. The usually reserved woman loses her inhibitions in her unconscious state. A sexy new Nora takes charge. She changes into a flashy green satin dress and saunters to John's home, where she flirts with him for a bit and then kisses him. John enjoys the visit, but Nora becomes stuffy and aloof with him once she awakens. She has no memory of her outing and thinks John is crazy for insisting that she kissed him. The sexy sleepwalking Nora has other similar nocturnal encounters with John, which serve to thoroughly confuse and frustrate the man. In the end, Nora comes to realize that she loves John and would prefer to marry him rather than Tim. John is way ahead of her. He produces a marriage license showing that she already married him during her last sleepwalking episode.

Alaska Seas (1954)

Jim Kimmerly (Brian Keith), a fisherman who heads a new canning cooperative, reminisces with a crew member about his old partner, Matt Kelly (Robert Ryan). Matt left town when the government imposed strict restrictions on the fisherman to preserve the dwindling salmon population. When Matt left town, he left behind a girlfriend, Nicki Jackson (Jan Sterling). Nicki is now engaged to Jim, although she occasionally thinks of Matt. Elsewhere, Matt has gotten himself into trouble for poaching seals and needs to quickly vacate his present environs. It is time to return to his old home. He visits Nicki, eager to resume their relationship. She makes it very clear to him that she intends to marry Jim. He doesn't take her engagement to Jim seriously. Next, he seeks out out Jim for work. Jim is glad to help his old friend, but Matt can't stay out of trouble for long. On his first day fishing with Jim, he causes an accident that destroys Jim's boat. The fishermen believe that he destroyed Jim's boat on purpose and refuse to have him in their co-op. Unable to work with the fishermen, Matt instead falls in with a criminal gang that is robbing the fishermen's traps.

Gun for a Coward (1957)

Will Keough (Fred MacMurray) plans to marry his girlfriend, Aud Niven (Janice Rule), once he has paid off the mortgage on his ranch. But, while Will is preoccupied with business, Aud becomes close to Will's younger brother, Bless (Jeffrey Hunter).

Eva (1962)

Letterboxd:

Best-selling author Tyvian Jones has a life of leisure in Venice, Italy, until he has a chance encounter with sultry Frenchwoman Eva Olivier. He falls for her instantly, despite already having wedding plans with Francesca Ferrara. Winning Eva's affection proves elusive; she's more interested in money than in love. But Tyvian remains steadfast in his obsession, going after Eva with a fervor that threatens to destroy his life.[450]

Dear Heart (1964)

Harry Mork (Glenn Ford), a middle-aged sales rep, is tired of lonely business travel and wants to settle down in one place with a wife. He impulsively asks a divorcee, Phyllis (Angela Lansbury), to marry him. But Harry becomes uncertain of his pending nuptials while spending a couple of days at a busy Manhattan hotel. He nervously and sneakily books a room at another hotel with a fun-loving gift shop clerk (Barbara Nichols). Later, he develops a closeness with Evie Jackson (Geraldine Page), who is visiting the hotel for a convention. Feeling guilty, Harry approaches Phyllis about his unfaithfulness. Phyllis, who has spent years devoted to household drudgery, is looking forward to a more leisurely life with her new business executive husband. She can't be bothered worrying about whether or not her husband is being faithful. She says, "Harry, you're a man. You've lived a great deal in the past, and I suppose you will live a great deal in the future. All I ask is that you don't tell me about it, because if I know, I'll have to do something. And Phyllis is done with doing. I think my attitude is very generous, Harry. Not many women would have it, you know." In the end, Harry breaks off his engagement with his nonchalant wife-to-be to pursue a romance with the loving and attentive Evie.

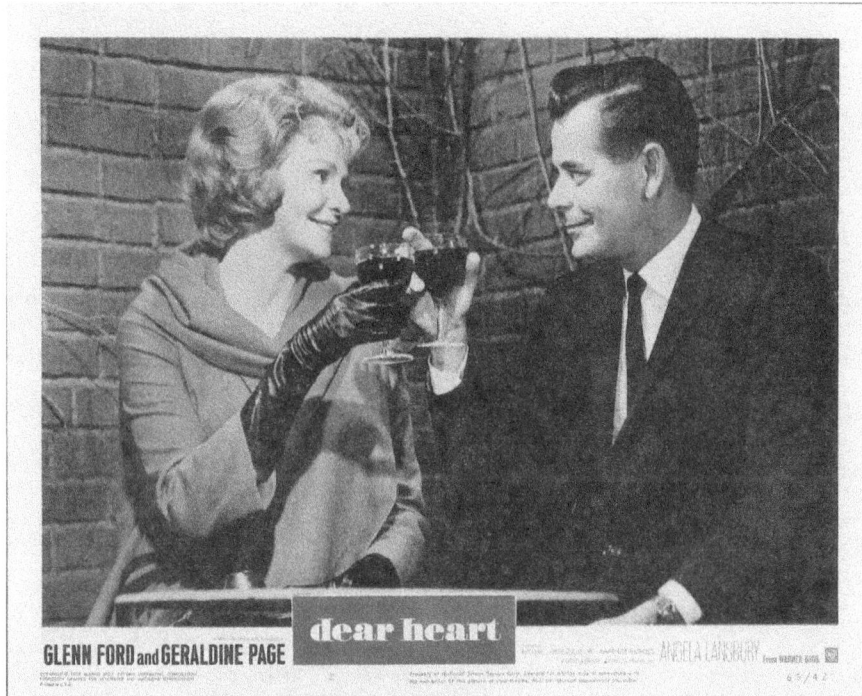

Geraldine Page and Glenn Ford in *Dear Heart* (1964)

The Last Kiss (2001)

The original Italian title: *L'ultimo bacio*

Carlo (Stefano Accorsi) is approaching his 30th birthday. He has a secure job at an advertising agency. He has been living with his girlfriend, Giulia (Giovanna Mezzogiorno), for three years. The couple is deeply in love. But Carlo's happy and stable life is upset when he learns that Giulia is pregnant. The news sends him into a panic, though he hides his feelings from Giulia. At a friend's wedding, Carlo is attracted to a beautiful 18-year-old student, Francesca (Martina Stella). She represents the freedom of youth that he suddenly desires. The next night, Carlo goes to a party with Francesca. She wants them to leave the party early to have sex, but Carlo cannot stop thinking about Giulia and has to decline this tempting invitation. Giulia understands that Carlo is at a bar with his friend Paola (Claudio Santamaria). She becomes suspicious when she encounters Paola. Where is Carlos? Paola struggles to lie to Giulia. She demands that he tell the truth, at which point he confesses that Carlo is with Francesca. Giulia is terribly distraught when Carlo arrives home. It is an intensely emotional confrontation between the couple. Giulia comes close to stabbing Carlo with a kitchen knife. Carlo is so infuriated with Giulia that he returns to Francesca and has sex with her. Carlo is remorseful in the morning. He pleads for forgiveness from Giulia, who strongly resists him for days before she finally takes him back.

The film was an international hit. It was remade in the United States five years later.

The Notebook (2004)

An old boyfriend, Duke Calhoun (Ryan Gosling), shows up as Allie Hamilton (Rachel McAdams) prepares for her wedding.

Allie: No, I made a promise to a man, he gave me a ring and I gave him my word.

Duke: And your word is shot to hell now, don't you think?

Allie: I don't. . . I don't know. I'll find out when I talk to him.

Duke: This is not about keeping your promise, and it's not about following your heart, it's about security.

Chapter Sixteen:
Therapeutic Cheating

Adultery is a cure for what ails you. Or is it? Many films have promoted the idea that adultery can be therapeutic. We saw already that an extramarital beachside romp was a great tension reliever in *About Mrs. Leslie*. We saw that a shipboard fling was a confidence-booster in *Now, Voyager*. Let us examine a few other films in which adultery was therapeutic.

A Woman's Face (1941)

Anna Holm (Joan Crawford) is embittered about her badly scarred face and has been led by her bitterness into a life of crime. She comes into possession of letters that a married woman, Vera Segert (Osa Massen), wrote to a lover. Ann demands payment from Segert for the return of the letters. Crawford falls in love with Vera's plastic surgeon husband, Gustaf (Melvyn Douglas), who demonstrates brilliance, affection and devotion in restoring Anna's beauty. Gustaf ends up leaving his faithless wife, Vera, for Anna.

Joan Fontaine, Ray Milland and Teresa Wright in *Something to Live For* (1952)

Something to Live For (1952)

Jenny (Joan Fontaine), a Broadway stage actress, has recently ended a bad relationship with her director. She figures to drink away her sorrows. Tony (Ray Milland), a counselor with Alcoholics Anonymous, is called to help her by Billy (Harry Bellaver), an elevator operator at Jenny's hotel. Tony is married with two children, but this doesn't stop him from becoming romantically involved with Jenny. Jenny has second thoughts about the relationship when, while visiting a museum, she and Tony encounter Tony's young son

(Lee Aaker), who is on a field trip with his class. Jenny feels deeply ashamed. She starts to avoid Tony, but she cannot stop thinking about him and he cannot stop thinking about her. On the opening night of her new play, Alan learns from Billy that Jenny has locked herself in her room and has gotten drunk. AFI notes:

> Alan rushes to the hotel and discovers Jenny passed out on the bed. After rousing her, he kisses her and cajoles her to admit that she loves him, as he loves her. He then declares that despite everything, they must find strength in their feelings, not sorrow. Bolstered by Alan's words, Jenny takes a cold shower and arrives at the theater moments before curtain call.[451]

Summertime (1955)

The film was directed by David Lean.

Jane Hudson (Katharine Hepburn), a middle-aged secretary from Ohio, is excited to be fulfilling her life-long dream of visiting Venice, Italy. Jane has been alone her whole life, without experiencing romance. So, she is caught by surprise by the romantic overtures of Renato de Rossi (Rossano Brazzi), a handsome antique dealer. At first, it panics her to see Renato staring at her from across the square. But she happens by chance to meet him again at his shop. After much resistance, she agrees to attend a concert with him. She falls in love with Renato and is devastated to learn that he is married.

Kelly wrote:

> Jane is morally outraged when she discovers the truth, but circumstances are such that her strict spin-sterish moral sense comes undone in the exotic Venetian night. When the train takes her away in the film's final moments it is with the audience's approval of her morally questionable but enlarging romantic adventure, as her adulterous lover waves fondly to her, so very unlike the character of [*The Indiscretion of an American Wife*'s Montgomery] Clift who finds himself sprawled on the gravel of the Rome Terminal Station, a picture of undignified injury as [Jennifer] Jones's train departs.[452]

Rossano Brazzi and Katharine Hepburn in *Summertime* (1955)

Brazzi played a straying husband in two other films, *Interlude* (1957) and *A Certain Smile* (1958).

Juliet Mills and Jack Lemmon in *Avanti!* (1972)

Avanti! (1972)

Wendell Armbruster, Jr. (Jack Lemmon) and Pamela Piggott (Juliet Mills) meet at a romantic island resort in Italy. The two are not there for sun and romance. Their parents, who had rendezvoused at the resort for extramarital relations, died in an automobile accident and the family has been summoned to claim their bodies.

Wendell regularly phones his wife Emily in Baltimore, but their conversations are always curt and businesslike. It figures why he'd be taken by the affectionate and free-spirited Pamela, especially considering the enchanting atmosphere of the island. Tony Macklin of The Journal Herald wrote, "When the rigid Armbruster warms up on a sunny rock and begins to shuck the cold, American, uptight existence for a lazier, livelier life, Wilder is telling us something that is more than just fun."[453] Since the Production Code is no longer in effect, the couple is allowed to wind up in bed together in the third act. Wendell and Pamela agree in the end to turn their happy adulterous romp into an annual ritual. Unlike most other adultery films, this one concludes with no pain, no fuss, and no mess.

Play It Again, Sam (1972)

Allan Felix (Woody Allen) manages to overcome his shyness with women by having an affair with his best friend's caring and sympathetic wife, Linda (Diane Keaton).

428 · ANTHONY BALDUCCI

Strange Occasion (1976)

The original French title: *Quelle strane occasioni*

Antonio Pecoraro (Nino Manfredi) is unexpectedly visited by Cristina (Jinny Steffan), the beautiful young daughter of an old friend, while his wife and children are away. He has no problem having sex with Cristina, but he is greatly upset when Cristina reveals that her father once had an affair with Antonio's wife Giovanna.

Cristina: To them, it was beautiful. A pure relationship.

Antonio: Of course, I know. . . What do you mean by "pure"?

Cristina: A purely physical relationship. A sexual attraction. Uncomplicated by sentiment.

Antonio is shocked by this revelation. He wants to know more about the affair and Cristina has no problem talking about it.

Cristina: Dad's marriage was in crisis then. And his relationship with your wife was very important. Important, because it was a purely sexual relationship. It was brief though. Only three months.

Antonio: So short? I thought it'd be more.

Cristina: No. Only for the three months, you were in Malmo for the trial. . . You did well because that saved my dad's marriage. After, he felt younger.

Antonio: Did he?

Cristina: Now his relationship with mom can be called perfect.

Antonio: Well, you can't imagine how glad I am.

Cristina: But it was important for your wife too.

Antonio: Really? Let's hear it, I'm interested.

Cristina: Before that, she had only been to bed with you.

Antonio: Right!

Cristina: She never knew another man's body. A mistake.

Antonio: Sure! Only making love to me would be a terrible mistake! She should throw herself out the window!

Cristina: No, this way, she could choose.

Antonio: And she chose me.

Cristina: And thus your marriage went well. Antonio. Today, I met a happy family.

Alan Alda and Ellen Burstyn in *Same Time, Next Year* (1978)

Same Time, Next Year (1978)

Never has a film about adultery been as cutesy and shallow as *Same Time Next Year*. The characters are not authentic, which is something the long-term story requires.

The way the couple first meet is an important part of the adultery story. The film opens at an inn restaurant in 1951. Doris (Ellen Burstyn), a 24-year-old housewife from Oakland, and George (Alan Alda), a 27-year-old accountant, are having dinner at separate tables. George takes notice of Doris and he is so mesmerized by her that he can't look away. She looks up and sees George. He smiles. She smiles. The whole time, a saccharine love song, "The Last Time I Felt Like This," is blaring on the soundtrack. We next see the couple sitting together at the same table and talking. We don't hear what they're saying. We hear, instead, the love song, which seems by now to be even more overwrought and sappy. The scene is handled with the subtly and nuance of a wine commercial. It would have been better if, like the play, the meeting was left to the viewer's imagination. Alda has no sensitivity in the role. He delivers his lines like he's auditioning a stand-up comedy set. It is never believable when, again and again, Alda bemoans his feelings of guilt.

After spending the night together, the couple agrees to meet once a year. Over the next 26 years, they develop an intimate and loving relationship.

IMDb critic MISSMOOHERSELF wrote:

Some of Miss Burstyn's transformations are a bit jarring - arriving one year to the reunion 8 months pregnant comes to mind, as does her transformation from a suburban housewife to a Berkeley University hippie chick. And Alan Alda's transformation from an uptight Goldwater Republican to the typical 1970s man who ditches the corporate life, grows a mustache, wears his hair longer and also uses every typical 1970s cliché in existence is also a bit jarring but it can be forgiven because Mr. Alda pulls it off so well.[454]

moonspinner554 of IMDb wrote:

> . . . [T]his role doesn't allow Burstyn any real personality: it's all processed, from the costume and wig changes down to the mannerisms, from youthful girlishness to flip, knowing womanhood. Opposite her, Alan Alda is serviceable though rather uncomfortable, flailing away at little sitcom routines like a fish caught in a net. . . Playwright/screenwriter Bernard Slade doesn't write for the ages, he's too impatient and wants to wring laughter out of every set-up. Therefore, the film is sniggering instead of intuitive, and artificially sentimental instead of human.[455]

Prince of Tides (1991)

Tom Wingo (Nick Nolte) meets with his sister's psychiatrist, Susan Lowenstein (Barbra Streisand), to work out the reason that his sister tried to kill herself. Tom and Susan are both married, but they are willing to disregard their marriages to have a bit of romance with each other. Tom has less reason to be committed to his spouse Sallie, who is having an affair and wants a divorce. As their feelings deepen, the couple gets together at Lowenstein's country home for an intimate weekend. Lowenstein helps Tom to cope with traumatic events of his past. Tom is contacted by Sallie, who is now interested in working on their marriage. He agrees. Tom says in the end:

> At the end of every day, I drive through the city of Charleston and, as I cross the bridge that'll take me home, I feel the words building inside me. I can't stop them or tell you why I say them. But as I reach the top of the bridge these words come to me in a whisper. I say them as prayer. As regret. As praise. I say. . . "Lowenstein. Lowenstein."

Yikes!

Bridges of Madison County (1995)

Carolyn (Annie Corley) and Michael (Victor Slezak) are settling the estate of their recently deceased mother Francesca (Meryl Streep) when they find a diary that they never knew about. In the diary, Francesca details a four-day love affair that she had while her husband and children were at a state fair. Her lover was a photographer, Robert Kincaid (Clint Eastwood), who had visited the area to create a photo essay of covered bridges. She talks about having planned to run away with Robert and travel the world.

Robert and Francesca spend most of the four days talking. Robert is as fond of Africa as Jean Gabin is fond of Tahiti in *La Marie du port*. He considers it to be an exciting place to live as a person never has to worry about other people passing judgment on them. He says:

> It seems to me there's too much of: "This is mine" and "He or she is mine." There's just too many lines being drawn.

Robert hears gossip in town about a woman named Redfield who had an affair with a married man named Delaney.

> Robert: I guess you got the whole story. The cashier at the grocery store was most generous. He's running for town crier next year. I know more about the Delaney affair than I knew about my mar-

riage. If it's going to be a problem for you to see me tonight, don't do so. I'm not too bright about people's reactions. I wouldn't want you to be put in a compromising situation.

Francesca: Yeah, I understand. That's very kind of you to think of that. Robert? I want to come. Okay? So I'll meet you at the bridge like we planned and don't worry about the rest.

Francesca realizes in the end that she can't bear to hurt her husband and children by leaving.

Francesca: They'll never be able to live through the talk. And Richard. . . Richard will never be able to get his arms around this. It will break him in half. He doesn't deserve that. He's never hurt anyone in his whole life.

Robert: He can move on. People move.

Francesca: His family has had this farm for over a hundred years. Richard doesn't know how to live anywhere else. And my kids. . .

Robert: They're practically grown. You said yourself they hardly talk to you.

Francesca: Yeah, they don't say much. But Carolyn is only 16. She's about to find out about all of this for herself. She's going to fall in love and she's going to try to build a life with someone. If I leave. . . what does that say to her?

Robert: What about us?

Francesca: You have to know deep down, the minute we leave here, everything will change.

Robert: Yeah, it could. . . It could get better.

Francesca: No matter how much distance we put between ourselves and this house I carry it with me. I feel it every minute we're together. And I will start to blame loving you for how much it hurts. And then, even these. . . even these four beautiful days will seem just like something sordid and a mistake.

Robert: Francesca. Do you think that what happened with us just happens to anyone? What we feel for each other? We're hardly. . . hardly two separate people now.

Francesca has made up her mind.

Francesca: I want to love you the way I do now for the rest of my life, but if we leave we lose it. And I can't make an entire life disappear to start a new one. All I can do is try to hold on to us. . . somewhere inside of me. You have to help me.

Robert: Don't lose us. Don't throw us away.

Francesca is in a truck with her husband and, while waiting at a stop light, she sees Robert standing beside his truck in the rain. He looks at her. She looks at him. She needs to make a choice - stay with her husband in the truck or open the door and run out to join Robert. She agonizes over what to do. She grips the door handle tightly and takes a heavy breath. But she remains in the car. She can't bring herself to leave. She murmurs, "Oh, no." Then she sobs, which confuses her unsuspecting husband.

The story provides direction to her children, who are struggling in their own marriages.

Michael: What do I do now? What's good enough for mom is good enough for me?

Carolyn: What gets me is I'm in my forties. I've been in this crummy frigging marriage for over 20 years because that's what I was taught. You stick things out. Normal people don't get divorced. I can't remember the last time my husband made love to me so intensely that he transported me to Africa, for Christ sake. Quite frankly, I don't think he ever did.

At the end of the film, Michael reconnects with his wife Betty (Phyllis Lyons) while Carolyn takes time off from her own marriage. Michael asks Betty, "Do I make you happy, Betty? Because I want to. More than anything." At their mother's request, the siblings scatter their mother's ashes at the covered bridge.

Peter Travers of Rolling Stone wrote:

"I live with dust on my heart," Robert tells Francesca after making the supreme sacrifice of giving her up to her husband and children. The sentiment is part of a tradition – not of poetry but of great romantic crocks, from Erich Segal's *Love Story* ("Love means never having to say you're sorry") to Pat Conroy's *Prince of Tides*, with its now notorious camp incantation of "Lowenstein, Lowenstein."[456]

Roger Ebert wrote:

[The novel's] prose is not distinguished, but its story is compelling: He provides the fantasy of total eroticism within perfect virtue, elevating to a spiritual level the common fantasy in which a virile stranger materializes in the kitchen of a quiet housewife and takes her into his arms. Waller's gift is to make the housewife feel virtuous afterward.

. . .

If the story had ended "happily" with them running away together, no one would have read Waller's book and no movie would exist. The emotional peak of the movie is the renunciation, when Francesca does not open the door of her husband's truck and run to Robert. This moment, and not the moment when the characters first kiss, or make love, is the film's passionate climax.

. . .

"The Bridges of Madison County" is about two people who find the promise of perfect personal happiness, and understand, with sadness and acceptance, that the most important things in life are not always about making yourself happy.[457]

Bonnie Brennen, a journalism professor at Marquette University, found that Kincaid dominates Francesca with a "magical shaman-like power."[458]

Marc Eliot, author of "American Rebel: The Life of Clint Eastwood," wrote that *The Bridges of Madison County*, like *Brief Encounter*, was "about the desperation, guilt, and temptations of two married people who meet, fall in love, commit adultery, and then separate forever."[459]

The film presents an extramarital affair as a safe antidote to the boredom of marriage. Francesca makes it clear in her diary that the affair gave her the strength to persevere as a wife and mother. John Leo of US News and World Report wrote, "All this lets readers have everything both ways - the thrill of a fantasy fling, the safety of marriage; the simultaneous commitment to rule breaking and rule keeping."[460]

The film aroused the curiosity of Dr. Larry Baas, professor of political science at Valparaiso University, and Dr. Dan Thomas, professor of political science at Wartburg College. A considerable number of *BOMC* viewers surveyed by the professors positively scored the following items:

I'm fed up with all these books about affairs. Why can't we just have romance within marriage, like it's supposed to be?

Francesca's attraction to Kincaid is described in such mystical, soul-partner terms. But might she have been fooled? I mean, she could simply have been lonely and bored, both with married life and with life on the farm.

Waller's depiction of Francesca's annual ritual commemorating her affair - with the cigarettes, love letter, brandy, photos and all - struck me as more sordid or perverse than as tender or loving.[461]

Meryl Streep and Clint Eastwood in *Bridges of Madison County* (1995)

Thomas and Baas concluded:

> To these readers, then, Francesca's behavior raises questions about the purity of her motives and the soundness of her judgment in entering into the affair in the first place. Moreover, despite the fact that Francesca's decision to say goodbye to Kincaid and remain in Iowa was the proper one for these readers, her compulsive reenactment of the initial scene of seduction is, in the absence of sufficient attention to defining elements of Mrs. Johnson's internal make-up, enough to raise serious questions about her emotional equilibrium and possibly even her sanity.[462]

The most popular film of the 1990s was a romantic drama, *Titanic* (1997), but science fiction was a far more popular genre of the decade. This was, after all, the decade of *Terminator 2: Judgment Day* (1991), *Jurassic Park* (1993), *Independence Day* (1996), *Men in Black* (1997), *Armageddon* (1998), *Star Wars: Episode 1: The Phantom Menace* (1999) and *The Matrix* (1999). Only two other romantic dramas were blockbusters at the box office during the decade. These films were *Ghost* (1990) and *The Bodyguard* (1992). Another successful genre of the period was the romantic comedy, which was represented by *Pretty Woman* (1990), *My Best Friend's Wedding* (1997), *There's Something About Mary* (1998) and *Runaway Bride* (1999). Not one of these films involved adultery. But that doesn't mean that Hollywood didn't have more adultery stories to tell. The 1990s produced six notable adultery films: *Prince of Tides, The Bridges of Madison County, The Age of Innocence, The Piano, The English Patient* and *Eyes Wide Shut*.

The *Bridges of Madison County* and *The English Patient* share distinct similarities. Like *Titanic* (which involves a young woman cheating on her fiancé), these films feature an adulterer who recounts their story (shown in flashback) to rapt, impartial listeners.

The Horse Whisperer (1998)

Tom Booker (Robert Redford), a sensitive horse trainer, helps a teenage girl Grace (Scarlett Johansson) and her horse, Pilgrim, to recover from a traumatic riding accident. The accident itself was jarring, but it is worse that a surgeon had to save Grace by amputating the lower half of one leg. Grace's mother, Annie (Kristin Scott Thomas), is distressed that her once vibrant daughter has become bitter and withdrawn. But Tom helps Grace to regain her confidence and peace of mind. In the meantime, Annie and Tom fall in love. But is this right? Annie has allowed her busy career to come between herself and her husband, Robert (Sam Neill). She doesn't feel that her needs are being met in her marriage, but it's no one's fault but her own.

Tom: [Your husband]'s a good man, Annie.

Annie: I never said he wasn't. I can't change the way I feel.

Tom: You gotta figure out what you want.

The couple finally kisses two hours into the film. But, afterward, they decide against pursuing a relationship. Tom provides love and acceptance, mostly in the form of a warm and steady gaze, to cure a variety of ills. He calms the nervous horse, he gets Grace to look beyond her physical disability and mental scars, and he persuades Annie to reconnect with her husband. Tom is, in his charming and rugged way, reminiscent of Clint Eastwood's Robert Kincaid from *The Bridges of Madison County*.

Lady Chatterley's Lover (2006)

Adultery was therapeutic to Lady Chatterley. The affair lifted the lady out of a terrible state of depression and confusion. The narrator spoke of the newly revived woman when he said:

That night, Constance was the perfect wife. The housewife every man dreams of. Modest yet attentive, with her big, clear eyes and calm gentleness which so well hid her intelligence.

Men in Hope (2011)

The original Czech title: *Muzi v nadeji*

Alice (Petra Hřebíčková) constantly bullies her husband, Ondřej (Jiří Macháček). Rudolf (Bolek Polívka), Ondřej's lusty and inhibited father-in-law, assures Ondřej that he would be healthier and happier if he engaged in an extramarital affair. Through Rudolf, Ondřej meets the lovely young Šarlota (Vica Kerekes). Šarlota, a bold and fun-loving woman, quickly persuades Ondřej to embark on an affair. Alice learns of the affair and comes to accept that she has been a bad wife.

A Young Man Receives Therapeutic Value From
Sleeping with An Older Woman

A Yank at Oxford (1938)

An Oxford student, Lee Sheridan (Robert Taylor), has an affair with Elsa Craddock (Vivien Leigh), the wife of a bookshop owner. This is an old "college widow" trope, which has to do with a woman in a college town who stalks the campus every year to find a new lover among the latest freshman class.

La Ronde (1950)

One of several storylines addresses adultery. A young man, Alfred (Daniel Gélin), has a tryst with Emma (Danielle Darrieux), the young wife of middle-aged businessman Charles (Fernand Gravey). That night, as she retires to bed, Emma starts a conversation with Charles about extramarital affairs. Charles admits that, as a young man, he was introduced to the ways of sex by an older married woman. He sees this as a common experience for young men. But he is not grateful to this woman for her instruction. He says, "Who wouldn't we be disgusted with love after the women we're condemned to start out with? But we have no choice." He worries about Emma associating with this type of woman.

Fernand Gravey and Danielle Darrieux in *La Ronde* (1950)

Charles: These women of dubious reputation often seek out the company of respectable women out of a sort of nostalgia for virtue. . . Their own unworthiness pains them. . . Think of their dreadful lives: trickery, lies, and constant danger. They pay dearly for the tiny bit of happiness. . . not even happiness. . .

Emma: Pleasure?

Charles: How can you call that pleasure?

Emma: I'm just guessing. Otherwise they wouldn't. . .

Charles: It's intoxication.

Emma: Intoxication?

Charles: Yes, intoxication.

Emma: But you enjoyed the benefit of it.

Charles: Yes, once.

Emma: Who was she? Was it long ago?

Charles: Very long ago. She's dead.

Emma: Dead?

Charles: Women like that all die young.

Emma: Are you sure?

Charles: It's a fact. It's justice.

Emma: Did you love her?

Charles: Darling, you don't love women like that. True love is only possible where there's truth and purity.

Tea and Sympathy (1956)

The film is set at Chilton College, an all-boys boarding school. Laura (Deborah Kerr), the wife of dormitory headmaster Bill Reynolds (Leif Erickson), feels compelled to help Tom Robinson Lee (John Kerr), a shy and sensitive freshman who is having difficulty adjusting to school. She starts out by giving him a dance lesson so that he will not be out of place at an upcoming school dance. But, when she sees the other students reject him for his less than masculine ways, she becomes more committed to providing him with motherly guidance (his actual mother is deceased) and improving his confidence. Their relationship becomes too serious in Bill's estimation. Bill destroys a book of poetry that Tom gave to Laura. He makes it clear to his wife that she is not to ever be alone with Tom. Laura becomes more deeply concerned when Tom, bullied by the other students, becomes suicidal. One day, Laura finds Tom alone in the woods. As she consoles him, Laura and Tom embrace and kiss. They are about to go beyond foreplay when the scene fades out.

The final scene is set ten years later. Tom has returned to Chilton for a reunion. He is now a bestselling author. His first book was a novel about his first year at Chilton and his relationship with Laura. Tom visits Bill, who is now living alone in the dormitory. He finds Bill collapsed in an easy chair. Understandably, Bill is not pleased to see Tom again. He has little to say to him. When Tom asks about Laura, Bill grimly gives him a letter that he found in Laura's belongings. Tom is surprised to see that the letter is addressed to him. He sits outside in the garden to read it alone. Laura explains in the letter that she wrote it on an impulse, but she knows that she will never have the nerve to mail it. She admits that she regrets their brief affair. She writes:

Deborah Kerr and John Kerr in *Tea and Sympathy* (1956)

You have romanticized the wrong we did and not looked at it clearly. At the end of the story, you say that the husband was far better off without his wife and the wife went on to her own happy life. You're quite wrong, Tom. As you'll know, I couldn't go back to Bill after that afternoon with you and pretend that nothing had happened, and my not going back ruined his life.

She admits to being sad and alone, but she still has affection for Tom.

Leif Erickson and Deborah Kerr in *Tea and Sympathy* (1956)

The epilogue with Laura's guilt-ridden letter was added to appease The Production Code Administration and The Catholic Legion of Decency.

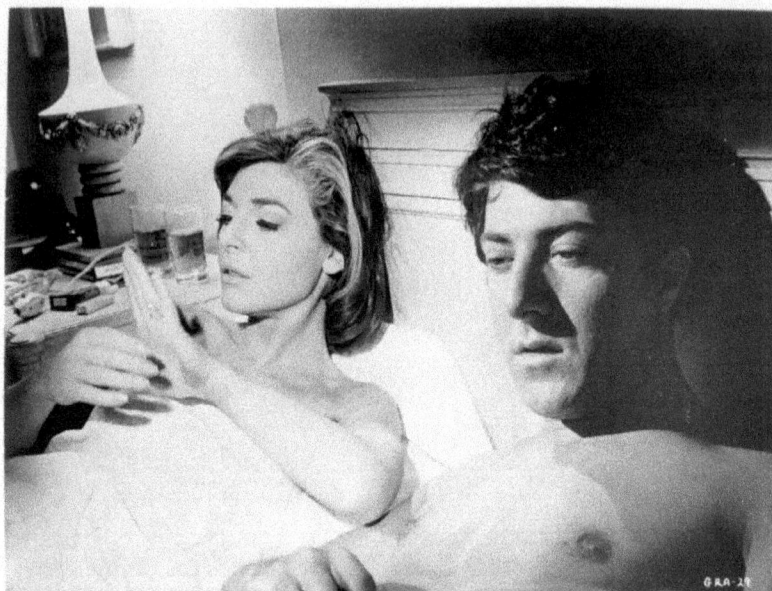

Anne Bancroft and Dustin Hoffman in *The Graduate* (1967)

The Graduate (1967)

Mrs. Robinson (Anne Bancroft) is perhaps the most famous seductress in film history. Mrs. Robinson dropped out of college and married after she unexpectedly got pregnant. She admits that, for the nineteen years that she has been married, she has never loved her husband. She and her husband now sleep in separate bedrooms. She drinks heavily to cope with feeling bored and unfulfilled. One night, she seduces her friends' son, Benjamin Braddock (Dustin Hoffman), who has just returned home after graduating from college. Peter Bradshaw of The Guardian wrote, "Basically, what is going on in Mrs. Robinson's head and heart is not of overwhelming interest: she is just a sexy, vampy older woman. . ."463 The vamp isn't seducing a married man this time. Rather, she is a married woman who seduces a wide-eyed, inexperienced youth.

At first, the affair gives Benjamin great confidence, which is something he desperately needs. It eventually becomes something that he regrets when he falls in love with Mrs. Robinson's daughter, Elaine (Katharine Ross).

The film is unique in that it gives the wronged husband, Mr. Robinson (Murray Hamilton), an opportunity to express to his wife's lover his grievances. Mr. Robinson is clearly agitated when he confronts Benjamin. He says:

Do you want to try and tell me why you did it? Do you have a special grudge against me? Do you feel a particularly strong resentment? Is there something I've said that's caused this contempt. . .?

He is appalled by this young man's disrespectful behavior. His anger builds. He finally says, "I do think you should know the consequences of what you've done. I do think you should know that my wife and I are getting a divorce soon. . . I think you are filth. I think you are scum. You are a degenerate!"

In film history, more men who slept with married women should have been confronted and told they were filth.

The Last Picture Show (1971)

The Last Picture Show presents adultery as an ideal cure for marital disappointment and depression.

Sonny Crawford (Timothy Bottoms), a high school football player, loses his virginity to his coach's despondent middle-aged wife, Ruth Popper (Cloris Leachman). Ruth's mood miraculously lightens once she has sex with Sonny. The film flips the *Tea and Sympathy* scenario. Now, a teenage boy resolves a middle-aged woman's suicidal despondency by having sex with her.

Sonny is eating Oreo cookies while Ruth is lovingly brushing his hair. It is a quiet respite in which the two are able to speak intimately. Sonny, who has never heard Ruth express affection for her husband, is curious to know the reason that she married him. She replies, "I don't know. My mother didn't like him. Maybe that was it. But I was 20 years old. I thought hairy-chested football coaches were about it." Sonny asks her what the coach would do if he found out about their affair. She responds casually, "Shoot us, probably. He's always glad to have an excuse to use his deer rifle." She is so blissful around Sonny that the idea of the coach shooting her dead doesn't bother her at all.

The film's director, Peter Bogdanovich, was a prominent member of New Hollywood. He was determined to portray infidelity in a more frank and realistic manner, reflecting the shifting social norms of the day.

Timothy Bottoms and Cloris Leachman in *The Last Picture Show* (1971)

The Summer of '42 (1971)

The film is based on an autobiographical novel by Herman Raucher. It tells the story of 15-year-old Raucher, then called Hermie, spending a memorable summer vacation on Nantucket Island.

When we first meet him, Hermie (Gary Grimes) is a bratty boy. In the novel, he lusts after Penny Singleton of the *Blondie* movies. From the novel: "He couldn't bear the thought of her bedding down with dumb Dagwood even though he knew that it was only a movie."[464] Coveting other people's wives becomes a habit for him. He sees a handsome young man carrying his beautiful young bride, Dorothy (Jennifer O'Neill), into a beach home. He is enchanted by Dorothy's beauty. From the novel: ". . .[H]is blood rushed dizzily at the very sight of her."[465] He cannot stop thinking about her.

The husband goes off to war, leaving his bride alone at the beach home. Hermie sees her struggling with her grocery bags and offers to help her carry the bags home. Eager to spend time with her, he continues to make himself helpful around her home. One day, he comes to visit her and finds her crying. He notices an empty bottle of whiskey nearby. A telegram on a table reports that her husband was killed in action. She puts on a romantic record (the film's theme "The Summer Knows") and dances slowly with Hermie. She embraces the boy tightly and kisses him. She leads him into the bedroom. They lie in bed together and hold one another. The scene fades out. The next morning, the two have nothing to say to one another. Wikipedia reports, "[Hermie] leaves, his last image of Dorothy being of her leaning against the railing, as she smokes a cigarette and stares into the night sky."[466]

Hermie starts out in the film as awkward and confused. But sex with an older woman has changed him. He says in a voice-over, ". . . [I]n a very special way, I lost Hermie. Forever." In other words, the boy Hermie had been replaced by the man Herman. Or something like that.

The film follows the older woman/younger man scenario that was seen before in *Tea and Sympathy*, *The Graduate* and *The Last Picture Show*. Like *Tea and Sympathy*, the film ends with the young man reading a farewell letter from his lover.

In the real story, Raucher was 14 years old. The author spoke at length about the experience in a 2002 interview. He said, "[Dorothy] had been drinking — heavily. . . She kept calling me 'Pete.' And I was not of a mind to slap her in the face and say, 'You've gotta cut this out.' I was just going to be Pete as best I could."[467] He admitted, though, that he and Dorothy never had sex. "We were mostly holding," he said. "In the movie we let you think what you want."[468] He also admitted that the experience was "hardly romantic."[469] "It was terrifying," he said. "I was really scared. I didn't know what to do.. . And no one has ever thought about that. Everybody thought, 'Oh, that's interesting. The kid grew up.' But it was a traumatic event."[470] Still, Raucher defended Dorothy. He said, "[Dorothy] had lost her husband. I think they were married [for] about seven months. And she was alone on an island and drinkin' and playing their favorite song and in walks this kid and — good grief! — the last thing in her mind was pedophilia. She just thought I was him."[471]

A precocious teenage boy stalks a married woman for weeks. Then, he takes advantage of her when she's drunk and distraught. Warren William would be proud.

Drive, He Said (1971)

Hector (William Tepper), a college basketball star, has an affair with a professor's strong-willed wife, Olive (Karen Black).

Love is Only a Word (1971)

The original German title: *Liebe ist nur ein Wort*

    Verena Angenford (Judy Winter), a banker's wife, falls in love with a college student, Oliver Mansfeld (Malte Thorsten). The wife enjoys a carefree romp, which allows her to feel young again. But her husband, Manfred (Herbert Fleischmann), is a strong-willed man who will not relinquish his wife to a kid. He bullies and humiliates Oliver, which causes the lovesick young man to commit suicide.

My Teacher's Wife (1999)

    A high school student, Todd Boomer (Jason London), has a romantic affair with his math tutor, Vicky (Tia Carrere). It turns out that Vicky is married to Todd's math teacher, Roy Mueller (Christopher McDonald).

Jason London and Tia Carrere in *My Teacher's Wife* (1999)

Chapter Seventeen:
Suicide

Many films about adultery climax with a suicide or at least attempted suicide. Take, for instance, the climax of *Counsellor at Law* (1933). George Simon (John Barrymore) is so distraught by his wife's cheating that he prepares to leap out of a window in his office. Just then, his loving secretary Regina Gordon (Bebe Daniels) rushes into the room and rescues him.

A suicide or attempted suicide is the resolution for so many other adultery films, including *Cynara* (1932), *Christopher Strong* (1933), *Dr. Monica* (1934), *Dreaming Lips* (1937), *I Take This Woman* (1940), *Brief Encounter* (1945), *Humoresque* (1946), *If Winter Comes* (1947), *They Won't Believe Me* (1947), *Daybreak* (1948), *The Passionate Friends* (1949), *A Life of Her Own* (1950), *The Heart of the Matter* (1953), *Hilda Crane* (1956), *Interlude* (1957), *This Is My Street* (1964), *Gypsy Moths* (1969) and *Ryan's Daughter* (1970).

Let's take a look at a few more.

Maisie (1939)

Ruth Hussey portrays the worst sort of adulterous wife. She only married her good-natured husband (Ian Hunter) for his money and seeks out sexual thrills from any good-looking man who comes along. Cliff, upset that his wife has cheated on him, commits suicide.

Nora Prentiss (1947)

Dr. Richard Talbot (Kent Smith) is called to the hospital to treat a woman injured in a car accident. The woman, Nora Prentiss (Ann Sheridan), is a beautiful nightclub singer. Talbot, who is bored with married life, finds himself enchanted by Nora. He becomes so obsessed with his charming new patient that he neglects his family and his practice. The distracted doctor becomes upset when he botches a surgical procedure. He wants desperately to run away with Nora, but he cannot bring himself to ask his wife for a divorce. Walter Bailey (John Ridgely), a patient with a heart condition, visits him at his office. Bailey is having great difficulty breathing. Before the doctor can help him, he collapses and dies. Talbot has an idea. He dresses the dead man in his clothing, puts his wedding band on the man's finger, and stuffs his wallet into the man's pocket. Then, he drives the man to the top of a cliff, where he sets the car on fire and shoves it over the cliff. Bailey is misidentified as Talbot just as intended. Now that he has been pronounced dead, he is free from his marital obligations. Talbot and Nora leave San Francisco to start their new lives together in New York City. So, it's a happy ending?

Old Movies Are Great noted:

Talbot drinks heavily and becomes increasingly paranoid and reclusive as he learns that his death is under investigation. After a fight with Nora's nightclub boss, Talbot crashes his car and his face is badly scarred. The police, not realizing that the man is Talbot, arrest him for Talbot's murder.[472]

In the end, Talbot chooses to be executed rather than shame his family.

They Won't Believe Me (1947)

Larry (Robert Young) plans to abandon his wife, Greta (Rita Johnson), and run away with his mistress, Verna (Susan Hayward). To finance his getaway, he plans to abscond with the funds from the marital bank account. But the idea of him robbing his wife of their savings is abhorrent to Verna, who makes it clear that she will not go away with him unless he leaves behind the money.

The incredible twists and turns of this story put Larry in the hot seat for murder. Police come to believe that Larry staged his wife's death and murdered his mistress to keep her quiet. Larry is sure, as the title suggests, that the jury won't believe his explanation for everything that has happened. The truth is that his mistress died in a car accident (a truck blew a tire and swerved into their lane) and his wife drowned herself. Matters are complicated by the strange circumstances under which his dead mistress, burned beyond recognition, was misidentified as his wife and his waterlogged wife was misidentified as his mistress. Before the verdict is read, Larry jumps out of a window and falls to his death. It is revealed in the end that the jury found him not guilty.

Anna Karenina (1948)

Anna Karenina (Vivien Leigh) is married to Alexei Karenin (Ralph Richardson), a cold-hearted government bureaucrat who is strictly focused on his career. Anna encounters a cavalry officer, Count Alexei Kirillovich Vronsky (Kieron Moore), at a train station. The two develop an immediate attraction to one another. At a ball, Vronsky pursues the married Anna, unconcerned that they are being closely watched by other guests. Gossip about the couple's ongoing relationship reaches Alexei, who threatens to bar Anna from seeing her son if she does not stop seeing Vronsky. Anna cannot keep away from Vronsky and eventually becomes pregnant with his child. Anna nearly dies during the delivery of the baby, which is stillborn. Anna remains obsessed with Vronsky and cannot bring herself to end their relationship. She becomes insanely jealous of the attention that he pays to other women. From the novel: ". . . [T]here's no help for it. He is everything for me, and I want him more and more to give himself up to me entirely. And he wants more and more to get away from me."[473] Fearful that Vronsky is planning to leave her for a rich society woman, she rushes to a railway station and throws herself beneath a passing train.

A 1935 version of *Anna Karenina* starring Greta Garbo inspired an early Production Code battle. It was important to Joseph Breen, Hollywood's chief film censor, that Anna be denied bliss for shamelessly neglecting her duties as a wife and mother. Breen was satisfied in the end. He found that "the matrimonial bond is positively defended - at least in the minds of those who take marriage seriously."[474] Andre Sennwald of the New York Times noted that Garbo "sins, suffers and perishes."[475] Leigh's Ann perishes, too. Anna has inevitably perished in every version of the story.

Anna's husband, Karenin, is depicted in the novel as cold and aloof. He tends to look down on Anna and treat her like a child. Filmmakers have been varied in their treatment of this character. Robert Short of Silver Screen Classics Blog wrote, ". . . [A]s portrayed by Basil Rathbone in the earlier [1935] presentation, Karenin was a tyrant, whereas Ralph Richardson's Karenin, while still a cold, emotionally sterile man, displayed a glimmer of humanity."[476]

Vivien Leigh in *Anna Karenina* (1948)

The opening of the novel includes the following passage:

Everything was in confusion in the Oblonskys' house. The wife had discovered that the husband was carrying on an intrigue with a French girl, who had been a governess in their family, and she had announced to her husband that she could not go on living in the same house with him.[477]

Stiva Oblonsky, Anna's brother, creates upheaval in his home with the affair. Spark Notes reports:

Stiva embodies the notion that life is meant to be lived and enjoyed, not repressed by duties. . . He is kind and jovial and genuinely loves his wife and family, yet he feels entitled to have sex with whomever he pleases.[478]

But his free ways cause destruction for himself and his family. Fortunately, though, Stiva lacks Anna's emotional intensity. Spark Notes continues:

His love affairs are trifles to him, whereas Anna's becomes a matter of life and death to her. Stiva is not a dynamic character in the novel — he does not change. He is never punished for his sins and never improves his behavior. In short, Stiva's constancy brings into relief the extraordinary changes — moral, spiritual, and psychological — that Anna undergoes.[479]

Vivien Leigh in *Anna Karenina* (1948)

The Astonished Heart (1950)

Noël Coward wrote both "The Astonished Heart" and "Still Life" as part of a collection of one-act plays called "Tonight at 8:30." It is hard to believe that one man in a single year wrote such radically different takes on adultery.

The Astonished Heart was originally shot with Michael Redgrave as Dr. Faber, but Coward found Redgrave's performance unconvincing and persuaded the producers to reshoot the entire film with himself in the lead.

A middle-aged psychiatrist, Dr. Christian Faber (Coward), irrationally destroys his happy life to pursue a romance with a frivolous young woman. He should have known better. He counsels a bank clerk named Burton who became so guilty about an affair that he tried to kill himself. He describes Burton as a "gentle little man." He finds that a combination of guilt and a "bizarre respectability" is "tearing him to pieces." He later treats another guilt-ridden adulterer, Mr. Lucas (Ralph Michael). He is desperate for Faber to cure him. He says, "I want peace of mind. The conflict within me is torturing me too much. I'm afraid of breaking down completely." Faber is strangely unsympathetic.

The story of the affair is, in the end, a story of madness. Faber has a loving wife, Barbara (Celia Johnson), and a thriving practice. His affair with Leonora (Margaret Leighton) starts out frivolously, with the couple bonding over their mutual disdain for a trite play. Leonora later admits that, when they first met, she was determined to trick him into loving her. But she develops doubts early on. She tells him, "I feel cheap. I feel frightened." He says, "Pangs of conscience are tiresome. They're also exceedingly bad for you." She asks about Barbara. He replies, "Barbara has nothing to do with this."

Faber is not home when Barbara returns from a trip. She casually checks his appointment book to see where he is. She sees the initials "LV" taking up a large portion of the day's page. She skims through the diary and finds the initials written over several large spaces in the book. It isn't hard to understand. LV. Leonora Vail. When Faber comes home, he finds Barbara playing the piano. She does not skip a note as she and her husband exchange banal greetings. She never, for a second, betrays the truth of the situation. In another scene, she is sitting alone in the dark when he arrives home from yet another rendezvous.

Faber's affair with Leonora goes on for a long while before Barbara finally speaks up about it. Barbara, her voice quivering, says:

> . . . [N]obody is having a good time. . . I hate her quite normally with all my feminine instincts. Sometimes, I get quite violent all by myself. . . I got over wanting to strangle her now. I just wish she'd never been born.

By now, Faber senses that Leonora has fallen out of love with him. She lies about going to a party when she really went to dinner with an old boyfriend. He becomes consumed with jealousy.

> Faber: You wanted me in the beginning didn't you? Whenever I came here, whenever I touched you, it was more important than anything in the world wasn't it? Wasn't it?
>
> Leonora: Yes, yes, it was.
>
> Faber: And now it isn't anymore.
>
> Leonora: Oh, Chris what's the use.
>
> Faber: Answer me. Do you still love me as much as you did in the beginning?
>
> Leonora: No.
>
> Faber: At last!
>
> Leonora: That was what you wanted, isn't it? The truth, well that's the truth.

Faber isn't satisfied. He wants to know more.

> Faber: When did it die? When did it die, this poor shabby love of yours?
>
> Leonora: A long time ago. You killed it yourself with your insane jealousies and cruelties. I can't even go back into my own memory now without finding you there jeering on every threshold. Walking with me through the empty rooms, making them tawdry, shutting them off from me forever. I hate you for that bitterly
>
> Faber: Sentiment for the dead at the expense of the living. Very interesting. Quite magnificent.
>
> Leonora: The dead have at least proper sense to be quiet.
>
> Faber: Long live the dead!
>
> Leonora: You're one of them now.

Faber: Did you mean that?

Leonora: Yes, I think I did.

Faber resents that, now that her passion has been spent, Leonora expects everything to be "tidied up and put back in the box." He concludes their discussion with a bitter speech.

> How does it feel to be so desirable, to be wanted so much? Tell me, please, I want to know, I want to know what your heart is doing now, your loving female heart. How enviable to be able to walk away into the future free of love, free of longing, a new life before you and the dead behind you. Not quite the dead. Let's say the dying. The dying aren't quite as sensibly quiet as the dead. They can be heard crying a little. You must walk swiftly out of their earshot and I implore you don't look back. . . You are a sane, thrilling animal without complications and the fact that my life has been wrecked on your loveliness isn't your fault. . . You see, I had a life to live and work to do and people to love and now I haven't anymore. Nobody could help me, those people I love and who love me. I can see them still straining to get to me, but they can't reach me anymore. It's too late. It's too late.

Faber seeks to end his torment by jumping off a roof. He finds emotional release as he is dying. Lenora comes to his bedside. Barbara becomes impatient when Lenora fails to come out after an hour. She decides to go into the bedroom, but she comes to the doors and is afraid to open them. The door is white and shines brightly from a window light. It has a divine look. The bedroom has become a private sacred sphere for two lovers. To enter through that door now would be a gross intrusion. But this is perverse. A husband and wife create the ultimate sacred sphere, upon which no one else has a right to enter. Leonora is the trespasser.

The Astonished Heart was poorly received. The film was not helped by Coward's performance, which *Brief Encounter* producer Anthony Havelock-Allan called "totally stilted."[480]

Gypsy Moths (1969)

Mike Rettig (Burt Lancaster) arrives in town as part of a death-defying skydiving show. Malcolm Webson (Scott Wilson), the youngest of the skydivers, arranges for his group to be guests at the home of his Uncle John (William Windom) and Aunt Elizabeth (Deborah Kerr). Elizabeth, who has become dissatisfied with her marriage, finds herself attracted to Mike. They have no concern about John when they make love in the living room while he is asleep upstairs. She does take the minor precaution of shutting the room's large oak doors. Is this enough to hide their wrongdoing? Later, she quietly enters her bedroom upstairs. The camera angle allows us to see what she can't: her husband lying awake in bed. His eyes are wide with sadness and desperation, indicating that he knows what happened downstairs. It is one of the most chilling moments in an adultery film. This is the pain and humiliation that adultery creates.

When Elizabeth refuses to leave town with Mike, Mike becomes depressed. During a skydiving stunt, he declines to pull the ripcord, which causes him to fall to his death

Aviators dejected by a failed infidelity commit a spectacular aerial suicide in *Christopher Strong* (1933) and *Dr. Monica* (1934). It was a trend at the time. Walter Connolly, unwilling for his daughter to marry a wealthy man to settle his debts, deliberately crashes his plane in *No More Orchids* (1932). Douglass Montgomery, an alcoholic playboy, crashes his plane to end his sad and useless life in *Five and Ten* (1931).

Chapter Eighteen:
A Midlife Crisis

We have already seen in *Dodsworth* (1936) that a midlife crisis can destroy a marriage.

The Power and Glory (1933)

Tom Garner (Spencer Tracy) has had a solid marriage with his wife Sally (Colleen Moore) for 30 years. But he suddenly becomes smitten with Eve Borden (Helen Vinson). His best friend, Henry (Ralph Morgan), defends Tom to his own wife. He says, "The man was kindly and honest and a square-shooter with [his wife] for 30 years. And then something happens that he couldn't help. Any more than. . . than. . . than. . . Well, he couldn't help."

Easy to Love (1934)

bkoganbing of IMDb wrote: "Adolph Menjou and Genevieve Tobin [star] as a married couple who are getting a bit stale. He's stepping out with Mary Astor so she decides to retaliate by doing a little stepping with Edward Everett Horton. That's the biggest problem with *Easy To Love*, buying Horton as a paramour."[481]

Hafer wrote, "*Easy to Love* is clearly an example of a Pre-Code film, as its theme is the joys of adultery. Practically everyone in the film is sleeping with someone else or at least wants to."[482]

There's Always Tomorrow (1934)

Les Adams of IMDb wrote:

[A] likeable and mild-mannered husband and father, Joseph White (Frank Morgan), begins to feel unneeded, unwanted by his family and generally over the hill. Alice Vail, who has been secretly in love with him for many years, begins an innocent friendship.[483]

It is, indeed, an innocent friendship. Joseph visits Alice (Binnie Barnes) once a week. They enjoy each other's company and see no need to have sex. But Joseph's children find out about the weekly visits and assume that something more is going on. They are determined to end this relationship. They visit Alice on the pretense that their car has stalled and they need to call a tow truck. Alice recognizes them, but she plays along with their ruse. As she drinks tea with her guests, she brings up the subject of love. She sees this as an opportunity to explain, in an oblique way, her relationship with their father. She tells them that she fell in love with her married boss. She says:

It was too hard seeing him every day. So, I cut and run. I thought I could forget that way. But it didn't work. So, I tried to take an interest in other men. Oh, yes, there were handsomer men and richer men. But none of them would do. I just seemed to miss him more and more. . . Have you ever tried running away from happiness? Well, I'll tell you now, it doesn't do any good. One night, when I couldn't bear it any longer, I went to find him. I made some silly excuse. And I did find him. I caught a glimpse of his children. And his wife. Otherwise it might have been a different story. I remember there was a party that night and he was sitting on the porch. Alone. I found that that was usual. He was always crowded out, I found out, too, that he was lonely. With all that big family. The thing I discovered that night made me wish that I hadn't been so foolish [to run away]. He was the forgotten man in that household.

The Woman in the Window (1944)

While his wife and children are on vacation, college professor Richard Wanley (Edward G. Robinson) spends time with his friends at his social club. Wanley has become enamored of an oil portrait displayed next door in a store window. He talks with his friends about the beautiful woman in the painting. Upon leaving the club, he goes back to admire the painting again. Alice Reed (Joan Bennett), the model for the painting, suddenly appears beside him and invites him to join her for drinks. The couple is enjoying a drink at Reed's home when her wealthy lover, Claude Mazard (Arthur Loft), arrives unexpectedly and jealously attacks Wanley. Mazard, possessed by an insane rage, grabs Wanley around the throat and attempts to strangle him to death. Desperate, Wanley takes hold of scissors and stabs Mazard repeatedly in the back. Mazard releases his grip and falls over dead. To avoid a scandal, Wanley and Reed dispose of Mazard's body in the country. It is a friend from Manley's club, district attorney Frank Lalor (Raymond Massey), who takes up the investigation of the murder. Wanley fears that Lalor, who is smart and determined, will inevitably figure out that he is the murderer. He takes a lethal dose of a prescription medication to end his life, but he suddenly awakens and realizes that his misadventure was nothing but a terrible dream.

An important scene occurs directly before Wanley meets Reed. The college professor speaks to fellow club members Lalor and Dr. Michael Barkstane (Edmund Breon) about middle-aged men desperately seeking to retrieve their youth by having affairs with young women.

Wanley: Well, look, I'm a middle-aged man. We all are. We are three old crocks. That sort of shenanigan is out for us.

Michael: Just a minute. I don't know if I like being described as an old crock.

Lalor: No, Michael, he's right, I'm afraid. And it's a darn good thing too. Men our age. . .

Wanley: I didn't say that. I didn't say it was a good thing. 'Cause I don't know that it is. All I know is that I *hate* it. I hate this solidity, the stodginess I am beginning to feel. To me it's the end of the brightness of life, the end of spirit and adventure.

Lalor: Don't talk like that. Men of our years have no business playing around with any adventure that they can avoid. We're like athletes who are out of condition. We can't handle that sort of thing anymore.

Wanley: Life ends at 40?

Lalor: In the district attorney's office, we see what happens to middle-aged men who try to act like colts. And I'm not joking when I tell you that I've seen genuine, actual tragedy issuing directly out of pure carelessness, out of the merest trifles. Casual impulse, an idle flirtation, one drink too many.

Wanley: You know, even if the spirit of adventure should rise up before me and beckon, even in the form of that alluring young woman in the window next door, I'm afraid that all I'll do is clutch my coat a little tighter, mutter something idiotic and run like the devil.

Scarlet Street (1945)

Chris (Edward G. Robinson) is walking home when he sees a young woman, Kitty March (Joan Bennett), being attacked by a man. He strikes the man in the head with his umbrella, which renders him unconscious. He invites Kitty to have a cup of coffee with him. She agrees. Chris is smitten with Kitty, who is so much more attractive than his shrewish wife Adele (Rosalind Ivan). It turns out that Johnny (Dan Duryea), the man who attacked Kitty in the street, is Kitty's boyfriend. He and Kitty are back together the next day. The two are joking with one another as if nothing happened. Kitty clearly isn't bothered at all that Johnny's violent behavior. Johnny instructs Kitty to pretend that she likes Chris to get money out of him.

Joan Bennett and Edward G. Robinson in *Scarlet Street* (1945)

Desperate to please Kitty, Chris steals money from his wife and his employer to pay her expenses and buy her lavish gifts. He pays for an apartment for Kitty and creates an art studio in a spare room. It is because of the art studio that he has paintings at Kitty's place. It was different in the original French film, in which Maurice had to hastily store his paintings with Lulu because his wife Adèle has threatened to throw them out.

Without Chris knowing, Johnny sells some of Chris' paintings to an art dealer. An art critic, David Janeway (Jess Barker), praises the paintings, which facilitates sales of the paintings. Johnny persuades Kitty to pretend that she's the artist.

Kitty has great success selling the paintings. Chris is delighted that his paintings are being so well-received. It doesn't even bother him that Kitty is getting credit for the paintings and keeping the money for herself. Chris becomes free to leave his wife when her ex-husband, who pretended to have drowned, turns up alive and well. Chris goes to propose marriage to Kitty, but he catches her in a loving embrace with Johnny.

Chris later speaks to Kitty alone. Kitty is clear that she has no interest in marrying him. She tells him that he's old and ugly and laughs at him. Enraged, he grabs an ice pick and stabs her to death.

Johnny, Kitty's criminal boyfriend, is the obvious suspect for Kitty's murder. But, on trial, he accuses Chris of murdering Kitty. He explains that Chris was the artist of the paintings that Kitty sold under her name. Chris is plain in his testimony: "I really can't paint."

Johnny is convicted and executed. Chris is consumed with guilt afterward. He attempts to hang himself, but a neighbor rescues him before the noose finishes its job.

Chris is fired for embezzling company funds. He ends up as a derelict, unable to feed himself and wandering the streets. Meanwhile, one of his old paintings is sold for $10,000 and he is unable to claim a cent.

He is tormented imagining Kitty and Johnny reunited in the afterlife. He hears their voices echoing in his head as they mock him mercilessly.

Chris' shrewish is played by Ivan, who so perfectly played Laughton's shrewish wife in *The Suspect* (1944).

Scarlet Street is a remake of a 1931 French film *La Chienne*. In the original film, the filmmakers made it clear that Lulu is a prostitute and her boyfriend is a pimp.

The film presents a midlife crisis story as well as a kept woman story. But who is really keeping who in this situation?

Edward G. Robinson in *Scarlet Street* (1945)

Pitfall (1948)

Bill Smiley (Byron Barr) was convicted for embezzling money from his employer. It becomes obvious to John Forbes (Dick Powell), an insurance investigator, that Smiley used the money to buy extravagant gifts for his beautiful girlfriend, Mona Stevens (Lizabeth Scott). Forbes visits Mona in hope of recovering the illicit gifts, but he finds himself attracted to Mona. He is a married man, but his wife and child are not on his mind while he is with Mona.

Forbes lets Mona keep the boat that Smiley gave her as a gift, but he reclaims everything else that Smiley purchased with his ill-gotten gains. A sleazy private eye, MacDonald (Raymond Burr), is angry that Mona spurned his advances. He turns up at Forbes' office with the bill of sale for the boat. He threatens to tell Forbes bosses that the insurance investigator is having an affair with Mona and did her a favor by letting her keep the boat. He warns Mac to keep away from Mona. Forbes goes back to Mona and arranges for the boat to be repossessed. But Mac is not done with Forbes. He takes him by surprise at his home and beats him brutally. He says, "I told you I like that girl." Forbes ends up in bed recovering from his injuries.

Mona finds that Forbes left his briefcase at her home. She goes to his office to return it, but she is told that he is home sick. She finds his home address in his briefcase and figures to bring him a meal. But, when she arrives, she encounters Forbes' heretofore unknown wife Sue (Jane Wyatt) talking with a doctor outside the home. Forbes is horrified that his wife and mistress nearly met. After he recovers, he visits Mona to end their relationship.

Lizabeth Scott, Dick Powell and Raymond Burr in *Pitfall* (1948)

Mac continues to stalk Mona. When she threatens to call the police, he tells her that he will tell Sue that she was fooling around with her husband. Forbes is angry to learn about this. He visits Mac and roughs him up, returning the beating that he himself had recently received.

Mac has one last trick in mind. He visits Smiley in prison and tells him about Mona's affair. Because Mona voluntarily returned Smiley's gifts, the authorities are persuaded to grant Smiley an early release. Mac welcomes Smiley back to the outside world. He takes this opportunity to supply Smiley with a gun so that he can get rid of Forbes. Forbes learns from Mona that Smiley is coming for him and he lies in wait for him at his home. He ends up shooting Smiley in self-defense. Mac expects that Forbes has been killed and Smiley has been arrested, so he sees nothing standing in his way with Mona. He arrives at Mona's home, but Mona is waiting with a gun and shoots him.

Come Back, Little Sheba (1952)

Doc Delaney (Burt Lancaster) is living in deep regret and despair. As a young man, he unintentionally got his girlfriend Lola (Shirley Booth) pregnant. Believing that he had a duty to care for mother and baby, he dropped out of medical school, married Lola, and got a job. When Lola lost the baby, he had to suffer with the knowledge that he gave up on his dream of being a doctor for nothing. Doc became so unhappy in his marriage that he frequently drank. His drinking got worse through the years. But, in recent days, he has finally found peace within himself. He has had the strength to remain sober since joining Alcoholics Anonymous a year earlier. Yet, he still struggles at times with depression. He becomes reinvigorated when a pretty college student, Marie Buckholder (Terry Moore), moves into their home as a boarder. He becomes obsessed with Marie, but she has two boyfriends and only sees him as a benign father figure. Frustrated, he begins to drink again. In a drunken rage, he threatens Lola with a knife. He passes out before he hurts her and two of his friends from AA take him to the hospital to dry out. When he returns home, Doc is remorseful for attacking Lola and begs his wife for forgiveness. He learns from Lola that Marie married her more reliable boyfriend, Bruce (Walter Kelley), and has moved out.

Shirley Booth and Burt Lancaster in *Come Back, Little Sheba* (1952)

Detour (1952)

The original German title: *Nachts auf den Straßen*

A married middle-aged truck driver, Heinrich Schlueter (Hans Albers), becomes besotted with Inge Hoffmann (Hildegard Knef), a beautiful young woman he encounters hitchhiking on the road one night.

Heinrich takes Inge shopping to buy clothes. She couldn't be happier trying on dresses. Heinrich is thrilled when she invites him to touch the soft fabric of her dress. The couple dances at a nightclub. Inge becomes smitten by Heinrich because he is a caring, decent man, unlike the other men that she has known in her life. Inge has a boyfriend, Kurt Willbrandt (Marius Goring), who has gotten involved in the black market to support a drug habit. He gets the idea to use Heinrich to smuggle stolen furs. He sees that his girlfriend is developing feelings for the truck driver and does his best to discourage these feelings. He tells her, "He loves his wife. With you he has fun."

Marius Goring, Hildegard Knef and Hans Albers in *Detour* (1952)

The strong performances of Albers and Knef make this a poignant film. seglora of IMDb wrote: "It is interesting to compare Albers in this role with his slightly younger French contemporary Jean Gabin, who also plays a family man and truck driver in Verneuil's film *Des gens sans importance* (1956), which features similarly a fateful encounter with a young woman."[484]

People of No Importance (1956)

The original French title: *Des gens sans importance*

The film depicts an affair between two very different people. Clotilde Brachet (Françoise Arnoul), a young woman, works as a waitress and a maid at a truck stop. She is lonely and unhappy. Jean Viard (Jean Gabin), a middle-aged truck driver, spends most of his waking hours on the road. His wife, Solange (Yvette Etiévant), is resentful that he is rarely home. In one scene, he comes trudging into his home after having been on the road for days. He is exhausted and thinks only of dragging himself into bed. Solange reacts unpleasantly to his appearance. She nags. She complains. Clotilde also has an unsupportive family. Her mother is similarly resentful when Clotilde comes home looking for a place to stay for a few days. Kindness is something that Jean and Clotilde have rarely experienced in their lives, so the kindness they show to one another creates an immediate bond between them. But, like Solange, Clotilde comes to resent Jean for never being around.

> Jean: The truck has been acting up. I only have 5 minutes left.

> Clotilde: Five minutes a week. At this rate, by the time we turn 80, we'll have spent about 3 days together.

Jean asks her to stop her constant complaining.

> Jean: You're a riot. It's not that simple! I have to keep earning. I still have a wife and kids. I can't just drop them. I've been with Solange 23 years. I have nothing against her.

> Clotilde: You're always throwing your wife and kids in my face.

> Jean: I still have to think about them! Don't tell me you're jealous of them.

> Clotilde: I don't know. I know that if I didn't care about you, I wouldn't get in this state.

The stress of the situation makes Jean short-tempered. He loses his job when, in a fit of anger, he assaults his manager.

Clotilde writes Jean a letter to inform him that she is pregnant, but she sends the letter to his garage not knowing he doesn't work there anymore. She assumes that he got the letter and chose not to answer it. She goes to see him at a truckers' dance and, after accusing him of ignoring her letter, she learns that he was fired. He asks her what she wrote in the letter. "You have enough problems," she says. "It was really nothing." She goes off on her own to have an abortion. Meanwhile, the letter is forwarded to Jean's home from the garage. Solange reads the letter and now knows about the affair. Clotilde phones Jean. She had difficulties with the abortion and is in great pain. Jean is frantic to get Clotilde to a hospital, but she dies on the way.

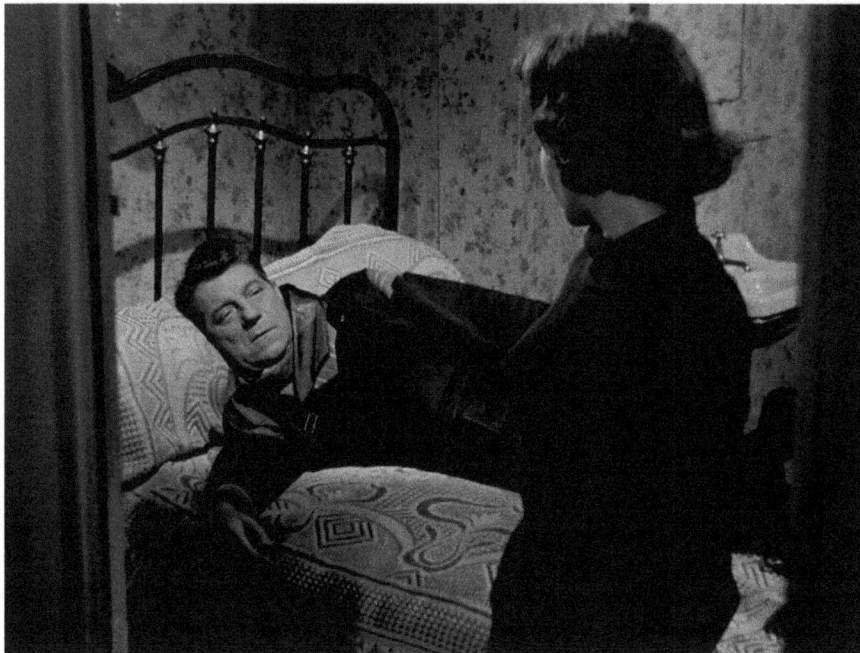

Jean Gabin and Françoise Arnoul in *People of No Importance* (1956)

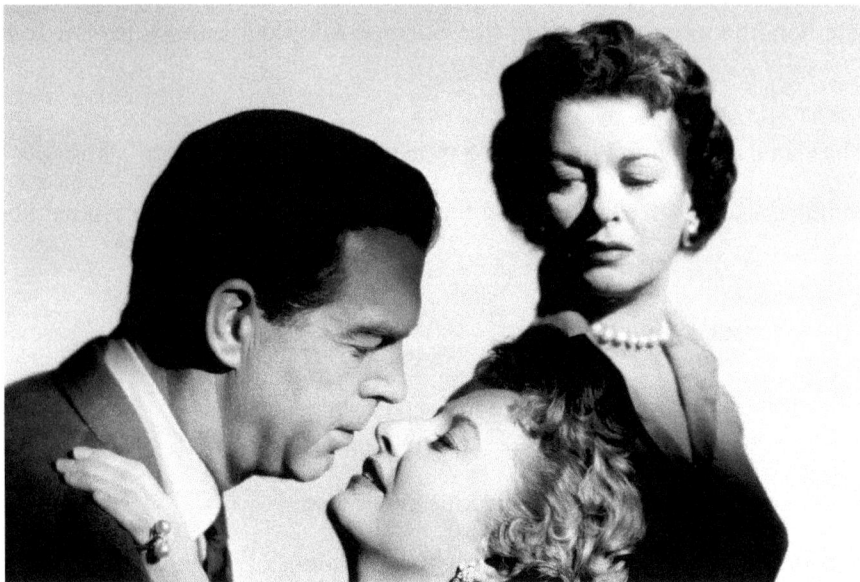

Fred MacMurray, Barbara Stanwyck and Joan Bennett in *There's Always Tomorrow* (1956)

There's Always Tomorrow (1956)

There's Always Tomorrow was remade in 1956. The film introduces us to a cruelly neglected husband, Clifford Groves (Fred MacMurray). Clifford is a highly successful toy manufacturer. He is an important man in the office, but his family shows no interest in him at home. Clifford's wife, Marion (Joan Bennett), is the worst, acting as if her husband doesn't exist. Clifford, frustrated, tells Marion:

> I am tired of the children taking over. I'm tired of being taken for granted. I'm becoming like one of my toys. Cliff, the walkie-talkie robot. Wind me up in the morning and I go to work. Wind me up again and I come home at night, eat dinner and go to bed. Wind me up the next morning and I work all day to pay the bills. . . I'm sick and tired of the sameness of it, day in and day out. Don't you ever want to get out, move around?. . . Every time I plan anything for us, you find some excuse. . . The children mean more to you than I do. When we were younger, we did so many things together. We had fun. No two days were alike. Life was an adventure but now. . .

"If life were always an adventure," Marion dryly replies, "it would be very exhausting." That's all she has to say to her husband after he has poured his heart out to her. She just doesn't care.

Samm Deighan points out in the Blu-ray commentary that this domestic melodrama places Clifford in a position usually occupied by a female character. She said, "You have a character who feels lonely and isolated and taken advantage of."[485] It is the same sort of abuse and suffering experienced by the standard melodrama heroine. The understated film provides a painfully realistic depiction of a moribund marriage.

Clifford has fun again when he meets an old friend, Norma Miller Vale (Barbara Stanwyck). Can the man be faulted if he takes this pleasant relationship further and has an affair with Norma? Deighan finds the film subversive for the subtle way that it makes a case for an affair.

Barbara Stanwyck and Fred MacMurray in *There's Always Tomorrow* (1956)

Clifford's adult son, Vinnie (William Reynolds), sees Clifford and Norma together at the Palm Valley resort. He tells his teenage sister, Ellen (Gigi Perreau), that their father is likely having an affair. Ellen, distraught, visits Norma at her hotel room and tearfully pleads with her not to take her father away. Norma realizes that Clifford cannot leave his wife without jeopardizing his relationship with his children. She tells him:

But you have a wonderful life with Marion and the children. What would you do the day we're together and you read in the paper that Vinnie Groves is about to graduate? You'll want to run from me and be with him, but you'll wonder if he'll see you again. Or the day you hear about the first professional recital of that of that young dancer, Frances Groves. You'll feel sick at not being invited. And I'll feel sick for you. And Ellen's wedding? "Oh, no, her father isn't here. He ran away with another woman, don't you remember? At his age! Oh, the poor kid!" Oh, face it, Cliff! I've had to face it! You know you'll want to see Marion again, hear her voice, quarrel with her over the bills and the children! She's the one who belongs in your life, your first love. And that's the way it should be. It's such a good life. What have I to give you to take its place? Be happy, Cliff. You will be happy.

She walks out into a rainstorm and takes a cab to the airport.

The adultery in this film never becomes more than spiritual. But marriage experts have broadened the definition of marital infidelity to include sexual infidelity (sexual exchange with no romantic involvement), romantic infidelity (romantic exchanges with no sexual involvement) and sexual and romantic involvement.

Woman in a Dressing Gown (1957)

One of the least glamorous depictions of adultery can be found in this British film.

The film opens introducing us to the Preston household. Amy Preston (Yvonne Mitchell), wife and mother, is so obsessed with a newspaper contest that she has burnt the toast. Frank Collins of Cathode Ray Tube wrote:

[Amy] push[es] into [her husband] Jim to sew a button on his shirt as he tries to eat his breakfast. The look on [Jim's] face and the developing tension is enough to foreshadow the crisis that is about to play out. . . Later, [when he steps outdoors]. . . she throws Jim's cigarettes to him and they end up in a puddle at his feet.[486]

Anthony Quayle in *Woman in a Dressing Gown* (1957)

Jim (Anthony Quayle) tells Amy that he is leaving her for another woman, Georgie (Sylvia Syms). Collins wrote, "Georgie is a clean, tidy, immaculate ideal and the calm antithesis to Amy." LaDonnaKeskes of IMDb wrote:

The cramped flat where they live is a suffocating mess, cabinets spilling debris, sinks filled with dishes, dustbins crammed, through which his bathrobe-clad wife drifts in a logorrheic, ash-dropping haze. By contrast, the young woman he is infatuated with is elegant and pristine, and their encounters are marked by a tranquility and privacy lacking in his domestic life. . .[487]

Amy is distraught by her husband's news.

Jim: No one's to blame, Amy, not one of us. Georgie's no home-breaker. It just. . . well, it just happened.

Amy: You read about this happening to other people. You never think one day it could be you.

Jim: It's not only Georgie. She's only part of it, you see. It's my whole life. It's leading nowhere. I feel I'm living in a blind alley.

Collins wrote, "There's a particularly moving scene which tips the film over into full blown tragedy as Amy crumbles emotionally in the dimly lit bathroom while, in juxtaposition, her son and his girlfriend dance to a raucous jazz record."[488]

Alone in the bathroom, Amy drops to her knees and sobs hysterically. She gets up early the next morning to iron the wrinkled clothes that have been piling up. She has herself convinced that this will fix everything wrong with their marriage. Amy implores Jim to bring Georgie to their flat so that she can talk to her.

Yvonne Mitchell in *Woman in a Dressing Gown* (1957)

Amy is determined to make a good appearance for her guest. She goes out to buy groceries and get her hair done at a salon. But everything goes wrong. Her hair gets ruined in the rain (she is the only person in sight without an umbrella), she tears her dress as she struggles with the zipper, and her dining room table collapses. She feels that she has nothing else to do at the point except to, as Collins wrote, "drown her sorrows in whisky."[489]

Georgie is well prepared to meet Amy when she arrives at their home. She is fully committed in her love for Jim and she realizes that he needs to leave his wife to be happy. She is calm, tender and reasonable throughout her visit.

Jim agonizes about leaving Amy. "If only she wasn't helpless," he says, "if only she was a bitch, it would all be so easy." Thompson cuts from a shot of Georgie withdrawing into the kitchen to Amy coming out of the bedroom. The contrast between the two women could not be greater. Georgie is immaculately dressed, her bright white blouse giving her an angelic appearance. A grim-faced Amy looks hellish in her dark, rumpled robe. Is Jim wrong to believe she's not a bitch? Is she, in fact, evil? She is selfish and manipulative. She has created this miserable home and demands that her husband lives in it with her. Isn't this evil? Or is this the marital commitment, holding and cherishing your spouse even in the worst of times and even if she is in a state of sickness?

Jim is upset that his teenage son, Brian (Andrew Ray), is behaving surly towards Georgie. He follows his son into his bedroom to talk to him. But Brian is furious with his father and doesn't care to hear what he has to say. He gets up from his bed and stands toe to toe with his father. He looks his father straight in the face. Jim is unsettled. He has never seen his son behave like this before. Brian starts, "Of all the bloody, dirty mean tricks. . ." But Jim cannot tolerate this behavior. Before Brian can say another word, he slaps his son hard across the face.

We learn during Amy's conversation with Georgie that Georgie lost a child. "Did you know we had another baby besides Bri? . . . We lost June. It's a terrible thing when you think of it. She only lived half an hour. It's when I lost my pretty figure. Women do. It happens sometimes when they've had children. You might lose yours if you have children!" Presumably, it is the child's death that has made her the way she is. Sometimes, a tragedy can send a person spiraling into a great depression from which they can never recover.

Jim, distressed by this highly emotional scene, reluctantly ends his relationship with Georgie and returns to Amy. Collins wrote, "[T]he family is patched back together. . . Thompson zooms in on Jim's face as for a moment he seriously considers what he may have lost by returning to the status quo." LaDonnaKeskes wrote, "[A]ll goes on exactly as before - only worse."[490]

Filmmaker Jean-Luc Godard said that Thompson's "lunatic"[491] direction was "as maddening as his heroine's behavior."[492] He found the director's "incredible debauch of camera movements"[493] to be "silly and meaningless."[494] He was displeased just as much by the many "cuts and changes in rhythm."[495] But Melanie Williams, a film studies professor, defended Thompson's direction. Collins wrote, "Williams suggests, the entire point was to emphasise the chaotic domestic environment and behaviour that Amy exhibits. There's a feverish, restless quality to these scenes that suggests the chaos that Amy surrounds herself with is simply the projection of underlying problems in a marriage that has slipped into suspended animation."[496]

Woman in a Dressing Gown is, despite Godard's complaints, a heart-wrenching drama.

Mitchell, a versatile actress, was rough and ruthless as a married man's kept woman in J. Lee Thompson's *Tiger Bay* (1959).

Redhead (1962)

The original German title: *Die Rote*

Franziska Lukas (Ruth Leuwerik) finds herself desperately bored with her life as she approaches forty. This creates great tension between herself and her husband, Herbert (Harry Meyen). She seeks a change by turning away from Herbert for an affair with his boss, Joachim (Richard Münch). When this fails to lift her spirits, she impulsively runs off to Venice in search of adventure. She wanders into a coffee shop after stepping off the train and meets a handsome historian, Fabio (Rossano Brazzi). Fabio wastes no time in flirting with the pretty lady. After leaving Fabio, she is approached on the street by Patrick O'Malley (Giorgio Albertazzi), who also expresses an attraction for Franziska. A woman as beautiful as Franziska cannot expect to be lonely for long. But Franziska is a lost lamb in Venice. She stumbles into an affair with Fabio and, through Patrick, becomes entangled with a fugitive war criminal. In the end, Franziska impetuously boards the next train leaving Venice. It doesn't matter to her where the train will bring her.

Family's Father (1967)

The original Italian title: *Il padre di famiglia*

Marco (Nino Manfredi) creates turmoil within his family as he struggles to cope with a midlife crisis. His struggle with his identity and his life choices drives him into an affair with a new woman. Marco is finally confronted by his wife, Paola (Leslie Caron), who demands that he discuss his grievances.

Marco: I'm not a hero, I'm just a family man. Maybe I could have become someone, but not anymore. I'm done. I sacrificed my chances when I got married. When you had me have all those kids. I was never a slave to anyone and became a slave to my family. I'm tired now.

Paola: You can do whatever you want. You want to quit a job that you like just to make more money. Do it if you want. But you must take the responsibility of what you're doing without using the excuse of the family and the children. Do you think I married you because you have brown eyes? I liked what was in your head. And now that after 14 years you change your mind, should I change my mind as well? You taught me to believe in things that are right. I'm sorry, but I'll keep on believing them. There's something else too. You can fall in love with someone else to get your satisfaction. But I can't fall in love anymore. If you change and become what you were telling me about, be careful. I don't know what's going to become of us. I don't know if I'll like you or not.

Paola collapses under the stress of the marital discord and has to be hospitalized. Marco has to care for his children while Paola recuperates. This allows him to reconnect with his family.

The Tiger and the Pussycat (1967)

The original Italian title: *Un tigre en la red*

Francesco Vincenzini (Vittorio Gassman) is upset that his teenage son tried to commit suicide over being rejected by a carefree young woman, Carolina (Ann-Margaret). He goes to see Carolina and suddenly finds himself drawn into an affair with her. He sends a farewell letter to his wife, letting her know that he is running off to Paris with Carolina. Wikipedia reports: "At the last minute, [Francesco] comes to his senses and decides to return home where Esperia [Eleanor Parker] pretends that she did not read his letter."[497]

Accident (1967)

Anna von Graz (Jacqueline Sassard), a student at Oxford, has a seductive effect on men around campus. She plans to marry a fellow student, William (Michael York), but she still has eyes for other men. She has an intense romance with a married professor, Charley (Stanley Baker). Stephen (Dirk Bogarde), a quiet and reserved professor, believes that the passion has gone out of his marriage to Rosalind (Vivien Merchant). Rosalind is certainly preoccupied being pregnant with their third child. Stephen lusts after Anna from afar. Rosalind is disgusted when Stephen tells her that Charley is sleeping with Anna.

Rosalind: How pathetic!

Stephen: What do you mean?

Rosalind: Poor, stupid, old man.

Stephen: He's not old!

Rosalind: Stupid bastard! I've never heard of anything so bloody puerile, so banal!

William promises to visit Stephen after a party, but he has become too drunk to drive. So, Anna drives the car instead and crashes it outside of Stephen's home. Stephen comes outside to investigate and finds Michael dead inside the car. He carries Anna inside his home and recommends that she remain hidden while the police examine the scene. Rosalind is away with the children, so he has the pleasure of being alone with Anna. He becomes aroused watching Anna asleep in his bed. He can no longer control his desire and forces himself on the traumatized woman.

The Babysitter (1969)

A married public prosecutor, George Maxwell (George E. Cary), has an affair with his teenage babysitter, Candy Wilson (Patricia Wymer). Maxwell is assigned to prosecute a brawny biker, Laurence Mackey (Robert Tessier), who has been charged with murder. Mackey's girlfriend, Julie Freeman, hopes to compromise the prosecution by finding a way to blackmail Maxwell. She has exactly what she needs when she photographs Maxwell and Candy kissing on a beach. But Candy enlists help from a couple of tough friends to force Julie to surrender the negatives of the photographs. But Julie has already sent copies of the photographs to Maxwell's wife Edith (Ann Bellamy) and boss Raymond Willas (Ken Hooker). Willas refuses Maxwell's resignation and advises him to be more concerned with how his wife will react to the photos. Edith is surprisingly awed by his extramarital activities. She tells him, "Maybe we do play too much bridge." Remember, this was the swinging sixties. You had sex with the babysitter? No problem.

We see this same attitude nearly two decades later in *Rita, Sue and Bob Too* (1987). Bob (George Costigan) is sexually frustrated with his wife, Michelle (Lesley Sharp). Rita (Siobhan Finneran) and Sue (Michelle Holmes) are high school students who babysit Bob and Michelle's children. While driving Rita and Sue home, Bob stops the car and asks the young ladies if they want to have sex with him. They are delighted to accept his proposal. The threesome carry on their relationship until Michelle finds out and ejects Bob from their home. Bob ends up happily living with Rita and Sue.

Primary Colors (1998) shows that you can sleep with the babysitter and still be president. Jack Stanton (John Travolta), the Governor of Arkansas, embarks on a campaign to be the President of the United States. The campaign is jeopardized when Stanton learns that he has gotten his 17-year-old babysitter pregnant. The governor is fully supported by his wife, Susan (Emma Thompson), while he arranges for staff members to tamper with the paternity test results.

Not every babysitter paramour is as fortunate as George, Bob and Jack. Take, for instance, Dennis Cromwell (Sam Bottoms) in *My Neighbor's Daughter* (1998). Dennis is a well-to-do banker and civic leader. He has a beautiful wife, Jill (Lisa Eichhorn) and newborn child. But he jeopardizes everything to have an affair with his 16-year-old babysitter. In the end, Jill kicks him out of his home, his boss fires him from the bank, and the police arrest him for statutory rape.

The Arrangement (1969)

Eddie Anderson (Kirk Douglas) is a wealthy advertising executive, but he finds his life stressful and unfulfilled. He wants to give up his job and live a more modest life, but his wife Florence (Deborah Kerr) doesn't understand this. He finds greater pleasure in his relationship with Gwen (Faye Dunaway), a research assistant at his agency. It doesn't matter to Eddie that Gwen has been promiscuous. She has a small son and doesn't know who the father is. It doesn't bother him that Gwen is engaged to Charles (John Randolph Jones). She is willing to continue her affair with Eddie after she is married. Eddie asks Florence for a divorce so that he can marry Gwen. This enrages her. Eddie becomes increasingly unstable. He acts suicidal. He attacks Florence. Finally, he is arrested for setting fire to his father's home in a dispute with his siblings, who want to commit their father to a nursing home. In court, he volunteers to check himself into a psychiatric hospital. He becomes comfortable at the hospital and is not sure that he wants to leave. But Gwen gets him to return to the world and start a new life with her.

Don't Let the Angels Fall (1969)

A married middle-aged businessman (Arthur Hill) copes with a midlife crisis by having an affair with a young woman (Sharon Acker).

I Walk The Line (1970)

The film is comparable to *Summer Storm* and *Dulcima* (1971). Gregory Peck, usually stoic and moral on screen, breaks loose when he meets the lovely young Tuesday Weld. Peck said, "[He falls] in love with her renewing youth," he said. "He wrecked his career, his family, his reputation, all for this vain obsession, and he's left with nothing."[498]

Peck, as Sheriff Henry Tawes, acts like a babbling idiot with the young woman. He says, "I have to see you. I have to see you all the time. I gotta see you too. I've been waiting every day to hear. . . I just couldn't wait no more."

The film was a failure with critics and audiences. Eldon Leslie, manager of Cookeville's Chamber of Commerce, told a newspaper writer, "A sheriff is a man who represents law and order, a man to be respected. That movie takes the sheriff and makes him a damn social derelict who blows his mind over a dumb blonde."[499] Harry Haun, a film critic with The Tennessean, wrote, "The character turns out to be not so much a product of Tennessee as he is a by-product of Tennessee Williams — a male equivalent to the playwright's fading Southern belles who consciously or unconsciously embrace their own destruction."[500]

The Los Angeles Times noted, "Peck's pre-existing heroic image made it difficult for him to appear flawed. Yet he conveys considerable anguish as a man who doesn't know what hit him."[501] In 1991, Charles Champlin of The Los Angeles Times wrote in retrospect, "It may be that in this instance, Peck as Mr. Imperfect was too much for audience's tastes."[502]

Tawes' wife, Ellen (Estelle Parsons), learns of the affair and wants to talk to him about their marriage and their life together. She remembers that, after they first met, they had a whirlwind courtship. She says:

Swept you clean off your feet in that whirlwind, didn't I? Before you knew it, you had Ellen Haney around your neck, didn't ya? Magazine I read said people never really know each other. Even married people it said. And I fully understand that people are entitled to their privacy. I mean, people who care about each other. . . can't even pretend to know everything about each other. Don't you agree?

Henry is unwilling to talk about it.

Ellen: She a pretty girl? If that's all then, well, from time to time a - a man your age does seek out a young girl sometimes. The Reader's Digest tells how -

Henry: Oh, that ain't it, Ellen Haney.

Ellen: Young though, huh?

Henry: That ain't it.

Ellen: Well, then what is it, Henry? Just somethin' different? Somethin' you need that bad, Sheriff?. . . I want you to know I've always tried to be honest with you. By that I mean I've never just wanted to be a diplomatic type, if you know what I mean. I know it's hard for you to hear me say how I feel. Maybe you never did feel the same way. Maybe I don't have much to give you anymore. But Sybil and me, we do have full respect for you. And we want you to know that, and we don't want you to be rash about doin' somethin'. Henry, tell me what to do! You want us to go to Aunt Carla's for a while?

Henry: Just do what you have to do, Ellen Haney.

Ellen: You're goin' off with her, ain't ya?

Henry: I don't know.

Ellen: Oh, God, Henry!

Parsons is sympathetic in her performance. The wife is far less sympathetic in the novel. She is an ambitious woman disappointed by her husband's business failures.

Last of the Red Hot Lovers (1972)

Barney Cashman (Alan Arkin) figures to get through a midlife crisis by experiencing a sexual adventure outside of his marriage. Barney dates three different women - Elaine (Sally Kellerman), Bobbi (Paula Prentiss), and Janette (Renee Taylor) - but none of these women are willing to sleep with him. So, instead, he goes home and sleeps with his wife.

Breezy (1973)

Middle-aged Bob Henderson (Roger C. Carmel) complains about his marriage to his best friend, Frank Harmon (William Holden).

The excitement's over. Yes, my wife just doesn't turn me on like she used to. Well, you know, you start wondering what it would be like to meet somebody new. Fall in love. To feel all that again. Because that's not all dead inside me, Frank. That's all still there. All the butterflies. You know what stops me? Fear. Oh, yeah. Scares the hell out of me. At my age, the thought of having to start all over again. Come on like I was 20. Doing all those numbers just to get laid.

Save the Tiger (1973)

Harry Stoner (Jack Lemmon), the owner of a struggling apparel company, seeks relief from his business problems by stepping outside of his marriage and having a one-night stand with a free-spirited young woman, Myra (Laurie Heineman).

Network (1976)

Network has the perfect wronged wife speech delivered with perfect anguish and fury by Beatrice Straight.

[G]et out. Go anywhere you want. Go to a hotel, go live with her, but don't come back! Because, after 25 years of building a home and raising a family and all the senseless pain that we have inflicted on each other, I'm damned if I'm gonna stand here and have you tell me you're in love with somebody else! Because this isn't a convention weekend with your secretary, is it? Or -- or some broad that you picked up after three belts of booze. This is your great winter romance, isn't it? Your last roar of passion before you settle into your emeritus years. Is that what's left for me? Is that my share? She gets the winter passion, and I get the dotage? What am I supposed to do? Am I supposed to sit at home knitting and purling while you slink back like some penitent drunk? I'm your wife, damn it! And if you can't work up a winter passion for me, the least I require is respect and allegiance! (sobbing) I hurt! Don't you understand that? I hurt badly!

In an emotion-packed confrontation, TV network news chief, Max Schumacher (WILLIAM HOLDEN), discusses a divorce with his wife, Louise (BEATRICE STRAIGHT), in MGM's "Network," a United Artists release.

Copyright 1976, United Artists Corporation, all rights reserved. Printed in U.S.A.   1931-55

Beatrice Straight and William Holden in *Network* (1976)

Her husband, Max (William Holden), hugs her. She asks, "Does she love you, Max?" He quickly dismisses Diana as shallow and work-obsessed:

I'm not sure she's capable of any real feelings. She's television generation. She learned life from Bugs Bunny. The only reality she knows comes to her from over the TV set. She has very carefully devised a number of scenarios for all of us to play, like a Movie of the Week. And, my God, look at us, Louise. Here we are going through the obligatory middle-of-act-two "scorned wife throws peccant husband out" scene. But don't worry, I'll come back to you in the end. All of her plot outlines have me leaving her and coming back to you because the audience won't buy a rejection of the happy American family. She does have one script in which I kill myself. An adapted for television version of Anna Karenina where she's Count Vronsky and I'm Anna.

Olivia de Havilland powerfully delivers a wronged wife speech in *Not as a Stranger* (1955). The actress plays an operating room nurse, Kristina Hedvigson. She falls in love with a medical student, Lucas Marsh (Robert Mitchum). Lucas is desperate for tuition money to finish medical school. He marries Kristina because she has scrupulously saved earnings over the years and can provide him with the money that he needs for tuition. Lucas graduates and becomes a skilled surgeon. He has never developed deep feelings for Kristina and begins an affair with a rich and sultry widow, Harriet Lang (Gloria Grahame). Kristina becomes pregnant, but she is afraid to tell Lucas because he has expressed an aversion to having children. Lucas' best friend, Dr. Alfred Boone (Frank Sinatra), is the film's voice of morality. He tells Lucas that Kristina is going to have his baby and needs his full support. Lucas apologizes to Kristina for his poor behavior and promises to be a better husband. But she vehemently rejects his apology. She says:

> You're always sorry. Every time you hurt me you're sorry. You always try to fix it by acting as though you love me. It doesn't work any more. I know where you were tonight. I can't forgive you. Nothing you can say will matter! From the beginning you never thought I was smart enough or attractive enough or woman enough to be your wife. You come crawling in here now because your friend told you I was going to have your child. Stop pretending! I'm sick of it! I don't need you to have this child! You had to have money, so you married me. Well, you made it - you're a doctor! You don't need me now! And I don't need the little you got to give me. I don't want to live with you, Luke. Please - get out of here! Go away! Get out of here, Luke! Please!

Middle Age Crazy (1980)

IMDb: "A married man (Bruce Dern) is turning forty and that's when the midlife crisis hits him. He becomes obsessed with young women and fast cars."[503]

A Change of Seasons (1980)

A middle-aged married couple, Adam and Karyn Evans (Anthony Hopkins and Shirley MacLaine), find themselves caught up in a midlife crisis. Adam, a college professor, has an affair with a student, Lindsey Rutledge (Bo Derek). Karyn, in turn, has an affair with a young carpenter, Pete Lachappelle (Michael Brandon).

All Night Long (1981)

All Night Long is similar to *The Tiger and the Pussycat*. George Dupler (Gene Hackman) is upset to learn that his son Freddie (Dennis Quaid) is having an affair with a married woman, Cheryl Gibbons (Barbra Streisand). George meets with Cheryl to persuade her to end the affair, but he ends up falling in love with her. Cheryl is more sunny and lively than George's stiff-lipped wife, Helen (Diane Ladd). He eventually leaves Helen to set up a new home with Cheryl.

Blame It on Rio (1984)

Matthew Hollis (Michael Caine) expects to vacation in Rio de Janeiro with his wife Karen (Valerie Harper) and teenage daughter Nikki (Demi Moore), but Karen tells him that she doesn't know if she wants to continue with their marriage and needs time alone to think. Victor Lyons (Joseph Bologna), Matthew's best friend, tells Matthew that he and his teenage daughter Jennifer (Michelle Johnson) can join him on his vacation. In the romantic atmosphere of Rio de Janeiro, Matthew is seduced by the sexually liberated Jennifer. The film is smutty and silly. Caine's jittery and guilt-ridden Matthew is a far cry from the slick and smooth adulterer that Cain played in *Alfie* (1966), which we will examine in Chapter Twenty-One.

Bernard Hill and Pauline Collins in *Shirley Valentine* (1989)

Shirley Valentine (1989)

Shirley Bradshaw (Pauline Collins), a middle-aged housewife, is given an opportunity to climb out of a rut when her best friend, Jane (Alison Steadman), wins a trip for two to an exotic Greek island. Shirley's husband, Joe (Bernard Hill), opposes the trip, but Shirley leaves anyway. Shirley feels uninhibited in Greece. She is not shy or hesitant while she is being wooed by an endearing tavern owner, Costas Dimitriades (Tom Conti). She enters into an affair with Costas with great amusement and curiosity. She has embarked on a mission of self-discovery and is willing now to approach her mission, and life in general, in a free and easy manner.

Being Julia (2004)

The film is based on the 1937 novel "Theatre" by W. Somerset Maugham.

The film, as the title of the novel suggests, is set in the theatre world. Michael Gosselyn (Jeremy Irons) produces plays for his theatrical grand dame wife, Julia Lambert (Annette Bening). The couple is comfortable in their longtime marriage. But do they love each other?

Michael is cool and practical, which makes him a good producer. Julia is vain, manipulative and imaginative, which makes her a good actress. She shows little personal substance off stage. In the novel, her son tells her, "When I've seen you go into an empty room I've sometimes wanted to open the door suddenly, but I've been afraid to in case I found nobody there."[504] She cannot walk into a room without imagining it as a set and figuring how she must play her part. W. Somerset Maugham acknowledged, "Some critics complained that Julia Lambert, my heroine, was not a creature of great moral character, great intelligence and nobility of spirit. . ."[505] But he believed that she was true to life. He wrote, "I feel a great affection for her; I am not shocked by her naughtiness, nor scandalized by her absurdities. . ."[506]

Julia has been bored with Michael for years, but she has remained with him due to their prosperous business relationship. In the novel, Julia is upset that Michael is no longer young. She feels disgusted to have this old man kiss her. But it bothers her more to look into a mirror and see that she, herself, is no longer young.

The novel includes an extended flashback to the couple's earlier years together. The flashback takes up roughly a third of the book, but not a trace of it is presented in the film. Michael is rendered fairly irrelevant as a result.

Annette Bening in *Being Julia* (2004)

Michael invites a young accountant, Tom Fennel (Shaun Evans), to have dinner with him and Julia. It turns out that Tom is a fan of Julia and invites her to have tea with him the next day. When he meets her at the theatre, he frets that they might draw too much attention by having tea at a public place. He recommends that they instead go to his apartment. She is flattered and amused by his unhidden ardor. He kisses her during tea, which leads them to have sex. She is amazed by the great passion she feels for her new young lover.

Julia presents Tom with lavish gifts, including large sums of money. Tom has become important to her as he has allayed her fear of getting old. But, as it turns out, Tom has only a passing interest in Julia. He suddenly shifts his affection to an ingénue, Avice Crichton (Lucy Punch). He has the audacity to ask Julia to give Avice a role in her upcoming play. Surprisingly, she agrees. But she has a plan. To regain her dignity, Julia needs to humiliate Tom and Avice. From the novel:

> It would be a satisfaction to turn the tables on Tom and Avice Crichton. She sat on, in the darkness, grimly thinking how she would do it. But every now and then she started to cry again, for from the depths of her subconscious surged up recollections that were horribly painful. Recollections of Tom's slim, youthful body against hers, his warm nakedness and the peculiar feel of his lips, his smile, at once shy and roguish, and the smell of his curly hair.[507]

Annette Bening and Shaun Evans in *Being Julia* (2004)

Julia is subdued during rehearsals, allowing Avice to dominate scenes. It looks to Michael and other observers that she is passing the torch to the younger actress. But, on opening night, Julia takes charge. She unleashes a formidable performance that makes a fool out of Avice and reduces the young actress to tears.

Julia dines alone to revel quietly in her triumph. She feels self-important, more so than usual. In the novel, she meditates:

> [I]t's we, the actors, who are reality. . . They are our raw material. We are the meaning of their lives. We take their silly little emotions and turn them into art, out of them we create beauty. . . Why, it's only we who do exist. They are the shadows and we give them substance. We are the symbols of all this confused, aimless struggling that they call life, and it is only the symbol which is real. They say acting is only make-believe. That make-believe is the only reality.[508]

Bening is splendid in the role.

Lili Palmer and Charles Boyer starred in an earlier film adaptation of "Theatre" called *Adorable Julia* (1962). *Adorable Julia* is a weak film. The direction is flat. Palmer, though charming and stately in the role, makes the wicked Julia warmer and more sympathetic than she deserves to be.

The Mosquito Net (2010)

The original Spanish title: *La mosquitera*

Miguel (Eduard Fernández) and Alicia (Emma Suárez) have grown distant as husband and wife. Miguel pays their immigrant teenage maid Ana (Martina García) for sex while Alicia has an affair with their teenage son's sly schoolmate, Sergi (Àlex Batllori). In the end, Miguel and Alicia give up their lovers to renew their commitment to their marriage.

Isabelle Huppert in *Paris Follies* (2014)

Paris Follies (2014)

The original French title: *La ritournelle*

The Lecanus, Brigitte (Isabelle Huppert) and Xavier (Jean-Pierre Darroussin), have a quiet and settled life as cattle farmers in picturesque Normandy. But things become a bit unsettled when Brigitte meets Stan (Pio Marmaï), a handsome young man, at a neighbor's party. The two take a stroll together. The two dance. Brigitte is excited to be in Stan's company and believes that she and Stan have made a connection. Brigitte wants to know more about Stan, but she has had too much to drink and becomes sick. As Stan goes to refresh their drinks, she rushes off to her home to vomit in ladylike solitude. Brigitte pretends to have a doctor's appointment so that she can visit Stan in Paris. She shows up unexpectedly at the store where Stan works and awkwardly arranges to meet the young man for dinner. Unfortunately, Stan's friend has an emergency and needs him to babysit for his two small children. Brigitte comes along, but it is not the romantic evening that she expected. She meets Stan for lunch the next day, but it becomes obvious to her that he isn't interested in her. Still, Brigitte remains determined to have the illicit romantic weekend that she dreamed about. So, instead of worrying about Stan, she has a fling with Jesper (Michael Nyqvist), a Danish businessman.

The film treats adultery in a light-hearted manner. Adultery is, in this context, nothing more than a passing amusement or a trivial form of soul-searching.

The film is, in many ways, similar to *Il seduttore*, which we will examine later. The protagonist sneaks away from their spouse for extramarital sex in Paris, but they are rejected by their intended partner and look to find a quick substitute. Alberto, the protagonist of *Il seduttore*, fails at both of his seductions. He is exposed as a fool for his Paris excursion. The failure of his ill-conceived seductions leaves him humiliated, defeated and diminished. In an odd contrast, *La ritournelle* becomes a female empowerment story.

Chapter Nineteen:
Wartime Affairs

The turmoil of World War II brought about many wartime affairs. The stock excuse for a wartime affair is simple: "There was a war on." George Brent's father uses this exact excuse in defending his unfaithful son to his daughter-in-law (Lucille Ball) in *Lover Come Back* (1946). This subject was addressed in a number of films during the 1940s.

Janet Wheeler (Eleanor Parker) discusses this matter with her younger sister, Molly (Andrea King), in *The Very Thought of You* (1944).

Molly: Don't you realize you can forget how a man really looks and talks and makes love? After two years, Freddy isn't real anymore.

Janet: I'd remember everything about Dave if we never saw each other again.

Molly: That's because you can still feel his arms around you. Wait a couple of months, baby, and you'll be making double dates with me just like we used to.

Janet: What do you think Freddy and all the other husbands and sweethearts are fighting for?. . . I'd like to know how Freddy feels, away on a carrier for two years, wondering why you don't write. How do you think he feels? And what if he knew you were spending his allotment on buying evening dresses for other fellas to enjoy? When he comes back, nobody would blame him if he beat your head off!

Molly confesses her infidelity to Freddy when he arrives home.

Molly: I worked in this place for about two weeks. Then I met this fellow. He was divorced. I started going out with him, just for laughs. I want to tell you everything before we go in. It got to be steady, this fellow and I, almost every night. The family and Jan gave me the devil, but I went out with him anyway. I let him kiss me, Freddy. He wanted me to marry him and ask you for a divorce. I started one of those "dear John" letters to you, but I never sent it.

Freddy: Why not?

Molly: Because I was all mixed up. I tried to bring you close to me at night, tried to remember us. But it's been so long, Freddy, so terribly long.

Freddy: I wish you knew how I thought and talked about you. I can't blame you, Molly, but I wish you had a better idea of what war is really like. Because it isn't all fighting, it's waiting. Days and nights of it. I had plenty of time to think of the night we first met. . . What you said, how you smiled, the way you put on your lipstick before you went into the house, how you loved me, how I loved you. It wasn't like the ads with me. You meant home. I was with you all those months I'd been away, but I guess you weren't with me.

Molly: Oh, Fred, please! I'm so terribly ashamed, if that makes any difference to you now. Anything you do to me, I deserve. Why don't you sock me or something?

Freddy: Maybe because I love you too much. I don't blame a guy for falling in love with you.

Molly: Will you take me back, Fred?

Freddy: You sure you want me?

Molly: Sure.

Divorce rates spiked in 1947, but steadily declined over the next ten years.

The Last Man (1916)

Lorna Harvey (Mary Anderson) falls in love with Lieutenant Horne (Jack Mower) while her husband, Major Harvey (William Duncan), is serving as an army surgeon in the Philippines.

Old Loves and New (1926)

Lord Geradine (Walter Pidgeon) seduces Elinor Carew (Katherine MacDonald) while her husband Gervas (Lewis Stone) is in military service during the First World War. When Gervas learns of his wife's infidelity, he divorces her and travels to Algiers to study medicine. Geraldine shows up in Algiers for health reasons. He is accompanied by his wife, Marny (Barbara Bedford). When Gervas catches Geradine beating Marny, he brings her to his home to keep her safe. The next day, Geradine bitterly goes looking for Gervas. But, while making his way across a field, he is trampled to death in a sudden elephant stampede. His death allows Gervas and Marny to marry.

Captured! (1933)

Captain Fred Allison (Leslie Howard), a British prisoner of war, is joined in the prison camp by a good friend, Lieutenant Jack Digby (Douglas Fairbanks Jr.). Fred doesn't realize that, while he has been in prison, Jack has been having an affair with his wife, Monica (Margaret Lindsay). Jack escapes from the prison camp and finds his way back to England. The German police suspect Jack of raping and murdering a young woman on the night of his escape. Colonel Carl Ehrlich (Paul Lukas), the camp commander, asks Fred to sign extradition papers so that Jack can stand trial. Fred refuses at first, but then Ehrlich shows him a letter that Monica wrote to Jack. It reads:

I want to be loyal to Fred, but it's no use - I love you, my dearest. The remembrance of our last night keeps haunting me - your arms around me, your kisses.

In England, Jack tells Monica that Fred is deeply in love with her. "When he spoke," he says, "it was you, you, you." The British military agrees to return Jack to Germany. During his trial, Jack accuses Allison of wanting him executed for his love affair with Monica. He says, "I condemned myself six months ago when I put my arms around a woman who was tired of a man she no longer loved. When I put my arms around her and kissed her for the first time, that was the death kiss. Wasn't it, Captain Allison?. . . That's why you asked that I be returned here. . . That was the real crime." Jack is convicted and sentenced to be shot by a firing squad. Allison learns that the real murderer wrote out a confession before hanging himself. He hesitates to reveal this information while Jack is led before the firing squad. But he imagines Monica pleading with him and races out to the firing squad commander, nearly coming within the line of fire. Allison has had to take the time to cope with his wife's infidelity and participate in a murder trial for his former best friend. Yet, he has still had time to plot a massive prison break. He takes control of a machine gun and sustains fire while his fellow prisoners steal planes. Every plane is in flight and on its way back to England by the time that Allison, who never expected to escape himself, is killed by a grenade. He essentially sacrificed his life so that his friend and wife could be together. It is similar to the fate of the cuckold husband in *Other Men's Women*.

Kiss of Araby (1933)

Les Adams of IMDb wrote, "While the commander of the British Army in Arabia, Major J. W. Courtney [Claude King], is out in the desert chasing marauding tribesmen, his wife [Claire Windsor] carries on an affair with Captain Randall [Theodore von Eltz]."[509]

Two Prisoners (1938)

The original Hungarian title: *Két fogoly*

Almády Miett (Gizi Bajor) turns to other men for affection and comfort while her husband, Dr. Takács Péter (Pál Jávor), is imprisoned in a Russian camp in Siberia.

Robert Donat and Deborah Kerr in *Vacation from Marriage* (1945)

Vacation from Marriage (1945)

A husband and wife, Robert (Robert Donat) and Catherine (Deborah Kerr), are bored with their marriage. We see in the opening scene that their life is drab and predictable. Robert looks worn and tired as he prepares for work. Catherine shuffles around the kitchen in a rumpled old bathrobe. She is weak and sickly. She has watery eyes and a stuffy nose. Her hair is uncombed. She wears no make-up. But their routine is suddenly shattered by world events. The onset of World War II draws them into military service. The Germans must be firing Cupid arrows at the British navy because both Robert and Catherine find romance in the war zone. She dallies with a naval architect while he dallies with a nurse. They are invigorated and liberated by their wartime affairs. The new and improved couple comes to dread their eventual reunion. Rotten Tomatoes notes: "Both are surprised by whom they find when they meet in a pub."[510] The film would fit well in the previous chapter on therapeutic value of affairs.

The director, Alexander Korda, greatly exaggerates the opening scene to hastily establish the dreariness of Robert and Catherine's marriage. It is also likely that he emphasizes the dreariness of the marriage to leave a strong impression on viewers, who need to sympathize with the protagonists as they stray from their marital vows. Due to the talents of Donat and Kerr, the film remains compelling despite its questionable message.

Waterloo Road (1945)

A soldier, Jim Colter (John Mills), goes AWOL to rescue his lonely newlywed bride, Tilly (Joy Shelton), from the charming and sleazy overtures of Ted Purvis (Stewart Granger), a petty criminal and draft dodger. To be excused from military service, Purvis paid a shady doctor to write a certificate claiming that he has a bad heart.

The film climaxes with a fistfight between Jim and Ted. Ted is much larger than Jim, but he begins to move unsteadily during the fight and is defeated. While he is receiving treatment for his cuts and bruises, the doctor determines that he does indeed have a bad heart, a likely consequence of his extravagant lifestyle. It is a gruesome twist ending, even though it is handled in a light and comic manner. Perhaps, the comic treatment makes it more gruesome. It's like having a smiling undertaker at a funeral.

The Best Years of Our Lives (1946)

The Best Years of Our Lives was condemned for an adultery subplot by the film board of the Roman Catholic Church.

During World War II, many American men swept up in the draft rushed to marry their girlfriends before they were shipped overseas. These hasty marriages quickly fell apart upon their return home. Fred Derry (Dana Andrews) is in this tough situation. He has come back from the war realizing that his own hasty pre-war marriage to Marie (Virginia Mayo) is not a solid union. Fred finds himself attracted to Peggy Stephenson (Teresa Wright), his friend Al's daughter. He has a pleasant lunch with Peggy. Afterward, he succumbs to a sudden urge to grab the young woman and kiss her. This upsets and confuses Peggy, who rushes to her car and drives away.

Peggy believes that she will be able to sort out her feelings if she can meet Marie. She brings along Woody (Victor Cutler) on a double date with Fred and Marie. Marie clearly does not show herself to be a loving and devoted wife. Woody tells Peggy that a marriage shouldn't be like Fred and Marie's marriage. Peggy asks him what is wrong with their marriage. "Nothing," he says, "except one slight detail. They just don't like each other."

After this outing, Peggy feels justified to save Fred from his marriage. She says:

Dana Andrews, Virginia Mayo and Steve Cochran in *The Best Years of Our Lives* (1946)

I'm going to break that marriage up. I can't stand seeing Fred tied to a woman he doesn't love. And who doesn't love him. It's horrible for him. It's humiliating, and it's killing his spirit. Somebody's got to help him.

Al (Fredric March) intervenes, insisting that Fred stop seeing his daughter. He says:

I don't like the idea of you sneaking around corners to see Peggy, taking her love on a bootleg basis. I give you fair warning, I'm going to do everything I can to keep her away from you, to help her forget about you and get her married to some decent guy who can make her happy.

Fred catches his wife at home with another man. This finally convinces him to divorce her.

Lover Come Back (1946)

professorharoldlloydhill of IMDb wrote: "Lucille Ball stars as Kay Williams, a woman who discovers her beloved husband [George Brent] wasn't faithful while away as a war correspondent and reacts by planting clues that she hadn't been faithful either."[511]

Homecoming (1948)

An army surgeon, Colonel Lee Johnson (Clark Gable), returns home to his wife Penny (Anne Baxter) after the war. He admits that, while away, he fell in love with a Red Cross nurse, Lt. Jane "Snapshot" McCall (Lana Turner). But he is mourning since Snapshot was wounded by a shell fragment and died days later in an army hospital. He says:

I'd seen a lot of people die, but somehow Snapshot - she was so active and alive, you somehow felt there was something indestructible about her. I was stunned. Finally, they told me that I could see her, but only for a few minutes. I don't think I was ever so shocked in my life. I'd been through almost three years of war with her. She'd stood up under everything that even men couldn't take. Then, to see her the way she was that day leaves you with something you can't ever forget.

He admits to his wife that her death remains a great loss to him. Penny understands that Lee had to bear many tragedies during the war and she promises to bear his grief with him and support him throughout his readjustment to civilian life.

The Good Die Young (1954)

An air force sergeant (John Ireland) learns that his wife (Gloria Grahame) cheated on him while he was away on military service.

The Man in the Gray Flannel Suit (1956)

Tom Rath (Gregory Peck), an army captain stationed in Italy during World War II, has a six-week affair with a young Italian woman, Maria Montagne (Marisa Pavan). He leaves Italy not knowing that Maria is pregnant with his son. It was clear in the novel that he was fairly sure he was abandoning a pregnant woman.

Tom had raced back to Maria's room, and it had been then she had told him she thought she was pregnant, she wasn't sure, but she thought she probably was. There had been no recriminations. She had asked nothing, and he had denied nothing. . . [She] had assumed he could do nothing much for her and had been surprised and grateful when he borrowed five hundred dollars from his friends and gave it to her, along with a jeepful of canned goods and cigarettes and chewing gum, all of which was worth a great deal.[512]

Tom returns home to his wife, Betsy (Jennifer Jones). Years later, he meets his old sergeant, Caesar (Keenan Wynn), who is now married to Maria's cousin. Caesar tells him that Maria gave birth to his son and is struggling to raise him on her own. Tom arranges to regularly send payments to Maria.

Another Time, Another Place (1958)

The film is set during World War II. An American reporter, Sara Scott (Lana Turner) has an affair with a British reporter, Mark Trevor (Sean Connery). Sara expects the two to marry until she learns that Mark is already married. Sara stays away from Mark at first, but she comes to have a change of heart. She is willing to stand by Mark until he can divorce his wife. Mark dies in a plane crash, which causes Sara to have a breakdown. Sara figures to work through her grief by visiting Mark's widow. But, rather than explain her relationship to Mark, she pretends that she's finishing a book that Mark started.

Doctor Zhivago (1965)

An adulterous affair between Yuri Zhivago (Omar Sharif) and Lara Guishar (Julie Christie) develops during the chaos of the Russian Civil War.

Hanna Schygulla in *The Marriage of Maria Braun* (1978)

The Marriage of Maria Braun (1978)

The original German title: *Die Ehe der Maria Braun*

The film opens in 1943 Berlin. Maria (Hanna Schygulla) marries Hermann (Klaus Lowitsch) during a bombing raid. Tim Brayton of Cinematheque wrote:

> *The Marriage of Maria Braun* opens with the muted sounds of a wedding ceremony barely audible under the screaming engines and thunderous explosions of an Allied bombing raid. . . An explosion rips a hole in the side of the building, giving us our first look at Maria herself, on the day of her wedding to Hermann Braun. The next few minutes present a cruelly hilarious travesty of the holy sacrament of marriage, with the newlyweds crouching on the ground in the rubble as they hastily sign the paperwork. . .[513]

This opening scene provides the absurdity of a Buster Keaton film. The soundtrack is dominated by harsh sounds. More audible than the screaming engines and thunderous explosions is the sound of a crying baby. Babies are certainly associated with marriage, but Maria's marriage will be a marriage without babies. Hermann is sent off to war two days later. Every day, Maria visits the train station with a cardboard sign featuring a photo of Hermann and the message "Who knows Hermann Braun?" But then Maria receives news that Hermann is dead. She gets a job at a bar for American soldiers. Maria's mother tells her daughter, "I just pray your soul doesn't come to any harm, my girl." Roger Ebert wrote: "Her mother alters the hem of her skirt while fretting that Maria's father would have been heartbroken to see his daughter as a bar girl; then she says she hopes somebody gives Maria some nylons."[514] Maria meets an American soldier, Bill (George

Byrd). They become lovers and Maria becomes pregnant. But Hermann isn't dead. He was interned for the last few years in a prison camp. He returns to find Maria with Bill. Hermann and Bill get into a scuffle. Maria strikes Bill in the head with a bottle, unintentionally killing him. It's an odd moment. It's as if Maria suddenly saw Bill as an obstacle between her and Hermann and needed to get rid of him. It is a cold and calculated act. Ebert explained plainly, "She settles the matter." Maria feels a great loyalty to Hermann. Whatever still exists of her soul lies within the sacred union that she formed with Hermann as the world went mad. Maria's mother (Gisela Uhlen) says, "The mistake people make is to love one person all their lives. If we don't have any potatoes, we eat turnips. If we don't have any turnips, we eat gruel. But in love, there's only one man, and when he goes to war and is dead five months later, you have to mourn for the rest of your life. Does that make sense?" Hermann takes the blame for Bill's death and is put into prison. Bill's baby is stillborn. Maria becomes the mistress of a wealthy industrialist, Karl Oswald (Ivan Desny). Karl visits Hermann at the prison. He offers to make Hermann and Maria his sole heirs if Hermann leaves the country after his release from prison. Hermann moves to Canada, but he regularly sends a red rose to Maria. Maria is willing to let Oswald have her body, but he cannot have her soul. She is committed to staying true to Hermann regardless of the situation. Brayton wrote, "[Schygulla] refuses to play Maria as a tragic soul and still less as an ice queen."[515] After Oswald dies, Hermann returns to Berlin for the reading of the will. On their reunion, Maria and Hermann are afraid that they will be able to resume the intimacy they once had together. When the will is read aloud, the executor quotes the stipulations of Hermann's deal with Oswald. This is the first time that Maria is learning about this. She is shattered that Hermann abandoned her for money. She turns on the oven jets in the kitchen, allowing the room to fill with gas. Then, she lights a match, which sets off a massive explosion. The wall of the kitchen bursts open much like the church wall did at the beginning of the film. The director, Rainer Werner Fassbinder, originally planned for Maria to kill herself in a car crash, but he decided that a more shocking and outlandish ending was appropriate.

Hanover Street (1979)

The film is set in London during the Second World War. An American B-25 bomber pilot, Lieutenant David Halloran (Harrison Ford), falls in love with a young British nurse, Margaret Sellinger (Lesley-Anne Down). Margaret never tells David that she's married. David is later assigned to assist a British agent, Paul Sellinger (Christopher Plummer), who turns out to be Margaret's husband.

Yanks (1979)

Like *Hanover Street*, *Yanks* is set in London during the Second World War. John (William Devane), an American captain, develops a romantic relationship with Helen (Vanessa Redgrave), an upper-class woman whose husband is away in the navy. John doesn't care that she's married. He doesn't think that she should care either. He tells her that she shouldn't worry about tradition and duty but instead trust her feelings. That sounds like the Devil speaking.

Some Kind of Hero (1982)

Eddie Keller (Richard Pryor) is held captive in a POW camp during the Vietnam War. He is finally released after six years and returns home, but he saddened to find that his wife Lisa (Lynne Moody) now has a new man in her life.

Another Time, Another Place (1983)

The film is set in Scotland during World War II. Janie (Phyllis Logan) is a young housewife married to an older man, Dougal (Paul Young). She has an affair with Luigi (Giovanni Mauriello), an Italian prisoner of war who has been assigned by military officials to work on her farm.

Rama Dama (1991)

The film is set in post-war Munich. A young mother, Kati Zeiler (Dana Vávrová), believes that her husband Felix (Johann Schuler) has died in battle and becomes romantically involved with Hans Stadler (Werner Stocker). However, Felix suddenly returns home to rejoin Kati.

The War Bride (2001)

Lily (Anna Friel) is lonely while her husband, Charlie (Aden Young), is away fighting in World War II. Lily becomes attracted to a young grocer, Joe (Loren Dean). Joe asks her if she still loves Charlie. She replies:

> I did once. God, I really loved him! Now I can't even remember his face, I can't remember what he looks like, I can't remember how he speaks. I can't remember anything about him, my husband!

Sylvia (Molly Parker) sees herself as unattractive because the lasting damage of childhood polio requires her to wear a leg brace. She is in love with Joe, but she is too shy to let him know. She is particularly self-conscious of the leg brace while attending a dance and watching Lily dance with Joe. Overwhelmed with grief, she loses her temper and calls Lily a slut. Lily is hurt by her outburst. Later that night, Lily asks Joe to drive her to the train station. She believes that she needs to find somewhere else to live. Outside, beside Joe's car, Lily and Joe speak of love. Joe embraces Lily and kisses her. Lily responds willingly at first, but she stops Joe when he pushes her down in the car and attempts to have sex. Peggy witnesses this scene from her bedroom window. Charlie arrives home unexpectedly and is told by Peggy of the canoodling. He is outraged at first, but Lily eventually convinces him of her remorse and he forgives her.

Chapter Twenty:
The Cuckold

The Merriam-Webster dictionary defines a cuckold as, simply, the husband of an unfaithful wife. But, in the minds of many, a cuckold is something more than that. A cuckold is a husband who has been tragically humiliated by his wife's indiscreet cheating. A cuckold is a husband whose wife has such little respect for him that she puts no real effort into keeping her illicit affair (or affairs) secret. A man is not a true cuckold unless he has been reduced to an object of derision by a wife who has abandoned decorum. In the most extreme instances, a cuckold lets his wife's cheating reduce him to a pitiable wreck of a man.

We have already seen horrible cuckolds - William B. Whitley in *The Heavenly Body* (1944), Pippo in *The Inheritance* (1976) and Paul in *Une affaire de femme* (1988). The best-known movie cuckold is Joseph Tura (Jack Benny) of *To Be or Not to Be* (1942). Tura, a vain and hammy Shakespearean actor, has a lovely wife who enjoys entertaining young airmen backstage while he is preoccupied performing "Hamlet." Let us now meet a few others.

Marlene Dietrich in *Blue Angel* (1930)

Blue Angel (1930)

Professor Immanuel Rath (Emil Jannings), a high school teacher, finds boys in his class passing around photos of a risqué cabaret singer, Lola Lola (Marlene Dietrich). Rath visits the Blue Angel cabaret expecting to catch students attending Lola Lola's show. But the visit has an unexpected effect on him. He is enchanted by Lola and visits her backstage, startled to catch her disrobing. Rath makes regular visits to the cabaret. He can no longer focus his attention on his job. His students, aware of Rath's nightly activities, draw a cartoon on the blackboard showing him strolling out of the cabaret. As the students hoot and howl, the principal enters the classroom to investigate the uproar. He is upset by what he finds and threatens to fire Rath.

Rath resigns from his job so that he can marry Lola and go on tour with her. To make money, he sells dirty postcards and performs in the magician's act as a clown. He is humiliated when the show returns to his hometown and old friends and acquaintances see him made up as a clown while the magician smashes eggs on his head.

Rath becomes enraged to catch Lola kissing the show's strongman. When he attempts to strangle Lola, he is subdued by other performers and bound into a straitjacket. He is taken away crowing like a mad rooster.

Wikipedia notes: "Later that night, Rath is released. He leaves and goes to his old classroom. Rejected, humiliated, and destitute, he dies clutching the desk at which he once taught."[516]

Smarty (1934)

Tony Wallace (Warren William) is deeply unhappy with his wife, Vicki (Joan Blondell). He can no longer tolerate either her constant flirting or her cruel put-downs. He implores her to stop behaving badly and, when she responds by mocking him, he loses his temper and slaps her. Upset, she arranges with her husband's friend and attorney Vernon (Edward Everett Horton) to secure a divorce for her. Vicki marries Vernon and treats him no better than Tony. She invites Tony for dinner and attempts to seduce him as soon as he arrives. Tony complains, "You can't commute between husbands. . . brutally, wantonly, swinishly." He understands that she left their marriage mostly because she was bored with him. "I was given the air, just like that. Take your dreams and toothbrush and clear out. Vickie wants to play another game." He tells Vickie that it's wrong to look upon flirting as "good clean fun."

My Life With Caroline (1941)

Anthony Mason (Ronald Colman) has a wife, Caroline (Anna Lee), who enjoys flirting with other men. He frequently travels on business and, while he is away, Caroline unsurprisingly seeks out attention from other men. Her latest lover is Paco Del Valle (Gilbert Roland).

bkoganbing wrote:

Colman proceeds to break the fourth wall and tell Roland will not be the first or last to fall for wife Caroline, the girl just can't help it and Colman can't help but put up with it. And as illustration Colman tells us about her last little flirtation with Reginald Gardiner and how that all ended up.[517]

Hafer wrote:

My Life with Caroline has a pretty shallow and impossible to believe plot. His wife is an apparently brainless idiot and falls in love at the drop of a hat with other men who pay attention to her. He[r] husband, Colman, is either completely cold and indifferent to her (leaving her alone for months at a time) or he is an ardent manipulator and suitor - a strange combination to say the least. None of this really makes sense and the characters seem. . . dumb.[518]

st-shot of IMDb wrote:

The limited Lee brings nothing but wide eyed confusion to the inane role of Caroline who seems to have the emotional maturity of a twelve year old. She seems committed to only her romantic delusions and completely out of touch with her fellow characters. Colman for his part looks distracted and uninvolved, his interplay with Lee patronizing more than intimate. The supporting cast offers none with a smarmy Reggie Gardner and a wheezing Charles Winninger unable to bring sly humor to surly character[s].[519]

Mason is far from the standard cuckold, who is typically helpless and miserable. He shows no real affection for his wife. How could he? What qualities does the wife have that a man could love? Love is needed for a true commitment. Caroline is shallow, dim-witted, and immature. But she's a pretty thing to have around. It's really a revenge film. Mason manipulates characters with an evil glee as he guides them to their downfall and humiliation.

The Maltese Falcon (1941)

Private investigator Sam Spade (Humphrey Bogart) is having an affair with his partner's saucy wife, Iva Archer (Gladys George).

They Were Sisters (1945)

Brian (Barry Livesey) loves Vera and wants to marry her, but there is a question if Vera (Anne Crawford) can be a faithful wife.

Brian: Asking you to marry me.

Vera: Darling, why look for trouble?

Brian: Because I love you.

Vera: But you see, I don't love you.

Brian: But I think I can make you.

Vera: Could you? I'm afraid you'd find me an awful handful. Lucy always says nothing lasts with me. That I pick things up and drop them like a monkey. I'd hate to do that to you, Brian.

Brian: I'm willing to take the chance if you are.

Vera believes that her warning to Brian gives her license to behave abominably as a wife. She openly engages with a steady succession of admirers. Brian walks past as she chats with a nameless admirer at a party. The admirer glances at Brian. "Who was that?" he asks. "My husband," she dryly responds. The admirer looks at a bouquet of roses on a table. "Oh, I see you got my roses," the man says. "Were they from you?" she asks. The camera casually passes away from this brief but telling scene.

Brian is annoyed to find one of her admirers wandering around the house. "Vera," he asks his wife, "when you finish with these admirers of yours, must you leave them about?" She reacts flippantly. "Will you grudge me my simple pleasures?" she asks. He responds, "I don't think I ever grudge you anything. Perhaps that is why our life is such a mess." He later takes the blame for the failure of the marriage. He says, "The trouble with me is. . . I could never help being a bore." Tony Williams, film studies professor at Southern Illinois University, wrote, "Brian loses his family due to masculine impotence."[520]

The cheating wife lives happily ever after with her latest lover. It is a perverse outcome indeed.
Flesh Will Surrender (1947)

Flesh Will Surrender is based on the 1891 novel "Giovanni Episcopo," which was written by Gabriele D'Annunzio.

The film involves a clerk, Giovanni Episcopo (Aldo Fabrizi), who finds himself humiliated when his wife Ginevra (Yvonne Sanson) has an affair with his manly friend Giulio Wanzer (Roldano Lupi). Giovanni, who is shy and modest, is a great mismatch for his wild, beautiful wife. A pair of young clerks snigger about this odd pairing. One tells the other, "Beautiful women, dear Novelli, one always pays for them. It's mathematics. Either with money, or being cuckold."

Only a Mother (1949)

A young woman, Rya-Rya (Eva Dahlbeck), creates an uproar in a Swedish farming community when she swims naked in a pond. Her boyfriend, Henrik (Ragnar Falck), is angry with her and ignores her at a dance. She goes off with another man, Nils (Max Sydow), and the couple finds a secluded spot in the woods to have sex. Rya-Rya becomes pregnant from this episode, but Nils is unwilling to marry her. She instead marries Henrik, not bothering to tell him that she's pregnant. This deception haunts Rya-Rya for the rest of her life. Years later, she asks her husband for forgiveness on her deathbed.

Cary Grant and Deborah Kerr in *The Grass is Greener* (1960)

The Grass is Greener (1960)

Victor (Cary Grant), a cash-strapped British earl, earns extra money by opening his ancestral estate to tourists. Among the latest batch of tourists is an oil tycoon, Charles Delaceo (Robert Mitchum). Charles leaves the tour to poke around in the private sections of the home. Hillary (Deborah Kerr), Victor's wife, is irritated when he suddenly appears in her study. He lies, telling her that he made a mistake and took a wrong turn. She snaps back, "Well, I don't call entering a door marked private making a mistake. I call that trespassing." Charles is instantly charmed by the beautiful and fiery Hillary. He admits to the truth. "Oh," he says, "it's quite simple really. As I had said, I spent a wonderful hour going through your beautiful home. . . Let's just say I was curious to see the people who live in them."

Charles is rude and brazen in his efforts to seduce Hilary.

Charles: I'm an American, I say what I think.

Hillary: And hesitate before you say it. A Frenchman would never have hesitated.

Charles: And an Englishman?

Hillary: Ooh, an Englishman would never have said it.

Charles: You mean an Englishman would never tell a married woman she was lovely?

Hillary: Oh, no, I don't mean that. It's just that he usually tells the husband first.

Charles: What's the point in that?

Hillary: Because he knows the husband will tell the wife. "Do you know what old George said to me last night, my dear? He said he thought you looked lovely."

Charles: I said very lovely.

Hillary: And so the wife is intrigued and the next time she's alone with George she sees to it that he tells her himself. It's an oblique approach but not a bad one, and very effective.

Hattie Durant (Jean Simmons) offers her old friend Victor advice on the situation. She tells him, " [Hilary's] paramount emotion at the moment, is neither her passion for Charles nor her love for you. It's a feeling of complete bewilderment that her values, her standards, her whole existence could be cockeyed in half an hour."

Hilary finds it difficult to resist Charles' charm.

Charles: Come here.

Hillary: No, and you stay where you are.

Charles: Why?

Hillary: Cause I can't think clearly when I'm near you.

Charles: What do you mean?

Hillary: You know exactly what I mean.

Victor challenges Charles to a duel by pistols. The duel ends with Charles shooting Victor in the arm.

Hillary: Do you realize that you might've been killed, or disabled for life, or put into prison for manslaughter?

Victor: You should be flattered I risked so much for you.

Cary Grant in *The Grass is Greener* (1960)

The Grass is Greener is talky, much like *When Ladies Meet* and *The Moment of Truth* (1952). But the talk is, in this case, uninteresting.

Marc Eliot wrote in "Cary Grant: A Biography," "Even Grant's most diehard fans stayed away, not wanting to see their idol compromised by, of all men, the swarthy, bullying Robert Mitchum."[521]

The Magnificent Cuckold (1964)

The original Italian title: *Il magnifico cornuto*

Andrea Artusi (Ugo Tognazzi) has a beautiful and amiable wife, Maria (Claudia Cardinale). But he has cheated on her with numerous women. He worries as he drives home from his latest hookup that he smells of his lover's perfume. He tries his best to waft it away. He projects his own devious desires onto Maria. He smells a strange soap scent on his wife. She explains that she visited an antique shop and touched dusty items, which required her to wash her hands at the shop. He gets a traffic ticket in the mail. The ticket shows that, late one night, Maria's car was parked in front of Murro del Castello. He takes this as evidence that Maria was out meeting a lover. The truth is that a watchman had borrowed the car to meet his girlfriend. Andrea's constant jealousy drives Maria into the arms of a sympathetic doctor (Philippe Nicaud). She enjoys being faithless and is soon driven into arms of other men. Improbably, this sweet and innocent woman becomes as sexually immoral as her philandering husband. A. H. Weiler of The New York Times praised a couple of fantasy scenes, including "one in which Miss Cardinale does a sensuous strip tease in black, filmy negligee before a covey of admirers, and another where Mr. Tognazzi does variations on nabbing her and her lover in flagrante delicto."[522] The cuckold was a fascinating figure in Italian cinema in the 1960s and 1970s.

Ugo Tognazzi in *The Magnificent Cuckold* (1964)

Help Me, My Love (1969)

Giovanni (Alberto Sordi) claims to have liberal views on marriage, but he is unable to cope when his wife Raffaella (Monica Vitti) admits to having passionate feelings for a handsome neighbor, Valerio (Silvano Tranquilli). Raffaella is appallingly immature. She is vain and selfish, incapable of thinking of anyone but herself and incapable of restraining her emotions. It likely corrupted her to be spoiled by her far too loving and far too generous husband. Giovanni has spoiled her terribly, letting her have anything that she wants. Why shouldn't he let her have a lover?

The couple listens on a car radio about a husband who found his wife strolling through a park with another man and instantly shot both of them. Giovanni insists that there needs to be trust and honesty in a marriage. He believes that a wife should simply be able to tell her husband if she has fallen in love with another man. She asks him how he would react in that sort of situation.

> Giovanni: It is quite simple, I'd have said: "Ramona, darling, you have been thrown off balance by this man. Very well, go out with him, get to know him better. If it is only an in-fatuation, then fine. If, on the other hand, you are really in love, then too bad, go with him and that's that."
>
> Raffaella: Why, that is typical reasoning for a man who doesn't love his wife.
>
> Giovanni: No, it's just that I can't bear deceit or hypocrisy. That's the only civilized way to behave.
>
> Raffaella: But that way marriage becomes no more than a lot of hot air.
>
> Giovanni: No more than hot air? My darling, if two people stop loving each other, let them separate.

The conversation resumes once they arrive at home. Raffaella, emboldened by Giovanni's philosophy, reveals to him that she has fallen in love with another man. Giovanni, startled while opening a can, cuts his finger. He becomes dizzy.

> Giovanni: Come on, Raffaella. You are behaving like a little girl. You have a ten year-old son. Aren't you ashamed at your age?

> Raffaella: No, don't say that. What's this got to do with age? It's an illness. It's like a microbe boring into my head and little by little paralyzing the whole of my body.

It only gets worse. Giovanni becomes enraged.

> Giovanni: I'm fed up. Stop mentioning the fellow. Do you understand? And furthermore, you know what? You won't see him ever again. God, you rotten slut. There, now my leg's going numb, too. I can't even walk. You're wicked. You're ruining my life. If you want to go off with him, all right, go. And don't set foot inside this house again.

> Raffaella: No, no, darling, don't scold me.

Alberto Sordi and Monica Vitti in *Help Me, My Love* (1969)

Raffaella openly carries on her affair with Valerio, eventually causing Giovanni to have a nervous breakdown.

Stronger husbands - Jean Gabin in *The Moment of Truth*, Paul Douglas in *Clash by Night* and Charles Boyer in *The Earrings of Madame* - do not allow themselves to be degraded by their cheating wives. They rightfully believe that it is their wives who should feel humiliated, not them.

The Seduction of Mimi (1972)

The original Italian title: *Mimì metallurgico ferito nell'onore*

    Mimi (Giancarlo Giannini) leaves his wife Rosalia (Agostina Belli) in Sicily to find work in Turin. He has an extramarital affair with Fiore (Mariangela Melato), a free-spirited young woman who doesn't care that he is married. Mimi and Fiore live together and have a child. By now, Mimi has lost interest in Rosalia. But then his employer transfers him to Sicily, which forces him to rejoin Rosalia. He pretends to be impotent to remain faithful to Fiore, but Rosalia can't believe that her virile husband is impotent and assumes that he has become gay. Rosalia confesses to Mimi that she had an affair with a police sergeant, Amilcare Finocchiaro (Gianfranco Barra). When he learns that Amilcare has gotten Rosalia pregnant, he resolves to seduce and impregnate Amilcare's wife as revenge. He sees this as the only way to remove the stain of being a cuckold and restore his dignity.

Come Home and Meet My Wife (1974)

The original Italian title: *Romanzo popolare*

    Giulio (Ugo Tognazzi), a 50-year-old factory worker, marries his beautiful 17-year-old goddaughter, Vincenzina (Ornella Muti). They become proud parents of a boy, Ciccio. Giulio, a dedicated communist, leads a political protest. He feels guilty when a member of his group injures a young police officer, Giovanni Pizzullo (Michele Placido). He invites Giovanni to his home to play poker with him and his friends. He sees Giovanni talking with Vincenzina and worries that his wife would prefer to be with a younger man. He has a nightmare in which he finds Vincenzina in bed with Giovanni. Giovanni drags him out of his home while Vincenzina screams, "Go away! You suck, you old fart! Throw him out! I don't want to see him again!" His dream is prescient. Giulio arrives home unexpectedly and overhears Vincenzina talking to Giovanni in the kitchen. She is telling him that they need to end their affair. Although he is deeply hurt by his wife's infidelity, Giulio doesn't want to handle the matter in a brutish way. So, he sits calmly with Vincenzina. He is loving. He is reasonable. He tells her how he feels and what he thinks. He tells her that he wants her to be happy. She is overjoyed by her husband's understanding and forgiveness. She suddenly leaps off her chair and throws her arms around his neck, which causes him to topple over backward in his chair. It is slapstick introduced to break up the tragedy. Vincenzina says, "I lost my mind! I was mad in love. I didn't know what I was doing." Giulio forgives her. He says, "When the blind man is given his sight back, he's happy to see, no matter what." Vincenzina is relieved. She swears to Giulio that she has learned from the experience. She says, "It was a big cold shower, Giulio!" Giulio responds, "More like a hammer." But then, days later, Giulio receives an anonymous letter taunting him about Vincenzina's infidelity. He becomes terrified that everyone he knows has found out about the affair. He calls the letter his "cuckold license." He can't eat. He can't sleep. He has a nightmare in which he sits in the break room at the factory and hears it loudly announced on the public address system that he is a cuckold. He runs out into the hallway in his pajamas and calls his fellow tenants out of their apartments. He lets them know that he is kicking out his unfaithful wife. Once Vincenzina departs, he turns the gas on in his oven to kill himself, but he changes his mind. He misses Vincenzina and regrets having thrown her out. He visits Giovanni to see if she has gone to him. Vincenzina arrived at Giovanni's home only minutes earlier. She panics hearing Giulio. She quickly grabs her baby and her bags, climbs out of the bathroom window, and runs off as fast as she can. Giovanni admits to Giulio that he wrote the cuckold letter. He doesn't regret it. He tells Giulio, "If a young woman doesn't love you anymore, be noble!" The story advances seven years. Vincenzina moved to another city and divorced Giulio. She has had a successful career as a manager in a factory. She has not been able to find herself another husband. Giulio has given up on women and gets pleasure from weekly poker games and playing in a boccia league. Giovanni has married another woman and they have had two kids together. He has taken up model airplanes as a hobby. Not surprising, the homewrecker has suffered the least amount of fallout. Ciccio (Gianmarco Tognazzi) asks his mother if his father can visit for lunch. She says in voice-over, "So, when Ciccio asked me if Giulio could come for lunch sometime I said. . . well, ok! Every other Saturday perhaps. . ." It is with this hopeful line that the film ends.

Giancarlo Giannini and Laura Antonelli in *The Innocent* (1976)

The Innocent (1976)

The original Italian title: *L'innocente*

Tullio Hermil (Giancarlo Giannini) neglects his wife, Giuliana (Laura Antonelli), to spend time with his fiery and sensuous mistress, Teresa Raffo (Jennifer O'Neill). Giuliana diminishes her anxiety and loneliness by taking sleeping pills. She lifts her spirit by having an affair with a sympathetic writer, Filippo d'Arborio (Marc Porel). Tullio is again interested in Giuliana now that she has a lover. He panics when he learns that Giuliana is pregnant with d'Arborio's child. He demands that his wife get an abortion, but she refuses. She says that abortion is a crime. He replies, "But you're quite happy to give my name and my family's affection to a stranger. Isn't that a crime?" d'Arborio contracts an infection and dies. Giuliana remains with Tullio and gives birth to a baby boy.

Tullio lays the baby by an open window to expose him to a chilly night breeze. The baby is dead by morning. He believes that he has now cleaned the slate and can begin his marriage again. He is like *The Se-*

duction of Mimi's Mimi in thinking that only a drastic deed can wash away the cuckold taint. But Mimi's drastic deed was to create a baby, not murder one. Giuliana will not allow the man who murdered her baby to keep his dignity. She tells him, "It's truly over. I loved and always will love that baby's father. To the end of my days, I can but hate you." Tullio becomes so distraught at Giuliana spurning him that he calmly walks onto a patio and shoots himself.

Laura Antonelli in *The Innocent* (1976)

I Know That You Know That I Know (1982)

The original Italian title: *Io so che tu sai che io so*

Vitti and Sordi returned to the roles of cheating wife and hysterical cuckold in *I Know That You Know That I Know*. Cavalli (Salvatore Jacono), a private investigator, is hired by a prominent financier to follow his wife, Elena (Micaela Pignatelli), who he suspects of having an affair. Elena loans her car to a neighbor, Livia Bonetti (Monica Vitti), which causes Cavalli to follow her by mistake. After learning that he filmed the wrong wife, Cavalli turns over a suitcase of films to Livia's banker husband, Fabio (Alberto Sordi). Fabio, who has been married to Livia for twenty years, believes that he knows his wife well and can trust her. But the films show him that his wife is not the person that he always imagined her to be. Among the many surprises is the fact that Livia is having an affair with a college student, Roman. Fabio gets a gun to shoot himself, but he changes his mind at the last moment. Instead, he runs through rain with the suitcase of films and tosses it into a river. At home, he loses control seeing Livia and attempts to strangle her. His adult daughter, Veronica (Isabella De Bernardi), calms her sobbing father and brings the family together once again.

Boogie Nights (1997)

Little Bill Thompson (William H. Macy) is married to a porn star (Nina Hartley), who openly has sex with other men. Little Bill reaches a breaking point when he discovers his wife having sex with another man during a New Year's Eve party. He shoots his wife and her lover. Then, with a happy grin, he shoots himself in the head. He's free at last.

Along Came Polly (2004)

While on his honeymoon, Reuben Feffer (Ben Stiller) catches his wife Lisa (Debra Messing) having sex with her scuba diving instructor, Claude (Hank Azaria).

The Squid and The Whale (2005)

Bernard and Joan Berkman (Jeff Daniels and Laura Linney) are embroiled in a bitter divorce. Bernard is resentful of Julia because she had multiple affairs during their marriage. When the couple gets into a heated argument, he can no longer contain his anguish and resentment. "You left all those fucking ticket stubs and letters lying around," he shouts. "You wanted me to know. It was fucking torture, Joan! Fucking torture!" Adultery is often an attention-seeking strategy that only causes pain.

Chapter Twenty-One:
The Man-Child

In his long-running series of short subjects for RKO, comedian Leon Errol played a married man who found it impossible to resist other women (especially if he has had a few drinks). His fans knew what to expect as soon as the title came up on the screen. They knew that the comedian would be mixing with a pretty young woman in films like *Panic in the Parlor* (1941), *Cutie on Duty* (1943), *Blondes Away* (1947) and *Wife Tames Wolf* (1947). Les Adams of IMDb summarized the plot of *Wife Tames a Wolf* as follows:

> Caught philandering (for the 1867th time, give or take a couple), Leon's wife (Dorothy Granger) announces (for the 1867th time, give or take a couple as she wasn't always his wife) that she is going to divorce him. His business partner hatches a scheme to cure Leon of his flirting with very pretty girls (and a few ugly ones) he meets, but the scheme has Leon faking a suicide.[523]

Leon did indeed hatch many wacky and desperate schemes to avoid having his exasperated wife divorce him. He has no regard for anyone but himself in these situations. He is willing to slide a woman under a bed or shove a woman onto a tenth-story ledge to hide her from his wife. Leon is a naughty little boy who can't keep himself out of trouble.

Leon is occasionally innocent of wrongdoing. In *Borrowed Blonde* (1947), Leon arrives home with a house coat that he has bought as a make-up present for his wife, who recently caught him fooling around with his secretary. A young woman who lives next door to the Errols is so taken by the house coat that she snatches it out of his hands and quickly tries it on. Leon attempts to remove the coat only to get his tie caught in the zipper. Of course, his wife comes along just at this moment and misconstrues the situation.

Madam Satan (1930)

The rich are prominent members of society. This should make them cautious about the way they behave. But it doesn't. *Madam Satan* makes the point that a wealthy man's indiscretion is bound to be exposed publicly by the press.

Angela Brooks (Kay Johnson), a prim and proper socialite, reads in the morning newspaper that her husband Bob (Reginald Denny) was brought into night court on a speeding charge. He was accompanied to court by his best friend, Jimmy Wade (Roland Young), and a beautiful showgirl, Trixie (Lillian Roth). Bob doesn't want Angela to know that Trixie is his mistress so he tells her the charming woman is Jimmy's wife.

Bob acts childishly as soon as we meet him. He has arrived home hopelessly drunk. Angela has to help him into the shower and then tuck him into bed. Bob whines a lot. He is a little boy who wants to play and resents anyone or anything that tries to stop him. He complains, "Marriage is a schoolroom and you're the teacher!" Presumably, it is because he sees his wife as a strict and chilly schoolteacher that he has lost interest in her.

Angela figures to win back Bob's affection by dressing as a sexy masked woman at an elaborate costume party being held aboard a tethered zeppelin. Bob finds this mysterious vamp, who calls herself Madam Satan, to be irresistibly sexy. It says much about Bob that he is most at home at a childish costume party.

A storm tears the zeppelin from its tethers. There's a mass panic. Guests scramble for parachutes and leap out of the unstable zeppelin. Trixie is alarmed as she cannot locate a parachute. Angela tells her that she can have her parachute if she promises to leave Bob alone. Trixie is more interested in having Angela's parachute than having her husband. She agrees to her terms, straps on the parachute and exits the zeppelin, at the same time exiting Bob and Angela's life forever. Bob now sees Angela unmasked and realizes that beneath his wife's cool exterior lies a dynamic lover. Bob relinquishes his parachute to Angela before taking a daring leap out of the zeppelin and landing safely in the Central Park reservoir. The couple is happily reunited before the final credits.

Gregory D. Black, Chairman of the Communications Department at the University of Missouri, wrote, "[Cecil B.] DeMille, with characteristic efficiency, had managed to put almost all of the objections of the reformers into one script. The script debunked virtue, justified adultery [and] made light comedy of drunken debauchery. . ."[524]

Week-End Marriage (1932)

Sandra Brennan of AllMovie Guide wrote: "In this comedy, a hard-working husband loses his job and his wife becomes the bread winner. The husband feels demeaned by his new role and takes a mistress to regain his lost manhood. The chastened wife eventually returns to the daily drudgery of home so her hubby can feel important and manly again. Marital bliss ensues."[525]

John Beal, Robert Montgomery and Helen Hayes in *Another Language* (1933)

Another Language (1933)

Victor (Robert Montgomery) returns from Europe with a new wife, Stella (Helen Hayes). Victor's family is not cordial towards the bride. Victor's callow nephew, Jerry (John Beal), foolishly develops an infatuation for his uncle's wife. Stella fails to recognize his infatuation. She takes a walk with Jerry, who expresses sympathy regarding her troubles with her new in-laws. AFI notes: "During the walk, Jerry confesses to Stella his romantic interest, but is soundly discouraged by her."[526] Later that day, Jerry reveals to the family that he is in love with Stella. Vicky believes his wife's innocence in the situation and defends her to his family. He pretends that he knew about Jerry's infatuation and laughed about it. Jerry storms out of the house in humiliation. By finally standing up for his wife, Victor has saved his marriage.

Riptide (1934)

A married woman, Mary (Norma Shearer), is passionately pursued by an old flame, Tommie (Robert Montgomery), while her husband, Lord Rexford (Herbert Marshall), is abroad for business. Their playful interactions at a large house party do not go unnoticed by the other guests. Wikipedia describes Tommie as "a good-time, heavy-drinking sort."[527] He has no real substance, indulging in immoral pleasure for pure hedonistic satisfaction. But Mary doesn't care. She says, "Tommie, you're a fool - but a nice one." Tommie is, in many ways, a Peter Pan type.

The couple slips out of a house party to frolic around together around a pool. They perform a comic ballet before diving into the pool in their evening clothes. Mary spurns a kiss from Tommie, who responds by pouting and calling her a "prude."

The wet couple sits by the pool for a quiet conversation. Tommie says, "Listen to those birds up there. They don't have to drink to be gay. They don't have to doll up and gab a lot of nonsense." One bird is particularly loud. He continues:

> He's a happy little fellow, isn't he? We could be happy too, Mary. Two people like us. . . [T]wo kindred spirits like you and me. They could sleep all day. They can get up just when the evening was gonna get gay and they could dance, and take long walks into the moonlight, then back and change, and out with the horses and riding into the dawn. Just when everybody else was waking up to face the day. They could be flitting in and out of warm shower baths and pulling down the blinds on trouble, and bores and telephones. Then they'd be up in the evening and drink steaming hot coffee and pull up the shades and let that old moon in again. It would be paradise, wouldn't it? They'd be children of the night.

The "children of the night" phrase was famously recited by the dark lord Dracula three years earlier. It is no wonder that Mary responds by calling Tommie "Satan."

Tommie says, "See me sometimes, Mary. Just like this. Forget all that solid routine they call living. Spread your wings and flutter with me sometimes." Yes, he could be talking about a vampire bat.

Mary: I've forgotten how to flutter.

Tommie: I can teach you. Wouldn't it be fun, wouldn't it be marvelous? Think of the thrill of knowing that just around the corner there was fun and laughter waiting to hold you.

Tommie's fanciful speech is effective in earning him a kiss. Mary enjoys the kiss, but she realizes that it was wrong and leaves. News of this episode gets back to Lord Rexford, who becomes furious with Mary. He tells his wife that he can longer trust her and he wants a divorce.

Rexford's mistrust, unjustified in Mary's view, drives her into Tommie's arms. One afternoon, she arrives at his lawyer's office to sign papers renouncing custody of her daughter. Wikipedia sums up the perfect happy ending: "As she leaves, Lord Rexford asks her to return to him, and as they happily reconcile, their little girl bursts into the room and embraces her parents."[528]

Forsaking All Others (1934)

The film again exposes the playboy as an irresponsible man-child.
We are familiar with the wedding vows:

Do you promise to love her, comfort her, honor and keep her for better or worse, for richer or poorer, in sickness and health, and forsaking all others, be faithful only to her, for as long as you both shall live?

So, this film about a faithless husband was given the sarcastic title *Forsaking All Others*.

Mary Clay (Joan Crawford) tosses aside conventional rules to have an affair with a married friend, Dill Todd (Robert Montgomery). We are introduced to Dill as he playfully tastes Mary's face cream. Mary says that Dill has been picking on her like this since they were children. Dill later enters a party proclaiming, "Eat, drink, and be merry." This is, by every indication, the motto of his life.

Dill, one of the idle rich, continues to act childishly throughout the film. He rides a bicycle recklessly around a farm, ultimately crashing into a pig pen. An old farmer who witnessed this foolish accident scratches his head and mutters to himself, "I don't know, maybe *I'm* wrong." He crashes his car because he stopped looking at the road to kiss Mary. He gets his comely companion to join him in a chorus of "Row, Row, Row Your Boat" as the pair, resembling an overgrown Jack and Jill, gaily stroll hand in hand down a dirt road. He nearly sets Aunt Paula's house on fire because he can't figure out where she keeps the wood for her fireplace (it's in a chest six feet away!) and instead uses an antique spinning wheel that we later learn is a family heirloom.

Mary intends to have an affair with Dill regardless if it is morally correct. She tells her friend, Jeffy Williams (Clark Gable), "I'm free, white and twenty-one and, if I want to, I'll kick my self-respect around until it's lost. I've played according to the book until now and where am I? From now on, I use my own rules." "You're talking like a fool," he says. "Fine," she insists, "fools have a lot of fun. They have a great time. I don't care whether or not I get a gold star for good behavior this week or any other week." He turns her over his knee and beats her backside with a hairbrush.

Mary sees her get-togethers with Dill as nothing more than "gay and friendly." But Dill doesn't see them the same way. When they arrive together at Aunt Paula's country home, he admits that his servant will not be showing up as planned. Mary now understands that Dill plans for them to be alone and intimate. She vehemently protests. To stop her from being upset, Dill promises to sleep on the lawn for the night.

The Production Code required Hollywood to remove the sex from their adultery films even though adultery, by its definition, includes sex as a component. It doesn't matter if, in these films, an affair does or doesn't explicitly involve sex. The lovers effectively share an adulterous passion and the writers clearly have adultery on their mind. But it would be technically more accurate to say these films address the broader topic of marital infidelity. So, adultery stories became infidelity stories, even though audiences understood what they really were about.

Jeffy isn't cross about a "Row, Row, Row Your Boat" duet when he confronts Mary at the country home. He tells her, "You're a spoiled, silly brat that needs a hairbrush every now and then." But, in the end, we have the sort of abrupt reversal described by Basinger. Mary admits "I was wrong yesterday. Fools don't have a lot of fun. I thought I could kick the rules over, but I guess I'm not the type. This isn't the answer." Jess talks to Dill's wife, Connie (Frances Drake), about the situation. He says, "I'm sure we can straighten this thing out. We're all grown up. Although, I must admit, there are times when Dill seems between the age of five and six." He adds, "We all know they were in the wrong. They acted like a pair of kids." So, the wrongdoers are forgiven and order is restored.

No More Ladies (1935)

Films of the period often featured an irresponsible young playboy who needs to mature before he can win the woman he loves. Robert Young plays such an irresponsible playboy in *Stowaway* (1936). Alice Faye encourages him to "grow up." "[B]eneath that too-smooth exterior," she says, "beats a heart of gold, I think." Young once joked that, while under contract with M-G-M, he was often assigned the roles that Robert Montgomery had rejected. That could have been the case with *Stowaway*. Montgomery held the patent on this sort of character. We saw that with Dill in *Forsaking All Others* and Tommie in *Riptide*. Now, we will see it again with Sherry in *No More Ladies*.

Marcia (Joan Crawford), a young socialite, shares her home with her grandmother, Fanny Townsend (Edna May Oliver). Unlike her friends, Marcia is a firm believer in marital fidelity. Yet, she has an on-again, off-again relationship with a charming womanizer, Sherry Warren (Robert Montgomery). In the opening scene, she informs Fanny that she has broken up with Sherry yet again. Fanny responds, "Here lies Sherry Warren. Man about town. Scamp. Heartbreaker. Worthless wreck. He was a nice guy, though. I kind of liked him." Fanny stands as the voice of reason throughout the film.

Robert Montgomery and Joan Crawford in *No More Ladies* (1935)

Sherry is strongly opposed to marriage. He remarks, "The rockbound coast is strewn with wrecks." He says of married couples, ". . . [T]hey think they're getting a slice of paradise and instead of that they're getting a kick in the pants." Marcia insists that a marriage can work if a husband and wife give it everything they got. She asks him to marry her and he accepts.

Sherry: I'll tell you one thing. It's going to be the most marvelous party in the world, or it's going to be a hell, so watch out. . . We're a pair of fools.

Marcia: Imbeciles.

Sherry: We haven't a chance.

Marcia: None on earth.

Sherry: Bound to be the most heartrending.

Marcia: Hideous.

Everyone who cares about her strenuously advises her against the marriage. Her friend, Jim Salston (Franchot Tone), does not hesitate to give his opinion. He says, "You ought to know what he is by now." Marcia becomes defensive. "I don't like your saying that to me," she says. Fanny is nearly speechless when she learns her niece intends to marry Sherry. She says, "Don't you realize, girl, I. . . Don't say I didn't wa. . . Oh, you little fool." Her friend, Edgar Holden (Charlie Ruggles), tells her, "I've got an important mission to perform. Marcia, I've got to save you from him. Oh, Marcia, Marcia, tell me it isn't too late for you to turn back to the right road."

Jim also wants to marry Marcia. But, even though he is a decent suitor, she prefers to marry a womanizer, believing that she can get him to behave like a proper husband once they marry.

Jim has a special dislike for Sherry. He once tried to shoot the cad for stealing his one-time fiancée, Lady Diana Knowlton (Vivienne Osborne). He tells Sherry, "You always fancied yourself as the dashing knight errant rescuing the beautiful misunderstood wife from the stodgy unappreciative husband."

It doesn't take long for Sherry's bad habits to create a crisis in the marriage. Sherry leaves a party with a friend's date, Theresa German (Gail Patrick), and doesn't return home until the following morning. The fact that he is apathetic when he is confronted by Marcia causes his wife to finally lose confidence in the marriage. He tries futilely to defend himself. "Marcia," he says. "I feel like a skunk. I'm as sorry as I can be. I could have lied to you." He tells her that the young lady is "ordinary" and he never intended to start anything serious with her. Fanny tells Marcia, "I suppose he's sorry." Marcia replies, "That's just it. He's not really. He'll do it again and again." Fanny says, "I told Sherry he'd be a fool to marry you. And that you'd be a bigger fool to marry him."

Marcia remains conflicted.

Marcia: It's something no one can do anything about but myself.

Fanny: Then do it, dear. You knew this was going to happen. Don't let yourself go through it a second time, Marcia. Get rid of him, now.

Marcia: No, I'm his wife. That doesn't seem to mean anything to anyone these days, but it does to me. Divorce is too easy, it's quitting.

Fanny: And besides. . . you love him.

The thought of losing Marcia panics Sherry, causing him to reconsider his actions. He ends up in tears as he begs his wife for forgiveness and vows to reform his reckless ways.

The Moment of Truth (1952)

The original French title: *La Minute de Vérité*

A physician, Pierre Richard (Jean Gabin), is called to a rooming house to treat Daniel Prévost (Daniel Gélin), who has attempted suicide. He sees a photo of his lovely actress wife, Madeleine (Michèle Morgan), on a bedside table. He learns from the landlady that the man, a bohemian painter, had carried on a lengthy affair with Madeleine.

Jean Gabin and Michèle Morgan in *The Moment of Truth* (1952)

The affair is portrayed in flashbacks. Pierre comes across at first as cold and aloof while, in contrast, Daniel appears to be passionate and attentive. But this is misleading. We find Pierre is in fact loving, but he expresses his love by caring for his family in a steady and responsible way. Daniel is temperamental and irrational. He is much like a bratty child, which may be the reason that Madeleine is attracted to him. Evidently, his childish emotionality, neediness and vulnerability arouse a maternal affection in her. She feels compelled to care for him.

Madeleine goes on a play tour to get away from Daniel, but she cannot stop thinking about him. She visits a church where he has captured her likeness in a stained-glass window. A church guardian (René Génin) suggests that Daniel is different than most people. He tells her, "He's a bit. . . like *that*, but he's still nice." She now has to see him. She says in voice-over, "Nothing could stop me. I had no qualms. Everything was suddenly simple, easy." She sheds her moral restraint as she marches out of the church.

Daniel Gélin and Michèle Morgan in *The Moment of Truth* (1952)

Pierre confronts Madeleine about the affair. She lets her husband know that it was a long time before she finally relented to sleep with him. He quickly responds, "Bravo! Well done. The rat asked you to bed, you didn't jump in. Such a force of character! Such willpower! Unbelievable!" He tells her, "You fought to be faithful but fate had the last word? You're defending yourself well." Pierre tells his wife he understands the reason that she has been cheating on him for years. He sees the problem simply. "I don't have charm," he says. "I don't paint horses."

Madeleine does not hesitate to defend herself. She clearly outlines her reasons for cheating. She was off-put by her husband's confidence. She resented his indifference. She became bored. She said that the peace-fulness of their marriage exasperated her.

Madeleine seemingly enjoys the fact that Daniel is mentally unstable. At one point, she enthusiastically cries out to him, "You're crazy!" Like a mother with a rambunctious child, she must always caution him to behave himself before they ever have to part. "Swear you won't do anything silly," she says.

Daniel demands that she tell Pierre, "It's over, we've played enough." Of course, this man-child sees a re-lationship between a man and woman as play. Madeleine tells him that it isn't easy to end a marriage. She reminds him that she has been with her husband for ten years. "He's had his share," he snarls. It is at this moment he plays a cruel prank on her, pretending to be phoning Pierre. He laughs when he sees her panic. He says, "Little Madeleine was scared, very scared."

Madeleine tells Pierre that she knows he had an affair with his nurse. He replies, "Oh, it's not the same for me. She had no power over me. She didn't cause a misunderstanding. She didn't poison things. She wasn't a danger or threat. I didn't have to run to get away from her. Oh, it wasn't a complicated drama like yours was! A short affair, very short."

A similar conversation occurred in *Who Is Killing the Great Chefs of Europe?* (1978). A business execu-tive (George Segal) resents his ex-wife (Jacqueline Bisset) for reminding him of his adulterous affair. He says, "Come on, you can't call a roll in the hay with your secretary 'adultery.'" She snaps back, "And what do you call it - shorthand?"

Madeleine is reminded of her husband's goodness when she watches him save a boy dying of meningitis. She ends her relationship with Daniel, which is the reason that he tries to kill himself.

Madeleine and Pierre reconcile. Madeleine smiles as she looks out the window and sees Pierre taking their young daughter to school.

Michèle Morgan and Jean Gabin in *The Moment of Truth* (1952)

The Layabouts (1953)

The original Italian title: *I Vitelloni*

I Vitelloni, written and directed by Federico Fellini, examines the empty lives of idle youth. Many young men in the post-war era were aimless. It was a trend that developed as a direct consequence of the war. Young men need encouragement and direction to become responsible adults, but the war had shattered traditional beliefs and created a society beset with fear and confusion.

Peter Bondanella wrote that the vitelloni is "an immature, lazy person without a clear identity or any notion of what to do with his life."[529] Fellini wrote, "They are the unemployed of the middle class, mother's pets. They shine during the holiday season, and waiting for it takes up the rest of the year."[530]

Fausto Moretti (Franco Fabrizi) is an appalling sort of man-child. He's lazy and deceitful. Fed up with the young man's layabout ways, his father gets him a job at a religious articles shop. He drops off his son at his new workplace like a parent dropping off a small child at school for the first time. His equally immature friends visit the store so that they can laugh at him through the display window. He sulks that he can't be outside playing with his friends.

Not that there's much to the young men's playing. Wikipedia notes: "Unemployed and living off their parents, Fausto's twenty-something friends kill time shuffling from empty cafés to seedy pool halls to aimless walks across desolate windswept beaches."[531]

Fausto considers joining an acting troupe. He says, "It wouldn't be a bad life. You travel, you're free, you have fun, no worries."

Alberto Sordi in *I Vitelloni* (1953)

Fausto is sitting in a movie theater with his wife when an attractive woman sits down next to him. He is so bold that he makes flirtatious glances at the woman while his wife is snuggled beside him. The woman smiles suggestively at Fausto and leaves the theatre. Fausto abandons his wife to eagerly follow her.

Fausto is attracted to his employer's wife, Giulia Curti (Lída Baarová). He makes a pass at Giulia in the storeroom, but she pushes him away before he can kiss her. Later, he grabs her more forcefully and kisses her. She tells him that he's a fool and slaps him. Her husband finds out about this and fires Fausto.

Fellini understood that womanizing was a form of immaturity. When Fausto's father learns that his son cheated on his wife, he removes his belt to give his son a good beating.

Angry at his boss for firing him, Fausto steals an angel statue from the shop, but no one is willing to buy it. Cinema Neorealismo Italiano noted, "Fausto ends up leaving the statue with a simple-minded peasant (Silvio Bagolini) who sets the angel on a mound outside his hovel, caressing it."[532]

The Seducer (1954)

The original Italian title: *Il seduttore*

Alberto (Alberto Sordi) fancies himself a ladies' man. Like Emma Bovary, he has been misled by romantic dreams. "Am I handsome?" he asks a co-worker. "No, I am not. But in men attractiveness does not matter. It's a question of blood." He likes to imagine that virility runs in his blood. He is Casanova. He is The Scarlet Pimpernel.

Alberto's wife, Norma (Lea Padovani), loves Alberto deeply, but she is too preoccupied running the family restaurant to rein in her errant husband.

Alberto arranges to rendezvous with a pretty French woman, Jacqueline (Jacqueline Pierreux), during his company's outing to Paris. But, to his dismay, he gets stood up by Jacqueline. He is now stuck in Paris with nothing to do for the next seven days. He meets his parish priest, Don Umberto (Dino Raffaelli), who is visiting Paris for an Easter observance, and asks for his advice (though he says the advice is for a friend). The priest, not as dense as the priest in *Madame Bovary*, instructs him in no uncertain terms to go home to his wife. But, instead, he meets another woman, Natalina Spencer (Lia Amanda), whose pilot husband is away on a flight. Natalina lives in a villa by the sea with her two young children. She agrees to rent a spare room to Alberto for the next few days. He sees this as a perfect opportunity to seduce her. But Natalina proves to be a faithful wife, with no interest in joining Alberto for a late-night frolic on the beach. Natalina's husband returns home in time to see Alberto drive away from the villa. He becomes suspicious and threatens to divorce his wife. Natalina travels to Norma's restaurant to persuade Alberto to speak to her husband. Meanwhile, Jacqueline turns up at the restaurant with her mother (Denise Grey) and her boyfriend (Mino Doro). Natalina notices Jacqueline wearing a hat that Alberto took away from the villa as a memento. Natalina and Jacqueline get into a discussion about the hat. Norma, suspicious, gets involved and learns that her husband is acquainted with both women. Alberto, unable to talk himself out of the situation, panics and runs off sobbing. But Norma forgives her foolish husband. In the final scene, Alberto is playing at the beach while his wife keeps a close eye on him. She says in voice-over: "Deep down he's a good boy. He just needs to get out of his head the idea of being a SEDUCER."

Alberto imagines that a sexual conquest outside of his marriage will be unquestionable proof of his virility. He possesses, according to film historian Andrea Bini, an "obsessive need to prove that his male power is still intact."[533] Bini wrote, "In order to understand the reason for Alberto's incorrigible behavior and final breakdown, we must ask why he needs so desperately to imagine himself a seducer. . . Throughout the movie, Alberto is frantically trying to create an image of himself as an irresistible *seduttore*, because this is the only way to reconstruct his masculinity jeopardized by recent history."[534] He noted that the film, along with similar Sordi films, depicts "childish and inept men striving to succeed in a society whose traditional moral and cultural coordinates have disappeared."[535] He added, "[T]he road to maturity has been jammed."[536]

The film lacks a single strong male. Bini observed, ". . . [P]ostwar Italy appears to be a country where father figures are either absent (Alberto and his wife do not have a father), old and powerless (the professor who eats every evening in the trattoria, the general who sublets two rooms in the villa), or swindlers (the insolvent commendatore, who blackmails Alberto in exchange for free meals at the trattoria)."[537]

The Seven Year Itch (1955)

Richard Sherman (Tom Ewell), a middle-aged book editor, is on his own while his wife and son spend the summer at the seashore. Sherman is excited by his sudden freedom. Like a little boy, he is led astray by mischievous impulses and an overactive imagination. He fantasizes about having an affair with a beautiful young woman (Marilyn Monroe) who lives upstairs from him. When the woman complains that it's hot in her apartment, he invites her into his air-conditioned apartment for a drink. The next night, the pair go to the movies together. Afterward, Richard lets the woman spend the night in his apartment. He dreams of his wife learning of his alluring female guest, which provokes her to shoot him. The dream, which remains vivid in his mind, makes him so fearful that he promptly forgets his thoughts of an affair.

Billy Wilder perfectly dissected the man-child philanderer in *The Seven Year Itch* and *The Apartment* (1960). Both films are discussed at length in my comedy man-child examination "I Won't Grow Up."

The Seven Year Itch shares plot elements with an Italian comedy, *The Adventuress from the Floor Above* (1941), in which a husband becomes entangled with a glamorous neighbor while his wife is away. Alberto Sordi starred in a remake of the film released three months before *The Seven Year Itch*.

Saturday Night and Sunday Morning (1960)

Alfred (Albert Finney), a young machinist in a bicycle factory, just wants to spend his free time drinking himself dizzy and fooling around with the ladies. "The rest is propaganda," he says. He has a girlfriend, Doreen (Shirley Ann Field), but she refuses to have sex with him until they get married. He finds an outlet for his sexual urges with a co-worker's wife, Brenda (Rachel Roberts). The adulterers are casual about their illicit relationship. They act like a pair of giggly children who have swiped animal crackers out of a cookie jar. But the relationship doesn't end with giggles. Brenda gets pregnant and Alfred has to arrange for an abortion. Alfred remains interested in Brenda. He sees her at a fair with her family and rushes after her when he spots her entering a ride alone. Brenda's brother-in-law sees Alfred with his arm around Brenda on the ride. He calls to a friend, who joins him to chase down Alfred. When they catch the rogue, they beat him severely. Alfred spends the next week recovering in bed while Doreen looks after him. In the end, he agrees to marry Doreen and buy a home with her.

Norman Rossington and Albert Finney in *Saturday Night and Sunday Morning* (1960)

Rachel Roberts and Albert Finney in *Saturday Night and Sunday Morning* (1960)

The Joker (1960)

The original French title: *Le farceur*

Les Adams of IMDb wrote, "Edouard Berlon (Jean-Pierre Cassel) is a happy-go-lucky rogue who takes nothing seriously and flits irresponsibly from one affair to another."[538] The film opens with Edouard clambering out of a skylight to escape an irate husband. He climbs into the window of a beautiful married woman, Hélène Larouch (Anouk Aimee). Edouard is charmed by Hélène and makes it his goal to seduce her. She continually rebuffs him, but she can't stay away from him. She finds him to be too appealing with his exuberance and eccentricity. Having an entertaining suitor causes her to grow bored and dissatisfied with her grave husband. She seems finally ready to relent to Edouard when he takes her to a country inn. But, when lovemaking is about to commence, she remains as cold as before. She lays in bed holding her fur coat tightly around herself, complaining that the room is dirty and cold. For the first time in the film, the happy-go-lucky Edouard appears to be glum. Frustrated, he abandons Hélène and goes to the dining room, where he enjoys a lively dance with a pretty young maid Aline (Irina Charitonoff). The camera tracks back until we are outside the inn and can see Edouard and Aline dancing through a window. The dance must go on. The film ends.

Jean Seberg in *Five Day Lover* (1961)

Five Day Lover (1961)

The original French title: *L'amant de cinq jours*

Madeleine (Micheline Presle), a wealthy couturière, provides generously to her kept man, Antoine (Jean-Pierre Cassel). Madeleine's friend Claire (Jean Seberg), a young married mother, meets Antoine at one of Madeleine's fashion shows and succumbs to his charms. Claire visits Antoine at his luxurious apartment every afternoon for the next five days. Claire tells Antoine that she is rich. She talks to him about her horses and gardens. But it's a lie. She is as imaginative as a little girl who has read too many fairy tales. The lovely, sweetly smiling Claire approaches adultery with a charming childlike innocence. She loves her husband Georges (François Périer), but he has too little time for the romance that she craves. Michael Coates-Smith and Garry McGee, authors of "The Films of Jean Seberg," wrote, "This is a man to whom nature has assigned the role of the buffoon, and he is too intelligent to imagine he can aspire to any other. . . [B]ut he constitutes the emotional anchorage without which [Claire's] existence would be impossible."[539] Georges is, according to Coates-Smith and McGee, "touching almost heroic."[540] The dutiful father explains his wife's absence to his children as he tucks them into bed. "You're wondering why mummy's late," he says. "It's because she wears high heels and they're difficult to walk on."

Determined to break up the affair, Madeleine invites Georges and Claire to a party. Claire arrives at the party unaware that Madeleine has also invited Antoine. Madeleine gets Claire alone and threatens to expose Antoine to Georges. Claire stands up to Madeleine and tells her that she loves Georges and they will always stand together. "You can't beat a happy man," she says. Despite her many snide comments, Madeleine can see that Antoine and Claire are not afraid of her threats and doesn't see that letting Georges know about his wife's affair will have the desired effect.

The next day, Claire tells Antoine that their relationship is "falling apart." He insists that they can start from scratch and put it back together. She replies, "It's impossible to start over." He asks her to leave her husband. He promises her that they will build back the relationship as something stronger. "We don't have to lie anymore," he says. But she will not consider it. "Love is a lie," she says. "It's like a bubble. When it reaches the ground, it's over." Antoine is brokenhearted as he watches Claire leave.

That night, Claire talks to Georges about her involvement with other men. She says that it's not safe for her to leave the house as men often approach her on the street. She ignores them, she says, but they continue to pursue her. She admits to being thrilled by these brief encounters, but she always closes her eyes and hopes that the man will be gone when she opens them again. She says that men are "true and beautiful," but also "terrible." "And you want me to go out?" she asks. Georges hesitates to respond. But then he tells her, "I don't want to put you in a cage. You were born to roam outside, free."

The final scene is telling. Claire is walking alone down the street when she is approached by a man. She smiles, happy to receive his attention. It seems inevitable that she will eventually go off with another man and have another passionate but fleeting affair.

Pauline Kael was not kind to Claire in her review of the film. She referred to the young woman as a "dreamy, role-playing nymphomaniac." She found her to be "heartlessly romantic and devious."[541]

Jean Seberg and Jean-Pierre Cassel in *Five Day Lover* (1961)

The film was a failure. Seberg said, "I'm sure if I had not had the two children they would have accepted [the lover]. But they felt it was outrageous. You would see me one second in the arms of my lover, and the next shot would be me holding the children. It became a bit shocking. . . [T]he film was a bit flippant, almost a parody of a comedy about the husband with the cheating little wife."[542]

François Périer in *Five Day Lover* (1961)

A Married Woman (1964)

The original French title: *Une Femme Mariée*

Charlotte (Macha Méril) is a spoiled and superficial young wife and mother. This coquettish brat acts nothing like a wife or mother. Film critic James Monaco wrote, "Charlotte is a concept rather than a human being. She's been formed and molded by the media that surrounds her - film, magazines, literature, records, ads, billboards, TV, radio."[543] Charlotte goes to the airport to meet her husband, Pierre (Philippe Leroy), who is returning home from a business trip. He has been nervous to leave her alone since finding out that she cheated on him with an actor, Robert (Bernard Noël).

Pierre: I hope you've been behaving yourself.

Charlotte: What's that supposed to mean?

Pierre: Nothing.

She swears that she ended her relationship with Robert, but she is plainly lying. Charlotte learns that she is pregnant, but she doesn't know if Pierre or Robert is the father. Robert has to fly out of town to perform in a play. She meets Robert at a hotel near the airport. They speak of love. She considers leaving Pierre to marry Robert, but she has doubts that Robert will make a good husband. She suspects that, as an actor, he has become well-trained at pretending to love a woman. Robert responds by reciting romantic dialogue from his play, which serves to confirm her worst fear. Charlotte decides that it's time to say farewell to Robert and focus her attention on her existing family. Charlotte's final line of dialogue is "C'est fini" ("It's over").

Alfie (1966)

Alfie Elkins (Michael Caine) is a compulsive womanizer who pursues women of every type. It matters little to him if they are married or single, young or old, glamorous or frumpy. Age, marital status, nothing matters to him. He should know by now that he is leading a shallow, empty life. His womanizing ways constantly cause him problems. He gets his girlfriend Gilda (Julia Foster) pregnant, but he refuses to marry her. He expects Gilda to put the baby up for adoption, but she decides to have the baby and raise him without Alfie. Alfie visits his child, Malcolm, and comes to love him. Gilda eventually marries Humphrey (Graham Stark), a bus conductor, who loves her and her son and treats them well. She tells Alfie that Malcolm is her son's father now and she doesn't want him to see the child any longer. This breaks Alfie's heart.

Alfie is diagnosed with tuberculosis and spends time in a convalescent home. Unable to repress his usual tendencies, he finds an outlet for his sexual urges by fooling around with one of the nurses.

Alfie befriends another patient, Harry Clamacraft (Alfie Bass). Alfie tells Harry that, if he wants to get well, he needs to stop worrying about his wife and worry more about himself. This single statement says much about Alfie. To him, selfishness is survival. He repeatedly tries to sell Harry on his rancid outlook of the world.

Alfie: Now, say your old woman picks up with a bloke and brings him home.

Harry: Not Lily. She wouldn't.

Alfie: Why not? She ain't bad. You know, she got a fair little figure. Not my type, of course, but still.

Harry remains unmoved, but Alfie persists.

Alfie: Harry, all I want is for you to see life, see what it is and what it does to you. I. . . I never wanted to hurt you, Harry. I never want to hurt anybody.

Harry: No, I suppose not. But you do, Alfie. You do.

Alfie gets better and is released from the home. He returns to visit Harry and meets Lily (Vivien Merchant). Harry asks Alfie to give his wife a ride home. Not surprisingly, Alfie has sex with Lily. He seduces her while comforting her about her sick husband. It doesn't seem as if it was something he planned. He really meant to console her. It is just something that came over him suddenly. But he refuses to give in to guilt. He says in voice-over: "Old Harry will never know and, even if he did, he shouldn't begrudge me." He believes that he helped the grieving wife with this romantic episode.

Vivien Merchant and Michael Caine in *Alfie* (1966)

Lily finds out that she's pregnant and tells Alfie that she needs to get an abortion to stop Harry from finding out about their one-night stand. Alfie meets the abortionist (Denholm Elliott) with Lily. The abortionist provides Lily with medication to induce premature labor. It takes time for the labor to begin. In the meantime, Lily is in great pain. Alfie tells us, "My understanding of women only goes as far as the pleasure. When it comes to the pain, I'm like every other bloke. I don't wanna know." Lily can tell that he's uncomfortable. She tells him, "You go. I'm better on my own. There's nothing you can do." The small, dark room has become suffocating by now. Alfie takes a walk to get fresh air. He is thinking about the abortion when he sees Gilda and Humphrey happily arriving at a church to get their newborn daughter baptized. The couple, together with their daughter and son Malcolm, is a picture-perfect family. Alfie returns to Lily. He cries staring down at his aborted child.

Alfie has compassion, but he doesn't let it take hold of him. He will not attach himself to any emotion that draws him away from his own self-interest. In the end, he continues to deny the obvious fact that his life is lonely and meaningless.

A Guide for the Married Man (1967)

Ed Stander (Robert Morse), a dedicated adulterer, encourages Paul Manning (Walter Matthau) to follow his example. He assures him that infidelity is great fun and will make him a happy and well-balanced husband. Paul winds up in a motel room with a sexy client, Jocelyn Montgomery (Elaine Devry), but he becomes apprehensive and can't bring himself to climb into bed. Just then, he hears a commotion coming from outside. He peeks through the window to see the cause of the commotion. A private investigator has burst into a room across the way and are taking photos of Ed in bed with a frisky neighbor, Irma Johnson (Sue Ane Langdon).

I Love My Wife (1970)

Richard Burrows (Elliott Gould), a surgeon, resents that his wife Jody (Brenda Vaccaro) stopped being an attractive and willing sexual partner once she became pregnant. He regularly works his charm on whatever nurse or patient is around for a quick romp at a nearby motel. Richard, overcome with regret, decides to stop his womanizing and reconcile with Jody. But Jody has returned from a weight loss center in a slimmer form and has decided to leave Richard for another man.

Bed and Board (1970)

Antoine Doinel (Jean-Pierre Léaud) has a charming wife, Christine (Claude Jade), and a rosy-cheeked baby boy. Inexplicably, he is drawn to a young Japanese woman, Kyoko (Hiroko Berghauer). Kyoko lacks charm and barely talks. Yet, he is willing to leave his wife and child for her. Kyoko is hip and stylish while she and Antoine are dating. On their first date, she wears a black leather mini-skirt, knee-high leather boots, and black stockings. But she changes once they are living together. She suddenly becomes a traditional Japanese woman, best exemplified by her wearing a kimono at home. A funny scene shows Antoine trying to adapt to Kyoko's short-legged Japanese-style dining table. Antoine misses Christine and gladly returns to her. What was the point of the affair?

Frank & Eva (1973)

Frank & Eva perfectly presents a man-child as an inveterate womanizer, although this womanizer is moral enough to avoid married woman and avoid becoming married himself. So, no marital vows are broken on either end of his many love affairs. Eva (Willeke van Ammelrooy) loves Frank (Hugo Metsers) so much that she is willing to tolerate his constant cheating. Frank is outraged to learn that Eva is pregnant because she stopped taking her birth control pill. He insists that her pregnancy is a plot to force him into marriage. He calls it a "nasty stunt." Eva turns to Frank's friend, Joop (Helmert Woudenberg), for support. Frank Swietek of Video Librarian wrote, "[Joop is] a more stable guy who has nonetheless long been Frank's pal and ena-bler. "[544] Frank has a close friendship with Max (Lex Goudsmit), a sickly old man who was as rakish as Frank in his youth. Max warns Frank to be civil with Eva. "You're doing the same stupid things that I did thirty years ago," he says. "You're a selfish, immature, pig-headed idiot!" In the opening scene, Frank is so busy groping a woman while driving that he crashes his car. Zeke Film reported, "Just as soon as Frank's totaled his vehicle, he panics, instructs the girl to take blame, and flees the scene on foot. A class act, in-deed."[545] Zeke Film added, "Metsers impressively manages to never sand off Frank's rough edges, all the while remaining that somehow-magnetic creep that Eva is drawn to."[546]

Pardon My Affair (1976)

The original French title: *Pardon Mon Affaire*

The film opens with its protagonist, a civil servant named Étienne (Jean Rochefort), indifferently standing on a seven-story ledge outside of an apartment house. We learn in flashback that the usually phlegmatic Étienne has lately become obsessed with a beautiful model, Charlotte, and took to pursuing her feverishly.

Étienne eventually persuades Charlotte to invite him to her home. After a night of lovemaking, Charlotte gets a call from her husband, who is about to return home early. In a panic, Charlotte drags Étienne out of bed and pushes him out onto the window ledge. We are now where the film started, with Étienne trapped seven stories above the street. A crowd has gathered, firemen have a safety net spread out to catch him, and a television crew is filming him. Étienne's wife Marthe (Danièle Delorme) and two small children watch Étienne on television while eating their breakfast. Étienne is about to leap for the safety net when he be-comes mesmerized by a lovely platinum-blonde woman photographing him for a newspaper. He leaps off the ledge and, during his slow-motion descent, thinks of his wife, of Charlotte and of the lovely photographer waiting for him below.

10 (1979)

George Webber (Dudley Moore), a forty-two-year-old composer, is going through a midlife crisis. His girlfriend, Samantha Taylor (Julie Andrews), resents his constant immature behavior. George becomes infat-uated with a young and beautiful newlywed, Jenny Hanley (Bo Derek), and ineptly pursues her while she is on her honeymoon in Mexico.

Separate Vacations (1986)

Richard Moore (David Naughton) is under great stress in his career as an architect. He arranges to take a break from work and family for a tropical vacation. Richard fails in his efforts to have sex with a local woman. But his wife, Sarah Moore (Jennifer Dale), takes their kids to a mountain resort, where she attracts the attention of a local ski instructor.

Adult Behavior (1999)

The original Swedish title: *Vuxna människor*

Frank Philgren (Felix Herngren), a young lawyer, has become bored with his wife Nenne (Karin Bjurström) after eight years of marriage. He begins to date a young art student, Sofia (Källa Bie). His friend, Georg (Mikael Persbrandt), is just as unhappy with his marriage to Rosie (Cecilia Ljung). A big problem is their bratty six-old son, who demands constant attention from his mother. The couple is never able to be alone. Georg has an affair with Nenne. Nenne is distressed over having to share Georg with Rosie and demands that he get a divorce. But he keeps putting her off. She becomes crazed when she catches Georg having sex with his son's babysitter, Kajsa (Annakarin Johansson). She rampages through his apartment, breaking everything that she can. Frank asks Sofia to marry him. Sofia looks uncomfortable as she listens to the proposal. She is as gentle as possible in turning him down, but he is left devastated nonetheless. This is a surprisingly poignant scene. Georg becomes despondent sitting among the wreckage that Nenne created. The destructiveness of his extramarital affairs cannot be any clearer than it is now. He confesses to Rosie about his unfaithfulness. He promises to devote himself to their marriage. Nenne and Frank reconcile. The film ends with the couple talking to a marriage counselor (Tone Helly-Hansen). Frank finds himself having sexual thoughts about the counselor.

Wonder Boys (2000)

English professor Grady Tripp (Michael Douglas) is unable to finish his latest book due to severe writer's block. He occupies much of his time having an affair with the university chancellor, Sara Gaskell (Frances McDormand), whose husband Walter (Richard Thomas) is the chairman of the English department. He is generally confused about life and doubts that he will ever be able to finish his novel. He is stunned to learn that Sara is pregnant with his child. He doesn't know what to do at first. But, after an event-filled evening, he reveals the affair to Walter and asks Sara to marry him. The film ends with Grady finishing up his book just as Sara and their baby arrive home from shopping.

Granny's Funeral (2012)

The original French title: *Adieu Berthe - L'enterrement de mémé*

Armand Lebrecq (Denis Podalydès) loves his wife, Hélène (Isabelle Candelier), but he has also fallen in love with Alix (Valérie Lemercier). Armand must figure out how to resolve this dilemma while organizing a funeral for his grandmother. A sad and awkward scene occurs early in the film. Alix sends Armand horny text messages ("I have a heart between my legs and it's beating") while he cuddles with Hélène in bed. Other messages stream on his phone as he listens to Hélène express deep and innermost feelings to him. "It's nice to have a family," she says. "We've come a long way. Do you realize that? All the shouting, all the arguments, all the joy. And all of it comes from the fact that one day during the exam I told you a formula."

She's Funny That Way (2014)

Arnold Albertson (Owen Wilson), a Broadway director, is married to an actress, Delta Simmons (Kathryn Hahn). The couple has two children. But, away from his family, Arnold frequents call girls. One of the call girls, Izzy Patterson (Imogen Poots), takes his advice to become an actress and unexpectedly shows up to audition for his latest play. This is particularly awkward as Delta is rehearsing to play a call girl in the play.

Chapter Twenty-Two:
For The Husband's Sake

The Cheat (1931)

Elsa Carlyle (Tallulah Bankhead), the wife of a reputable stockbroker, is desperate to pay off a debt that she has incurred from her compulsive gambling. She uses money that she has collected for a charity to invest in a stock deal, but the deal goes wrong and she loses all of the charity funds. Hardy Livingston (Irving Pichel), a wealthy rake, is ready to exploit the woman's predicament to satisfy his lecherous and sadistic desires. He brazenly offers to restore Elsa's losses in exchange for sexual favors. In this instance, a married woman has sex outside of her marriage unwillingly.

There are other films in which a woman cheats on her husband out of a desperate need to help herself or her husband out of a fix. The type of story goes back as far back as *Forbidden Fruit* (1915), in which a wife provides sexual favors to her husband's business partner to prevent the man from turning her spouse over to the police for forgery. There were other films of this sort.

The Virtuous Sin (1930)

The film is set in St. Petersburg, Russia, in 1914. Marya Ivanovna (Kay Francis) agrees to marry Victor Sablin (Kenneth MacKenna), but she does not consent to marriage out of love. She feels no more than affection and friendship for him. She marries him solely to aid him in his valuable medical work. But his work is interrupted when he is inducted into the Russian army. Sablin openly expresses a greater interest in saving lives than in ending lives. General Gregori Platoff (Walter Huston) charges him with insubordination. At trial, he is sentenced to death by firing squad. Marya becomes a singer in a brothel so that she will have the opportunity to meet Platoff, who is known to be a frequent client. Marya expects to bed the general, who will hopefully reward her affections by pardoning her husband. She is surprised when she falls in love with the general. Platoff is upset to learn of Marya's motives, but she convinces him that she truly loves him and he forgives her.

Victor is freed, but he is upset to learn that Marya has left him for Platoff. He threatens to kill the general. But Marya confesses to Victor that she never loved him and only acted out of loyalty to him. She tells Victor, "To be loyal, I had to be disloyal. To find love, I had to go where no love should have been."

The reviews for this film weren't good. Time reported, "*The Virtuous Sin* falls between burlesque and melodrama."[547] Film Daily noted, "Trite story material and dialogue put this Russian melodrama in weakling class, slow and obvious stuff."[548] Certainly, the acting is hammy.

No More Orchids (1932)

An heiress, Annie Holt (Carole Lombard), is forced to marry into royalty to save her banker father Bill (Walter Connolly), but she falls in love with another man (Lyle Talbot) while on a cruise.

Splendor (1935)

The Lorrimore family, once wealthy and highly admired, are now bankrupt financially and morally. The debt-ridden family will resort to any means to keep themselves solvent. The cold-hearted matriarch, Emmeline Lorrimore (Helen Westley), exerts great pressure on her handsome young son, Brighton (Joel McCrea), to court a wealthy young woman even though he doesn't love her. Marc Slope of IMDb wrote: "[Westley] is a multilayered and quite frightening monster-mother, alternately loving and manipulating her children. . ."[549] Andre Sennwald of The New York Times wrote, "The unpleasant Lorrimores are acted with poisonous effectiveness by Helen Westley as the embittered dowager, Katharine Alexander as the scornful daughter and David Niven as the useless son."[550] But Brighton, who values love more than wealth, runs off and marries a woman of far less means, Phyllis Manning (Miriam Hopkins). Phyllis is snubbed by the family, but she gives the family hope when she arouses the affection of a well-to-do cousin, Martin Deering (Paul Cavanagh). Deering is willing to give Brighton a high-paying job if Phyllis will sleep with him.

Conquest (1937)

Imagine cuckolding your husband to save your country. Napoleon Bonaparte is upset that his wife, Josephine, is unable to produce an heir. He takes an interest in a married woman, Countess Marie Walewska (Greta Garbo). IMDb reviewer Arthur Hausner wrote:

[Marie] ignores [Napoleon's] frequent letters and flowers until a few grim Polish leaders led by Senator Malachowski urge her to give into his desires as a personal sacrifice in order to save Poland. She goes to him despite the humiliation of her husband. . .[551]

Napoleon divorces Josephine and devotes himself to Marie. Marie is prepared to tell him that she's pregnant, but he has bad news for her. His advisors have arranged a highly beneficial political marriage for him with Archduchess Marie Louise of Austria.

Lady of the Tropics (1939)

While visiting Saigon, American playboy Bill Carey (Robert Taylor) dates a French-Vietnamese woman, Manon DeVargnes (Hedy Lamarr). The couple falls in love almost instantly and marries. The marriage infuriates Pierre Delaroch (Joseph Schildkraut), a powerful local businessman who had planned to marry Manon. Delaroch uses his influence to prevent Manon from getting a passport, which traps the couple in Saigon. He then blocks Carey's efforts to find employment, which leaves the couple without an income. Delaroch knows that, stuck in Singapore without money, Manon will eventually be at his mercy and be forced to concede to his whims. She secretly meets with him and agrees to have an affair with him in exchange for a passport.

Sterling Hayden and Barbara Stanwyck in *Crime of Passion* (1957)

Crime of Passion (1957)

Kathy (Barbara Stanwyck) gives up a job as a newspaper columnist to marry a police officer, Bill Doyle (Sterling Hayden). She finds herself bored and unfulfilled as a suburban housewife. Dan Callahan, author of "Barbara Stanwyck: The Miracle Woman," wrote, "Hayden installs Stanwyck into a hellish suburbia. . . [She] rages against the mediocrity all around her."[552]

Kathy is bothered by Bill's lack of ambition and believes it's her job as a wife to push him to greater heights.

Kathy: I want you to be somebody! Not for my sake, but for yours! For yours!

Bill: Kathy, Kathy, you listen to me. Try to understand. I love you, Kathy. All these jobs, positions, ratings, it's all nothing. I do this because it gives us a living. Because it makes it possible for us to live in peace and security. Because it makes it possible for us to be together. That's what's important. That's all that matters.

The truth is that Kathy is frustrated to have given up her career ambitions and is now determined to achieve success through her husband. It doesn't matter to her that Bill isn't interested in career advancement. She ignores Bill's wishes. She engages in a sexual relationship with her husband's boss, Police Inspector Tony Pope (Raymond Burr), in hope that he will recommend her husband for a promotion. Not long after, Pope announces his retirement. He surprises Kathy when he refuses to recommend Bill as his replacement. He insists that Bill lacks the necessary qualifications.

Tony: I'm not putting Bill in for the job.

Kathy: But you promised, Tony. You promised.

Tony: Pillow talk. I've got a responsibility to the department. I won't sell that out for something we both stole. Bill's not good enough for the job.

Barbara Stanwyck in Crime of Passion (1957)

Kathy is devastated to have demeaned herself for nothing. Enraged, she steals a gun from the evidence room at the police station and goes to Pope's home to shoot him.

Cinema Cities noted, "*Crime of Passion* is a showcase for Barbara Stanwyck to do what Barbara Stanwyck does best, which is to craft and bring to life a complex and dynamic character whose emotions blaze across the screen."[553]

Indecent Proposal (1993)

David Murphy (Woody Harrelson), a young architect, is having financial difficulties and is about to lose his home. He assures his wife, Diana (Demi Moore), that he will find a way resolve their debt. He manages to obtain $5,000 from his father. He figures that he could increase this money at the casino. A billionaire, John Gage (Robert Redford), takes notice of David and Diana at the gaming tables. Gage is enamored of Diana. He asks her to join him at the craps table for good luck. After a big win, the billionaire pays for the Murphys to stay in a luxurious suite and buys Diana a dress that she likes. That night, he offers David one million dollars to spend the night with Diana. David is stunned. He doesn't know what to say. David and Diana talk about the proposal while lying in bed that night.

Diana: I'd do it for you.

David: For me? I can't believe we're even talking about this.

Diana: Think about what this money could do for us. What it could do for our future. You could finish your house. You could pay your dad back. Get rid of our debt. After all, it wouldn't mean anything. It's just my body. It's not my mind. It's not my heart.

The couple accepts the proposal, but they come to regret it.

Chapter Twenty-Three:
Revenge

Two-timed spouses enact revenge schemes in many films, including *Freaks*, *The Goose and the Gander*, *Fear*, *Crucible*, *The Accident*, *A Woman's Revenge* and *An Affair To Die For*. But the schemes rise to mad heights in six films.

Gérard Oury lurks in the shadows in *Back to the Wall* (1958).

Back to the Wall (1958)

The original French title: *Le dos au mur*

Jacques Decrey (Gérard Oury) returns home early from a business trip. He is shocked to see his wife Gloria (Jeanne Moreau) kissing a strange young man, Philippe Nicaud (Yves Normand), outside the front gates of their home. Decrey determines to exact revenge. He writes an anonymous letter to Gloria demanding a substantial sum of money to keep quiet about her affair. Gloria sells her furs and jewels to pay the blackmail money. Decrey hires a private investigator, Mr. Mauvin (Jean Lefebvre), to pose as a music agent. The private investigator pretends to hire Phillipe, a piano player, for a job and pays him off with a portion of the blackmail money. Gloria recognizes the money from the serial numbers and assumes that Phillipe is the blackmailer. She is stone-faced as she confronts him with a gun. He asks her what she is doing. She shoots him. She is determined to recommit to her marriage and be a good wife, but she finds paperwork that shows that Oury rented the post office box where the blackmail money was delivered. She sends evidence of Oury's plot to the police before she kills herself.

Michael Caine Laurence Olivier *Sleuth* (1972)

Sleuth (1972)

Andrew Wyke (Laurence Olivier), a famous crime novelist, invites his wife's lover, Milo Tindle (Michael Caine), to his home. He tells Milo that he can have his wife's jewelry, but he has to help him to stage a burglary so that he can collect on an insurance policy. Milo is hesitant at first, but he finds Wyke's offer too tempting to resist. Once the staging is complete, Wyke startles Milo by producing a gun. He says that he can now kill Milo and tell the police that he interrupted Milo during a burglary. Milo breaks down in tears. He says, "If it hadn't been me, it would've been somebody else.. . . Why me? I must know why!" Wyke replies, "Above all, I hate you because you're a cowing, blue-eyed wop. And not one of me. A creeping, hairdressing seducer of silly women. A jumped-up pantry boy, who doesn't know his place! Did you really believe I'd give up my wife and jewelry to you? That I'd make myself that ridiculous?. . . Whether I love her or not, I found her. I've kept her. She represents me." Wyke fires the gun at Milo, but nothing happens. The gun was loaded with blanks. This entire scene was nothing more than a prank to frighten Milo. Milo designs his own elaborate ruse to get revenge on Wyke. He fools Wyke into thinking that he murdered his mistress (Wyke isn't faithful either) and has planted evidence to frame him for the murder. The ruse unhinges Wyke and causes him to shoot Milo for real. While Milo is near death, the police arrive and arrest Wyke. The unfaithful wife is only present in a portrait painting. The director, Joseph L. Mankiewicz, periodically cuts to the painting as if the wife is silently watching over her rival lovers' humiliation games. The ruses that the rivals played on one another have led to their mutual destruction.

She-Devil (1989)

Bob Patchett (Ed Begley Jr.), an accountant, cheats on his homely, overweight wife Ruth (Roseanne Barr) with a glamorous romance novelist, Mary Fisher (Meryl Streep). When Bob leaves her, Ruth plots an elaborate revenge scheme. First, she gets a job at a nursing home where Mary's mother Mrs. Fisher (Sylvia Miles) lives and coaxes the old woman to reveal unsavory secrets about her daughter's past to a reporter. She befriends Bob's secretary Olivia Honey (Maria Pitillo). Olivia, who was recently jilted by Bob, is happy to expose Bob's embezzlement practices.

She-Devil was based on the 1983 novel "The Life and Loves of a She-Devil" by British author Fay Weldon. The novel was faithfully adapted into a 1986 miniseries. Unlike the film, the book and miniseries emphasized the dark, demented and repugnant aspects of Ruth's obsession for revenge. Ruth is truly the villain of the story. She allows envy to transform her into a diabolic creature. Bob and Mary are sympathetic by comparison. Bob got Ruth pregnant when they were teenagers and married Ruth because he thought it was right thing to do. He never loved her and found her increasingly unattractive as she failed to attend to her fitness and appearance. He never embezzled money. Ruth embezzled the money and made Bob appear to be the guilty party. Bob didn't thoughtlessly seduce and abandon his secretary. The secretary was specifically hired by Ruth to seduce Bob and help to frame him for the embezzlement. Mary did not have an unsavory past. Ruth gets a job in the nursing home to create mischief for Mary's mother, Pearl, to get the old woman expelled from the home. One of her tricks is to empty Pearl's bedpans onto the old woman to make it look like she has become incontinent. Bob and Mary are now forced to take Pearl into their home and care for her. Also, Ruth sets her home on fire, which leaves her children homeless and forces Bob and Mary to take responsibility for them. And the worst was yet to come. But it would be redundant to describe more of Ruth's inexcusably wicked deeds.

Revenge (1990)

Michael Cochran (Kevin Costner), a retired U.S. Navy aviator, visits a friend, Tibey Mendez (Anthony Quinn), in Mexico. Mendez, a powerful crime boss, lives in a lavish hacienda with his beautiful young wife, Miryea (Madeleine Stowe). Michael and Miryea find themselves attracted to one another. During a party, the couple sneaks off into a closet to have sex. Miryea tells Mendez that she is going to visit her sister in Miami when, in truth, she has made arrangements to rendezvous with Michael at an isolated cabin. Mendez finds out about his wife's true plans and shows up unexpectedly at the cabin with several armed henchmen. The men viciously beat the lovers. Mendez uses a large knife to ruin Miryea's beautiful face. He calls her a "faithless whore" and tells her that she will be brought to a brothel, where she will be "fucked fifty times a day." Michael, covered from head to toe in blood, is left for dead. But he miraculously survives and goes on a savagely vengeful search for Miryea. A drug addict, Antonio (Alfredo Cienfuegos), is tasked with keeping Miryea drugged so that she won't resist the brothel clients having sex with her. When Mirya learns that Antonio has AIDS, she gets him to share a needle with her so that she will contract AIDS and die. Michael rescues Miryea from a convent's hospice, but she soon dies in his arms.

Revenge is reminiscent of *Toys in the Attic* (1963), in which a betrayed husband hires goons to slice his wife's face and beat up her lover. *Revenge* is surely one of the darkest and goriest adultery films ever made. Not surprisingly, audiences kept away.

The Other Woman (2014)

Carly Whitten (Cameron Diaz) learns that her boyfriend of eight weeks, Mark King (Nikolaj Coster-Waldau), has a wife. Carly has been happy with Mark, but she is unable to tolerate his deceit. Carly is approached by Mark's wife, Kate (Leslie Mann). The wife and mistress bond over drinks. Kate asks how often Carly had sex with Mark.

> Carly: Okay, fine. Gun to my head, fifty.
>
> Kate: Fifty times?! Fifty times?! You had sex with my husband fifty times?! Don't you have a job?! Or hobbies?! What is wrong with you?!

Carly's assistant, Lydia (Nicki Minaj), asks her why she broke up with Mark.

> Carly: He has a wife, okay? He's married.
>
> Lydia: But I think a married guy is a perfect fit for you. . . You need a guy with something to keep him busy.
>
> Carly: Not a wife!

Gone Girl (2014)

Amy Dunne (Rosamund Pike) is enraged to learn that her husband, Nick (Ben Affleck), is having an affair. As revenge, she mysteriously disappears, leaving behind clues that make it look as if Nick murdered her. The police find evidence of a struggle in Amy and Nick's home. They find bloodstains. And, most of all, they find a diary that clearly implicates Nick in his wife's sudden disappearance. Amy hides out in the Ozarks while police assemble the many false clues. She is ecstatic to see the police investigation bring Nick closer and closer to death row.

Chapter Twenty-Four:
The Offbeat Adultery Film

The Woman Between (1931)

Victor Whitcomb (Lester Vail), upset that his father plans to remarry so soon after his mother's death, flees to Europe for an extended absence without bothering to meet his father's intended bride. On his return home, Victor has a shipboard romance with Julie Whitcomb (Lili Damita), unaware this beautiful young woman is his new stepmother. He is shocked to be introduced to Julie at his homecoming party. Victor's sister, Doris (Miriam Seegar), catches Paul in a lie and susses out that Julie is the woman that he met on the ship. She writes a letter to her father, John (O.P. Heggie), to expose the affair. Victor wants to return to Europe with Julie, but Julie chooses to reject his offer and remain with John. John and Julie agree to forget about what has happened and go off together for a jaunt to the Riviera.

Many shipboard affairs were depicted in films during this period. Take, for instance, *Forbidden* (1932), *Bachelor's Affairs* (1932), *Chained* (1934), *One More River* (1934), *I Take This Woman* (1940) and *Now, Voyager* (1942).

This is the Night (1932)

IMDb Plot Summary: "An affair is almost exposed when Claire's husband unexpectedly returns early from Summer Olympics."[554]

Lovely Thelma Todd is cheating on her charming Olympic athlete husband Cary Grant with droll, pint-sized milquetoast Roland Young (described by IMDb reviewer utgard14 as "the mousy, mumbly guy from Topper"[555]). utgard14 exclaimed: "On what planet, I ask you. . . on what planet!?! Anyway, to cover for their affair, Young hires Lili Damita to pose as his wife. Gradually he and Damita fall for each other."[556]

The Wrecker (1933)

The Wrecker shows how a manly action hero handles an adultery situation. The poster features a colorful image of a square-jawed Jack Holt carrying Genevieve Tobin out of a collapsed building. Holt is the boss of a wrecking crew. He loses his wife Mary (Tobin) to his best friend, Tom Cummings (Sidney Blackmer). An earthquake traps the unfaithful couple under the wreckage of a school. An act of God? Holt jumps into action, operating a backhoe to lift off the rubble.

The Masquerader (1933)

John Chilcote (Ronald Colman), a member of Parliament, is secretly struggling with drug addiction. He needs to hide away on his own to recover, but he has too many obligations that need his constant attention. Ron Kerrigan of IMDb refers to Chilcote's "clinging mistress, discarded wife [and] demanding party bosses."[557] A solution arises when he encounters his lookalike cousin, John Loder (also Colman). Loder agrees to masquerade as Chilcote while his cousin recovers his health. Loder is a much kinder man than Chilcote, which surprises both his wife Eve (Elissa Landi) and his mistress Lady Diana Joyce (Juliette Compton). Lady Diana looks with disdain at this kind man, who she quickly realizes must be an impostor. Meanwhile, John and Mrs. Chilcote fall in love.

Enchanted April (1935)

Unaware that they share a man (Frank Morgan), a wife (Ann Harding) and a mistress (Jane Baxter) become friends while staying at a holiday villa in Italy.

The Tender Enemy (1936)

The original French title: *La tendre ennemie*

An engagement party is attended by two ghosts. The first ghost is the bride-to-be's father, Dupont. The second ghost is a lion tamer, Rodrigo, who was a lover of Dupont's wife.

Call It a Day (1937)

Love is in the air on the first day of Spring. The screenwriters create a world in which a normal reaction to temperate weather and the scent of flowers in bloom is to aggressively pursue a romantic entanglement with your neighbor's spouse. It is unusual for a filmmaker to examine rampant adultery with a light comedy approach.

Red Roses (1940)

IMDb: "A man poses as a mysterious admirer to find out whether his wife would cheat on him."[558]

Day of Wrath (1943)

The film is unique in that it climaxes with a cheating wife being condemned as a witch. . . a literal witch.

The story takes place in a Danish village in 1623. Anne (Lisbeth Movin) is married to a much older pastor, Absalon Pederssøn (Thorkild Roose). The home is made tense at times by the constant presence of Absalon's strict, domineering mother, Meret (Sigrid Neiiendam), who does approve of her son's young wife.

Years earlier, Anne's mother had been accused of being a witch. Absalon, who wanted to marry young Anne, intervened to spare Anne's mother. Not surprisingly, the young woman married him out of a sense of gratitude and obligation. Absalon now sees that he abused his influence as a pastor to secure Anne as his wife.

Lisbeth Movin in *Day of Wrath* (1943)

Anne hides her mother's old friend Marte (Anna Svierkier), who church officials have accused of practicing witchcraft. Marte tells Anne that her mother had the power of life and death. She says, "She had the power of calling. . . She could call the living and the dead, and they had to come. If she wished someone dead, they died."

Absalon watches impassively as the inquisitors torture Marte on the rack. She curses the pastor, telling him that his death is imminent.

Absalon's son, Martin (Preben Lerdorff Rye), returns home and becomes close to Anne. It becomes obvious to Absalon that his wife enjoying being in Martin's company. He hears her laughing for the first time since they married.

Anne inevitably falls in love with Martin. Martin is having trouble accepting that his father's wife could belong to him. She tells him that she never loved Absalon and he never loved her. She suggests that the two of them could have a happy life together if only his father was dead.

Martin: You wish him dead?

Anne: No. I only said "if". . .

At that moment, Absalon falters suddenly in making his way along a blustery path. He tells a companion, "[I]t was as though death brushed my sleeve." Later that night, Anne confesses to Absalon that she is in love with Martin.

Anne: You have taken my best years, and you have taken my joy. I have burned for somebody I could love. I have dreamt of a child to hold in my arms. You haven't even given me that. Have I ever wished you dead? I have wished it hundreds of times. I have wished you dead when you were with me and when you were away from me. But never as intensely as since Martin and I. . .

Absalon: Martin and you?

Anne: Yes, Martin and I. Now you know. That's why at this very moment I wish you dead. Dead!

526 · ANTHONY BALDUCCI

Absalon collapses and dies.

Meret comes forward at her son's funeral to denounce Anne as a witch. Anne reaches out to Martin in a pleading manner, but he coldly pulls away from her. Anne, devastated, refuses to defend herself. She lays across her husband's coffin and says, "So you got your revenge after all. Yes, I murdered you with the help of the evil one. And I have lured your son into my power with the help of the evil one. Now you know. Now you know."

A similar plot turns up in *Crucible* (1957), a film that is set in 1692 Salem. A young maid, Abigail (Mylène Demongeot), is angry to be cast aside by her married lover, John Proctor (Yves Montand). She seeks revenge by accusing Proctor's wife Elisabeth (Simone Signoret) of being a witch.

Madonna of the Seven Moons (1945)

A young wife, Maddalena Labardi (Phyllis Calvert), struggles to cope with the memory of a rape. She is finally able to escape her trauma by developing an alternate personality. It is under her second identity as a free-spirited gypsy that she flees from her dull but loving husband, Giuseppe Labardi (John Stuart), and has an ardent affair with the fiery Nino (Stewart Granger). Both men justifiably claim Maddalena as their woman, for she is truly two women. The author evidently saw no way for Maddalena to reconcile her two personalities or her two lives and came to see killing off the troubled woman as the best resolution. Giuseppe and Nino mourn at her bedside together as she draws her final breath.

A suitable companion film to *Madonna of the Seven Moons* is *Strange Madame X* (1951). A woman doesn't need a psychological crisis to drive her into a double life. Irene (Michele Morgan), a secretary, marries her wealthy boss, Jacques Voisin-Larive (Maurice Escande). Jacques expertly schools Irene on how to be a high-society lady. But she still has many of her old interests. One day, she visits a soccer stadium and meets a handsome young cabinetmaker, Etienne (Henri Vidal). She doesn't want Etienne to know her true identity, so she tells him that she is a chambermaid. As she alternates between Jacques and Etienne, Irene develops two separate personalities. Ironically, her false chambermaid identity may be closer to the person that she really is. She isn't entirely sympathetic. She comes across at times as calculated and controlled. She likes to weigh her options to best serve her own interests. Jeanette (Arlette Thomas), one of Etienne's co-workers, once dreamed of marrying Etienne. She is devastated to lose her dream lover to Irene. Jeanette, an honest and selfless young woman, offers a great contrast to Irene. A friend, Roland (Roland Lesaffre), tells her that she is uniquely innocent and pure. Irene isn't at all innocent and pure. Everything changes when Irene learns that she has become pregnant. She never considers that this might be Jacques' child, which suggests that she and Jacques haven't been having sex. She casually informs Jacques of Etienne and her pregnancy. She refuses when he advises her to get an abortion. So, instead, Jacques arranges for her to spend the next few months in seclusion in Switzerland. She tells Etienne that she has to go to Switzerland to attend to her mistress, Madame Voisin-Larive (who is her!). She returns from Switzerland with a baby girl, Agnès. She is by now determined to divorce Jacques and marry Etienne. While she was away, Etienne found a new apartment with room for a nursery. On New Year's Eve, Agnès becomes sick and has to be taken to the hospital. Etienne rushes off to find Irene at the Voisin-Larive mansion. On his arrival, he looks through a window and sees that a New Year's Eve ball is in progress. Then, he sees an elegantly dressed Irene dancing with Jacques. He is shocked, but he has to think about Agnès now. He leaves Irene a message about their baby and hurries to the hospital. Irene goes to Etienne's home. A neighbor doesn't recognize the elegant Irene in fur and jewels. Agnès dies before Irene arrives at the hospital. Etienne refuses to forgive her. He regrets having believed her many lies. He tells her, "I've been listening to you for too long. Our love is dead and buried. It is like Agnès: at the bottom of a hole." He leaves town. Irene sadly returns to her false and empty aristocratic life.

The Chase (1946)

Chuck Scott (Robert Cummings), a World War II veteran with post-traumatic stress disorder, is haunted by bizarre dreams. He gets a job as a chauffeur for a gangster, Eddie Roman (Steve Cochran). Roman is a possessive husband, locking his wife Lorna (Michèle Morgan) in her room every night. Scott feels sorry for Lorna. The couple soon falls in love and makes plans to run away together to Havana. Roman finds out about their plans and arranges to have them murdered. A shadowy assassin hired by Roman trails the couple to Havana. The assassin fatally stabs Lorna in a nightclub and Chuck, left poised over the bloody body, is assumed to be the killer. But the assassin, as it turns out, is just something that Chuck dreamed about. He still has a chance to safely leave the country with Lorna.

Les Parents Terribles (1948)

The French title translates into *The Terrible Parents*, but the film was released to English-speaking audiences under the title *The Storm Within*.

Michel (Jean Marais) tells his parents, Georges (Marcel André) and Yvonne (Yvonne de Bray), that he is in love with a girl, Madeleine (Josette Day). But, much to his dismay, Georges recognizes the girl, who was until recently his mistress. Georges confides about his dilemma to Yvonne's spinster sister, Léonie (Gabrielle Dorziat). Léonie plots with Georges to discourage Madeleine and get her to end her relationship with Michel.

The Interrupted Journey (1949)

The film brings a supernatural element to the adultery story.

Dan Stumpf of Mystery File wrote: "Richard Todd plays a struggling young writer whose wife wants him to get a job. He elects to run off with a wealthy married woman who flatters him, but as they're preparing to leave he finds himself persecuted by doubts, nagging conscience, and the strange feeling they're being followed."[559]

The couple boards a train headed to Plymouth, a port city in South West England. As the train nears his neighborhood, John (Richard Todd) suddenly changes his mind and pulls the emergency cord. He jumps off the train and races back to his home. The stalled train is struck by another train traveling on the same line. It is originally believed that he caused the crash by pulling the brake cord, but it is later found that the accident was actually caused by a failed signal.

Police Inspector Waterson (Ralph Truman) determines that John's companion, Susan Wilding (Christine Norden), was shot in the heart. He believes that John murdered her before he jumped off the train. His theory is nearly proven when the police recover a gun from John's garden pond. John suspects that Susan's husband, Jerves Wilding (Alexander Gauge), followed them onto the train and murdered Susan. But the police identify Wilding's body as one of the bodies found at the crash site.

John does his own investigation to find out if anyone else had a motive to kill Susan. He comes to suspect that Wilding, the only person likely to have killed Susan, is still alive and hiding from the authorities. A series of clues allow him to track Wilding to a hotel in Plymouth. Wilding is not happy to be found. He shoots John in the head, at which time John suddenly awakens back on the train with Susan. Wikipedia notes:

> Instead of pulling the cord, John returns to Susan and expresses his doubts about what they are doing. Now, she pulls the cord and tells him to go back to his wife. He jumps from the train and arrives at his house, and he and his wife embrace. Then he hears the sound of a train whistle, but it is just the train he stopped moving off again.[560]

The Killer That Stalked New York (1950)

Adultery becomes an issue in the middle of a smallpox epidemic. Sheila (Evelyn Keyes) is shocked to learn that her younger sister, Francie (Lola Albright), is having a passionate affair with her husband, Matt (Charles Korvin). Francie commits suicide.

Little Big Horn (1951)

Adultery crops up in the strangest places. An adultery subplot gets mixed up with a dramatization of Custer's Last Stand.

The film gets fairly melodramatic early on when Captain Phillip Donlin (Lloyd Bridges) walks in on his wife, Celie Donlin (Marie Windsor), in the arms of Lt. John Haywood (John Ireland). Bridges assumes an odd ramrod pose.

Phillip: That's pretty plain.

Celie: Phil!

John: I know I should say "Let me explain," Phil, but you've heard about everything there is to hear.

Celie: I don't want to ruin anyone's life, let alone your's, Phil. I loved you once, but now I can't stand what little I do see of you.

Phillip parts with a quip: "I came over to kiss my wife goodbye, but it seems that's been taken care of for me."

The scene is strangely campy, as if meant to be a spoof old melodramas.

Diary of a Country Priest (1951)

The original French title: *Journal d'un curé de campagne*

A young priest (Claude Laydu) feels isolated in his new community. He is a faithful Christian who finds himself living among faithless parishioners. He is uneasy, withdrawn, and sorrowful. Roger Ebert wrote, "The young priest only smiles once. It is on the day he leaves the cruel country town to catch a train and see a doctor. A passing motorcyclist gives him a lift to the station, and as he climbs on behind him we see a flash of the boy inside the sad man. It is a nice day, it's fun to race though the breeze, and he is leaving behind the village of Ambricourt."[561]

The priest finds more distress when he counsels a governess, Miss Louise (Nicole Maurey), about her affair with her ward's father. The priest finds himself drawn into a nasty domestic conflict. Miss Louise's lover, The Count (Jean Riveyre), is an arrogant and steely man. He refuses to talk to the priest about the affair. The count's daughter, Miss Chantel (Nicole Ladmiral), strongly opposes this affair. Unable to tolerate his daughter's dissent, the count demands that she leave his home. Miss Chantel is in an agitated state when she goes to see the priest. He tries to keep her calm, but his efforts are futile. The girl is infuriated and, according to Frédéric Bonnaud, "bursting with wicked intentions."[562] She raves about Miss Louise:

> She is as sly as an animal! I trusted her. You get used to her eyes. You imagine they're kind. Now I'd like to tear out those eyes of hers and stamp on them with my foot!. . . [A]ll I ask is justice. Ever since that beastly woman came to the house —

The priest is appalled. "I heard them last night," she tells him. "I was under their window. They don't even draw the curtains!"

Claude Laydu in *Diary of a Country Priest* (1951)

The priest speaks to the Countess (Rachel Bérendt) on the matter. The woman has grown cold and distant since the death of her young son. She doesn't care about her husband's affair and has no sympathy for her daughter. She says:

> My husband can keep whomever he likes here. Besides, the governess has no money. Perhaps he's been too attentive, too familiar. . . but suppose I don't care? After putting up all these years with countless infidelities, suffering absurd humiliations, shall I now, as an old woman — to which I'm well resigned — open my eyes, put up a fight, take chances? For what? Shall I care more about my daughter's pride than my own? Let her put up with it as I have.

She tells him of her great love for her son.

The Countess: Love is stronger than death. Your scriptures say so.

The Priest: We did not invent love. It has its order, its law.

The Countess: God is its master.

The Priest: He is not the master of love. He is love itself.

The priest helps the bitter woman to reconcile with God and find an inner peace. That night, she quietly dies in her sleep. The Count believes that the priest's meeting with his wife upset her and brought about her death. He seeks to get the priest expelled from the parish.

The adultery film often has a voice of morality. It's usually a friend, or a parent, or a sibling. But, this time, it's a priest. Who better to be the voice of morality? And, for a change, the moral authority is the main character. The cheating husband is a cold man who feels no remorse for his illicit behavior. His wife has become hardened about her husband's infidelities. She feels pain about her son's death. The affair doesn't affect her. The daughter expresses hatred over the affair, but it is doubtful that she really cares. The priest tells her, "You'll always find someone to hate. But the only person you really hate is yourself." It is only the priest who endures grief over the infidelity. Later, a priest was the voice of morality in *The Heart of the Matter* (1953), *The Seducer* (1954) and *Ryan's Daughter* (1970).

Folly to Be Wise (1952)

"The Brains Trust" was a popular BBC radio series at the time. The series featured a panel of experts that were tasked with answering questions sent in by listeners. The entertainment director at a military camp, Captain William Paris (Alastair Sim), creates his own brain trust for a camp show. He has no idea that one panelist is having an affair with the wife of another panelist. Tensions rise as the panel stumbles through a question about the benefits of marriage.

The Wonderful Country (1959)

A U. S. Army commander, Major Stark Colton (Gary Merrill), hires Brady (Robert Mitchum), a mercenary with connections to the Mexican government, to help him to acquire Mexico's assistance in putting down an Apache uprising. Brady is attracted to Colton's unhappy wife, Ellen (Julie London). Ellen and Brady have a brief affair. Colton is fatally wounded in a skirmish with the Apaches. It is understood in the final scene that Brady is on his way to reunite with Ellen.

The 400 Blows (1959)

Antoine Doinel (Jean-Pierre Léaud), a young boy, wanders through Paris while cutting school with his friend, René Bigey (Patrick Auffay). He glances to one side in time to see his mother (Claire Maurier) kissing a strange man on a street corner. The mother looks terrified. The son looks stunned. This is a very real moment. No melodrama. No plot device. Just a moment of chilling authenticity.

The House in Marsh Road (1960)

Roku: "An adulterer's plot to murder his wife is foiled by a watchful poltergeist."[563]

Phaedra (1962)

Phaedra (Melina Mercouri) travels from Greece to London to meet her estranged stepson, Alexis (Anthony Perkins), for the first time. She falls in love with Alexis and, unable to control her desires, seduces him.

The Pink Panther (1963)

Inspector Jacques Clouseau (Peter Sellers), who is on the trail of a notorious jewel thief known as The Phantom, is unaware that his wife Simone (Capucine) is having an affair with The Phantom. Wikipedia: "[Simone] has become rich by acting as a fence for the Phantom under the nose of her amorous but oblivious husband."[564]

Luv (1967)

Stockbroker Milt Manville (Peter Falk) sets up a romance between his wife Ellen (Elaine May) and suicidal college buddy Harry Berlin (Jack Lemmon) so that his wife will consent to a divorce, freeing him to marry his mistress.

Adultery Italian Style (1968)

The original Italian title: *Adulterio all'italiana*

Marta threatens to leave her husband for his infidelity unless he allows her to betray him in kind with a lover of her choice. She really has no interest in having an affair. She just wants her husband to realize how wrong he was to cheat and, at the same time, make sure he sees that she is desirable to other men. She looks to fulfill her objectives by inventing a lover.

Stolen Kisses (1968)

Antoine Doinel (Jean-Pierre Léaud) starts a job as a hotel clerk. A visitor, Monsieur Henri (Harry Max), inquires about a woman who checked into the hotel. He explains that she missed a dinner date and he is worried that she took sleeping pills. A man who has accompanied Monsieur Henri is pacing around nervously. Monsieur Henri rushes Antoine to the room and gets him to let him inside with his pass key. They interrupt a couple naked in bed together. It turns out that Monsieur Henri is a private investigator and his nervous companion is the woman's husband. The husband rips apart the couple's clothing while the wife sits naked in bed, rebuking her angry spouse with mild indignation. Antoine is fired by the hotel manager for being fooled by the private investigator.

Claude Jade and Jean-Pierre Léaud in *Stolen Kisses* (1968)

Antoine later gets a job as a sales clerk at a shoe store. He becomes smitten by his boss' alluring wife, Fabienne Tabard (Delphine Seyrig). Fabienne overhears two salesgirls talking in the stockroom about Antoine's infatuation with her. One of the young women repeats Antoine's starry-eyed assessment of Fabienne: "She is not a woman. She's an apparition!" Fabienne invites Antonie to have tea with her. Antoine is nervous and

Jean-Pierre Léaud and Claude Jade in *Stolen Kisses* (1968)

leaves abruptly. Afterward, he sends her a letter apologizing for his behavior and letting her know that he is quitting his job. He writes: "I dreamed that a feeling might exist between us. But that is as impossible as Felix's love for Madame de Mortsauf. Farewell." She recognizes this as a reference to "Lily of the Valley," a book of which is very fond. She makes a surprise visit to Antoine's apartment. She lets the young man know that she enjoyed his letter. She tells him, "I'm not an apparition. I'm a woman." She proposes that they meet for a passionate sexual experience. "We'll spend a few hours together," she says, "and then, whatever happens, we'll never meet again."

The Bliss of Mrs. Blossom (1968)

Popular true crime stories often feature a cheating spouse as either a murder suspect or murder victim. Readers are intrigued by crime stories with elements of love, betrayal and murder. But arguably the most bizarre story in this genre centers on Dolly Oesterreich.

Dolly was 14 years old when she met Fred Oesterreich, who was 17. The couple married three years later. Fred opened a shoe store, which was a big success. He opened other stores. Eventually, he got into manufacturing. His factory produced aprons and ladies undergarments.

Fred was a generous husband by Dolly's own admission. He bought her jewelry and clothing and provided her with a limousine. But she was not satisfied. It could be assumed that having a busy husband left her feeling bored and lonely. But it is clear by the numerous affairs that Dolly had during the marriage that the woman was bedeviled by prodigious sexual urges.

Dolly entered into her most fateful affair while she was in her thirties. She asked her husband to send a handyman from his factory to fix her broken sewing machine. A shy 17-year-old Otto Sanhuber arrived at the Oesterreich home greeted by Dolly, who was dressed alluringly in a silk robe and stockings.

Otto, who lost his parents at a young age, grew up feeling lonely and unloved. He quickly became enchanted with Dolly. He later said that Dolly was the only person who ever showed him love.

Dolly and Otto found it inconvenient to meet at hotels and Dolly was worried that nosy neighbors would spot Otto if he made frequent visits to her home. So, she came up with the idea of creating a hideaway for Otto in her attic. Dr. Kate Lister, a specialist in the history of human sexuality, reported, "Otto cut off all contact with the outside world and hid himself away, relying on Dolly for food, water, and clothes. Later reports claimed she would bring Otto out to have sex with him multiple times every day."[565]

Otto slept on a mattress on the floor. He amassed a collection of books, which he read using an electric reading lamp. He also spent his free time cleaning the house, writing erotica, and mixing up bathtub gin.

Otto managed to keep out of sight whenever Fred was home. But there were still traces of his presence. Addison Nugent of the Atlas Obscura blog wrote, "[Fred] heard inexplicable noises coming from the attic, his cigars kept going missing, and he could swear that strange shadows passed outside his bedroom door some nights."[566]

Otto remained in the attic for almost 10 years. But he finally revealed himself to Fred on August 22, 1922. That day, Otto heard his hosts violently arguing and worried that Fred might hurt Dolly. He came out of hiding armed with a pistol. He later told the police that Fred became excited and shouted, "What are you doing here, you dirty rat?" Fred lunged after him and struggled for the gun. "It was his life or mine," Otto said. "I was certain of that. Finally, I got him with a lucky shot to the head." Apart from the lucky shot, Otto shot him two more times in the chest. Working quickly, Otto and Dolly staged the scene to look like a botched burglary.

The neighbors heard the shots and called the police. One neighbor reported to police that she saw the shadow of a man on the window curtains of the Oesterreich home.

Lister reported:

> Dolly inherited Fred's money and bought herself a new house. . . with an attic. Even though Dolly and Otto were now free to live openly, they continued to stick to their old arrangement. Otto would later say he was Dolly's sex slave.[567]

Dolly became bored with the enslaved and obsessed Otto and took on new lovers. One lover was Roy Klumb, a motion picture producer. Klumb told the police that Dolly had given him a pistol and told him to get rid of it for her. He tossed it in the Labrea tar pits, but came to regret this. The fact that the gun was the same caliber as the gun that killed Fred led to Dolly's immediate arrest.

Dolly insisted that she was innocent. She told the police that she and Fred got along well. She said, "We had many arguments over religion, but they were never violent quarrels." Was Fred preaching religion to his licentious wife?

While in custody, Dolly became worried about Otto. She explained to her attorney, Herman Shapiro, that she had "a vagabond half-brother" living in a secret room in her attic. She implored him to bring him food. She said that Otto would come out from hiding if Shapiro entered her clothes closet and tapped on the wall with his nails. Shapiro entered the home and, rather than tap on the wall, he loudly whistled. Otto promptly emerged out of a hidden panel. Being starved for human contact, he was happy to meet Shapiro and spoke to him at great length about his relationship with Dolly. Shapiro decided immediately to get rid of the odd little man. He had him pack up his belongings. He then drove him out to San Fernando Valley, where he dumped him off.

The district attorney, Asa Keyes, was convinced that Dolly had murdered her husband, but he wasn't sure that he could prove it to a jury. Then, Keyes got was indicted in a graft scandal and completely lost interest in the case.

Dolly started to date Shapiro upon her release. But this is where Dolly got herself into trouble. She had claimed that the burglar got away with Fred's diamond watch. So, Shapiro was startled when Dolly presented him with the watch as a gift. He questioned her about this, but she told him that she found the watch under a seat cushion.

Dolly was not faithful to Shapiro for the seven years that they were together. Shapiro was appalled when, in 1928, Dolly was sued for alienation of affection by a lover's wife. After a volatile breakup, the disgruntled ex-boyfriend reported to police that Dolly had a man living in her attic at the time of her husband's murder.

The police located Otto in San Francisco in 1930. He cried and trembled when the police took him into custody. Otto's defense attorney implied to the jury that Klumb was the actual murderer. But Otto was still convicted. Unfortunately, the statute of limitations had expired by then and the judge had to order his release.

Dolly was also acquitted and freed. She eventually found a new husband and remained married until her death in 1961.

Los Angeles Times reported in 1930, "Nothing in fiction is more dramatic than the story of the sudden quarrel in the hallway, the popping out of an armed jack-in-the-box, the struggle, the slaying. . . and the mysterious disappearance of the slayer back into his cubbyhole."[568]

The Oesterreich story became the basis of *The Bliss of Mrs. Blossom*. The film provides an outrageously comic take on the grim and lurid story. Today, the work is appreciated more for its psychedelic visuals than its strange characters, juvenile humor and off-putting plot.

Robert Blossom (Richard Attenborough), a brassiere manufacturer, is so busy at his factory that he rarely has time for his wife, Harriet (Shirley MacLaine). The scriptwriters, Alec Coppel, Denis Norden and Josef Shaftel, evidently imagined that bras were funnier than aprons.

Robert sends a young employee, Ambrose Tuttle (James Booth), to his home to repair his wife's sewing machine. Bored and lonely, Harriet becomes attracted to this shy young man and musters her feminine charms to seduce him. Afterward, Harriet arranges to hide Ambrose in the attic so that he will be readily available for further sexual encounters.

Robert plays a more interesting role in the story than his real-life counterpart. He is unnerved by mysterious noises that he frequently hears at night. Fearful that he is losing his mind, he visits a psychiatrist. He eventually admits in a therapy session that he is unhappy because he would rather be producing symphonies than producing bras.

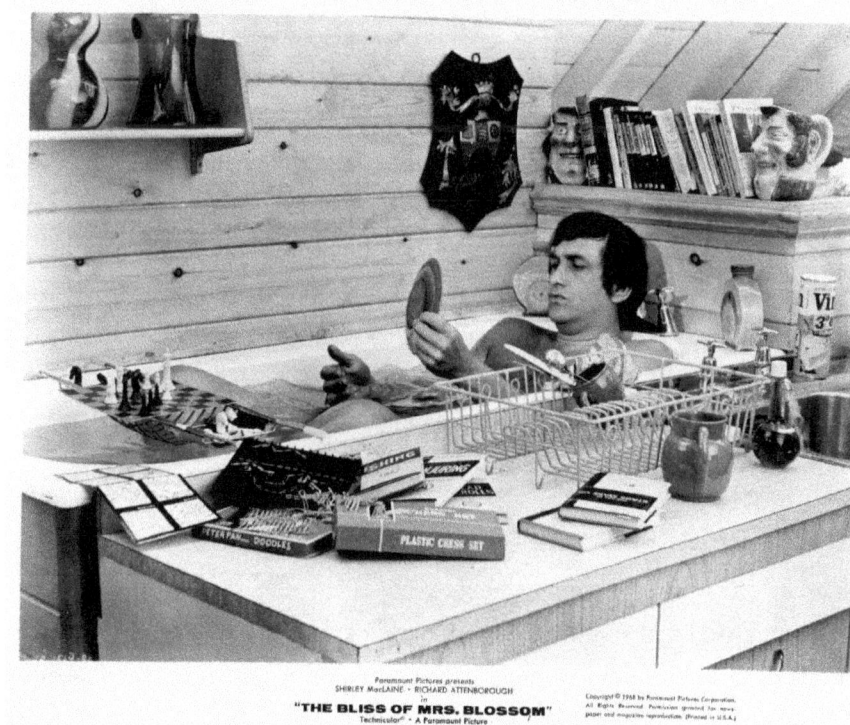

James Booth in *The Bliss of Mrs. Blossom* (1968)

Ambrose spends his time alone in the attic reading. He applies his growing book knowledge and natural creativity to a variety of projects. To start, he reads up on interior decoration, which allows him to beautifully redesign his modest living space into a colorful and plush environment.

Robert, also creative, invents an inflatable brassiere. He plans to move to Geneva, Switzerland, once he has successfully launched the new brasserie. This panics Harriet and Ambrose because the homes in Switzerland have no attics, which means the move will end their current living arrangement. So, Ambrose sets about to sabotage the unveiling of the new bra at an apparel convention. He reworks the bra so that it will over-inflate and cause its wearer to float high off the ground.

Ambrose is successful in destroying Robert's business opportunity. But the financial tide turns in Robert's favor despite his professional humiliation. Ambrose, who has read up on investments and banking, passes stock market tips to Robert through Harriett. As a result, Robert earns a fortune in the stock market.

Robert is angry when he first learns about Ambrose. But he comes to see this as an ideal opportunity for himself. He consents to divorce Harriet so that she can marry Ambrose and presents the factory to the couple as a wedding present. He is now free to pursue a career in music.

Wikipedia describes the final scene as follows: "Ambrose, soberly dressed for the office, has breakfast with Harriet and leaves her for a day of business. Harriet stamps on the floor, and Robert ascends [on a platform] from the basement. . ."[569] Robert is dressed in a white Nehru jacket with a string of black beads hanging around his neck. This was fashionable attire for rock musicians at the time. The couple passionately embraces.

Strangely, the murder story no longer includes a murder.

A more serious retelling of the Dolly Oesterreich story was scripted by former *Hart to Hart* writers Duane Poole and Tom Swale. The result was a television movie called *The Man in the Attic* (1995). Dolly became Krista, Otto became Edward, and Fred became Joseph. The film emphasizes Krista turning her young lover into her personal slave. Edward is not only a sex slave. He is also a work slave. He secretly presses Joseph's suits and cooks his meals. In one scene, he lovingly polishes Krista's toenails as she lounges on a settee.

In 1990, the American public became fascinated with a similar true-life murder story. Again, a married woman seduced a naive teenage boy. Again, the lover fatally shot the husband. Again, the wife and her lover staged the murder scene to look like a botched burglary. The woman, Pamela Smart, became one of the most notorious news figures of the 1990s. But, unlike Dolly, Pamela carefully arranged her husband's murder. She found an opportunity to recruit teenage Billy Flynn to carry out the bloody deed. It was easy to gain control of Flynn by luring him into a sexual relationship. At that point, she simply had to threaten to stop having sex with him to coax him into her murder scheme. The lurid story was dramatized in the 1995 film *To Die For*, which starred Nicole Kidman as a Pamela Smart stand-in called Suzanne Stone.

Platonov (1971)

The film is based on an 1878 play by Anton Chekhov.

At a country house, a married and somewhat unprincipled schoolmaster Mikhail Platonov (Rex Harrison) stimulates the affections of three different women, each of whom becomes eager to steal him away from his wife.

Platonov is a charming and witty rogue. He enjoys mocking other people. Women lavish their affections on him. He says, "I love everybody. Everybody. . . Ever so many of you, I love you all and you love me. Sometimes I am beastly to you and still you love me, you know." One woman complains that he is "rude and impertinent," yet this is exactly what she finds so thrilling and seductive about him. Another woman tells him with a wry smile, "Well, either you're completely above the ordinary or you're a scoundrel, one or the other." Anna (Siân Phillips) praises him for his "sinful soul." Yet, she senses that he has a genuine warmth for her.

Platonov fears that he is taken over too easily by lust. "I do struggle" he says, "but I am weak, terribly weak." He claims to be in "the sway of a monstrous passion." He feels great guilt about cheating on his wife. He says, "It is hard to deceive somebody who believes in you so completely. It makes you sweat and blush."

The demands of his many admirers cause him to drink excessively. He is distressed when one of his mistresses, Sofia, announces to him that she has told her husband about their affair. She promises him a new life. "I don't want your new life," he cries out. "I don't know what to do with the old one as it is."

Platonov's wife, Sasha (Patsy Byrne), is so upset to learn of his infidelity that she poisons herself. Nicolai Triletski (Clive Revill), Sasha's brother, mockingly repeats what his sister told him about Platonov: "And they like him here, he's such an interesting fellow, so original!" The news panics Platonov, who loves his wife deeply.

Sofie fatally shoots Platonov when she finds him in the arms of a chemistry student, Maria Grekova (Bridget Armstrong).

The play is a precursor to *The Norman Conquests* (1977). It was noted on The Real Chrisparkle blog:

Platonov himself is a truly Ayckbournian creation – like Norman, in *The Norman Conquests*, attractive to women beyond all reasonable expectations without going out of his way to pursue them; just being playfully irreverent, primarily taking care of himself at the expense of others, wheedling his way out of awkward situations, loving others but not as much as he loves himself.[570]

Norman (Tom Conti), a puckish librarian, is bored with his marriage and arranges an illicit weekend with his shy sister-in-law, Annie (Penelope Wilton). Annie is isolated on a country estate caring for her demanding and difficult old mother and the idea of a romantic retreat is very appealing to her.

Annie confesses the affair to her sister-in-law, Sarah (Penelope Keith).

Annie: It was just wham, thump and there we both were on the rug.

Sarah: Rug? Which rug?

Annie: The brown nylon fur one in the lounge. . . [*She starts to giggle.*]

Sarah: [*irritated*] What? Why are you laughing?

Annie: [*unable to control herself*] Does it matter which rug?

Sarah cannot believe that Anne was willing to go off with Norman for a weekend.

Sarah: But how could you even think of it?

Annie: He asked me.

Sarah: What is that to do with it?

Annie: Well, I want the holiday. . .

Sarah: Yes but – this wouldn't be just a holiday. . . I mean, I mean, you just don't go off on holiday with your sister's husband.

Annie: It was only a weekend. I needed a holiday.

Sarah: Well, you could have gone on your own.

Annie: [*slightly angry*] I didn't want to go on my own. I'm always on my own.

Sarah: But did you realize what you were getting yourself into?

Annie: Well – the way Norman puts it - it sounded simple. Just the weekend.

Sarah: Norman will put it anyway which suits Norman.

Sarah confronts Norman about his illicit plans.

Sarah: In this house. With your wife ill upstairs – rolling about with her sister on this very rug.

Norman: Oh, that – that was just festive fun.

Sarah: And if that isn't enough, planning to sneak off with her for some sordid weekend.

Norman: There's nothing sordid about East Grinstead. She wanted to come. I wanted to go. Don't you see? It would have been something different for her – exciting. And for me. She's stuck here, all on her own, day after day looking after that old sabre-toothed bat upstairs.

He clarifies that he was only borrowing Annie.

Sarah: Make her sound like one of your library books.

Norman: She was borrowing me, too. It was mutual. It was a friendly loan. We never intended to upset anybody. We both agreed. That was the joy of it, don't you see? Nobody need ever have known. If Annie hadn't gone and told you – nobody.

Norman asks Annie why she had to tell Sarah about their plans. She says:

Things were getting very complicated, you see. I mean, when we were planning it, last Christmas and on the phone and things – well – it was simple then, wasn't it? It was easy just to forget about Ruth and - Tom. Not that Tom's all that important but after all you are married to Ruth and she is my sister, even if I'm not very fond of her, but I don't think I'm very good at pretending for very long. Sarah got it out of me and no time.

She admits that their plan seemed innocent and harmless at first. She says:

Far better we go away quietly to a little hotel somewhere, get it all off our chests – out of our system – God, I'm making it sound like a laxative – you know what I mean – work it all off, that's what I mean. Then you go back to Ruth and live happily ever after – or as happily as you can seeing it's Ruth and I come back to mother and - and – look after her.

Annie's mother is a nagging and bossy Gorgon. It's hard not to feel sorry for Annie.

The Heartbreak Kid (1972)

Lenny Cantrow (Charles Grodin), who has barely started his honeymoon, finds himself regretting having gotten married. He falls in love with a stunningly beautiful young woman, Kelly Corcoran (Cybill Shepherd), on the second day of his honeymoon.

Dirty Weekend (1973)

BFI: "A married man plans his clandestine week-end with his girl-friend when he is kidnapped with her by a gang of bank robbers and his story ends up on the front page of the newspaper and on television."[571]

Ash Wednesday (1973)

IMDb: "After getting plastic surgery in Switzerland to help rejuvenate her shaky marriage, Barbara Sawyer has an affair with a younger man while waiting for her husband's arrival from the U.S."[572]

The film is surprisingly weak considering it stars two legendary actors: Elizabeth Taylor and Henry Fonda.

How Funny Can Sex Be (1973)

The original Italian title is *Sessomatto* (the English translation of which is *Sex Nut*)

This anthology comedy features nine stories, three of which involve adultery. The first story, "Due cuori e una baracca" ("Two Hearts and a Shack") involves marital mistrust. Celestina (Laura Antonelli) is angry at her husband, Cesaretto (Giancarlo Giannini), because she found lipstick on the collar of his shirt. He sees that she has a new dress and accuses her of wearing the dress to go on a date. Their jealous quarrel escalates to physical violence, but the violence turns out to be effective foreplay for the couple. "Non è mai troppo tardi" ("It's never too late") examines gerontophilia. A lawyer, Enrico (Giannini), is married to a beautiful young woman (Antonelli), but he finds himself desperately attracted to his ninety-year-old mother-in-law, Esperia (Paola Borboni). The film ends with "L'ospite" ("The Guest"). Vittorio (Duilio Del Prete), invites a business associate, Doctor Bianchi (Giannini), to his home for dinner. Bianchi is pleasantly surprised when Vittorio's beautiful wife, Tiziana (Antonelli), persists in trying to seduce him. Vittorio has too much to drink and dozes off. Bianchi becomes overwhelmed with passion. He is madly groping Tiziana when Vittorio suddenly awakens from his drunken nap. He grabs hold of Bianchi and brusquely escorts him to the door. It turns out that Tiziana teases dinner guests to get Vittorio excited. Rosario (Carla Mancini), the maid, enters the home with most of her dress torn off. She remarks, "He's a raging lunatic! Why do the dinner guests always molest me?"

The Two Worlds of Jennie Logan (1979)

Jennie Logan (Lindsay Wagner), is working with her husband Michael (Alan Feinstein) to save their marriage after her husband strayed into a brief affair with another woman. Jennie finds an old Victorian dress in the attic of their new home. When she tries on the dress, she finds herself transported back in time to 1899, where she meets and falls in love with an artist named David Reynolds (Marc Singer). Jennie repeatedly travels back and forth between 1899 and present-day. She learns that David was killed in a duel and desperately looks for a way to prevent his death.

Sunday Lovers (1980)

IMDb: "Armando, an Italian whose wife goes away, and while she's away, he finds his old address book and decides to call his old girlfriends and see if any of them want to hook up."[573]

The French Lieutenant's Wife (1981)

Anna (Meryl Streep) and Mike (Jeremy Irons) have an extramarital affair while acting together in a film.

Betrayal (1983)

The film begins as Jerry (Jeremy Irons) and Emma (Patricia Hodge) end an affair. The story of their ill-fated affair is told in reverse, with each scene taking place further back in time. The final scene shows the couple at the beginning of the affair.

Jerry and Emma rent an apartment as a love nest. In time, Emma becomes dissatisfied with the apartment. She says that, early in the relationship, they were determined and inventive in arranging their time together at the apartment, but now they can't ever find an opportunity to be there. Jerry says, "I know what you wanted, but it could never actually be a home. You have a home. I have a home. . . with curtains, etc. And children. Two children. In two homes. . . So, it's not the same kind of home." This infuriates Emma. She responds, "You didn't ever see it as a home in any sense, did you?" He says that he simply saw it as a flat. "For fucking," she snaps.

The film lacks human warmth. The characters are dull and unexpressive. The dialogue is cold and calculated. Emotional restraint is not what an audience expects from an adultery film.

Patricia Hodge and Jeremy Irons in *Betrayal* (1983)

Between Us (1983)

The original French title: *Entre Nous*

Lena Korski (Isabelle Huppert), the wife of a prosperous garage owner, is captivated by Madeleine Segara (Miou-Miou), an actor's wife that she meets at her daughters' school. Lena and Madeleine form a tight bond that excludes their husbands. Madeleine has a brief affair with her former art teacher. Léna enjoys her first orgasm when she allows a dashing soldier to grope her during a train ride. But the women can find no true intimacy or comfort with men. It is only with each other that they can find a deep affinity.

Just Between Friends (1986)

Sandy (Christine Lahti) and Holly (Mary Tyler Moore) become friends at a gym. But, when Sandy comes to Holly's house for dinner, she is shocked to discover that Holly's husband Chip (Ted Danson) is her boyfriend. Sandy knew that Chip was married, but being friends with his wife is terribly awkward for her. The situation is made even more awkward by a series of events - Chip dies in car accident, Sandy learns that she is pregnant, and Holly finds that the baby's father is Chip. So what happens now? Sandy is happy to have the baby. Holly volunteers to help Sandy through her pregnancy and help her to raise her child. The film is reminiscent of the Bette Davis classic *The Great Lie* (1941).

Too Beautiful for You (1989)

The original French title: *Trop belle pour toi*

Bernard Barthélémy (Gérard Depardieu) is a wealthy businessman with a young beautiful wife. His wife, Florence, is played by a former Bond girl, Carole Bouquet. But Bernard is willing to upend his life when he falls in love with his chubby, middle-aged secretary, Colette Chevassu (Josiane Balasko). This is a strange and incomprehensible film. Honkon of IMDb wrote, "Not one for the viewer who likes to sit back and be told a straight story but for the rest of us, a joy from start to finish."[574]

Enchanted April (1991)

Four women spend a month at a beautiful Italian villa, which soon begins to have a magical effect on them. The villa is an Eden that washes away their various sins and vices - the depression of Rose Arbuthnot (Miranda Richardson), the anxiety of Lottie Wilkins (Josie Lawrence), the priggishness of Mrs. Fisher (Joan Plowright), the avarice of Mellerish Wilkins (Alfred Molina), and the adulterous lust of Frederick Arbuthnot (Jim Broadbent).

Demi Moore in *The Butcher's Wife* (1991)

The Butcher's Wife (1991)

The great success of *Ghost*, *Pretty Woman* and *Green Card* in 1990 encouraged the studios to turn out several romantic films the following year. Those earlier films were unusual to say the least. *Ghost* involved a continuing romance between a woman and her deceased lover. *Pretty Woman* involved an unlikely romance between a millionaire and a prostitute. *Green Card* involved a romance between a prim woman and a gregarious illegal alien. But *The Butcher's Wife*, an attempt to derive lighthearted romance from extramarital hanky-panky, was even more unusual.

Marina (Demi Moore), a beautiful young woman with clairvoyant powers, lives on a small island off the coast of North Carolina. In the script, Marina speaks of her parents being a bad match, which is the reason she believes her mother ran off with a Portuguese sailor. She is unwilling to make the same mistake. She longs to find her soulmate.

Marina comes across a series of objects that she perceives as omens. She is walking along the shore when she comes across a snow globe with the Manhattan skyline. She sees a twin-tailed comet in the night sky. Preparing dinner, she slices open the belly of a mullet and finds a wedding band inside. She calls the wedding band "an undeniable sign that I would soon meet my mate." She dreams of a man smiling at her. Well, not the entire man, just the smile. "It was a lustrous, glowing smile," she says. One morning, she sees a rowboat heading for shore and rushes out to greet it. Inside the rowboat is Leo Lemke (George Dzundza), a portly middle-aged butcher from Greenwich Village. From the script: "Leo is a middle-aged New York butcher who's spent so much of his time around sides of beef, he's come to resemble one."[575] Marina is convinced that this man is meant to be her husband. She takes a leap of faith by accepting this side of beef as her soulmate. In a single heady moment, she is willing to trust the signs that have been laid out before her. She is willing to believe with all her heart that she will find a lifelong romance with this unromantic figure. Marina says in voice-over, "Love is the leap that won't be denied." But, as we will soon learn, she is wrong.

Marina happily leaps into the rowboat and kisses Leo. She kisses him with quick little pecks like a mother kissing a newborn baby. He does no more than look at her in shock. The couple is never shown engaged in a mutual kiss. No mildly affectionate kiss. No passionate kiss. No lip-locking at all. We would have seen them kissing if the film included a wedding scene. But the film skips from their meeting to their arrival as newlyweds in Greenwich Village. The couple is never shown to be physically affectionate in any way. They are never shown in bed together. It is questionable if they have had the time to consummate the marriage. In this way, we never get the sense that they are married. Marjorie Nielsen, who co-wrote the script with Ezra Litwak, spoke to the author for this book. She was asked if, in her mind, the newlyweds ever had sex. She said, "We never considered or discussed if she and the butcher slept together."[576]

The script was consulted for further insight. In the script, Leo gives Marina "an affectionate swat on the butt."[577] But we don't see anything like this in the film. Leo puts on a Bessie Smith record, which gets him in the mood to dance. The script reads, "[Leo] sweeps Marina up in his arms, gives her a big kiss and twirls her around to the music."[578] But, in the film, Leo gently leads Marina in a dance. That's all. He doesn't sweep her up in his arms, he doesn't give her a big kiss, and he doesn't twirl her around. He may be about to kiss her when the scene cuts to a seashell-encrusted clock and other island mementos strewn across the bed. What does this shot mean? Does a ticking clock suggest lovemaking in the same way a train speeding through a tunnel suggests lovemaking in other films? In the script, the bed is free to be occupied by the newlyweds. Marina hops into the bed and motions for Leo to join her. Once he is the bed, she kisses him and turns off the light. That's where the scene ends.

The executives at Paramount Pictures very much wanted John Goodman to play Leo, but Goodman was tied up working on *Rosanne*. The director Terry Hughes briefly considered shooting Goodman's scenes during the actor's downtime on weekends, but he saw this as becoming a logistical nightmare. Hughes also considered Bob Hoskins for the role. But, in the end, the role went to Dzundza.

Dzundza was 45 years old, which made him significantly older than 28-year-old Moore. And he was substantially overweight, unlike the film's fit and shapely leading lady. It may have been the filmmakers' intention to make the couple look obviously mismatched from the start. Why risk getting your audience emotionally invested in the couple when they are soon to be torn apart by an extramarital affair? The audience has to recognize without hesitation that Marina is making a big mistake and the marriage will be unable to hold together. Perhaps, it is meant for viewers to react in the way that *Madame Bovary*'s Rodolphe reacts to seeing Emma Bovary with her husband Charles. Rodolphe thinks to himself, "She is very pretty, this doctor's wife." It upsets him that a woman as beautiful as this could have married a "fat fellow."[579] Certainly, in his mind, these two don't belong together.

Roger Ebert wrote, "So, obviously, in the Hollywood mind, [Leo] has not evolved high enough on the ladder of personal attractiveness to deserve Demi Moore. A mistake must have been made. The plot develops a compulsion to reassign her to a more handsome man, and that's where the movie goes wrong."[580] Ebert saw this as outright cruel. Nielsen wrote, "Yeah, Ebert took that personally, that the butcher never got the star. But he got Mary Steenburgen! His mate meant to be."[581] More on the Steenburgen plot turn shortly.

The community changes upon the arrival of this enchanting woman, who uses her clairvoyant powers to advise people on their love lives. A big part of the film is what Ebert calls "partner reassignment."[582] Marina sorts out mismatched couples, shifting people from a wrong partner to a right partner.

Leo is dissatisfied with Marina. He comes to resent that she married him just because of her dreams. And, more important, he finds it creepy that she has visions. He meets a timid choir teacher, Stella Keefover (Mary Steenburgen), and falls in love. Stella is introduced in the script in a therapy session with her psychiatrist, Dr. Alex Tremor (Jeff Daniels). She says that she fantasizes being Anna Karenina or Madam Bovary, although she realizes that both women "offed themselves."[583] She reluctantly admits that, in her romantic pursuits, she has on occasion been involved with a married man. None of this dialogue is included in the finished film.

Alex starts out as Marina's adversary. Desson Howe of The Washington Post wrote, "The uptight practitioner isn't happy about [the newcomer's fortunetelling]. Moore is transforming - and complicating - the lives of his clients. People aren't supposed to be cured this easily. Shrink and mystic battle each other for control of the neighborhood's collective psyche."[584] As it turns out, her psychic matchmaking is more encouraging and reassuring than Alex's tough-love psychiatric care. Janet Maslin of The New York Times wrote, "Mr. Daniels, as the doctor who is alternately exasperated and entranced by Marina, makes himself comically and convincingly frazzled in her presence."[585]

At night, a young man eagerly watches as Marina walks barefoot across a rooftop in a diaphanous gown. It is reminiscent of the scene in *The Summer of '42* in which a young man finds cover in sand dunes while spying on a beautiful young bride outside of her beach house. Moore's alluring wardrobe was designed by three-time Oscar nominee Theodora Van Runkle. It is a highlight of the film.

Nielsen was surprised that the film was to be included on a book about adultery films. She wrote, "The script had gone through so many drafts and incarnations, but adultery was never in mind. The movie was about finding your soulmate, as the characters stumbled their way to their true partners. Yes she was married, but I believe we made it innocent enough, never secretive or underhanded. We never intended for the relationship between Demi Moore and Jeff Daniels to be *adulterous*. . . but to more innocent and self aware so neither went very far until all was resolved. Is that adultery?"[586]

The time that the couple spends together is innocent. A key scene shows them roller-skating in the park, which is reminiscent of Cary Grant and Loretta Young ice skating in *The Bishop's Wife*. Nielsen wrote that she and Litwak purposely made this outing innocent. She said that romantic comedies of the period were "fairly innocent, sexually."[587] We have already discussed the sexless extramarital romances in *The Bishop's Wife*, *Forsaking All Others* and *There's Always Tomorrow*.

The script is not as innocent as the film. Marina is a changed person after spending a day with Alex. She no longer feels connected to Leo. A single image in the script shows this: "Marina and Leo sleep soundly on opposite sides of the bed."[588] Marina gets out of bed and wanders out of the apartment. She shows up at Alex's apartment still dressed in her diaphanous nightgown. She tells Alex that she dreamed about him. From the script: "She kisses him with enormous pent up passion. Alex succumbs completely for a few erotic moments."[589] But he suddenly comes to his senses and, according to the script, "extricates himself from her grasp."[590] Marina is confused that Alex is rejecting her when she is sure that he loves her. She kisses him again. He tells her that she is only kissing him to spite her husband for having an affair with another woman. She is shocked to hear this. Despite her clairvoyant powers, she didn't know about Leo and Stella. She storms out of the office. Later, Alex shows up at her home. He sees that she is alone. The script reads, "He pushes the door open and steps in. Overwhelmed by her sparkling beauty, he kisses her with total abandon then sweeps her off to the bedroom as they tear at each other's clothes. Alex and Marina make passionate love."[591] The couple, according to the script, "doze off in post coital bliss."[592] Eugene, a helper at the shop, catches the couple in bed together. Alex panics, but Marina doesn't seem to care. From the script: "A love-dazed Marina wakes slowly and happily watches a nude Alex hunt madly all over the room for his scattered clothes."[593]

Did Marina misinterpret a snow globe and two-tailed comet as mystical signs out of a desperate longing or a brash confidence? Or was she guided exactly as the cosmic forces intended? If she didn't follow Leo to Greenwich Village, she would have never met her true love Alex and she would have never persuaded Stella to sing a blues song at a local bar, which is how she and Leo ended up meeting and falling in love. And her presence in Greenwich Village allowed her to match up a second couple and help Eugene to open up his own art studio. But this means that the cosmic forces have such little respect for marital vows that they are willing to bring about a false marriage for a wider and more ambitious purpose. Or should we realize that omens are the bunk and a woman shouldn't marry a man because a wedding band rolls out of a mullet's belly?

Howe wrote, "*The Butcher's Wife* is a fantasy spin on 'A Midsummer Night's Dream,' by obvious way of *Moonstruck*."[594] Jill Rachlin of Entertainment Weekly thought that the film, which was essentially *Moonstruck* for carnivores, should have been called *Meatstruck*.[595] *The Butcher's Wife* could have benefited from a greater sprinkling of *Moonstruck*'s fairy dust. It is unlikely that audiences would have been so easily charmed by *Moonstruck* if Cher's Loretta and Danny Aiello's Johnny were married rather than simply engaged. *Moonstruck* focused a great deal on religious morality and family fidelity, which is sorely lacking in *The Butcher's Wife*.

It needlessly complicated the film to bring marriage into the equation. The couple could have become engaged. Marina could have traveled to Leo's home in Greenwich Village to meet his family and arrange a marriage ceremony at the family's church. Strangely, Leo never mentions bringing Marina to see his family. Does he have a family?

It must be noted that *The Butcher's Wife* has an undeniable charm despite its flaws.

Spanking the Monkey (1994)

Ray Aibelli (Jeremy Davies) gives up a medical internship to care for his mother, Susan Aibelli (Alberta Watson), who has injured her leg. Susan is lonely as her husband has to frequently travel on business. She is glad to have Ray around to keep her company. Ray has to massage his mother's leg and help her to shower. He becomes disturbed to be developing sexual thoughts about his mother. But Susan seems to be intent on encouraging those thoughts. In time, she seduces Ray into having sex with her. The guilt over what he has done causes him to try hanging himself. But Susan stops him. Ray is torn between opposing passions of anger and lust. He wildly kisses Susan at first, but then he starts to strangle her. He stops short of killing her. He now sees this as a hopeless situation. He quickly packs his bags and leaves. The final scene shows him on the highway hitchhiking.

Dream Lover (1994)

Ray Reardon, a wealthy architect, marries a beautiful and enigmatic woman, Lena (Mädchen Amick). He becomes unsettled over Lena's suspicious comings and goings. He becomes convinced that Lena is having an affair, but he finds it odd that she is leaving many obvious clues. Can she possibly be that sloppy about her illicit activities? He doesn't realize that Lena is attempting to drive him to violent paranoia so that she can have him committed to a mental institution and run off with his money. She intends to start a new life in New Zealand with her boyfriend, Larry (Fredric Lehne).

Black Day Blue Night (1995)

Hallie Schrag (Mia Sara) follows her husband Bo (Tim Guinee) to a hotel. She watches Bo check into a room with a waitress, Rinda Woolley (Michelle Forbes). She breaks into the room with a gun drawn. "I'm gonna kill you both," she announces. Rinda assures Hallie that she didn't know that Bo was married. Hallie changes her mind about killing anyone. The incident convinces Rina that she needs to change her life. She quits her job to go on a road trip. Hallie begs Rinda to let her come along. Rina hesitates for a moment, but then she lets Hallie get into the car. During the trip, the two women pick up a good-looking hitchhiker (Gil Bellows), who they later learn is being pursued by the police.

The Daytrippers (1996)

Metacritic: "When a happily married woman discovers a love letter written by her husband to an unknown party, she enlists her dysfunctional family to discover the truth."[596]

Beautiful Mother (1999)

On his wedding day, Antoine (Vincent Lindon) realizes that he is in love with his mother-in-law, Léa (Catherine Deneuve).

Pushing Tin (1999)

Nick Falzone (John Cusack) and Russell Bell (Billy Bob Thornton) are highly competitive air traffic controllers. Their contentious relationship gets worse when Nick seduces Russell's despondent wife, Mary (Angelina Jolie). Mary confesses to Russell about the affair. Nick becomes terrified that Russell might seduce his own wife, Connie (Cate Blanchett), as revenge. But one day, when the air traffic control facility receives a bomb threat, Nick and Russell set aside their differences and figure out a way to work together to route the incoming planes.

One Hour Photo (2002)

Sy Parrish (Robin Williams) is a technician at a one-hour photo lab. He is lonely and develops a fascination with a model family that regularly has photos developed at his lab. He secretly copies their photos and puts them around his home as if they are his own family. Sy becomes distraught when a roll of photos shows that Will Yorkin (Michael Vartan), who he always saw as the perfect father, is having an extramarital affair with Maya Burson (Erin Daniels). He follows Will to the hotel where he regularly meets Maya. He holds a knife on the lovers and forces them to pose in sexual positions while he photographs them.

The Secret Lives of Dentists (2002)

David Hurst (Campbell Scott) goes to see his wife, Dana (Hope Davis), act in a play. He slips backstage afterward and sees Dana kissing another man in a dressing room. He doesn't know how to handle the situation and is desperate for advice. His imagination conjures up a personal adviser who looks a lot like a disgruntled former patient, Slater (Denis Leary). David and his imaginary friend banter a great deal about the situation. David finally resolves to confront Dana. He has one question for her: "Are you leaving or staying?" She tells him that she is staying. He says, "I don't want to know who he was or what you did." He leaves the room. The story ends.

Code 46 (2003)

Code 46 was oddly marketed as a futuristic *Brief Encounter*. But it would be better to describe the film as a futuristic *Pitfall*. The film is set in a future where citizens live under a totalitarian government. William (Tim Robbins), a government investigator, travels to Shanghai to track down the supplier of fake identification cards. This is a serious matter as the government relies on identification cards to closely monitor its citizens. William, though married, falls in love with Maria Gonzales (Samantha Morton), who is the likely source of the illegal identification cards. Their relationship is obviously improper in a professional context. But it creates a greater issue under government regulations, which only allow a man and a woman to have sex if they possess a compatible genetic code.

Five Times Two (2004)

The film depicts the disintegration of a marriage in five scenes arranged in reverse order.

It is often difficult and sometimes impossible to engage in the story. The main characters of the film, Gilles (Stéphane Freiss) and Marion (Valeria Bruni Tedeschi), act in ways that are strange and inexplicable.

On his honeymoon night, Gilles drunkenly passes out in bed. The disappointed bride wanders around outside the hotel. She sits down in a dark garden on the hotel grounds. She is startled by a man who comes rustling through the shrubbery. After the shortest amount of small talk, the man grabs hold of her and repeatedly kisses her. She strenuously resists him at first, but soon acquiesces. Is this rape? It may be, but many critics see her as a willing party. jotix100 of IMDb wrote, "Marion is ready to consummate her marriage, even if it's not with her own man!"[597]

Gilles and Marion share many of the same flaws. They are both remote and both suffer from insecurities.

Gilles, who is also selfish and aloof, is the worst of the two. Marion experiences great distress during a pregnancy. She is rushed to the hospital for an emergency Caesarean, but her husband learns about it and doesn't seem to care. He can't even be bothered to come to the hospital.

jotix100 ideally described the ending, which depicts the couple's first meeting:

> . . . [Gilles] turns up at a remote spot on the beach where Marion is sunbathing. When Gilles asks her if she would like to swim, Marion answers she has been told not to attempt to go into the water because of the dangerous tides. Obviously, neither Marion, nor Gilles, heed the advice of the native wisdom and we watch them getting in the water slowly walking and then swimming into the sunset![598]

The tides of marriage are certainly dangerous for bad swimmers.

Man About Town (2006)

Jack Giamoro (Ben Affleck), a Hollywood talent agent, learns that his wife Nina (Rebecca Romijn) is having an affair with his most important client, Phil Balow (Adam Goldberg). Jack confronts Nina about the affair.

Jack: If you really loved me, no matter what I did, no matter what we were going through, you would not have done what you did.

Nina: Okay, you're right. I'm human. I'm flawed. I'm a flawed piece of shit, Jack. Is that what you want to hear? Do you want to hear me beg? 'Cause I will. I'll beg. It's not in my nature, but I'll do it. I'll beg. I'm asking for forgiveness. I'm asking you to somehow look inside yourself and. find the place that will allow you to focus on all the incredible good that's happened between us. If you really love me, then why is that so goddamn hard?

Jack isn't willing to forgive her at first. He demands that she leave. But he later finds her sobbing inside her car. This softens him enough to reconcile with her.

The Valet (2006)

Gossip circulates that a billionaire businessman, Pierre Levasseur (Daniel Auteuil), is cheating on his wife Christine (Kristin Scott Thomas) with a supermodel, Elena Simonsen (Alice Taglioni). Levasseur pays a parking valet, François Pignon (Gad Elmaleh), to pretend to be Elena's boyfriend while he can arrange a divorce settlement with his lawyer.

Notes on a Scandal (2006)

Barbara Covett (Judi Dench), an elderly history teacher, becomes infatuated with a younger teacher, Sheba Hart (Cate Blanchett). She becomes jealous when she witnesses Sheba having sex with a 15-year-old student, Steven Connolly (Andrew Simpson). She secretly reveals the relationship to Sheba's husband, Richard (Bill Nighy). She is not surprised when Richard kicks Sheba to the curb and is ready to welcome Sheba into her home. Sheba learns the truth of Barbara's betrayal when she reads her friend's diary.

Game of Four (2007)

Lisa (Mathilde Seigner) and Thomas (Roschdy Zem) have embarked on an affair, never suspecting that their trusting spouses Carole (Alice Taglioni) and Lionel (François Cluzet) will ever find out.

Lisa and Thomas are not at all discreet, having sex in an RV outside of their children's school. A group of elementary school students gathers around the vehicle to observe the commotion going on inside. It is reminiscent of the brazen wife in *Shadows on the Wall* kissing her lover in a car outside her apartment building. Lisa shows little foresight as she indulges her sexual passion. She claws Thomas' back so badly during sex that he cannot take his shirt off in front of his wife.

Carole visits her new gynecologist, who happens to be Lionel. It surprises them to realize that they have met before at the school. Another surprise occurs when they go to complete paperwork and see that they both own a novelty pen adorned with a flamenco dancer. Carole explains that her husband bought her pen while visiting Seville. Lionel says that his wife bought him his pen while she, too, visited Seville. It turns out that their spouses were in Seville the same day. This coincidence and others draw them to the conclusion that their spouses are having an affair. The wronged spouses team up to break up the hanky-panky.

Carole and Lionel get an idea of how to keep their spouses apart. Lionel tells Lisa that, in examining Carole, he found that she has a yeast infection. Thomas immediately gets tested for the infection, but he's told that he has to wait ten days for the test results. This creates ten days of abstinence. It gives the schemers time to rekindle the passion in their marriages or, if that doesn't work, create a bit of mischief.

The two couples attend a dinner party at the home of a mutual friend. On the way home, Lionel casually mentions to Lisa that Thomas comes across as the type of man who likes to fool around with younger women. Carole similarly tells Thomas, "I bet [Lisa] cheats on [her husband] like crazy. . . She's the kind of woman who finds a docile husband, then jumps the first lifeguard she meets."

On their next meeting, Lisa and Thomas accuse each other of being untrustworthy.

Lisa: You lie to your wife, why not to me?

Thomas: I could say the same about you. How do I know you're not screwing your yoga teacher? Or your lifeguard? You like athletes, don't you? Quickies in the shower? I know you do.

Carole hires a man, Damien (Philippe Lefebvre), to interrupt Lisa and Thomas during a romantic dinner to denounce her for not returning his calls.

In the end, Carole and Lionel manage to destroy their spouses' affair while starting an affair of their own.

This story could have gone an entirely different way, as revealed by *An Affair To Die For* (2019). IMDb summarized the film as follows: "A man cheats on his wife. A woman cheats on her husband. And then everything goes bad, quickly."[599] Holly Pierpoint (Claire Forlani) travels to Aspen for a romantic weekend with Everett Alan (Jake Abel). But their spouses, Russell (Titus Welliver) and Lydia (Melina Matthews), are secretly waiting for them. Holly and Everett's two-timed spouses have teamed up to put the adulterers through a twisted and dangerous game. They are taken captive, tormented, and manipulated. Only one of these people survive the bloody weekend. The convoluted plot lacks the wit of *Sleuth* and the chills of *Saw*, though it tries its best to emulate both films.

Blame It on Mum (2009)

The original French title: *Quelque chose a te dire*

Alice Celliers (Mathilde Seigner) paints nightmarish images of sad, drug-addicted women. She falls in love with a solitary, world-weary cop, Jacques de Parentis (Olivier Marchal), who is married to Valérie (Gwendoline Hamon). Their relationship is jeopardized when Jacques learns that Valérie is pregnant.

Alice: Good. This story was doomed from the start.

Jacques: Don't say that. That's not true. We're going to be fine.

Alice: No, I don't think so.

But Alice is wrong (and probably most of the audience is wrong). Jacques is unwilling to end the affair despite having a child on the way. Shockingly, he manages in the end to dump his very sweet, very beautiful and very pregnant wife. For a depressed and neurotic woman. And this is presented as a happy ending. Really.

A number of actresses, from Irene Dunne to Kristin Scott Thomas, have specialized in extramarital cheating on screen. Another one of those actresses is Seigne. LaSalle wrote:

> In *Mariages!* (2004), [Seigne] cheats on her husband - at a wedding! - and isn't terribly pleasant with her lover, either. In *Palais royal!*, Valerie Lemercier's satirical take on the life of Princess Diana, she is the sleazy longtime mistress of the Prince. In *Détrompez-vous* (2007), she is utterly shameless as a married woman having an affair with a married man (Roschdy Zem). In *Quelque chose a te dire* (2009), she is a talented painter who has had "one abortion after another" and busts up a man's marriage. . . A hallmark of Seigner's interpretation of these roles is that she never shows the slightest moral uncertainty.[600]

Extract (2009)

Joel (Jason Bateman) hires a man to seduce his wife Suzie (Kristen Wiig) so that he won't have to feel guilty to have an affair with an attractive new employee, Cindy (Mila Kunis).

Brownian Movement (2010)

This is a creepy take on the adultery story.

Charlotte (Sandra Hüller) has a respectable career as a doctor. She seems by all appearances to have a happy marriage. But she secretly rents an apartment to have sex with an unusual variety of patients. The Hollywood Reporter noted:

> Charlotte is introverted and complex, unsatisfied with her seemingly "perfect" life with her attentive, handsome husband Max (Dragan Bakema) and young son Benjamin (Ryan Brodie), even though she and Max continue to enjoy rewarding intimacy. Her dissatisfaction manifests itself in impulsive sexual experimentation, as Charlotte picks up men — most of them physically unprepossessing — at her hospital, taking them back to a rented, sterile apartment.[601]

Mike Goodidge of Screen Daily wrote:

> The men are never of a type. One is overweight, one hairy, one very old. While these encounters are one-offs and never entail emotional engagement, they bring her a fulfillment she cannot get in her marriage.[602]

The situation goes awry when she is confronted by one man who wants to continue their relationship. She panics and strikes him repeatedly. The incident requires police involvement, exposing Charlotte's affairs. In therapy sessions, Charlotte is unable to explain the reason for her behavior. Her motives remain incomprehensible by the end of the film. Jeremy Heilman of Movie Martyr wrote, "*Brownian Movement* feels unnecessarily coy at times, as if it understands what makes Charlotte tick, but opts instead to obfuscate in the name of art."[603]

The Dilemma (2011)

The film's disturbing situations, which involve adultery, blackmail, a gambling addiction and gun violence, undermine the filmmakers' efforts to get laughs.

Ronny Valentine (Vince Vaughn) and Nick Brannen (Kevin James), longtime best friends, are hardworking partners in an auto-design firm. Persuasive and fast-talking Ronny is the sales director and technical genius Nick is the chief engineer. The pair is under great stress to produce the first electric muscle car for automotive giant Dodge. The deal is a once-in-a-lifetime dream opportunity that will expire if the two fail to meet their deadline. But the situation is complicated when Ronny visits a botanical garden and sees Nick's wife, Geneva (Winona Ryder), passionately kissing another man (Channing Tatum). Ronny is afraid to tell Nick about his wife's unfaithfulness as Nick, who is already buckling under the pressure of the Dodge project, may be devastated by the news and be unable to complete his work. Ronny tries to convince Geneva to end the affair, but she resents his interference and draws him into a dark adversarial relationship. Geneva becomes wicked, Ronny becomes desperate, and Geneva's hunky boy toy becomes violent. Are you laughing yet?

The Descendants (2011)

Matt King (George Clooney) struggles to cope after a boating accident leaves his wife, Elizabeth (Patricia Hastie), in a coma. It complicates matters when Alex (Shailene Woodley), Matt's teenage daughter, reveals to her father that Elizabeth was having an affair with a real estate agent, Brian Speer (Matthew Lillard). Matt finds out from Elizabeth's best friend that his wife felt neglected and planned to divorce him. He argues that Elizabeth was a spoiled daddy's girl who was selfish and demanded lots of attention. He says to Elizabeth as she lies comatose in bed, "Isn't the idea of marriage to make your partner's way in life a little easier? For me, it was always harder with you, and you're still making it harder." Matt sets out to find Brian to let him know that Elizabeth is dying. When they finally meet, he tells him, "Elizabeth is dying. Oh, wait. Fuck you. And she's dying." Brian is married and has two small children. He explains to Matt, "It was an affair, an attraction. It was sex. She got carried away with the whole thing, and I went with it. At least, I didn't say no to things that I should have. I love my family."

Silver Linings Playbook (2012)

Pat Solitano Jr. (Bradley Cooper), a teacher who suffers with bipolar disorder, becomes violent when he finds his wife Nikki (Brea Bee) in the shower with another man. He is convicted for brutally beating the man and is committed to a mental health facility. The film traces Pat's return to a normal life after being released from the facility. The novel, written by Matthew Quick, provides intriguing facts omitted from the film. Nikki, a literature teacher, educates her students on two adultery novels: "The Scarlet Letter" and "The Great Gatsby." Pat figures that it would make Nikki happy if he reads these books. In regards to "The Scarlet Letter," he wonders if Nikki "hypes up the racy stuff in her class. . ."[604] He hopes that some day he, like the adulteress' lover Arthur Dimmesdale, can stand in a public place with the unfaithful wife and "apologize for being such a jerk."[605] He thinks, "[Nikki] says 'The Great Gatsby' is the greatest novel ever written by an American, and yet it ends so sadly. One thing's for sure, Nikki is going to be very proud of me when I tell her I finally read her favorite book."[606] Where did a married woman get the idea that it's acceptable to invite a lover into your shower? Novels, novels.

Locke (2013)

The story centers on Ivan Locke (Tom Hardy). Ivan had a one-night stand with a co-worker, Bethan (Olivia Colman), seven months earlier. Bethan ended up pregnant from their hookup. Tonight, Locke learns that Bethan has gone into premature labor. Locke's wife and children are waiting for him at home to watch a football game, but Locke is determined to drive from Birmingham to London to be present for the birth.

Ine Marie Wilmann and Simon J. Berger in *Homesick* (2005)

Homesick (2015)

The original Norwegian title: *De nærmeste*

Charlotte (Ine Marie Wilmann) meets her half-brother Henrik (Simon J. Berger) for the first time. They find themselves oddly attracted to one another and, though Henrik is married with children, they embark on a sexual affair. IMDb noted, "[I]t becomes an encounter without boundaries between two people who don't know what a normal family is."[607]

Maggie's Plan (2015)

Maggie Hardin (Greta Gerwig) is attracted to John Harding (Ethan Hawke), who is a married man. Maggie persuades John to leave his wife, Georgette Nørgaard (Julianne Moore), and move in with her. Soon after, Maggie gives birth to a daughter, Lily. After three years, Maggie realizes that her relationship with

John isn't working and he was probably better off with Georgette. She figures to get the exes back together. She starts by visiting Georgette, who immediately becomes suspicious. She says:

Greta Gerwig and Ethan Hawke in *Maggie's Plan* (2015)

Oh, I see. I see. So you are tired of your little affair? You're all done with it. Now you want to make sure you don't feel guilty so you're going to manipulate us all into some absurd happy ending. I have met a lot of control freaks in my life - in fact, I thought I was one - but you make me look like an amateur. Have the decency to leave him and face the fact that you poisoned my life and my children's life, and probably John's life with your own selfishness. That's your burden. You earned it.

John and Georgette reconcile. Lily demonstrates an early math aptitude. Maggie suspects that her actual father is Guy Childers (Travis Fimmel), a math major that she dated before she met John. In the final moments of the film, Maggie is playing with Lily at an ice rink when she happens to see Guy walking in her direction. Fate has restored order in the universe.

Melora Walters and Tracy Letts in *The Lovers* (2017)

The Lovers (2017)

Mary (Debra Winger) and Michael (Tracy Letts) have grown distant in their marriage. Mary has found affection and intimacy with Robert (Aidan Gillen), a writer, while Michael has gotten cozy with a dancer, Lucy (Melora Walters). It distresses their lovers to see Mary and Michael suddenly renew their feelings for one another. The couple divorces and moves in with their respective lovers, but the final scene shows them whispering on the phone to arrange a date.

Alibi (2017)

Grégory Van Huffel (Philippe Lacheau) runs a company that provides alibis for cheating spouses. He is shocked when his new girlfriend, Flo Martin (Élodie Fontan), introduces him to her father, Gérard (Didier Bourdon), who is one of his best customers.

Beaux-parents (2019)

The English translation of this French title is *Parents-In-Law*.

Harold Becker (Bénabar) travels out of town to attend a corporate meeting. The boss' wife, Chloé Fleury (Gwendolyn Gourvenec), shows up at his hotel room just as he is getting ready for bed. She is drunk and tries to seduce him, but she vomits and passes out on his bed. Harold leaves and spends the night in another room. His wife, Garance (Charlie Bruneau), phones the room and is shocked when Chloé answers. She assumes, without a moment's doubt, that Harold is cheating. She does not accept Harold's explanation. No one can reason with her. She ejects Harold from their home. Garance's parents are fond of Harold, who they regard as a son, and continue to see him while struggling to keep it a secret from Garance.

Lockdown all'italiana (2020)

The lockdown forces a pair of adulterers and their respective spouses to live together in a modest apartment in Rome.

My Donkey, My Lover and I (2022)

Antoinette Lapouge (Laure Calamy), an elementary school teacher, is dating Vladimir Loubier (Benjamin Lavernhe), the married father of a young pupil. Antoinette is preparing to join Vladimir on a romantic getaway while his wife and daughter are away at the seaside. She is giddy at the thought of spending a full week alone with her lover. But Vladimir's wife abruptly changes her plans, insisting that the Loubier family visit a hiking trail in Cévennes National Park. Antoinette cannot bear to be alone on her vacation and figures that, if she travels to Cévennes, she might be able to spend time with Vladimir.

Antoinette, a novice hiker, embarks on her trip loaded down with hastily assembled hiking gear. She joins other hikers at a guest house at the starting point of the trail. A nosey woman asks her many questions during breakfast. She lies to the woman at first, but she becomes exhausted squirming around the truth and finally blurts out that she is out to find her married lover. This evokes awkward reactions among the hikers.

Laure Calamy in My Donkey, My Lover and I (2022)

Antoinette ends up on the trail with an uncooperative donkey named Patrick. In time, Patrick settles down and serves as a faithful companion. We get insight into Antoinette as she confides to Patrick about her bad history with men. She says that she feels relaxed around Vladimir and they laugh all of the time. She insists that it doesn't feel they are doing anything wrong and she sees no reason to be ashamed.

It becomes common knowledge along the trail that Antoinette is searching for her married lover. One woman becomes hostile toward her, but the others are either amused or sympathetic. One young woman admires her. She tells her, "You're a local hero. I think you're amazing. You're so brave."

After two days, Antoinette finally encounters Vladimir and his family at a stopover point. At night, while his wife Elénore (Olivia Côte) and his daughter Alice (Louise Vidal) are asleep in a dormitory, Vladimir follows Antoinette into a field and has sex with her.

Elénore has been acting friendly towards Antoinette, but she is wise to Antoinette's relationship with her husband. She gets her alone on the trail and has it out with her.

Elénore: How long has it been going on?

Antoinette: Pardon?

Elénore: I see you didn't plan to meet up. I know my husband. The poor thing. He's in such a state. Look at him.

Antoinette insists that she barely knows Vladimir. Elénore ignores her. She suggests that Antoinette gets excitement out of dating a married man - waiting for him, meeting him, and knowing that he won't stay around long. Elénore becomes brutally frank as she concludes her rebuke.

Elénore: Did he say we no longer fuck? If it was up to him, it'd be every night. In 10 years, he tried to jump me every day. Surprisingly, he has a big sexual appetite. Have you noticed? He just has to fuck. I'm grateful to you really. You and the others. You're not in love, are you?

Antoinette: I don't know what you're thinking, but I've never seen him outside school.

Elénore: He won't leave me. Do you know that? He won't.

Antoinette: Well, that's great. I'm pleased for you.

Elénore: We're so different, we never agree, but we have a bond. If ever we're apart, we call each other non-stop. We tell each other everything. We're a loving couple, dammit!

It is like cold water has been splashed into Antoinette's face. She realizes that she has been wasting her time with Vladimir and needs to stop seeing him. She meets a handsome young man on the trail. He convinces her to spend a few extra days at the park.

In the end, adultery is tragic but also silly. Its silliness is exposed in a scene from *Hannah and Her Sisters* (1986). Lee (Barbara Hershey) finds it unsettling when her brother-in-law, Elliot (Michael Caine), suddenly announces to her that he loves her. She insists that he shouldn't have told her this. He assures her that his marriage is "in the last stages." He explains that he and her sister, Hannah (Mia Farrow), are "going in different directions." He begs Lee to say that she loves him. Lee admits that she has "certain feelings" for Elliot, but she refuses to say anything else.

Lee: Elliot, please, I can't be a party to this. I'm suddenly wracked with guilt just talking to you.

Elliot: Your guilt is because you feel the same.

Lee: Oh, please, I have to go. I have to get my teeth cleaned.

Elliot: I have my answer. I have my answer. I'm walking on air!

Elliot sounds like a silly, needy, selfish child.

Let's allow Richard Taylor, the author of "Love Affairs: Marriage & Infidelity," to have the final word:

People who have. . . stayed together through the years. . . do have a justified basis for pride in what they have managed. . . And why should this not be praised? Surely, it seems, the world would be better if more married people did this, if they settled for what they had, instead of becoming discontented and abandoning their marriages. . . They swore to a lifetime commitment, so now let them do it.[608]

[1] "Adultery in literature," *Wikipedia*. https://en.wikipedia.org/wiki/Adultery_in_literature.

[2] Jeffbert, "QUICKSAND, in films, TV, novels, & reality," *Science Fiction & Fantasy Chronicles*, February 16, 2017. https://www.sffchronicles.com/threads/567203/.

[3] Daniel Engber, "Terra Infirma: The rise and fall of quicksand," *Slate*, August 23, 2010. http://www.slate.com/articles/health_and_science/science/2010/08/terra_infirma.html.

[4] Roxana Robinson, "Teaching 'Madame Bovary,'" *The New Yorker*, November 5, 2017. https://www.newyorker.com/culture/culture-desk/teaching-madame-bovary.

[5] Hal Erickson. "Remorques (1939)," *AllMovie Guide*. https://www.allmovie.com/movie/remorques-v47051.

[6] "Melodrama," *Wikipedia*. https://en.wikipedia.org/wiki/Melodrama.

[7] Richard Dyer, *Brief Encounter (BFI Film Classics)*, United Kingdom: British Film Institute (December 27, 1993).

[8] The Sexperts, "The History Of Dating in America," *SexInfo Online*, March 23, 2018. https://sexinfoonline.com/the-history-of-dating-in-america/.

[9] Alain de Botton, "How Romantic Ideas Destroy Your Chance at Love," *Time*, June 2, 2016. https://time.com/4354465/romanticism-relationships/.

[10] *Ibid.*

[11] *Ibid.*

[12] David Lutz, "The Institution of Marriage and the Virtuous Society," *Institute for Family Studies*, February 15, 2021). https://ifstudies.org/blog/the-institution-of-marriage-and-the-virtuous-society.

[13] David Kelly, "Fidelity and Adultery at the Movies: From F.W. Murnau's Sunrise to David Lean's Brief Encounter," *Sydney Studies in English*, Vol. 42, January 1, 2016. pp. 102-138.

[14] "The Motion Picture Production Code of 1930 (Hays Code)," Joseph Smith Foundation. https://josephsmithfoundation.org/docs/the-motion-picture-production-code-of-1930-hays-code/.

[15] *Ibid.*

[16] *Ibid.*

[17] Jeanine Basinger and Sam Wasson, *Hollywood: The Oral History*, New York City: Harper, November 8, 2022, p. 2.

[18] *Ibid.*

[19] Hehir, Colleen, "Movies And TV Shows Love To Romanticize Cheating And It Is Ruining Real People's Perceptions," *Odyssey*, August 6, 2018. https://www.theodysseyonline.com/movies-romanticize-cheating.

[20] Leo Tolstoy, "Epilogue to The Kreutzer Sonata," The University of Minnesota. http://lol-russ.umn.edu/hpgary/russ1905/epilogue%20to%20kreutzer%20sonata.htm.

[21] "La Grande Bretèche," *The Moving Picture World*, Volume 5 Number 25, December 18, 1909) pp.889. https://ia600607.us.archive.org/BookReader/BookReaderImages.php?id=moviewor05chal&itemPath=%2F9%2Fitems%2Fmoviewor05chal&server=ia600607.us.archive.org&page=leaf000895.

[22] "La Grande Bretèche," *Wikipedia*. https://en.wikipedia.org/wiki/La_Grande_Bret%C3%A8che.

[23] *Ibid.*

[24] *Ibid.*

[25] Oscar Cooper, "The Unfaithful Wife," *Motion*

Picture News, December 18, 1918, page 83.

[26] *Ibid.*

[27] "Photoplays from Essanay's Coming Features," *Motography*, Vol. VIII, No. 10, November 9, 2012). pp. 372. https://ia800304.us.archive.org/BookReader/BookReaderImages.php?id=motography78elec&itemPath=%2F7%2Fitems%2Fmotography78elec&server=ia800304.us.archive.org&page=leaf000734.

[28] "The Cameraman's Revenge (1912)," *IMDb*. https://www.imdb.com/title/tt0001527/plotsummary.

[29] Red-Barracuda. "At home with The Beetles" (User review), *IMDb*, April 2, 2012. https://www.imdb.com/title/tt0001527/reviews?ref_=tt_urv.

[30] Lon & Debra Davis, *CHASE! A Tribute to the Keystone Cops*, BearManor Media, Florida: Orlando, 2020.

[31] Les Adams, "Damaged Goodness (1917)," *IMDb*. https://www.imdb.com/title/tt0321884/plotsummary?ref_=tt_ov_pl.

[32] Pamela Short, "The Soul Market (1916)," *IMDb*. https://www.imdb.com/title/tt0007377/plotsummary?ref_=tt_ov_pl.

[33] Laurence Reid, "Heart's Haven," *Motion Picture News*, August 12, 1922.

[34] Imogen Sara Smith, "Husbands and Lovers," *San Francisco Silent Film Festival* (2019). https://silentfilm.org/husbands-and-lovers/.

[35] Gordon Gassaway, "Introducing Every Woman's 'Little Devil,'" *Picture-Play Magazine*, Volume XII, No. 6,August, 1920). pp. 64. https://ia600309.us.archive.org/BookReader/BookReaderImages.php?id=pictureplaymagaz12unse&itemPath=%2F0%2Fitems%2Fpictureplaymagaz12unse&server=ia600309.us.archive.org&page=leaf000597.

[36] Frank Fob, "The Marriage Whirl (1925)," *IMDb*. https://www.imdb.com/title/tt0016093/plotsummary?ref_=tt_ov_pl.

[37] David Kelly.

[38] "Filmsite Movie Review: Sunrise (1927)," *Filmsite*. https://www.filmsite.org/sunr.html.

[39] *Ibid.*

[40] Roger Ebert, "Sunrise," *Roger Ebert Website*, April 11, 2004. https://www.rogerebert.com/reviews/great-movie-sunrise-1928.

[41] "Sunrise Review," *TV Guide*. https://www.tvguide.com/movies/sunrise/review/2000048416/.

[42] Martin Scorsese, *A Personal Journey with Martin Scorsese Through American Movies Part II*, British Film Institute (1995).

[43] Ebert.

[44] Ann Toplovich, "Marriage, Mayhem, & Presidential Politics: The Robards-Jackson Backcountry Scandal," *Alabama Trails*. http://alabamatrailswar1812.com/Rachel%20and%20Andrew%20Jackson.htm.

[45] James Parton, *Life of Andrew Jackson In Three Volumes: Volume 1*, New York: Mason Brothers (1860), 148.

[46] Ann Toplovich.

[47] *Ibid.*

[48] *Ibid.*

[49] *Ibid.*

[50] *Ibid.*

[51] *Ibid.*

[52] *Ibid.*

[53] Charles Hammond, "View of General Jackson's

Domestic Relations, " as quoted in Norma Basch, "Marriage, Morals, and Politics in the 1828 Election," 905.

54 *Ibid.*

55 Ellen Eineck, "Political Agent: Emma Hamilton's many identities," *Royal Museums Greenwich*, March 7, 2018. https://www.rmg.co.uk/stories/blog/curatorial/political-agent-emma-hamiltons-many-identities.

56 Jean Giono, *Blue Boy*, Redditch, Worcestershire: Read Books Ltd., April 26, 2013, 1.

57 Walter Walsh, *The Greater Parables of Leo Tolstoy*, London: C. W. Daniel, 1906, 146.

58 "The Baker's Wife (film)," *Wikipedia*. https://en.wikipedia.org/wiki/The_Baker%27s_Wife_(film).

59 Frank Pittman, *Private Lies: Infidelity and the Betrayal of Intimacy*, New York City: W. W. Norton & Company (1990), p. 122.

60 "Ni tuyo, Ni mía (2020)," *IMDb*. https://www.imdb.com/title/tt4057720/.

61 planktonrules, "Mr Illington is married and didn't even know it!," *IMDb*, January 23, 2019. https://www.imdb.com/review/rw4601284/?ref_=tt_urv.

62 Hal Erickson, "A Letter to Three Wives (1949)," *AllMovie Guide*. https://www.allmovie.com/movie/a-letter-to-three-wives-v29115.

63 Jessica Burke, ""Open Marriage' Is Just Another Term For Adultery, And Just As Selfish," *The Federalist*, May 15, 2017. https://thefederalist.com/2017/05/15/open-marriage-just-another-term-adultery-just-selfish/.

64 Hal Erickson, "Illicit (1931)," *AllMovie Guide*. https://www.allmovie.com/movie/illicit-v96301.

65 David Parkinson, "La Séparation," *Radio Times*. https://www.radiotimes.com/movie-guide/b-hii291/la-sparation/.

66 Jim Tritten, "The Road to Singapore (1931)," *IMDb*, August 1, 2003. https://www.imdb.com/review/rw0008417/.

67 "The Vampire," *The Film Index*, October 29, 1910. pp. 11.

68 "Manufacturers Advance Notes," *The Moving Picture World*, Vol. 18, No. 1, October 4, 1913. pp. 51.

69 "The Siren's Reign (1915)," *IMDb*. https://www.imdb.com/title/tt0229728/.

70 "The Destroyer (1915)," *IMDb*. https://www.imdb.com/title/tt0229333/plotsummary#synopsis.

71 "Stories of the Films," *The Moving Picture World*, April 24, 1915, 616. https://ia600703.us.archive.org/BookReader/BookReaderImages.php?id=movingpicturewor24newy&itemPath=%2F3%2Fitems%2Fmovingpicturewor24newy&server=ia600703.us.archive.org&page=leaf000648.

72 "Comments on the Films," *The Moving Picture World*, March 14, 1914, 1385. https://ia802904.us.archive.org/BookReader/BookReaderImages.php?id=movingpicturewor19newy&itemPath=%2F9%2Fitems%2Fmovingpicturewor19newy&server=ia802904.us.archive.org&page=leaf0001427.

73 "Manufacturers Advance Notes," *The Moving Picture World*, February 28, 1914, 1106. https://ia802904.us.archive.org/BookReader/BookReaderImages.php?id=movingpicturewor19newy&itemPath=%2F9%2Fitems%2Fmovingpicturewor19newy&server=ia802904.us.archive.org&page=leaf0001142.

74 "Siren's Charms Lead Her to Death," *Motography*, Vol. XII, No. 8, August 22, 1914, 1. https://ia600701.us.archive.org/BookReader/BookReaderImages.php?id=motography12elec&itemPath=%2F20%2Fitems%2Fmotography12elec&server=ia600701.us.archive.org&page=leaf000299.

[75] *Ibid.*

[76] *Ibid.*

[77] "Stories of the Films," *The Moving Picture World*, October 30, 1915), 866. https://ia600702.us.archive.org/BookReader/BookReaderImages.php?id=moviwor26chal&itemPath=%2F5%2Fitems%2Fmoviwor26chal&server=ia600702.us.archive.org&page=leaf000890.

[78] *The Moving Picture World*, November 13, 1915, 1266. https://ia800309.us.archive.org/BookReader/BookReaderImages.php?id=movinwor26chal&itemPath=%2F4%2Fitems%2Fmovinwor26chal&server=ia800309.us.archive.org&page=leaf000228.

[79] Fritzi Kramer, "A Fool There Was," *Movies Silently*, November 1, 2015. https://moviessilently.com/2015/11/01/a-fool-there-was-1915-a-silent-film-review/.

[80] *Ibid.*.

[81] "A Fool There Was (1915)," *AFI Catalog of Feature Films*. https://catalog.afi.com/Catalog/moviedetails/18193.

[82] Leo Tolstoy, *The Kreutzer Sonata and Other Stories*. United Kingdom: Oxford University Press (1998), 157.

[83] Leo Tolstoy, "Epilogue to The Kreutzer Sonata," The University of Minnesota. http://lol-russ.umn.edu/hpgary/russ1905/epilogue%20to%20kreutzer%20sonata.htm.

[84] "The New York Peacock," *Motography*, February 17, 1917, 375.

[85] Edward Weitzel, "The New York Peacock," *The Moving Picture World*, February 24, 1917), 1207.

[86] "Intoxication (1919)," *IMDb*. https://www.imdb.com/title/tt0010612/plotsummary?ref_=tt_ov_pl.

[87] Janiss Garza, "The Wild Goose (1921)," *All-Movie Guide*. https://www.allmovie.com/movie/v117036.

[88] *Ibid.*

[89] Laurence Reid, "The Wild Goose," *Motion Picture News*, May 21, 1921, 3225. https://ia601306.us.archive.org/BookReader/BookReaderImages.php?id=motionpicturenew23moti_7&itemPath=%2F2%2Fitems%2Fmotionpicturenew23moti_7&server=ia601306.us.archive.org&page=leaf000363.

[90] "Foolish Wives," *Wikipedia*. https://en.wikipedia.org/wiki/Foolish_Wives.

[91] "Through the Box-Office Window," *The Moving Picture World*, December 3, 1927. pp. 27.

[92] Imogen Sara Smith (2019). Audio Commentary: *It Always Rains on Sunday* (1947). [Film; Blu-ray]. Kino Lorber.

[93] *Ibid.*

[94] "gold digger," *Merriam-Webster*, https://www.merriam-webster.com/dictionary/gold%20digger.

[95] "Gold Digger," *Wikipedia*. https://en.wikipedia.org/wiki/Gold_Digger.

[96] Hal Erickson, "They Knew What They Wanted (1940)," *AllMovie Guide*. https://www.allmovie.com/movie/they-knew-what-they-wanted-v49414.

[97] Hal Erickson, "The Secret Hour," *AllMovie Guide*. https://www.allmovie.com/movie/the-secret-hour-v109278

[98] planktonrules, "Not ANOTHER Kay Francis adultery film!!!!," *IMDb*, December 24, 2006). https://m.imdb.com/review/rw1553236/?ref_=tt_urv.

[99] Janiss Garza "The Next Corner (1924)," *All-Movie Guide*. https://www.allmovie.com/movie/next-corner-v103855.

[100] "The Next Corner," *Wikipedia*.

https://en.wikipedia.org/wiki/The_Next_Corner.

[101] "The Iron Man (1931 film)," *Wikipedia*. https://en.wikipedia.org/wiki/Iron_Man_(1931_film).

[102] *Picture Play Magazine*, October 1932, 60.

[103] Kim Luperi, "Pre-Code Bachelor's Affairs Are Never Dull, That's for Sure!," *I See a Dark Theater*, July 27, 2015). https://www.iseeadarktheater.com/bachelors-affairs.

[104] Scott Nye, "Bachelor's Affairs (1932)," *Letterboxd*, March 8, 2015. https://letterboxd.com/film/bachelors-affairs/.

[105] frankfob2, "Love Bound," *IMDb*. https://www.imdb.com/title/tt0023155/plotsummary.

[106] "One Hour with You (1932)," *IMDb*. https://www.imdb.com/title/tt0023303/?ref_=fn_al_tt_1.

[107] John Oswalt, "One Hour with You (1932)," *IMDb*. https://www.imdb.com/title/tt0023303/?ref_=fn_al_tt_1.

[108] "Black and White Beaded Chemise Dress From the Wardrobe of Theda Bara Circa 1925," *Doyle*. https://doyle.com/auctions/0205221-couture-textiles-and-accessories/catalogue/105-black-and-white-beaded-chemise.

[109] nnnn45089191, "Has to be seen to be believed," *IMDb*, January 31, 2007. https://www.imdb.com/review/rw1587324/.

[110] "Red-Headed Woman," *Wikipedia*. https://en.wikipedia.org/wiki/Red-Headed_Woman.

[111] "Downstairs (film)," *Wikipedia*. https://en.wikipedia.org/wiki/Downstairs_(film).

[112] Hal Erickson, "Flesh (1932)," *AllMovie Guide*. https://www.allmovie.com/movie/flesh-v91710.

[113] "Sins of The Fathers (1928)," *AFI Catalog of Feature Films*. https://catalog.afi.com/Film/1683-SINS-OFTHEFATHERS?sid=93623deb-d809-41ba-a534-46673bbcf88c&sr=0.1106916&cp=1&pos=0.

[114] *Ibid.*

[115] Britannica, "A Lost Lady." https://www.britannica.com/topic/A-Lost-Lady.

[116] SuperSummary, "A Lost Lady." https://www.supersummary.com/a-lost-lady/summary/.

[117] James Leslie Woodress, *Willa Cather A Literary Life*, Lincoln: University of Nebraska Press, 1987, p. 346.

[118] SuperSummary.

[119] Britannica.

[120] Indianapolis Times, October 20, 1934, p. 14.

[121] The Sexperts.

[122] bkoganbing, "The Elliot Sisters of Broken Bow," *IMDb*, September 13, 2007. https://www.imdb.com/review/rw1729305/?ref_=tt_urv.

[123] "The Women (1939 film)," *Wikipedia*. https://en.wikipedia.org/wiki/The_Women_(1939_film).

[124] "Gone with the Wind." *Purity and Precision*. http://www.purityandprecision.com/2015/04/gone-with-wind.html.

[125] Hal Erickson, "Marriage Is a Private Affair (1944)," *AllMovie Guide*. https://www.allmovie.com/movie/marriage-is-a-private-affair-v101688.

[126] Sandra Brennan, "Divorce (1945)," *AllMovie Guide*. https://www.allmovie.com/movie/divorce-v89601.

[127] "The Egg and I (1947)," *AFI Catalog of Feature Films*.

https://catalog.afi.com/Catalog/moviedetails/2515 3.

[128] "East Side, West Side, DVD Overview," *Warner Archives*, February 7, 2017. https://www.barnesandnoble.com/w/dvd-east-side-west-side-barbara-stanwyck/3873022.

[129] "Licensed Film Stories," The Moving Picture World,August 1, 1914. p. 732. https://ia802802.us.archive.org/BookReader/Book ReaderImag- es.php?id=movingpicturewor21newy&itemPath= %2F20%2Fitems%2Fmovingpicturewor21newy& serv- er=ia802802.us.archive.org&page=leaf000756.

[130] "Born to be Bad (1950 film)," *Wikipedia*. https://en.wikipedia.org/wiki/Born_to_Be_Bad_(1 950_film).

[131] Mel Gordon, *Theatre of Fear and Horror: The Grisly Spectacle of the Grand Guignol of Par- is,1897-1962*, Port Townsend, WA: Feral House, August 9, 2016.

[132] "Grand Guignol," *Wikipedia*. https://en.wikipedia.org/wiki/Grand_Guignol.

[133] "Good Lord Without Confession," *Wikipedia*. https://en.wikipedia.org/wiki/Good_Lord_Without _Confession.

[134] Thomas O. Harris, The Kingfish: Huey P. Long, Dictator, Gretna, Louisiana: Pelican Pub- lishing Company (2001), page 4.

[135] "The Earrings of Madame de... (1953)," *Wik- ipedia*. https://en.wikipedia.org/wiki/The_Earrings_of_M adame_de%E2%80%A6.

[136] *The Criterion Collection DVD (2008), The Earrings of Madame de. . . DVD Liner Notes, The Criterion Collection.* pp 23.

[137] Terrell-4, "One of Max Ophuls most elegant and saddest films," *IMDb,*February 6, 2008). https://www.imdb.com/review/rw1815125/?ref_=t t_urv.

[138] Chamberlain, John,October 17, 1935). "Books of the Times," The New York Times.

[139] John O'Hara, *BUtterfield 8*, Penguin Books (2013). pp. 3. First published by Harcourt, Brace and Company in 1935.

[140] Henry Gonshak, "Resurrecting a Minor Writer: BUtterfield 8 and The New York Stories by John O'Hara," *The Quivering Pen*, December 5, 2013). https://davidabramsbooks.blogspot.com/2013/12/r esurrecting-minor-writer-butterfield-8.html.

[141] Liz Locke, "BUtterfield 8," *Cinema Sips*, Oc- tober 14, 2019). https://cinemasips.com/2019/10/14/butterfi eld-8/.

[142] "Zandalee," *IMDb*. https://m.imdb.com/title/tt0101004/plotsummary/? ref_=kw_pl#synopsis.

[143] "Say Nothing (2001)," *IMDb*. https://www.imdb.com/title/tt0288808/.

[144] "Exile (1917)," *IMDb*. https://www.imdb.com/title/tt0007907/plotsumma ry?ref_=tt_ov_pl.

[145] "Jack Holt in Vengeance," *Weekly Kinema Guide: London suburban reviews and pro- grammes*, December 1, 1930, page 14.

[146] *Ibid.*

[147] A. F. Botsford, "What the Picture Did for Me," *Exhibitors Herald-World*, March 29, 1930, page 55.

[148] Les Adams, "White Heat (1934)," *IMDb*. https://www.imdb.com/title/tt0025985/plotsummar y?ref_=tt_ov_pl.

[149] "The Heart of the Matter (1953)," *IMDb*. https://www.imdb.com/title/tt0047066/?ref_=fn_al _tt_1.

[150] Ruth Prawer Jhabvala, *Heat and Dust*, New York: Harper & Row, 1976, page 17.

[151] Sheila O'Malley, "Other Men's Women (1931)," *The Shelia Variations,*October 9, 2010. http://www.sheilaomalley.com/?p=28355.

152 "Guinevere or Gwenhwyfar, Gwenivar, Guenevere, or Guenever - Queen of Camelot," A Land of Myth and A Time of Magic. https://alandofmythandatimeofmagic.weebly.com/guineviere.html.

153 "Bed and Sofa," *Wikipedia*. https://en.wikipedia.org/wiki/Bed_and_Sofa.

154 "Vampire Reviews," *TV Guide*. https://www.tvguide.com/movies/vampire/review/2030093774/.

155 "Guest in the House (1944)," *AFI Catalog of Feature Films*. https://catalog.afi.com/Film/1378-GUEST-INTHEHOUSE?sid=b48129e8-a831-4a8a-b265-b322a348e1be&sr=11.623656&cp=1&pos=0.

156 Tony Williams, *Structures of Desire: British Cinema, 1939 to 1955*, Albany: State University of New York Press (2000).

157 *Ibid.*

158 *Ibid.*

159 Janiss Garza "A Private Scandal (1921)," *All-Movie Guide*. https://www.allmovie.com/movie/a-private-scandal-v131065.

160 Edith Wharton, *Ethan Frome and Other Short Fiction*, New York, NY: Random House Publishing Group, September 25, 2007. pp. 108.

161 *Ibid.*

162 "Ethan Frome," *Wikipedia*. https://en.wikipedia.org/wiki/Ethan_Frome.

163 Rita Kempley, "Ethan Frome," *Washington Post*, March 19, 1993. https://www.washingtonpost.com/wp-srv/style/longterm/movies/videos/ethanfromepgkempley_a0a367.htm.

164 "Freaks (1932 film)," *Wikipedia*. https://en.wikipedia.org/wiki/Freaks_(1932_film).

165 Hal Erickson, "Pitfall (1948)," *AllMovie Guide*. https://www.allmovie.com/movie/pitfall-v38247.

166 "Agamemnon (Play)," *World History Encyclopedia*. https://www.worldhistory.org/Agamemnon_(Play)/.

167 "Up for Murder.," *Wikipedia*. https://en.wikipedia.org/wiki/Up_for_Murder.

168 Molly, "Death Becomes Her: The Kiss Before the Mirror (1933)," *Dreaming in The Balcony*, July 19, 2017. https://dreaminginthebalcony.wordpress.com/2017/07/19/death-becomes-her-the-kiss-before-the-mirror-1933/.

169 "The Kiss Before The Mirror (1933)," *Obscure Hollywood*, https://obscurehollywood.net/the-kiss-before-the-mirror-1933.html.

170 *Obscure Hollywood.*

171 "Stories of Films," *The Moving Picture World*, January 22, 1916. pp. 672. https://ia802800.us.archive.org/BookReader/BookReaderImages.php?id=movingpicturewor27newy&itemPath=%2F26%2Fitems%2Fmovingpicturewor27newy&server=ia802800.us.archive.org&page=leaf000716.

172 Pamela Short, "Plot Summary of Playing with Fire (1916)," *IMDb*. https://www.imdb.com/title/tt0007190/plotsummary.

173 Alexander Walker, *Bette Davis: A Celebration*, Boston, MA: Little Brown & Co, January 1, 1986, p. 264.

174 Farran Smith Nehme, "The Letter (1940)," *Self-Styled Siren*, March 3, 2008. http://selfstyledsiren.blogspot.com/2008/03/letter-1940.html.

175 Jan Herman, *A Talent for Trouble: The Life Of Hollywood's Most Acclaimed Director, William Wyler*, New York: Da Capo Press, August 22, 1997, page 78.

176 Nehme.

[177] Herman, page 185.

[178] hitchcockthelegend, "Anodyne affected affairs of the heart," *IMDb*, August 29, 2013. https://www.imdb.com/review/rw2859867/.

[179] Linda Rasmussen, "Double Indemnity (1944)," *AllMovie Guide*. https://www.allmovie.com/movie/double-indemnity-v14457.

[180] "Summer Storm (1944 film)," *Wikipedia*. https://en.wikipedia.org/wiki/Summer_Storm_(1944_film).

[181] Hal Erickson, "Black Angel (1946)," AllMovie. https://www.allmovie.com/movie/black-angel-v85153.

[182] brogmiller,"Naughty baby," *IMDb*, June 12, 2020. https://www.imdb.com/review/rw5818096/?ref_=tt_urv.

[183] "La Verité sur Bébé Donge (Lost & Found for Sight & Sound)," *The Self-Styled Siren*, June 1, 2015. http://selfstyledsiren.blogspot.com/2015/06/la-verite-sur-bebe-donge-lost-found-for.html.

[184] Lola Walser, *Goodreads*, December 4, 2019. https://www.goodreads.com/book/show/9748532-la-verit-su-b-b-donge.

[185] Hal Erickson, "Blowing Wild (1953)," *AllMovie*. https://www.allmovie.com/movie/blowing-wild-v6216.

[186] Paul Gordon, *Dial 'M' for Mother: A Freudian Hitchcock*, Vancouver: Fairleigh Dickinson University Press, April 1, 2008. p. p 216.

[187] melvelvit-1, "A James Hadley Chase 'noir' that puts a new spin on old favorites," *IMDb*, March 15, 2014. https://www.imdb.com/review/rw2979993/.

[188] "Cinema: The Man Who Understood Women," *Time*, October 19, 1959.https://content.time.com/time/subscriber/article/0,33009,869337,00.html.

[189] "Station Six Sahara (1963)," *AFI Catalog of Feature Films*. https://www.tcm.com/tcmdb/title/91350/station-six-sahara#synopsis.

[190] "A Woman for All Men," *IMDb*, https://www.imdb.com/title/tt0316900/.

[191] Roy Stafford, Adapting Highsmith #1: Deep Water," *The Case for The Global Film*, September 2, 2016. https://itpworld.wordpress.com/2016/09/02/adapting-highsmith-deep-water-eaux-profondes-france-1981/.

[192] Desson Howe, "'Faithful' to a Fault," *The Washington Post*. https://www.washingtonpost.com/wp-srv/style/longterm/movies/videos/faithful.htm.

179 John Bingham, *Five Roundabouts to Heaven*, New York City: Simon & Schuster, July 17, 2007, page 41.

[194] H. H. Niemeyer, "The Great Gatsby," *St. Louis Post-Dispatch*, November 15, 1926, p. 17.

[195] Epes W. Sargent, "The Great Gatsby," *Moving Picture World*, December 4, 1926, p. 365.

[196] Patrick McGilligan, editor, *Backstory 1: Interviews with Screenwriters of Hollywood's Golden Age*, Los Angeles: University of California Press, 1986, p. 280.

[197] *Ibid.*

[198] F. Scott Fitzgerald, *The Great Gatsby*, Peterborough, Ontario: Broadview Press, March 26, 2007, p.117.

[199] Fitzgerald, p. 133.

[200] *Ibid.*

[201] gftbiloxi, "Memorable But Flawed Version of the Stage Classic," *IMDb*, March 29, 2005. https://www.imdb.com/review/rw1049343/?ref_=tt_urv.

[202] Melanie Novak, "Come and Get It (1936): Bad

Adaptation, Great Film," *Melanie Novak*, February 15, 2022. https://melanienovak.com/2022/02/15/come-and-get-it-1936-bad-adaptation-great-film/.

203 Sandra Brennan, "Brief Ecstasy (1937)," *All-Movie Guide*. https://www.allmovie.com/movie/brief-ecstasy-v85986.

204 Kat Ellinger, Audio Commentary Track for *Singapore* Blu-ray, Kino Lorber, April 26, 2022.

205 *Ibid.*

206 Disgustipated, "The Passionate Friends," *Letterboxd*, October 27, 2016. https://letterboxd.com/karmanoodle/film/the-passionate-friends/.

207 "Untamed (1955)," *IMDb*. https://www.imdb.com/title/tt0048767/?ref_=nv_sr_srsg_0.

208 "A Summer Place (1959)" *Rotten Tomatoes*. https://www.rottentomatoes.com/m/summer_place.

209 Jorge Amado, *Dona Flor and Her Two Husbands*, New York City: Knopf Doubleday Publishing Group, September 12, 2006, p. 102.

210 Amado, p. 473.

211 Amado, p. 548.

212 Ada Pîrvu, "François Truffaut's Heroines: Part II," *The Big Picture*, February 22, 2020. http://thebigpicturemagazine.com/franc%CC%A7ois-truffauts-heroines-part-ii/.

213 moonspinner55, "Handsome, but dull, vapid example of the Woman's Picture," *IMDb*, April 28, 2006. https://www.imdb.com/review/rw1354311/?ref_=tt_urv.

214 Roger Ebert, "Violets Are Blue," *RogerEbert.com*, April 25, 1986. https://www.rogerebert.com/reviews/violets-are-blue-1986.

215 Mick LaSalle, *The Beauty of the Real: What Hollywood Can Learn from Contemporary French Actresses*, Stanford, CA: Stanford General Books, May 9, 2012, 139.

216 Shelia O'Malley, "Both Sides of the Blade," *RogerEbert.com*, July 8, 2022. https://www.rogerebert.com/reviews/both-sides-of-the-blade-2022.

217 derek-duerden, "So Much Dialogue," *IMDb*, January 4, 2023. https://www.imdb.com/review/rw8778875/?ref_=tt_urv.

218 John Serba, "Stream It Or Skip It: 'Tonight You're Sleeping With Me' on Netflix, a Dull, Passionless Polish Rom-Dram," *Decider*, March 1, 2023. https://decider.com/2023/03/01/stream-it-or-skip-it-tonight-youre-sleeping-with-me-on-netflix-a-dull-passionless-polish-rom-dram/.

219 *Ibid.*

220 Stacey Laura Lloyd, "The Real Reasons Why Men Cheat," *The List*, May 4, 2022. https://www.thelist.com/32353/real-reasons-men-cheat/.

221 Perel, Esther, "Why Happy People Cheat", *The Atlantic*, October, 2017. https://www.theatlantic.com/magazine/archive/2017/10/why-happy-people-cheat/537882/.

222 planktonrules, "Definitely Pre-Code in its sensibilities," *IMDb*, January 21 2019. https://www.imdb.com/review/rw4598199/?ref_=tt_urv.

223 "Unfaithful (1931)." *AFI Catalog of Feature Films*. https://catalog.afi.com/Catalog/moviedetails/6394.

224 lbbrooks3, "Only Dunne Saves This Potboiler!," *IMDb*, January 20, 2017. https://www.imdb.com/review/rw3630885/?ref_=tt_urv.

225 "MOVIE #71 Easy Living (1949)," *Everything Lucy*. https://everythinglucy.youns.com/movies/movie-71.html.

226 bkoganbing, "The Rise And Fall Of A Marriage," *IMDb*, June 16, 2010. https://www.imdb.com/review/rw2265317/?ref_=tt_urv.

227 Adrian Danks, "Petulia, mon amour," *Senses of Cinema*, August 2008. https://www.sensesofcinema.com/2008/cteq/petulia/.

228 *Ibid.*

229 Dennis Schwartz, "Petulia," *Dennis Schwartz Movie Reviews*, August 5, 2019. https://dennisschwartzreviews.com/petulia/.

230 Walt Mundkowsky, "Time Capsule Cinema: Petulia," *Traveling Boy*. https://travelingboy.com/travel/time-capsule-cinema-the-knack-how-to-misuse-it/.

231 *Ibid.*

232 "Diary of a Mad Housewife," *Wikipedia*. https://en.wikipedia.org/wiki/Diary_of_a_Mad_Housewife.

233 Roger Ebert, "Ju Dou," *RogerEbert.com*, April 12, 1991. https://www.rogerebert.com/reviews/ju-dou-1991.

234 "The Piano," *StudioCanal*. https://www.studiocanal.com/title/the-piano-1993/.

235 Joanna Di Mattia, "The Heart Asks Pleasure First: Economies of Touch and Desire in Jane Campion's The Piano (1993)," *Senses of Cinema*, September 2017. https://www.sensesofcinema.com/2017/cteq/the-piano/.

236 Josh Larsen, "The Piano," *Larsen on Film*, October 16, 2021. https://www.larsenonfilm.com/the-piano.

237 Artemis-9, "A Modern Eve (1907)," *IMDb*. https://www.imdb.com/title/tt1032908/plotsummary?ref_=tt_ov_pl.

238 Bruce Calvert, "Too Wise Wives (1921)," *All-Movie Guide*. https://www.allmovie.com/movie/too-wise-wives-v50408.

239 Owen, "The Marriage Circle (1924)," *Letterboxd*, August 29, 2014. https://letterboxd.com/owene73/film/the-marriage-circle/.

240 Isabella McNeill, "Nuanced Complexity: The Marriage Circle (Ernst Lubitsch, 1924) and the Early Days of the 'Lubitsch Touch'," *Senses of Cinema*, CTEQ Annotations on Film, Issue 83, June 2017. https://www.sensesofcinema.com/2017/cteq/the-marriage-circle/.

241 "The Coast of Folly (1925)," *AFI Catalog of Feature Films*. https://catalog.afi.com/Film/3361-THE-COASTOFFOLLY.

242 Ed Lorusso, "Gloria Swanson and The Coast of Folly," *Silent Room*, July 25, 2018. https://silentroomdotblog.wordpress.com/2018/07/25/gloria-swanson-and-the-coast-of-folly/.

243 "Sin Takes a Holiday (1930)," *IMDb*. https://www.imdb.com/title/tt0021377/?ref_=nv_sr_srsg_0.

244 Curtis Yarvin, "Why the bums always lose," *Gray Mirror*, February 2, 2021. https://graymirror.substack.com/p/why-the-bums-always-lose.

245 "Forbidden (1932 film)," *Wikipedia*. https://en.wikipedia.org/wiki/Forbidden_(1932_film).

246 "Lord of the Manor (film)," *Wikipedia*. https://en.wikipedia.org/wiki/Lord_of_the_Manor_(film).

247 planktonrules, "A Pre-Code comedy about the wacky world of adultery," *IMDb*, April 11, 2011. https://www.imdb.com/review/rw2412360/?ref_=tt_urv.

248 Arthur Hausner, "Our Betters (1933)," *IMDb*. https://www.imdb.com/title/tt0024421/plotsummary.

249 Roger Ebert, "The Rules of the Game," *Roger-Ebert.com*, February 29, 2004. https://www.rogerebert.com/reviews/great-movie-the-rules-of-the-game-1939.

250 dougdoepke. "Women Behaving Badly," *IMDb*, January 21, 2010). https://www.imdb.com/review/rw2194962/?mode=desktop&ref_=m_ft_dsk.

251 jery-tillotson-1, "Darling Julie," *IMDb*, June 14, 2017. imdb.com/review/rw3730692/?ref_=tt_urv.

252 *Ibid.*

253 "Darling (1965 film)," *Wikipedia*. https://en.wikipedia.org/wiki/Darling_(1965_film).

254 White Mischief, *IMDb*. https://www.imdb.com/title/tt0094317/plotsummary/.

255 pfgpowell-1, "Extremely good and faithful version of Waugh's classic satire," *IMDb*, October 24, 2009. https://www.imdb.com/review/rw2146049/.

256 Roger Ebert, "The Ice Storm," *Roger Ebert*, October 17, 1997. https://www.rogerebert.com/reviews/the-ice-storm-1997.

257 "The Ice Storm," *Wikipedia*. https://en.wikipedia.org/wiki/The_Ice_Storm.

258 "Your Friends and Neighbors," *Wikipedia*. https://en.wikipedia.org/wiki/Your_Friends_%26_Neighbors.

259 *Ibid.*

260 Philip French, "Keep your shirt on. . .," The Guardian, September 12, 1999. https://www.theguardian.com/film/1999/sep/12/philipfrench.

261 Robert Temple, "Absolutely delightful in every way," *IMDb*, October 6, 2011. https://www.imdb.com/review/rw2499085/.

262 *Ibid.*

263 "Othello," *Spark Notes*. https://www.sparknotes.com/nofear/shakespeare/othello/.

264 "Wives Under Suspicion," *Amazon Prime*. https://www.amazon.com/Wives-Under-Suspicion-Warren-William/dp/B000SAO3AK.

265 "I Take This Woman (1940)," *AFI Catalog of Feature Films*. https://catalog.afi.com/Catalog/moviedetails/5063.

266 "Unfaithfully Yours (1948 film)," *Wikipedia*. https://en.wikipedia.org/wiki/Unfaithfully_Yours_(1948_film).

267 "Never Say Goodbye (1956 film)," *Wikipedia*. https://en.wikipedia.org/wiki/Never_Say_Goodbye_(1956_film).

268 Andrew Pragasam, "Jubal," *The Spinning Image*. https://www.thespinningimage.co.uk/cultfilms/displaycultfilm.asp?reviewid=10696.

269 Charlot47, "An ancient story that reflects Spain of its time," IMDb, March 15, 2014. https://www.imdb.com/review/rw2979675/?ref_=tt_urv.

270 EdgarSTR, "Genre and the 180° rule," *IMDb*, February 15, 2018. https://www.imdb.com/review/rw4062725/?mode=desktop&ref_=m_ft_dsk.

271 John Flaus, "Back Street," *Senses of Cinema*, May, 2002. https://www.sensesofcinema.com/2002/feature-articles/back_street/.

272 Tim Dirks, "Best Film Deaths Scenes: 1930-1933," *Filmsite*. https://www.filmsite.org/bestdeaths2.html.

273 Rick Reynolds, "Is it Love or Infatuation?," *Affair Recovery*. https://www.affairrecovery.com/newsletter/founder/an-affair-is-it-love-or-infatuation.

274 Richard Taylor, *Love Affairs: Marriage & Infi-*

delity, Buffalo, NY: Prometheus Books, 1997, p. 34.

275 pitcairn89,"A pretty good Pre-Code film," IMDb, September 10, 2011. https://www.imdb.com/review/rw2486362/?ref_=tt_urv.

276 AlsExGal, "The grass is always greener," IMDb, December 14, 2014. https://www.imdb.com/review/rw3141295/?ref_=tt_urv.

277 "Dr. Monica (1934)," *AFI Catalog of Feature Films*. https://catalog.afi.com/Catalog/MovieDetails/3960.

278 Mark Waltz, "Living by principals, not desires," *IMDb*, April 24, 2020. https://www.imdb.com/review/rw5672210/?ref_=tt_urv.

279 "Main Street (novel)," *Wikipedia*. https://en.wikipedia.org/wiki/Main_Street_(novel).

280 Robert Allerton Parker, "Dramas: Plays So Serious and No So Serious," *The Independent and The Weekly Review*, October 29, 1921, 112.

281 Max Holleran, "The Secluded Self: Sinclair Lewis's 'Main Street'," *Public Books*, September 24, 2020. https://www.publicbooks.org/the-secluded-self-sinclair-lewiss-main-street-100/.

282 Sinclair Lewis, *Main Street: The Story of Carol Kennicott*, New York: Grosset & Dunlap, March 10, 2008. p. 366. First published by Harcourt, Brace and Company in October 1921.

283 Cliff Aliperti, "I Married a Doctor (1936): Attempts to Update Main Street," *Immortal Ephemera*, March 14, 2014. https://immortalephemera.com/48521/i-married-a-doctor-1936.

284 Holleran.

285 *Ibid*.

286 Lewis, p. 32.

287 Lewis, p. 240.

288 Mark Schorer, "Main Street," *American Heritage*,October, 1961). https://www.americanheritage.com/main-street.

289 "Mayerling (1936)," *ClassixQuest*, July 20, 2014. https://classixquest.wordpress.com/2014/07/20/mayerling-1936-4/.

290 "In This Our Life," *Rotten Tomatoes*. https://www.rottentomatoes.com/m/in_this_our_life.

291 Geoffrey Nowell-Smith, *Luchino Visconti*, New York City: Viking Press, 1973.

292 "Ossessione," Cinema Neorealismo. https://cinemaneorealismo.wordpress.com/home/obsession/.

293 *Ibid*.

294 *Ibid*.

295 *Ibid*.

296 James Naremore, *Letter From An Unknown Woman*, London: Bloomsbury Academic, March 25, 2021).

297 garykmcd, "Letter from an Unknown Woman (1948)," *IMDb*. https://www.imdb.com/title/tt0040536/.

298 D for Doom, "Beyond the Forest (1949)," *Classic Movie Ramblings*, March 5, 2011. http://dfordoom-movieramblings.blogspot.com/2011/03/beyond-forest-1949.html.

299 TCh, *Time Out*,September 10, 2012. https://www.timeout.com/movies/beyond-the-forest.

300 "Beyond the Forest (1949)," *Filmsite*. https://www.filmsite.org/beyo.html.

301 David Melville, "Scary Monsters (and Super Tramps) – Beyond the Forest David Melville"

Senses of Cinema, CTEQ Annotations on Film, Issue 68, August 2013. https://www.sensesofcinema.com/2013/cteq/scary-monsters-and-super-tramps-beyond-the-forest/.

302 Melville.

303 Mary Webb, *Gone to Earth*, New York, New York: E.P. Dutton & Company, 1918, p. 8.

304 Samm Deighan, Audio Commentary Track for *Images* Blu-ray, Arrow Films, March 20, 2018.

305 *Ibid.*

306 Webb, p. 91.

307 Michael Barrett, "The Primal Instinct That Drives Wild Things in Gone to Earth and The Wild Heart," *Pop Matters*, August 20, 2019. https://www.popmatters.com/gone-to-earth-wild-heart-2639846140.html.

308 Webb, p. 248.

309 Webb, p. 316.

310 Bosley Crowther, "THE SCREEN IN REVIEW; 'September Affair,' With Joan Fontaine and Joseph Cotten, Opens at the Music Hall," *The New York Times*, February 2, 1951. https://www.nytimes.com/1951/02/02/archives/the-screen-in-review-september-affair-with-joan-fontaine-and-joseph.html.

311 Laura, "Tonight's Move: September Affair (1950)," *Laura's Miscellaneous Musings*, May 15, 2011. https://laurasmiscmusings.blogspot.com/2011/05/tonights-movie-september-affair-1950.html.

312 "Sister Carrie: Summary and Analysis Chapters 20-21," *CliffNotes*. https://www.cliffsnotes.com/literature/s/sister-carrie/summary-and-analysis/chapters-2021.

313 Theodore Dreiser, *Sister Carrie*. New York, New York: Grosset & Dunlap, 1907, 239.

314 "Sister Carrie: Summary and Analysis Chapters 20-21," *CliffNotes*. https://www.cliffsnotes.com/literature/s/sister-carrie/summary-and-analysis/chapters-2021.

315 PiPiWiki, "Sister Carrie." https://www.pipiwiki.com/wiki/Sister_Carrie.

316 *Ibid.*

317 Dreiser.

318 *Ibid.*

319 *Ibid.*

320 *Ibid.*

321 *Ibid.*

322 "The Way of All Flesh (1927)," *IMDb*. https://www.imdb.com/title/tt0019553/?ref_=nv_sr_srsg_0.

323 Kelly.

324 bmacv, "Not tiger but tigress Alexis Smith walks away with the movie," *IMDb*, August 29, 2002. https://www.imdb.com/review/rw0053501/?ref_=tt_urv.

325 Vanessa Keys , "The tragic real story behind The Deep Blue Sea," *The Telegraph*, August 31, 2016. https://www.telegraph.co.uk/theatre/national-theatre-live/the-deep-blue-sea/.

326 Josephine Botting, "Vivien Leigh adrift: The Deep Blue Sea," *BFI*, November 26, 2013. https://www.bfi.org.uk/news-opinion/news-bfi/features/vivien-leigh-adrift-deep-blue-sea.

327 NowVoyager88, "The Deep Blue Sea (1955)," *Letterboxd*, August 23, 2015. https://letterboxd.com/nowvoyager88/film/the-deep-blue-sea-1955/.

328 Rinella, Michael D., *Margaret Sullavan: The Life and Career of a Reluctant Star*, Jefferson, NC: McFarland and Company, Inc., July 29, 2019.

329 *Ibid*

330 *Ibid.*

331 *Ibid.*

332 Michael Billington, "Great performances: Penelope Wilton in The Deep Blue Sea," *The Guardian*, May 25, 2015. https://www.theguardian.com/stage/2015/may/25/great-performances-penelope-wilton-the-deep-blue-sea.

333 "From the Terrace," *Wikipedia*. https://en.wikipedia.org/wiki/From_the_Terrace.

334 Boyd van Hoeij, "Il Deserto Rosso (Red Desert, Michelangelo Antonioni, 1964)," *Senses of Cinema*, CTEQ Annotations on Film, Issue 101, May 2022. https://www.sensesofcinema.com/2022/cteq/il-deserto-rosso-red-desert-michelangelo-antonioni-1964/.

335 Roger Ebert, "Interview with Claudia Weill," *RogerEbert.com*, October 20, 1980. https://www.rogerebert.com/interviews/interview-with-claudia-weill.

336 Roger Ebert, "It's My Turn," *RogerEbert.com*, October 28, 1980. https://www.rogerebert.com/reviews/its-my-turn-1980.

337 Simon Abrams, "'Possession': In which Isabelle Adjani's sex scene with a monster isn't the odd part," *Politico*, December 2, 2011. https://www.politico.com/states/new-york/albany/story/2011/12/possession-in-which-isabelle-adjanis-sex-scene-with-a-monster-isnt-the-odd-part-067994.

338 Paul Attanasio, "Stifling 'Soffel," *The Washington Post*, February 9, 1985.

339 *Ibid.*

340 *Ibid.*

341 Pauline Kael, "Fever Dream," *The New Yorker*, January 7, 1985, page 66. https://www.newyorker.com/magazine/1985/01/07/fever-dreamecho-chamber.

342 *Ibid.*

343 Hal Hinson, 'Enemies, A Love Story,' *Washington Post*, January 19, 1990. https://www.washingtonpost.com/wp-srv/style/longterm/movies/videos/enemiesalovestoryrhinson_a0a92e.htm.

344 *Ibid.*

345 Robert S. Leventhal, "Narcissism, Masochism, and Love after the Holocaust: Paul Mazursky's Film Enemies, A Love Story, " University of Virginia, 1995. http://www2.iath.virginia.edu/holocaust/enemies.html.

346 Josephine Hart, *Damage*, First Pegasus Crime, New York City: Simon & Schuster, January 2023.

347 *Ibid..*

348 theodarsey, "A brilliant but misunderstood film," *IMDb*, January 13, 2004. https://www.imdb.com/review/rw0307215/.

349 Derek Elley, "Une Femme Francaise a French Woman," *Variety*, April 3, 1995. https://variety.com/1995/film/reviews/une-femme-francaise-a-french-woman-1117903908/.

350 *Ibid.*

351 jhclues,"A Magnificent Motion Picture," *IMDb*, July 29, 2002. https://www.imdb.com/review/rw0383104/?ref_=tt_urv.

352 Roger Ebert, "Post Coitum," *Roger Ebert*, May 01, 1998. https://www.rogerebert.com/reviews/post-coitum-1998.

353 *Ibid.*

354 Leo Tolstoy, *Anna Karenina*, Translated by Constance Garnett, Canterbury Classics, December 3, 2012.

355 Christy Lemire, "Plush," *RogerEbert.com*, September 13, 2013. https://www.rogerebert.com/reviews/plush-2013.

356 "The Office Wife (1930 film)," *Wikipedia*. https://en.wikipedia.org/wiki/The_Office_Wife_(1930_film).

357 "Jewel Robbery," *Wikipedia*. https://en.wikipedia.org/wiki/Jewel_Robbery.

358 *Ibid.*

359 Norbert Lusk, "The Screen in Review," *Picture Play Magazine*, October 1932. https://ia800306.us.archive.org/BookReader/BookReaderImages.php?zip=/6/items/picturep37stre/picturep37stre_jp2.zip&file=picturep37stre_jp2/picturep37stre_0732.jp2&id=picturep37stre&scale=4&rotate=0.

360 David Melville, "Voices from an Empty Room: Ernst Lubitsch and Angel (1937)," *Senses of Cinema*, CTEQ Annotations on Film, Issue 93, March 2020. https://www.sensesofcinema.com/2020/cteq/angel-1937/.

361 *Ibid.*

362 Richard Brody, "Angel," *The New Yorker*. https://www.newyorker.com/goings-on-about-town/movies/angel.

363 "Dreaming Lips (1937 film)," *Wikipedia*. https://en.wikipedia.org/wiki/Dreaming_Lips_(1937_film).

364 Robert Temple, "Pouting Lips," *IMDb*, September 20, 2009. https://www.imdb.com/review/rw2129770/?ref_=tt_urv.

365 Richard W. Nason, "Dreaming Lips," *The New York Times*, November 1, 1958. https://www.nytimes.com/1958/11/01/archives/dreaming-lips.html.

366 Kat Ellinger, "Audio Commentary," *Madame Bovary* (1991), Arrow Video, February 22 2022.

367 Robinson.

368 Gustave Flaubert, *Madame Bovary: Provincial Manners*. W.W. Gibbings (1901), p. 310.

369 Joe McElhaney, "Looking for a Path: Clash by Night and Fritz Lang," *A Companion to Fritz Lang*, Hoboken, NJ: Wiley-Blackwell, January 27, 2015. https://www.academia.edu/19486306/Looking_for_a_Path_Fritz_Lang_and_CLASH_BY_NIGHT, 514-535.

370 William Ahearn. "Clash by Night," *William Ahearn*, 2013. http://www.williamahearn.com/clashnight.html.

371 Megan Abbott, "Clash by Night (1952)," *Noir of the Week*, April 10, 2009. https://www.noiroftheweek.com/2009/04/clash-by-night-1952.html.

372 "Odets' 'Clash by Night' on Screen," *The New York Times*, June 19, 1952. https://www.nytimes.com/1952/06/19/archives/odets-clash-by-night-on-screen.html.

373 McElhaney.

374 Patrick McGilligan, *Fritz Lang: The Nature of the Beast*, New York City: St. Martin's, 1997.

375 *Ibid.*

376 McElhaney.

377 Sam Hamm, "Sam Hamm on STRANGERS WHEN WE MEET," *Trailers for Hell* (YouTube channel), October 16, 2013. https://www.youtube.com/watch?v=FhLGKyePa9o.

378 Jacqueline T. Lynch, "Strangers When We Meet (1960)," Another Old Movie Blog, June 19, 2008. https://anotheroldmovieblog.blogspot.com/2008/06/strangers-when-we-meet-1960.html.

379 *Ibid.*

380 *Ibid.*

381 Cammmalot, "Strangers When We Meet (1960)," *Letterboxd*. https://letterboxd.com/film/strangers-when-we-meet/.

382 Lynch.

383 *Ibid.*

384 *Ibid.*

385 JamesHitchcock, "The Golden Couple of the Sixties," *IMDb*, November 19, 2010. https://www.imdb.com/review/rw2341015/?ref_=tt_urv.

386 Charles Champlin, "Irish Coast Has Best Lines in Lean's 'Daughter'," *Los Angeles Times*, Calendar, November 15, 1970, 1.

387 Lina Das, "The final affair of Roman Polanski's murdered wife Sharon Tate," *Daily Mail*. https://www.dailymail.co.uk/femail/article-478867/The-final-affair-Roman-Polanskis-murdered-wife-Sharon-Tate.html.

388 Jane Fryer, "Saucy secret letters that brought my love for Larry back to life: She was 18, he was 53. Now Sarah Miles reveals the truth about her illicit affair with Sir Laurence Olivier," *Daily Mail,* May 17, 2019. https://www.dailymail.co.uk/femail/article-7043061/Sarah-Miles-reveals-truth-illicit-affair-Sir-Laurence-Olivier.html.

389 Geoffrey MacNab, "Brief encounters: How David Lean's sex life shaped his films," *Independent*, June 29, 2008. https://www.independent.co.uk/arts-entertainment/films/features/brief-encounters-how-david-lean-s-sex-life-shaped-his-films-854957.html.

390 "Brief encounters: How David Lean's sex life shaped his films," *Independent,* June 29, 2008. https://www.independent.co.uk/arts-entertainment/films/features/brief-encounters-how-david-lean-s-sex-life-shaped-his-films-854957.html.

391 *Ibid.*

392 Kevin Brownlow, *David Lean: A Biography*, New York, New York: St. Martin's Press, August 15, 1996, 556.

393 *Ibid.*

394 *Ibid.*

395 Jack Beatty, "Hunting, Hunting, Hunting," *The Atlantic*, 1997. https://www.theatlantic.com/past/docs/unbound/polipro/pp9702.htm.

396 "Cousin Cousine," Wikipedia. https://en.m.wikipedia.org/wiki/Cousin_Cousine.

397 writers_reign, "You CAN Go Home Again (But I Wouldn't Bother)," IMDb, October 22m 2005. https://www.imdb.com/review/rw1198842/?ref_=tt_urv.

398 LaSalle.

399 I Am Love (film), *Wikipedia*. https://en.wikipedia.org/wiki/I_Am_Love_(film).

400 "Art's Revolt: 'I Am Love'," The Niles Files, July 15, 2010. https://nilesfilmfiles.blogspot.com/2010/07/i-am-love.html.

401 Be Kind Rewind, "12 Days of Actress 2022," December 23, 2022. https://www.youtube.com/watch?v=ZdxouFb1snU.

402 "Partir (2009)," IMDb. https://www.imdb.com/title/tt1315962/plotsummary#synopsis.

403 LaSalle.

404 Taylor, p 15.

405 Kerby Anderson, "Adultery," *Probe*, October 1, 2014. https://probe.org/adultery/.

406 "Christopher Strong," *Wikipedia*. https://en.wikipedia.org/wiki/Christopher_Strong.

407 "Films Classified in Catholic List," The New York Times, July 7, 1934.

408 Sonya Roberts, "Dodsworth (1936)," *IMDb*. https://www.imdb.com/title/tt0027532/plotsummary.

409 Mark Deming, "Dodsworth (1936)," *All Movie Guide*. https://www.allmovie.com/movie/v14183.

410 Roberts.

411 ccthemovieman-1, "7 reasons why Intermezzo works," *IMDb*, April 16 2005. https://www.imdb.com/review/rw1061152/?ref_=tt_urv.

412 "Now, Voyager (1942)," *IMDb*. https://www.imdb.com/title/tt0035140/?ref_=nv_sr_srsg_0.

413 Olive Higgins Prouty, *Now, Voyager*, Feminist Press at CUNY,August 10, 2012), 3.

414 Emma Rice, *Brief Encounter*, London, United Kingdom: Bloomsbury Publishing, May 11, 2018.

415 Kevin Brownlow, 200.

416 Kelly.

417 *Ibid.*

418 "Still Life (play)," *Wikipedia*. https://en.wikipedia.org/wiki/Still_Life_(play).

419 Brian McFarlane, *The Never-ending Brief Encounter*, Manchester, United Kingdom: Manchester University Press, August 28, 2019.

420 Jeanine Basinger, *I Do and I Don't: A History of Marriage in the Movies*, New York City: Knopf Doubleday Publishing Group, January 29, 2013, p. 149.

421 Hal Erickson, "The Facts of Life (1960)," *All-Movie Guide*. https://www.allmovie.com/movie/v90859.

422 Kamlesh Tripathi, "THE LADY WITH THE DOG by Anton Chekov," *Kamleshsujata Blog*, July 12, 2019. https://kamleshsujata.blog/2019/07/12/the-lady-with-the-dog-by-anton-chekov/.

423 Robert Fulford, "Surprised by love: Chekhov and 'The Lady with the Dog'," Queen's Quarterly, Volume 111, Issue 3, Fall 2004.

424 Hal Erickson, "A Touch of Class (1973)," *All-Movie Guide*. https://www.allmovie.com/movie/a-touch-of-class-v50537.

425 dglink, "Two Top Comedic Performances in Half a Hysterical Film," *IMDb*, November 5, 2005. https://imdb.com/review/rw1209344/.

426 The Scarlet Letter (1995 film), *Wikipedia*. https://en.wikipedia.org/wiki/The_Scarlet_Letter_(1995_film).

427 Nathaniel Hawthorne, *The Scarlet Letter*, New York City: Columbia University Press, 2000, page 109.

428 *Ibid.*

429 Carina Chocano, "A disturbance in the playing fields," *The Los Angeles Times*, October 6, 2006. https://www.latimes.com/archives/la-xpm-2006-oct-06-et-little6-story.html.

430 "Someone I Loved (Je L'Aimais) 2009," *Phoenix Cinema*, May 22, 2011. https://phoenixcinema.wordpress.com/2011/05/22/someone-i-loved-je-laimais-2009/.

431 Gerard Gilbert, "A fare to remember: David Nicholls reveals the inspiration for his new BBC drama The 7.39," The Independent, January 1, 2014. https://www.independent.co.uk/arts-entertainment/tv/features/a-fare-to-remember-david-nicholls-reveals-the-inspiration-for-his-new-bbc-drama-the-7-39-9033061.html.

432 Paula Dumas, "Marriage Tested by Chronic Illness? Why Some Men Leave," *Migraine Again*, March 24, 2020. https://www.migraineagain.com/chronic-illness-in-marriage/.

433 Karen Bruno, "7 Ways to Keep Your Relationship Strong Despite a Chronic Illness," *WebMD*, November 22, 2012. https://www.webmd.com/sex-relationships/features/chronic-illness-seven-relationship-tips.

434 Judith Graham, "When Caring For A Sick Spouse Shakes A Marriage To The Core," *KHN*,

November 7, 2019. https://khn.org/news/when-caring-for-a-sick-spouse-shakes-a-marriage-to-the-core/.

435 "Thunder Below (1932)," *AFI Catalog of Feature Films.* https://catalog.afi.com/Film/6738-THUNDER-BELOW.

436 planktonrules, "Apart from the plot seldom making any sense. . ," *IMDb*, May 20, 2017. https://www.imdb.com/review/rw3712251/.

437 GrandeMarguerite, "In a nutshell: terrible" (User review), *IMDb*, July 14, 2010. https://www.imdb.com/review/rw2279151/.

438 ccmiller1492, "Sexual healing?. . . a menage a trois goes horribly wrong," IMDb, January 26, 2007. https://www.imdb.com/review/rw1582958/.

439 "Madeline, Study of a Nightmare (1974)," *IMDb.* https://www.imdb.com/title/tt0125896/?ref_=nv_sr_srsg_0.

440 Roger Ebert, "Story of Women," *RogerEbert.com*, February 14, 1990. https://www.rogerebert.com/reviews/story-of-women-1990.

441 D. H. Lawrence, *The Works of D. H. Lawrence: Three Great Novels*, World Publications, December 1995, 72.

442 "Lady Chatterley's Lover," *Wikipedia.* https://en.wikipedia.org/wiki/Lady_Chatterley%27s_Lover.

443 "Lady Chatterley's Lover," *SparkNotes.* https://www.sparknotes.com/lit/ladychatterley/characters/.

444 Lawrence.

445 *Ibid.*

446 *Ibid.*

447 Jeanine Basinger, *A Woman's View: How Hollywood Spoke to Women, 1930-1960*, New York City: Knopf Doubleday Publishing Group, September 4, 2013.

448 Les Adams, "Paris Frills (1945)," *IMDb.* https://www.imdb.com/title/tt0035853/?ref_=nv_sr_srsg_0.

449 José Arroyo, "La Marie du Port (Marcel Carné, France, 1950)," *Notes on Film*, August 8, 2019. https://notesonfilm1.com/2019/08/08/la-marie-du-port-marcel-carne-france-1950/.

450 "Eva (1962)," *Letterboxd.* https://letterboxd.com/film/eva-1962/.

451 "Something to Live For (1952)," *American Film Institute Catalog of Feature Films.* https://catalog.afi.com/Film/50660-SOMETHING-TO-LIVE-FOR?cxt=filmography.

452 Kelly.

453 Tony Macklin, "Avanti's incongruities give pleasure," *The Journal Herald,*February 12, 1973). http://tonymacklin.net/content.php?cID=214.

454 MISSMOOHERSELF, "A Sheer Delight," *IMDb*, January 2, 2005. https://m.imdb.com/review/rw0990114/?ref_=ur_urv.

455 moonspinner554, "A sit-com in soft-focus," *IMDb*, July 4, 2007. https://www.imdb.com/review/rw1686823/.

456 Peter Travers, "The Bridges of Madison County," *Rolling Stone*, June 2, 1995. https://www.rollingstone.com/movies/movie-reviews/the-bridges-of-madison-county-99082/.

457 Roger Ebert, "The Bridges of Madison County," *Roger Ebert*, June 2, 1995. https://www.rogerebert.com/reviews/the-bridges-of-madison-county-1995.

458 Brennen, Bonnie, "Bridging the Backlash: A Cultural Materialist Reading of The Bridges of Madison County," Marquette University, October 1, 1996.

459 Marc Eliot, *American Rebel The Life of Clint Eastwood*, New York City: Harmony Books, October 6, 2009, p. 291.

460 John Leo, "A bodice ripper goes mainstream," *U.S. News and World Report*, August 9, 1993.

461 Dan Thomas and Larry Baas, "Reading the Romance, Building the Bestseller: A Q-technique Study of Reader Response to Robert Waller's The Bridges of Madison County," *Operant Subjectivity*, No. 17, November 8, 1993, p. 17-39.

462 *Ibid.*

463 Peter Bradshaw, "The real Mrs. Robinson is no Anne Bancroft in The Graduate," *The Guardian*, January 13, 2010. https://www.theguardian.com/film/filmblog/2010/jan/13/graduate-mrs-robinson-affair.

464 Herman Raucher, *Summer of '42*, New York City: Diversion Books, May 3, 2015.

465 *Ibid.*

466 "Summer of '42," *Wikipedia*. https://en.wikipedia.org/wiki/Summer_of_%2742.

467 Louis Hillary Park, "Herman Raucher Interview," TCPalm.com, May 2002. https://web.archive.org/web/20060206230410/http://web.tcpalm.com/specialreports/summerof42/raucher.html.

468 *Ibid.*

469 *Ibid.*

470 *Ibid.*

471 *Ibid.*

472 "Nora Prentiss (1947)," Old Movies Are Great,April 17, 2017). https://oldmoviesaregreat.wordpress.com/2017/04/17/nora-prentiss-1947/.

473 Leo Tolstory, *Anna Karenina*, Translated by Constance Garnett, Redditch, Great Britain: Read Books Limited, September 8, 2020.

474 Gregory D. Black, *Hollywood Censored Morality Codes, Catholics, and the Movies*, Cambridge, United Kingdom: Cambridge Univer-

sity Press, 1994, p. 216.

475 Black, p/ 217.

476 Robert Short, "A Look At Two Versions Of Anna Karenina (1935 and 1948)," Silver Screen Classics, April 3, 2020. https://silverscreenclassicsblog.wordpress.com/2020/04/03/a-look-at-two-versions-of-anna-karenina-1935-and-1948/.

477 Tolstory.

478 "Anna Karenina Characters: Stiva Oblonsky," *Spark Notes*. https://www.sparknotes.com/lit/anna/character/stiva-oblonsky/.

479 *Ibid.*

480 Philip Hoare, *Noel Coward A Biography*, Chicago, IL: University of Chicago Press, May 22, 1998, p. 383.

481 bkoganbing, "Not so easy to buy Edward Everett Horton as a paramour," *IMDb*, September 21, 2012. https://www.imdb.com/review/rw2677091/?ref_=tt_urv.

482 planktonrules, "A Pre-Code comedy about the wacky world of adultery," *IMDb*, April 11, 2011. imdb.com/review/rw2412360/?ref_=tt_urv.

483 Les Adams, "There's Always Tomorrow (1934)," *IMDb*. https://www.imdb.com/title/tt0025876/?ref_=nv_sr_srsg_0.

484 seglora, "excellent forgotten film from post war Germany," *IMDb*, April 5, 2016. https://www.imdb.com/review/rw3446242/?ref_=tt_urv.

485 Samm Deighan, Audio Commentary Track for *There's Always Tomorrow* Blu-ray, Kino Lorber, August 25, 2020.

486 Frank Collins, "British Cult Classics: Woman in a Dressing Gown," *Cathode Ray Tube*, July 11, 2012.

https://www.cathoderaytube.co.uk/2012/07/british
-cult-classics-woman-in-dressing.html.

487 LaDonnaKeskes, "Unforgettable (Possible
spoiler)," *IMDb*, January 29, 2004).
https://www.imdb.com/review/rw0063187/.

488 Collins.

489 *Ibid.*

490 Collins.

491 Jean-Luc Godard, *Godard on Godard*, Boston,
MA: Da Capo Press, March 22, 1986, 85–86.

492 *Ibid.*

493 *Ibid.*

494 *Ibid.*

495 *Ibid.*

496 *Ibid.*

497 "The Tiger and the Pussycat (1967)," *Wikipedia*.
https://en.wikipedia.org/wiki/The_Tiger_and_the_
Pussycat.

498 Gerard Molyneaux, *Gregory Peck: A Bio-
bibliography*, Westport, CT: Greenwood Press,
June 30, 1995.

499 Ken Beck, ""I Walk the Line' laid an egg in
1970," *The Wilson Post*, October 26, 2020.
https://www.wilsonpost.com/community/i-walk-
the-line-laid-an-egg-in-1970/article_344a4cb2-
1346-11eb-9680-2792d3a367a1.html.

500 *Ibid.*

501 *Ibid.*

502 Charles Champlin, "Mr. Peck, After All These
Years : After 50 years in the spotlight, America's
favorite good guy shares memories of his many
successes - and a few failures," The *Los Angeles
Times*, October 20, 1991.

503 Middle Age Crazy (1980), *IMDb*.
https://www.imdb.com/title/tt0081157/?ref_=fn_al
_tt_1.

504 W. Somerset Maugham, *Theatre*, Kingswood,
Surrey: The Windmill Press, 1957, p. 262.
https://archive.org/stream/in.ernet.dli.2015.149229
/2015.149229.Theatre_djvu.txt.

505 Maugham, viii.

506 Maugham, xii.

507 Maugham, p. 205.

508 Maugham, p. 294.

509 Les Adams, "The Kiss of Araby," *IMDb*.
https://www.imdb.com/title/tt0024223/.

510 "Vacation from Marriage (1945)," *Rotten Tomatoes*.
https://www.rottentomatoes.com/m/vacation_from
_marriage.

511 professorharoldlloydhill, "often times silly, but
not dull," *IMDb*, January 23, 2013.
https://www.imdb.com/review/rw2744829/?ref_=t
t_urv.

512 Sloan Wilson, *The Man in the Gray Flannel
Suit*, New York City: Arbor House, 1955, page 82.
https://archive.org/details/maningrayflanne00wils.

513 Tim Brayton, "The Recovering Romantic:
Fassbinder's THE MARRIAGE OF MARIA
BRAUN," Cinematheque, November 28, 2018.
https://cinema.wisc.edu/blog/2018/11/28/recoverin
g-romantic-fassbinders-marriage-maria-braun.

514 Roger Ebert, "The mind of the married woman," *RogerEbert.com*, April 24, 2005.
https://www.rogerebert.com/reviews/great-movie-
the-marriage-of-maria-braun-1979.

515 *Ibid.*

516 "Blue Angel," *Wikipedia*.
https://en.wikipedia.org/wiki/The_Blue_Angel.

517 bkoganbing, "A George Burns Moment,"
IMDb, August 4, 2011.

https://www.imdb.com/review/rw2468979/?ref_=t
t_urv.

518 planktonrules, "This film is salvaged strictly because of Colman's effortless and wonderful performance," *IMDb*, April 19, 2007. https://www.imdb.com/review/rw1640308/?ref_=t
t_urv.

519 st-shot, "Lifeless," *IMDb*, August 31, 2011. https://www.imdb.com/review/rw2482220/?ref_=t
t_urv.

520 Williams.

521 Marc Eliot, *Cary Grant: A Biography*, New York City: Crown Publishing Group, February 4, 2009, p. 335.

522 A. H. Weiler, "'The Magnificent Cuckold' at Fine Arts Theater Brings Back 'Conjugal Bed' Hero," *The New York Times*, April 20, 1965. https://www.nytimes.com/1965/04/20/archives/the
-magnificent-cuckold-at-fine-arts-theater-brings-
back-conjugal.html.

523 Les Adams, "Wife Tames Wolf (1947)," *IMDb*. https://www.imdb.com/title/tt0236872/?ref_=nv_s
r_srsg_0.

524 Black, 57.

525 Sandra Brennan, "Week-End Marriage (1932)," *AllMovie Guide*. https://www.allmovie.com/movie/v116208.

526 "Another Language (1933)," *AFI Catalog of Feature Films*. https://catalog.afi.com/Film/7296-
ANOTHER-LANGUAGE.

527 "Riptide (1934 film)," *Wikipedia*. https://en.wikipedia.org/wiki/Riptide_(1934_film).

528 *Ibid.*

529 Peter Bondanella, *The Cinema of Federico Fellini*, Princeton, NJ: Princeton University Press, 1992, 90.

530 Alpert Hollis, *Fellini: A Life*, New York, New York: Paragon House, 1988, 81.

531 "I Vitelloni," *Wikipedia*. https://en.wikipedia.org/wiki/I_Vitelloni.

532 "I Vitelloni," *Cinema Neorealismo Italiano*. https://cinemaneorealismo.wordpress.com/director
-profile/film/i-vitelloni/.

533 Andrea Bini, *Male Anxiety and Psychopathology in Film: Comedy Italian Style*, London, United Kingdom: Palgrave Macmillan, September 10, 2015, 93.

534 Bini, 94.

535 Bini, 84.

536 Bini, 82.

537 Bini, 96.

538 Les Adams, "The Joker," *IMDb*. https://www.imdb.com/title/tt0053814/.

539 Michael Coates-Smith and Garry McGee, *The Films of Jean Seberg*, Jefferson, NC: McFarland & Company, Inc., 2012, p. 59.

540 *Ibid.*

541 Pauline Kael, *5001 Nights at the Movies*, New York City: Henry Holt and Company, August 2, 2011, p. 247.

542 Coates-Smith and McGee, p. 58.

543 James Monaco, *The New Wave Truffaut, Godard, Chabrol, Rohmer, Rivette (Thirtieth Anniversary Edition)*, Sag Harbor, New York: Harbor Electronic Publishing, 2004, page 152.

544 Frank Swietek, "Frank & Eva," *Video Librarian*, August 23, 2018. https://videolibrarian.com/reviews/classic-
film/frank-eva/.

545 "Sexed-up Dutch Drama Charts a Couple Living Apart Together," *Zeke Film*, June 5, 2018. https://www.zekefilm.org/2019/04/30/frank-eva-
1973-blu-ray-review/.

546 *Ibid.*

547 Time Staff, "Cinema: The New Pictures," *Time*, November 10, 1930. https://content.time.com/time/subscriber/article/0,33009,740677,00.html.

548 "The Virtuous Sin," *Film Daily*, October 26, 1930, 10. https://ia800504.us.archive.org/BookReader/BookReaderImages.php?id=filmdailyvolume55354newy&itemPath=%2F3%2Fitems%2Ffilmdailyvolume55354newy&server=ia800504.us.archive.org&page=leaf0001144.

549 Marc Slope, "A surprise from 1935," *IMDb*, October 12, 2015. https://www.imdb.com/review/rw3333942/.

550 Andre Sennwald, "Rachel Crothers and Samuel Goldwyn Collaborate on 'Splendor,' the New Film at the Rivoli Theatre," *The New York Times*, November 23, 1935. https://www.nytimes.com/1935/11/23/archives/rachel-crothers-and-samuel-goldwyn-collaborate-on-splendor-the-new.html.

551 Arthur Hausner, "Conquest (1937)." https://www.imdb.com/title/tt0028739/plotsummary.

552 Dan Callahan, "B-Noir at Film Forum," *Slant Magazine,* May 5, 2006. https://www.slantmagazine.com/film/b-noir/.

553 Cinema Cities, "4 Must Watch Underrated Film Noir Classics part 2," *YouTube* video, January 29, 2023. https://www.youtube.com/watch?v=e4_YWSU2Jwk&ab_channel=CinemaCities.

554 "This is the Night (1932)," *IMDb*. https://www.imdb.com/title/tt0023584/.

555 utgard14, "I'm just a young girl living by her hips," *IMDb*, December 2, 2014. https://www.imdb.com/review/rw3134785/?ref_=tt_urv.

556 *Ibid.*

557 Ron Kerrigan, "The Masquerader (1933)," *IMDb*. https://www.imdb.com/title/tt0024308/.

558 "Red Roses (1940)," *IMDb*. https://www.imdb.com/title/tt0031878/?ref_=nv_sr_srsg_0.

559 Dan Stumpf, "A Movie Review by Dan Stumpf: INTERRUPTED JOURNEY (1949)," *Mystery File*, March 4, 2011. https://mysteryfile.com/blog/?p=8587.

560 "The Interrupted Journey," *Wikipedia*. https://en.wikipedia.org/wiki/The_Interrupted_Journey.

561 Roger Ebert, "The solitary journey of the 'little priest,'" *RogerEbert.com*, January 1, 2011. https://www.rogerebert.com/reviews/great-movie-diary-of-a-country-priest-1951.

562 Frédéric Bonnaud, The Criterion Collection, "Diary of a Country Priest," February 2, 2004. https://www.criterion.com/current/posts/313-diary-of-a-country-priest.

563 "The House in Marsh Road." *Roku*. https://www.roku.com/whats-on/movies/the-house-in-marsh-road?id=68b2a41dd4de5fa0a1d55fa67d0d4495.

564 "The Pink Panther (1963 film)," *Wikipedia*. https://en.wikipedia.org/wiki/The_Pink_Panther_(1963_film).

565 Dr. Kate Lister, *Whores of Yore*. https://twitter.com/whoresofyore/status/1583435650866458625.

566 Addison Nugent, "The Married Woman Who Kept Her Lover in the Attic," *Atlas Obscura*. https://www.atlasobscura.com/articles/the-married-woman-who-kept-her-lover-in-the-attic.

567 Lister.

568 Nugent.

569 "The Bliss of Mrs. Blossom," *Wikipedia*. https://en.wikipedia.org/wiki/The_Bliss_of_Mrs._Blossom.

570 "Review – Platonov, Ivanov, The Seagull – Young Chekhov, Festival Theatre Chichester, 31st October 2015," *The Real Chrisparkle*. https://therealchrisparkle.com/2015/11/03/review-platonov-ivanov-the-seagull-young-chekhov-festival-theatre-chichester-31st-october-2015/.

571 "Mordi e fuggi (1973)," *BFI*. https://www2.bfi.org.uk/films-tv-people/4ce2b6b0c76ff.

572 "Ash Wednesday (1973)," *IMDb*. https://www.imdb.com/title/tt0069736/plotsummary.

573 "Sunday Lovers (1980)." *IMDb*. https://www.imdb.com/title/tt0081591/plotsummary.

574 Honkon, "Bravo Blier," *IMDb*, April 7, 2004. https://www.imdb.com/review/rw0276329/.

575 Ezra Litwak and Marjorie Nielsen, *The Butcher's Wife* (script revisions), May 9, 1990. p. 5.

576 Marjorie Nielsen, Interview by e-mail, Conducted by Anthony Balducci, December 6, 2022.

577 Litwak and Nielsen, p. 21.

578 Litwak and Nielsen, p. 22.

579 Flaubert, p. 142.

580 Roger Ebert, "The Butcher's Wife," *RogerEbert.com*, October 25, 1991. https://www.rogerebert.com/reviews/the-butchers-wife-1991.

581 Nielsen.

582 Ebert, "The Butcher's Wife."

583 Litwak and Nielsen, p. 10.

584 Desson Howe, "A 'Wife' with a Meat-Cute Tale," *The Washington Post*, October 25, 1991. https://www.washingtonpost.com/archive/lifestyle/1991/10/25/a-wife-with-meat-cute-tale/55783ff2-0265-40ef-847b-b2227534c052/.

585 Janet Maslin, "A Sea-Sprite's Advice to the Lovelorn," The New York Times, October 25, 1991. https://www.nytimes.com/1991/10/25/movies/review-film-a-sea-sprite-s-advice-to-the-lovelorn.html.

586 Nielsen.

587 *Ibid.*

588 Litwak and Nielsen, p. 88.

589 Litwak and Nielsen, p. 90.

590 *Ibid.*

591 Litwak and Nielsen, p. 112.

592 *Ibid.*

593 Litwak and Nielsen, p. 113.

594 Howe.

595 Jill Rachlin, "The Butcher's Wife," *Entertainment Weekly*, May 15, 1992. https://ew.com/article/1992/05/15/butchers-wife/.

596 "The Daytrippers (1996)," *Metacritic*. https://www.metacritic.com/movie/the-daytrippers.

597 jotix100, "Gilles and Marion," IMDb, June 16, 2005. https://www.imdb.com/review/rw1104404/.

598 *Ibid.*

599 "An Affair to Die For," *IMDb*. https://www.imdb.com/title/tt8620646/plotsummary/.

600 LaSalle, 146.

601 THR Staff, "Brownian Movement: Berlin Review," *Hollywood Reporter*, February 14, 2011. https://www.hollywoodreporter.com/movies/movie-reviews/brownian-movement-berlin-review-99508/.

602 Mike Goodidge, "Brownian Movement," *Screen Daily*, February 10, 2011.

https://www.screendaily.com/brownian-movement/5023429.article.

603 Jeremy Heilman, "Brownian Movement (Nanouk Leopold, 2010)," *Movie Martyr*. http://www.moviemartyr.com/2010/brownianmovement.htm.

604 Matthew Quick, *The Silver Linings Playbook*, New York City: Farrar, Straus and Giroux, April 27, 2010, p. 57.

605 Quick, p.58.

606 Quick, p. 9.

607 Homesick (2015), *IMDb*. https://www.imdb.com/title/tt3166500/.

608 Taylor, p 28.

Ingram Content Group UK Ltd.
Milton Keynes UK
UKHW030933110723
424927UK00013B/290

9 798218 231262